To Eva

A DICTIONARY
OF POLITICS

A DICTIONARY OF POLITICS

Walter Laqueur, the editor of this dictionary, is Director of the Institute of Contemporary History in London and co-editor of the *Journal of Contemporary History*. Professor Laqueur has written extensively on nineteenth and twentieth century history and his books include *Russia and Germany*, *Young Germany*, *The Fate of the Revolution* (a study of the outcome of the Russian Revolution) and *Europe Since Hitler*.

A DICTIONARY
OF POLITICS
Revised Edition

Edited by
WALTER LAQUEUR

with the assistance of
Evelyn Anderson
Ernest Hearst
Bernard Krikler
and
Lawrence Silverman

THE FREE PRESS
A Division of Macmillan Publishing Co., Inc.
NEW YORK

The Free Press
A Division of Macmillan Publishing Co., Inc.
866 Third Avenue, New York, N.Y. 10022

Originally published in England by
George Weidenfeld & Nicolson
Reprinted by arrangement with Pan Books Ltd.

Library of Congress Catalog Card Number: 74–9232

This edition published by The Free Press in hardcover, 1974

Printed in the United States of America

printing number
     3 4 5 6 7 8 9 10

PREFACE

It is the object of this DICTIONARY OF POLITICS to present concise up-to-date information about the facts, the changes in terminology and the historical background of contemporary politics for the student and general reader. It is a work of reference, not a handbook of political science, and it concentrates on developments since 1933. (All entries have been updated to 1971 and in some cases to early 1973.) There are narrow limits to the amount of information that can be compressed into a single volume and the main difficulty facing those instrumental in preparing the dictionary was the problem of selection. Almost every entry was originally longer and had to be cut to provide for the inclusion of others to make this volume as comprehensive as possible. The general concept was my own but most of the organizational work and arrangement of the Dictionary was done by Bernard Krikler and Ernest Hearst to whom my special thanks are due. A number of people outside the Institute of Contemporary History also helped in the preparation of the Dictionary. In particular, the Dictionary owes a great deal to Mrs Evelyn Anderson who contributed and accepted editorial responsibility for all the material on Russia, Eastern Europe and all the entries which deal with communism and the communist world. I would also like to thank Dr Silverman of Reading University who undertook to edit the USA entries and prepare a vast amount of additional material on the United States. Geoffrey Pridham assisted Bernard Krikler in the work of revision as well as contributing a large section of the Dictionary. Aileen Stevenson also worked unstintingly as editorial secretary and research assistant. A special word of thanks is due to Mr Ze'ev Ben Shlomo whose encyclopaedic knowledge proved invaluable to the editors and contributors. Additional material was contributed by Martin Stoll. The staff of this Institute also deserve thanks for their help and patience.

To make dictionaries, Dr Johnson said, is dull work. On another occasion he compared them with watches: the best cannot be expected to go quite true. But he also added: the worst is better than none. We hope that the present volume will be of some use in a world that has become more complicated and bewildering at an alarming pace.

WALTER LAQUEUR
London, June 1970

LIST OF CONTRIBUTORS

WALTER LAQUEUR, editor of the dictionary, is co-editor of the *Journal of Contemporary History* and Director of the Institute of Contemporary History (the Wiener Library). He has written extensively on recent European and Middle-Eastern history and his books include *Europe Since Hitler, The Fate of the Revolution* (a study of the outcome of the Russian Revolution), *Russia and Germany, Young Germany, Communism and Nationalism in the Middle East, The Middle East in Transition* and *The Road to War 1967: the origins of the Arab-Israel conflict.*

EVELYN ANDERSON has written on developments in various communist countries and on inter-communist relations. Her published work includes *Hammer or Anvil: The story of the German working class movement.*

ROBERT GALLUCI is instructor in history at Lasell Junior College.

RICHARD GRÜNBERGER is the author of *Germany 1918–1945* and the forthcoming *Social History of the Third Reich.*

ERNEST HEARST is a senior member of the staff of the Institute of Contemporary History.

BERNARD KRIKLER is Assistant Director of the Institute of Contemporary History and the Wiener Library.

GEOFFREY PRIDHAM is Assistant Lecturer in European Politics at the University of Bristol.

LAWRENCE SILVERMAN is Lecturer in Politics at the University of Reading.

A DICTIONARY
OF POLITICS

A

AAPSO. Afro-Asian People's Solidarity Organization – a communist front organization sponsored by the World Peace Council to mobilize 'neutralist' and 'pacifist' groups in the ⇨ Third World. Headquarters were established in Cairo from where it organized Afro-Asian Solidarity Conferences – Conakry 1960, Beirut 1960, Bandung 1961, Moshi 1963, Algiers 1964, Winneba 1965. The activities of AAPSO have been disrupted by Sino-Soviet polemics.

Abbas, Ferhat (1900–). Leader of movement of Algerian independence, he proclaimed his Manifesto of the Algerian People in 1943 and founded the *Union Démocratique du Manifeste Algérien* in 1946. He supported the ⇨ FLN after the outbreak of the Algerian War (1955) and was Prime Minister of the 'provisional government' in exile in Tunisia (1958–61). After independence he was President of the National Assembly (1962–63) but resigned after growing differences with ⇨ Ben Bella.

Abdication Crisis (U K 1936). Caused by King Edward VIII's wish to marry Mrs Simpson, a twice-divorced American commoner. ⇨ Baldwin advised the King either to renounce Mrs Simpson or abdicate. A morganatic marriage (Mrs Simpson would become the King's wife but not his Queen) was advocated in some quarters including the ⇨ Beaverbrook press and Winston ⇨ Churchill. Edward chose to abdicate (Dec. 1936) and was succeeded by his brother, the Duke of York, who became King George VI.

Abdul Rahman, Tunku (1903–). Prime Minister of ⇨ Malaysia 1963–70) Prime Minister of ⇨ Malaya (1957–63) and leader of the United Malays' National Organization (⇨ UMNO) and now of the Alliance Party. A leading figure in the movement for Malayan independence, he helped found the UMNO after World War II and became Chief Minister when Malaya was granted ministerial government in 1955. His policy included 'Malayanization' of the public services and the encouragement of foreign, especially British investment. He promoted the plan for the Federation of Malaysia but insisted on the political superiority of the Malays over the Chinese. In Sept. 1970 he resigned and was succeeded by Tun Abdul Razak.

Abdullah, King (1882–1951). King of ⇨ Jordan (1949–51) after being Emir of Transjordan from 1921 and later King. He maintained the traditionally close connexions with the British and during World War II was a strong opponent of the ⇨ Axis powers. During the 1948 war with Israel he annexed territory from Palestine on the West Bank of the River Jordan but his ambitions to establish an Arab federation under a member of his dynasty came to nothing and he was assassinated by an Arab nationalist in 1951.

Abu Dhabi. ⇨ Trucial States.

Abyssinia. ⇨ Ethiopia.

ACDA. United States Arms Control and Disarmament Agency – an ⇨ Independent Agency established by Act of Congress in 1961 to support and conduct research into problems of arms control and disarmament, and to advise the President and the ⇨ Secretary of State in these matters. It prepares drafts for, and sends representatives to, disarmament negotiations. The 1963 ⇨ Nuclear Test-ban Treaty was negotiated on the basis of a draft prepared by this agency; and the ACDA also took the initiative in establishing the ⇨ 'Hot Line' to Moscow. The Agency is headed by a Director appointed by the President with the consent of the ⇨ Senate.

Acheson, Dean G. (1893–1971). US Secretary of State (1949–55). He entered government service in 1933 as Under-Secretary of the Treasury only to resign the same year over a policy disagreement. Appointed Assistant Secretary of State (1941–45) and then Under-Secretary of State (1945–47), he prepared the Acheson-Lilienthal Plan for international control of atomic energy. As Secretary of State, Acheson was instrumental in establishing ⇨ NATO and implementing the Korean policy.

ACLU. American Civil Liberties Union – an association in the USA dedicated to the protection and promotion of ⇨ Civil Liberties, regarding which it adopts a broad and liberal interpretation. Apart from propaganda, its principal method of action is through the courts, and it provides legal assistance and representation for private citizens seeking to establish their rights in this way. It occasionally gives evidence before ⇨ Congressional Committees. In like manner, it has also contributed to the ⇨ Civil Rights Movement.

Action Française. French right-wing royalist movement founded during the Dreyfus controversy. Led by such accomplished writers as Charles Maurras and Léon Daudet, its violently anti-republican, anti-German and anti-semitic views gained an air of intellectual distinction before World War I, while its corps of activists, the *Camelots du Roi* became notorious for their brutality. Anticipating and inspiring much of the later Fascist ideology, the movement, again active in the inter-war years, was banned in 1936. Its paper, permitted to continue, opposed France's entry into the war and after her defeat supported all-out collaboration.

ADA. Americans for Democratic Action – an influential group associated with the ⇨ Democratic Party, of liberal, but not radical, persuasion.

Adams, Sherman (1899–). Former Governor of New Hampshire, USA (1949–53) and close adviser to President ⇨ Eisenhower. He was elected to the New Hampshire House of Representatives as a Republican (1941) and became its Speaker (1943–44). After serving in the US House of Representatives (1945–47), he returned to State politics, and was elected Governor (1949). During his term as Governor, he was Chairman of the North-Eastern Governors Conference (1951–52). In 1953, Dwight D. Eisenhower, the first Republican in the White House for twenty years, made him his chief of staff and relied heavily on his advice as Assistant to the President in all matters of domestic policy. He resigned in 1958, after being connected with a scandal involving improper soliciting of public officials by a businessman, so as to save embarrassment to the President and his party and despite the President's public avowal of his full confidence in him.

Aden. ⇨ South Yemen, People's Republic of.

Adenauer, Konrad (1876–1967). First Chancellor of the ⇨ German Federal Republic (1949–63), founder and leader of the Christian Democratic Union ⇨ CDU, Germany's largest party. Mayor of Cologne and speaker of the Prussian Diet in the ⇨ Weimar era, he was dismissed by the Nazis (1933) and imprisoned after the 20 July plot (1944). Reinstated and then removed as mayor of Cologne by the British, he founded the CDU (1945) and as its leader became on a majority of one vote the first Chancellor of the newly-established Federal Republic (Sept. 1949). Re-elected in 1953, 1957 and 1961, he not only initiated Germany's spectacular economic recovery but, departing from the traditional patterns of German policies, also committed her unequivocally to the West, joining the abortive EDC (1952), ⇨ NATO (1955) and the ⇨ EEC (1957). This uncompromising Western alignment, critics alleged, deepened the division of Germany and vitiated relations with her Eastern neighbours. A life-long advocate of Franco-German reconciliation, Adenauer regarded the conclusion of the Franco-German friendship treaty (1963) as one of his crowning achievements. He resigned his chancellorship (Oct. 1963) and his party leadership (1966) to be succeeded in both by Professor ⇨ Erhard.

AEC. United States Atomic Energy Commission – an ⇨ Independent Agency set up under the 1946 Atomic Energy Act to administer the Federal Government monopoly in the development of atomic energy. The Commission was established to ensure civil rather than military control of the nuclear programme; its five commissioners are appointed by the President with the consent of the ⇨ Senate for five years each, and its operations are continuously reviewed by a joint ⇨ Congressional Committee. The AEC has been responsible both for the development of the US nuclear arsenal, and peaceful uses of atomic energy in the USA and friendly foreign countries under the ⇨ 'Atoms for Peace' programme. The 1954 Atomic Energy Act went some way to ending the government monopoly, empowering the AEC to license private enterprises and permitting the latter to patent inventions. The 1964 Act went still further, envisaging that in future the function of the AEC will be to regulate but not operate the industrial atomic energy programme of the USA. A number of nuclear power stations were licensed, but their operations have been increasingly criticized as infringing standards laid down in recent environment-protection legislation.

Afghanistan. *Area* – 250,000 sq. miles. *Population* (1969 est.) – 16,516,000. *Head of State* – King Mohammad Zahir Shah (1933–). *Prime Minister* – Dr Abdul Zahir (1971–). *Constitution* (1964) – Constitutional monarchy with a bicameral Legislature of a House of the People elected for four years by universal suffrage and House of Elders whose members are partly nominated by the King and by the provisional councils and elected by the residents of each province. The Prime Minister and Cabinet are responsible to the Legislature. Each of the 28 provinces has its own Legislature and Executive, which are directly responsible to the Ministry of the Interior.

A buffer state between British India and Russia. Afghanistan was under British influence until the UK recognized her independence in 1919. During the 1920s the rulers (who changed their title from Emir to King in 1926) began a process of modernization of the country including economic and social reforms, but this Westernization policy, influenced by the example of Kemal ⇨ Ataturk, e.g. monogamy, European clothing and the emancipation of women, led to a revolt by the Mullahs, the Moslem clergy, in 1929 and the resignation of King Amanullah. The policy of modernization continued under Mohammad Nadir Shah, who was assassinated in 1933, and his successor, Mohammad Zahir Shah, who has ruled since then. Until 1963 the King had virtually unlimited powers particularly as the Prime Minister was chosen from his family. Daoud was replaced in that year by M. Yussuf, the first non-royal head of government, and this was followed in 1964 by a new constitution establishing a constitutional monarchy. The first elections were held in 1965 but voting was by personal choice of candidate although the formation of parties is allowed. Afghanistan has followed a neutralist course, remaining uncommitted in World War II, and has accepted economic aid from both the West and the East. Relations with the USA (aid since 1951 and visit of the US President 1959), the USSR (aid since 1955 and extension of the Neutrality Treaty in 1965), China (Friendship and Economic Agreement 1960 and boundary agreement 1963) and India (Friendship Treaty 1950) have been generally good. Only with Pakistan have relations been soured over a border dispute since 1947. Afghanistan claims 'Pakhtunistan', the territory in West Pakistan west of the river Indus and down to the Arabian Sea and has been supported by India and the USSR in her claim.

Aflaq, Michel (1910–). One of the leaders of the Syrian radical movement. In 1943 he established his own left-wing nationalist group, the *Ba'ath*, of which for many years he was the chief ideologist. Aflaq was Secretary-General of the ⇨ *Ba'ath* Party until 1965 and wrote a book on its history and ideology. During the period preceding the federation of Egypt and Syria (⇨United Arab Republic), Aflaq supported the idea of negotiating with Nasser 'on equal terms'. Aflaq was arrested in Feb. 1966 after the left-wing *Ba'athist* Party came to power. He subsequently emigrated to South America, but later returned to Iraq and Lebanon.

AFL–CIO. American Federation of Labor and Congress of Industrial Organizations – Trade union organization in the USA and Canada, formed by the merger of the AF of L and the CIO in 1955. The former was founded in 1881 by representatives of craft unions, and it continued primarily to represent the interests of craft workers into recent times. In 1936 the CIO, which had been formed within it the previous year to represent the interests of general industry-wide unions, was expelled, and there followed a period of inter-union conflict. The AF of L was more conservative on matters of union organization and relations than the CIO, and this was reflected in its more cautious dealings with the ⇨ Democratic Party and its refusal to join the World Federation of Trade Unions. With the passage of the ⇨Taft-Hartley Act in 1947 and the advent of a Republican Administration in 1952, reasons for co-operation became stronger. When the two organizations merged in 1955, AF of L President George ⇨ Meany became President of the combined body, whilst CIO President Walter ⇨Reuther became head of the section comprising all the industrial unions participating. The combined membership was then about 16 million, more than 9½ million having been members of the AF of L; but membership has since declined to about 13 million, and is still declining, despite a continuing increase in the working population. This is said to be due to America's having entered a 'post-industrial age'. However, the AFL–CIO remains one of the most powerful associations in American public life. It maintains an influential ⇨ Lobby in Washington, and is often called upon to give evidence before ⇨ Congressional Committees and advice to the Administration. It opposed President ⇨ Nixon's 'new economic policy', introduced in Aug., 1971, including the ninety-day wage-price-rent freeze. And though it at first co-operated in 'Phase II' of the policy, begun Dec. 1971, its representatives on the President's Pay Board, which had been instituted at Meany's suggestion, resigned in Mar. 1972, declaring that the Board offered 'no hope for fairness, equity or justice' to labour. The leadership also came into conflict with Democratic presidential nominee, George ⇨ McGovern, at the convention in July 1972, and, in a most unusual action, declined to endorse the Democratic candidate.

Africa. See references to specific territories.

African National Congress. ⇨ ANC.

Afro-Asian Conference. ⇨ Bandung Conference.

Afro-Asian People's Solidarity Organization. ⇨ AAPSO.

Agnew, Spiro T. (1918–). Vice-President of the USA (1969–). Of Greek-American extraction, he attended Johns Hopkins University and obtained his law degree from the University of Baltimore. He was elected Governor of Maryland on the Republican ticket in 1966, and although he gained a considerable local reputation for his conduct of the office, he was virtually unknown to most Americans when he was chosen by Richard ⇨ Nixon as his Vice-Presidential running-mate in the 1968 elections. As Vice-President, he gained a reputation rather different from the one he had previously enjoyed in his own State. In his distinctive alliterative style, he attacked all opponents of the Administration, from the Press to anti-war demonstrators, generating still more opposition in the process. He proved something of an embarrassment to the President during the 1970 mid-term Congressional elections and it was widely thought that he would not be the Vice-Presidential candidate again in 1972. The President, however, continued to support him, and he was nominated and held office for a second term.

'Agonizing Reappraisal'. Threat of a possible shift in the foreign and defence policies of the USA made by Secretary of State John Foster ⇨ Dulles at the NATO Council session in Paris (14.10.1954) to encourage speedy French ratification of the EDC ⇨ treaty. In fact, no significant changes followed French rejection of the treaty, and the threat can be regarded as an instance of Dulles' rhetoric, another example being ▷ 'Rollback'.

Agrément. Formal acceptance of a foreign country's diplomatic representative who thereby becomes *persona grata*.

AID. United States Agency for International Development – an agency within the ▷ State Department established in 1961 to replace the ▷ ICA and to administer the ▷ Development Loan Fund. It is responsible for the non-military aspects of the ▷ Mutual Security Program, and also co-ordinates military assistance programmes implemented by the ▷ Defense Department. In administering economic and technical aid, the Agency seeks to promote the social advance and political stability of the countries receiving assistance, in support of defence and security requirements.

Aitken. ▷ Beaverbrook, Lord.

Ajman. ▷ Trucial States.

Albania, People's Republic of. *Area* – 11,101 sq. miles. *Population* (1969) – 2,079,800. *Chairman*, Presidium of the People's Assembly – Haxhi Lieshi. *Prime Minister* – Mehmet Shehu. *First Secretary*, Albanian Workers' Party – Enver ▷ Hoxha. The highest organ of state power is the uni-cameral People's Assembly elected by universal suffrage from a single list of candidates. Effective power is concentrated in the leadership of the (communist) Albanian Workers' Party, headed by its First Secretary, Enver Hoxha.

The smallest communist country, Albania was for several years in the centre of the controversies sparked off by the ▷ Sino-Soviet Conflict. Apart from ▷ Yugoslavia, it is the only communist country in Europe ruled by a regime which does not owe its power to the Soviet armies.

Dominated in the inter-war period by tribal chieftains and landowning beys, Albania was an object of prolonged dispute between Italy, Greece and Yugoslavia. On 7 April 1939, Mussolini annexed Albania, and during World War II a resistance movement developed in the country. It was led by communist intellectuals who had been educated abroad and who founded (Nov. 1941) the Albanian Communist Party, renamed Albanian Workers' Party (1948). In consultation with the communist partisan movements in ▷ Yugoslavia and ▷ Greece, they founded a National Liberation Front LNC (Sept. 1942), which organized guerrilla war against the Italians. After Mussolini's fall (1943), the LNC attracted widespread popular support and succeeded in liberating most of Albania. In Sept. German troops occupied the country, but, after initial setbacks, the LNC successfully fought back. In 1944, they followed ▷ Tito's example in setting up a provisional government headed by

Enver Hoxha. Under growing pressure on other fronts, the Germans evacuated Albania in the autumn of 1944, leaving Enver Hoxha in control. After the war, Albania was proclaimed a People's Republic, with close economic, political and military links with Yugoslavia. Hoxha increasingly regarded this association as a form of dependence, aggravated by the existence of a sizeable Albanian minority in Yugoslavia. He used the occasion of Tito's expulsion from the ⇨Cominform to break off relations and has ever since denounced the Yugoslav communists as his country's worst enemies. He purged the Workers' Party of all suspected sympathizers with Yugoslavia, including his principal rival, Koci Xoxe, Vice-Premier and Minister of the Interior, who was executed (June 1949).

Relations with the USSR deteriorated as a result of ⇨Khrushchev's reconciliation with Tito and his subsequent denunciation of ⇨Stalin. This emerged at the Bucharest conference of communist parties in June 1960, when only the Albanians sided with ⇨China against the USSR, and at the larger Moscow conference in Nov. 1960, when Hoxha delivered a bitter personal attack on Khrushchev. In the spring of 1961, Albania secured a Chinese economic aid agreement, which, repeatedly renewed and extended, has helped to sustain Albania ever since. At the 22nd CPSU Congress (Oct. 1961), Khrushchev for the first time attacked Albania publicly, followed by similar attacks from foreign communist delegations and strong protests against such attacks from ⇨ Chou En-lai. Most of the many subsequent Soviet polemics against Albania were in fact indirect attacks on China, while Albania, for a time, served as a public mouthpiece for Chinese views until China and the USSR began to engage in direct polemics. Albania itself was, at the same time, subjected to a sharp Soviet campaign of revenge, complete with the cancellation of all aid agreements, severe economic sanctions and a breach in diplomatic relations, reminiscent of Stalin's campaign against Yugoslavia in the late 1940s. Though not formally expelled, Albania has since 1961 been excluded from both ⇨CMEA and the ⇨Warsaw Pact and has ever since then lived in total political isolation as China's lonely outpost in Europe. Some of the European communist countries re-established bi-lateral trade and diplomatic relations with Albania in the mid-1960s. Albanian-Soviet relations reached a new low after the invasion of ⇨ Czechoslovakia when Albania, as a gesture of protest, formally withdrew from the Warsaw Pact (12.9.1968). The intervention in Czechoslovakia caused Albania also to normalize its relations with Yugoslavia.

Aldermaston. ⇨CND.

Algeria. *Area* – 850,000 sq. miles. *Population* (1970 est.) – 13,547,000.

Prime Minister – Col. Houari ⇨ Boumedienne (1965–). *Constitution* (1963) – A one-party state with an executive President and a uni-cameral National Assembly. The functions of the President are (since June 1965) exercised by Boumedienne's Revolutionary Council.

Algiers, a French colony from the mid-nineteenth century, was unaffected by nationalist movements until well after the First World War. Messali Hadj's *Parti Populaire Algérien* (PPA), founded in 1936, called for total independence from France and the establishment of a socialist government, whereas Ferhat ⇨ Abbas' Federation of Muslim Councillors, founded in 1930, presented a platform of complete integration into France for Algerians. Encouraged by the latter the ⇨ Popular Front proposed the Blum-Viollette Plan (1936) to enfranchise certain small groups of Muslims, but *colon* (settler) intransigence forced the plan to be dropped, encouraging the growth of the PPA. The fall of France put a halt to reform movements but after the 1942 Allied landings Abbas urged reforms as promised in the ⇨ Atlantic Charter. The Free French administration's rejection of his Manifesto of the Algerian People (1943) and later proposals for an independent Algerian state were followed by the enactment of a Statute for Algeria (March 1944) – merely a revived Blum-Viollette plan. This failure to grant any measure of independence led to the savagely repressed Sétif riots (May 1945) in which well over 2,000 Muslims died. As a result, despite electoral success (March 1946), Abbas' moderate Democratic Union of the Algerian Manifesto (UDMA) gave way to Hadj's radical Movement for the Triumph of Democratic Liberties (MTLD). A new statute was enacted in 1947 giving full French citizenship to Muslims, but the separation of Europeans and Muslims into different electoral colleges, vote-rigging, etc. rendered the statute ineffective and the MTLD powerless. Hence the National Liberation Army (ALN) of the Cairo-based National Liberation Front (⇨FLN) invaded Algeria and was soon active throughout the country. 400,000 French troops failed to stop the increasingly savage war, although reprisals (1957) involving the torture and internment of Muslims forced the ALN to abandon city terrorism. The continued intransigence of the *colons* and their strong lobby in France, together with the FLN's refusal to negotiate after ⇨Ben Bella's arrest (Oct. 1956), led to a stalemate. In France ⇨Mollet fell (May 1957) and the *Bourgès-Maunoury* reform proposals were rejected. In Algeria paratroopers under General ⇨Salan seized power (22.4.1961) and the settlers' hurriedly-formed Committee of Public Safety, supported by Jacques ⇨ Soustelle, demanded the return of General ⇨ de Gaulle with emergency powers. Though de Gaulle's success (4.10.1958) was followed by his call for a 'peace of the brave', the war continued, despite both General Challe's successes (early 1960) and the ALN's heavy losses. Growing war-weariness and opposition at home and abroad prompted de Gaulle to put settlement proposals to a referendum (Nov. 1960). The abstention of 50% of the electorate finally persuaded him to negotiate directly with the FLN from May 1961. A cease-fire and settlement were completed at Evian on 18 March 1962. *Colon* hostility to any such settlement had already expressed itself after an unsuccessful army revolt (21.4.1961) in the formation of the *Organisation de l'Armée Secrète* (⇨OAS) which, by violent raids, tried unsuccessfully to goad the FLN into breaking the cease-fire. A referendum (1.7.1962) showed 91% in favour of independence which was declared on 3 July 1962. The accession to power of the FLN provisional government (GPRA), led by Ben Khedda, was followed by a party split and the seizure of power by Ben Bella who, having himself elected President, suppressed all opposition and introduced a new constitution. His major problem was the economic chaos caused by the departure of 80% (800,000) of the European population. Large-scale aid was forthcoming from China, Russia, America and above all France, whilst nationalization and the requisitioning of property left by the French (in contradiction to the Evian agreement) were enforced as part of Algeria's socialisation plan. After border disputes and an open clash with ⇨Morocco (Oct. 1963) a settlement was reached and Ben Bella was able to concentrate on improving Algeria's standing in the ⇨Third World especially in view of the forthcoming Afro-Asian Conference in Algiers (26.9.1965). It was indefinitely postponed, however, by Ben Bella's deposition in a bloodless coup (19.6.1965) led by Boumedienne. Since the coup, long-term agreements, particularly for the exploitation of Algeria's oil and natural gas, have been negotiated with France. Ties with Russia have been strengthened. Boumedienne's three visits to the USSR and his visits to Cairo were coupled with his efforts for Arab unity, emphasized by Algeria's declaration of war on Israel (5.6.1967).

Algiers Conference of Afro-Asian States. ⇨ Bandung Conference.

Alliance for Progress. *Alianza para el Progreso* – established 1961 at a meeting of 20 American countries at Punta del Este (Uruguay). The Alliance aimed at encouraging economic and social development, with American aid providing funds for the implementation of necessary social reform, e.g. land redistribution, fairer division of wealth, assistance in programmes of literacy, and at 'accelerating the integration of Latin America'. Despite the financial resources of the United States Agency for International Development (⇨ AID) the political and economic realities of Latin America have presented severe obstacles to the

achievement of the Alliance's programme. Its opponents have con-
demned it as another example of Yankee imperialism in the Cold War
context. Envisaged by some as a form of 'Marshall Aid for South
America', the relative absence of reformist but democratic governments
in Latin America is an indication of the difficulties faced by the Alliance.
Its members are: Argentina, Barbados, Bolivia, Brazil, Chile, Colombia,
Costa Rica, Dominican Republic, Ecuador, El Salvador, Guatemala,
Haiti, Honduras, Mexico, Nicaragua, Panama, Paraguay, Peru,
Trinidad and Tobago, USA, Uruguay, Venezuela.

Allon, Brig.-Gen. Yigal (1918–). Deputy Prime Minister and Minister
of Education of Israel (July 1968–), Minister of Labour (1961–69). A
former Secretary-General of the *Achduth Ha-avodah* (Socialist Party),
he entered the *Knesset* after a distinguished military career, having been
C.-in-C. of *Palmach* shock troops (1945–48).

Amer, Field-Marshal Abdel Hakim (1919–67). C.-in-C. of the Joint
Arab Forces (1964–67) and until his arrest (Sept. 1967) ⇨UAR head of
the UAR Armed Forces. A close friend and collaborator of ⇨ Nasser,
dating back to the Free Officers' Association and Officers' Coup of
1952, he was accused in *Al Ahram* of plotting Nasser's overthrow,
arrested and his suicide announced later.

**American Federation of Labor and Congress of Industrial
Organizations.** ⇨AFL–CIO.

American Legion. Largest ex-servicemen's organization in the USA
with between two-and-a-half and three million members, and more
inclusive than ⇨VFW. Apart from promoting veterans' special interests,
it gives evidence before ⇨Congressional Committees on matters affecting the internal and national security of the USA. It adopts a generally
conservative position.

American Samoa. *Area* – 76 sq. miles. *Population* (1970) – 27,769. An
unincorporated territory of the USA, the eastern section of the Samoan
Islands is administered by the US Department of the Interior through
the Governor. The Legislature, consisting of two houses, has limited
law-making powers.

Amin, General Idi. President of ⇨ Uganda (1971–).

Amri, General Hassan (*c.* 1916–). Prime Minister of the ⇨ Yemen
1965, 1965–66 and 1967–69. He took part in the revolution of 1962, held
various Cabinet appointments and was Vice-President from 1963–66.
Re-elected Prime Minister in Aug. 1971, he failed to form a Cabinet and
was exiled on 1 Sept. after killing a photographer in an argument.

Anarchism. A radical political philosophy which sees state authority as
the chief obstacle to freedom and aims, therefore, at its abolition.
Anarchists, divided among themselves as to how this is to be achieved,

are also divided on the question of the type of property relations that should be established in a future stateless society. Anarchist aims have themselves inhibited effective political organization and they have wielded little influence or power compared to other radical movements. However, anarchist influences have been noticeable in the development of the ⇨ New Left and student protest movements in Western Europe and the USA.

ANC. African National Congress – the oldest non-White political organization in ⇨ South Africa (founded 1912), it was banned in 1960 after ⇨ Sharpeville. Its leaders have included Chief Albert ⇨ Luthuli and Nelson Mandela (⇨ Treason Trials). It was committed to the creation of a multi-racial society and welcomed the alliance of White liberals. Following the suppression of the Communist Party and the South African Government's spate of discriminatory legislation (⇨ *Apartheid*) and in danger of losing members to more militant African nationalist groups, it was itself forced to adopt more radical policies in later years. Its leaders in exile, in alliance with other exiled South African political organizations, have continued to draw attention to political repression in South Africa.

Andean Development Corporation. ⇨ LAFTA.

ANF. Atlantic Nuclear Force – a British-sponsored scheme (Dec. 1964) for a NATO-controlled nuclear deterrent in lieu of the American-backed Multilateral Force (⇨ MLF) which had failed to gain general acceptance. Under the ANF plan NATO members were to assign part of their atomic weapons, delivery systems and operating crews to an independent NATO-controlled force, thus overcoming the existing NATO dependence on American nuclear power – and the concomitant American veto on its development – without giving Germany or Germans control over atomic weapons. Although not formally rejected, the scheme was abandoned.

Anglo-Egyptian Sudan. ⇨ Sudan.

Anglo-German Naval Treaty, 1935. Allowed Germany to build a fleet up to 35% of the strength of the British navy and submarines up to 45% of British submarine strength. Although a limitation on naval arms, it was regarded with its recognition of Germany's rearmament as an open repudiation of the Treaty of Versailles.

Angola. ⇨ Portuguese Overseas Provinces.

Ankrah, General J. A. (1915–). Leader of the National Liberation Committee and President of ⇨ Ghana (1966–69). A distinguished soldier (World War II and with UN forces in the Congo) he was dismissed by Dr ⇨ Nkrumah (July 1965). He led the successful military coup against Nkrumah and ruled the country through a National

Liberation Committee. In 1969 a new constitution took effect and a civilian government was elected.

Anschluss. Union of the two German-speaking states of ⇨Austria and Germany. Forbidden by the Allies after World War 1 (and even in an economic form by France in 1931) it was carried out by Hitler and his Austrian *Gauleiter* Seyss-Inquart in March 1938 and apparently received wide popular support in both countries (⇨Schuschnigg).

Anti-Comintern Pact. Agreement concluded (Nov. 1936) between Germany and Japan for the ostensible purpose of combating international communism. Italy joined the Pact in Nov. 1937. The Anti-Comintern Pact was the forerunner to the military ⇨Tripartite Pact concluded Sept. 1940. (⇨Hitler-Stalin Pact.)

Anti-Hitler Plot. ⇨Twentieth July.

Anti-Party Group. Term applied in the USSR to a number of top-ranking communist party leaders, headed by ⇨Malenkov, ⇨Kaganovich and ⇨Molotov, who made an abortive attempt at ousting N. S. ⇨Khrushchev from the party leadership (June 1957). According to subsequent revelations, the 'anti-party group' also included N. A. ⇨Bulganin and K. E. ⇨Voroshilov.

Anti-Poverty Program. General title for a series of Federal Government measures aimed at eliminating the causes and effects of poverty in the USA. The programme was initiated by President ⇨Kennedy as an important aspect of his 'New Frontier', and was extended by President ⇨Johnson who proclaimed a 'War on Poverty' as part of his vision of a 'Great Society'. Major Acts were passed by ⇨Congress in the early 1960s, to deal with the location of industry, regional development, technical training, and other matters affecting poverty, and increasing funds were voted for the programme. Particularly noteworthy was the Economic Opportunity Act of 1964, which sought to deal with the problem of providing those most affected by it with the means to overcome it for themselves. The Office of Economic Opportunity was established within the ⇨Executive Office of the President to co-ordinate the programme, and Sargent Shriver, director of the ⇨Peace Corps, was appointed by the President to head it. Under his leadership, ⇨VISTA was organized as a 'domestic peace corps' working in the most impoverished areas of the United States. Further measures were introduced to deal with education and housing problems among the poor, and with the special problems of rural poverty. In the later 1960s, due largely to the mounting cost of the Vietnam War, additional funds for the poverty programme were not so readily voted. Moreover, a substantial proportion of the funds that were voted appeared to be 'lost' before reaching those they were intended to benefit. As the impetus of the programme diminished, disappointment with its achievements grew. This feeling, especially among Negroes who constituted so large a proportion of the poor, may have contributed to the trend towards greater political militancy during this period, exemplified by the ⊳Black Power movement and the increasingly violent opposition of the ⊳New Left to American involvement in Vietnam.

Anti-semitism. Hostility towards or hatred of Jews. The term although a misnomer – it is a political force in the Arab world today – indicates the important nineteenth-century transition from religious to racial persecution of Jews. From the turn of the century onwards, the racial concept put forward by the French Count Gobineau and a Germanized Englishman, Houston Stewart Chamberlain, prefigured Nazi and similar ideologies. Based on supposedly 'genetic characteristics', modern anti-semitism offered its victims no escape by recantation or conversion. Anti-semites identified 'the Jew' with their respective national enemy; to the French (Dreyfus Affair) he was pro-German, to the German he was a Francophile before World War I and a Bolshevik afterwards, while to the Soviet establishment he became a 'cosmopolitan Zionist' in league with the forces of imperialism. Nourished by powerful irrational forces and the allegedly dominant role of Jews in economic life, anti-semitism flourished despite the obvious contradictions in its mythology. A forgery concocted by Tsarist police, *The Protocols of the Elders of Zion*, purporting to reveal a Jewish conspiracy to enslave the world, won widespread attention. Published in Russia to divert attention from the 1905 military defeat (Russian-Japanese War) and social unrest, the *Protocols* were an almost literal translation of a political satire against Napoleon III, i.e. M. Joly's *Dialogues aux enfers entre Machiavell et Montesquieu*, Brussels 1864. They reached the West in the wake of the 1917 Russian revolution and, although a transparent forgery, were and still are widely believed. Hitler was greatly impressed by them.

As the source of Nazi ideology, anti-semitism reached a terrible climax in Hitler's Germany and the countries under Nazi occupation. The process of legal discrimination, degradation, segregation, spoliation, etc. (⊳Nuremberg Laws, ⊳Crystal Night, ⊳Holocaust), culminated in the slaughter of six million Jews. Anti-semitism as a political weapon has recently been revived in Eastern Europe in the guise of anti-Zionism and Jewish bourgeois cosmopolitanism. In parts of the Arab and Moslem worlds, the mythology of the Protocols has been resurrected in anti-Israeli propaganda.

One of the justifications of religious anti-semitism was removed when the Vatican Council II (Oct. 1965) formally absolved the Jews from the charge of 'deicide'. Anti-semitism gave rise to the Zionist movement, and powerfully affects Israeli attitudes.

Antonescu, General. ⇨ Rumania.

ANZUS Treaty. Security treaty signed by Australia, New Zealand and the USA at San Francisco (1951) to co-ordinate defence against armed attack in the Pacific. Each party recognized that an attack on the other parties would threaten its own peace and safety and agreed to develop their capacity to resist attack by 'continuous self-help and mutual aid'. This was the first step to a more comprehensive system of regional security in the Pacific, further developed by the formation of SEATO in 1954. It also represented a reorientation in defence policy by Australia and New Zealand towards the USA and away from the UK.

Apartheid. (Afrikaans – Apartness). South African doctrine and practice of racial segregation, first propounded in the victorious 1948 election campaign of Dr ⇨ Malan's ⇨ National Party. Although segregation had long been accepted political practice in ⇨ South Africa (by a predominantly White electorate (⇨ Smuts, ⇨ Hertzog)), the Nationalists claimed that only their concept of *Apartheid* could ensure the future of 'White civilization' in South Africa. Its supporters claimed that *Apartheid* was based not on repression, but on a sense of trusteeship for the African (Bantu) population allowing for their separate development along their own lines. It envisaged the creation of separate, closed, racial societies in South Africa as sanctioned, according to Dutch Reformed Church spokesmen, by Christian precept and the scriptures. In practice – with the South African economy dependent on Black labour, and with 70% of the land reserved for White (12% of the population) occupation – all internal opposition to 'White supremacy' has been suppressed and the Africans' role as a disenfranchised politically powerless labour force has been 'legally' endorsed. The outline of the South African political and economic structure can be discerned in the spate of discriminatory legislation enacted under Nationalist Premiers (Malan, ⇨ Strijdom, ⇨ Verwoerd, ⇨ Vorster) since 1948: e.g. the Prohibition of Mixed Marriages Act (1949), the Suppression of Communism Act (1950) – so broadly defining communism as to make opposition to the government illegal, the Group Areas Act (1950), the General Law Amendment Act (the Ninety Day Law) (1963) – giving the police the right of arbitrary arrest and the right to hold suspects in solitary confinement without recourse to the courts. *Apartheid* doctrine, particularly as put forward by Verwoerd and Vorster, envisaged (as an answer to its critics, including the UN) a programme of separate development, creating self-governing African states (*Bantustans*) in South Africa. However, the provisions for the administration of the first *Bantustan*, 'The Transkei', with power in the hands of the chiefs and close government supervision, indicate a very limited 'independence'. Their real creation would require substantial funds (voted by the White electorate elsewhere) for their development. The *Verligtes* (⇨ National Party) have argued that petty discrimination which exacerbates African ill-will should be replaced by a positive *Apartheid* that benefits the non-Whites. However, the heart of the doctrine with its '*Herrenvolk*' ideology of necessity makes justice for the individual dependent on his race (as defined by the government).

Appeasement. Conceding territories, preferably of other nations, and/or shirking treaty obligations in the hope of placating a hostile power and avoiding war. The term acquired this derogatory meaning in the thirties when nations and principles were sacrificed in the hope of buying off the dictators, particularly ⇨ Hitler. The dismemberment of Czechoslovakia (29.9.1938) under the ⇨ Munich Agreement has come to be regarded as the prototype of the dishonesty and the futility inherent in appeasement policies. Reference to these 'discredited policies' has been used to justify firmness in supposedly, although not actually, similar confrontations (⇨ Suez, ⇨ Korea, ⇨ Vietnam).

Appropriation. Procedure whereby the United States Congress in legislation involving government funds must first pass the legislation and then in a separate process approve the allocation of the necessary funds. Where insufficient funds are made available this process can weaken already enacted legislation.

APRA (⇨ Peru). *Alianza Popular Revolucionaria Americana* (also referred to as *Partido Aprista*), founded in 1924 by the exiled leader ⇨ Haya de la Torre. The party was outlawed from 1931 to 1945 and again from 1948 until 1956. Though influenced by Marxism and nationalism (especially in its early years, advocating the political and economic emancipation of the Indian *indigenistas*), as is and was the case with other Latin American political parties (e.g. *Peronistas* in ⇨ Argentina or ⇨ MNR in ⇨ Bolivia), comparison with European political parties can be misleading and it is best understood as a response to specific South American conditions. For its members APRA constitutes a state within the state with its own student, professional and sporting associations and even its own welfare schemes and community centres. The prestige of its leader has cemeneted loyalties, but there have been splits and internal political differences. From 1945 until 1948 *Aprista* factions opposed Bustamante despite earlier electoral agreements. In the elections of 1962 and 1963 Haya de la Torre seemed less concerned with revolution than with allaying the fears of a growing middle class.

Arab-Israeli Conflict (1948–68). The onset of World War II temporarily arrested the conflict between Arab and Jew in Palestine. It was violently resumed after 1945, escalating into open warfare in the chaotic period following Britain's announcement (April 1947) of her determination to relinquish the Mandate in 1948. The Arab states, totally opposed to the creation of a Jewish state, rejected the UN Partition Plan (29.11.1947). King ⇨ Abdullah of Trans-Jordan, with British connivance, intended to take over part of the proposed Palestinian State (i.e. the West Bank of the Jordan). The Egyptian government was forced into a war-like stance both through internal pressures and anxiety about Abdullah's territorial ambitions. With the proclamation of the State of ⇨ Israel and the termination of the British Mandate (14/15.5.1948), Palestine was invaded by the Egyptian army in the south, the armies of ⇨ Syria and ⇨ Lebanon in the north and the Trans-Jordanian Arab Legion in the east. The war was fought at company level – the Israelis lacked the resources for larger engagements while the Arabs (except for the Arab Legion) were deficient in organization and military leadership. While the Israeli forces (*Haganah* and *Palmach* shock troops) blocked advancing Egyptian and Syrian units, they could not prevent the Arab Legion from establishing control of the West Bank of the Jordan and the old city of Jerusalem. Both sides welcomed the truce (11.6.1948).

With the renewal of hostilities (9.7.1948), though interrupted by further truces, the *Haganah* (strengthened by the purchase of arms from Czechoslovakia) was transformed into an efficient army, and was able to go over to the attack, so that by March 1949, Israel was a unified state, with the Negev secured as well as the port of Eilat in the Straits of Tiran. UN-supervised armistice agreements were signed between Israel and Egypt (24.2.1949), Trans-Jordan (3.4.1949) and Syria (20.7.1949). Jordan formally annexed the West Bank (April 1950).

Ironically, the war produced opposite results from those intended by the invading Arab states. The new State of Israel, and its sense of nationhood, were strengthened not weakened by the experience of war. The Israeli Defence Forces, utilizing that experience, developed into the most effective military force in the area. Israeli territory was extended beyond the area envisaged in the UN partition resolutions, and the war (together with the Jordanian annexations) also prevented the formation of an independent Arab Palestinian state as envisaged in the resolutions. One legacy of the war was the continuing tragedy of the Arab refugees.

The armistice lines did not imply recognition of Israel by her neighbours and difficult to defend and easy to infiltrate, they contained the germs of future conflict.

The continued harassment of Israeli settlements by Egyptian-supported *fedayeen*, especially from 1955, provided the occasion for the next clash. Though a state of belligerency had existed, trade with Israel including firms trading with her was boycotted by Arab states, and from 1953 an Egyptian blockade on Israel-bound shipping through Suez restricted commerce to the port of Eilat. On 29 Oct. 1956 this conflict between Egypt and Israel was complicated by collusion between the UK, France and Israel (⇨ Suez Crisis). Although Israel had the advantage of powerful allies and their air-cover, nevertheless the speed of the Israeli advance – overrunning the Sinai peninsula in six days – demonstrated the superiority of their forces.

As a result of UN pressure, UNEF (United Nations Emergency Force) was established on Egyptian territories and Israel subsequently withdrew, although freedom of navigation to Eilat was assured.

The effect of the Sinai campaign on Arab-Israeli relations (the whole Suez crisis had far wider repercussions) can be briefly analysed: from Israel's point of view, 1) Israel's immediate aim of securing her frontiers with Egypt and preventing *fedayeen* invasion was obtained; 2) she incurred the odium of world opinion through her collusion with France and Britain – and provided the Egyptians with an alibi for their defeat. From Egypt's point of view – despite defeat, Nasser and the Egyptian Government emerged with enhanced reputations; Nasser was regarded as the hero of the Arab world's struggle against imperialism and the diplomatic victory strengthened Nasserism throughout the Middle East. However, it also marked an increasing dependence on the Soviet Union whose encroachment in the area has complicated inter-Arab and Arab-Israeli relations. From 1957 to 1965, although armed clashes occurred between Arabs and Israelis, these were mainly confined to the Syrian/Israeli border. Syria confirmed her reputation as the most openly anti-Israeli and intransigent of the Arab states, all of whom reiterated their opposition to Israel. It seemed to be accepted, especially in Egypt, that another war, though inevitable, could only take place at some future date when the Arabs had become strong enough to be assured of victory. Thus, at the 1964 Cairo Conference the Arabs expressed their opposition to Israel's use of the Jordan Waters for irrigation schemes. Although attempts were made to set up an Arab Unified High Command and to mobilize Palestinians through the PLO (Palestine Liberation Organization) and the PLA (Palestine Liberation Army), the defeat of Israel was seen as a long-term aim. From 1965 onwards incidents were on the increase and mainly Syrian-inspired. There were severe Israeli reprisals, particularly on the Jordan village of Samu (13.11.1966), and in April 1967 six Syrian fighter aircraft were shot down by the Israeli air-force. However, it is not possible to establish precisely why or when the Arab states and particularly Nasser decided that the military balance had swung in their favour and that a direct confrontation was possible, nor is it possible to know the precise role played by Egypt's ally the USSR in escalating the conflict. In May 1967, Israel's Prime Minister and the C.-in-C. of the armed forces warned Syria of the dangerous consequences of their continued aggression. In the events that followed, Nasser claimed (after the war) that he had not envisaged aggressive action but had merely come to the assistance of his ally Syria. However, his speeches at that time and statements in the Egyptian press indicate that Nasser apparently believed that an Arab victory was now possible (e.g. Nasser's speeches to UAR air-force (25.5.1967), to Arab trade unions (26.5.1967), press statement (28.5.1967), speech to National Assembly (29.5.1967), and in addition an *Al Ahram* article (26.5.1967) stating that an armed clash with Israel was inevitable). Egypt claimed that it had been informed by the USSR of an Israel troop build-up threatening Syria. However, UNTSO observers denied (18.5.1967) the existence of a large Israeli build-up and the Russian ambassador did not avail himself of Premier ⇨ Eshkol's invitation to visit the areas in the north of Israel and see for himself that such troop movements were not taking place. In May (16/17) a state of emergency was proclaimed in Egypt and her forces mobilized. As the situation developed and UNEF was withdrawn (19 May) at Egypt's request, with Nasser's prestige soaring and claims that the destruction of Israel was at hand, it is possible that events generated a momentum which Egypt was either unwilling or unable to control. There was a rapid build-up of UAR forces (80–100,000) in Sinai and on 23 May Egypt announced that Sharm el Sheikh had been closed to Israeli shipping and on 24 May that the Straits had been mined. Arab states announced their support for Egypt's actions and on 30 May King Hussein, until shortly before the subject of violent Egyptian invective, was welcomed in Cairo and a mutual defence pact between Jordan and the UAR signed. Israel's Foreign Minister Eban's diplomatic activity failed to produce the assurance either for the Israeli Government or Israeli public opinion that Israel's right of passage in the Straits of Tiran would be internationally guaranteed. Under pressure of public opinion General ⇨ Dayan was appointed Minister of Defence in a Government of National

Unity (1 June). With each succeeding day the Arab position grew stronger and Israeli military opinion (at least until Dayan's appointment) feared that the indecision of the politicians threatened Israel's survival. The Six Day War began on 5 June with Israeli air attacks on Arab air-fields in Egypt, Syria, Jordan and as far afield as Iraq. The Arab air-forces were virtually destroyed on the ground, later resulting in unfounded Arab charges of Anglo-US collusion. The success of the air attacks destroyed the possibility of an Arab victory. Israeli forces advanced rapidly to the Suez Canal (7 June), completely destroying the Egyptian armour on the way. Following Jordanian intervention, Israeli forces successfully occupied the West Bank of the Jordan and the old city of Jerusalem (7 June). On the final day of the war (9 June) Israeli forces captured the Golan Heights in Syria, capturing Kuneitra, and advancing 30–40 miles into Syrian territory. The cease-fire finally agreed to on 9 June left Israeli forces in occupation of the Sinai peninsula, the West Bank of the Jordan and the Syrian Heights. Egypt's unwillingness to announce the full extent of her losses delayed acceptance of a cease-fire to her own disadvantage. The political results of the war are difficult to assess. The Suez Canal is still closed (1973), and the prospects of permanent peace are still a long way off. The Security Council Resolution (Nov. 1967), although accepted by the Arab states – except Syria – and Israel, is differently interpreted. A constantly changing element in the situation is the terrorist activity organized by Arab guerrilla groups, e.g. *Al ⇨Fatah*, Palestine Liberation Front.

Arab League (The League of Arab States). Was formed with British blessing in 1945 following discussions between Egypt and ⇨ Iraq (1944). The founding members were Egypt (⇨ UAR), Iraq, ⇨ Syria, ⇨ Lebanon, Trans-Jordan (⇨ Jordan), ⇨ Saudi Arabia and ⇨ Yemen. Special provision was made to include a representative of the Palestine Arabs. Members who joined subsequently were ⇨ Libya (1953), ⇨ Morocco (1958), ⇨ Sudan (1956), ⇨ Tunisia (1958), ⇨ Kuwait (1961) and ⇨ Algeria. The League, a voluntary association, aimed at strengthening the links between member states and co-ordinating policies. In 1945 the League supported Syria and Lebanon in their conflicts with France. Strongly opposed to ⇨ Israel, invaded by Arab League countries (1948), the League has boycotted Israel as well as foreign countries trading with Israel. Despite common hostility to Israel, and the establishment of a number of inter-Arab organizations – e.g. Arab Postal Union (1954), Arab Development Bank (1957), since renamed Arab Financial Institute, Arab Common Market (1965) – unity is continually threatened by political rivalries. These rivalries have grown in intensity since 1957 and have reflected hostility between the 'revolutionaries' (Nasser's UAR) and the 'conservatives' (Saudi Arabia, Jordan). For a short period (1962–63) the UAR boycotted League meetings, while in 1961 Iraqi hostility was increased by the stationing of League forces in Kuwait. The PLA is financed by the League and since 1967 there have been attempts to close ranks, e.g. the UAR and Jordan have been compensated by other members for their war losses.

Aref, General Abdul Rahman (1916–). President of ⇨ Iraq (1966–68), he succeeded his brother, Abdul Salam ⇨ Aref, after the latter's accidental death. He was formerly Chief of Staff (from 1964) and was deposed in 1968.

Aref, Colonel Abdul Salam (1921–66). President of ⇨ Iraq (1963–66), who advocated Arab unity and closer ties with the UAR. He established a military dictatorship, founded the Arab Socialist Union Party (1964) and suppressed the communists. Most of his policies were a reversal of those of his predecessor, General ⇨ Kassem, whom he overthrew in 1963. Aref had been co-leader with Kassem of the revolution which overthrew the Iraqi monarchy in 1958, was deputy Prime Minister in Kassem's government until personal rivalry and differences over Kassem's pro-communist and anti-UAR policies led to Aref's arrest. In 1966 he was killed in an air crash.

Argentina. *Area* – 1,072,745 sq. miles. *Population* (1970) – 23,360,000. *President* – Lt.-Gen. Alejandro Agustin Lanusse (1971–). *Constitution* (1853) – Federal, modelled on the US, with a President and Congress. Extensively modified, most recently by 'Charter of the Revolution' (29.6.1966) which banned political parties.

Despite its constitutional development, wealth and economic potential, Argentina's history over the last 30 years has reflected the failure of successive governments, civilian and military, to heal its deep social divisions. In the 1930 Depression, radical President Irigoyen's government was deposed by a military coup. Irigoyen failed to implement necessary radical reforms. In particular, and as was to be the case for the next decade, the needs of a growing urban proletariat were ignored. From 1930 to 1937 Conservative oligarchies, increasingly Fascist in outlook, maintained themselves in power against growing Liberal and Left opposition. In 1937 the radical Dr Ortiz, at the head of a Liberal and Conservative coalition, became President (after an obviously government-manipulated election). Hope of reform was cut short when ill health forced him to resign in favour of the Conservative Dr Castillo. Military intervention (1943), followed by an internal revolt within the junta, secured power for a group of colonels including Juan ⇨ Perón, who placed himself at the head of the Secretariat of Labour and Social Security. Combining propaganda with badly-needed social reforms, raising the living standards of industrial workers, Perón won mass support, assisted by the radio actress Eva Duarte whom he later married. Their success was demonstrated when Perón was arrested in an attempted army coup. His followers, the *descamisados* (shirtless ones), took over the streets (17.10.1945) enforcing his release. Now certain of his popularity, Perón, at the head of his new *Partido Laborista*, held elections and won a decisive victory (Feb. 1946). Benefiting from the nationalism (which he assiduously fostered), Perón was helped rather than hindered by the US Government's attempt to sway the electorate by the publication of a Blue Book recording his attachment to the Axis cause. (Argentina entered the war in March 1945 after four years of pro-Axis neutrality.) Perón's presidency, this time in a manipulated election, was re-confirmed (1951). His political acumen was less sure after Eva's death (1952) and his regime became increasingly totalitarian. Threatened by economic crises, Perón offered an American company a contract for the exploration and exploitation of Argentinian oil, a defeat for his policy of nationalism and economic self-sufficiency. He also collided with the Church, which had previously supported the regime. After two uprisings (June and Sept. 1955) he was forced to flee the country. One result of Perón's rule – the emergence of the previously alienated urban working class as a political force – decisively affected Argentinian politics. Since 1955, attempts to re-establish constitutional democracy have failed in the face of the determination of military and conservative groups to exclude organized labour from participation in government. In Feb. 1958, after two military administrations, ⇨ Frondizi (leader of the *Union Civica Radical Intransigente* (UCRI – Intransigent Radicals) with the support of *Perónistas* (whose own organization had been banned) was elected President. Through a programme of austerity and modernization, Frondizi attempted to cure the country's economic and political malaise. Conservative irritation was inflamed by his lenient attitude (in the ⇨ OAS) to ⇨ Castro and his permitting the Perónist *Partido Justicialista* to stand in the 1962 elections. Their resounding success (30% of the vote followed by Frondizi's UCRI with 25%) was too much for the military. Frondizi was deposed and in an attempt to preserve the facade of democracy Dr Guido was appointed President. Unsure of themselves, the military leaders held elections the following year (1963) during which Frondizi was held under arrest and *Perónista* candidates banned. In an atmosphere of economic stagnation and indecision, the new President Dr Illia failed to achieve his aim of national reconciliation. If his own leadership was a factor in this failure, so was the impatience with democracy of both the traditional Right and the *Perónistas*. Though in the 1965 congressional elections Illia's UCRP

(*Union Civica Radical del Pueblo*) increased its vote, over 28% of the poll, the Perónist *Union Popular* managed over 31%. (The rest of the votes were split among numerous parties, including a much weakened UCRI which lost votes to a new Frondizi-led faction.) The President's inability to achieve an overall majority was again to provide the pretext for a coup. He was deposed (1966) and replaced by General Ongania, whose authoritarian regime promised extensive reforms. Political parties were abolished, special liberties of the universities, guaranteed in the constitution, were withdrawn and initially the press was threatened and antisemitism encouraged. Ongania was deposed in an Army coup in 1970 by Brig.-Gen. Robert Marcelo Levingston, in turn deposed in a bloodless coup by Lt.-Gen. Lanusse who has restored political parties and promised a return to democratic government.

Armed Forces Policy Council. A high-level body in the ⇨ Defense Department of the USA sometimes called its 'little Cabinet'. Members are the Secretary and Deputy Secretary of Defense, the Secretaries of the Army, Navy and Air Force Departments, the Director of Defense Research and Engineering, and the Chairman and members of the ⇨ JCS.

Armenia. One of the 15 Federal Soviet republics constituting the USSR. *Capital* – Erevan.

Arrow Cross. ⇨ Hungary.

Arzhak, Nikolai. Pseudonym of Yuli ⇨ Daniel.

ASA. Association of South-East Asia – founded in 1961 by the Declaration of Bangkok to promote economic social and cultural co-operation in the region. Its members are Malaysia, the Philippines and Thailand, and its main administrative body is the Foreign Minister's Conference and the Standing Committee which is responsible for the continued operation of projects between the annual meetings of the Conference. Progress has been hindered by the Indonesian-Malaysian ⇨ Confrontation and the Filipino claim on ⇨ Sabah.

ASEAN. Association of South-East Asian Nations – established in 1967 to accelerate economic progress and increase the stability of South-East Asia. Members include Indonesia, Malaysia, the Philippines, Singapore and Thailand, and its organization consists of a Ministerial Conference of the Foreign Ministers of the member states and a Standing Committee. This is the third attempt at establishing a regional organization after the failure of ⇨ ASA and ⇨ Maphilindo and followed ⇨ Sukarno's fall from power in Indonesia, the most important member.

Asia. See references to specific territories.

ASPAC. Asian and Pacific Council – a consultative association of nine non-communist countries in the Asian and Pacific region (Australia,

Republic of China [Taiwan], Japan, South Korea, Malaysia, New Zealand, Philippines, Thailand and South Vietnam) established in 1966 to foster solidarity and further regional cooperation in the economic, cultural and social fields.

Assemblée Nationale. The Lower House of Parliament in the French ⇨ Fourth and ⇨ Fifth Republics, with Deputies elected for a period of five years. The June 1968 general elections, held after the student disturbances and anti-government strikes of May 1968, gained the ruling Gaullist parties an unprecedented majority of nearly three-quarters of the seats.

As-Shaabi, Qahtan (*c.* 1920-). President and Prime Minister of the People's Republic of ⇨ South Yemen (1967–69). He was one of the founder-members of the National Liberation Front (NLF) and as its Secretary-General led the NLF delegation in talks with the UK Government in Geneva.

Associated States. ⇨ West Indies Associated States.

Atassi, el, Noureddine (1929-). President of ⇨ Syria (1966–70). Formerly Minister of the Interior (1963) and deputy Prime Minister (1964), he was a leader of the military 'left wing' branch of the ⇨ *Ba'ath* Party which seized power in 1966 after ousting the old party leadership. His foreign policy and antagonism towards Israel contributed to the crises culminating in the ⇨ Arab-Israeli War of 1967.

Ataturk. Mustapha ⇨ Kemal.

Atlantic Charter. Joint declaration on peace aims issued by President ⇨ Roosevelt and Prime Minister ⇨ Churchill at their mid-Atlantic meeting (Aug. 1941). It listed eight basic principles: no territorial aggrandizement; no territorial changes without consent of the populations concerned; self-government by all nations; international cooperation; freedom from want and fear; equal access to essential raw materials; freedom of navigation on the high seas; total disarming of the Axis powers and general disarmament after the war. Later subscribed to by all nations fighting the Axis, these principles were finally incorporated in the ⇨ United Nations Charter.

Atoms for Peace. Civil aspects of the nuclear programme of the USA administered by ⇨ AEC. Unlike the military aspects of the programme, it provided a field for international cooperation in research and development.

Attlee, first Earl, Clement Richard (1883–1967). Prime Minister of the UK (1945–51), leader of the Parliamentary ⇨ Labour Party (1935–55), deputy Prime Minister in ⇨ Churchill's war-time government (1940–45) and Leader of the Opposition from 1935 to 1940 and again from 1951 to 1955. His socialism sprang from personal concern rather than from abstract political theory, and he became involved with the Labour Party as a result of his experience as a social worker in the East End of London. Later his refusal to become entangled in doctrinal disputes or to be associated with either extreme wing of the Labour Party served him well as its leader. Before he entered Parliament, as Major Attlee in 1922, he had served with distinction in Gallipoli and on the Western Front during the war. The opinions he developed as a member of the Simon Commission on ⇨ India (1927) were given practical expression when he became the Prime Minister under whom India was granted independence (1947). A minister in ⇨ MacDonald's second Labour Government, he remained loyal to his party and refused to serve in MacDonald's coalition ⇨ National Government (1931). He succeeded Lansbury as Leader of the Parliamentary Labour Party in 1935. In 1940 Labour leaders indicated their willingness to serve in a coalition under Churchill – but not, and it was a crucial factor in his resignation, under ⇨ Chamberlain. In 1945 Attlee, but not the Labour Party, was prepared to continue in Churchill's coalition, and he later led Labour to its landslide election victory (June 1945). Under his guidance the post-war Labour administration carried out its intensive programme of nationalization and welfare legislation, and began the process of de-colonization. Defeated in the 1951 elections, he received the Order of Merit, and accepted an earldom on his retirement (1955). In the ensuing controversy over the Party leadership he supported ⇨ Gaitskell.

Attorney General of the USA. The principal law officer of the Federal Government. He is head of the Department of Justice, and a member of the President's ⇨ Cabinet. The office was established at the time the Constitution was adopted and is considerably older than the Depart-ment, which was established in 1870. The Attorney General is ap-pointed by the President with the consent of the ⇨ Senate, and is removable by him at any time. He advises the President and his agents on legal matters, and the published *Opinions* of the Attorney General carry great legal authority. He lays down broad lines of policy for the Justice Department, and has general responsibility for the conduct of its business. This includes the initiation of Federal investigations and prosecutions. For conducting investigations, the Department includes the ⇨ FBI. The chief prosecuting officer, under the Attorney General, is the Solicitor General, and it is usually he who represents the Federal Government before the ⇨ Supreme Court. Coming under the Attorney General, also, are the United States Marshals and District Attorneys who act for the Federal Government and the Justice Department in their several districts. Through its various divisions, the Department insti-tutes proceedings, not only in ordinary criminal cases, but also in cases involving Federal anti-trust laws and laws administered by such Federal agencies as ⇨ ICC, Federal tax law and Federal laws pertaining to internal security and ⇨ Civil Rights. In all these matters the Attorney General can play an important policy-forming role if he chooses to do so. The Department includes the United States Immigration and Naturalization Service to administer the law in those areas, and a Bureau of Prisons to operate the Federal penitentiaries and other correctional establishments. The Attorney General is more directly concerned with the work of the former of these two agencies through the Department's Board of Immigration Appeals, and with that of the latter through the Parole Board. He also has responsibility, in conjunction with the Pardon Attorney, for making recommendations to the President in the exercise of his power of pardon under the Constitution. In addition to performing important executive and administrative functions, the Attorney General can play a major part in government and politics. It was as Attorney General to his brother, President John F. ⇨ Kennedy, that Robert F. ⇨ Kennedy attained his greatest eminence. It is in fact usual for an incoming President's campaign manager to be made Attorney General, as happened in the Kennedy case. Richard M. ⇨ Nixon's campaign manager, John N. Mitchell, became Attorney General in 1969, and returned to managing the Nixon campaign in 1972, only to resign after allegations of spying on the Democratic organization were supported by his wife.

Auriol, Vincent (1884–1966). Was the ⇨ Fourth Republic's first President (1947–54). A socialist Deputy in the thirties, he was interned by the ⇨ Vichy government (1940–42). He joined ⇨ de Gaulle's Committee of National Liberation (1943–45) and served as Minister of State in his Provisional Government (Nov. 1945–Jan. 1946). Before being elected to the presidency of the Republic, he presided over the National Assembly (Nov. 1946–Jan. 1947). After disagreement with its Secretary-General, Guy ⇨ Mollet, he resigned from the Socialist Party in 1959.

Auschwitz. ⇨ Holocaust.

Australia. *Area* – 2,968,000 sq. miles. *Population* (1971 est.) – 12,881,100. *Prime Minister* – Gough Whitlam (1972–). *Constitution* – ⇨ Commonwealth Dominion (1901) consisting of a federation of six states (New South Wales, Victoria, Queensland, South Australia, Western Australia and Tasmania), its sovereignty confirmed by the Statute of ⇨ Westminster (1931). Legislative power is vested in the Federal Parliament of a six-year term Senate (with equal representation for the states), and a three-year term House of Representatives elected in proportion to the population. Both chambers are elected by universal adult suffrage. The Prime Minister is responsible to Parliament and the Queen is represented by the Governor-General, who is advised by the Executive Council of Ministers. The powers of the Federal Parliament are limited and include defence, foreign affairs and finance. Each of the six states has a Governor representing the Queen, a Parliament and a Cabinet led by a Premier. Attempts to increase the powers of the Federal Government at the expense of the states were frustrated by a referendum in 1944. To prevent rivalries between the state capitals a Federal capital was created in Canberra where Parliament House was officially opened in 1927.

A British settlement from the late eighteenth century, later a British colony, then a dominion, Australia has a predominantly White population as a result of her restrictionist 'White Australia' immigration policy.

The Great Depression severely disrupted Australia's economy, but during the premiership (1932–39) of Joseph Lyons (leader of the United Australia Party) economic recovery, now benefiting from rising gold and (after 1933) wool prices, was rapid. In World War II, as in World War I, Australians immediately rallied to Britain's cause. Following the UK's declaration of war (3.9.1939), the Australian Government at once declared war on Germany. During the war Australia made an important contribution to the Allied campaign in the Pacific and worked in close cooperation with the USA.

The country had been governed since 1949 by a coalition of the Liberal and Country parties led by Robert ⇨ Menzies (1949–66), Harold ⇨ Holt (1966–67), John ⇨ Gorton (1968–71) and William McMahon (1971–72). The Liberal Party – conservative, strongly anti-communist, for free enterprise and loyalty to the throne – was founded in 1944 as successor to the United Australia Party. The smaller Country Party is the spokesman of agricultural interests. The Labour Party, out of power from 1949–72 (Joseph Chifley was Prime Minister from 1945 to 1949), was weakened by splits in the 1950s. In 1967 Gough Whitlam succeeded Arthur Calwell as Leader of the Opposition (1960–67). In the 1969 general election the Liberal and Country Parties were returned with a diminished majority, winning 66 seats to the Labour Party's 59. A cabinet crisis in March 1971 led to the resignation of John Gorton as Prime Minister and his replacement by William McMahon. In the 1972 election Gough Whitlam became the first Labour Prime Minister since 1949. Australia's defence policy since the war has been based on collective security – she is a member of the ⇨ANZUS Pact and ⇨SEATO. While maintaining strong links with the Commonwealth (the UK is still her chief trading partner and the main source of her immigration) Australia has formed a closer relationship with the USA. This is especially true of defence matters, for she has a strong interest in containing communism in Asia. Australia participated in the ⇨Korean War, assisted ⇨Thailand against Laotian guerrillas and supported ⇨Malaysia in her ⇨Confrontation with ⇨Indonesia. She was the only Commonwealth country, apart from New Zealand, to send troops to support the USA in Vietnam (1965–72). This tendency towards a closer alliance with the USA was accelerated by the UK's withdrawal ⇨East of Suez. Australia administers a number of external territories including ⇨New Guinea, Papua, Norfolk Island, Christmas Island and the Australian Antarctic Territory.

Austria. *Area* – 32,376 sq. miles. *Population* (1970 est.) – 7,391,000. *President* – Franz ⇨Jonas (1965–). *Chancellor* – Dr Bruno ⇨Kreisky (1970–). *Constitution* (1920) – Federal Republic composed of nine provinces. Executive power is vested in the President, elected for six years by universal suffrage, who chooses the Chancellor. The Legislature consists of the National Council (*Nationalrat*) elected by universal suffrage for four years, and the Federal Council (*Bundesrat*) which consists of representatives from the provinces.

The Austrian Republic, established in 1919, was the much diminished 'successor state' to the vast Habsburg Empire. She now had a population of six million which was almost entirely German-speaking, having lost control over all the non-German lands. One-third of this population lived in Vienna, which was geared to be the industrial centre of a large state. Austria suffered economically from the break-up of the Empire, for she was deprived of much of her raw materials, her markets and access to the sea. For these reasons the idea of a union with Germany (⇨ *Anschluss*) enjoyed wide support, although it was forbidden by the Western powers (the failure of the projected customs union (1931) was due in part to pressure from France). Austria suffered heavily from the world economic crisis, and the Nazis' 'seizure of power' in Germany (1933) strengthened their Austrian counterparts. The domestic scene was marked by conflict between the two main parties: the Catholic Christian Social Party representing the rural, conservative and clerical forces, and the Social Democrats representing the urban working class. Chancellor ⇨Dollfuss' (1932–34) attempt to meet the deteriorating situation by introducing authoritarian rule – ⇨ Austro-Fascism (suspension of Parliament and the constitution, government by decree) – met with violent Social Democratic opposition. In Feb. 1934 a socialist strike was suppressed and the Social Democratic Party was dissolved. In view of her enclosed position in Central Europe, Austria needed protection from other powers, and for a time sought this in an alliance with Italy and Hungary (Rome Protocols,

March 1934). When Dollfuss was assassinated during the Nazi coup, (July 1934), it was the concentration of Italian and Yugoslav troops on the frontier which prevented possible German intervention. Dollfuss's successor, ⇨ Schuschnigg, continued Dollfuss' policies, but the German-Italian rapprochement resulting in the ⇨ Axis agreements removed Austria's last support. Schuschnigg was compelled to follow a policy of ⇨ Appeasement towards Germany (German-Austrian Agreement, July 1936). In Feb. 1938 Hitler coerced Schuschnigg, after a humiliating interview, into lifting restrictions on the Austrian Nazis and appointing Nazis to his Cabinet. In March Schuschnigg's announcement of plans for a plebiscite to articulate support for Austrian independence prompted Hitler to take action. Schuschnigg rejected a German ultimatum demanding the postponement of the plebiscite, resigned and was replaced by ⇨ Seyss-Inquart. German troops invaded Austria and on 13 March the *Anschluss* was proclaimed. Austria participated in World War II as an integral part of the German *Reich*. By the Moscow Declaration (1943) the Allies agreed on the restoration of an independent Austria after the war. In 1945 the Allied occupation of Austria led to the division of the country into four occupation zones. Elections later that year produced a coalition government under Leopold ⇨ Figl (1945–53) of the People's Party (OVP – successor to the Christian Social Party) and the Social Democrats (SPO). Karl ⇨ Renner, a veteran Social Democrat leader, became President (1945–50). This set a pattern of OVP Chancellors (Julius ⇨ Raab 1953–61, Alfons Gorbach 1961–64 and Josef Klaus 1964–70) and SPO Presidents (Theodor Korner 1951–57, Adolf Scharf 1957–65 and since 1965 Franz Jonas). In 1946 Karl Gruber (Foreign Minister 1946–53) negotiated a ⇨ South Tyrol agreement with the Italian Government, but the problem has continued to plague relations between the two countries partly because of the alleged non-implementation of the agreement by Italy. After protracted negotiations and obstruction by the Russians, the ⇨ Austrian State Treaty was finally signed (May 1955) restoring complete sovereignty to Austria and the occupation troops were withdrawn. Austria pledged herself to permanent neutrality and renounced the use of major offensive weapons. In 1955 Austria joined the UN and in 1958 ⇨ EFTA. In 1961 she announced her decision to seek closer economic relations with the ⇨ EEC (political relations are not allowed under the Treaty) and in 1972, along with other EFTA members, she concluded a trade agreement with the EEC. The Soviet Union expressed its opposition on the grounds that this was tantamount to an 'economic *Anschluss*'.

The controversy over whether to allow Otto von ⇨ Habsburg to return to Austria has divided the two main parties and weakened the coalition. In April 1966 the coalition came to an end when the People's Party gained an absolute majority (it won 85 seats to the SPO's 74) and reintroduced party government for the first time in Austria's post-war history.

After the November 1971 elections, the Socialists (SPO) won under Chancellor Kreisky an absolute majority in Parliament.

Austrian State Treaty. Agreement signed by the USA, the USSR, France, the UK and Austria (May 1955) by which Austria regained her sovereign independence (July 1955) after ten years of occupation by Allied forces which were then withdrawn. Austria promised to maintain permanent neutrality and renounce the use of major offensive (including nuclear) weapons. A political or economic union with Germany was forbidden (⟡ *Anschluss*) and the four powers gave up their claims to reparations.

Austro-Fascism. Name given to the authoritarian rule in ⟡ Austria of the Christian Social Party Chancellors ⟡ Dollfuss (1932–34) and ⟡ Schuschnigg (1934–38) which included the suspension of constitutional government, curtailment of the freedom of the press, the suppression of the Social Democrats (when they opposed this), corporatism in economic matters and elements of clericalism and monarchism. It therefore contained much that was similar to the Fascist governments in Italy and Germany, but a major reason for its adoption was to check the growing chaos of political life, which resulted in part from the increasing threat from the National Socialists, and it included the suppression of the Austrian Nazi Party. Eventually, with the end of support from Italy it paved the way for Nazi rule after the ⟡ *Anschluss.*

Avon, Lord (1897–). Formerly Sir Anthony Eden, British Prime Minister and leader of the Conservative Party (1955–57) and one of Britain's longest-serving Foreign Secretaries (1935–38, 1940–45 and 1951–55), first appointed to that office at the early age of 38. Although publicly identified with support for the League of Nations – in 1935 he had been made first Minister for League Affairs – his period in office was marked by the powerlessness of the League in the face of aggression by the ⟡ Axis powers: the Italian occupation of ⟡ Ethiopia and the German march into the Rhineland. During the ⟡ Spanish Civil War Eden supported non-intervention but failed to enforce it. In 1938 he resigned after policy disagreements with ⟡ Chamberlain – the latter sent a lukewarm reply to Roosevelt's proposal for an international conference without consulting Eden, who opposed Chamberlain's plan for further discussions with Italy. Eden opposed ⟡ Appeasement but rejoined the Chamberlain Government on the outbreak of war as Secretary of State for Dominion Affairs. After ⇨ Churchill became Prime Minister (1940) he was reappointed Foreign Secretary. During the war, Eden established a close association with Churchill, whom he accompanied to conferences with other Allied leaders, e.g. ⇨ Teheran and ⇨ Yalta. Eden also made visits to Moscow, Greece and Washington. He served a third time as Foreign Secretary after the Conservatives were returned to power in 1951. He took part in ending hostilities in Indo-China (⇨ Geneva Agreements 1954) and in the London Conference (1954) which ended the occupation of West Germany and admitted her to ⇨ NATO. The basis of Eden's policy was the Anglo-American partnership and this helped to account for his lack of enthusiasm for plans for European federation, e.g. the failure of the European Army project (⇨ EDC). Long regarded as Churchill's successor – Eden was deputy Leader of the Opposition (1945–51) and deputy Prime Minister (1951–55). Succeeding Churchill (1955), his short term as Premier was overshadowed by the failure of the Anglo-French invasion of ⇨ Suez (Oct./Nov. 1956), and the consequences of that event. Troubled by ill health, he resigned in Jan. 1957 and retired from Parliament.

Awolowo, Chief Obafemi (1909–). Yoruba chief prominent in the Nigerian independence movement and the first Prime Minister (1954) of the Western Region of Nigeria. Arrested (1962 ⇨ Nigeria), he was released in 1966 and has since played an active part in politics, representing the Federation of Nigeria at the ⇨ OAU Assembly (Algiers, Sept. 1968) as a strong opponent of Biafran secession.

Axis, Berlin-Rome. Term denoting the common Nazi-Fascist approach to international problems. It was coined by ⇨ Mussolini after signing the October Protocols (Oct. 1936) in which Germany and Italy pledged themselves to oppose the Spanish Republican Government and communism in general. These aims were more specifically spelled out in the Italian-German Pact of Steel (May 1939) in which the signatories promised to support each other in case of war. The Berlin-Rome Axis was extended to Tokyo when Japan, already a member of the ⇨ Anti-Comintern Pact (Nov. 1936) acceded to the Tripartite Pact (Sept. 1940) which Russia had refused to join.

Azerbaidjan. One of the 15 Federal Soviet republics constituting the USSR. *Capital* – Baku. Azerbaidjan comprises one autonomous republic and one autonomous province.

Azikiwe, Dr Benjamin Nnamdi (1904–). Pioneer of Nigerian nationalism. Prime Minister of the Eastern Region of ⇨ Nigeria (1954–59), first Governor-General of the Federation of Nigeria (1960–63), and after it became a republic (1963), Nigeria's first President. From 1966 he acted as adviser to the Eastern Region's military government and from 1967 as a roving ambassador for Biafra. In this capacity he was probably instrumental in securing Tanzanian recognition, followed by that of three other African states.

B

Ba'ath Party. Pan-Arab movement whose full name is The Party of Arab Renaissance. The *Ba'ath* is not confined to any single Arab state and until 1958 was a rival to Nasserism and communism in the Middle East, but now includes both pro-communist and pro-Egypt factions. Founded in Syria in 1941 by Michel ⇦⊳ Aflaq and Salah Bitar, it originally aimed at giving a more unified direction to the Arab liberation movement in World War II, and now has branches also in Iraq, Jordan, the Lebanon and the Gulf sheikdoms. Its programme of 1947 defined the aims of the *Ba'ath* as unity (of the whole Arab nation), freedom (for Arabs from foreign interference) and socialism. The divorce between its doctrine and reality was illustrated when the party rose to prominence in the 1950s and eventually came to power in Iraq and Syria – in both cases weakened by its dependence on the military, for which it often acted as a cover. In Iraq it participated with General ⊳ Kassem in the overthrow of the monarchy but quickly lost favour with the new regime. When that in turn was overthrown in 1963, the *Ba'athists* enjoyed nine months of power, only to lose the support of the new ruling military clique. It was also plagued by divisions and this was again typical of the party in Syria, where it has enjoyed a longer period of office. Its influence there was first shown with Syria's decision to form a union with Egypt in the ⊳ United Arab Republic (1958), but disillusionment with Egyptian dominance exposed the latent conflict between the pro-Nasser and anti-Nasser elements in the party. The *Ba'ath* came to power after a military coup in 1963 and in 1966 the old leadership was replaced in office by the younger and more extreme wing of the party. The new *Ba'ath* Party in Syria was more doctrinaire and formed a close relationship with the communists both at home and abroad. The conflict here of its professed aims, i.e. Arab 'freedom' and dependence on outside assistance, is again strikingly shown in its attitude towards the UAR. On the one hand it attacked Nasser (in apparent contrast to its pursuit of Arab 'unity') and on the other made a military alliance with him (1966) as a logical consequence of its militant policy towards Israel. Mainly a movement supported by military groups, the middle classes and intellectuals, the *Ba'ath* has not succeeded in clarifying political issues, nor has it (so far) brought greater stability in those countries where it has achieved power. Its ideological commitments have been affected by personal, class, local and ethnic rivalries.

Backbencher. Ordinary Member of UK Parliament as opposed to Ministers and members of the ⇨ Shadow Cabinet who occupy the front benches. With increasing pressure of government business and the dominance of the Cabinet and party leaders, the backbenchers' power to initiate legislation (Private Member's Bill) tends to exist in theory rather than in practice.

Baghdad Pact. Mutual defence pact (1955) for the Middle East signed originally by Iraq and Turkey but soon after joined by the UK, Pakistan and Iran. The purpose of the pact was to resist possible aggression by the Soviet Union and was open to any member of the ⇨ Arab League. The USA declined formal membership but from 1956 participated in the military and economic committees. After Iraq withdrew from the organization in 1959, it was reconstituted as ⇨ CENTO.

Bahrein, State of. *Area* – 245 sq. miles. *Population* (1971) – 216,000. *Ruler* – Isa bin Sulman al-Khalifa (1961–). An independent Arab state, it was under British protection until 1971. Three-quarters of its income comes from oil (discovered in 1932).

Bakr, Major-General Ahmed (*c.* 1916–). President and Prime Minister of ⇨ Iraq since July 1968. He was formerly Prime Minister of the *Ba'athist* Government (1963) after the overthrow of the ⇨ Kassem regime, but fell when the *Ba'ath* Party lost power. Bakr was a noted opponent of President Abdul Salam ⇨ Aref and of his brother Abdul Rahman ⇨ Aref, and succeeded the latter after he was deposed. Mass trials and public hangings have occurred during his presidency.

Balaguer, Joaquin (1906–). President of the ⇨ Dominican Republic (1966–).

Balance of Terror. A balance of nuclear strength between two nations in which neither can launch a first strike nuclear attack upon the other without suffering unacceptable damage in a retaliatory second strike by the other's surviving nuclear force. A balance exists between two nations, then, when neither has a 'first strike capability', and both have a 'second-strike capability'. Simple or 'passive' deterrence in this context is usually thought of as the ability of a nation to suffer an attack upon its nuclear forces ('counterforce targeted') and still be capable of a retaliatory strike at the opponent's population centre ('countervalue targeted') that would cause intolerable destruction.

Baldwin, Stanley, First Earl of Bewdley (1867–1947). UK Conservative Prime Minister (1923–24, 1924–29) and subsequently Prime Minister of the National Government (June 1935–May 1937). As Lord President of the Council in Ramsay ⇨ MacDonald's previous ⇨ National Governments he had exercised considerable influence behind the scenes. Baldwin won the general election of Nov. 1935 as a supporter of the ⇨ League of Nations and ⇨ Collective Security, but his prestige sagged with the publication of the ⇨ Hoare-Laval Plan (10.12.1935). Later accused of leaving Britain unprepared in the face of growing German re-armament, he claimed that the country had been too pacifist at the time of the 1935 general election to have voted in favour of re-armament. His reputation was enhanced by his astute handling of the ⇨ Abdication Crisis. He resigned the following year (27.5.1937) and was succeeded by Neville ⇨ Chamberlain.

Balewa, Sir Alhaji Abubakar Tafawa (1912–1966). First Prime Minister of the Federation of Nigeria (1951–60) and of an independent Nigeria from 1960 to 1965 and from 1965 until his assassination the following year. He was a founder of the country's largest political party, the Northern People's Congress.

Balfour Declaration. British Government statement, issued in the form of a letter signed by Foreign Secretary Balfour and addressed to Lord Rothschild (2.11.1917). A crucial document in Zionist history legitimizing Jewish claims to settlement in ⇨ Palestine, the ambiguity of the Declaration led to heated controversy and different interpretations of its intention on the part of Jews and Arabs. While it declared 'His Majesty's Government's . . . sympathy with Jewish Zionist aspirations . . .' and viewed 'with favour the establishment in Palestine of a National Home for the Jewish People' it included the proviso that 'nothing shall be done which may prejudice the civil and religious rights of existing non-Jewish communities in Palestine . . .'

Balkan Entente. Alliance established in 1934 between ⇨ Yugoslavia, ⇨ Greece, ⇨ Rumania and ⇨ Turkey, chiefly directed against ⇨ Bulgaria's claims to territories incorporated in these countries since World War I. (⇨ Balkans.)

Balkan Federation. Abortive plan for a federation of Balkan and Danubian states, promoted in 1947 by President ⇨ Tito of ⇨ Yugoslavia and Georgi ⇨ Dimitrov, the Prime Minister of ⇨ Bulgaria, but subsequently vetoed by ⇨ Stalin.

Balkan Pact. Military alliance, concluded (Aug. 1954) between ⇨ Greece, ⇨ Turkey and ⇨ Yugoslavia, pledging mutual aid in case of aggression against a member country. The Treaty was concluded for 20 years and has never been formally cancelled, but since 1955 Yugoslavia has claimed that the Treaty has become a dead letter.

Balkans. Geographically, a peninsula in South-East Europe; politically, the collective name for ⟱ Bulgaria, ⟱ Yugoslavia, ⟱ Rumania, ⟱ Greece, ⟱ Albania and (European) ⟱ Turkey. The Balkans have a long history of wars, conquests and migrations and of disputes over frontiers and the claims of national minorities. The successive repartitions of the area resulting from the Balkan wars of 1912 and 1913 and from World War I led to substantial territorial gains for Rumania at the expense of Hungary (⟱ Transylvania) and of Bulgaria (⟱ Dobrudja); for Yugoslavia (formerly Serbia) at the expense of Bulgaria (⟱ Macedonia) and of Hungary; and for Greece at the expense of Bulgaria. The territorial losses suffered by Bulgaria and Hungary gave rise to claims for frontier revisions, sometimes described as ⟱ Revisionism, which, in turn, led to the conclusion of defensive alliances against revisionist claims, such as the ⟱ Balkan Entente and the ⟱ Little Entente. In the interwar years, the Balkans were the scene of an intense rivalry for influence between ⟱ France, ⟱ Great Britian, ⟱ Germany, the ⟱ USSR and, to a lesser extent, ⟱ Italy, with German influence gradually becoming preponderant. During World War II, Germany overran the whole of the Balkans, as a consequence of which Bulgaria occupied nearly all Macedonia, while Hungary re-annexed large areas from Rumania and Yugoslavia. As a result of the wartime agreements between ⟱ Roosevelt, ⟱ Churchill and ⟱ Stalin, after the war the Balkan countries, with the exception of Greece and Turkey, became a Soviet sphere of influence and frontiers were once again re-drawn by a series of awards from Moscow. Since then, attempts at inter-Balkan cooperation have alternated with fresh outbreaks of tension. In 1947, ⟱ Tito and ⟱ Dimitrov made a pact providing for close cooperation and an eventual customs union between Bulgaria and Yugoslavia as the nucleus of a future Federation of Balkan and Danubian states – a project which was vetoed by Stalin. Yugoslavia's hitherto preponderant influence in Albania was broken in 1948 as the result of Tito's expulsion from the ⟱ Cominform. The expulsion also gave rise to fresh tension between Bulgaria and Yugoslavia over Macedonia. The reconciliation between Yugoslavia and the USSR in the mid-1950s served as the starting point for renewed attempts at inter-Balkan cooperation, promoted especially by Rumania but supported by all the communist countries in the area, with the exception of Albania. Yet another turn came with the renewed deterioration in Soviet-Yugoslav relations beginning in 1967, which revived some of the old tensions between Bulgaria and Yugoslavia and produced a new flare-up of Yugoslav-Bulgarian polemics over Macedonia. Yugoslav-Bulgarian relations improved again after Mr ⇨ Brezhnev's visit to Belgrade in Sept. 1971, while Yugoslavia's relations with Albania were normalized as a result of their common opposition to the Soviet-led intervention in Czechoslovakia (Aug. 1968).

Baltic States. Collective name for Lithuania, Latvia and Estonia. Formerly part of the Tsarist Empire, the three countries became independent states after World War 1. After the conclusion of the ⇨ Hitler-Stalin Pact (Aug. 1939), the Baltic States were re-annexed by the USSR (1940) and transformed into Soviet Republics.

Banda, Dr Hastings Kamuzu (1906–). President (1966–) of ⇨ Malawi.

Bandaranaike, Mrs Sirimavo (1916–). Prime Minister of ⇨ Ceylon (1970–) and leader of the Sri Lanka Freedom Party, she succeeded her husband, Solomon Bandaranaike, who was assassinated in 1959. She was also Prime Minister from 1960 to 1965.

Bandung Conference. The first large-scale gathering of Asian and African states held in April 1955 on the initiative of the ⇨ Colombo Powers. Following the settlement of the Sino-Indian conflict over Tibet, China and India concluded a trade agreement (29.4.1954) incorporating 'The Five Principles of Peaceful Co-existence'. These were: mutual respect for territorial integrity and sovereignty; non-aggression; non-interference in each other's internal affairs; equality and mutual benefit; peaceful co-existence and economic cooperation. These Five Principles, which were re-affirmed during exchange visits later in the year by the Chinese Premier ⇨ Chou En-lai and ⇨ Pandit Nehru, were recommended as the guidelines for the Bandung Conference in the following spring. The preparatory meeting at Bogor was marred by conflicts over whom to invite and not to invite. In the end it was decided to exclude Israel as well as the two Korean States and Taiwan (Formosa). The Bandung Conference was attended by Afghanistan, Burma, Cambodia, Ceylon, China, Egypt, Ethiopia, the Gold Coast (Ghana), India, Indonesia, Iran, Iraq, Japan, Jordan, Laos, Lebanon, Liberia, Libya, Nepal, Pakistan, the Philippines, Saudi Arabia, Sudan, Syria, Thailand, Turkey, North Vietnam, South Vietnam and the Yemen, i.e. a collection of states with pronounced differences in interests and policies. These differences came to the fore in various conflicts over procedure and formulations. China and the neutralist nations favoured broad generalities, conveying a picture of unity. Other participants insisted on the discussion of controversial current topics. Conflicts also arose over the definition of terms such as 'colonialism', which, according to some participants, should include a reference to the new Soviet type of colonialism through force, infiltration and subversion as well as to Western imperialism, and over 'the right to collective self-defence' as a general principle. Chiefly as a result of the conciliatory efforts of Chou En-lai who dominated the proceedings, a compromise was eventually achieved in the form of Ten Principles incorporating both the original Five Principles of Peaceful Co-existence and the main principles proposed by the anti-communist states.

The tenth anniversary of the Bandung Conference was to be celebrated by a second Afro-Asian Conference, sponsored jointly by China and Indonesia and to be held in Algeria in June 1965. By that time, Chinese policies had undergone a radical change and the 'second Bandung' project was over-shadowed by the ⇨ Sino-Soviet Conflict. The USSR (which did not attend Bandung) claimed the right to attend the second conference as an 'Asian' power – a claim which was supported by India and many other Afro-Asian states but contested by China, Indonesia and their supporters. The preparatory stage was beset by a number of other difficulties, and many of the invited states had announced in advance that they would not attend. Then, on the eve of the conference, President Ben Bella of Algeria was overthrown in a *coup d'état*. Most of the would-be participants of the conference thereupon urged its postponement against the opposition of China, Indonesia, North Vietnam and North Korea. The conference was first postponed until November. In the end the project was abandoned altogether after China, by then anticipating being outvoted on all issues, had reversed its original position and proposed an indefinite adjournment.

Bangladesh. *Area–*55,000 sq. miles. *Population–*63,000,000. *President–*Abu Chowdhury (Jan. 1972). *Prime Minister* – Sheikh Mujibar Rahman. *Constitution* – the Provisional Constitution of 1972 established Bangladesh as a parliamentary democracy and in Apr. 1972 it was admitted into the ⇨ Commonwealth. Formerly the State of East ⇨ Pakistan, Bangladesh achieved independence in the Indo-Pakistan war of Dec. 1971.

Bao Dai. ⇨ Vietnam.

Barbados. *Area* – 166 sq. miles. *Population* (1969 est.) – 253,633. *Prime Minister* – E. W. Barrow (1966–). *Constitution* (1966) – Independent Dominion within the ⇨ Commonwealth – (the Queen is represented by the Governor-General) – the Prime Minister is responsible to a bicameral Parliament of a partly-appointed and partly-elected Senate and an elected House of Assembly. There is universal adult suffrage.

Densely populated (most of its people the descendants of Negro slaves) with a plantation economy (more diversified in recent years), Barbados was a British colony from the early seventeenth century. In attitude it has remained the most British of the former West Indian colonies. From the nineteen-fifties Barbadians, led by Sir Grantley Adams, favoured federation, and in 1958 Adams became the Prime Minister of the ⇨ West Indies Federation. With its dissolution (1962) attempts were made to form an Eastern Caribbean Federation centring on Barbados, but (except for agreement on currency and certain common services) it was never established. Barbados became self-governing in 1964. Following the 1966 elections (resulting in a victory for E. W. Barrow's Democratic Labour Party), Barbados attained full independence (30.11.1966). Barbados has joined ⇨ Guyana and Antigua in a trading alliance and has joined the ⇨ OAS (1967).

Barber, Anthony Perrinott Lysberg (1920–). Chairman UK Conservative Party (1967–70) and since 1970 Chancellor of the Exchequer. An MP from 1951, Minister of Health (1963–64) and Chancellor of the Duchy of Lancaster (June–July 1970).

Barrientos Ortuno, General René (1920–69). Vice-President of ⇨ Bolivia (1964), elected President (1966) by a two to one majority, earlier led the military coup that deposed ⇨ Paz Estenssoro (1964). Initially popular with Indians, his army occupied the mines (1967) and crushed a guerrilla uprising (⇨ Guevara). Killed in an air-crash (April 1969).

Baruch, Bernard Mannes (1870–1965). US financier, philanthropist and 'elder statesman'. He was a US economic adviser at Versailles, and again entered government service during World War II, becoming special adviser to the Office of War Mobilization (1943). In 1946 President Harry S. ⇨ Truman appointed him United States representative to the UN Atomic Energy Commission where he proposed the 'Baruch Plan' for control of atomic energy.

Barzel, Dr Rainer (1924–). Leader of the opposition ⇨ CDU since 1971. Minister of All-German Affairs under ⇨ Adenauer (1962) and the party's Chief Whip (1966), his temporary refusal to support ⇨ Brandt's ⇨ *Ostpolitik* rocked the Government compelling it to dissolve Parliament prematurely.

Basutoland. ⇨ Lesotho.

Batlle Y Ordonez, José (1856–1929). President of ⇨ Uruguay (1903–7 and 1911–15), leader of the *Colorados*. An idealist and admirer of Swiss democracy, he set out to eradicate corruption and excessive personal power (which he regarded as the two great evils of South American politics). His governmental reforms made possible the social legislation of his own and later administrations.

Battle of Britain. ⇨ World War II.

Baudouin. ⇨ Belgium.

Bay of Pigs. Site of an abortive invasion of ⇨Cuba on 17 April 1961 by refugees from Dr Castro's regime living in the USA. The plan of attack was devised by the ⇨CIA (which had also formed and trained the exiles' military units) and approved by the ⇨JCS, and included provision for limited air strikes by US forces before and after the landing. When the plan was submitted to President ⇨Kennedy for his approval, he acquiesced in the invasion, but refused US air support for it. It was expected, on the basis of CIA reports, that there would be a general uprising in Cuba against Castro following the invasion, but the President finally disallowed direct US military support even in this eventuality. In fact there was no uprising and the invasion was immediately defeated. The President assumed full responsibility for the fiasco, but resolved to bring the CIA under presidential control once more.

Beaverbrook, Lord (Max Aitken) (1879–1964). Created a peer 1917 – Canadian-born British Press lord and spokesman for radical Toryism and imperialism. Minister of Information in 1918. A close friend of ⇨Churchill, with whom he supported the claims of ⇨Edward VIII (for a morganatic marriage) during the ⇨Abdication Crisis. Served in War Cabinet as Minister of Aircraft Production (1940–41) and Minister of Supply (1941–42). Lord Privy Seal (1943–45).

Bechuanaland. ⇨Botswana.

Belaunde Terry, Fernando (1913–). President of ⇨Peru (1963–68), founded the AP (*Accion Popular*) which emerged as a strong force in the 1962 elections. Belaunde's administration was seriously concerned with improving the material and social conditions of the Peruvian Indians. He was opposed by a hostile Congress and later arrested in a military coup (1968).

Belgian Congo. ⇨Congo, Democratic Republic of.

Belgium. Kingdom. *Area* – 11,799 sq. miles. *Population* (1970 est.) – 9,691,000. *Head of State* – King Baudouin. *Prime Minister* – Edmond Leburton (1973–). *Constitution* – Belgium, a constitutional monarchy, gained independence from the Netherlands in 1830. Executive power is exercised by the King through a Cabinet responsible to a bi-cameral Parliament. The Lower House, the Chamber of Deputies (212 members), is quadrennially elected by universal and compulsory suffrage based on proportional representation. Only half the membership of the Upper Chamber (Senate) is so elected; the other half is made up of members appointed by provincial councils and those co-opted by the elected and appointed Senators.

Belgium, after being invaded in World War I, abandoned her traditional neutrality, concluded a military alliance with France (Sept. 1920) and became a co-signatory of the Locarno Treaty (Oct. 1925).

But after the remilitarization of the Rhineland – demonstrating France's inability to contain Nazi Germany – Belgium reverted to a position of strict neutrality (Oct. 1936). In the context of the smouldering conflict between the Flemings (55%) and the French-speaking Walloons (45%), this was a popular move, because the French alliance was regarded by the Flemings as a symbol of Walloon domination. With the Flemings fighting for linguistic and political equality – Flemish was only recognized as an official language in 1920 – the embittered relations between the two national communities remains one of Belgium's chief internal problems.

In World War II the country was once more invaded by German forces (May 1940). After resisting for 18 days, the army under King Leopold III capitulated. The King, disregarding ministerial advice, refused to leave Belgium and follow Hubert Pierlot's coalition government to London. On its return to liberated Brussels (Sept. 1944), the government had to pass a Regency Bill in order to replace the King (interned in Germany) by his brother Prince Charles. However, even after victory, the entire Left and the Liberals (particularly among the Walloons) were so adamantly opposed to the King that the regency had to be extended (July 1945). The controversy about the King's person and war record was further aggravated by inter-communal resentments with the more conservative, religious and Germanophile Flemings favouring his return. But hostility to his person was so strong that even after a plebiscite (March 1950) and a parliamentary majority had recalled him from exile (June 1950), threats of widespread civil disobedience finally persuaded him to transfer power to his son Baudouin who acceded to the throne in July 1951. Throughout the post-war era, frequent government changes reflected the varying electoral fortunes of the three main coalition parties, the Social Christians, Socialists and Liberals. The sudden loss of the ⇨Congo (July 1960) necessitated strict austerity measures but the steady growth of the ⇨EEC economy in the later sixties accelerated Belgium's spectacular recovery. Communal strife flared up again over the attempt to expel the Walloons from Louvain University (1966), and also prevented the consideration of constitutional reforms to which the Boeynants government was committed. It led to the downfall of the Boeynants government, new elections (March 1968) and the formation of the Eyskens Christian Social-Socialist coalition government. Without greatly altering traditional party patterns, the elections showed increasing support for the linguistically-orientated (federal) parties. The Fleming *Volksunie* obtained 9·7% and the francophone *Rassemblement Wallon* 5·9% of the vote. Responding to the clamour for decentralization on linguistic lines, the government appointed two separate Ministers of Education and of Culture for the two regions, as well as two ministers for relations between the communities. It seems, however, to have been unable to resolve the basic conflict (federalist v. unitary state), which now seems to engulf also the status of Brussels. Like other small nations Belgium actively supports all efforts to enlarge the area of international co-operation. A UN member, she played a leading part in establishing ⇨ BENELUX, ⇨ EEC, ⇨ WEU, ⇨ NATO, etc. Brussels, the seat of many EEC commissions, also became the home of NATO head-quarters (March 1967) when on de Gaulle's insistence it had to leave France.

In 1972 the Eyskens government resigned and a new coalition government of Socialists, Social Christians and Liberals was formed under Edmond Leburton, the first Socialist Prime Minister since 1958.

Belgrade Conference (1961). Conference of non-aligned nations, sponsored by Yugoslavia, India and the UAR, seeking to enhance the international influence of the participants vis-à-vis the Great Powers and the existing military alliances. A second larger conference of non-aligned nations was held in Cairo in 1964.

Belgrade Declaration. Joint Soviet-Yugoslav government statement issued on 2 June 1955, at the end of a Soviet visit which had begun with ⇨ Khrushchev's public apology to ⇨ Tito for the wrongs inflicted by the USSR on ⇨ Yugoslavia. The preamble of the Belgrade Declaration formally endorsed the view, until then only upheld by Yugoslavia, that 'questions of the internal social order, differences in the social system and differences in the concrete forms of the development of socialism are exclusively matters for the peoples of the countries concerned'.

Ever since 1955, Yugoslavia has insisted on using the Belgrade Declaration as the basis for all its foreign relations. Mr L. ⇨ Brezhnev was thus obliged formally to re-endorse the Declaration when he visited Yugoslavia (Sept. 1971) in order to mend Soviet-Yugoslav relations. The Declaration was formally re-endorsed for a second time during President Tito's visit to the USSR in June 1972.

Belorussia. One of the 15 Federal Soviet republics constituting the USSR, sometimes called White Russia. *Capital* – Minsk.

Ben Barka, Mehdi. Exiled Moroccan left-wing revolutionary whose kidnapping (Oct. 1965) and murder in France by Moroccan agents with the complicity of French police officials, made him the centre of a political scandal after his death. The central figure behind the plot was General Mohammed Oufkir, the Moroccan Minister of the Interior, for whom Ben Barka was a dangerous political rival. Coming shortly after de Gaulle's close re-election as President of ⇨ France, the sensational revelations involving the French underworld the following January, caused a public outcry. It was evident that members of his Government were informed before the election. The scandal soured Franco-Moroccan relations, which were not helped by Oufkir's alleged connection with the American ⇨ CIA (Ben Barka is said to have been an associate of Fidel ⇨ Castro). The incident also threatened de Gaulle's effort to court favour with the Third World. Trials of the alleged kidnappers were held in 1966 and 1967 but resulted in the acquittal of all except two who received prison sentences. By that time the scandal had ceased to be the centre of public interest.

Ben Bella, Mohammed (1916–). First Prime Minister of ⇨ Algeria. A revolutionary leader from his formation of the *Organisation Spéciale* (OS) in 1947, he was arrested (1950) but escaped (1952) to Cairo where he formed first the CRUA (Revolutionary Council for Unity and Action) and then the ⇨ FLN (National Liberation Front). On flight to Tunis his plane was forced to land at Algiers and he was arrested (22.10.1956) and taken to France. Released (18.3.1962) he seized the FLN leadership from Ben Khedda, becoming Prime Minister of Algeria (26.9.1962) and President (13.4.1963) until his deposition (19.6.1965) by his former right hand man Col. ⇨ Boumedienne.

BENELUX. Short for Belgium, the Netherlands and Luxembourg and the economic, non-political union these countries entered into under the Benelux Treaty of Nov. 1960.

Beneš, Dr E. (1884–1948). Former President of ⇨ Czechoslovakia. The closest associate of T. G. Masaryk, the founder President of the Czechoslovak Republic, Benes was its Foreign Minister from its foundation in 1918 until Masaryk's death in 1935, when he became President. He resigned from the presidency after the ⇨ Munich Agreement (Sept. 1938) and, after the outbreak of World War II, became the head of the London-based Czechoslovak government-in-exile. Determined to maintain close relations with the USSR in the post-war period he concluded an agreement (April 1945) with the Czechoslovak communists, headed by Klement ⇨ Gottwald, and was re-elected President of the Republic (1946). Having refused to sign the new Soviet-type constitution introduced after the communist coup of Feb. 1948, he resigned from the presidency in May 1948 and died shortly afterwards.

Ben Gurion, David (1886–). As Chairman of the ⇨ Jewish Agency (1935–48), proclaimed the independence of ⇨ Israel and became its first Prime Minister (1948–53). Like ⇨ Weizmann, Ben Gurion's life story is indissolubly linked with the history of ⇨ Zionism and later with the history of Israel. His capacity for leadership was confirmed in desperate times during the last years of the Mandate and the emergence of the new state. Ben Gurion came to ⇨ Palestine in 1906 and served in the Jewish Legion in World War I. He was a founder member of *Mapai* (Israel Labour Party) and until 1965 its leader. He was again Prime Minister from 1955 until 1963, which included the period of the ⇨ Suez Crisis and Israel's invasion of Sinai. In 1965 he emerged from retirement to form *Rafi* (Israel Labour List) – a breakaway group of former *Mapai* members.

Benn, Anthony Wedgwood (1925–). UK Labour politician and Minister of Technology (1966–70). He was formerly Postmaster-General (1964–66) and in 1963 successfully fought a campaign to renounce the title inherited from his father, Lord Stansgate.

Beria, L. P. (1899–1953). Soviet Secret Police Chief. A ⇨ Bolshevik from 1917, Beria made his career in Georgia, where he first specialized in Secret Police activities and later worked in the Communist Party *apparatus*. In Dec. 1938, he succeeded ⇨ Yezhov as People's Commissar for Internal Affairs, in which capacity he was responsible for all subsequent Secret Police activities until ⇨ Stalin's death (March 1953). For a brief time a member of the post-Stalin ⇨ Collective Leadership, he was swiftly ousted by his colleagues and executed in 1953.

Berlin. Former German capital, since May 1945 under Allied control, whose post-war history reflects, often in accentuated form, the East-West tensions which kept the former Allies as well as Germany divided. The Four Power Statute (June 1945) vested authority over Berlin in the Allied *Kommandantura* made up of the generals commanding the city's four occupation zones. Under its supervision an elected town council was to attend to the day-to-day administration, but the feebleness of communist representation (they polled only 20% at the Oct. 1946 elections) provoked continuous Soviet vetoes, e.g. Russia's refusal to recognize the election of E. Reuter as Berlin's mayor (June 1947). Disagreement over German policies, particularly over the currency reforms the Western Allies had recently introduced, led to the Berlin Blockade (March 1948–June 1949). Russian attempts to force the issue by cutting the surface supply lines to West Berlin and its garrison were defeated by the Berlin Airlift. During the confrontation Russia withdrew from the *Kommandantura* (June 1948), thus making joint government impossible. Zonal boundaries hardened into definite frontiers when, within days of each other, the USSR and the Western Allies introduced separate currencies into their respective sectors (June 1948). The split was formalized after communist demonstrations against and

occupation of the city parliament (Sept. 1948) resulted in the establishment of separate municipal administrations in East and West Berlin
(Nov./Dec. 1948). Although after the lifting of the blockade, the Paris
Foreign Ministers Conference (June 1949) confirmed Allied access
rights to and freedom of movement within Berlin, it failed to reunite the
divided city. Indeed the rift deepened when the ⇨ GDR made East
Berlin its capital (Oct. 1949) and the Federal Republic gave West Berlin
Land status (Oct. 1950), at least economically, since its 22 *Bundestag*
delegates have no voting rights, which are also withheld from the East
Berlin guest deputies in the GDR's *Volkskammer*. With the Federal
Republic's admission to NATO, West Berlin was given a large measure of
independence although the *Kommandantura*, in order to emphasize
legal continuity, remained the ultimate source of power. After a period
of comparative calm, Russia renewed pressure on West Berlin (Nov.
1958) when she demanded that within six months the unworkable Four
Power statute must be replaced by new agreements providing for the
creation of a demilitarized free city. The Allied refusal to countenance
the unilateral abolition of international agreements led ⇨ Khrushchev
partly to implement his threat to hand over control of all access routes
to Berlin to the GDR by allowing the East German authorities to build
the Berlin Wall (Aug. 1961), thus physically separating the eastern from
the western sector. The Western Allies, denouncing the wall as 'illegal',
failed to demolish it after an 'eyeball to eyeball' confrontation of
American and Soviet tanks across the zonal border. Nor could they
prevent a Soviet declaration (Oct. 1962) denouncing the Four Power
Statute as no longer valid. The Allied military presence, underlined by
President Kennedy's visit (Aug. 1963), demonstrated Western determination to hold on to West Berlin. It remains, however, an extremely
sensitive area, always exposed to probing pressures on its vulnerable
communications with which the East German authorities interfered in
1965 and again in March 1968. Within the wider context of Chancellor
⇨ Brandt's ⇨ Ostpolitik, West Berlin's inviolability has been re-
affirmed by the Four Power Agreement (September 1971) between
France, the UK, USA, and USSR.

Berlin Airlift. ⇨ Berlin.
Berlin Blockade. ⇨ Berlin.
Berlin Wall. ⇨ Berlin.
Bessarabia. Claims to this area (north-west of the Black Sea) were for
long disputed between ⇨ Rumania and Russia. It has a mixed population of Rumanians, Ukrainians, Russians and others, with Rumanians
predominating. Since World War 1, Bessarabia has repeatedly changed
hands. It was annexed by Rumania (1918) but again yielded up to the

USSR (July 1940) after a Soviet ultimatum. As Germany's ally in the war against the USSR, Rumania reconquered Bessarabia (1941) while the USSR, in turn, reconquered it in 1944, since when Bessarabia has formed part of the Moldavian Soviet Socialist Republic.

Betancourt, Romulo (1908–). President of ▷ Venezuela (1959–64). Organizer of the anti-communist Left and founder and leading member of AD (*Accion Democratica*). Exiled by Vicente Gomez and again from 1939 to 1941 and from 1948 to 1958. President of military-backed junta (1945–47), who in turn deposed AD government (1948). A strong opponent of 'guerrilla subversion', his prestige as a political leader extends beyond the borders of Venezuela.

Bevan, Aneurin (1897–1960). Welsh miner's son who became deputy Leader of the UK ▷ Labour Party (from 1959) and its Treasurer (from 1956). As Minister of Health (1945–51), he was the chief architect of Britain's National Health Service. Minister of Labour (1951) until his resignation over Health Service charges (▷ Gaitskell). Entered Parliament in 1929; briefly expelled from his party (1939) for supporting ▷ Cripps' advocacy of a united front of all parties opposed to ▷ Chamberlain. An outstanding orator, he was a strong opponent of Labour's defence policies. The champion of the constituencies' section and the left wing of the Labour Party he failed in his bid to achieve the leadership of the party (1955). Subsequently Shadow Cabinet spokesman first for Colonial and then for Foreign Affairs.

Beveridge Report (UK 1942). Sir William Beveridge's plan for universal social security in Britain ('from the cradle to the grave'). It aimed at abolishing the causes of want (poverty, unemployment) by a system of insurance benefits, anticipating some of the social legislation of the ▷ Attlee Government (1945–51).

Bevin, Ernest (1881–1951). UK Foreign Secretary (1945–51), member of ▷ Churchill's War Cabinet and Minister of Labour and National Service (1940–45); his authority stemmed from his prominent position in the Trades Union movement. He organized the Transport and General Workers' Union (General Secretary 1921–40) and was a member of the General Council of the ▷ TUC (1925–40; Chairman 1937). A dominating figure in ▷ Attlee's Cabinet, who contributed decisively to the establishment of the system of Western alliances (e.g. Brussels Pact, ▷ NATO), his period as Foreign Secretary was somewhat overshadowed by the failure of his Palestine policy and the strife which accompanied the end of the Mandate (▷ Israel).

Bhutan. *Area* – 18,000 sq. miles. *Population* (1972 est.) – 1,010,000. *Head of State* – King Druk Gyalpo Wangchuk. A semi-independent state with an absolute monarchy, Bhutan's status depends largely on her close relations with India. By the Treaty of Friendship (1949) India recognized Bhutan's autonomy but assumed the former role of the UK (Bhutan had been a British Protectorate) in subsidizing the country and guiding her external affairs. Increased tension on the northern frontier, especially after the Chinese invasion of India (1962), has made this relationship with India more important for Bhutan (which has only a militia with which to defend herself) and India gave her the assurance that an invasion of Bhutan would be regarded as an invasion of India. China still claims part of Bhutan. The present king, who has ruled since 1952, has carried out reformist measures at home including the abolition of slavery and the caste system.

Bhutto, Zulfikar Ali (1928–). President of ⇔ Pakistan (1971–), was appointed after Pakistan's defeat by India in Dec. 1971. A former Foreign Minister (1963–66) he promoted close relations with the People's Republic of China and favoured a stronger line towards India over Kashmir. In 1967 he formed the opposition People's Party and won popular support, especially from the students. As president, Bhutto initiated social and political reforms including state control of the country's major industries.

Biafra and Biafran-Nigerian Conflict. ⇔ Nigeria.

Bidault, Georges (1899–). Prominent French politician, bitter opponent of ⇔ de Gaulle, one of the outlawed ⇔ OAS leaders, fled to Brazil. A distinguished Resistance leader during World War II, he led the Paris uprising (19.8.1944) and became Foreign Minister in de Gaulle's provisional and subsequent governments (1944–48). Member of the moderate left wing MRP (*Mouvement Républicain Populaire*) and in 1949 its President, Bidault was one of the most prominent politicians of the ⇔ Fourth Republic, serving twice as Prime Minister (1946; 1949–50). Identifying himself increasingly with the Algerian settlers, he left the MRP, founded (1959) the *Rassemblement pour l'Algérie Française*, presided over the Algerian *Conseil National de la Résistance* (1962) and belonged to the terrorist OAS Executive. He returned to France (June 1968) when the warrant against him was withdrawn.

Bierut, B. E. (1892–1956). A member of the Polish Communist Party from 1921, in the inter-war years Bierut divided his time between underground political work in Poland and lengthy visits to the USSR. Jailed in Poland, he survived the dissolution of his party by the ⇔ Comintern and the execution of many leading Polish communists in the USSR in the late 1930s. After the outbreak of the war, he made his way to the USSR where he was put in charge of communist party work in the Soviet-sponsored Union of Polish Patriots. Parachuted into Poland in 1943, Bierut was the chief organizer of the ⇔ Lublin

Committee and became the first President of the post-war Polish Republic. The most powerful communist leader with ⇨ Stalin's backing, he replaced ⇨ Gomulka in 1948 as the First Party Secretary and retained that position until his sudden death in Moscow in March 1956.

Bill of Rights. In the USA the first ten amendments (in fact, addenda) to the Constitution, adopted in 1791, which guarantee certain basic ⇨ Civil Rights and ⇨ Civil Liberties to the citizens. Some of them are of little importance now; but the ⇨ First Amendment and the ⇨ Fifth Amendment are of continuing importance, as are the Fourth (against 'unreasonable searches and seizures'), the Sixth (speedy and fair trial), the Seventh (trial by jury), and the Eighth (against 'cruel and unusual punishments'). Other rights and liberties not specifically mentioned in the Bill of Rights are, in accordance with the Ninth Amendment, nevertheless not denied. Some are specified in later amendments, notably the Thirteenth, ⇨ Fourteenth, and Fifteenth – the 'Civil War Amendments' – which rule against slavery and guarantee civil equality. The Fifteenth Amendment, which extends the right to vote to all citizens without regard to race or colour, has provided the basis for the Negro ⇨ Civil Rights Movement. Still other rights and liberties have been specified from time to time by the ⇨ Supreme Court, exercising the power of judicial review – for example, the 'right to travel', in 1958 and 1964. Though not strictly part of the Bill of Rights, such additional guarantees are made possible by the existence of that instrument. It should be noted, however, that the requirement for ⇨ Due Process of Law excepted, these guarantees do not necessarily hold against the several States.

Bipartisan Foreign Policy. Generally, aspects of the foreign policy of the USA supported by both the ⇨ Democratic Party and the ⇨ Republican Party. There is a widespread conviction that 'politics should stop at the water's edge'. More particularly, it refers to the view on foreign policy, associated with Democratic President Franklin D. ⇨ Roosevelt and Republican Senator Arthur Vandenberg, and supposed to have been operative from 1942 to about 1950, which held that on matters of foreign policy the President should act in collaboration with the responsible leaders of both parties in ⇨ Congress, that both parties should generally support the position adopted by the President, and that differences should not be made into inter-party issues in electoral campaigns. In practice, whilst there was less inter-party conflict over foreign policy after the Second World War than after the First, there was never a fully-developed bipartisan foreign policy, certainly not in the 1950s and 1960s. Such agreement as there was related mainly to

Europe. There was little agreement respecting the Far East. This is not to say, however, that there were profound differences between the parties on the general lines of United States foreign policy. The lines of division between the parties are, if anything, even less clearly drawn on foreign than on domestic policy questions, though each party may sometimes have a distinctive style or emphasis in its approach to foreign policy. Consequently, whilst United States foreign policy may not be strictly bipartisan, it can often be non-partisan, appealing to major sections of Congress and the public regardless of party. This was perhaps most true immediately after the war and during the presidency of Dwight D. ⇨Eisenhower. On the other hand, President ⇨Johnson's attempt to place foreign policy on a basis of 'consensus' was far from successful, though the attack on his policies, especially in the Far East, from inside and outside Congress, came as much from members of his own party (Senator ⇨ Fulbright, Chairman of the important Senate Foreign Relations Committee, being a notable example) as from his party's opponents.

Black Muslims. American Negro movement, insisting on Negro superiority and racial separation. It has countered 'White racism' with 'Black racism'. Totally rejecting 'White' values, its members have adopted the forms of Islam. One of its most influential leaders was ⇨Malcolm X, assassinated in Feb. 1965. He created a climate favourable to the spread of ⇨Black Power ideas among Negroes in the USA. The movement also has its adherents in the UK.

Black Panther Party (USA). Its name derives from the symbol used by ⇨Black Power candidates organized by Stokeley ⇨Carmichael to fight elections in Lowndes County, Alabama, in 1966. In the same year Carmichael became Chairman of ⇨SNCC, and the two bodies worked closely together for a time. Subsequently, while SNCC declined, the Black Panther Party, under the leadership of 'Minister of defense', Huey P. Newton, and 'Minister of information', Eldridge Cleaver, became more prominent, especially in Oakland, California. In recent years, its Black nationalist ideology has been affected by 'Marxist' thinking and ideas current in the ⇨New Left. Its members carry arms – they claim for the protection of Black communities. In 1968, Cleaver went into virtual exile, first in Cuba, and finally in Algeria, when his parole from prison in California was revoked. Arrests and 'shootouts' with police – instigated, according to some, by the police, and according to others, by the Panthers themselves – thinned the active ranks of the organization, though these had never exceeded 2,000. Splits among leaders and members developed, particularly between a more concilia-tory Newton faction and a more uncompromising Cleaver faction, and by mid-1971 the organization was in serious disarray. At that time, the House of Representatives Internal Security Committee (successor to ⇨HUAC), which had been investigating the organization for two years, reported that although it was 'subversive' it was not a 'serious threat to security'. Black political activity has in recent years been increasingly directed to using the 'System' rather than overthrowing it.

Black Power. Slogan of Negro militants in the USA, used by Stokeley ⇨ Carmichael and others from about 1965, and adopted by a number of ⇨ New Left organizations, including ⇨ SNCC and the ⇨ Black Panther Party. It advocates a rejection of ⇨ Integration as a solution to the race problem, though it is seldom used in reference to full separation as advocated by the earlier ⇨ Black Muslims. Those who use it are sometimes accused of being Black racists, but claim rather to be Black nationalists whose aim is to win for their own people their rightful place in America without seeking to denigrate or dominate other groups. Their demands range from securing for Black citizens an influence and benefits proportionate to their numbers in accordance with American ⇨ Pluralism, to establishing control by Black people over all agencies and facilities in their own areas.

Blum, Léon (1872–1950). With Jaurès, co-founder of the French Socialist Party (1902) and from 1920 its leader. Headed the first ⇨ Popular Front government (1936–37), introducing social welfare measures and proposing nationalization schemes which contributed to the downfall of his government. Served as vice Prime Minister in the Chautemps Cabinet (June 1937–Jan. 1938) and again as Prime Minister (March–April 1938) without, however, gaining the necessary Senate approbation. In the wake of the French defeat he was 'tried' by the ⇨ Vichy authorities on a war guilt charge at the ⇨ Riom Trials and interned by the Germans in Buchenwald and Dachau concentration camps. After the war he went to the US to negotiate economic assistance for ⇨ France and headed a socialist minority caretaker government (Dec. 1946–Jan. 1947). For a short time editor and frequent contributor to the socialist *Le Populaire*, he also wrote books on political and general subjects (*Du Mariage, A l'Echelle Humaine*). His humanism and literary interests made him the classic representative of an intellectual and middle-class socialist tradition.

Bogoraz-Daniel, Larissa. Wife of Yuli ⇨Daniel (⇨Dissent – Eastern Europe).

Bolivia. *Area* – 424,160 sq. miles. *Population* (1970 est.) – 4,658,000. *President* – Gen. Hugo Banzer (1971–). *Constitution* – There have been a number of constitutions since the first one was promulgated in 1826. Under the present 1947 Constitution (revived in 1964), executive power is vested in the President. There is a Congress of a Senate and Chamber of Deputies. A decree (1952) abolished the selective franchise based on literacy, giving the vote to all adult citizens, literate and illiterate.

Deprived of access to the sea after a series of disastrous local wars, Bolivia emerged into the twentieth century as one of the poorest countries in South America. Its hierarchical society – the Indian majority dominated by a *mestizo* élite – was threatened by the disastrous ⟡Chaco War (1932–35). Demobilized soldiers formed the nucleus of a discontented proletariat. Radical demands were thwarted by military coups, though General Busch's administration (1936–39), which nationalized Standard Oil, combined authoritarian rule with social reform. In the forties an inflated economy, stimulated by World War II, contributed to political unrest. (Pro-Axis sentiment delayed Bolivia's declaration of war until 1943.) After a brutally suppressed miners' strike, General Villarroel, backed by the *Movimiento Nacional Revolucionario* (MNR), headed a successful revolt (1943). Support for the MNR, formed by ⟡Paz Estenssoro in 1941, ranged from the extreme Left to some army officers and the radical Right and from liberal intellectuals to mine labourers. With the MNR leaders in exile, following Villarroel's assassination (1946), traditionalist parties returned to power. In the 1951 presidential elections, Paz, in exile in Argentina, secured a majority, but was prevented from taking office by military intervention. The following year the MNR, helped by defecting *carabineros* (police militia), staged a short, bloody but successful revolt. Peasant land ownership through the division of large estates, the enfranchisement of the whole population and mine nationalization destroyed the old political structure. Despite these measures, and the anti-imperialism of the MNR left wing, the regime received massive doses of US aid. Increasingly authoritarian, after his 1964 election victory Paz modified the constitution to keep himself in power and maintain his hold over the disintegrating MNR. Vice-President General ⟡Barrientos, claiming to protect the revolution, staged a coup (1964), then shared the presidency with General Ovando (1965) before resigning to compete successfully in the 1966 presidential elections. Barrientos was strongly opposed by the miners, particularly the Trotskyist POB – *Partido Obrero Revolucionario*, and the mines were occupied by the army (1967). In the same year there was an outbreak of guerrilla warfare in which Régis Debray was captured and Che ⟡Guevara killed. Following the overthrow of the Government by Gen. Condia, he was ousted by Gen. Torres after an army coup. In August 1971 Gen. Banzer replaced Torres following a takeover by right-wing elements in the army.

Bolsheviks. Name originally applied to the section of the All-Russian Social Democratic Workers Party which was founded and led by Lenin. The term Bolsheviks (meaning literally Majoritarians) was first adopted in 1903 after the 2nd Congress of the Russian Social Democratic Workers' Party, at which Lenin's faction received a majority vote against the faction led by Martov, thereafter called Mensheviks (Minoritarians). In 1912, the Bolshevik faction set itself up as a separate party. After its victory, it changed its name (1918) to All-Russian Communist Party (Bolsheviks); in 1925, to All-Union Communist Party (Bolsheviks); and in 1952 to its present name, Communist Party of the Soviet Union (CPSU). After the foundation of the ⇨Communist International, the term Bolshevik was widely used as a synonym for communist and Leninist. (⇨Bolshevism.)

Bolshevization. A slogan proclaimed at the 5th World Congress of the ⇨Communist International (1924) in the context of ⇨Stalin's battle against ⇨Trotsky. The slogan was designed to make the condemnation of Trotsky and Trotskyites obligatory for all sections of the Comintern and to subject them generally to the changing requirements of the Soviet leadership.

Bolshevism. The influence of ⇨Marxism on Russia's revolutionary intelligentsia led towards the end of the 19th century to the foundation of a Russian Social Democratic Party. The Party subsequently split over the problem of how to apply ideas evolved in the context of West European capitalism to Tsarist Russia which was still overwhelmingly a peasant country ruled by a pre-bourgeois autocracy. Originally they all accepted the Marxist view that socialism could only develop from a bourgeois-capitalist society and that the immediate aim therefore was a bourgeois-democratic revolution. But Lenin convinced himself early on that the Russian bourgeoisie was too weak and indecisive to bring about that revolution. Even a bourgeois-democratic revolution, he concluded, could in Russia only be achieved by the small, newly emerging working class, supported by the mass of the peasantry. Yet, the workers, according to Lenin, lacked political class-consciousness and were thus merely a potentially revolutionary force. Political class-consciousness, he insisted, can be brought to the workers only from without by a vanguard of revolutionary Marxists. The revolutionary vanguard, according to Lenin, should be closely linked to the working class but should itself play the role which the Jacobin clubs played in the French Revolution. To exercise effective leadership, Marxists must turn themselves into professional revolutionaries, knit together in a conspiratorial, strictly centralized and tightly disciplined organization. The Menshevik opposition to these ideas argued that the ⇨Bolshevik organization, which Lenin created on these principles, was taking onto itself the role of the initiator of revolutionary change which, according to Marx, belonged to the proletariat as a class.

Lenin's chance came after the overthrow of the Tsar in Feb. 1917. By then he had come to share ⇨ Trotsky's opinion that, in view of the seemingly imminent revolutions all over Europe, the Russian democratic revolution could be almost immediately transformed into a socialist-proletarian revolution. By the time it emerged that the European revolutions had failed to materialize, the Bolsheviks were already firmly in power and were thus faced with the alternative of abdicating in favour of a bourgeois-capitalist regime (which they never even considered) or embarking on a hitherto never envisaged enterprise, the construction of socialism in a single and still largely pre-capitalist country.

The Bolsheviks had seized power (7.11.1917) through the medium of the ⇨ Soviets which, after February, had spontaneously sprung up all over Russia. Like others at the time, Lenin then still believed that his slogan 'All Power to the Soviets' would lead to the establishment of a revolutionary 'direct' democracy of the overwhelming majority of the population on the model of the Paris Commune of 1871 – the authentically Marxian 'dictatorship of the proletariat'. Yet, almost immediately after the Bolshevik victory, the soviets began to lose power to the dictatorship of the Bolshevik Party. One by one, the workers' and peasant parties represented in the soviets were outlawed until, by the end of the Civil War, the soviet regime had become a mere façade for the communist one-party state. This happened originally under the pressure of circumstances rather than by deliberate design. But it followed, with an inner logic of its own, from the very concepts which had guided Lenin in the creation of the Bolshevik Party. Established as a self-appointed élite, 'linked' to the working class rather than part of it, the Party had, even before its victory, laid claim to a monopoly of political wisdom and leadership. Their victory provided the Bolsheviks with the chance of translating this claim into an immutable fact of political power, which they later used to transform their country by an uninterrupted series of 'revolutions from above' without the need to enlist popular consent. At a still later stage, Lenin's heirs elevated the fact of monopolistic political rule to the central new dogma of communism. In its contemporary formulation this new dogma is usually expressed in the slogan of the paramount duty of all communists to maintain 'the leading role of the party'. (⇨ Bolsheviks, ⇨ Bolshevization, ⇨ Communist International, ⇨ Marxism, ⇨ USSR, ⇨ World Communism.)

Bonn. Capital of German Federal Republic (⇨ Germany, Federal Republic of).

Borneo. The third largest island in the world (287,000 sq. miles), Borneo consists of four political regions. Kalimantan, the largest part (about 70% of the area) belongs to ⇨ Indonesia, which also claims the rest of the island. On the northern coast are ⇨ Brunei (a British protected sultanate), Sabah and Sarawak (formerly British colonies but now part of the Federation of ⇨ Malaysia). Borneo was occupied by the Japanese during World War II. After the formation of the Federation of Malaysia in 1963 the island became the base for Indonesia's policy of ⇨ Confrontation.

Bosch, Juan (1909–). President of the ⇨ Dominican Republic (1963), overthrown by a military coup. A democratic socialist he lived in exile from 1937 to 1961 and again from 1963 to 1966, and again since 1966. President and founder of the PRD (*Partido Revolucionario Dominicano*).

Botswana. *Area* – 222,000 sq. miles. *Population* (approx.) – 540,000 African, 4,000 European, 3,900 Coloured (mixed descent) and Asian. *President* – Sir Seretse ⇨ Khama (1965–). *Constitution* – Executive power is vested in the President elected by the National Assembly. The Cabinet, appointed by the President, is responsible to a National Assembly elected by universal adult suffrage, for a five-year term. Matters affecting the constitution must be referred to the House of Chiefs.

Botswana, formerly the British Protectorate of Bechuanaland (⇨ High Commission Territories), is economically dependent on ⇨ South Africa, and its policies affected by the need to live on reasonable terms with this powerful neighbour. It uses South African currency and the railway, its economic life-line, is jointly operated by ⇨ Rhodesia and South Africa. (Even the capital of Bechuanaland was in South African territory until 1964, when, with the help of one and a half million pounds donated by Britain, work was started on a new capital city at Gaberones.) Political development is hampered by years of economic neglect and the consequent lack of capital and technical resource endemic in the ⇨ Third World. Chronic underemployment forces half the working population to seek work in South Africa. Botswana's links with Britain go back to 1885 when a tribal chief, fearing Boer encroachment, appealed to Queen Victoria for British protection. Tribal loyalties are important in Botswana and Sir Seretse Khama, though committed to modernization, must still take them into account. Seretse Khama, despite six years of exile and his forced renunciation of the chieftainship, triumphantly returned to power when his Bechuanaland Democratic Party swept the polls in the general election of March 1965. Internally self-governing from March 1965, Bechuanaland became an independent republic within the Commonwealth, changing its name to Botswana (30.9.1966). Botswana's strategic position ensures that it is and will be profoundly affected by developments in neighbouring states. At the moment, it serves as a buffer rather than a bridge between Black ⇨ Zambia and 'White' South Africa, nor can it risk friction with ⇨ Smith's Rhodesia. These considerations, rather than its own initiatives, are likely to affect its policies in the near future.

Boumedienne, Col. Houari (1925–). Prime Minister of ⇨ Algeria. A former teacher, he organized and commanded the National Liberation Army (ALN) of the ⇨ FLN from 1960. He helped ⇨ Ben Bella to seize power (1962) and was his Minister of Defence and (from 1963) deputy Prime Minister, until he deposed him (19.6.1965) to become President of the newly-formed Revolutionary Council, and a month later, Prime Minister.

Bourguiba, Habib (1902–). President of ⇨ Tunisia. Educated at Paris University and a member of the Destour Party from 1921, he broke away and formed the ⇨ Neo-Destour in 1934. Imprisoned by the French from 1934 to 1936 and 1938 to 1942, he was released by the Nazis, but refused offers of cooperation from them or the Italians. The post-war repression of nationalism led him to flee to Cairo (1945) from where he campaigned for Tunisian independence. Imprisoned by the French from 1952 to 1954, he became the first Prime Minister (8.4.1956) and President (8.7.1957) of the Tunisian Republic. Notable for his seeming moderation, he has called for a more realistic approach to their problems by Arab leaders. In 1964 he appointed his son Habib Bourguiba Jr. his Foreign Minister.

Bow Group. Organization of reformist younger members of the UK ⇨ Conservative Party acting as a ginger-group to modernize party policy. Its publications tend to be associated with the 'left wing' of the Conservative Party.

Brandeis, Louis Dembitz (1856–1945). US jurist, Supreme Court Justice (1916–39). Acquiring a reputation as a liberal, he acted as counsel for the people in disputes over government power to regulate the hours and wages of workers, and was appointed an Associate Justice of the Supreme Court by President Wilson. During the early 1930s his liberal views were reflected in the many cases in which he dissented from the opinion of the Court's conservative majority. He resigned in 1939 and devoted himself to the Zionist movement until his death in 1945.

Brandt, Willy (1913–). Chancellor of the German Federal Republic, previously Foreign Minister (1966–69), became internationally known as West ⇨ Berlin's fighting mayor (1957–66) who resisted East German and Russian encroachments. A life-long socialist, he fled to Norway to escape Nazi persecution. Returning to Berlin after the war, he quickly rose in the party hierarchy to become a member of the ⇨ SPD's Executive (1962) and since 1964 its leader. The opposition's choice for Prime Minister, he failed to win the 1961 and 1965 general elections. A pragmatist, he supported the party efforts to shed its class basis and Marxist dogmatism (*Godesberger Programm*, Nov. 1959). As Foreign Minister Brandt renewed the dialogue with the East; diplomatic relations were established with Rumania in 1967 and resumed with Yugoslavia in 1968. In August 1970, as Chancellor, Brandt signed a treaty with the Soviet Union (*Gewaltverzicht*) and initiated his conciliatory ⇨ *Ostpolitik*; ratification of this (May 1972) eroded his parliamentary majority, compelling him to hold a premature general election in Nov. 1972 at which he was, however, reelected.

Brazil. *Area* – 3,286,000 sq. miles. *Population* (1970) – 93,215,301. *President* – Gen. Emilio Garrastazu Medici (1969–). *Constitution* – Federal Republic established 1891. Subsequent amendments and revisions have increased the power of the Union (Central Government) at the expense of the states. The latest revision (1967) has diminished the authority of the Legislature and increased executive power. The Legislature consists of a bi-cameral National Congress – Federal Senate and a Chamber of Deputies. Senate members are elected from each state and the Federal capital. In a system of proportional representation, the Deputies are elected by compulsory adult suffrage for a four-year term – men and employed women – with a literacy qualification. Executive power is vested in the President, now voted into office by an electoral college representing both houses of the National Congress. Each state elects its own governor and has its own internal administration with its powers defined by the constitution.

In the 1930s, the Brazilian economy, heavily dependent on a single product – coffee, was particularly hard hit by the Depression. With dissatisfaction increased by a manipulated presidential election, the defeated candidate, Getulio ⇨ Vargas, supported by the army and acclaimed by the city population, overthrew the government and assumed the presidency. For the 15 years (1930–45) of his first, and from 1937 dictatorial regime, Vargas based his authority on: a wide coalition of previously neglected group interests (from industrialists to urban workers), an elaborate government-directed political machine, and an increasingly centralized administration which created a vast army of dependent civil servants. In some of its attitudes and effects on the country, the Vargas government anticipated *peronismo* in

⇨ Argentina and ⇨ Paz Estenssoro's rule in ⇨ Bolivia. Brazil's economy, stimulated by the war, was transformed. (In 1942 Brazil declared war on the Axis.) Rapid industrialization was reflected in the increasing political importance of a rising middle class and emergent urban proletariat as well as in a (still continuing) architectural revolution and a new nationalism. Vargas proclaimed his corporate *Estado Novo* (1937) after suppressing a left-wing revolt. His power was entrenched in a new constitutional amendment repealing the law forbidding the President's re-election. Despite economic development (the government established a state-controlled steel industry (1941)), and educational and social reform including advanced (but not always effective) labour legislation (1943), opposition to the dictatorship increased. After the war the military intervened and forced Vargas to resign (Oct. 1945). Two political parties (the Labour PTB – *Partido Trabalhista Brasileiro* and the PSD – *Partido Social Democratico*), appealing to different elements among Vargas' supporters, were formed and General Dutra was elected President. The next elections (1950) following recurrent economic crises, restored the presidency to the still popular Vargas. Plagued by economic failure and the threat of military intervention, Vargas' second presidency ended in suicide (1954). By the end of ⇨ Kubitschek's presidency (1955–60), a period of staggering economic expansion, Brazil was easily the most powerful industrial nation in South America. Kubitschek's extravagance (he founded the new capital, Brasilia), though cushioned by a booming economy, was set against a background of rising inflation and increasing corruption. His successor, Quadros, swept into office (1960) to clean out corruption, resigned within a year. He was succeeded, against the wishes of the army, by his Vice-President ⇨ Goulart (1961). Thwarted by a hostile Congress, Goulart's attempts (though unsuccessful) to outbid the Left only increased the hostility of industrialists and the army. In 1964, an army coup, described by its leaders as a revolution, installed Marshal Branco as President. Direct presidential elections – the constitutional device which in Brazil most nearly reflected the popular will – were abolished. In 1965 only two specially-constituted political parties – the government party (ARENA – *Aliança Renovadora Nacional* and in opposition the MDB – *Movimento Democrático Brasileiro*) – were officially recognized. Marshal Costa e Silva, approved only by ARENA, became President in 1967. The 'revolution' has increased the power of the central government and its theme has been restraint – economic and political. Opposition, from the extreme Left to liberals anxious for a return to civilian government, has been curbed. The army, claiming to represent the people's will and meet its needs, has stepped out of the wings onto the centre of the political stage. Gen. Medici became President in Oct. 1969.

Brazzaville Conference (1944). Called by General de Gaulle to revise the relationship between France and her overseas territories. Regarded as the first step in post-war constitutional advance of France's African colonies, its provisions included social and economic reform of the overseas territories (while adhering to their indivisibility with France), and the election of territorial assemblies. The main recommendations were incorporated in the second French constitution of 1946 and provisions made for election of representatives of the overseas territories to the French National Assembly and Senate.

Brazzaville Group (1959–61). Comprising the former colonies of ⇨ French Equatorial Africa, the ⇨ *Conseil de l'Entente*, ⇨ Cameroun, ⇨ Mauritania, ⇨ Malagasy Republic and ⇨ Senegal – sought economic and political cooperation (in the first place in relation to ⇨ Algeria) and was superseded by UAM and later ⇨ OCAM.

Brezhnev, L. I. (1906–). Secretary-General, ⇨ CPSU Central Committee, Brezhnev joined the ⇨ Komsomol in 1923 and the CPSU in 1931. An engineer by training with a flair for organization, he made his career in the Ukraine as a protégé of ⇨ Khrushchev. A full-time party official from 1938, he served during the war as a political administrator on various sectors of the Ukrainian front. A member of the Ukrainian Central Committee from 1949 and, for a time, First Secretary of the Moldavian Party Committee, he took his place in the central party leadership in 1952, when he was simultaneously promoted to the CPSU Central Committee and its Secretariat. In 1954, Khrushchev put him in charge of the ⇨ Virgin Land Campaign in Kazakhstan. Back in Moscow in 1956, he was brought back into the Secretariat and, in 1957, he became a member of the Presidium (now the Politbureau). In 1960, he replaced ⇨ Voroshilov as Chairman of the Presidium of the USSR Supreme Soviet (Head of State), a post he relinquished in July 1964 to become Khrushchev's Deputy in the party Secretariat. Three months later, he replaced Khrushchev as First Secretary, a post he has retained ever since, changing its name back to Stalin's old title of Secretary-General (April 1966). Since the early 1970s, his personal status has outstripped that of his colleagues in the country's 'collective leadership'. In his subsequent dealings with foreign statesmen, includ. Pres. ⇨ Tito (Sept. 1971), Pres. ⇨ Pompidou (Oct. 1971) and Pres. ⇨ Nixon (May 1972), he was treated and acted as the *de facto* new one-man ruler of the USSR.

Brezhnev Doctrine (also described as the 'doctrine of limited sovereignty'). A term coined outside the USSR after the invasion of

⇨Czechoslovakia (Aug. 1968) for the thesis advanced by L. I. ⇨Brezh-
nev and other Soviet spokesmen in justification of the intervention, i.e.
that socialist countries are entitled to intervene in other socialist
countries if and when the preservation of socialism is deemed to be
threatened.

Bricker Amendment. A proposed amendment to the Constitution of
the USA, sponsored by Senator John Bricker of Ohio in 1953. It would
have limited the power of the Federal government to make treaties and
⇨ Executive Agreements by requiring that, in order to have effect
within the USA, their terms would have to conform to the Constitution.
As international treaties and agreements are, with the Constitution, the
'supreme law of the land', Federal legislation may be valid by their
terms even though it would not have been valid by the terms of the
Constitution itself. The Administration strongly opposed any such
amendment, on the grounds that it would limit the freedom of action of
the President in foreign affairs and hamper United States foreign
relations. A version of the proposal failed by one vote to receive the
necessary two-thirds majority in the ⇨ Senate in 1954. In 1957, the
⇨ Supreme Court ruled that treaties and agreements were subordinate
to the Constitution, but it may still be possible for the Federal Government to extend its powers through these instruments into fields otherwise reserved to the States.

Britain. ⇨ United Kingdom of Great Britain and Northern Ireland.

British Cameroons. ⇨ Cameroun.

British Caribbean Federation Act. ⇨ West Indies Federation.

British Commonwealth. ⇨ Commonwealth.

British East Africa. Prior to their independence, consisted of ⇨ Kenya,
Tanganyika (⇨ Tanzania) and ⇨ Uganda. Until recently (Kenya 1966,
Uganda and Tanzania 1967), shared a common currency. They are still
linked by a transport system (railways, harbours and air services)
administered in common by the three states.

British Empire. ⇨ Commonwealth.

British Guiana. ⇨ Guyana.

British Honduras. *Area* – 8,866 sq. miles. *Population* (1969 est.) –
122,000. *Governor* – Richard Neil Posnett (1972–). *Prime Minister* –
George Price (1965–). *Constitution* (1964) – The Governor is the Queen's
representative and retains certain powers (e.g. defence, internal
security). Executive authority is vested in a Prime Minister and Cabinet
responsible to a bi-cameral National Assembly consisting of an appointed Senate and an elected House of Representatives.

From 1871, British Honduras was a Crown Colony administered by
a Governor-in-Council. A minority of the Council was elected from

1936 until 1954 when a Legislative Assembly with a majority of elected members was established. The colony became internally self-governing under a new constitution in Jan. 1964; full independence had been anticipated by 1968 but to date (1973) it retains its colonial status. Political development has been complicated by ⇨ Guatemala's territorial claims. The dispute was discussed at the UN (1946) and Britain (opposed by Guatemala) proposed that the matter be put before the International Court of Justice (⇨UN). The People's United Party won 16 seats in the elections (1965). The opposition National Independence Party (two seats 1965) fear that the Prime Minister is not sincere in claiming that he will keep British Honduras in the Commonwealth after independence. Their anxiety has not been decreased by the proposal to rename the territory Belize.

British Somaliland. ⇨ Somalia.

British Union of Fascists (U K). Founded by ⇨Mosley in 1932 with a programme for a British corporate state involving a strong government, the abolition of the party system and restrictions on political freedom. The Union imitated the Italian Fascists, adopting their salute and their blackshirt uniform, but it never achieved the mass support of some of its European counterparts. The public became increasingly alienated by its political violence, especially after the maltreatment of hecklers at a meeting at Olympia in June 1934, its anti-semitism and admiration for Hitler – symbolized by the change of name to 'British Union of Fascists and National Socialists'. Continuing violence led to the Public Order Act (1936) allowing the police to restrict demonstrations. On the outbreak of war its leaders and many of its members were arrested.

Broederbond. The secret society which has decisively influenced South African politics since the early thirties. Led by Calvinist intellectuals, dedicated to achieving a White Afrikaaner Republic, the *Broeders* united the chronically schismatic ⇨ National Party. Through the *Broederbond* Dr ⇨Verwoerd and his allies established a power network resulting in a virtual dictatorship over party and country for the *Volksleier* (people's leader). Sectarian, pro-Nazi, militantly anti-British and antisemitic during the war (policies now carefully forgotten), including Prime Ministers and most Cabinet Ministers among its membership, it has been the government within the government since 1948.

Brosio, Manlio (1897–). Italian politician and diplomat who became NATO's Secretary-General in Aug. 1964. An anti-Fascist imprisoned by Mussolini, he served as deputy Prime Minister (June–Nov. 1945) and Defence Minister (Dec. 1945–June 1946) before joining the diplomatic service as ambassador in Moscow (1946–51), London (1952–55), Washington (1954–61) and Paris (1961–64).

Brown, George (1914–). Deputy Leader of the UK Labour Party (1960–70) and a leading member of the Wilson Cabinet (1964–68). He also held the position of deputy Prime Minister. As Minister for the new Department of Economic Affairs (1964–66) he was responsible for creating the machinery to implement the Government's prices and incomes policy. By conviction an economic expanionist, Brown nearly resigned over the Government's restrictionist measures of July 1966. Appointed Foreign Secretary (July 1966) he resigned in March 1968. His period at the Foreign Office was marked by Britain's second unsuccessful attempt to negotiate entry into the ⇨EEC. Brown had held junior ministerial posts under Attlee and was Minister of Works in 1951. He later became a strong Gaitskellite and defended ⇨Gaitskell in his fight against the unilateralists in the Labour Party in the early 1960s. He lost his seat in the 1970 general election and entered the House of Lords as Lord George-Brown.

Brown v. Board of Education (of Topeka, Kansas, USA). An historic legal action in which the ⇨Supreme Court, in 1954, decided that racial segregation of schools in the South violated the guarantee of 'equal protection of the laws' contained in the Fourteenth Amendment to the Constitution. In 1955, the Court ordered that schools be integrated with 'all deliberate speed'. By thus declaring ⇨Segregation unconstitutional, and reversing the earlier ⇨'Separate but Equal' ruling, the Court justified opposition to ⇨Jim Crow Laws in the South and gave a strong impetus to the Negro ⇨Civil Rights Movement. In many subsequent decisions the Court invalidated measures taken by States to perpetuate segregation in schools, and endorsed such measures as ⇨'Busing' for promoting integration, but with diminishing determination after 1969.

Brunei. *Area* – 2,226 sq. miles. *Population* (1971 est.) – 137,000. A British-protected state on the north coast of ⇨Borneo. The 1959 constitution granted the Sultan additional powers in local affairs. A Legislative Council was established but the UK retained control over foreign and defence matters.

The country has an oil-based economy. There is one political party, the Independence Party, which is an amalgamation of all former parties, and although there has been pressure to democratize the state (elections to the Legislature were finally held in 1962), the Sultan retains a large measure of control over the affairs of the country. In 1963 Brunei, unlike neighbouring ⇨Sabah and ⇨Sarawak, declined to join the newly formed Federation of ⇨Malaysia. Islam is the official religion of the country.

Bucharest Meeting. Conference of communist party delegations attending the Rumanian Communist Party Congress of June 1960, which became the occasion for the first Sino-Soviet clash in front of other communist parties. (▷ Sino-Soviet Conflict and ▷ World Communism.)

Bukharin, N. I. (1888–1938). Soviet communist. A ▷ Bolshevik since the age of 18, Bukharin became one of the leading and most influential Soviet communists. Linked in ▷ Lenin's Testament with ▷ Pyatakov as the two ablest men among the younger generation of Bolsheviks, Bukharin was, according to Lenin, not only a most valuable and most distinguished Party theoretician, but also 'rightly regarded as the darling of the entire Party'. In the factional struggles after Lenin's death, Bukharin first sided with ▷ Stalin against the 'left' and became ▷ Zinoviev's successor as the head of the ▷ Communist International. In 1929, when Stalin suddenly reversed his previous policies and embarked on compulsory collectivization, Bukharin became the leader of the 'right' opposition to Stalin, supported by ▷ Rykov and Tomsky. In 1938, Bukharin was the leading defendant in the last of the three ▷ Moscow Trials. He was convicted and executed as a traitor.

Bukovsky, Vladimir (1941–). Soviet writer and spokesman of the Soviet civil rights movement. Arrested in 1963 for contributions to clandestine journals, he was for 18 months confined in the mental ward of a prison hospital. On his release, he agitated for a fair trial for his fellow-writers ▷ Sinyavsky and ▷ Daniel; re-arrested, he was again forcibly confined to a mental prison hospital. Discharged after a year, he was re-arrested in 1967 and sentenced to 3 years in a forced labour camp. On his release in 1970, he appealed to Western psychiatrists to concern themselves with the widespread Soviet practice of imprisoning dissenters in mental institutions. This appeal and other activities on behalf of the Soviet civil rights movement earned him a fresh sentence (in 1971) of another 7 years imprisonment in a 'strict regime labour camp' to be followed by 5 years of exile.

Bulganin, Marshal N. A. (1895–). Former Premier of the USSR. A ▷ Bolshevik from 1917, Bulganin served his apprenticeship in the ▷ Cheka, but later made his career as an administrator. He rose to prominence after the great purges and distinguished himself during the war as an economic and military organizer. Created a Marshal after the war he became deputy Premier, Minister of Defence and a member of the party's Politbureau. Confirmed in these posts after Stalin's death, he subsequently joined ▷ Khrushchev in a number of widely publicised foreign visits. In 1955, he replaced ▷ Malenkov as Premier, but fell into disgrace in 1957, when Khrushchev routed the ⇨Anti-Party Group. In 1958, Khrushchev succeeded him as Premier, after which Bulganin retracted his earlier support for the 'Anti-Party Group'. He has lived in retirement since 1960.

Bulgaria, People's Republic of. *Area* – 42,823 sq. miles. *Population* (1966) – 8,256,800. *Chairman*, State Council (head-of-state) – Todor ⇨Zhivkov. *Prime Minister* – Stanko Todorov. *First Secretary, Communist Party Central Committee* – Todor Zhivkov. By a decision taken in July 1968, a new constitution is being prepared. Pending its completion, the highest organ of state power is the National Assembly, the unicameral Legislature elected by universal suffrage from a single list of candidates. Effective power rests with the leadership of the Communist Party, headed by its First Secretary, Todor Zhivkov.

For the greater part of the inter-war period Bulgaria was dominated by repressive dictatorial regimes and beset by repeated insurrections, *coups d'état* and outbreaks of terroristic violence. A semi-democratic interlude between 1931 and 1934 ended with a military *coup d'état*, led by Damian Velchev and Kimon Gheorghiev. They, in turn, were overthrown in 1935, when King Boris III established his own royal dictatorship which he maintained until his death in 1943. Traditionally pro-German and intent on regaining the territories lost to Yugoslavia, Greece and Rumania in the Balkan War of 1913 and after World War I, Bulgaria joined the ⇨Tripartite Pact in March 1941. In the following month the German armies were given facilities to use Bulgaria as a base for their attack on ⇨ Yugoslavia. In the aftermath Bulgaria was rewarded with the permission to annex Thrace from Greece and ⇨Macedonia from Yugoslavia. Later, Bulgarian troops helped in the occupation of further areas in Greece and Yugoslavia conquered by Germany. An active belligerent against its ⇨Balkan neighbours and in a state of war with the Western powers, Bulgaria remained officially neutral in Germany's war against the USSR. Its internal policies, at the same time, increasingly followed the Nazi model, complete with anti-Jewish persecutions and the close cooperation of the two countries' political police forces in the brutal repression of democrat and communist opponents.

The best-known communist leader, Georgi ⇨ Dimitrov, was then living in the USSR. Inside Bulgaria, communist resistance against the regime was directed by Traycho ⇨ Kostov until his arrest in 1942. Other communists still at liberty, among them Anton Yugov, took the initiative in organizing the underground Fatherland Front – an anti-Fascist, republican coalition between their own party, the left wing of the influential Agrarian Union, led by Nikola Petkov, the left wing of the

Social Democrats, led first by Cheshmedjiev and, after his death, by Kosta Lulchev, and *Zveno*, a group led by Velchev and Gheorghiev who had ruled Bulgaria from 1934 to 1935. From the summer of 1943 onwards, the Fatherland Front organized partisan resistance against (Bulgarian) police and army units. The partisans were controlled by communists and later received help from the Yugoslavs. After King Boris' death in 1943, a Regency Council was set up which appointed a new government. In the summer of 1944, this government made peace with the Western Allies. A few days later (5 Sept.), the USSR declared war on Bulgaria. Bulgaria immediately asked for peace terms and declared war on Germany (6 Sept.). On 8 Sept. the Red Army entered Bulgaria without meeting resistance and the Fatherland Front seized power in Sofia (9 Sept.). The imprisoned communists were freed; Gheorghiev became the new Premier, and Anton Yugov, the communist Resistance leader, took over the Ministry of the Interior and the control of the police. The Bulgarian army then helped the Yugoslav partisans in the final liberation of their country from the Germans. Nazi collaborators and the erstwhile persecutors of the communist and democratic opposition were arrested and tried. Having executed or imprisoned many thousands of their enemies, the communists then turned on their allies in the Fatherland Front. Their proposal for a single joint list of candidates for the elections of Oct. 1946 was turned down both by Petkov for the Peasant Party and Lulchev for the Social Democrats. They both contested the elections, despite the personal intervention of the Soviet deputy Foreign Minister, A. Y. ⇨Vyshinsky, growing police terror and the imprisonment of large numbers of peasant party and socialist leaders. Faked results confirmed the communists in power, and Georgi Dimitrov, just back from the USSR, became the new Premier. In 1947, the extermination of surviving opposition leaders culminated in the ⇨Show Trial and execution of Nikola Petkov. The surviving social democrats were compelled to fuse with the communists. ⇨Sovietization was completed in Dec. 1947 with the adoption of a Soviet-type constitution.

During his brief tenure as Premier, Dimitrov was almost wholly occupied with international affairs and his abortive scheme for a ⇨ Balkan Federation. The Communist Party was rent by factional strife between the ⇨Home Communists, led by Traycho Kostov, and the ⇨Muscovites, led by Vlko ⇨Chervenkov. Dimitrov died shortly after ⇨Stalin's break with ⇨Tito, and Chervenkov succeeded him as Premier. Backed by Stalin, his first act was to oust Kostov who, after a Show Trial, was executed (Dec. 1949). In 1950, Chervenkov became party leader as well as Premier and remained Bulgaria's unchallenged dictator until after Stalin's death. Though demoted in stages from 1954 onwards, he remained a powerful influence and continued to be publicly honoured until after ⇨ Khrushchev's second denunciation of Stalin at the 22nd ⇨ CPSU Congress (Oct. 1961). Chervenkov's successor as party leader, and, later also as Premier, was his protégé, Todor Zhivkov. After a series of purges (with Khrushchev's backing) of his many factional rivals, including Anton Yugov, Zhivkov eventually established himself as Bulgaria's acknowledged leader. An invariable supporter of all Moscow's policies Bulgaria, under Zhivkov's leadership, participated in the invasion of ⇨ Czechoslovakia (Aug. 1968) and has remained (together with East Germany) one of the only two communist-ruled states which has never acted in defiance of Soviet wishes.

Bullitt, William Christian (1891–1967). A State Department assistant to President Woodrow Wilson at Versailles. In 1933 President Franklin D. ⇨ Roosevelt appointed him a special assistant to the Secretary of State and then the first US Ambassador to the Soviet Union (he had been a strong advocate of its recognition). From 1936 to 1941 he was United States ambassador to France. Bullitt was a strong and outspoken advocate of American aid to France and Britain and eventually of American entry into the war. During the early years of World War II he served as special assistant to the Secretary of the Navy and in 1944, unable to enlist in the United States Army, he joined the Free French as Chief of the Psychological Warfare Division. After the war he advocated aid to Chiang Kai-shek.

Bundestag. The ⇨ German Federal Republic's Lower House of Parliament in Bonn. Its 518 Deputies (Sept. 1965) are elected by universal suffrage for a period of four years; among them are 22 West ⇨ Berlin Deputies who have no voting rights.

Bundestag was also the name given to the Austrian Parliament under the authoritarian ⇨ Dollfuss and ⇨ Schuschnigg regimes (1934–38); since 1945 known, as previously in Austrian history, as the *Nationalrat*.

Bureau of the Budget. An agency of the Federal Government in the USA, established in 1921 in the Treasury Department and transferred to the ⇨ Executive Office of the President in 1939. It is responsible for co-ordinating the budgets of other Federal agencies, each of which prepares its own estimates with the aid of a budget officer who works closely with the Bureau. Agreed proposals are submitted to the President for approval, and his final decisions are contained in the Budget Message which he sends to ⇨ Congress early in each session. Congressional action is required to authorize both the purposes for which funds are requested and, separately, the ⇨ Appropriation of the necessary funds; and at both stages the President's requests can be wholly or partially refused. Thus the executive does not have full control over budgeting, and an important task of senior members of the Bureau of the Budget is persuading ⇨ Congressional Committees to accept the President's proposals. In practice, the President's budget is largely accepted by Congress, whilst the Bureau's disapproval of proposals coming from members of Congress is often sufficient to prevent their enactment. In addition to its primary functions, the Bureau has responsibility for organization and management throughout the Executive, for scrutinizing the legislative proposals of Federal agencies, and for maintaining statistical records. It is headed by a Director appointed by the President with the consent of the Senate.

Burger, Warren L. (1907–). Chief Justice of the USA (1969–). Graduated from the University of Minnesota, he attended night-school to obtain his Law qualifications. He was appointed Assistant Attorney General by President Eisenhower (1953), and then (1956) to the US Circuit Court of Appeals for the District of Columbia (Washington). He was often a conservative dissenter from the judgements of a generally liberal court. Appointed Chief Justice by President Nixon – an appointment that gained easy confirmation in the Senate – he has tended, unlike his predecessor, Earl ⇨ Warren, to favour a strict constructionist position regarding the interpretation of the Constitution by the ⇨ Supreme Court.

Burma. *Area* – 261,789 sq. miles. *Population* (1970 est.) – 27,584,000. *Prime Minister* – General ⇨ Ne Win (1962–). *Constitution* – An independent Republic since 1948, Burma has been ruled by a military government since the constitution was suspended in 1962. Executive and legislative power is held by General Ne Win who heads the Revolutionary Council. The Union of Burma consists of Burma Proper and the five states of Chin, Kachin, Karen, Kayah and Shan.

Burma was formerly a British colony and until 1937 a part of British India, in which she was given some measure of self-government. During the 1930s popular pressure for independence led to anti-British riots, militant student strikes and the formation of political private armies, e.g. the Thakin Army which was trained in Japan. During World War II Burma was occupied by the Japanese (1942–45), who set up a puppet government composed largely of Thakins under Ba Maw. British rule was re-established after the Japanese defeat but in 1948 independence was granted to Burma, which became a republic with a President elected by the two Houses of Parliament. The first Prime Minister was U ⇨ Nu, who held the office until 1962 with two breaks (1956–57, 1958–60). The governing party was the Anti-Fascist People's Freedom League (AFPFL), a loose confederation of many interests including the (Marxist-Leninist) Socialist Party, the Peasants' Organization, the Trades Union Congress and communal organizations. The AFPFL won 85% of the vote in the first election (1951) and followed a socialist programme, e.g. nationalization and the establishment of a welfare state. Government efforts to bring about political and communal harmony were jeopardized by armed risings of communists and Karen tribesmen (who had formed the most effective wartime resistance) and the situation was further confused by acute balance of payments problems resulting from the sharp drop in the world price of rice, on which Burma mainly depended. U Nu established Buddhism as the official religion in an attempt to heal political divisions, but in the 1956 election the AFPFL majority was greatly reduced. In 1958 a split in the governing party led to a crisis when U Nu handed over power to a military government under General Ne Win which restored order but earned increasing unpopularity. In the 1960 election U Nu was returned with a sweeping victory but he failed to fulfil his promises and in order to check the growing threat of separatism by the national minorities the army overthrew him in 1962. Ne Win became Prime Minister and imposed military rule, abolishing the 1947 constitution, replacing it with a Revolutionary Council and prohibiting parties. Ne Win introduced a policy of nationalization, e.g. the banks and trade (1963), and of centralization to defeat separatism (the Shan and other states are not Buddhist like Burma Proper). In foreign relations Burma has been neutralist. She declined to join the ⇨ Commonwealth and has not joined ⇨ SEATO and non-communist regional organizations like ⇨ ASA and ⇨ ASEAN although she is a party to the ⇨ Colombo Plan. Maintenance of good relations with her neighbour China is necessary for Burma's security. In the early 1950s international tension was caused by the presence of Chinese Nationalist troops in Burma who made forays across the Chinese border and Burma insisted on their removal. In 1956 Chinese troops invaded Burma but later withdrew, and in 1960 a Treaty of Friendship and Non-Aggression was signed between the two countries. This was supplemented by a border agreement the same year. Foreign policy has not changed with the military government (foreign aid is still accepted from both China and the USA) and in recognition of the country's neutrality a Burmese (⇨ U Thant) was chosen as UN Secretary-General in 1961.

Burnham, Lindon Forbes Sampson (1923–). Prime Minister of ⇨ Guyana (1964–). A socialist (leader of the PNC and previously with ⇨ Jagan a leader of the PPP), Burnham's administration depends on the support of the right-wing UF. Burnham has accepted an International

Commission of Jurists' recommendation to recruit more Indians for the public services. Unless Burnham can conciliate the East Indian community (about half the population and with the fastest rate of increase), the determined exclusion of the PPP from office threatens further unrest. He was re-elected (Dec. 1968).

Burundi. *Area* – 10,000 sq. miles. *Population* (1969 est.) – 3,475,000. *President* – Colonel Michel Micombero (1966). *Constitution* – Without one since the declaration of a Republic – Nov. 1966. Like ⇨ Rwanda, formerly part of the Belgian-administered Trust Territory of Ruanda-Urundi, Burundi became independent on 1 July 1962. It has a recent history of tribal strife, Belgian and Chinese involvement in its affairs and a rapid turnover of governments. Its first Prime Minister was assassinated a month after the UN-supervised general election (Sept. 1961). Following further assassinations and uprisings, with the King in exile, army leader Micombero proclaimed a Republic on 28 Nov. 1966. Relations with Peking were severed in Feb. 1965. In May 1972 widespread fighting broke out between the governing Tutsi tribe and the much larger Hutu tribe with bloody massacres by both.

Busia, Dr K. A. (1913–). Prime Minister of ⇨ Ghana (1969–72). A University lecturer and leading opponent of Dr ⇨Nkrumah, Busia lived in exile in Britain from 1959 until 1966 when he returned to Ghana to become political adviser to the National Liberation Committee. With the restoration of constitutional rule, Busia was elected Prime Minister in Sept. 1969. His government was overthrown by a bloodless military coup led by Gen. Acheampong, while Busia was in hospital in London, on 13 Jan. 1972. An attempt to regain power in July 1972 was unsuccessful.

Busing. In the USA, a method of achieving a 'racial balance' among children in different schools in a State or district in pursuance of the policy of ⇨ Integration. Numbers of children, Black and White, are sent by bus to schools at some distance from their homes, rather than to the neighbourhood schools to which they would otherwise go, in order to overcome the effects of the concentration of families of the different races in separate neighbourhoods. These measures were upheld by the ⇨ Supreme Court on appeal as proper means of ending school ⇨ Segregation in accordance with rulings in ⇨ Brown v. Board of Education. However, popular opposition to busing steadily grew, mainly, though not exclusively, among White parents, and spread from the South to the rest of the country. It was taken up by George ⇨Wallace in the 1968 presidential election campaign, when there was much talk of an impending ⇨ 'White Backlash'. After the elections, the new President, Richard ⇨ Nixon, used his authority to support opponents of busing, and, despite strong pressures from the ⇨ Civil Rights Commission, delays in enforcing court orders in favour of busing were countenanced by Federal officials. Following the mid-term elections of 1970, Congress began to consider a possible 'moratorium' on busing, and demands for Congressional action became urgent in 1972 after George Wallace, campaigning on the issue for the Democratic presidential nomination, won the Florida ⇨ Primary Election. In June 1972, Congress incorporated into the Higher Education Amendments legislation provisions postponing till 1974 court orders requiring busing. At the same time it voted $2,000 m. to aid in desegregation among $19,000 m. appropriations for higher education.

Bustamante, Sir William Alexander (1884–). First Prime Minister of an independent ⇨ Jamaica (1962) until ill-health forced his retirement (1965). As a trades union leader (from 1937) he was a pioneer of the political movements which ultimately led to Jamaican independence. At a trial (1939) for organizing a strike in war-time, he was defended by his cousin (later his main political opponent) Norman ⇨ Manley, and was interned (1940–42). His Jamaican Labour Party (1943) owed its success to his personal style of leadership, and was supported by business as well as union interests. His opposition to the ⇨ West Indies Federation was largely responsible for a referendum (1961) which resulted in the Federation being dissolved.

Butler, Richard Austen (1902–). UK Conservative but reformist politician, distrusted by the party stalwarts and twice passed over for the party leadership (1957 and 1963). Though a supporter of ⇨ Chamberlain's ⇨ Appeasement policy, he later became Minister of Education (1941–45) in Churchill's government and was responsible for the Education Act of 1944 raising the school-leaving age. After the Conservative election defeat of 1945 he played a crucial part in modernizing the party's organization and policies. In the 1950s his critics claimed that there was little difference between Butler's conservatism and Gaitskell's socialism, hence the term 'Butskellism' to describe the two. He held many important government posts, including Chancellor of the Exchequer (1951–55), Home Secretary (1957–62) and later deputy Prime Minister and Foreign Secretary. In 1965 Butler retired from politics and became Master of Trinity College, Cambridge.

Byrnes, James Francis (1879–1972). US Secretary of State (1945–57). In the House of Representatives (1911–25) and as a Senator (Democrat, South Carolina, 1931–41), he at first advocated but later opposed ⇨ New Deal programmes. Never having broken with President ⇨ Roosevelt, he was appointed to the Supreme Court (1941) but resigned after one year to direct the Office of Economic Stabilization and then War Mobilization (1943–45). As Secretary of State he played a significant role in the negotiations of the peace treaties at Paris and in the establishment of the UN Atomic Energy Commission. Byrnes was elected Governor of South Carolina (1950–55) and became a leader of conservative southern Democrats.

C

Cabinet. In the USA, the heads of the 12 major executive departments acting as a body of advisers to the President. They are, in order of rank: the ⇨Secretary of State, the Secretaries of the Treasury and of Defense (head of the ⇨Defense Department): ⇨Attorney General; Postmaster General; and the Secretaries of the Interior; Agriculture; Commerce; Labor; Health, Education and Welfare; Housing and Urban Development; and Transportation. They are appointed by the President with the consent of the ⇨Senate, are responsible to him, and are removable by him at any time. The Vice-President and the Ambassador to UNO are sometimes also included. Whilst the Cabinet can be important as an advisory body, it is not a decision-making body comparable to the British Cabinet. Some Presidents make much use of the Cabinet, some prefer to deal with its members individually, and others rely on informal groups of personal advisers who may be known as a 'kitchen cabinet'. (⇨UK Constitution and ⇨Shadow Cabinet – UK.)

Cadre. In communist usage a term for Communist Party members trained to exercise leading functions within the Party or in other institutions under Party control.

Caetano, Professor Marcello (1906–). Prime Minister of ⇨Portugal since Sept. 1968. A close collaborator of Dr ⇨Salazar, he helped draft the 1933 constitution, became Minister for the Colonies (1944–47), President of the National Union and deputy Prime Minister (1955–58).

Cairo Conference (1964). ⇨Belgrade Conference.

Callaghan, James (1912–). UK Labour Party politician, responsible, as Chancellor of the Exchequer (1964–67), for the policy of economic restraint. He resigned the chancellorship after devaluation of the pound, and was Home Secretary 1967–70. In 1963 Callaghan stood unsuccessfully against ⇨Wilson and ⇨Brown for the leadership of the Labour Party.

Cambodia. *Area* – approx. 70,000 sq. miles. *Population* (1972 est.) – 7,100,000. Formerly a Kingdom under the leadership of Prince

Sihanouk, Cambodia was proclaimed a Republic after a *coup d'état* (March 1970). The new leader was Marshal Lon Nol who declared a state of emergency and assumed the office of President (March 1972).

In 1941, while Cambodia was still a French Protectorate within Indochina, the French chose Prince Sihanouk, then only 19 years old, over the head of his father, to succeed as King on the death of his grandfather. Soon afterwards, the Japanese established their overlordship over all Indochina. In 1945, on the eve of their surrender, the Japanese empowered King Sihanouk to proclaim Cambodia's independence. After the end of World War II, King Sihanouk concluded an agreement with France transforming Cambodia into an autonomous Kingdom within the ⇨ French Union, but he continued to agitate for full independence. As a result of the ⇨ Geneva Agreements of 1954, Cambodia – like ⇨ Laos – became a fully independent state committed to a policy of neutrality.

In Cambodia, as in Laos, pro-communist groups, with the assistance of the ⇨ Viet Minh, had set up their own organization – the Khmer People's Party – which took up arms against the authorities. In contrast to Laos, however, these forces had been largely subdued by the time the Geneva Conference met. At Geneva, Cambodia, again like Laos, undertook to re-integrate the opposition forces into the general community and to hold elections by 1955. King Sihanouk adhered to this undertaking by abdicating in the spring of 1955 and forming a party under his own leadership, the Popular Socialist Community, which in the subsequent elections for a National Assembly won all the seats. Having styled himself Prince Sihanouk since that time, he was overthrown during a trip abroad. In Sept. 1970 he established an exile counter-government in Peking, which, by the summer of 1972, had gained the *de jure* recognition of 16 non-aligned states and 7 communist states (Albania, China, Cuba, N. Korea, Rumania, N. Vietnam, Yugoslavia). The remaining communist powers (Bulgaria, Czechoslovakia, East Germany, Hungary, Poland, USSR) maintain diplomatic relations with the Republican government, while recognizing Prince Sihanouk as the legitimate Head-of-State. The *coup d'état* involved Cambodia in an increasingly bitter civil war, in which both North and South Vietnamese forces intervened in strength. By mid-1972, most of the countryside was held by forces loyal to Sihanouk, while Marshal Lon Nol's troops controlled most towns.

Cameroun, Federal Republic of. *Area* – 180,000 sq. miles. *Population* (1970) – 5,836,000. *President* – Ahmadou Ahidjo (1960–). *Constitution* – Federal, with an elected President, Vice-President and Federal Assembly. The Eastern and Western Provinces each have their own Prime Minister and Legislative Assembly.

In 1919, Kamerun (a German colony from 1902) was divided and administered by Britain and France under League of Nations Mandate. In plebiscites (1961) the Northern Cameroons (British) voted to join ⇨ Nigeria and the Southern Cameroons (British) voted to join the Cameroun Republic, established, after five years of rebellion and civil disorder in the French Cameroons, on 1 Jan. 1960. Cameroun is a member of ⇨UDEAC, ⇨OCAM and the ⇨OAU.

Canada. *Area* – 3,852,000 sq. miles. *Population* (1972 est.) – 21,689,578. *Prime Minister* – Pierre Elliott ⇨ Trudeau (1968–). *Constitution* – Independent Dominion within the ⇨Commonwealth, its sovereignty confirmed by the Statute of ⇨Westminster (1931). The British North America Act (1867) provided that the constitution should be 'similar in principle to that of the UK' – the Queen is represented by the Governor-General who appoints the Prime Minister who is responsible to Parliament. Parliament consists of the Senate, whose members are appointed for life by the Governor-General on a regional basis, and the House of Commons, elected for five years by universal adult suffrage. Canada is a confederation of ten Provinces (Alberta, British Columbia, Manitoba, New Brunswick, ⇨ Newfoundland, Nova Scotia, Ontario, Prince Edward Island, Quebec and Saskatchewan) with two Territories (Yukon and the North-west Territories). Each Province has its own Lieutenant-Governor, Parliament and Administration and regulates its local affairs, e.g. education, health, justice, taxation, but the powers not expressly granted to the provincial governments are reserved to the Federal Government.

Canada is the world's second largest state (in area) and one of its leading industrial nations. Both English and French are official languages with about 70% of the population English-speaking and about 30% French-speaking. Of the two main parties, the Liberal Party, which draws its main strength from French Canada and the Prairie Provinces, favours a diminution of UK and US influence, and supports comprehensive social security, held office from 1935 to 1957 (1935–48 under William L. Mackenzie ⇨ King and 1948–57 under Louis St. Laurent) and has been in office since 1963 (under Lester ⇨ Pearson 1963–68 and since April 1968 under Pierre Trudeau). The Progressive Conservative Party, which draws its main support from the Anglo-Canadian Eastern Provinces and supports free enterprise with selective public ownership and increased trade with the Commonwealth, ruled from 1930 to 1935 (under Richard Bennett) and from 1957 to 1963 (under John ⇨ Diefenbaker). The party is now led by Robert Stanfield (1973). Other parties include: the New Democratic Party (a Labour party founded in 1961 supporting major economic planning and a non-nuclear role for Canada), the Social Credit Party (based on Alberta) and the Creditists (based on Quebec). At the general election in June 1968 the Liberals increased their seats to 154, the Conservatives won 71, the New Democratic Party 23 and the Creditists 15. Canada's pre-war aloof attitudes to world affairs have changed radically since 1939 and her important contribution to the Allied cause in World War II. Apart from her military effort, Canada became the fourth-largest producer of war materials (after the USA, Britain and the Soviet Union) and her rich sources of uranium ores and hydro-electric engineering contributed to the manufacture of the atom bomb. In 1940 she signed the Ogdensburg Agreement with the USA for the defence of North America and formed a joint defence board with that country. Canada emerged from the war with an enhanced international position and her new industrial expansion, depending on the exploitation of vast natural resources, formed the basis of her post-war prosperity. Canada was a founding member of ⇨NATO, sent forces to Korea in 1950 and in the same year joined the ⇨ Colombo Plan to aid the development of South-East Asia. Cooperation with the USA was a mainstay of Canadian foreign policy (exchange of defence and atomic information, the North American Air Defence Command (NORAD) agreement of 1958 (extended 1968)), although she did not support US opposition to accepting Communist China into the UN and has been critical of American policy in ⇨Vietnam. Despite growing economic involvement with the US – 72% of Canada's imports came from the USA in 1966 and US investors controlled 74% of the oil industry and 60% of the manufacturing industry in 1963 – Canada has continued to play a major role in the Commonwealth (the first Commonwealth Secretary-General is a Canadian) and trade links with its members, especially the UK, are important. Also a strong UN supporter, Canadian contingents served with UNEF (United Nations Emergency Force) in the Middle East (1956–67). Canadian domestic politics have been affected by the growth of ethnic rivalries in recent years. The Catholic French Canadians have maintained their own culture partly through regional concentration – some $4\frac{1}{2}$ of their 6 million live in the Province of Quebec. By 1967, separatist parties in Quebec secured popular support for a separate Province, which was encouraged by ⇨de Gaulle's visit that summer and his apparent support for 'le Quebec libre'. Regionalism was growing in other parts of the country and later in 1967 a Royal Commission on bi-lingualism and bi-culturalism was appointed. This was followed early in 1968 by a constitutional conference, which recommended bi-lingualism at all levels of administration throughout the country. Legislation to make Canada officially bi-lingual was introduced in the autumn of 1968. One sign that a solution might be reached was the increased support given in the 1968 general election to the Liberals, whose new leader Trudeau, although himself a French Canadian, campaigned on the issue of national unity. He was reelected in 1972.

Cape Verde Islands. ⇨ Portuguese Overseas Provinces.

Capitol. USA – the building in which a Legislature meets (hence a term for the legislative branch of government), applied particularly to the building on Capitol Hill in Washington DC where the US ⇨ Senate and ⇨ House of Representatives meet. The ⇨ White House, where the President resides, is a mile distant, thus symbolizing the ⇨ Separation of Powers.

Caradon, Lord (1907–). UK representative at the UN 1964–70, he was formerly, as Sir Hugh Foot, Governor-in-Chief of Jamaica (1951–57) and Governor and Commander-in-Chief of Cyprus (1957–60).

Cardenas, Lazaro (1895–). President of ⇨ Mexico (1934–40), the champion of the poor and the Indians, he attempted to give practical effect to the ideals of the Mexican revolution. Large estates were divided and land redistributed among the peasants. A socialist (but not a Marxist and an opponent of Soviet communism), he encouraged trades-unionism. The railways were nationalized (1937) and foreign oil companies expropriated (1938) (though they were later compensated). Unlike previous Presidents and leaders of the revolution (whose socialist principles had not prevented their personal enrichment), he set an example of honesty and financial probity. In accordance with the constitution, and his aim of turning Mexico into a modern democracy, he did not seek re-election for a second term. He served as Minister of Defence (1943–45).

Caribbean Federation. ⇨ West Indies Federation.

Carmichael, Stokely (1942–). Leading ⇨ Black Power advocate in the USA. Born in Trinidad, and taken to the United States at the age of 11, Carmichael rejected the traditional deferential stance of the American Negro and the pacifism of the early ⇨ Civil Rights Movement. During 1965 he organized a Black group to contest elections in Lowndes County, Alabama, under the symbol of the Black Panther, although the claim that he founded the ⇨ Black Panther Party is contested by the leaders of the organization using the name established in Oakland, California, the following year. In any case, his position is unlike that of such leaders of the Black Panther Party as Eldridge Cleaver, inasmuch as he is a Black Nationalist of the kind of ⇨ Malcolm X, and not a Marxist revolutionary. He first gave public currency to the 'Black Power' slogan whilst on a Civil Rights march with the Rev. Luther ⇨ King in 1967, but he denied Dr King's charge of seeking to replace

White supremacy by Black supremacy. Shortly afterwards, however, he declared, 'Our only hope is to destroy the government or be destroyed'. In 1966 he had become chairman of ⇨ SNCC and converted it from a moderate protest organization seeking ⇨ Integration into a militant Black Nationalist organization. In 1967 he was replaced as chairman by the still more militant H. Rap Brown, and his public importance has since declined.

Carol, King. ⇨ Rumania.

Casablanca Conference (14–24 Jan. 1943). Meeting in Morocco between President ⇨ Roosevelt and Prime Minister ⇨ Churchill to plan Allied war strategy after the North African campaign (⇨ World War II). ⇨ Stalin was invited but declined because the USSR wished to follow up the victory at Stalingrad. Important decisions were taken on the future conduct of the war. Offensive action in the Mediterranean was to be continued and Italy invaded to prevent her further participation in the war; the US air force was to join the British bombing of Germany in preparation for the invasion of Western Europe; the UK resources were to be transferred to the Far East after the defeat of Hitler; and meanwhile the USA was to take full responsibility for the campaign against Japan. The Conference is known for Roosevelt's statement, agreed with Churchill, that the Allies demanded the 'unconditional surrender' of the Axis Powers. The phrase, an expression of the Allies' confidence that they would win the war, expressed their determination to rid Germany of Nazism and Europe of the German threat to peace once and for all. The Allies hoped thereby to prevent a repetition of the situation after World War I, when the negotiated peace with Germany on the basis of the Fourteen Points led to inter-Allied disputes and later German charges that the Allies were not fulfilling their promises (which assisted the growth of nationalism in Germany). 'Unconditional surrender' has since been much criticized because its proclamation is said to have stiffened German resistance and so prolonged the war.

Castle, Barbara (1911–). UK Labour Party politician and a leading member of the ⇨ Wilson Cabinet. Minister for Overseas Development (1964–65) and Transport (1965–68); from April 1968 until June 1970 Minister of the new Department of Employment and Productivity with responsibility for implementing the Government's prices and incomes policy. Previously, as an Opposition MP, she was associated with the left wing of the Labour Party.

Castro, Dr Fidel (1926–). Prime Minister of the Republic of ⇨ Cuba. Castro served his political apprenticeship in the revolutionary student movement at Havana University, where he enrolled in 1945 to read law.

By 1952, when a *coup d'état* brought Batista back to power, Castro was a practising lawyer, but soon afterwards abandoned his career to devote himself wholly to revolutionary activities. He staged his first unsuccessful armed rising against the Batista regime on 26 July 1953 – a date commemorated in the name of the movement developing under his leadership. Sentenced to a long prison term after the failure of his rising, he was set free under a general amnesty and left for Mexico. There he collected a group of supporters with whom he spent the next 15 months in military and political training and collecting arms and money from sympathisers. Much of the money was spent on purchasing the small yacht *Granma*, on which Castro, with 82 armed companions, set out in Nov. 1956 to sail to Cuba. They landed on 2 Dec. but only 15 are said to have survived, including Fidel Castro, his brother Raoul and Che ⇨Guevara. The survivors made their way to the Sierra Maestra where they established their headquarters and whence they conducted their guerrilla campaign which, within two years, brought them to power. Though an ardent revolutionary from his early youth and later influenced by general socialist ideas, Castro was not yet a Marxist when he started his guerrilla war and remained for long very critical of the Cuban communists. His own 'July 26 Movement' never developed into an organized party. It consisted of a band of individualistic, undisciplined, but utterly devoted followers held together by the magnetism of Castro's own reckless personality and the quality of his leadership. Castro developed into a communist only after his seizure of power though even then he adhered to his own interpretation of communism. The image he is said to have of himself as a man of destiny entrusted by history with the mission to bring revolution to the whole of Latin America has made him an uncomfortable ally of earlier and more tradition-bound communists elsewhere in the world.

Caucus. Generally, any meeting of the members of a political party or faction. Nowadays in the USA it particularly refers to Democratic and Republican Congressmen's meetings which attempt to arrive at common party decisions on legislative proposals and the selection of congressional leaders. In this sense, 'conference' is often used instead.

CCP. Chinese Communist Party.

CDU. *Christlich-Demokratische Union* – together with the affiliated but regionally independent Bavarian CSU (*Christlich-Soziale Union*) West Germany's largest and, for twenty years, her governing party. It emerged after the war as a successor to the ⇨Weimar Republic's mainly Roman Catholic *Zentrum*, the only bourgeois party to have consistently opposed the Nazi rise to power. Although still most strongly entrenched in the traditionally Roman Catholic regions, it now represents the broad stratum of conservative though not radical opinion rather than denominational views. The party's Ahlener Programme (1947) still envisaged the nationalization of basic industries (mining, etc.) as well as workers' profit sharing schemes, ideas which under Professor ⇨ Erhard were subsequently replaced by the concept of a 'socially responsible market economy' (1949), pragmatically combining the virtues of free enterprise with demands for social justice, job security, etc. Although it ran almost neck and neck with the ⇨ SPD in the Federal Republic's first (1949) elections – CDU 31·2%; SPD 29·2% – the CDU forged ahead and with 50·2% gained an absolute majority in the 1957 elections. It still holds a commanding lead after winning 47·6% to the SPD's 38·3% in the 1965 elections. The party's main achievement is to have aligned the broad middle stratum of German society behind the liberal and democratic institutions of the Federal Republic, preventing the fragmentation and disillusionment of the bourgeois centre, which led to the downfall of the Weimar Republic. Having dropped its share of the vote to 46% in the Sept. 1969 elections and unable to form a coalition with the liberals (FDP), the CDU found itself excluded from power, and in opposition.

Ceausescu, Nicolae (1918–). President of ⇨ Rumania. Ceausescu joined the Rumanian Communist Party in 1936 by way of the Union of Communist Youth. A protégé of ⇨ Gheorghiu-Dej after the communist seizure of power in Rumania, he rose rapidly in the Communist Party. Elected to the Central Committee in 1952, he became a member of its Secretariat in 1954 and a member of the Politbureau in 1955. By 1957 he had become the most important party leader after Dej and, upon Dej's death (March 1965) he succeeded him as the Party's General Secretary. In Dec. 1967 he took over the state presidency and has since become known as a forthright and skilful champion of Rumania's national interests.

CENTO. Central Treaty Organization – mutual defence pact for the Middle East between Iran, Pakistan, Turkey and the UK. It replaced the ⇨ Baghdad Pact in 1959 after Iraq had withdrawn from that organization following its revolution of 1958. With the Soviet threat in mind, the pact permits the accession of any member of the ⇨ Arab League and any other state concerned with security in this region. The pact also provides for political and economic cooperation. Its organization, with headquarters at Ankara, consists of the Council (made up of senior ministers of the member countries meeting once a year), the Secretariat and various committees, e.g. military, counter-subversion and economic. The USA is a member of these three committees although she has not joined the organization and signed bilateral agreements for military and economic cooperation with Iran, Pakistan and

Turkey in 1959. There is no provision that an attack on one member is regarded as an attack on the others; military cooperation takes the form of special inter-state agreements. Among the projects sponsored by CENTO have been the Permanent Military Telecommunications System linking Turkey, Iran and Pakistan, the development of the Turkish port of Trabzon and various rail and road links between the member countries.

Central African Federation. ⇨Rhodesia and Nyasaland, Federation of.

Central African Republic. *Area* – 240,000 sq. miles. *Population* (1968) – 2,255,536. *President* – Colonel Jean-Bedel Bokassa (1966–). *Constitution* – suspended. The President governs through a Revolutionary Council.

As Oubangui-Chari, formerly part of ⇨ French Equatorial Africa, the Central African Republic became a self-governing member of the ⇨ French Community in 1958 under Barthélemy Boganda (died 1959) – ⇨ UDEAC is a vestige of his hoped-for French-speaking African federation. In 1960 the Republic attained full independence, remaining in the Community. The first President, M. David Dacko (whose recognition of Communist China was withdrawn by the present government), was ousted by the military coup of the pro-French Col. Bokassa (1.1.1966). The CAR is a member of ⇨ OCAM and ⇨OAU.

Central Committee. ⇨USSR.

Centre–PDM. The label under which J. ⇨ Lecanuet's *Centre Démocrate*, The French Progress and Modern Democracy group, and J. Duhamel's CNI (*Centre National des Indépendents et Paysans*) contested the June 1968 elections. They polled 1·14 m. votes and gained 33 seats, as against 41 in the 1967 elections.

CERN. European Organization for Nuclear Research – set up in Geneva (1954) to promote joint non-military, nuclear research (e.g. building large-scale apparatus like the two synchrocyclotron particle accelerators) beyond the financial resources of individual member countries. These are: Austria, Belgium, Denmark, France, Germany, Great Britain, Greece, Italy, Netherlands, Norway, Spain, Sweden, Switzerland. For financial reasons Poland, Turkey and Yugoslavia are observers and not represented on the Council.

Cernik, O. (1921–). Ex-Premier of ⇨ Czechoslovakia. A Communist Party member since 1945 and for many years active in local and regional party work, Cernik became a member of the Party Secretariat in 1956. He left the Secretariat in 1960 to become Minister of Fuel and Power. In 1963 he was promoted Deputy Prime Minister and Chairman of the State Planning Commission. A member of the Party's Presidium since 1966 and Prime Minister since April 1968, Cernik was one of the advocates of radical economic reforms and of far-reaching democratisation until the Soviet intervention of August 1968. He tried to follow a middle-of-the-road course but was deposed in 1970.

Ceylon. *Area* – 66,000 sq. miles. *Population* (1971) – 12,747,755. *Prime Minister* – Mrs Sirimavo ⇨Bandaranaike (1970–). Constitution (1972) – An independent republic within the ⇨ Commonwealth, Ceylon, now renamed Sri Lanka, was a British colony until the Ceylon Independence Act of 1947 and was an independent state within the Commonwealth until 1972. It is governed by a uni-cameral National Assembly elected for six years and has a titular president.

Ceylon has a mixed population – three-quarters are Sinhalese and Buddhist, but over 20% are Hindu Tamils. A new constitution (1931) provided for universal adult suffrage, an elected Legislature with limited powers and an Executive Council which included some Ceylonese ministers. The country has been governed since independence by two main parties – the conservative United National Party (UNP), representing the English-speaking middle class, which was in office from 1948 to 1956 (under D. S. Senanayake, Dudley Senanayake and Sir John Kotewala) and again from 1965 to 1970 under Dudley Senanayake, this time in coalition with several smaller groups; and the Sri Lanka Freedom Party (SLFP), a socialist party based on the Sinhalese-speaking element which ruled from 1956 to 1960 (under Solomon Bandaranaike and W. Dahanayake) and from 1960 to 1965 (under Mrs Sirimavo ⇨ Bandaranaike). In the 1970 election the SLFP won 90 seats against 17 for the UNP. The political stability of the first decade after independence was threatened in the late fifties by communal disturbances following government moves to establish Sinhalese as the official language in place of English. There were riots by the Tamils which lasted into the sixties and in 1959 Bandaranaike was assassinated. Although Tamil was recognized as the official language in the northern and eastern provinces, this period has not yet passed. The communal problem has not been helped by the rapid growth of population which has more than doubled since 1920. In foreign policy Ceylon has followed a neutral course which is recognized by the two main parties – she is not a member of ⇨SEATO, although she signed a mutual defence pact with the UK in 1947, and received aid from the West, China and the USSR. In 1963 the USA suspended aid after a dispute over compensation for nationalized US oil interests on the island.

CGT. *Confédération Général du Travail* – the French trade unions' central organization which exerted considerable influence on the Third, Fourth and Fifth Republics. The communists, who had split it (1921), rejoined the CGT under the impact of the 1934 Fascist conspiracy. By successfully negotiating the highly advantageous Matignon agreements (1936) in the first months of ⇨ Popular Front rule, the CGT vastly increased its membership and prestige. After the outbreak of war in 1939 it expelled its communist members and was itself dissolved by ⇨ Vichy (1940). Communist control of the CGT when reconstituted after liberation, led to the establishment of the independent break-away *CGT–Force Ouvrière*, which in terms of membership and influence remains, however, much the weaker.

Chaban-Delmas, Jacques (1915–). Prime Minister of ⇨ France (1969–72) he was formerly President of the National Assembly (1958–69). A 'liberal Gaullist' and former Resistance leader, he was a minister in de Gaulle's government (1945). Chaban-Delmas led the Gaullist group in the National Assembly (1953–56) but accepted office in governments of the Fourth Republic (Minister of Public Works (1954–55), Minister without Portfolio (1956–57) and Minister of Defence (1957–58)). From 1947 he was also Mayor of Bordeaux.

Chaco War (1932–35). War between ⇨ Bolivia and ⇨ Paraguay over the possession of the Chaco, a sparsely populated plain at the foot of the Andes. The territory had been disputed since 1810, but the discovery of oil there precipitated the war, particularly as Bolivia needed access to the Paraguay River to ship the oil to the sea. Although Paraguay won the war, it cost 100,000 lives and had a disrupting effect on the economies and politics of both countries. The 1938 treaty granted three-quarters of the area to Paraguay, but Bolivia gained access to the river and the right to construct a port.

Chad. *Area* – 495,000 sq. miles. *Population* (1969 est.) – 3,510,000. *President* – François Tombalbaye (1960–). *Constitution* (1963) – Elected President responsible to a uni-cameral National Assembly. Since 1963 a one-party state.

Formerly part of ⇨ French Equatorial Africa (established as a colony 1913) Chad became self-governing within the ⇨ French Community in 1958 and achieved full independence in Aug. 1960, remaining in the Community. Chad is a member of ⇨OCAM, ⇨OAU and ⇨UDEAC. (In World War II, Félix Eboué, Negro governor of Chad, ensured French Equatorial Africa's loyalty to the Free French.)

Chamberlain, Neville (1869–1940). British Prime Minister (1937–40) whose name is particularly associated with the policy of ⇨ Appeasement, first entered Parliament in 1918 at the age of 50. Chancellor of the Exchequer in 1923; Minister of Health (1924–29) and again Chancellor from 1931 to 1937. A dominant figure in the ⇨ Conservative Party and in the ⇨ MacDonald and ⇨ Baldwin governments and a forceful administrator in Home Affairs, it was his and the country's misfortune that he held the highest office when foreign affairs were of crucial importance. His belief that the maintenance of peace overrode almost all other considerations – 'How horrible, fantastic, incredible, it is that we should be digging trenches and trying on gas-masks here because of a quarrel in a faraway country between people of whom we know nothing' (28.9.1938) – was, at the time, probably shared by the majority of his countrymen. Chamberlain's determination to appease ⇨ Hitler rested on the assumption that the dictator's grievances were reasonable and limited and therefore could be satisfied by timely concessions. When the Czech crisis pushed Europe to the brink of war, he (three times – 15, 22 and 29.9.1938) flew to meet Hitler. On the third occasion (using ⇨ Mussolini's good offices), the Czechs were forced to cede territory to Germany (⇨ Munich Agreement). Failure to guarantee independence of the rump of ⇨ Czechoslovakia (March 1939) led to a dramatic reversal of the Appeasement policy (⇨ UK, ⇨ France). Despite the loyalty of most of his party, Chamberlain at last resigned (May 1940), following the defeat of British forces in ⇨ Norway. He lingered on in ⇨ Churchill's government as Lord President of the Council until ill health forced his resignation the following October.

Chambre des Députés. The Lower House of Parliament of the French ⇨ Third Republic.

Chamoun, Camille (1900–). President of the ⇨ Lebanon (1952–58). His policy of close relations with the USA (in 1957 he accepted the ⇨ Eisenhower Doctrine) led to discontent and to serious riots in 1958.

Chapultepec, Act of. The Act of Chapultepec of 6 March 1945 promulgated at the Mexico City Inter-American Conference, instituted an inter-American system of collective security. The declaration provided that in the event of any aggression against a North or South American State, the threatened country could call for collective action against the aggressor. The Mexico City Conference was limited to those 'cooperating in the war effort' to exclude ⇨ Argentina which had been cooperating with the Axis powers. To prevent Argentina from establishing its own bloc and exerting strong pressure on many Latin American states, the United States convened (1947) at Rio de Janeiro the Inter-American Conference for the maintenance of continual peace and security, which adapted the act to peacetime conditions by forming the Organization of American States. (⇨ OAS, ⇨ Good Neighbour Policy.)

Charter of Punta del Este. Signed (17.8.1961) to set up the ⇨ Alliance for Progress.

Chebab, General Fuad (1902–). President of the ⇨ Lebanon (1958–64). Formerly Commander of the Lebanese Army (from 1945) and Prime

Minister (1952), he succeeded as President after the riots against the pro-Western policy of President ⇨Chamoun and managed to calm the conflict between the Moslem and Christian communities.

Checks and Balances. Institutional arrangements, especially as exemplified in the USA, designed to distribute governmental authority so as to prevent the concentration of political power in one place or in the hands of one person or group. The most important checks and balances established in the United States Constitution are: first, federalism, which divides authority between the Federal and State governments; secondly, the ⇨Separation of Powers, which divides Federal authority between the Executive (the President and his agents), the Legislature (⇨Congress), and the Judiciary (primarily the ⇨Supreme Court); and thirdly, bi-cameralism, which divides legislative authority (including power of ⇨Appropriation) between the ⇨Senate and the ⇨House of Representatives. In practice, power and authority in the United States have been increasingly concentrated in the presidency as the Federal Government has acquired a larger role within the United States, and the United States has acquired a larger role in the world. Even so, the President of the USA is subject to more checks and balances than most other heads of state.

Cheka. Russian abbreviation for Extraordinary Commission. (⇨USSR State Security Service.)

Chen Po-ta (1904–). Chinese communist. A ⇨CCP member from 1927 and, for some years, a student at the Moscow Sun Yat-sen University, Chen made his way to ⇨Mao's headquarters at Yenan after the outbreak of the Japanese war (1937). He became Mao's political secretary, and their association has remained close ever since. In 1949 Chen was appointed Deputy Director of the CCP Central Committee's Propaganda Department, and in 1958 he became the editor-in-chief of the leading CCP journal, *Red Flag*. Promoted to Head of the Central Committee's newly established Cultural Revolution Group (1966), at the 9th party congress in April 1969 he was confirmed in his position as a member of Mao's new top hierarchy by his election to the Politbureau's 5-men Standing Committee. During the following year he fell into disgrace. He has not appeared in public nor been mentioned since 1 Aug. 1970.

Chervenkov, V. (1900–). A founder-member of the Bulgarian Communist Party. In 1925, at a time of severe police persecutions, Chervenkov escaped to the USSR where he remained until his return in 1944 in the wake of the Soviet army. He was immediately elected to the party's Politburureau but achieved real power only after ⇨Tito's expulsion from the ⇨Cominform and ⇨Dimitrov's death. The chief engineer of the trial and execution of ⇨ Kostov (Dec. 1949), Chervenkov became

(1950) both party leader and premier. Attempting to adapt himself to the pattern set by the post-Stalin Soviet leadership, he formally resigned from the party secretaryship in 1954 in favour of his protégé, T. ▷ Zhivkov, while retaining the premiership and the real leadership of the country. From 1956 onwards, he was demoted in stages, but remained a powerful influence until, with Khrushchev's backing, he was publicly denounced for his misdeeds and expelled from the party (Nov. 1962).

Chetniks. ▷ Yugoslavia.

Chiang Ching (1913–). Wife of ▷ Mao Tse-tung and Member of the ▷ CCP Central Committee's Politbureau. An actress before she went to Yenan in 1937, Chiang Ching became Mao's third wife (1939) against the opposition of the Central Committee, which is said to have given its eventual consent on the condition that she kept out of politics. She did so until 1965, since when she has played an increasingly important role as a leader of the Cultural Revolution. Since 1966 she has been listed as a member of Mao's new top hierarchy. The 9th party Congress of April 1969 confirmed her in this position by electing her as one of the 21 full members of the Central Committee's new Politbureau.

Chiang Kai-shek (1887–). Leader of the Chinese Nationalists. In 1928 he became head of the ▷ Kuomintang Government and Generalissimo of the Nationalist Army and since 1950 he has been President of the Republic of ▷ China (Taiwan). He came into prominence as military aide to Sun Yat-sen, first leader of the KMT, who sent him to Moscow to study Russian military methods. After his return to China he founded the Whampoa Military Academy at Canton (1924) and in 1926 led the Northern Expedition which wrested control of China from the war-lords. Having succeeded Sun Yat-sen (who died in 1925) as leader of the KMT, Chiang Kai-shek became head of the Nationalist Government set up in Nanking (1928), a post he held until his defeat by the communists in the Civil War of 1945–49. His rejection of Sun Yat-sen's policy of cooperation with the communists led to civil war with them which only ceased temporarily (1937–40) during the Japanese invasion. Chiang Kai-shek was China's leader during World War II, but in spite of his international prestige (he was Supreme Commander of the Allied Forces (China theatre) 1942–45, represented his country at the Cairo Conference in 1943, and was counted as one of the Big Five), his domestic position was weakened by internal corruption, growing un-popularity and the strength of the communists. Following defeat in the Civil War (▷ Chinese People's Republic) Chiang Kai-shek established his nationalist government in Taiwan. He has continued, with support from the USA, to claim recognition as the only official representative of China.

Chichester-Clark, Major James (1923–). Prime Minister of ⇨Northern Ireland and leader of the Unionist party (1969–71). Formerly Minister of Agriculture (1967–69) and Leader of the House of Commons (1966–69) he succeeded Captain Terence ⇨O'Neill, as Prime Minister. Following the growing disorders in Northern Ireland, he resigned in March 1971 and was succeeded by Mr Brian Faulkner. He was later made Lord Moyola.

Chile. *Area* – 286,396 sq. miles. *Population* (1971 est.) – 10,000,000. *President* – Dr Salvador Allende Gossens (1970–). *Constitution* (1925) – Unitary Republic with an executive President who cannot be immediately re-elected, and a bi-cameral Legislature (Congress) of a Senate and Chamber of Deputies. There is universal adult suffrage, subject to a literacy qualification. The Church was disestablished in 1925.

Chile's continuing political problems derive from: economic stagnation following a period of extensive industrialization between the wars, vast social inequalities, and especially from a rapidly expanding urban population recruited from a depressed peasantry. Yet Chile's history since 1891 has been noticeable (compared with many South American countries) for its lack of violence and, with only brief exceptions, for its adherence to constitutional government. Neither political antagonisms in the twenties nor the economic strains of the Depression produced radical change in its political structure. Economic developments stimulated by the left Popular Front Government (1938–42) – itself weakened by internal dissensions – were not consolidated by succeeding administrations. The continued failure of the political establishment to activate the economy, or to satisfy the needs of urban workers and to meet the demands of a vocal professional middle class, resulted in the emergence (1958 elections) of two new parties. The candidate of one – FRAP (*Frente de Accion Popular*) – was only narrowly defeated – and the other, the Christian Democrat PDC (*Partido Democrata Christiano*), led by Eduardo ⇨Frei Montalva, was successful in the subsequent elections (1964). FRAP, a 'Marxist' coalition, is weakend by doctrinal disputes (it included pro-Moscow, pro-Chinese and Castroite factions) and it split into two main groups in 1968. The PDC is committed to the maintenance of democracy and economic reform, though Frei's presidency was increasingly marked by frustrating conflict between the Administration and Congress. Dr Allende, leader of a socialist coalition elected President Sept. 1970.

Chiltern Hundreds. Accepted formality whereby a British Member of Parliament, by applying for the Chiltern Hundreds, resigns his parliamentary seat. He may only resign if disqualified from holding his seat by accepting an office of profit under the Crown. The 'hundreds' (administrative districts) are Stoke, Burnham and Desborough in Buckinghamshire and their stewardship is an obsolete office given up after acceptance.

China, Republic of (Taiwan). *Area* – 13,885 sq. miles. *Population* (1970) – 14,746,375. *Head of State* – President ⇨ Chiang Kai-shek (1950–). *Constitution* (1947) – Combines both presidential and parliamentary features. Modelled on the five-power system of Sun Yat-sen, it consists of a President with large powers elected for six years by the National Assembly and the Five *Yuans*: the Executive *Yuan* (Cabinet), responsible to the Legislative *Yuan* (elected by universal suffrage), the Judicial, Examination and Control *Yuans*.

The Republic of China consists of the island of Taiwan (Formosa), the nearby Pescadores Islands and the islands of Quemoy and Matsu close to the Chinese mainland. Formerly part of the Chinese Empire, Taiwan became a Japanese possession in 1895 but was returned to China after the Japanese defeat in World War II in 1945. Following the communist takeover of power in China (1949) the Nationalist forces under Chiang Kai-shek withdrew to Taiwan where they proclaimed the Republic in 1950. The Republic's policy since then has been based on her claim to represent the whole of China and so has depended entirely on the USA for political, military and economic support. A threatened invasion of the island by Chinese communists in 1950 was averted when President Truman ordered the US Seventh Fleet to patrol the Formosa Strait and after repeated attacks by mainland China on the offshore islands of Quemoy and Matsu the US Government signed a mutual security pact with Formosa (1954) by which the USA pledged the protection of the Republic. Communist forces resumed their attacks on the two islands in 1958 and meanwhile the Nationalists received training and equipment from the Americans. The USA also exerted pressure on the Nationalist Government to pass agrarian reforms. Considerable American aid resulted in the revival of the economy after the war to such an extent that the USA has been able to diminish its grants (from $69 million in 1961 to $600,000 in 1967). The political question of the two Chinese governments centred on representation in the United Nations, where the Nationalist Government held a seat from 1945–71 and, as the government of one of the five wartime Great Powers, was a permanent member of the Security Council. Pressure for representation of the Peking Government increased with the admission of the newly independent developing nations and the USA postponed discussion of the China issue by a moratorium until 1961 when discussion was permitted with the ruling that it was 'an important matter' requiring a two-thirds majority for a change. In 1971 the Chinese People's Republic was admitted to the UN and the Nationalist Government expelled. American defence of Taiwan is part of the US policy of checking communism in Asia, e.g. the Korean and Vietnam Wars, and as such has taken on symbolic as much as strategic importance. The USA has undertaken no commitment to help the Nationalist Government return to the mainland and clearly its future depends largely on what happens after Chiang Kai-shek's death.

Chinese-Japanese War. Beginning with the seizure of Mukden (Sept. 1931), the Japanese annexed the whole Chinese province of Manchuria and transformed it (Feb. 1932) into a Japanese puppet state called Manchukuo. In 1935, the Japanese began to advance further into northern China and, in July 1937, launched a full-scale invasion, leading to the occupation of all important north-Chinese cities and ports, which reverted to China only after the end of ⇨ World War II.

Chinese People's Republic (CPR). *Area* – 3,768,100 sq. miles. *Population* (approx.) – 700,000,000. *Head of State* – the former President of the CPR, ⇨ Liu Shao-chi, has been ousted without a successor being nominated. *Prime Minister* – ⇨ Chou En-lai. *Chairman, Communist Party* (CCP) – ⇨Mao Tse-tung. *Constitution* – Like all other former laws and institutions has, for all practical purposes, been suspended since the onset of the Cultural Revolution in the mid-1960s.

Before the communist victory over ⇨Chiang Kai-shek in the autumn of 1949, China was for almost four decades a country without a central authority. After the proclamation of a Chinese Republic (Jan. 1912) under the provisional presidency of Sun Yat-sen, effective government was in the hands of the 'war-lords' – provincial governors and generals, each commanding his own army, who, by their misrule and their constant civil wars, immersed China in growing anarchy. The large coastal cities were dominated by foreign powers with extra-territorial privileges. The nominal government in Peking was manned by changing war-lord combinations and, from the early 1920s onwards, a rival national-revolutionary centre, established by Sun Yat-sen in South China, strove to unify the country and liberate it from both foreign encroachments and its own feuding and repressive war-lords. From 1923 onwards, Sun Yat-sen's nationalist 'People's Party', the ⇨ Kuomintang (KMT), received large-scale Soviet support in the form of funds, military equipment and a host of political and military advisers. On Moscow's orders, the members of the CCP (founded 1921) joined the KMT individually, while keeping their own party in being, so as to ensure that the KMT would continue to cooperate loyally with the USSR.

Cooperation began to break down soon after Sun Yat-sen's death in 1925 and the ascendancy of Chiang Kai-shek to the KMT leadership and his appointment as Commander-in-Chief of the KMT government's National Army. The total break came in 1927 when Chiang and his associates, in a series of separate moves, crushed the communist party organizations, followed by large-scale massacres of their leaders, members and sympathizers.

Comintern policies had driven the Chinese communists into an unparalleled disaster. Among those who escaped with their lives was Mao Tse-tung who, with a small communist force, took refuge in a remote mountain area. He was joined there later by other communist contingents brought by Chu Teh, the outstanding military leader of the civil war to come. In 1929, Mao and Chu moved to the province of Kiangsi. With the support of the local peasants, they transformed part of the province into a self-contained 'base-area', later to be proclaimed as the first Chinese Soviet Republic. It was in that period that Mao began to develop his strategy for a communist conquest of power with an army of revolutionary peasant guerrillas operating from rural base areas. Though a founder-member of the CCP, Mao was at that time a mere provincial party official whose ideas and activities were still unacceptable to the party's underground headquarters in Shanghai and its superiors in Moscow. In the early 1930s, police searches drove the remaining communist leaders in Shanghai to seek refuge in Kiangsi. They arrived in the midst of a series of 'encirclement campaigns' launched by Chiang Kai-shek. The fifth and last of these campaigns, started in Oct. 1933, against the communist stronghold, all but succeeded. Unable to hold out, the communists secretly evacuated Kiangsi and other smaller base areas meanwhile established in the south (Oct. 1934). They set out on their legendary Long March which took them from the south right across to the north of China. Fighting battle after battle, they marched for a whole year with the barest minimum of rest until their decimated columns reached the province of Shensi (Oct. 1935). Shensi became their new base area and Yenan their headquarters in the area. It was only during the Long March that the Chinese communist Politbureau acknowledged Mao's qualities by electing him their Chairman (Jan. 1935) – a post he has held ever since.

Meanwhile, in the autumn of 1931, Japan had invaded Manchuria. The end of the Long March coincided with further Japanese advances into North China and also with the new turn towards world-wide united front tactics taken by the Comintern at its 7th World Congress (1935). For both reasons the CCP took the initiative in appealing to the KMT to end their hostilities and to collaborate in a patriotic front against the

Japanese invaders. Chiang Kai-shek agreed to this proposal after Japan's full-scale invasion of China (July 1937). The two sides made a pact, based on mutual concessions, under which each maintained its separate forces and institutions but undertook to support the other side against Japan. By the end of 1937 Peking and most major cities in North China together with their railway and other links were in Japanese hands. The vast rural areas in between constituted a no-man's land in which the communist forces, by experience and training, had a marked advantage over their Japanese enemies and their Nationalist allies, both wedded to methods of positional warfare and unfamiliar with the mobile guerrilla tactics in which the communists excelled. Though supplied with a certain amount of equipment by Chiang Kai-shek, the communists acquired their main supplies themselves in guerrilla attacks on isolated Japanese units or from the stores left behind by routed Nationalist Army units. As they advanced militarily, they established new regional base areas. The governments in all their base areas were united front coalitions, from which landlords and right-wing elements were excluded and which were dominated by the CCP, although communist membership in all administrative units was limited to one-third. Agrarian reforms in all base areas were designed to secure the support of the middle as well as the poor peasants. Prodigious production drives, encouraged by the army's participation in all forms of work and by the establishment of mutual aid teams among the peasantry, helped to sustain the areas economically.

Military, political and economic successes, and the propaganda campaigns accompanying them, attracted growing numbers of outsiders, especially students and other intellectuals, from the coastal cities to Mao's headquarters at Yenan. Mao, Chou En-lai and others had established an 'Anti-Japanese Red Army University' at Yenan to provide future party and army leaders with political and military training. Various forms of political and military training were also provided for the new rank-and-file recruits to the army and the party. A high proportion of the newcomers were prisoners-of-war, deserters from the Nationalist and various war-lord armies and former bandits. The rest were recruited from the peasantry in the base areas under communist control or from other rural areas infiltrated by communist guerrilla forces. They had joined up because they favoured military action against the Japanese, approved of the agrarian and other social reforms sponsored by the CCP, and were impressed by the absence of corruption among the CCP leaders and by their evident dedication and courage. But the newcomers were no communists.

As early as 1929 Mao had proposed that new recruits should be educated or re-educated by means of 'rectification campaigns'. From 1942 onwards, such rectification campaigns (*Cheng Feng*) became an established and characteristic Chinese practice. They had the dual purpose of imparting a minimum of 'Marxist-Leninist' knowledge as developed in the USSR to the newly recruited illiterate peasants and ex-mercenaries and of reforming them morally. Rectification of thought, as conceived by Mao, was above all a means of transforming selfish individuals into dedicated revolutionaries, prepared to sacrifice their personal interests and ambitions and, if need be, their lives to the collective goals of the Chinese nation as interpreted by the CCP leadership. The successful conduct of such rectification campaigns depended, according to Mao, on the consistent application of the 'mass line' by the party and army leadership. The 'mass line' was defined as a continuous process of interaction between communist party cadres and non-party workers and peasants, designed to secure and maintain communist leadership, to arouse maximum popular participation, and to prevent the degeneration of the party cadres into an isolated, merely commanding bureaucracy. These and related concepts and practices, all developed long before victory was in sight, were to play a crucial part in the Cultural Revolution of the 1960s.

Since America's entry into the war against Japan (Dec. 1941) both the communists and the Nationalists had begun to spend rather greater efforts on consolidating and expanding the areas under their control than on fighting the Japanese. Both realized that their 'alliance' was a mere truce and, with America bearing the brunt of the war against Japan, both sides concentrated on improving their positions for a new civil war. Even before the Japanese surrender (14.8.1945) there had been serious new clashes between Nationalist and communist forces. After the surrender, full-scale civil war developed almost immediately. Four years of fighting ended with the communists in control of all mainland China and Chiang Kai-shek's retreat with the remnants of his forces to Taiwan (⇔ China, Republic of).

The Chinese People's Republic, formally proclaimed on 1 Oct. 1949, with Mao Tse-tung as its Head of State, was defined as a 'People's Democratic Dictatorship' over the reactionaries. The 'reactionaries' were the landlord class and the bureaucratic (pro-KMT) bourgeoisie, while the 'people' comprised the petty and the national (anti-imperialist and anti-KMT) bourgeoisie as well as the workers and peasants. Mao made it plain from the outset that the People's Democratic Dictatorship was to be a mere stage in a continuous process of revolutionary transformation required to achieve the gradual establishment of socialism and the eventual triumph of a classless communist society.

The first phase of communist rule was devoted to the reconstruction of the country's war-torn economy. It included a successful programme to eliminate inflation, the completion of land distribution and the beginning of the socialization of private industry and trade. Externally, it coincided with the outbreak of the war in ⊏>Korea, in which Chinese 'People's Volunteers' intervened from Oct. 1950 onwards. At the same time, the Chinese People's Liberation Army (PLA) also began to occupy ⊏>Tibet which the government claimed as an integral part of Chinese territory.

The second phase began with the launching of the first Five Year Plan (Jan. 1953). Following the Soviet model and aided by considerable Soviet technical assistance, including technical experts, the plan was geared to the development of heavy industry. The collectivization of agriculture began in 1955 under the slogan of cooperization and was practically completed by the end of 1957. The existing system of rule was formalized in a complex constitution (1954) based on single-list elections of a hierarchy of administrations, which left all effective power in the hands of the communist leadership. During the same period, and for the first time in the modern era, China began to emerge on the world scene as an independent nation and a potential great power. The combination of political consolidation and economic progress at home with the military successes achieved in Korea imbued the Chinese leaders with a new sense of self-confidence. China's delegation to the 1954 Geneva Conference, led by Chou En-lai, played an important part in the formulation of the ⊏> Geneva Agreements. Chou En-lai's subsequent visits to India and Burma, his sponsorship of 'The Five Principles of Peaceful Co-existence' and the dominant part which he played at the ⊏>Bandung Conference of 1955 all helped to enhance China's role as a would-be spokesman for all Asia.

In the following year, ⊏>Khrushchev's denunciation of ⊏>Stalin at the 20th CPSU Congress produced the first sharp differences between the Chinese and Soviet leadership. In the autumn of 1956, China actively supported the Soviet repression of the Hungarian revolution, while restraining Khrushchev from taking similar action against ⊏>Poland. This was the first time that China intervened in European affairs and in a field hitherto regarded as an exclusive Soviet prerogative.

The growing sense of self-confidence mirrored in these international initiatives expressed itself internally in the so-called 'Hundred Flowers Campaign' launched in May 1956. Based on the assumption of broad popular support for CCP policies, the slogan 'Let a hundred flowers bloom, let a hundred schools contend' was designed, as Mao explained (Feb. 1957), to promote uninhibited free debate. The newly encouraged freedom produced unexpected results. Critical intellectuals began to attack the very system of communist party rule and even Mao personally. This, in turn, drove Mao to the opposite extreme. Beginning with a violent campaign against 'rightists' of every description, Mao performed a sharp general turn to the 'left' culminating in the simultaneous aggravation of the incipient ⇨ Sino-Soviet Conflict and the adoption (1958) of radical domestic innovations under the slogan of the Great Leap Forward. The innovations included the establishment of huge rural Communes, ordered to combine an upsurge in farm output with the development of light industries, the organization of large-scale construction projects, the operation of steel furnaces in their backyards and of small-scale coalmines in their neighbourhood. All this was to be achieved by extreme forms of regimentation and accompanied by a decrease in consumption, the abolition of material incentives and incessant exhortations to greater efforts and displays of enthusiasm. The Communes were also presented as a short-cut to the full-scale communist society to be ushered in in the immediate future.

The Great Leap Forward ended in disastrous failure. It was first modified in Dec. 1958, at the time when Mao announced his intention to step down from his post as China's Head of State in favour of Liu Shao-chi, and was finally abandoned in 1961. By that time China appeared to be on the verge of economic ruin. The chaos engendered by the Great Leap Forward had been aggravated by three successive years of natural disasters and the sudden withdrawal (Aug. 1960) of all Soviet technical experts and assistance. There were signs, too, of increasing conflict within the Chinese party leadership, produced, on the one hand, by Mao's Great Leap Forward and, on the other, by the aggravation of the dispute with the USSR. In Aug. 1959, the Minister of Defence, Marshal Peng Te-huai, was ousted after criticizing Mao's policies and leadership on his return from a visit to Eastern Europe with the alleged encouragement of Khrushchev. He was replaced by Marshal ⇨ Lin Piao who, in the following decade, was to become China's most powerful leader after Mao. Between 1961, when the Great Leap Forward was finally liquidated, and the onset of the Cultural Revolution in 1965, continuing or growing extremism in foreign affairs – generally merely verbal except for the Sino-Indian War of 1962 – went hand in hand with a return to a more moderate course in domestic policies. The stress was once again on a sustained form of all-round economic growth to be achieved by incentives designed to promote efficiency and the development of technological and managerial expertise. It emerged only later that this turn towards internal moderation and economic rationality had been achieved over Mao's head and against his opposition.

In 1961 and 1962, covert attacks on Mao began to appear in certain Peking publications in the form of allegorical plays and stories. Mao, at the same time, began to prepare his own counter-offensive for which he increasingly relied on Lin Piao and the PLA. Lin Piao took the lead in promoting an ubiquitous and ever-expanding cult of Mao's personality and 'thought'. In the early 1960s, the study of 'Mao's thought' was made compulsory for the entire PLA. In Feb. 1964, the CCP and the rest of China's population were urged to learn from the 'advanced ideological work' of the PLA. This development probably sharpened the hidden opposition to Mao among his colleagues in the top leadership. Mao's final counter-attack, which culminated in the Great Proletarian Cultural Revolution, began in Nov. 1965 with the publication of an article in a Shanghai paper, written on his personal initiative; it denounced the author, an important official in the Peking party organization, of one of the earlier allegorical attacks on Mao. A second similar denunciation, appearing in May 1966, became the final curtain-raiser to a large-scale purge of the Peking CCP Committee, including its Secretary, Polit-bureau member Peng Cheng. In Aug. 1966, Mao presided over the first of a large number of open-air rallies attended by millions of 'Red Guards', newly formed groups of youths whom Mao and Lin Piao encouraged to take matters into their own hands.

Since then, the Cultural Revolution has engulfed the whole of China in a series of different though overlapping campaigns. Officially designed to eliminate 'revisionism', to counter the degeneration of the Chinese people into 'bourgeois' habits and bourgeois modes of thought and to create guarantees for keeping China 'eternally red' and revolutionary, the Cultural Revolution developed from an outsize 'rectification campaign' into a vast purge of most of the senior party and state leaders. It culminated, in the autumn of 1968, in the ousting from all his party and state posts of Liu Shao-chi, Mao's former second-in-command and China's Head of State but, since the late 1950s or early 1960s, apparently Mao's leading opponent. The purge, conducted in the name of the Cultural Revolution, has led to the virtual destruction of the hitherto ruling Communist Party. In embarking on this enterprise Mao has relied on characteristically different methods from those employed by ⇨ Stalin in the great Soviet purges of the 1930s. Reverting to practices based on the 'mass line', developed during the Yenan period, Mao attempted to isolate and defeat his powerful adversaries in the party and state hierarchy by inciting, first the students, and later the masses of workers and peasants to exercise their own initiative in a gigantic upheaval designed to paralyse and unseat the entrenched anti-Maoist authorities. This purpose was eventually achieved but at the price of propelling China into a state bordering on anarchy and of dividing, not only the party stalwarts, but the population as a whole into bitterly hostile camps engaged in endless factional strife. The maintenance of industrial and agricultural production and the restoration of a semblance of order had increasingly to be left to the party-soldiers of the PLA, which appeared to be the only organized force left to retain a measure of cohesion throughout the Cultural Revolution. In the course of 1967 and 1968 new Revolutionary Committees were set up all over China to replace the former provincial or municipal party and state authorities. Most of them contain a sprinkling of former party leaders, but the overwhelming majority of them are dominated by military leaders and party commissars attached to the PLA. Since the late summer of 1968, repeated calls have appeared in the Chinese press for a rebuilding of the Communist Party on uncompromisingly Maoist lines. By Oct. 1968 Mao and Lin Piao had regained sufficient power to call an 'enlarged' CCP Central Committee meeting, composed of the minority of Central Committee members who had not fallen victim to the purges and newcomers who had distinguished themselves during the Cultural Revolution as staunch Maoists.

At the end of this meeting it was announced that Liu Shao-chi, hitherto only anonymously attacked as the 'Khrushchev of China' had been exposed as a 'scab, renegade and traitor' and been deprived of all his party and state posts. The overdue 9th party congress was held in April 1969. It adopted a new party constitution, which named Lin Piao as Mao's official successor, and elected the 9th Central Committee which, in turn, elected the 9th Politbureau and its Standing Committee. Of the 174 surviving full and alternative members of the 8th Central Committee (elected in 1956 and 1958) only 52 were included in the 9th Central Committee. Of the 21 full and 4 alternative members of the new Politbureau, roughly half had been members of the 8th Politbureau, the remainder being newcomers. Conspicuous among the latter were a number of leading military commanders and certain formerly obscure party members who had distinguished themselves by their particular ardour in the Cultural Revolution, such as the two leaders of the new Shanghai Revolutionary Committee, Chiang Chun-chiao and Yao Wen-yuan, and Mao's wife, Chiang Ching. The new 5-men Standing Committee of the Politbureau, the highest party executive consisted, on the other hand, only of members of the old-established leadership, i.e. Mao, Lin Piao, Chou En-lai, Chen Po-ta and Kang Sheng. Within the next three years, the party leadership was further decimated by purges. Among their most prominent victims were Chen Po-ta (probably ousted in August 1970) and Mao's appointed successor, Lin Piao, who, together with his wife and 4 top military leaders vanished in the autumn of 1971. These events left Chou En-lai in effective charge, and they were accompanied by both visible improvements in China's economy and the establishment of diplomatic relations between the CPR and a growing number of nations, culminating in the CPR's admission to the UN (Oct. 1971) and leading up to President ⇨ Nixon's visit to Peking (Feb. 1972).

Chinese Revolution. ⇨ Chinese People's Republic.

Chornovil, Vyacheslav (193?–). Soviet journalist, sentenced (1967) to 18 months hard labour for distributing documents exposing repression in the Ukraine and the methods of the Soviet Secret Police.

Chou En-lai (1898–). Prime Minister of the ⇨ Chinese People's Republic. A revolutionary since his early youth, Chou went as a student to Europe and became a founder-member of the French branch of the CCP (1921). Back in China in 1924, he became one of the Party's top organizers in Shanghai and, in the late 1920s, took part in the series of Comintern-sponsored communist uprisings. In 1931, he escaped to the Kiangsi Soviet area where he was for a time placed above ⇨ Mao Tse-tung and became the Political Commissar of the Red Army. In that capacity he took a leading part in the Long March, during which he and others ceded the leadership to Mao. Since then Chou has been one of Mao's closest associates, siding with him at all critical political turns. Prime Minister since the foundation of the CPR (1949) and also Foreign Minister (1949–58), Chou has travelled widely abroad and become internationally a more familiar figure than any other Chinese leader. The only leader whose standing was not affected by the Cultural Revolution, he played an outstanding part in bringing it to an end and in reactivating China's economy and the CPR's relations with the outside world. After the disappearance of ⇨ Lin Piao (Sept. 1971) he acted in the – informal – capacity of China's single most important leader.

Christian Democrats. Name given to major parties in the Catholic countries of Western Europe and in the Federal Republic of Germany which have in common a general allegiance to Catholic political doctrines, e.g. the questions of confessional schools and divorce and an acceptance of the need for social welfare ('social catholicism'). These parties originated in the Catholic movements of the nineteenth century but have relinquished their association with traditional ultramontanism, although perhaps their support for European integration reflects a concern for Catholic universality: three of the main architects of European union were Christian Democrats, i.e. ⇨ Schuman (France), ⇨ De Gasperi (Italy) and ⇨ Adenauer (West Germany). The CDs came to prominence after World War II when they adopted programmes of social reform from which they benefited electorally. In some cases CD parties had long periods in office although often in coalition with left-wing parties, e.g. the ⇨CDU (*Christlich Demokratische Union*) has been the governing party in the German Federal Republic since its foundation in 1949 but it formed coalitions with the liberal FDP (1953–57, 1961–66) and the Social Democrats (since 1966). In Italy the DC (*Democrazia Cristiana*) led a centre coalition from 1948 and formed a coalition with the socialists in 1963, and in Austria the Christian Social Party allied with the socialists in the first coalition after the war. The Christian Democrats not only broadened their policy (they also accepted economic planning) but also in some cases broadened their support, e.g. the West German CDU includes several Protestants among its leaders, one of whom was Chancellor ⇨Erhard. In spite of their modifications of policy the Christian Democratic parties reject socialist egalitarian ideas and share a common policy of anti-communism, which is also true of those Christian Democratic parties which have been formed in countries outside Europe, e.g. the PDC which came to power in ⇨Chile in 1964.

Churchill, Sir Winston Leonard Spencer (1874–1965). Achieved greatness as Britain's war-time Prime Minister (1940–45) after more than 40 years of public life, for the last ten of which he had been out of office and his advice rejected by his party. The son of Lord Randolph Churchill, whose radical Toryism he admired, he entered Parliament as a Conservative in 1900. He had already experienced military service (India, Cuba, Sudan), and as a war correspondent in South Africa had been captured by the Boers. In 1904, a believer in Free Trade, he left the ⇨Conservative Party and joined the ⇨Liberal Party. Promoted to the Cabinet (1908) he was closely associated with ⇨Lloyd George in supporting and introducing welfare legislation before being appointed First Lord of the Admiralty (1911). A dynamic First Lord, he mobilized the fleet before the outbreak of war (1914). Following the failure of the Dardanelles expedition, which he had advocated, he resigned (1915) and served in the army on the Western Front. Appointed Minister of Munitions (1917), he held Cabinet posts until 1922 when he left the Liberal Party, re-entering Parliament (1924) as a Conservative, and was appointed Chancellor of the Exchequer (1924–29). His chancellorship was marked by Britain's return to the Gold Standard which helped precipitate the economic crisis and General Strike (1926). His posture of total opposition to the strikers reflected an inability to comprehend the aspirations of many of his countrymen or the resentments bred from social injustice – a weakness revealed again in 1945 when he failed to understand (despite his war-time leadership) why a majority of Englishmen preferred the programme of the ⇨Labour Party. From 1930, his opposition first to the Government's India policies and later to ⇨ Appeasement – shown in his concern that the country should prepare itself against the menace of Hitler's Germany – kept him out of office until he was appointed First Lord of the Admiralty on the outbreak of war (3.9.1939). On 10 May 1940, the one man capable of vigorous leadership, he became Prime Minister of the coalition government. In the first stage of his premiership, against a background of defeat, he never doubted ultimate victory, while from 1941 his main concern was the successful maintenance of the alliance against the enemy (even when his own views differed from ⇨ Roosevelt's, e.g. ⇨ Yalta). While Leader of the Opposition (1945–51) he delivered his Fulton 'Iron Curtain' speech (1946). Again Prime Minister (1951–55) he retired from Parliament in 1964. A gifted leader, parliamentarian and orator, he was extolled in a *Times* obituary as 'The greatest Englishman of his time'.

Winston Churchill – Chronology from 1900:

1900	Elected to Parliament
1905–08	Under-Secretary of State for Colonies
1908–10	President of the Board of Trade
1910–11	Home Secretary
1911–15	First Lord of the Admiralty
1915	Chancellor of the Duchy of Lancaster
	Serves on the Western Front – France
1917–19	Minister of Munitions
1919–21	Secretary of State for War and Air
1921	Secretary of State for Colonies and Air
1921–22	Secretary of State for Colonies
1924–29	Chancellor of the Exchequer
1939–40	First Lord of the Admiralty
1940–45	Prime Minister and Minister of Defence
1951–55	Prime Minister
1951	Order of the Garter
1963	Granted Honorary Citizenship USA
1964	Retired from Parliament

Publications include:

Marlborough: His Life and Times (4 vols.), London, George G. Harrap & Co. Ltd. 1933–38.

The Second World War (6 vols.), London, Cassell & Co. Ltd. 1948–54.

A History of the English Speaking Peoples (4 vols.), London, Cassell & Co. Ltd. 1956.

as well as collections of his speeches including:

War Speeches (3 vols.), compiled by Charles Eade, London, Cassell & Co. Ltd. Definitive Edition 1952.

Chu Teh, Marshal (1886–). (Chinese People's Republic.) A professional soldier before becoming a communist in 1925, after the communist defeats of 1927, Chu joined ⟡ Mao in his mountain hide-out and has been close to him ever since. As Commander-in-Chief of the Chinese Red Army from 1931 onwards, Chu was the main military leader of the Long March and the principal architect of the communist victories in the war against Japan and in the civil war. A member of Mao's inner circle of top leaders since the proclamation of the CPR, he has in recent years only appeared on rare ceremonial occasions.

CIA. United States Central Intelligence Agency – an agency of the Federal Government established by the National Security Act of 1947 in pursuance of the policy of integrating the defence and security arrangements of the USA. It operates under the direction of ⟡ NSC, and is headed by a Director who is appointed by the President with the consent of the ⟡ Senate and who reports directly to the President. The CIA co-ordinates the intelligence operations of other agencies, but its own world-wide activities are of primary importance. Very little information is made available, even to ⟡ Congress, regarding the working of the agency, and its appropriations are concealed within the general budget. It is believed to duplicate many of the activities of the ⟡ State Department – its budget is estimated to be two to four times as large – and it has been called an 'invisible government'. The CIA has played an important, and largely independent, part in foreign affairs, not always with the results anticipated – as in the case of the ⟡ Bay of Pigs. As a result of that incident, President ⟡ Kennedy sought to restrict the CIA more to its intelligence function. He used the President's Foreign Intelligence Advisory Board, which included the heads of other agencies engaged in intelligence, to keep the work of the CIA under continuous review. It was later revealed that the CIA had disbursed considerable sums to educational and cultural institutions at home and abroad; though, given the difficulty of making direct budgetary provision for such purposes, this was perhaps because the agency's appropriations could most easily be used to secure the necessary funds.

CIO. Congress of Industrial Organizations – Trade Union organization in the USA and Canada. It was formed within the American Federation of Labor (AF of L) in 1935 to promote labour organization on an industry rather than a craft basis, and it was expelled from the parent organization the following year. For two decades there was conflict between them, with the ⟡ NLRB keeping an uneasy peace. In 1955, under the presidency of Walter ⟡ Reuther, it re-emerged with its rival to form the AFL–CIO. At that time it had about six million members.

Civil Liberties. Immunities from State interference in certain spheres of action secured to the citizen by law (or the absence of law). The most important are the freedoms of conscience, speech, worship, publication (the Press), association, assembly, and peaceful demonstration, protest, or petition. It is common for these to be guaranteed in constitutional documents (which may not be respected, however). The USA provides the prime example of legally enacted Civil Liberties in the ⇨ Bill of Rights, enforced by the ⇨ Supreme Court. In Great Britain, by contrast, Civil Liberties are guaranteed largely by the 'silence of the law'. The Universal Declaration of Human Rights expresses a broad international consensus (not always acted upon) regarding Civil Liberties. Civil Liberties are usually associated with ⇨ Civil Rights.

Civil Rights. Rights, such as the vote and trial by jury, legally conferred upon the citizen by the State. In democratic theory, they are granted to all citizens equally, on terms that are universal and hence non-discriminatory, though it is common for some groups to be discriminated against in otherwise democratic countries. Strictly, Civil Rights concern relations between citizen and State, but the term has been extended, especially in the USA, to cover relations between groups of citizens. In the USA, securing Civil Rights has come to mean preventing discrimination against minority groups, particularly Negroes, by any body whatever, public or private. The legal and extra-legal means used to prevent such discrimination constitute the ⇨ Civil Rights Movement. Civil Rights are usually associated with ⇨ Civil Liberties.

Civil Rights Commission. In the USA, a temporary agency of the Federal Government established originally for two years by the Civil Rights Act of 1957, and extended by subsequent Acts. It has responsibilities for investigating allegations concerning the denial of the right to vote and of the 'equal protection of the laws' to citizens, and for appraising Federal action and informing the President and ⇨ Congress respecting the enforcement of ⇨ Civil Rights. The six Civil Rights Commissioners are appointed by the President with the consent of the ⇨ Senate.

Civil Rights Movement. In the USA, the movement (sometimes involving Civil Disobedience) to secure Civil Rights for all citizens, especially Negroes. The guarantees contained in the ⇨ Bill of Rights were extended to the former slaves by the Thirteenth, Fourteenth, and Fifteenth Amendments to the Constitution, the last expressly forbidding Federal or State curtailment of the right to vote 'on account of race, colour or previous condition of servitude'. Until recently, however, this provision was generally disregarded in the South, where poll taxes, literacy tests, and other devices were used to deny Negroes the vote; and this was but one aspect of the systematic denial of Civil Rights to Negroes under ⇨Segregation. Effective action to alter the situation was given a legal basis by the ⇨ Supreme Court decision in ⇨ Brown v. Board of Education (1954) against segregation in schools. Enforcement of the desegregation decision required Federal action, including the despatch of troops to Little Rock, Arkansas, by President Eisenhower (1957). In the same year the first of a series of Civil Rights Acts was passed by Congress. The 1957 Act established the ⇨ Civil Rights Commission to safeguard voting rights, and its provisions were reinforced by the 1960 Act. In 1964, the Twenty-fourth Amendment, prohibiting the use of poll and other taxes to deny the vote, was added to the Constitution, and a further Civil Rights Act was passed to extend anti-discrimination laws to public accommodation and employment. The 1965 Voting Rights Act prohibited the use of ⇨Literacy Tests as a means of depriving people of the vote in States where this was common. In the meantime, Southern Negroes had resorted to 'direct action' to further the Civil Rights Movement, beginning with ⇨ Sit-ins, and leading up to the 'March on Washington' (Aug. 1963) headed by Martin Luther ⇨ King. Thereafter, action became increasingly militant, with outbreaks of violence in the cities. This trend, culminating in the call for ⇨ Black Power, was reinforced by the growing dissidence of the White ⇨ New Left associated with the escalation of the Vietnam War after 1964. Resistance to the Civil Rights Movement and Black militancy – the ⇨White Backlash – increased simultaneously. This state of affairs contributed heavily to President ⇨Johnson's decline in popularity and his decision not to stand for re-election in 1968. In the election campaign all candidates proclaimed the necessity of maintaining 'law and order'. The Nixon Administration proved more equivocal than its predecessors on Civil Rights issues, particularly as regards Federal enforcement of such measures as ⇨ 'Busing'.

For Soviet civil rights movement ⇨Dissent (in Eastern Europe).

'Clause 4'. The clause of the UK ⇨Labour Party constitution of 1918 which advocated 'the common ownership of the means of production'. The debate over the revision of the clause was at the centre of the internal party disputes which followed defeat in the 1959 general election and the attempt by ⇨ Gaitskell to 'modernize' the party and remove its doctrinaire image.

'Clear and Present Danger'. A legal doctrine in the USA relating to free speech. In a decision of 1919, the ⇨Supreme Court held that freedom of speech, as guaranteed in the ⇨ First Amendment to the Constitution, was not absolute, but might be restricted when words

'. . . are used in such circumstances and are of such a nature as to create a clear and present danger that they will bring about the substantive evils that Congress has a right to prevent.' The precise meaning of the doctrine has never been settled, and it has not always been applied. In recent times, ⇨ Congress and the Court have tended to treat many things as constituting a 'clear and present danger', particularly where the Communist Party is involved, as is exemplified by the ⇨ Smith Act, the Act establishing the ⇨ Subversive Activities Control Board, and the ⇨ Communist Control Act.

Clifford, Clark (1906–). US lawyer and statesman who served as special counsel to President ⇨ Truman (1946–50) and played a vital role in shaping policy (⇨ Truman Doctrine, 1947) and reorganizing the ⇨ Defense Department (1947). After a period of government service, he was appointed to the Foreign Intelligence Advisory Board by John F. ⇨ Kennedy (1961), and later to its chairmanship (1963–68). Always a close adviser to President ⇨ Johnson, Clifford was chosen to replace Robert ⇨ McNamara as Secretary of Defense (1968) and played a significant part in determining American policy in Vietnam. Although he shunned a 'hard-line' label, he favoured continuing US nuclear superiority over the Soviet Union, thus rejecting his predecessor's policy of establishing nuclear parity.

Closed Primary. Form of ⇨ Primary Election in the USA.

CMEA. Council for Mutual Economic Assistance – an economic organization of East European communist states, set up in Moscow (Jan. 1949) by Bulgaria, Czechoslovakia, Hungary, Poland, Rumania and the USSR. Albania became a member in Feb. 1949 but was again excluded in 1961. The German Democratic Republic joined in 1950, Mongolia in 1962, and Cuba became a member in 1972. Until the late 1950s, CMEA did little beyond endorsing bi-lateral trade agreements between member-states. Attempts at turning CMEA into a centre of multi-lateral economic cooperation date from the Moscow summit meeting of May 1958. In 1960, CMEA adopted its first constitution, the CMEA Charter. The charter vested supreme authority in the all-member Council in Session which must take all decisions unanimously. Since then, the USSR and certain other member states have advocated the transformation of CMEA into a unified, supra-national planning organ. In 1962, they introduced amendments to further these designs, providing for a new Executive Committee with potentially far-reaching supra-national powers. ⇨ Rumania opposed these Soviet-sponsored moves as incompatible with national sovereignty and as injurious to the interests of the economically less developed member-states. As a result of this opposition, the 1962 Amendments have not been ratified although an Executive Committee was set up and has directed CMEA activities since 1962.

CND. Campaign for Nuclear Disarmament – mass protest movement in the UK which advocated the unilateral renunciation of atomic weapons. Launched in Feb. 1958 by Lord Bertrand Russell, its president, and Canon John Collins, the CND organized annual Easter marches from Aldermaston, site of the Atomic Weapons Research Establishment, to Trafalgar Square, where it held mass rallies. CND influence on the Labour Party reached its peak at the Labour Party's annual conference in Oct. 1960 when the left wing succeeded in carrying a resolution which favoured unilateral disarmament. ⟡Gaitskell, determined to 'fight and fight and fight again', had the resolution reversed the next year. The movement was weakened by the variety of its supporters, ranging from Christian pacifists to communists, and disagreement over the tactics of its militant section, the Committee of 100.

Collective Leadership. Term in communist usage to distinguish real or alleged joint group decisions, based on debates and voting majorities, from the autocratic decisions of a supreme individual leader.

Collective Security. The maintenance of international peace and security by the concerted efforts of the nations, especially the peace-keeping operations of international organizations such as the League of Nations and the United Nations. The collective power of the great majority of nations would be used to prevent or punish aggression by any one state or group of states. However, since World War II, American politicians have used this phrase with its universal peace-keeping connotations to describe specifically American alliances such as SEATO and NATO. (⟡Mutual Security Program.)

Collectivization. In communist countries, the compulsory transformation of individually-owned peasant farms into commonly-owned and commonly-directed large-scale 'collective farms'. In ⟡Yugoslavia and ⟡Poland, where peasants were allowed to stay out of or opt out of the collective farm system, the overwhelming majority adhered or reverted to private farming.

College of Commissioners. Government of the ⟡Congo (Kinshasa) established by Colonel ⟡Mobutu (14.9.1960) and recognized by the UN (Nov. 1960). Made up of university graduates, it lasted less than a year and executive power seems to have remained in the hands of Mobutu and ⟡Kasavubu.

Colombia. *Area* – 455,335 sq. miles. *Population* (1970 est.) – 22,000,000. *President* – Dr Misael Pastrana Borrero (1970–). *Constitution* (1886– frequently amended up to and including 1967) – Unitary Republic with executive power vested in an elected President. The presidency alternates between the Liberal and Conservative parties, who must also be equally represented in a bi-cameral Congress – Senate and House of Representatives. The President has power to rule by decree. Voting – universal adult suffrage.

As with some other Latin American countries Colombian political life has a violent tradition. *Violencia* (lawlessness, banditry, guerrilla warfare) and its urban counterpart, mob violence, has become a dominant theme in Colombian politics. Despite foreign investment and new agricultural projects, the socio-economic factors making for instability and violence persist: over-dependence on a single product – coffee, a small powerful financial oligarchy, peasant production strangled by an archaic system of land tenure and consequent migration to already over-crowded urban slums. The Church, as an opponent of change, has also played a crucial part in government failure to alleviate mass poverty. The Depression of 1930 dislocated the economy and reduced the effectiveness of earlier reforms. The Liberal administration of Alfonso Lopez (1934–38) curbed the power of the Church and enacted social welfare legislation. But between 1938 and 1945 effective government and the implementation of necessary reforms were thwarted by Conservative opposition and violent party disputes. Following the assassination of Gaitan (1948), the one leader with powerful mass support, Colombia was plunged into a wave of violence and civil war. Chaos was temporarily arrested by the military dictatorship of Rojas Pinilla (1953–57) until it too was disrupted by renewed violence. Order was restored by a Liberal-Conservative National Front coalition (1958). In 1962 there was a resurgence of guerrilla warfare, now Castroist in character, and Rojas Pinilla returned to power briefly (1962–63). Despite new political alliances and continued discontent, the National Front survived and in 1966 a Liberal, Dr Carlos Lleras Restrepo, was elected President. The Pope's visit to Colombia in Aug. 1968 focused attention on the social problems of Colombia and South America. He appealed for peace and social justice. However, his own encyclical on birth control, especially as it relates to South America, affected by the highest rate of population growth in the world, has become a subject of major controversy. Dissatisfaction with the Church's past policies has already expressed itself in Catholic circles. Some parish priests openly favour revolutionary change.

Dr Borrero, elected (April) took office (Aug. 1970) as President at the head of dual Liberal-Conservative Government.

Colombo Plan (1951). Plan for the cooperative effort of both developed and developing countries for economic development in South and

South-East Asia. This effort consists of aid, e.g. capital aid, experts, technical training and equipment, provided under bi-lateral agreements between member governments. The Plan is directed by the Consultative Committee and there is also a Council for Technical Cooperation. It was originally formulated by the Commonwealth Nations Meeting at Colombo but the members now consist of six nations outside the area (Australia, Canada, Japan, New Zealand, the UK and the USA) and 17 within (Afghanistan, Bhutan, Burma, Cambodia, Ceylon, India, Indonesia, Laos, the Maldive Islands, Malaysia, Nepal, Pakistan, the Philippines, Singapore, South Korea, South Vietnam and Thailand).

Colombo Powers. A group of Asian states which, at a meeting in Colombo (Ceylon) in April 1954, agreed on close cooperation among themselves and other newly independent nations in Asia and Africa. The Colombo meeting was attended by government leaders of India, Pakistan, Burma, Ceylon and Indonesia. After the formation of ⇨SEATO later in 1954, Pakistan left the group. On the initiative of Pandit ⇨Nehru and President ⇨Sukarno, the Colombo Powers played a leading part in the organization of the ⇨Bandung Conference of 1955.

A second Colombo Conference, attended by Burma, Cambodia, Ceylon, Ghana, Indonesia and the UAR, was held (Dec. 1962) to attempt mediation in the armed conflict which had meanwhile broken out between India and China.

Colon. ⇨Algeria, ⇨France.

Colonialism. Strictly referred to the policies and methods by which an imperial power maintained or extended its control over other territories or peoples; now more frequently used in a pejorative sense, often synonomous with ⇨Imperialism. Resentment of their colonial status has been an important factor in the growth of nationalist and independence movements of the ⇨Third World.

Comecon. Frequently used abbreviation for ⇨Council for Mutual Economic Assistance.

Cominform. The Cominform (Communist Information Bureau) was set up (Sept. 1947) on Soviet initiative at a meeting in Poland, attended by communist party leaders from Bulgaria, Czechoslovakia, France, Hungary, Italy, Poland, Rumania, the USSR and Yugoslavia. Its foundation followed the announcement of the ⇨Truman Doctrine (spring 1947) designed to forestall further Soviet expansion, and the Soviet veto against Poland's and Czechoslovakia's participation in the Marshall Plan. The main speaker at the inaugural meeting was the ⇨CPSU delegate Andrei A. ⇨Zhdanov who confirmed the final break between the USSR and its war-time allies by once again declaring the world to be divided into two irreconcilably hostile camps and by foreshadowing a new world-wide communist offensive. The Information Bureau, to be located in Belgrade, was charged with the official task of organizing the exchange of information and, where necessary, the co-ordination of the activities of the nine communist member parties.

The only notable action taken by the organization concerned ⟐ Yugoslavia. After ⟐ Tito's conflict with ⟐ Stalin, a Cominform meeting at Bucharest in June 1948 denounced the Yugoslav leaders and called for their replacement. Following ⟐ Khrushchev's bid for a reconciliation with Yugoslavia, the Cominform was dissolved in April 1956.

Comintern. ⟐ Communist International.

Commerce Clause. A clause in the Constitution of the USA (Article 1, Section 8) giving to ⟐ Congress the power 'to regulate commerce with foreign nations and among the several States . . .' The first element in this, the regulation of foreign commerce, has been the legal basis for United States tariff policy. Traditionally, United States trade policy was protectionist; but beginning with the Trade Agreements Act of 1934, Congress has given the President increasing authority to negotiate tariff reductions with foreign countries. This process was carried further by the ⟐ Trade Expansion Act of 1962, which led to the ⟐ Kennedy Round of tariff negotiations of 1964–67. The second element in the clause – the regulation of interstate commerce – has been of even greater importance within the United States. It has provided the basis for the progressive extension of the regulatory power of the Federal Government over most phases of the American economy, including industrial relations. Up to 1937 the clause was interpreted rather narrowly by the ⟐ Supreme Court, which maintained that it did not cover manufacturing. On this basis, the Court had restricted the scope of action under the ⟐ Sherman Antitrust Act and invalidated some important ⟐ New Deal legislation. For similar reasons, the powers and functions of such Federal agencies as ⟐ ICC and ⟐ FTC were very limited. Since 1937, however, the Court has interpreted the clause more and more broadly, giving the Federal Government greater and greater legal authority over many matters that are only very indirectly interstate and only remotely connected with commerce. Thus, on the basis of a broad construction of the Commerce Clause, the Court has upheld the right of the Federal Government to act against discrimination by all sorts of undertakings in the field of ⟐ Civil Rights. This, naturally, provokes a strong reaction from the upholders of ⟐ States' Rights.

Common Market. ⟐ EEC.

Commonwealth. Is made up of independent countries comprising:

Her Majesty's Dominions of:

	Date of Independence
THE UNITED KINGDOM	
CANADA	
AUSTRALIA	
NEW ZEALAND	
JAMAICA	5.8.1962
TRINIDAD and TOBAGO	31.8.1962
MALTA	21.9.1964
BARBADOS	30.11.1966
MAURITIUS	12.3.1968
TONGA	7.6.1970
FIJI	10.10.1970

Republics:

INDIA	15.8.1947
CEYLON (renamed Sri Lanka in 1972)	4.2.1948
GHANA	6.3.1957
CYPRUS	16.8.1960
NIGERIA	1.10.1960
SIERRA LEONE	27.4.1961
TANZANIA	9.12.1961
UGANDA	9.10.1962
KENYA	12.12.1963
MALAWI	6.7.1964
ZAMBIA	24.10.1964
GAMBIA	18.2.1965
SINGAPORE	16.10.1965
GUYANA	26.5.1966
BOTSWANA	30.9.1966
BANGLADESH	17.4.1972

Monarchies:

WESTERN SAMOA	1.1.1962
The Federation of MALAYSIA	16.9.1963
Kingdom of LESOTHO	4.10.1966
Kingdom of SWAZILAND	6.9.1968

and Her Majesty's Dependent Territories comprising:

In Africa SOUTHERN RHODESIA (granted responsible government in 1923) in rebellion since its UDI (1965). In the Far East the Protected State of BRUNEI, the Colony and Leased Territories of HONG KONG. In the Indian Ocean the Colonies of British Indian Ocean Territory and SEYCHELLES. In the Mediterranean the Colony of GIBRALTAR. In the Atlantic Ocean the Colonies of BRITISH ANTARCTIC TERRITORY, the FALKLAND ISLANDS and ST HELENA (including ASCENSION and TRISTAN DA CUNHA. In the West Indies the Colonies of the BAHAMAS; BERMUDA; BRITISH HONDURAS; BRITISH VIRGIN ISLANDS; CAYMAN ISLANDS; MONTSERRAT; and the TURKS AND CAICOS ISLANDS; the Associated States of ANTIGUA; ST CHRISTOPHER, NEVIS, ANGUILLA; DOMINICA; GRENADA; ST LUCIA; ST VINCENT. In the Pacific the GILBERT AND ELLICE ISLANDS; the Protectorate of the BRITISH SOLOMON ISLANDS; the Anglo-French Condominium of the NEW HEBRIDES.

The following countries have left the Commonwealth: ⇨The Republic of Ireland (1949), ⇨South Africa (1961), ⇨Burma (1947), ⇨Sudan (1956), British Somaliland (since 1960 part of the ⇨Somali Republic), Southern Cameroons (since 1961 part of the ⇨Cameroun Federal Republic), People's Democratic Republic of South Yemen – formerly Aden – (1967), and Pakistan (1972) after the recognition of Bangladesh.

The Commonwealth evolved from the nineteenth century British Empire. In 1931 the Statute of ⇨Westminster gave formal recognition to the independence of the 'old' dominions (which then consisted of ⇨Australia, ⇨Canada, ⇨Newfoundland (which has since lost its independence and become part of Canada), ⇨New Zealand and ⇨South Africa). The increasing number of states which have become independent since 1947 has radically altered the structure and unity of the Commonwealth. It remains as a loose informal association with no constitutional provision for enforcing common policies. Citizens of Commonwealth republics no longer owe allegiance to the crown but accept the monarch as the symbol of their free association within the Commonwealth. Open warfare has occurred between Commonwealth members (⇨India, ⇨Pakistan) and disagreements within the Commonwealth have been emphasized by the contradictory attitudes of its members to recent events (e.g. ⇨Suez, ⇨UDI in ⇨Rhodesia, ⇨Arab-Israeli Conflict, ⇨Commonwealth Immigration into UK, ⇨Nigeria-Biafra conflict). The most obvious division within the Commonwealth is between the 'old white' dominions with their Western standards and the emergent nations of the ⇨Third World. Since 1944, Commonwealth

Prime Ministers have met in London nearly every year. (In Jan. 1966 a special meeting was convened in Lagos specifically to discuss the problem of UDI). The meeting of March 1961 preceded South Africa's departure from the Commonwealth. A Commonwealth secretariat to assist in internal cooperation, but with no executive power, was established in June 1965. (Secretary-General Arnold C. Smith since 1965 – Canada.) The changed nature of the Commonwealth led to the establishment in the UK of the Commonwealth Office, replacing the old Colonial office and the Commonwealth Relations Office. The Commonwealth Office (since Oct. 1968 merged with the Foreign Office) is responsible for Britain's remaining dependent territories (but not for their internal administration) and for relations with the Maldive Islands, Rhodesia and the Republic of Ireland.

Commonwealth Development Corporation. Set up (1948) to help the economic development of British Colonies. Originally the Colonial Development Corporation, its name was changed by the Commonwealth Development Act (1963) which also extended its role to cover independent Commonwealth countries.

Commonwealth Immigration Acts (UK). The 1962 Act demanded that Commonwealth immigrants to Britain must have a job to come to or must possess some 'special skill' useful in Britain. This was a departure from the previous uncontrolled entry of Commonwealth citizens. Although attacked by the Labour Opposition, British policy did not change after the Labour Party came into power in 1964 and the annual intake of immigrants was even reduced. The 1968 Act, aimed specifically at the sudden immigration of Asians from Kenya, tightened the controls of the 1962 Act and applied them to UK citizens holding UK passports who had not been born, adopted or naturalized in Britain.

Communes. ⇨ China.

Communism. Term covering a multitude of movements, institutions and ideas; among them (1) the characteristics distinguishing communist parties from other political parties (⇨ Bolshevism, ⇨ Democratic Centralism, ⇨ Communist International); (2) the methods of government prevailing in countries dominated by communist parties (⇨ USSR etc.); (3) the concept or ideal of a classless society based on the common ownership of the means of production which, according to Marx and his disciples, will be ushered in by the victorious revolutionary proletariat, after a transitional period of the dictatorship of the proletariat, and which will lead to the 'withering away' of the state and provide limitless opportunities for the unfolding of human potentialities and the development of productive forces (⇨ Marxism).

Communist Control Act, 1954. An Act of Congress in the USA which outlawed the Communist Party, declaring it to be '. . . in fact an instrumentality of a conspiracy to overthrow the Government of the United States . . .' and, as such, '. . . not entitled to the rights, privileges and immunities attendant upon legal bodies . . .' This unprecedented measure was enacted by ⇨ Congress against the background of recent war in Korea and ⇨ McCarthyism at home, but it has never been fully enforced. Its chief effects have been to prevent official communist candidates contesting elections, and to extend to Communist Party members as such the provisions of the 1950 Act which established the ⇨ Subversive Activities Control Board. It is regarded by some as carrying the doctrine of ⇨ Guilt by Association to new lengths. The position of the ⇨ Supreme Court regarding this legislation has varied, but the tendency has been to modify the ⇨ 'Clear and Present Danger' doctrine to accommodate the provisions of the Act.

Communist Information Bureau. ⇨ Cominform.

Communist International. The Communist International (Comintern) came into being to replace the Second International which, in Lenin's opinion, betrayed socialism when most of the leaders of its member parties supported their respective governments at the outbreak of World War I. The Comintern foundation congress (Moscow, March 1919) adopted a number of general revolutionary theses and manifestos, the most important of which were drafted by Lenin, ⇨ Trotsky, ⇨ Bukharin and ⇨ Zinoviev. It set up an Executive Committee (ECCI) with headquarters in Moscow and elected Zinoviev as its first President.

The major decisions on the structure and functions of the Comintern were taken at its 2nd Congress in the summer of 1920. This Congress met after a year of revolutionary upheaval in Europe and at a moment when the Red Army had triumphed in the war of intervention and was advancing towards Warsaw. In the opinion of the Bolshevik leaders, all Europe was on the verge of a proletarian revolution. The essential requirement for final victory, as they saw it, was to provide the revolutionary movements with a single-minded effective leadership on the model of their own ⇨ Bolshevik organization. This was to be achieved by the Statutes, which defined the Comintern as a single world party in which national parties had the status of mere sections, and by the 21 Conditions of Admission, which effectively kept out sympathizers judged to be undesirable or who themselves refused to submit to the Bolshevik concept of centralized direction. By means of the 21 Conditions of Admission, the Comintern enforced splits in a number of socialist mass organizations in Europe which either (like the Italian Socialist Party) had already decided to join the Comintern or (like the

German Independent Socialist Party and the French Socialist Party) were considering doing so.

By the time these splits had been carried out, Russian hopes that the revolution might spread to the rest of Europe were already beginning to fade. They were finally buried with the failure of the Red Army to win popular support in Poland and the quick collapse of an attempted communist insurrection in Germany in March 1921, which compelled the Comintern to abandon its original objective. In its search for an alternative purpose, the Comintern experimented for a few years with various forms of united front tactics increasingly adapted to the changing domestic needs of the USSR. Beginning with the 5th World Congress in 1924, the Comintern was gradually transformed into an auxiliary of the factional struggles within the Soviet communist leadership between ⇨ Stalin and his various adversaries. The step-by-step elimination of Trotsky, Zinoviev, Bukharin and their associates from the Soviet party leadership was accompanied and finalized by corresponding purges in the Comintern leadership and in all the national Comintern sections. The process was completed between 1928 and 1930, when the last groups of leaders associated with any of the anti-Stalin factions were expelled from all communist parties. In between, Comintern policies produced in 1923 a serious débâcle for the German Communist Party and, in 1927, a disastrous defeat for the Communist Party of ⇨ China, surpassed, in its consequences, only by the policies later pursued by the German section of the Comintern at the time leading up to Hitler's advent to power. In the period between the 6th World Congress of the Comintern in 1928 and its official dissolution in May 1943, the only function left to the Comintern was that of organizing support for Soviet foreign policies. This exclusive purpose was demonstrated on the eve of World War II, when Comintern propaganda, after the conclusion of the ⇨ Hitler-Stalin Pact, suddenly switched from an anti-Nazi to an anti-Western line.

Communist Parties. ⇨Bolshevism, ⇨Bolshevization, ⇨Communist International, ⇨USSR, ⇨World Communism, ⇨Sovietization.

Community Relations Service. In the USA, an agency established within the Commerce Department by the Civil Rights Act of 1964, and brought under the purview of the ⇨ Attorney General in 1966. It has the task of improving race relations by means of conciliation at the local level, and it cooperates with Federal courts in efforts to secure voluntary compliance with laws against ⇨ Segregation before legal enforcement becomes necessary.

Concentration Camps. Introduced by the British during the Boer War, are now generally associated with the approximately 2,000 camps the

Nazis established in Germany and occupied Europe to detain political, racial or social 'undesirables' under conditions calculated to prevent prolonged survival. Set up in Germany immediately after ▷ Hitler's seizure of power (1933) in such places as Dachau, Buchenwald, Sachsenhausen, the concentration camps soon became a byword for unspeakable outrage which, cunningly publicized, was used by the Nazis to intimidate dissenters. After the outbreak of the war, a new class of camp was added to those which began to spring up all over occupied Europe. These, the so-called 'extermination camps' like Auschwitz, Sobibor, Treblinka, etc. carried specialized installations for the mass slaughter of Jews (▷ Holocaust) and others who were killed there in their millions. More than eight million people are believed to have perished in Nazi concentration camps, among them about six million Jews.

Concordat. Signed (20.7.1933) by the ▷ Third Reich and the Vatican. It protected the German Catholic educational system, Church property and freedom of worship, but excluded the clergy from politics. Broken later by Hitler, its importance at the time was that it weakened Catholic resistance to the Nazis and increased the prestige of the new regime through the implied recognition of the Papacy. In 1957 the West German Federal Constitutional Court upheld its continued validity.

CONEFO. Conference of New Emerging Forces proposed by President ▷ Sukarno of Indonesia with the backing of China as a 'revolutionary' alternative to the UN for the Afro-Asian and Latin American peoples. Suggested at the time of closer Sino-Indonesian relations, it received less credibility after the fall of Sukarno and his replacement by a more moderate government in Indonesia and when it became clear that China intended to use it as a means of strengthening her position both in the communist camp and among the developing countries.

Confédération Général du Travail. ▷ CGT.

Confrontation. Policy of President ▷ Sukarno of ▷ Indonesia towards ▷ Malaysia (1963–66), deriving from his opposition to the formation of the new federation on the grounds that it was 'neo-colonialist' and also because he objected to a stronger neighbour, especially to the Malaysian incorporation of the territories in North ▷ Borneo – Sabah and Sarawak. Sukarno ceased trading with ▷ Singapore, expropriated British property in Indonesia, broke off diplomatic relations with Malaysia and Indonesian troops raided Sabah and Sarawak and even the Malayan mainland. Malaysia received military support from the UK and Australia, but the conflict only ended with Sukarno's fall from power.

Congo (Brazzaville), Republic of. *Area* – 139,000 sq. miles. *Population* (approx.) – 1,000,000. *President* – Major Marien Ngouabi (1969–). *Constitution* (1970) – replaced National Assembly by regional people's councils. Chairman of the Congolese Workers Party was *ex officio* Head of State and President of Council of State.

As the Middle Congo (formerly the French Congo), a colony of ⇨ French Equatorial Africa from 1910 (Brazzaville was de Gaulle's Free French Capital), with internal self-government from 1956, and as the Republic of the Congo an autonomous member of the ⇨ French Community from 1958, it attained full independence in Aug. 1960, remaining in the Community. The Republic's first President, the Abbé Youlou, who alienated support through his pro-French policies, active friendship with Moise ⇨ Tshombe and suppression of opposition parties (April 1963), was forced to resign in Aug. 1963. Massamba-Débat's new government, with a revised constitution (adopted by referendum – Dec. 1963) curbing presidential power, repudiated Youlou's policies, established friendly relations with China and the Soviet Union and from 1966 with France (relations were severed for some months in 1965). A military coup (1966) was overcome with the aid of Cuban troops attached to the President. The Congo Republic has no diplomatic relations with the USA (severed by the USA 1965) nor with the UK (severed by the Congo over ⇨UDI). Two years later, in a confused situation, with the army challenging the President (July/Aug. 1968), the presidential powers were drastically reduced by the *Acte Fondamental* (Aug. 1968) replacing the 1963 constitution. The President (believed to be under arrest) was deposed (14.9.1968) and Captain Raoul became Head of State the following day and formed a provisional government. Raoul was replaced by Marien Ngouabi in Jan. 1969. The country's fragile political stability was threatened by several attempted coups during the early 1970s.

Congo (Kinshasa), Democratic Republic of. (Renamed Zaire.) *Area* – 895,348 sq. miles. *Population* (1969) – 17,100,000. *President* – General ⇨ Mobutu Sese Soko. *Constitution* (June 1967) – Executive power is vested in an elected President and his appointed Council of Ministers. There is a uni-cameral National Assembly elected by universal suffrage.

An international scandal caused by the savage exploitation of the territory compelled King Leopold II to cede his control of the Congo Free State (1885–1908) to the Belgian Parliament when the administration of the colony – from 1908 to 1960 the Belgian Congo – was reformed. A few large companies (e.g. *Union Minière du Haut Katanga*), granted extensive concessions, continued to monopolize economic development. Administrative policies (in a vast colony made up of many tribes largely dependent on a subsistence economy) have been blamed for some of the difficulties later inherited by the Congo Republic. Public services were expanded and Africans trained for employment in the lower echelons of the administration, industry and the *Force Publique*, but political organizations were repressed and political development retarded. (Almost no provision was made for higher education or for professional and advanced technological training for Africans.) Until the late fifties, when the Congo could no longer be shielded from the impact of African nationalism, administrative policies did not aim at Congolese self-government. Following riots in Leopoldville (Jan. 1959), the Belgian Government invited Congolese leaders to a Round Table Conference in Brussels (20.1.1960) and June 30 was agreed as the date for independence. This abrupt reversal of previous policies, precipitated by threatened disorder and the demands of the recently formed Congolese political parties, left the politicians little time to achieve national rather than local and tribal support. In the elections (May 1960) ⇨Lumumba's MNC (*Mouvement National Congolais*) emerged as the strongest party and he was appointed Prime Minister and ⇨ Kasavubu, leader of the *Abako* party (*Alliance des Bas-Kongo*), President. Within a week of its foundation (30 June 1960), as crisis followed crisis, the new Republic was threatened with disintegration. Following a mutiny (4 July) of the *Force Publique* (still officered by Belgians), including attacks on civilians in Leopoldville (Kinshasa), Thysville and Elizabethville, Belgian troops intervened and Lumumba and Kasavubu, convinced that independence was threatened, appealed to the UN. On 13 July – two days after ⇨ Tshombe, apparently with Belgian support, had declared Katanga's independence – the Security Council agreed to Secretary-General ⇨ Hammarskjöld's request for a UN force to be sent to the Congo. On 5 Sept. Kasavubu dismissed Lumumba who, dissatisfied with UN reluctance to intervene in Katanga, had appealed for and accepted Russian aid (transport planes). On 14 Sept. Colonel Mobutu, with his ANC (*Armée Nationale Congolaise*, formerly the *Force Publique*) entrenched in Leopoldville, established a new government – the ⇨ College of Commissioners. Reversing Lumumba's policies Mobutu immediately severed relations with the USSR and Czechoslovakia and later with Ghana and the UAR. Following UN recognition of the Mobutu/Kasavubu government (Nov.) ⇨ Gizenga organized a rival Lumumbist government in Stanleyville. (The 'Mining State' – Baluba – following Katanga's example had seceded in Aug.) With the government increasingly concerned to arrest the process of fragmentation, new alliances (e.g. with Tshombe then with Gizenga) were continually being formed and broken. Tshombe's employment of 'white' mercenaries had already inflamed

African opinion which was further outraged by Lumumba's murder (Jan. 1961) – (though Leopoldville had delivered Lumumba to Katanga). Nor did the deed prevent Kasavubu's later appointment of Tshombe as Prime Minister of the Congo – (⊳Lumumba, ⊳Kasavubu, ⊳Tshombe). The outbreak of hostilities (Aug. 1961) between Katangese and UN forces bitterly divided world opinion. (In Sept. 1961 Dag Hammarskjöld was killed in a plane crash on his way to negotiate with Tshombe.) Tshombe's army was forced to retire (Dec. 1961) but Katanga's secession only came to an end in June 1963 after another round of fighting. Leopoldville and Stanleyville were temporarily united by the struggle against Katanga. A new government, with UN backing, had been formed (Aug. 1961) under Kasavubu with Adoula as Prime Minister and Gizenga as deputy Prime Minister. In 1962 Adoula moved against Gizenga and the Lumumbists and in 1963 (Oct.), following a vote of no confidence, Kasavubu suspended Parliament. With the Government again unable to exert its authority in the provinces, Tshombe returned from exile and Kasavubu appointed him Prime Minister (10.7.1964). The Lumumbists had re-established their rival state – 'People's Republic of The Congo' (4.9.1964) in Stanleyville. Tshombe again called on his mercenaries. The Belgian Government dispatched paratroopers to Stanleyville (with Tshombe's approval) to rescue their nationals (estimated at over 1,000). Their capture of the city also fatally undermined the authority of the rebel government. OAU attempts at mediation failed. While the USA supported Tshombe and Belgian intervention, many African states supported the rebels and Algeria and the UAR sent arms to Stanleyville. Before the rebels were defeated, barbarous acts were again committed by both sides. In Leopoldville (Kinshasa) political rivalries continued unabated. Following Kasavubu's dismissal of Tshombe (Oct. 1965) General Mobutu staged a second *coup d'état* in Nov. 1965. His presidency secured by the loyalty of the ANC, a year later (Oct. 1966) he also took over the premiership. On 27 Oct. 1971 the name of the Democratic Republic of the Congo was changed to the Republic of Zaire.

Congress. The Federal Legislature of the USA in which, in accordance with the doctrine of the ⊳ Separation of Powers, all legislative powers granted by the Constitution (Article 1) are vested. Its meeting-place is the ⊳ Capitol. Congress is bi-cameral; and the two houses – the ⊳ Senate and the ⊳ House of Representatives – have similar powers, this being part of the system of ⊳ Checks and Balances characteristic of American government. Elections for the House and a third of the Senate take place in November of all even-numbered years, and each Congress lasts for a two-year period beginning the following January.

The 93rd Congress, elections for which were held on 7 Nov. 1972, began on 3 Jan. 1973. Virtually all seats in all congressional elections are won by candidates of the ⇨ Democratic Party and the ⇨ Republican Party. The Democrats have won majorities in both houses at most elections since the period of the ⇨ New Deal.

The legislative and other powers specifically granted to Congress by the Constitution are extensive, and they have been further extended by decisions of the ⇨ Supreme Court. Congress regulates foreign and interstate commerce under the ⇨ Commerce Clause. It has considerable fiscal powers, also, including the power to tax, to borrow on credit, and to coin money; these powers have provided the basis for the ⇨ Federal Reserve System and other means of regulating the national economy. Congress alone has the power to declare war, though the President, acting as Commander-in-Chief, can make ⇨ Executive War. All treaties are subject to ratification by a two-thirds vote of the Senate; but the President increasingly makes ⇨ Executive Agreements to avoid the need for formal treaties. Congress legislates for the establishment, maintenance, and regulation of the Armed Forces; and it is the source of their funds. Its powers extend also to the ⇨ National Guard. It has direct responsibility for the District of Columbia (D C) and U S territories other than the states. In the rare event of the ⇨ Electoral College being unable to decide on the election of a President and Vice-President, the election of the former passes to the House of Representatives, and that of the latter to the Senate. Finally, in conjunction with its legislative powers, Congress has control over ⇨ Appropriations, and hence the 'power of the purse'. Some powers, by contrast, are specifically denied to Congress by the ⇨ Bill of Rights – e.g. to legislate for an 'establishment of religion' (the ⇨ First Amendment) or to infringe 'the right of the people to keep and bear arms' (Second Amendment). Moreover, by the same instrument, powers not 'delegated to the United States' (and hence to Congress) are reserved to the states or the people (Tenth Amendment). However, successive decisions of the Supreme Court have loosened restrictions on the legislative competence of Congress.

Much of the work of Congress is done by ⇨ Congressional Committees. Standing committees hold ⇨ Hearings on legislative proposals and committees also hold ⇨ Congressional Investigations into the conduct of administration and other matters.

The principal officers of Congress, including the President *pro tempore* of the Senate and the Speaker of the House of Representatives, are chosen by the majority party in their respective houses. The influential chairmen of the legislative committees are also chosen from the majority party in each house on the basis of the ⇨ Seniority Rule, with the result that they tend to come from states and districts where one party predominates, and are often conservative. When the majority is Democratic, which it most frequently is, a high proportion of the most important committee chairmen are Southerners, or ⇨ 'Dixiecrats'. The leading party officials in Congress, the ⇨ Majority Leader, ⇨ Minority Leader, and Whips in each house, are also influential. The Senate Majority Leader in particular can greatly help or hinder a President seeking to carry through a legislative programme, especially when (as in the case of ⇨ Nixon) the President belongs to the other party. It was in this position that Lyndon B. ⇨ Johnson established his political reputation. However, though individual party leaders are powerful in Congress, the parties themselves are far from strong. The members of each party in each house constitute a ⇨ Caucus or 'conference' which chooses party officers, approves assignments of members to congressional committees, and considers questions of policy. But party organs, though sometimes established by law and provided with considerable funds and staff, have relatively little power over members, largely because of the relative strength of the members' local ties. It is regarded as only proper that Senators and Congressmen should put the interests of their constituents before all other considerations, including party unity. Consequently, the congressional parties lack cohesion and discipline, and there is no clear and consistent party policy; cross-party voting is common, and the outcome of debates is by no means dependent on party strength alone.

For reasons that include the loose party structure and the separation of powers, Congress remains markedly independent in its relations with the President; and the balance between the legislative and executive branches of government has shifted less in favour of the latter in the USA than in other countries.

Congressional Committees. Special bodies set up within the US ⇨ Congress to carry on various aspects of its business which could not be conveniently conducted by all members of either or both of its houses. The present system of committees is regulated by the provisions of the Legislative Reorganization Act of 1946. Apart from the Committee of the Whole of the ⇨ House of Representatives, which is the House itself operating under modified rules, there are four kinds of congressional committees.

Standing committees, of which there are 18 in the ⇨ Senate and 21 in the House of Representatives, are the most important kind. They are permanent bodies, each specializing in some aspect of public affairs in which its members tend to become expert. They are sometimes called the 'little legislatures'. All legislative proposals must be referred to the appropriate committees, where they become the subject of often extensive ⇨ Hearings, and cannot be proceeded with further until reported by the committees to their parent bodies. The committees have the power to amend or reject proposals as they see fit, and they virtually control the legislative process. Membership is formally determined by vote of the respective house but, by convention, it is settled in advance by the parties. For this purpose, each party has a 'committee on committees' in each house. The ⇨ Republican Party 'conference' elects such a body in the Senate and the House, whilst the ⇨ Democratic Party makes use of its steering or policy committee in the Senate and its members on the Ways and Means Committee in the House, these being chosen by the party ⇨ Caucus. The assignment of party members to committees is governed by the ⇨ Seniority Rule, the more senior members being placed on the more important committees of their choice. The party with a majority in the parent body has a majority on all its committees; and the chairman of a committee, who has a large measure of control over the committee's business, is the member of the majority party with the longest continuous service on the committee. Particularly prominent committees are, in the Senate, Foreign Relations, Government Operations, Armed Services, Finance, and Appropriations, and in the House of Representatives, Appropriations, Ways and Means, and the ⇨ Rules Committee.

Special or *select committees* are established to deal with specific, non-recurrent matters, though sometimes they are continued from year to year, becoming indistinguishable from standing committees. They do not have the same legislative powers as standing committees, however, and are used rather to conduct occasional ⇨ Congressional Investigations. They have been used less since 1946 than before.

Joint Committees are composed of members of both houses. They are established either by statute or by concurrent ⇨ Resolutions of Congress, usually to deal with some aspect of public business not specifically covered by standing committees. There are few of them, two of the most important being the Joint Economic Committee, which scrutinizes the ⇨ Economic Report of the President, and the Joint Committee on Atomic Energy, which oversees the ⇨ AEC.

Conference committees are joint committees established for the purpose of harmonizing legislation in the Senate and the House when they have passed a Bill in other than identical terms, this being required for enactment.

Congressional Investigations. Inquiries conducted by ⇨ Congressional Committees or subcommittees in the USA in connexion with proposals for legislation, oversight of administration, or other proceedings within the competence of ⇨ Congress. The powers of investigation granted to Congress by the Constitution are considerable, though the ⇨ Supreme Court in 1957 declared, as on previous occasions, that they were limited by the ⇨ First Amendment. They include the power to subpoena witnesses who, if they refuse to testify, may be punished for contempt of Congress, subject to the protection of the ⇨ Fifth Amendment. However, Congress has not attempted to enforce its claimed authority to compel executive officials, including the President, to testify. Apart from the regular ⇨ Hearings of standing committees considering legislative proposals, many special investigations are conducted by special or select committees. The purpose of some investigations is political; they are undertaken partly to embarrass the Administration or some section of Congress, or to provide publicity for those conducting them. Others render a public service that could not be performed in any other way, and can be compared to the investigations of a ⇨ Royal Commission in Britain. Particularly noteworthy in recent years have been the investigations into 'internal subversion' instigated, and later conducted, by Senator Joseph ⇨ McCarthy and by ⇨ HUAC, those conducted by the Kefauver Committee into crime in interstate commerce, and the investigations by the Foreign Relations Committee of the ⇨ Senate (Chairman Senator ⇨ Fulbright) into the conduct of the Vietnam War.

Congress Party. The governing party of ⇨ India. Founded in 1885, it was reorganized by ⇨ Gandhi after World War I into a nationalist movement, which pursued civil disobedience campaigns during the 1920s and 1930s. It won increasing popular support and after the 1937 provincial elections established itself as the governing party in most states. The British tried to conciliate it by concessions which stopped short of full independence for India, and for this reason Congress leaders refused to help the UK during World War II and were imprisoned. Originally supported by Moslems as well, Congress became a Hindu movement while the ⇨ Moslem League represented the minority Moslem population. In 1947 British India was partitioned on independence into the states of India and ⇨ Pakistan. Congress has been continuously in power since then under ⇨ Nehru (1947–64), ⇨ Shastri (1964–66) and Mrs ⇨ Gandhi from 1966. Its absolute majority decreased in the 1960s, especially after the death of Nehru, and in many states it lost power to coalitions of opposition groups, the strongest being the communists.

Conseil de l'Entente. An association for economic and political co-operation founded in 1959 consisting of ⇨ Dahomey, ⇨ Ivory Coast,

⇨Niger, ⇨Upper Volta and joined by ⇨Togo in 1965. The Council – Heads of State, Presidents and Vice-Presidents of the Legislative Assemblies of member-countries – has executive authority and meets bi-annually. It has a Regional Defence Council and aims at achieving identical constitutional and administrative procedures for each member state and at establishing a common bank and diplomatic corps. In 1965 an attempt by ⇨Houphouet-Boigny to introduce dual citizenship in the Entente was thwarted by tribal rivalries. (⇨Mali – Federation.)

Conservative Party. British political party which grew out of the nineteenth-century Tory Party. Originally the aristocratic party, the modern Conservatives are largely committed to free enterprise and the defence of established institutions. Its electoral strength rests on a broad coalition, ranging from the upper classes, banking and business interests, the professions, right through to sections of the working class. The Party's continuing electoral appeal stems partly from its ability to adapt itself to changing conditions. Except for the minority Labour governments of 1924 and 1929–31, ⇨Churchill's war-time coalition (there was no General Election between 1935 and 1945) and the Labour governments (1945–51), the Conservative Party either on its own or as the dominant partner of the National Governments (1932, 1935), held office from 1922 to 1964. Party prestige suffered badly from the failure of ⇨Chamberlain's appeasement policies and despite Churchill's personal popularity the Party was decisively rejected in the first post-war election (1945). It emerged from defeat to win three successive elections (1951, 1955, 1959), the last only three years after Eden's (Lord ⇨Avon) ⇨Suez policies threatened to disrupt the Party. After ⇨Macmillan's retirement, an influential section in the Party expressed dissatisfaction with ⇨Douglas-Home's leadership and the manner in which he had been chosen, and two years later, Conservatives followed Labour's example of allowing M Ps to choose the Leader. On a first ballot ⇨Heath secured 150 votes, ⇨Maudling, who then stood down in Heath's favour, 133, and Enoch ⇨Powell 15. The party was returned to office in June 1970 winning 330 seats to Labour's 287, Liberal's 6 and 6 independents.

Leaders of the Conservative Party from 1937:

1937–40	Neville Chamberlain
1940–55	Winston Churchill
1955–57	Anthony Eden (Avon)
1957–63	Harold Macmillan
1963–65	Sir Alec Douglas-Home
1965–	Edward Heath

Conservative Party Election Results:

	MPs elected	Votes polled
1945	189	9,988,306
1950	298	11,166,026
1951	321	13,718,069
1955	344	13,311,938
1959	365	13,750,965
1964	303	11,980,783
1966	253	11,418,433
1970	330	13,106,965

Constantine XIII (1940–). Became King of ⇨ Greece in 1964 but fled the country (Dec. 1967) following his unsuccessful counter-coup against the military government that had seized power in April of that year. In 1965 he was involved in a serious conflict with his Prime Minister, George ⇨ Papandreou, over an investigation into a secret army organization.

Consultative Assembly. ⇨ Council of Europe.

Containment (of communism). A persistent theme of American foreign policy since World War II, and the basic Cold War objective of the USA, containment means confining communist control and influence within existing limits. It contrasts with the policy of ⇨ Rollback, but is consistent with that of ⇨ Massive Retaliation. Successive Presidents and other leaders of both parties have subscribed to and acted upon it with varying degrees of consistency and intensity; but at no time, even during periods of 'peaceful co-existence', has it been wholly neglected. Much of the effort involved has taken the form of economic and technical assistance to non-communist countries, exemplified by the ⇨ European Recovery Program and the ⇨ Mutual Security Program. But direct military action, as in Korea and Vietnam, has also been a feature of the policy.

CORE. Congress of Racial Equality – political association in the USA, founded in 1942 to fight against racial discrimination by non-violent means. With the beginning of ⇨ Sit-Ins in 1960 (the technique had been used by CORE members in 1942 and 1949) it became more active in the Negro ⇨ Civil Rights Movement, working closely with ⇨ SNCC and ⇨ NAACP against ⇨ Segregation in the South.

Corrective Labour Camps. ⇨ Forced Labour Camps.

Cosmopolitanism. As used in the USSR after World War II – a term of abuse with strongly anti-semitic overtones, directed against Jewish non-conformist intellectuals.

Costa e Silva, Marshal Artur Da (1902–). President of ⇨ Brazil (1967–69) and a leader of the 1964 'revolution'. The army had intervened in politics before, but since the enforced resignation of ⇨ Vargas (1945), direct army initiatives (though it exercised considerable pressures on governments) had been followed by restoration of civil authorities. The significance of the 1964 coup lies in its seeming permanence and a new political role for the army at the centre of political power.

Costa Rica. *Area* – 19,653 sq. miles. *Population* (1972 est.) – 1,800,000. *President* – Dr José Figueres Ferrer (1970–). *Constitution* (1949) – Unitary Republic; executive power is vested in an elected President and two Vice-Presidents. The President cannot serve successive terms. There is a uni-cameral National Assembly elected by proportional representation, through compulsory universal adult suffrage. (A committee has been established (1967) to draft proposals for constitutional reform.)

Compared with many Latin American countries, twentieth-century Costa Rica has provided an example of political stability and, with brief exceptions, adherence to constitutional government. One reason for this has been the absence of military intervention in politics. Since an unpopular military dictatorship (1917–18), the power of the army has been continually reduced, culminating in its formal abolition (1944) and its formation is expressly forbidden by the constitution (1949). Present political alignments were profoundly affected by the events of 1947–48, when a left-wing Congress refused to accept the validity of the new President's election. He was returned to power (1949) following civil war and rebellion by his supporters. In Costa Rica official political parties are state-sponsored – i.e. they can reclaim their election campaign funds. This does not apply to the unofficial parties of the communist-oriented Left, whose strongest supporters are the rural workers on the large fruit plantations. Disputes with Nicaragua and accusations of Nicaraguan interference in Costa Rican politics (1948) flared up again in 1955. Costa Rica was backed by the ⇨ OAS and military support from the US before a settlement was reached.

Coty, René (1882–1962). Second and last President of the French ⇨ Fourth Republic (1954–59), he was succeeded by General ⇨ de Gaulle, on whom he called to form a government (29.5.1958) when the ⇨ Pflimlin administration bowed to the military insurrection in Algiers and the right-wing demand for the General's return to power. From the time he relinquished the presidency to his death, he was a member of the Constitutional Council of the ⇨ Fifth Republic.

Council for Mutual Economic Assistance. ⇨ CMEA.

Council of Europe. Established (London, May 1949) to achieve in the words of its Statute 'a greater unity between its members for the purpose of safeguarding and realizing the ideas and principles which are their common heritage and facilitating their economic and social progress'. The founding countries were Belgium, Denmark, France, Great Britain, Ireland, Italy, Luxembourg, The Netherlands, Norway and Sweden; Greece, Iceland and Turkey joined in 1949/50, the German Federal Republic 1951, Austria 1956, Cyprus 1961, Switzerland 1963, Malta 1965. Any European country willing to respect human rights and fundamental freedoms (Article 3 of the Statute) is eligible for membership, from which the Iberian and ⇨ Iron Curtain dictatorships are excluded. The Committee of Ministers is the Council's Executive. Composed of the Foreign Ministers of member states meeting once or twice yearly and their deputies (permanent officials) who meet eight to ten times a year, it alone can conclude agreements, make recommendations to governments, etc. The Committee can also set up commissions to deal with specialized tasks such as the Council for Cultural Cooperation (CCC) or the Committee on Legal Cooperation.

The Consultative Assembly (Strasbourg), although lacking legislative or executive power, provides a parliamentary forum in which European issues can be discussed independently of established national policies. Its 147 deputies, appointed by the member countries, form national delegations whose sizes vary according to population. Thus England, France, Germany and Italy have 18 deputies and Malta, Cyprus and Luxembourg 3. The delegations (made up of active parliamentarians) are so composed as to reflect party strength in their respective countries, sit and vote according to party (Christian-Democrat, Socialist, Liberal) rather than national affiliations. The Assembly can only submit recommendations or resolutions to the Committee of Ministers; the former needs a two-thirds majority, the latter a simple one.

The European Commission and Court of Human Rights is one of the Council's special agencies, set up after the European Convention for the Protection of European Rights and Fundamental Freedoms had been ratified by 15 of the 18 member countries. The Commission (established April 1955) can hear complaints between member states and also (subject to the provisions of Article 25) individual complaints, 43 of which out of the 3,500 so far received have been regarded as 'admissible'.

Couve de Murville, Maurice (1907–). Prime Minister of ⇨ France (1968–69). An ardent supporter of ⇨ de Gaulle whom he joined in Algiers (1943), he served as ambassador in Cairo (1950–54), Washington (1955–56) and Bonn (1956–58). De Gaulle, upon assuming office in the Fifth Republic (June 1958), appointed him Foreign Minister, a position he held for ten years. After the reshuffle of the ⇨ Pompidou Cabinet following the May 1968 riots, he became Minister of Finance (May 1968) and succeeded Pompidou as Prime Minister (July 1968). He was not included in President Pompidou's first government (June 1969) and defeated in a by-election (Oct 1969) had to withdraw temporarily from politics.

CPP. Convention People's Party – ⇨ Ghana.

CPR. ⇨ Chinese People's Republic.

CPSU. Communist Party of the Soviet Union.

Cripps, Sir Richard Stafford (1889–1952). Brilliant barrister and left-wing socialist who was expelled from the UK Labour Party (1939) for earlier urging a United Front with the communists (re-admitted in 1945). In 1940 he was sent to Moscow as British Ambassador in the belief that as a socialist he might enlist Russia as an ally in the war. In 1942 he headed an unsuccessful mission to India with plans for self-government in return for cooperation in the war against Japan. President of the Board of Trade (1945–47) and Minister of Economic Affairs (1947–50), he was particularly associated with 'austerity' and his strict economic measures (continuation of war-time levels of taxation, voluntary trade-union wage-freeze, etc.) contributed greatly to the slowing-down of inflation in the years of reconstruction after the war.

Croix de Feu. The largest of the French right-wing ex-servicemen leagues. Founded in 1927 as an association of World War 1 veterans decorated with the *Croix de Guerre*. Under the guidance of the politically ambitious Colonel de la Rocque, it accepted any ex-servicemen and later, in affiliated organizations, all 'patriotic' citizens, sharing the Colonel's anti-parliamentarian, right-wing views. Its 260,000 members – a quarter of them in the Paris area – took an active part in the Paris riots (6.2.1934) which led to the dissolution of the organization under the ⇨ Popular Front government. Colonel de la Rocque thereupon reconstituted the movement as the *Parti Social Français* (PSF).

Crossman, Richard (1907–). UK Labour politician and member of the Wilson Cabinet – Minister of Housing and Local Government (1964–66), Leader of the House of Commons (1966–68) and 1968–70 Secretary of State for Social Services. A former assistant editor of the *New Statesman*; during the war Crossman was a Director of Psychological Warfare and from 1945 to 1946 was a member of the Anglo-American Commission of Enquiry on Palestine. He was editor of the *New Statesman* from 1970 to 1972.

CRS. *Compagnie Républicaine de Sécurité* – is a special branch of the French police with specific responsibilities for the maintenance of state security. The fully motorized force, stationed in strategically-placed barracks throughout France, consists of about 500 officers, 2,000 NCOs and 15,000 men. During the May 1968 'student' riots the CRS acquired a reputation for brutality.

Crystal Night (Nov. 1938). ⇨ NAZI euphemism for the anti-semitic pogroms organized to demonstrate 'popular fury' at the murder of the German consular official (von Rath) in Paris by a Polish Jew (Grynszpan). Almost all synagogues were burned down, more than 26,000 Jewish men and boys were sent to ⇨ Concentration Camps and a fine of RM 1000 million was imposed on Jewish communists under Nazi rule. The riots were followed by a spate of legislation barring Jews from all economic activities and enforcing complete segregation.

Cuba, Republic of. *Area* – 44,178 sq. miles. *Population* (1970) – 8,553,395. *President* – Osvaldo Dorticos Torrado (1959–). *Prime Minister* – Dr Fidel ⇨ Castro Ruz (1959–). *Constitution* – The former constitution has been suspended; a new socialist constitution has been in preparation since 1965.

Having gained formal independence at the beginning of this century, Cuba remained under US domination for several decades. In 1934, the USA renounced its right of intervention, but retained a naval base in Cuba, and American economic and diplomatic influence remained powerful. Except for an interval between 1944 and 1952, the dominating personality in Cuba between 1933 and 1958 was General Batista who, throughout this period, ruled Cuba, either indirectly through puppet Presidents, or directly as President. During the last years of his rule, following a military *coup d'état* in 1952, the democratic constitution was suspended and the methods of government became increasingly repressive.

In Dec. 1956, Fidel Castro and a small group of supporters (including Che ⇨ Guevara) established a secret base in the mountain range of the Sierra Maestra as the core of a gradually expanding revolutionary guerrilla force and a centre of propaganda for social justice and the re-establishment of democratic liberties. Their campaign gained in popularity proportionate to the increasing disenchantment with Batista and the demoralization of his army. Castro's final offensive in the summer of 1958 met with little effective resistance. On 31 Dec. Batista fled, and on 1 Jan. 1959 the victory of the revolution was proclaimed.

The new regime, headed by Castro as Prime Minister, carried out a series of nationalization measures and a radical land reform amounting to an agrarian revolution from above. With the progress of this social transformation, Castro and his followers, the 'July 26 Movement', gradually abandoned their originally libertarian political programme, as a result of which many of his former democratic supporters joined his enemies in seeking refuge in the USA. In the course of 1960, nationalization measures were greatly stepped up and increasingly affected American-owned firms. Washington took a series of counter-measures and, by the end of 1960, Cuba and the USA were in a state of economic war, followed by a breaking off of diplomatic relations (Jan. 1961). In the meantime, Havana had established economic as as well as diplomatic relations with Moscow. The break with the USA made Cuba economically wholly dependent on the USSR and other communist countries. At about the same time, Castro began to cooperate internally with the 'Socialist People's Party' – the Cuban communists who had played practically no part in the revolution. The abortive invasion of Cuba in April 1961 by exiles in the USA, who attempted a landing on the ⇨ Bay of Pigs, accelerated Castro's rapprochement with the communists. In the early summer of 1961, he took the first steps towards the amalgamation of his 'July 26 Movement' with the (communist) 'Socialist People's Party'. In Dec. 1961, Castro called himself a Marxist-Leninist for the first time and succeeded soon afterwards in ousting his most powerful would-be rival among the communist 'old guard' (Anibal Escalante) and in establishing his ascendancy over the rest of the old communist party leadership. In the spring of 1962, the new 'United Party of the Socialist Revolution' (renamed, in 1965, 'Communist Party of Cuba') was set up under Castro's leadership as the only legal political party, in command of all aspects of life in the country. Soon afterwards, Castro's political relations with the USSR deteriorated sharply as a result of the ⇨ Cuban Missile Crisis, which was resolved over his head. The same event led to a temporary rapprochement between Havana and Peking. Relations with Moscow were later patched up, but, despite Cuba's continuing economic dependence on the USSR and its allies and, to a far lesser extent, on China, Castro has, since the mid-1960s, increasingly dissociated himself from both China and the USSR, attempting to establish his own rival communist hegemony over the revolutionary movements in Latin America. The lack of success of these movements, in combination with Cuba's own economic failures, produced a new rapprochement between Cuba and the USSR. Having publicly approved of the Soviet intervention in ⇨ Czechoslovakia (Aug. 1968), Castro paid friendship visits to Eastern Europe and the USSR in 1972. After these visits Cuba became a member of ⇨ CMEA.

Cuban Missile Crisis. On 16 Oct. 1962 President ⇨ Kennedy of the USA learnt from u-2 aerial photographs that the USSR, contrary to formal undertakings, was installing ballistic missiles and atomic weapons in ⇨ Cuba. On 22 Oct. President Kennedy, in a television broadcast, told the world about the Soviet missiles in Cuba and announced that the USA, as an initial counter-step, was going to impose a quarantine so as to prevent further shipments of offensive weapons to

Cuba. Having obtained the unanimous support of the Organization of American States and of the member countries of NATO for this step, President Kennedy, in an exchange of letters with the Soviet Premier Khrushchev, warned the USSR against attempts at breaking the block-ade and requested the Soviet Government to remove its offensive missiles from Cuba. For six days, while Moscow seemed unwilling to fulfil the American request, the world hovered on the brink of a nuclear war. On 28 Oct., the USSR agreed to withdraw its missiles under UN supervision in exchange for an American undertaking to lift the blockade and to give assurances against an invasion of Cuba. Though welcomed by most of the world's nations, this solution added further fuel to the ⇨ Sino-Soviet Conflict and was sharply attacked by ⇨Castro who had not been consulted and who refused the UN inspection team, appointed to verify the removal of the missiles, entry into Cuba.

Cultural Revolution. A Chinese movement launched by ⇨ Mao Tse-tung in 1965 to purge the country's institutions of his adversaries and to revolutionize people's thoughts and attitudes. (⇨ Chinese People's Republic.)

Curtin, John (1885–1945). Prime Minister of ⇨ Australia (1941–45) and leader of the Labour Party (1935–45). He was concurrently Minister of Defence from 1942 and organized Australia's defence policy during World War II. Although this was based on strong cooperation with the USA he hoped for a closer organization of the ⇨ Commonwealth but his proposals were rejected at the Prime Ministers' Conference (1944).

Curzon Line. A line of demarcation first proposed to Poland in 1920 by Lloyd George and later elaborated by the British Foreign Secretary, Lord Curzon, as an ethnically fair frontier between Poland and Russia. Rejected by Poland at the time, the Curzon Line became, with minor variations, first, the boundary between the German and Soviet zones of occupation after their partition of Poland in Sept. 1939 and, subsequently, the post-war Soviet-Polish frontier.

Cyprus. *Area* – 3,572 sq. miles. *Population* – 633,000 (including 463,000 Greek Cypriots and 108,000 Turkish Cypriots). *Head of State* – Archbishop ⇨ Makarios (1960–). *Constitution* (1960) – Independent state in the ⇨ Commonwealth. The 1960 constitution (which has proved unworkable since independence) vested executive authority in the President (a Greek) and a Vice-President (a Turk), both elected for five years by their respective communities. The Vice-President was given the right of veto over decisions of the President in important matters, e.g. foreign affairs, questions of security or defence. A Council of Ministers (seven Greek, three

Turkish) was to assist them both. Legislative authority was vested in the House of Representatives, elected by universal suffrage for five years and consisting of 35 Greek members and 15 Turkish. Communal questions such as religion, education and welfare came within the jurisdiction of separate Greek and Turkish Communal Chambers. Greek and Turkish were both recognized as official languages and posts in the public service, the police and the armed forces were proportioned between the two races.

Originally a Turkish possession, Cyprus was administered by the UK from 1878 and became a Crown Colony in 1925. The movement among the Greek population for *Enosis* (political union with Greece) led to riots in 1931 – the Legislative Council was suspended and two Greek bishops exiled (the Greek Orthodox Church in Cyprus spearheaded the attack on British rule). The movement temporarily lost some of its momentum in the 1930s, when Cyprus depended on British protection against the threat of an Italian attack, and during ⇨World War II when the UK and Greece fought on the same side. In 1943 permission was granted for the formation of political parties and in 1946 the British Labour Government promised to summon a Consultative Assembly to establish a constitution and a central Legislature but this came to nothing – the proposals were rejected by the Greek Cypriots because they did not alter the political status of the country. Instead they demanded a plebiscite and in 1950 the bishops cooperated with the communists, who controlled the majority of trade unions, in holding an unofficial one among the Greek population, 96% of whom favoured *Enosis*. Popular pressure for *Enosis* increased during the fifties and in 1955 erupted into a campaign of violence which lasted for four years. This followed unsuccessful efforts at the UN by the Greek Government, which now openly supported *Enosis*. Acts of sabotage against the British by ⇨EOKA, the Greek terrorist organization under General ⇨Grivas, developed into communal strife with the turks, who created their own guerrilla organization, the *Volka* (later the TMT). By 1959, 600 people had been killed and 1,300 wounded. A state of emergency was imposed on the island and in 1956 Archbishop Makarios III, the temporal as well as spiritual leader of the Greek Cypriots and ardent advocate of *Enosis*, was exiled on the grounds that he was implicated in EOKA terrorism. The London Conference (Aug.–Sept. 1955) had shown that the positions of the UK, Greece and Turkey were wide apart and the ensuing warfare between Greek and Turkish Cypriots increased tension between the three powers. The Turks preferred British rule for the protection it offered and because neither *Enosis* nor independence would favour them as a minority. When the latter became more likely, the Turks pressed for the partition of Cyprus. By 1959 Makarios had renounced the idea of *Enosis*, the British were willing to abandon their political control over Cyprus and the Turks to give up the idea of partition. Compromise agreements were made by the three powers and the two Cypriot communities at Zurich and London (Feb. 1959) and Cyprus was granted independence in 1960 while the UK retained sovereignty over her military bases. A Treaty of Guarantee was signed between Cyprus, Greece, Turkey and the UK and a Treaty of Alliance betweeen Cyprus, Greece and Turkey, by which Greece kept a force of 950 and Turkey one of 650 men on the island (soon to be the cause of trouble). Makarios was elected President and ⇨ Kuchuk, leader of the Turkish Cypriots, Vice-President of Cyprus. In the 1960 elections the Patriotic Front (supporting Makarios) won 30 seats, the Turkish Nationalists 15 and the Akel (Greek Communist Party) 5 seats. The compromise settlement of majority rule with safeguards for the minority (1960 constitution) did not solve the old antagonism between the two communities and civil violence broke out again (Dec. 1963) when Makarios introduced constitutional changes in municipal government. This led to the intervention of a UN Peacekeeping Force (April 1964) which enforced an armed truce but could not effect a political settlement. The Turkish Cypriots withdrew from the Council of Ministers and the Parliament. Violence erupted again (Nov. 1967) when the Greek Cypriot National Guard under Grivas (who had never given up *Enosis*) raided two Turkish villages. Greece and Turkey came close to war but the crisis was again patched up by international diplomacy. This feud had important international repercussions as it added greatly to insecurity in the eastern Mediterranean and weakened NATO, of which Greece and Turkey are both members. After the latest conflict Cyprus seemed further from a political solution than before. The Turkish Cypriots formed their own 'Transitional Administration' (Dec. 1967) with Kuchuk as President. Although he and Makarios were re-elected to their offices as Vice-President and President (Feb. 1968), normal parliamentary politics had ceased to exist.

Cyrankiewicz, J. (1910–). Prime Minister of ⇨ Poland. A member of the Polish Socialist Party in the inter-war period, during World War II Cyrankiewicz worked actively in the underground resistance in the German-occupied part of Poland until his arrest in 1941 when he was taken to Oswiecim (Auschwitz) concentration camp, and later transferred to Mauthausen (1945) from where he was liberated a few months later by the Americans. Having become a communist during his years of detention, after the war Cyrankiewicz played the decisive part in enforcing the socialist-communist merger leading to the foundation of the 'Polish United Workers' Party'. He was appointed Prime Minister in 1947 and, except for a short period between 1952 and 1954 when ⇨ Bierut assumed the premiership, he remained in that post until 1972.

Czechoslovakia (Czechoslovak Socialist Republic). *Area* – 49,357 sq. miles. *Population* (1970) – 14,361,557. *President* – Ludvik ⇨ Svoboda (1968–). *Prime Minister* – Lubomir Strougal 1970. *First Secretary, Communist Party* – Gustav ⇨ Husak (1969–). Constitutional changes were introduced on 1 Jan. 1969 when the country became a Federation with equal rights for the Czech and Slovak nations. Further constitutional changes have been envisaged. Meanwhile the highest organ of state power remains the Federal National Assembly, elected by universal suffrage from a single list of candidates, and effective power continues to rest with the leadership of the Communist Party.

Founded in 1918 by Thomas Garrigue Masaryk, the multi-national Czechoslovak Republic was the only state in Central Europe which maintained political democracy and free institutions right up to the moment when they were crushed from outside. Internal tensions arose mainly from the centralization of the Republic's unitary administration, which concentrated power in the hands of the Czech majority and caused considerable grievances among the large Slovak as well as the German and the smaller Hungarian, Polish and Ukrainian minorities. After Hitler's advent to power in Germany a strong Nazi movement developed among the (Sudeten) German population of the Republic, while Slovakia came increasingly under the influence of the separatist, Fascist Slovak People's Party. Under Hitler's growing pressure, Britain, France, Germany and Italy concluded the ⇨ Munich Agreement (Sept. 1938) which forced Czechoslovakia to cede a large part of its territory to Germany, Hungary and Poland. In March 1939, Hitler occupied the remainder of Czechoslovakia, dividing it into three areas – the German Protectorate of Bohemia and Moravia; the nominally independent vassal state of Slovakia; and Sub-Carpathian Ruthenia, which later became a centre of Ukrainian nationalism and was after the war ceded to the USSR. Between 1939 and 1945, with the country subdued by Nazi terror, active resistance developed mainly in Slovakia and led, in the autumn of 1944, to the Slovak armed uprising under largely communist leadership.

Early in 1945 the Soviet army entered Czechoslovakia, followed by the return of Eduard ⇨ Benes, the former President and, between 1940 and 1945, the Head of the London-based Czechoslovak Government-in-exile, and his Foreign Minister, Jan ⇨ Masaryk, the son of the 'Liberator-President'. Determined to establish close relations with the

USSR, Benes agreed from the outset to give the communists a leading role in the post-war administration. In the first post-war People's Front Government (a coalition of independent parties) communists took over the key Ministries of the Interior (controlling the Security Police), Defence (controlling the Army), Information (controlling all media of publicity) and Agriculture (controlling the distribution of the land of the three million Germans who, after the war, were expelled from Bohemia). Free and fairly-conducted elections in May 1946 resulted in a big communist success. With 38% of the poll, they emerged from it as the strongest single party, but not nearly strong enough to govern alone. A new coalition government was formed on the model of the first, but now under the premiership of Klement ⇨ Gottwald, the foremost communist leader since 1929, who had spent the war in the USSR. In July 1947, his government accepted an invitation to the Paris conference called to organize the ⇨ Marshall Plan. Threatened with an ultimatum from ⇨ Stalin, the acceptance was withdrawn three days later. Thereafter friction between the communists and their coalition partners mounted. Despite express Cabinet instructions to the contrary, the communists, with the connivance of the Minister of the Interior, proceeded to replace all non-communist police officers with their own men. On 21 Feb. 1948, 12 Ministers resigned in protest. Their resignations relieved the communists of the need to oust them unconstitutionally. Under the pressure of the Soviet Deputy Foreign Minister, V. A. Zorin, who at this crucial moment arrived in Prague and stayed throughout the crisis, and of communist-staged mass demonstrations, President Benes accepted the resignations and empowered Gottwald to form a new government of his own choice.

Three months after the establishment of the new regime, a Soviet-type constitution was introduced (9.5.1948). President Benes refused to accept it and resigned. In June 1948, he was replaced by Gottwald as the country's new President, while another veteran communist leader, Antonin Zapotocky, took over the premiership. There followed the reorganization of the economy and of all institutions on the Soviet model, complete with mass purges, treason trials, executions or long prison sentences directed first against hundreds of thousands of non-communists and, later, also against communists. The most notorious purge of communists culminated in the ⇨ Show Trial (Nov. 1952) of the Party's ex-Secretary-General, Rudolf ⇨ Slansky and 13 other high-ranking communists, which differed from similarly fantastic show trials elsewhere mainly in its strongly anti-semitic flavour.

Gottwald survived Slansky by only a few months. He died a week after Stalin, in March 1953. His successor as party leader – and later also as President of the Republic – was Antonin ⇨ Novotny who remained the country's effective ruler until his overthrow in Jan. 1968. Under his rule, Czechoslovakia functioned for many years as Moscow's model satellite, performing all the required turns of policy with due circumspection and without risky experiments. His bureaucratic conservatism worked for a time thanks mainly to the fact that Czechoslovakia had been a prosperous industrial country before the war and had suffered little damage during the war. But after a time, the Soviet type of centralized planning, designed for the modernization of backward countries, began to show its drawbacks for countries with developed and complex industries. By the early 1960s the initial advantages were exhausted and Czechoslovakia's economy began to grind to a halt. Industrial output first failed to grow and then declined; food shortages appeared and the neglected transport system began to break down. The mounting economic difficulties coincided with ⇨ Khrushchev's second onslaught on Stalin at the 22nd CPSU Congress (Oct. 1961) which, in Czechoslovakia, had far stronger repercussions than his first anti-Stalin speech of 1956. This emerged from the increasingly open expression of Slovak grievances against the rigidly centralized regime which had neglected both their national aspirations and their economic development and which had made martyrs of some of their notable communist leaders, including the former Foreign Minister, Vladimir Clementis (executed after the Slansky Trial) and Laco Novomesky and Gustav Husak who, with others, were sentenced in 1954 to long prison terms as 'bourgeois nationalists'. Another symptom of the smouldering discontent was its increasingly bold expression by writers, artists and scientists, demanding truth, freedom and all-round reforms. Alternating between half-hearted concessions to these multiple pressures and acts of repression, Novotny managed to keep them under control until the communist party leadership itself revolted against him.

On 5 Jan. 1968, a majority of the Party's Central Committee forced Novotny to resign as First Secretary and elected in his place the Slovak party leader Alexander ⇨ Dubček. Events moved fast – extensive democratic reforms were instituted, including freedom of speech and press, the complete rehabilitation of the victims of political persecution, the restoration of the rule of law and the independence of judges, the assurance of equal rights for Czechs and Slovaks in a new federal state, and the speeding up of the previously promised far-reaching economic reforms. These reforms were accompanied by certain changes in personnel, including Novotny's eventual replacement as President of the Republic by General Ludvik Svoboda and the appointment of Oldrich Cernik to the premiership.

The changes were unreservedly welcomed by ⇨Yugoslavia, ⇨Rumania and all non-ruling communist parties in Europe, but they came under increasing attack from Czechoslovakia's other ⇨ Warsaw Pact partners, especially East Germany, the USSR and Poland. The press in these countries mounted a campaign against Czechoslovakia, heaping abuse on its most outstanding and popular reformers and publishing invented reports of alleged collusion between 'imperialist revanchists' and Czechoslovak reformers. Despite the increasingly menacing pressure and a number of direct threats and confrontations, Dubček and his supporters refused to abandon the path of reform, while issuing countless reassurances about their unswerving loyalty to the Warsaw Pact alliance. On the night of 20/21 Aug. armed forces of the USSR, Bulgaria, East Germany, Hungary and Poland invaded and occupied Czechoslovakia. On the morrow, Dubček, Cernik and other leaders were arrested and taken to the USSR. Unable to find any collaborators in Czechoslovakia willing to form a Soviet puppet administration, Moscow attempted to negotiate with President Svoboda who successfully insisted on the release of Dubček and the other arrested leaders as a condition for talks. Some form of compromise was eventually achieved under duress in the shape of a Soviet-Czechoslovak Treaty, legalizing the 'temporary' presence of Soviet troops in Czechoslovakia in return for a Soviet undertaking not to interfere in domestic matters. Soviet and allied pressures nevertheless continued. Under this pressure most of the newly instituted reforms had to be revoked, while the most popular liberal-minded leaders were, one by one, ousted from their positions. They included the Communist Party's First Secretary, Alexander Dubček, who in April 1969 was replaced by Dr Gustav Husak.

D

DAC. Development Assistance Committee – within the ⇨OECD, its members are Belgium, Denmark, West Germany, France, Britain, The Netherlands, Italy, Japan, Canada, Norway, Austria, Portugal, Sweden, USA and the ⇨EEC Commission. DAC, by collecting and transmitting relevant statistics and information to member countries, tries to co-ordinate and rationalize their contributions. These represent 90% of all development aid and amounted to $8,710 m. in 1964, which also saw the despatch of 80,000 technical experts and teachers.

Dachau. ⇨Concentration Camps.

Dahomey. *Area* – 45,000 sq. miles. *Population* (1969 est.) – 2,640,000. *President* – Justin Ahomadégbé (1972–). *Constitution* (1960) – An elected President and an elected National Assembly – suspended (Dec. 1965).

A province of ⇨French West Africa from 1904, Dahomey achieved self-government within the ⇨French Community in Dec. 1958. A member of the ⇨*Conseil de l'Entente*, Dahomey became fully independent, outside the Community, on 1 Aug. 1960. Lacking resources, heavily dependent on French aid, the country has been beset by economic and political crises. In 1963 popular discontent led to the overthrow of the President and General Soglo headed a caretaker government. The second civilian administration (Jan. 1964) was undermined by economic crisis and political rivalries and was overthrown by General Soglo's bloodless military coup (1965). Political parties were banned and a five-year plan declared Soglo's aim to stop political strife and build a sound economy. Two years later (Dec. 1967) Soglo was deposed in a military coup led by Lt.-Col. Alley, who became President. A draft constitution providing for a civilian one-party rule was approved by referendum in March 1968. May elections (which had been promised) were successfully boycotted through opposition to army attempts to select the candidates. Eventually, in a stalemate situation, Col. Alley, who had announced the army's wish for a return to civilian rule, appointed a former Cabinet Minister, Dr Emile D. Zinsou to the presidency, an appointment approved by referendum (July 1968).

In 1969 a coup overthrew Dr Zinsou and for five months a military *directoire* ruled. After abortive elections in 1970 a Presidential Council was set up, comprising MM Maga, Ahomadégbé and Apithy, with Maga as President, succeeded in 1972 by Ahomadégbé, to be followed in 1974 by Apithy.

Daladier, Edouard (1884–1970). French Prime Minister at the outbreak of ⟡ World War II and co-signatory of the ⟡ Munich Agreement. A prominent member and sometime leader of the Radical Socialists, he served in numerous Cabinets from the late twenties until the fall of ⟡ France. A supporter of the ⟡ Popular Front and Minister of War in its various Cabinets, he became Prime Minister (18.4.1938) when the Popular Front began to disintegrate. After Munich, he lost the support of the Socialists and increasingly had to rely on the Right. Ineffectual as a war leader, he was replaced by Paul ⟡ Reynaud (21.3.1940) under whom he continued to serve as Minister of War. The ⟡ Vichy authorities prosecuted him on a war guilt charge (⟡ Riom Trials) and the Germans interned him in the Buchenwald and Dachau concentration camps (1943–45). A member of the National Assembly from 1946 to 1958 and leader of the Radical Socialist Party in 1957/58.

Daniel, Yuli (1925–). Soviet poet and translator (⟡ Dissent).

Danquah, Dr. ⟡ Ghana.

Danzig. German city at the mouth of the Vistula, which after World War I was made a 'Free City' under ⟡ League of Nations auspices. It gave the newly-created, land-locked Poland an outlet to the sea with special extra-territorial privileges. Their denial and the city's incorporation into ⟡ Germany (1.9.1939), a chief cause of ⟡ World War II, provided ⟡ Hitler with an issue sufficiently remote to enable the Western Nazi and Communist sympathizers of the ⟡ Hitler-Stalin Pact to question the necessity of 'dying for Danzig' (⟡ *Mourir pour Danzig?*). After the war the Germans were expelled and Gdansk (formerly Danzig) came under Polish administration.

Darlan, François (1881–1942). C.-in-C. of the French navy (1939–40), the Admiral supported Marshal ⟡ Pétain and collaboration with Germany, particularly after the British attack on the French fleet (3.7.1940). Following ⟡ Laval's dismissal (13.12.1940) he became Vice-President of the Council of Ministers and Pétain's successor-designate (Feb. 1941). After their landings in North Africa, he joined the Allies, allegedly on the secret instructions of Marshal Pétain, who publicly denounced this betrayal and stripped him of his offices. Contesting General ⟡ de Gaulle's leadership and claiming to represent the legally constituted authority he was assassinated by an anti-Vichyist supporter of the General.

Darnand, Joseph (1897–1945). French Fascist and collaborator, shot as a traitor. In the thirties he led the extreme right-wing militants, *Les*

Camelots du Roi, and was intimately associated with such other strong-arm organizations as the *Cagoulards* and the ⇨ *Action Française*. Achieving ministerial rank under ⇨Vichy (Feb. 1944), he organized the hated ss-like militia which, in cooperation with the Nazi police, hunted down Resistance fighters, Jews and other political suspects.

Davies, Joseph Edward (1876–1958). US lawyer and statesman. Chairman, Federal Trade Commission (1915–16) and adviser to President Wilson at Versailles (1918), he was appointed ambassador to the Soviet Union (1936–38). He served for two years as ambassador to Belgium and minister to Luxembourg (1938–40) and attended the Potsdam Conference as an adviser (1945). His book, *Mission to Moscow* (which accepted the Stalinist version of the purges) did much to foster American sympathy for the Soviet cause against Germany.

Davis, Angela Y. Black militant in the USA, tried and acquitted (1972) on a charge of complicity in a courtroom shooting incident at San Rafael, California, in Aug. 1970, in which the judge and three prisoners were killed. A student at Brandeis University and the Sorbonne, she became a philosophy instructor under Herbert Marcuse, having joined the Communist Party and been dismissed for that reason from a post in the University of California at Los Angeles (UCLA). She was charged on the basis of having purchased the weapons used in the courtroom shooting, which was connected with an attempt to kidnap the judge to draw attention to the case of the 'Soledad Brothers', with one of whom, George Jackson, her name was linked at the trial. Her acquittal was variously described as a demonstration of the fairness of American justice and a victory for the people over the oppressive American system.

Dayan, General Moshe (1915–). ⇨Israel Minister of Defence (1967–), famous as the 'Victor of Sinai', began his military career in *Haganah*. Imprisoned by the British (1939), he was released (1941) to act as a scout for the British forces occupying ⇨Syria. A colonel noted for his daring in Israel's War of Independence (1948–49) he was appointed Chief of Staff (1953–58) and commanded the 1956 Israel Sinai campaign. Entered politics as a *Mapai* (Israel Labour Party) member of the *Knesset* (1959) and served as Minister of Agriculture (1959–64). He joined ⇨ Ben Gurion's breakaway *Rafi* (Israel Labour List) in 1965, but in the critical days of May 1967 public opinion demanded his recall to the government, and his appointment as Minister of Defence (1.6.1967) immediately boosted civilian and army morale.

DC. District of Columbia, USA – an area of Federal territory on the Potomac River between Maryland and Virginia comprising the city of Washington, capital of the USA and seat of the Federal Government.

Déat, Marcel (1894–1955). As ⇨Vichy's Minister of Labour and State

Security responsible from March 1944 for the deportation of French workers to Germany, the enrolment of French volunteers in the *Waffen SS* (⇨ss) and the organization of the French security police. He was a socialist Deputy in the thirties and briefly (1936) Minister of Aviation. A radical pacificist, he became a supporter of ⇨ Appeasement and is credited with coining the catch-phrase ⇨ *Mourir pour Danzig?* Sentenced to death after liberation, Déat escaped and lived incognito in Northern Italy.

Debré, Michel (1912–). First Prime Minister of the French ⇨ Fifth Republic (1959–1962). A devoted follower of ⇨ de Gaulle, whom he joined in Algiers, he was a prominent member of the General's ⇨RPF (*Rassemblement du Peuple Français*) in the Senate (1948–58). After his accession to power de Gaulle appointed him his Minister of Justice (June 1958–Jan. 1959). Debré rejoined the Cabinet (Jan. 1966) as Minister of Finance. He became Foreign Minister after the reshuffle of the ⇨ Pompidou Cabinet following the May 1968 riots, a post he continued to hold when ⇨ Couve de Murville became Prime Minister after the July 1968 elections. He became Minister of Defence in President Pompidou's first two cabinets of June 1969 and July 1972.

Declaration of Lima. 1942 declaration by the members of the ⇨Pan-American Union expressing their common determination to resist any external intervention in the affairs of the Western Hemisphere. It internationalized the traditional foreign-policy stance of the United States known as the Monroe Doctrine.

De Facto Recognition. ⇨ Recognition.

Defense Department (United States Department of Defense). A major department of the Federal Government established in 1949 to unify the defence forces of the USA as envisaged in the National Security Act of 1947. It incorporated the older Departments of War (which included the Air Force) and the Navy, and contains subordinate Army, Navy and Air Force Departments, each headed by a civilian Secretary who is advised by a military Chief of Staff. The Secretaries and their Chiefs of Staff are members of the ⇨ Armed Forces Policy Council, the Department's 'little Cabinet', and the latter form the ⇨ JCS. The Secretary of Defense, who heads the Department, is a ⇨Cabinet member, appointed by the President with the consent of the ⇨ Senate, and removable by the President at any time. He is also a member of ⇨NSC.

The Department was established to overcome the problems inherent in the division of the defence effort of the USA among the several armed services. Its basic task was to co-ordinate their operations, and establish and maintain an integrated defence capability. In this it has been only partially successful; and in the light of continuing inter-service rivalries, further action has had to be taken to enforce unification, notably the Defense Reorganization Act of 1958. This Act reinforced the authority of the Secretary of Defense over the subordinate Departments and their civilian and military personnel, and provided for greater integration of the services. It did not, however, end the right of the civil and military heads of the services to appeal directly to the President and ▷Congress and to contradict the advice offered by the Department and the Secretary – a practice that President ▷ Eisenhower had called 'legalized insubordination'. But the Act provided a legal basis for the 'revolution' carried through by Defense Secretary Robert S. ▷ Mc-Namara with the backing of Presidents ▷ Kennedy and ▷ Johnson. This was based on new management techniques which demanded closer cooperation among the services.

The principal offices of the Department are located in the ▷ Pentagon which has given its name to the Department and the military establishment generally.

De Gasperi, Alcide (1881–1954). Prime Minister of ▷Italy (1945–53), Foreign Minister (1944–46, 1951–53) and leader of the Christian Democratic Party. He led various coalition governments but his party won an absolute majority in 1948. De Gasperi was a fervent supporter of European integration and in 1949 his country joined ▷NATO. He was a Catholic Deputy in the National Parliament (1921–24), opposed Mussolini, was arrested (1926) and from 1929 to 1943 worked in the Vatican Library, from where he continued to organize the Christian Democrats.

De Gaulle, Charles (1890–1970), General. ▷World War II leader and organizer of French Resistance and liberation forces (1940–44), head of first post-war French government (1944–46), leader of the ▷RPF (*Rassemblement du Peuple Français*) (1947–53), Prime Minister (1958), architect and first President of the ▷ Fifth Republic (1959–69). A professional officer, de Gaulle served with distinction under ▷Pétain in World War I and in the inter-war years developed new ideas about the deployment of armoured forces. As the commander of an armoured division, he led one of the few successful French counter-attacks during the Battle of France (1940) and shortly before the final collapse became Under-Secretary of War in the ▷ Reynaud government. When Pétain took over, he escaped arrest and after reaching London, broadcast his historic appeal '. . . the flame of French resistance must not be extinguished; it shall not be extinguished' (18 June 1940). It not only established the Free French movement but also gave the General his sense of mission. '*C'était à moi d'assumer la France*' – it fell upon me to become France – is how his memoirs describe the experience of being called to represent the soul of France. The France of his vision could not 'be France without greatness'. This certainty of his mission, what Roosevelt called the 'Jeanne d'Arc complex', made de Gaulle a difficult ally. After de Gaulle's triumphal return to Paris (Aug. 1944) his leadership of France could no longer be disputed. However, the France over which he presided was not even invited to the ⇨ Yalta Conference (Feb. 1945) where the post-war fate of Germany was settled.

At this stage de Gaulle was haunted by the twin spectres of a resurgent Germany and of an American dominated Europe. He tried to deal with these threats by drawing closer to Britain, but ⇨ Churchill proved unwilling to sacrifice the 'special relationship' with the US to closer links with France. France also failed to enlist Russian support. Stalin opposed French schemes for the dismemberment of Germany which would have left France in control of the Rhine, Ruhr and Saar industries. While de Gaulle's attempts to establish Paris as the pivot of a new balance-of-power combination miscarried, the increasing reluctance of the Constituent Assembly to grant him the powers he regarded as 'the necessary condition for responsible and dignified government', led to his abrupt resignation (Jan. 1946).

Once relinquished, power could only be regained via the ballot. Hence the Gaullist RPF was founded (1947) with the single objective of returning France to de Gaulle, otherwise the party was to sabotage Parliament and the ⇨ Fourth Republic. The RPF became temporarily (1951) France's strongest party but de Gaulle severed all links with it when some of its members accepted ministerial appointments (1953). De Gaulle returned to power when the army, dissatisfied with the conduct of the Algerian War, rebelled and insisted that de Gaulle take over the government (May 1958).

This time de Gaulle received power on his own terms, and through the constitution of the Fifth Republic secured for himself the authority he demanded. Once in office he unhesitatingly disowned the diehard defenders of French rule in Algeria who had brought him to power, when he realized that the rebels could not be militarily defeated. Undeterred by two abortive army rebellions and numerous attempts on his life, he conceded Algerian independence in the Evian treaties (March 1962). As chief executive, de Gaulle set out to restore French greatness. He offered French leadership of the neutralist powers as an alternative to US-USSR domination. By decolonizing the French empire and granting generous development aid to former French possessions he tried to gain the goodwill of the Third World. He visited South America (1964) and Cambodia (1966). Similarly, his recognition of Communist China, his denunciation of American intervention in Vietnam and of Israeli policies during and after the Six Day War were aimed at winning the support of the Third World. Efforts to transform the revitalized Europe of the sixties into a power bloc truly independent of the Americans led not only to the creation of the nuclear ⇨ Force de Frappe but also to the conclusion of the Franco-German Friendship Treaty (1963), French withdrawal from the military commitments to ⇨NATO (1966–67), and the exclusion of Britain – still regarded as an American bridgehead in Europe – from the Common Market (1963, 1967). To gain room to manoeuvre, de Gaulle also wooed the Communist Bloc. But his vision of a Europe 'from the Atlantic to the Urals', propounded during his state visits to Russia (1966), Poland (1967) and Rumania (1968) failed to impress his hosts.

While France benefited from stable government and economic growth, many Gaullist hopes were unfulfilled. Lack of French support for German reunification soon reduced the friendship treaty to a mere formality. The refusal to admit Britain to the Common Market led to friction among the Six and inhibited further integration. The attempted détente with the East produced no tangible results. America's nuclear umbrella, particularly after the invasion of ⇨ Czechoslovakia (Aug. 1968), acquired a new significance. Although Gaullist parties dominated the Assembly, often commanding absolute majorities, when de Gaulle presented himself for re-election (1965) he failed to gain an absolute majority in the first ballot. Investment in a nuclear deterrent of doubtful credibility deprived the state of funds needed for education, health and other social services. Discontent erupted in the 1968 May riots. Starting as a students' protest they soon involved workers in nation-wide strikes which threatened the survival of the Fifth Republic. General concessions, substantial wage increases and the dissolution of Parliament saved de Gaulle, whose supporters in the subsequent June elections won the biggest majority so far achieved. But confidence in the President and his policies was badly shaken and when he made approval of his complex schemes for popular participation in government through regional institutions and reform of the Senate a question of confidence, the vote went against him. De Gaulle promptly resigned the presidency (April 1969) to be succeeded by Georges ⇨ Pompidou, his former Prime Minister (June 1969).

De Jure Recognition. ⇨ Recognition.

Demirel, Suleyman (1924–). Prime Minister of ⇨ Turkey (1965–71) and leader of the Justice Party since 1964.

Democracy. Derived from the Greek 'people' and 'power', originally referred to the right of the citizens of the Greek city states to participate directly in the act of government. Nowadays, in the West, the term is usually reserved for political systems that accept certain basic assumptions (often written into the constitution) but which may also be the result of custom and tradition – e.g. the British Constitution. These are:

- the government should reflect the people's will and the people's choice – hence the constitutional provision of regular elections, by secret ballot, with representatives of at least two parties standing for election. Citizens, therefore, have the right to combine to achieve common aims – provided these aims do not jeopardize the rights of others.
- the Rule of Law (i.e. no imprisonment or restriction of a citizen's liberty without a fair trial). The protection of ⟱ Civil Liberties including freedom of conscience.
- the ⟱ Separation of Powers – i.e. an independent Judiciary and an Executive separately elected or responsible to an elected Legislature.

Critics of democracy have drawn attention to its apparent contradictions – liberty of the individual v. equality, government by the majority v. minority rights – but its supporters have claimed that despite its deficiencies it remains the best defence against arbitrary government and tyranny.

As democracy is almost universally a term of approbation, most states, including those with one-party governments and those who deny ⟱ Civil Rights to most or some of their citizens, claim to be democratic.

The term People's Democracy is used in the Communist Bloc to describe the political systems of Eastern Europe, where the voter's choice is limited to a single list of candidates selected and approved by the Communist Party. This does not satisfy the conditions listed above, but the leadership of the Communist Party is justified as being 'objectively' correct and as being in the true interests of the people. In Africa the emergence of single-party governments has been claimed to suit local conditions better than multi-party systems (including a permitted opposition) based on European models.

Democratic Centralism. The principle governing the organizational structure of the Soviet Communist Party (CPSU) and other parties modelled on the CPSU. The CPSU Statutes of 1961 define democratic centralism as meaning: (1) that leading organs (officials) of the party from the lowest to the highest are elected; (2) the periodic accounting of party organs to both their party organization and superior party organs;

(3) strict party discipline and the subordination of the minority to the majority; (4) the unconditional application of decisions by higher party organs to lower party organs. This official definition provides no details about electoral procedures. In the CPSU and most other parties committed to democratic centralism, elections offer no choice of alternatives but are an opportunity for the endorsement of a single list of candidates drawn up by leading party officials. Earlier definitions of the same principle laid more stress on the overriding importance of strict centralization. The 21 Conditions of Admission to the ⇨ Communist International, for instance, included a passage declaring that 'the Communist Party will be able to fulfil its duty only if its organization is as centralized as possible, if iron discipline prevails, and if the party centre, upheld by the confidence of the party membership, has strength and authority and is equipped with the most comprehensive powers'. (⇨ Bolshevism and ⇨ USSR.)

Democratic Party. One of the two major political parties of the USA, the other being the ⇨ Republican Party. It traces its origins back to the Republican (or Democratic-Republican) party of Thomas Jefferson (President, 1801–09). The party assumed its present name under the leadership of Andrew Jackson (President, 1829–37). It maintained an ascendancy over a succession of rivals until the Civil War, when the party split over the issue of slavery. Thereafter, the ascendancy passed to the newly-organized Republican Party, beginning with the presidency of Abraham Lincoln (1861–65). From then until the Great Depression, only two Democrats were elected President – Cleveland in 1884 and 1892, and Wilson in 1912 and 1916. The Democrats regained the ascendancy with the election of Franklin D. ⇨ Roosevelt (President, 1933–45) who introduced the ⇨ New Deal to meet the problems of the Depression. Since World War II, the two parties have been equally successful in Presidential elections, the Democrats winning in 1948 (Harry S. ⇨ Truman), 1960 (John F. ⇨ Kennedy) and 1964 (Lyndon B. ⇨ Johnson), and the Republicans in 1952, 1956, 1968 and 1972. However, in elections for ⇨ Congress, the Democrats have been markedly more successful than the Republicans. They have won or held a majority of seats in both the ⇨ Senate and the ⇨ House of Representatives at all but two (1946 and 1952) of the 21 congressional elections since 1932. This has not meant, however, that Democratic Presidents have always been backed, or Republican Presidents always blocked, by majorities in the two Houses of Congress. Party organization, cohesion and discipline in Congress are notoriously weak; and the Democratic Party has always included a body of Southern Democrats, or ⇨ Dixiecrats, who have by no means always seen eye to eye with their party colleagues from other parts of the country. Very often the majority in Congress has consisted of a coalition of such conservative Democrats and Republicans, as apt to oppose a Kennedy, or support an Eisenhower, as the opposite.

The loose structure of the party in Congress reflects the conditions in which the American parties operate. First, because of the ⇨ Separation of Powers, party unity in Congress is not required for maintaining a government, as is the case in the British ⇨ House of Commons. Secondly, because of the great size and diversity of American society and the resulting ⇨ Pluralism and because, further, of the common commitment of both parties and most citizens to the Constitution and the 'American Way of Life', the party lacks a distinctive ideology or programme such as might serve to maintain internal unity and discipline. On the other hand, the institution of a single, popularly elected, national Chief Executive (the President) creates the need for some sort of national popular political organizations, however loosely structured, to conduct nation-wide electoral campaigns. The Democratic Party is, in fact, a national electoral alliance of many diverse local, State and regional interests, existing primarily for the purpose of fighting presidential elections and only secondarily for purposes connected with Congress, whether fighting congressional elections or maintaining congressional alignments. That this is so is indicated by the character of such national party organs as exist.

The ⇨ National Convention is a delegate assembly, representing State and local party organizations, that meets for a few days every four years for the prime purpose of nominating the party's candidate for the presidency. Between Conventions, the national business of the party is conducted by a National Committee, which heads the party's national headquarters. When in full operation, the national organization disposes of very large sums of money, running into millions of dollars, subject to the ineffectual provisions of the ⇨ Hatch Act. But it is not in continuous operation. The National Committee has some continuing authority when the ⇨ White House is occupied by the other party, but scarcely any when the party's own nominee is President. In fact, the party's national organization, inside and outside Congress, is rudimentary, although at State and local levels party organization is often more highly developed and more important, reflecting the true locus of power in the party.

These remarks apply equally to the Republican Party, which operates in the same basic conditions. However, though the parties are markedly similar, they are not identical. The distinctiveness of each party lies in the particular combination of interests it represents. The Democratic Party has the support of the majority of industrial workers, skilled and unskilled, members and non-members of Trade Unions. This means that its main strength lies in the major urban centres, though its support extends to lower-income, limited-education, newly arrived groups in all parts of the country. With the support of immigrants and minority groups the party combines the support of the bulk of American intellectuals and the majority of young voters. And with all this, at least until recently, it has managed to retain the almost undivided support of the conservative South and the Border States. This combination makes it impossible to characterize the Democratic Party as either definitely liberal or definitely conservative. However, since Roosevelt's New Deal it has generally leaned towards new-style liberalism, favouring social welfare, economic regulation, international cooperation, and, not least, ⇨ Civil Rights. The position adopted by successive Democratic presidential candidates on Civil Rights has in recent years alienated Southern voters in presidential elections (though not so much in congressional elections), as was shown by the candidacy of George ⇨ Wallace, former Governor of Alabama, in 1968 and 1972. Despite recent defections, the Democratic Party remains, nationally, the majority party. The combination of interests on which it is based, and the vague but strong convictions that inform and sustain that combination, are in the mainstream of American political life. They can be traced back through successive periods of the party's and the country's history, and are quite discernable in the successful coalition that formed behind Andrew Jackson in the second and third decades of the previous century. The Democrats have not always had the 'winning combination' – far from it – but they have had the advantage for some time, and seem likely to retain it for some time to come except, perhaps, in the race for the Presidency.

Denmark, Kingdom of. *Area* – 16,600 sq. miles. *Population* (1969 est.) – 4,879,187. *Head of State* – Queen Margrethe. *Prime Minister* – J. Otto ⇨ Krag (1971–). *Constitution* – Constitutional monarchy – since 1953 succession rights restricted to the descendants of King Christian x, allowing for female succession (daughters rank after sons). Executive power is vested in the King, acting through a Prime Minister and ministers responsible to Parliament. The 179-member uni-cameral Parliament (*Folketing*) is elected for a period of four years by universal suffrage on a system of proportional representation. It must include two members each from ⇨ Greenland and the self-governing ⇨ Faeroe Islands. On certain topics one-third of the *Folketing* can demand a plebiscite. A public affairs commissioner (*Ombudsman*) is appointed by Parliament to investigate complaints against abuses of authority.

In spite of the economic crisis of the early thirties, rendering one-third of the registered labour force unemployed, Denmark made considerable progress under the Social Democrat-Radical Liberal coalition which ruled the country from 1929 to 1940. Its *Sozialreform* (1933) provided the country with one of the most advanced social services and pioneered the ⇨welfare state. A dispute with Norway over the territorial right to East Greenland was submitted to the Permanent Court of International Justice, which found in Denmark's favour (April 1933). Traditionally neutralist and without a significant armed force, Denmark signed a non-aggression pact with Germany (May 1939), which did not prevent German forces from invading the country a year later (April 1940). Unable to resist militarily, the King and government accepted 'under protest' the German offer to respect Danish political independence and territorial integrity, provided the country's occupation was not opposed. However, though the Danes tried to acquiesce and even joined the Anti-Comintern Pact (Nov. 1941), resistance increased. The Danish government refused to introduce anti-resistance legislation and the Germans, declaring martial law, disarmed the army (the navy to avoid capture scuttled itself) and in effect interned the King and took over the administration. This further provoked the resistance, which succeeded in smuggling Denmark's 7,000 Jews into Sweden (Oct. 1943) and in cutting the important rail link to Norway after D-Day (June 1944). A general strike (organized by the Resistance) first in Copenhagen and then throughout the country (Sept. 1944), led to the disarming of the Danish police and their subsequent internment in concentration camps. After the war, Denmark, unable to conclude an effective defence pact with her Scandinavian neighbours (Jan. 1949), joined ⇨ NATO (April 1949), and subsequently the Council of Europe, the Nordic Council (Dec. 1951) and ⇨ EFTA (Nov. 1959). After ⇨ Iceland had opted for independence under the 1918 agreement (June 1944), Denmark accorded the Faroe Islands complete local autonomy (March 1948), and in the 1953 constitution made Greenland an integral part of the realm. The Danish government also signed an agreement with the German Federal Republic on the rights of the Danish minority in South Slesvig (1955) after having specifically rejected conservative pressure to annex the territory (1947). For long periods Denmark has been ruled by coalitions led by the Social Democrats – continuously in office from 1957 until their defeat in the 1968 elections. They regained their leading position in the September 1971 elections, forming a government under party-chairman J. O. Krag. Although divided on the EEC issue, the Social Democrats pursued under Krag the Common Market policies initiated by the Baunsgaard administration (1968–71) and signed the Brussels treaty of accession (January 1972).

Destalinization. Term which came into use after ⇨ Khrushchev's denunciation of ⇨ Stalin's crimes and ⇨ Personality Cult at the 20th CPSU Congress (Feb. 1956) and which is applied to either the actual or the desired reforms of the Soviet and other communist regimes aiming at the establishment of the rule of law, individual and cultural freedom and economic rationality.

De Valera, Eamon (1882–). President of the Republic of ⇨ Ireland since 1959, he was three times Prime Minister (1932–48, 1951–54 and 1957–59) and a former leader of the movement to achieve Irish independence. He refused to recognize the 1921 treaty with the UK and founded the *Fianna Fail* party – of which he was President (1926–59) – to win complete independence from the UK, achieve union with ⇨ Northern Ireland and revive the Irish language and culture. During his long years in office he succeeded in the first of these aims.

Development Loan Fund. A US agency established under the Mutual Security Act of 1957 to promote economic development in friendly countries on a basis of self-help and mutual cooperation. It can supply investment capital for specific projects, public and private, at low interest and on generally favourable conditions, including repayment in local currencies. It can also guarantee investments by private US citizens in enterprises abroad. The agency, together with other aspects of the ⇨ Mutual Security Program, was incorporated in ⇨ AID in 1961.

Dewey, Thomas Edmund (1902–71). US lawyer and Republican politician, Governor of New York State (1942–44). He established a national reputation for his successful prosecution of racketeers. In 1944, he ran unsuccessfully against Franklin D. ⇨ Roosevelt as the Republican presidential candidate and was again defeated in 1948 by Harry S. ⇨ Truman.

Dewline or **DEW.** US Distant Early Warning system (in case of nuclear attack) – a radar network which extends across Arctic Canada from Alaska to Greenland.

Dialectical Materialism. ⇨ Marxism.

Diaz Ordaz, Gustavo (1911–). President of ⇨ Mexico (1964–70).

Diefenbaker, John (1895–). Prime Minister of ⇨ Canada (1957–63) and leader of the Progressive Conservative Party (1956–67). Although it did not win a clear victory in 1957, it received 75% of the seats in the 1958 election, a remarkable achievement for a party which had not been in power for over 20 years. His government fell in 1963 after a controversy over defence policy. He was Leader of the Opposition (1963–67).

Diem Ngo Dinh. ⇨ Vietnam.

Dimitrov, G. (1882–1949). Bulgarian communist who spent most of his life in the service of the ⇨ Communist International. On a Comintern mission in Berlin at the time of the *Reichstag* fire he was arrested (March 1933) on the charge of having started it together with other communists. His courageous defence at his subsequent trial earned him world-wide fame (although, according to some sources, he knew in advance that he would be acquitted). He was eventually extradited to the USSR, which had given him Soviet citizenship, and became the new General-Secretary of the Comintern until its dissolution in 1943. He returned to Bulgaria after 22 years of exile (Nov. 1943) and, following the 'elections' of Oct. 1946, became the new Premier. In 1947, Dimitrov visited ⇨ Tito in Bled and agreed with him on the outlines of a future ⇨ Balkan Federation, which, as he later explained during a visit to Rumania, was, in addition to the Balkan countries, also planned to include Poland and Czechoslovakia. Sharply attacked by ⇨ *Pravda* in Jan. 1948, Dimitrov and other Bulgarian and Yugoslav communists were summoned to Moscow and forced by ⇨ Stalin to abandon their plans. A personal friend of Tito, Dimitrov took no active part in the ⇨ Cominform campaign against ⇨ Yugoslavia which started almost immediately afterwards. He went back to the USSR towards the end of 1948 and again in 1949 for medical treatment and died there in July 1949.

Direct Primary. ⇨ Primary Election.

Dissent (in Eastern Europe). Overt dissent on a major scale first erupted in Eastern Europe in direct response to ⇨ Khrushchev's 'secret' speech at the 20th CPSU Congress (Feb. 1956). His onslaught on the myth of Stalin's infallibility produced a wide-spread crisis of confidence in which everything hitherto taken for granted began to be questioned. Isolated rebels had emerged even before, outstanding among them Milovan ⇨ Djilas, then still Vice-President of Yugoslavia, who, in a series of articles published in the winter of 1953/54, called for full freedom of thought and free democratic institutions. Djilas' direct influence on other dissenters in Eastern Europe remained negligible, but his views and demands largely anticipated what later emerged as the general pattern of dissent in Eastern Europe. The pattern is comparatively simple and clear-cut. Almost without exception dissenters in Eastern Europe have sought to reform rather than abolish the socialist system prevailing in their countries. They have called for the realization, in terms of practical policies, of the liberal values in Europe's humanist tradition. They have objected to the narrow limits which the Soviet and other communist rulers imposed on the process of de-Stalinization. The rebels have sought to widen these limits and carry de-Stalinization to its logical conclusion. This overall purpose has been expressed in a series of specific demands which, in one form or another, have been raised over and over again. Outstanding among them are: (1) the demand for the full unvarnished truth about the Stalinist past and for convincing explanations of its origins; (2) the demand for full freedom of expression and artistic creation without censorship or other forms of state and party intervention; and (3) the demand for the practical implementation of those individual and national rights and liberties which are theoretically guaranteed by the constitutions of the countries concerned.

The impact of dissent on Eastern Europe has varied from country to country. In the three countries where dissent among writers, artists, students and other intellectuals was most intense and most widespread – in ⇨ Poland and ⇨ Hungary in 1956 and, from 1962 onwards, in ⇨ Czechoslovakia – the ferment among the intelligentsia acted as a catalyst for nation-wide movements for radical reforms in all fields. Nowhere else did the quest for intellectual liberty and full-scale de-Stalinization produce comparable consequences, but manifestations of intellectual dissent were also widespread in East Germany in 1956/57 and, from 1962 onwards to a lesser extent, in Bulgaria.

In the USSR developments have been more complex. During the Khrushchev era brief periods of comparative freedom alternated with periods of renewed attempts at enforcing conformity. A turning point came with the publication (after Khrushchev's personal intervention) (Nov. 1962) of Alexander Solzhenitsyn's *One Day in the Life of Ivan Denisovich*, the first truthful literary work on Stalin's forced labour camps to be legally published in the USSR. The tremendous impact made by this novel was apparently too much for the authorities. Of the many hundreds of memoirs, novels, stories and poems on the same theme which immediately afterwards flooded the Soviet publishing houses hardly any were allowed to appear in print. Deprived of the chances of legal publication, they increasingly sought other outlets – secret publications in the form of typescripts circulating from hand to hand. Underground typescripts of that kind were first known to have appeared in the USSR in 1958. They differed widely from one another in subject matter, genre and style, sharing only their authors' refusal to conform to the standards laid down by officialdom. From the early 1960s onwards there was a steady increase in underground literature of all types and in the number of works by Soviet authors smuggled abroad for publication under pseudonyms – in particular the works of 'Abram Tertz' who, after his arrest (Sept. 1965), was identified as Andrei Siniavsky.

The arrest and subsequent trial – ending in sentences of long terms of hard labour – of Siniavsky and his fellow-writer Yuli Daniel (who had published abroad under the pseudonym of Nikolai Arzhak), led to the first outbreaks of public protests in the USSR and set in motion a chain reaction of persecution resulting from open defiance and vice versa. The travesty of justice committed by the trial of Siniavsky and Daniel (Feb. 1966) was exposed in the 'White Book' compiled by Alexander Ginzburg. The circulation of this White Book and other underground literature led to the arrest and eventual trial and conviction in Jan. 1967 of Ginzburg, Yury Galanskov (editor of the underground literary magazine *Phoenix 1966*) and others. Though designed to frighten off would-be imitators, the arrests and convictions of these young writers only served as a stimulus for further protests. There were (small-scale) public demonstrations, floods of appeals and protest letters to the Soviet authorities from eminent Soviet scientists, writers, artists, students and people in other walks of life, and renewed counter-measures in the form of fresh arrests or (as on many previous occasions) the confinement of particularly awkward dissenters to mental asylums. The Ginzburg-Galanskov trial also led to the composition of an 'Appeal to World Public Opinion' by Pavel Litvinov (grandson of the former Soviet Foreign Minister) and Larissa Bogoraz-Daniel (wife of the imprisoned Yuli Daniel) in which they called on their fellow-citizens to join them in protests against the gross violations of justice committed by the authorities and which they openly distributed to foreign correspondents on the last day of the Ginzburg-Galanskov trial. Following their participation in a demonstration in Moscow's Red Square against the invasion of ⟐ Czechoslovakia (25.8.1968), Pavel Litvinov and Larissa Bogoraz-Daniel were arrested and, after a trial (Oct. 1968), sentenced to terms of banishment and prison. Small-scale but open manifestations of dissent have continued ever since, leading to the emergence of a small, openly defiant civil rights movement. Since 1968, supporters of this movement have published a bi-monthly 'Chronicle of Current Events' – a factual record of Soviet violations of human rights, political persecutions, trials, sentences, protest actions and the fate of individual victims of persecution. As part of the civil rights movement a growing number of Soviet Jews applied for visas to emigrate to Israel, while members of other nationalities and/or religions have openly pleaded for the practical observation of their constitutionally guaranteed rights. The authorities reacted to the multiplication of these and other expressions of dissent with ever-spreading persecutions and political trials aimed especially at the eradication of the production, distribution and possession of *samizdat*, the Russian term for the now ubiquitous phenomenon of typewritten underground literature of every description.

Dixiecrat. Term coined in the 1948 US presidential elections when Southern Democrats opposed to the ⟐ Democratic Party's liberal economic and ▷ Civil Rights policies, formed their own States' Rights Democratic Party in the hope of ensuring the defeat of Truman. However, the party only captured 39 electoral votes and Truman was elected. Thereafter, the name was applied to dissident Southern Democrats generally. In Congress, the Dixiecrats sometimes combine with conservative mid-western Republicans to block liberal legislation, and until recently they were successful in blocking Congressional Civil Rights legislation. The tendency of most Southerners to vote Democratic enabled their Senators and Congressmen to gain seniority, thereby securing important committee posts from which to defeat civil rights legislation. (▷ Seniority Rule, ▷ States' Rights.)

Djilas, Milovan (1911–). Yugoslav revolutionary. Born in Montenegro and a member of the illegal Yugoslav Communist Party from 1932, Djilas became one of its leading writers and theoreticians. A Partisan leader during the war and one of ▷ Tito's closest associates, he later became a Secretary of the Communist Party's Politbureau and Vice-President of the new Federal Republic. He fell out with Tito after the publication (1953) of articles criticizing the ruling bureaucracy and advocating radical democratic reforms. Deprived of his Party and government posts, he was jailed in 1957 after the publication abroad of *The New Class*, followed in 1962 by *Conversations with Stalin*. With brief interruptions, he spent almost eight years in jail. He was released in 1966, and in 1968 was again allowed to travel abroad.

Dobrudja. Claims to this area on the western coast of the Black Sea were for long disputed between ▷ Bulgaria and ▷ Rumania. Though inhabited mainly by non-Rumanians, Dobrudja was acquired by Rumania in 1878 in return for the cession of ▷ Bessarabia to Russia. The acquisition was upheld by the Peace Treaties concluded after World War I, despite pressing Bulgarian claims to the area. In 1940, combined German-Soviet pressure compelled Rumania to cede Southern Dobrudja to Bulgaria. The cession was subsequently upheld by the Paris Peace Treaty of 1947.

Doctors' Plot. ▷ USSR.

Doenitz, Karl (1891–). Grand Admiral and the ▷ Third Reich's last head of Government (2–23 May 1945), appointed by ▷ Hitler in his eve-of-suicide testament; he and his government were later arrested by the Allies. Commander of the German submarine fleet (from 1936) Doenitz's tactics of massed 'wolf-pack' attacks played havoc with Allied shipping. Sentenced to ten years' imprisonment by the Nuremberg Allied Military Tribunal, he was released from Spandau in 1956.

Dollar Diplomacy. Condemnatory term for diplomatic activities of the USA thought to serve the interests of American business and to further the 'economic penetration' of other countries by the United States.

Dollfuss, Engelbert (1892–1934). Chancellor of ⇨ Austria (1932–34) and leader of the Christian Social Party who established a 'corporative' state. He suspended Parliament (March 1933) and introduced a 'corporative' constitution (May 1934). Sometimes called Fascist, his policy aimed at checking the growing strength of the Austrian Nazi party (which he banned in June 1933). Dollfuss hoped, by relying on the support of Mussolini, to preserve Austrian independence, threatened by Nazi Germany. Strongly anti-socialist and under pressure from Mussolini, he suppressed the Social Democrats after a workers' strike in Vienna (Feb. 1934). On 25 July 1934 Dollfuss was assassinated by Austrian Nazis during an unsuccessful coup.

Dominican Republic. *Area* – 18,700 sq. miles. *Population* (1970 est.) – 4,012,000. *President* – Dr Joaquin Balaguer (1966–). *Constitution* (1966) – Unitary Republic with an executive President and a bi-cameral Congress of a Senate and Chamber of Deputies elected by universal suffrage.

The Dominican Republic occupies the eastern part of the island of Hispaniola. The remainder, smaller in area but with a larger population, is occupied by ⇨ Haiti. Relations between the two countries have been almost continuously strained. From 1930 until 1961 the Dominican Republic was ruled by Rafael ⇨ Trujillo. Under his corrupt and despotic regime all opposition was suppressed. In 1960, at a meeting of the ⇨ OAS, Trujillo was denounced by Romulo ⇨ Betancourt for his interference in Venezuelan domestic affairs, and the OAS imposed an oil embargo on the Dominican Republic. He also lost the support of a US government anxious to win Latin American goodwill. Trujillo was assassinated (1961) by officers of his own following. The effects of 30 years of cynicism, brutality and political stagnation and the creation of a privileged repressive, economically burdensome army continued to plague the Republic's development. Dr Joaquin Balaguer, who had been closely involved with the Trujillo regime, headed an interim government until, as a result of mounting opposition and OAS pressure, elections were held (1962) – the first free elections for nearly 40 years. The social reformist leader of the PRD (*Partido Revolucionario Dominicano*), Dr Juan ⇨ Bosch was elected President. Handicapped by his adherence to democratic methods and by the opposition of the extreme left and right, Bosch was ousted by a military coup (1963). At first opposed to the junta, the US was soon reconciled and aid resumed. Colonel Caamano Deno's attempted pro-Bosch insurrection was defeated by US military intervention (1965). To restore their prestige, badly damaged by this intervention, the US Government appealed to the OAS for (retrospective) approval of its action, only just securing the necessary majority. (Six countries – Chile, Ecuador, Mexico, Peru, Uruguay, Venezuela – refused to endorse the American intervention.) But an inter-American force was organized (to join the US Marines) until elections could be held (1966). Through OAS mediation a provisional government was formed. In the subsequent elections (1966) Balaguer (despite his tarnished reputation as an associate of Trujillo) defeated Juan Bosch. Army support remains a crucial factor in Dominican politics, while Bosch's defeat appears to have attracted additional support to the extreme left. Dominican politics have been dominated by a small Spanish-descended white élite (about 15% of the population). Their attitudes shared by other sections of the population have been affected by fears of Haitian French-Negro domination. A history of violence and corruption (in both countries) has contributed to their mutual suspicions (⇨ Haiti and ⇨ Trujillo, 1937 massacre). Relations severed (1963), improved after Bosch's defeat, but have again (since 1967) deteriorated.

Dominion (literally government, sovereignty; the territory of a particular monarch or government). Used to refer to the independent states of the ⇨ Commonwealth, particularly those states whose independence was confirmed by the Statute of ⇨ Westminster (1931) and who have remained in the Commonwealth, i.e. ⇨ Australia, ⇨ Canada, ⇨ New Zealand. Used less frequently since the rapid post-World War II increase in the number of independent Commonwealth states, the term (implying allegiance to the British Crown) is not applicable to those states who remained in the Commonwealth but chose a republican form of government on independence (e.g. ⇨ India, ⇨ Pakistan).

Douglas, William Orville (1898–). US jurist appointed to the ⇨ Supreme Court in 1939. A leading liberal on the Court, he has written significant opinions on the power of the government to protect natural resources and regulate the economy, and has often dissented from the majority to argue for the preservation of individual freedom in questions of government infringement.

Douglas-Home, Sir Alexander Frederick (1903–). Renounced his peerage (1963) to assume the leadership of the UK ⇨ Conservative Party, but the manner in which he was chosen led to the reform of the system of electing the Conservative Party Leader. Some Conservative Cabinet Ministers (⇨ Powell and ⇨ Macleod) resigned on his appointment to the leadership and his party was defeated in the General Election of 1964. Continuing dissatisfaction led to his resignation from the party leadership (22.7.1965) and he was succeeded by ⇨ Heath. From 1965 until 1970 he was Opposition spokesman on Foreign and Colonial

Affairs. Critical of the Government's Rhodesian policy, he visited Ian ⇨ Smith (Feb. 1968) and on his return claimed to have proposals which could solve the crisis. From 1937 to 1939 – which included the period of the ⇨ Munich Agreement – he was Neville Chamberlain's Parliamentary Private Secretary. Re-appointed Foreign Secretary in 1970.

Doves. ⇨ Hawks.

Draft Board. In the USA, civilian boards consisting of three or more local residents who administer the ⇨ Selective Service System in their own areas.

Dubai. ⇨ Trucial States.

Dubček, A. (1921–). Former First Secretary, Czechoslovak Communist Party. Born in Slovakia, Dubček emigrated as a small boy with his parents to the USSR where they remained until 1938. Back in Slovakia, he joined the Communist Party in 1939 and took an active part in the anti-German resistance movement and the Slovak uprising of Aug. 1944. A full-time party official since 1949, he was sent to the USSR in 1955 for further training at the Higher Party School in Moscow where he remained for three years. Rapidly promoted after his return in 1958, he became the First Secretary of the Slovak Communist Party and a member of the Czechoslovak Party Presidium (1963). Though by then one of the top leaders, he kept out of the limelight until the Central Committee meeting of Dec./Jan. 1967/68 which, after prolonged debates, elected him in ⇨ Novotny's place as the party's new First Secretary. Under his leadership, the Party launched a programme of far-reaching democratization and radical reforms, symbolized by his own phrase 'socialism with a human face'. Propelled into the role of a popular hero by both the confidence of his own people and the Soviet and allied attacks on his path of reform, he attempted for a time to save what could be saved of the original reform programme. Unable to stand up to the mounting Soviet pressure against his leadership, he was eventually compelled to resign from his post as First Party Secretary. His resignation was announced in April 1969 when Dr Gustav ⇨ Husak was installed as his successor.

Dubinsky, David (1898–). US labour leader who became President of the International Ladies Garment Workers' Union (1932) which, with John L. ⇨ Lewis' United Mine Workers, formed the nucleus of the ⇨ CIO. Dubinsky became known as a vigorous opponent of racketeering in unions.

Due Process of Law. A legal doctrine in the USA, based on the use of these words in the ⇨ Fifth Amendment to the Constitution, and again in the Fourteenth Amendment, protecting citizens against arbitrary deprivation of life, liberty and property. What constitutes 'due process' has never been fully determined, but it clearly entails all that is implied by 'fair trial'. Since about 1880, the ⇨ Supreme Court has interpreted it as applying to the substance as well as the administration of law; and up to 1937 it was used by the Court as grounds for declaring unconstitutional many important measures of social and economic reform, most notably in the period of the ⇨ New Deal. The Court still construes the expression in this way with reference to legislation in the ⇨ Civil Liberties field, but not any longer in other fields. Basing its action on this interpretation and on the fact that the Fourteenth Amendment applies to the States as well as to the Federal Government, the Court has argued, especially since 1964, that the requirement for due process of law extends almost all the other provisions of the ⇨ Bill of Rights to the States.

Dulles, John Foster (1888–1959). US ⇨ Secretary of State (1953–59). He served with the World Trade Board during World War I and was later appointed counsel to the United States delegation to the reparations commission at Versailles. A leading international lawyer, he advised Governor ⇨ Dewey on foreign policy matters during the latter's unsuccessful campaign for the presidency (1944). In 1945 Dulles was named adviser to the US delegation to the UN conference at San Francisco, and in 1949 was chosen to fill a vacant seat in the Senate, which he subsequently lost in a special election. As adviser to Secretary of State Dean ⇨ Acheson he successfully negotiated the peace treaty with ⇨ Japan and was appointed ⇨ Eisenhower's Secretary of State (1953). A staunch opponent of communism, he was responsible for the policy of brinkmanship, i.e. willingness to go to the verge of war without going over the 'brink'. The term ⇨ 'Massive Retaliation' was coined by the Secretary of State in reference to the nuclear character of the Western defensive response. In the course of his six years in office, Dulles exerted a dominant influence on American foreign policy.

Dumbarton Oaks. Venue, in Washington, ⇨ DC, of the conference between representatives of the USA, USSR, UK and China held in 1944 to discuss the possible organization of UNO. It was agreed that the 'Big Five' (the four participating countries plus France) should be permanent members of a Security Council with primary responsibility for preserving international peace. This initial agreement was further elaborated at the ⇨ Yalta Conference the following year.

Dunkirk, Evacuation of (June 1940). Occurred when the British Expeditionary Force and the French First Army of over 300,000 men – cut off following the surrender of Belgium in the north and the advance of German tank forces in the south – were evacuated from Dunkirk to

Britain. The evacuation, hailed as a triumph, softened the blow of military defeat and raised the morale of war-time Britain.

Dunkirk Treaty, 1947. Treaty of alliance between France and the UK signed at Dunkirk (March 1947); marked the re-emergence of France as a major European power after the war.

Duvalier, Dr François (1907–71). President of ⇨ Haiti (1957–71). He was succeeded by his 19 year old son, Jean-Claude Duvalier.

E

Eagleton, Thomas F. (1929–). US Senator from Missouri, and briefly Democratic Vice-Presidential candidate in 1972. A liberal Catholic, he was Missouri State Attorney General (1960–64) and Lt. Gov. (1964–68) before being elected to the Senate in 1968. In the Senate he served as Chairman of the District of Columbia Committee, and was chosen as Sen. George ⇨McGovern's running-mate at the Democratic Convention in Miami Beach, July 1972, only to resign within a month following revelations of his having had psychiatric treatment.

EAM ⇨ Greece.

Eastern Aden Protectorate. ⇨ South Yemen, People's Republic of.

East Germany. ⇨ Germany, German Democratic Republic.

East of Suez. Refers to the controversy over Britain's planned military withdrawal from the Far East following the decision of the ⇨Wilson Government (1967) that Britain's military contribution must be commensurate to her economic strength. Because of the need for cuts in defence expenditure, this withdrawal is to be accelerated and most British troops had left the Far East by the end of 1971, except for Hong Kong and the five-power arrangement based on Singapore.

Eban, Abba (1915–). Became ⇨Israel's Foreign Minister (1966) after a distinguished ambassadorial and ministerial career.

ECA. United States Economic Cooperation Administration – an agency established in 1948 to administer the ⇨ European Recovery Programme. In 1951, with the extension of the ⇨ Mutual Security Program to cover friendly countries not included in the ⇨Marshall Plan, the functions of ECA were transferred to the Mutual Security Agency.

Economic Report of the President. An annual message of the President of the USA to ⇨Congress giving information and making recommendations regarding national economic affairs, as required by the Employment Act of 1946. The Report is prepared by the Council of Economic Advisers, which is part of the ⇨ Executive Office of the President, and is scrutinized by the Joint Economic Committee, a

⇨ Congressional Committee composed of seven members of each House of Congress.

Economism. A polemical term first used by Lenin and other Russian revolutionaries at the turn of the century to denigrate social democrats who relied on those trade unionist movements which the working classes develop spontaneously in response to their living and working conditions and which tend to exhaust themselves in struggles for immediate economic and social improvements instead of advancing the cause of revolution. The term 'economism' was revived in ⇨ China in 1967 to denounce workers and peasants who had used the Cultural Revolution as an opportunity for seeking to secure better living and working conditions for themselves through strikes and other spontaneous economic actions.

ECSC. European Coal and Steel Community – the oldest and most completely supra-national of the three Common Market Communities came into being as the result of French Foreign Minister ⇨ Schuman's proposal (May 1950) to pool Franco-German coal and steel resources in order to prevent future wars and create a basis for Europe's economic and ultimate political unification. With Belgium, Italy, Luxembourg and The Netherlands joining the scheme, the Paris Treaty (April 1951, ratified July 1952) formally established the ECSC. It specifically aims at stimulating the growth of the coal and steel industries in member countries by rationalizing production and distribution, eliminating tariffs, quotas and restrictive practices and thereby establishing the economic basis for eventual political integration.

Executive power is vested in an independent High Authority which was merged (July 1967) together with the ⇨ EEC and ⇨ EURATOM Commissions into a single Commission. Its members, although they must be nationals of member countries, do not represent national governments or interests. They decide on a simple majority vote. The High Authority was originally responsible to a specially constituted Common Assembly whose functions have been taken over by the ⇨ European Parliament to which it now submits its annual report. If unsatisfactory, the European Parliament can, on a two-thirds majority, censure the Commission, thereby forcing the collective resignation of its members.

Liaison between the Commission and member states is provided by the Council of Ministers (one from each country). Its role is mainly consultative; it can, however, exercise a veto on matters not covered by the Paris Treaty (e.g. investments outside the coal and steel industry, etc.).

A Consultative Committee of no less than 30 and no more than 51

members, representing in equal numbers workers, producers and con-
sumers, is appointed by the Council of Ministers and attached to the
Commission, which is required to consult it on specified social and
economic issues.

A Court of Justice composed of seven judges – now also shared by the
other two Communities – adjudicates between the Commission and individual litigants, firms, the Council of Ministers and member states.

By levying a quarter per cent on the industry's sales, ECSC is financially independent and has been able to make important contributions
to the industry's welfare and research projects. It created a European
Labour Pass bringing about a free labour market within the Community
for 118 categories of skilled miners and steel workers.

Britain is formally associated with the ECSC by the 1954 agreements,
which provide for regular consultations between members of the then
High Authority and British Government, Coal and Steel Board representatives. Major tariff reductions between the two producing areas
were negotiated in 1957.

Ecuador. *Area* (approx.) – 104,500 sq. miles. *Population* (1970 est.) –
5,589,000, of whom about 40% are *Mestizo* and 40% Amerindian.
President – Gen. Rodriguez Lara (1972–). *Constitution* (1945) – Re-
introduced in 1972 after Gen. Lara's coup.

In Ecuador's recent history a succession of military coups (even more
than in any other Latin American country) alternating with periods,
frequently curtailed, of presidential rule, reflects a political pattern in
which political success has rested on personal appeal rather than on
party loyalties or programmes. Slow economic progress, resulting
largely from a little-changed feudal social structure, was not helped by
defeat in a war with Peru (1941), when she was forced to cede a large
part of her eastern territory, thus losing her outlet on the Amazon.
Without benefit of party attachment, José Maria Velasco Ibarra (1893–),
since he first appeared on the political scene nearly 40 years ago, has
been five times elected to the presidency. He was first elected President
in 1934 but overthrown a year later. In 1939, returning from exile, he
was defeated in the elections and, after an unsuccessful attempt to
organize a revolt, exiled to Chile. Elected (*in absentia*) 1944, he held
office till his presidency was ended by a military coup (1947). In 1952,
returning from abroad, he was elected for a third time and served his full
term. Re-elected (1960) he was again deposed by a military coup (1961).
There was further military intervention in 1963 and rule by a junta. But
he was again elected, after exile in Argentina, in June 1968, to start his
new term in Sept. In 1972 the threat of a free general election promised
by President Ibarra in which at least one left-wing presidential candidate

would stand was too much for the army to tolerate. Ibarra was again deposed and the elections were cancelled.

EDC. European Defence Community – abortive French attempt to create an integrated ⇨Common Market defence force, by acquiescence in Germany's rearmament. First suggested by Premier René Pleven (Oct. 1950), the treaties setting up the force, although signed by all member countries (May 1952), were repudiated by the French National Assembly (Aug. 1954).

Eden, Anthony. ⇨Avon, Lord.

EDES. ⇨Greece.

Edward VIII. ⇨Windsor, Duke of and ⇨Abdication Crisis.

EEC. European Economic Community – generally known as the Common Market, was set up under the ⇨Rome Treaties (25.3.1957) by Belgium, France, the German Federal Republic, Italy, The Netherlands and Luxembourg, and became operative on 1 Jan. 1958. During a 12 year transitional period, internal customs and other restrictions on the free movement of capital and labour, goods and services were to be phased out while disparate external tariffs were to be harmonized. Finally, a common market with a single, common external tariff was to 'establish the foundation of an ever closer union among the European peoples'.

The EEC's decision-making power rests with the Council of Ministers (one for each country) merged with ⇨Euratom's and ⇨ECSC's ministerial councils (1.7.1967). It proceeds on a system of weighted votes, which gives France, Germany and Italy four votes each; two votes each to Belgium and the Netherlands and one to Luxembourg. Except for a few contingencies subject to the unanimity rule (e.g. new admissions), any 12 out of the total of 17 votes will carry a resolution. To prevent big power rule, the stipulated 12 votes must in certain specified cases (proposals not tabled by the Commission) represent at least four countries.

The Commission (originally a separate EEC institution, was integrated with ECSC's High Authority and the Euratom Commission into a single Commission (1.7.1967)) is the Community's policy-making body. Its 14 members, appointed with the unanimous approval of all member states by the national governments, but not responsible to them, serve a four-year term. Not more than two Commission members can be the citizens of any one country. The Commission exercises administrative as well as executive functions. By proposing lines of action to the Council of Ministers it initiates policies which if acceptable to the Council it then implements. In formulating its policies, the Commission can modify its proposals up to the moment of vote-taking by the Council, a procedure facilitating consensus by providing opportunities for last-minute compromises; the Council, on the other hand, can only modify Commission proposals on a unanimous vote. The Commission is ultimately responsible to the ⇨European Parliament, to whom it submits annual reports and by whom it can be censured. Parliament must also be consulted before certain decisions are taken, a constitutional privilege it does not enjoy in the ECSC. Certain consultative functions are given to the Economic and Social Committee whose 101 delegates represent trade unions, employers and general interests.

With the adoption of a common external tariff and the removal of the last internal customs barriers on industrial goods (1.7.1968) the EEC came significantly nearer to complete economic integration.

To facilitate coordination EEC has set up a number of specialized consultative agencies, among them: the Monetary Committee with the important task of coordinating national monetary policies; the Short- and Medium-Term Economic Policy Committees set up to harmonize Community and national planning; the European Social Fund established under the Rome Treaties to prevent or alleviate economic dislocations caused by the creation of the Common Market and to assist with redeployment and retraining schemes; the European Investment Bank has independent status and backs investment in the Community's more underdeveloped areas (e.g. Southern Italy) and recently also in associate countries. It assists in modernizing old and in setting up new industries. Capital has been underwritten on a weighted ratio by member countries, who can be called upon for further loans; the European Development Fund administers the Community's development aid to the 18 associate African members. (Associate membership was attained by Greece (1.11.1962), Turkey (28.10.1964), France's Overseas Territories – ⇨ French Community (1.6.1964) and those of the Netherlands (1.10.1964) as well as by the now independent Belgian and French colonies (Yacoundé Convention, July 1963): Burundi, Cameroun, Central African Republic, Chad, Congo (Brazzaville), Congo (Kinshasa), Dahomey, Gabon, Ivory Coast, Madagascar, Mali, Mauritania, Niger, Rwanda, Senegal, Somalia, Togo, Upper Volta.)

Britain's efforts to join the Community (autumn 1961–Jan. 1963; Jan.–Oct. 1967) were frustrated by a French veto which also barred applications from other ⇨EFTA members. This was withdrawn under President ⇨Pompidou. The Brussels Treaty of Accession (Jan. 1972) admitted – subject to ratification by the various parliaments – Denmark, Ireland, Norway and the United Kingdom into the EEC but, as a result of a referendum, Norway did not join.

The Community more than doubled intra-market trading between 1958 and 1964, spectacularly raised exports to the rest of the world, in-

creasing the Community's GNP by 38% and real wages by 30%.
EFTA. European Free Trade Association (Geneva) – was set up under
the Stockholm Convention (July 1959) by Austria, Denmark, Great
Britain, Norway, Portugal, Sweden, Switzerland, with Finland becoming an associate member (June 1961). Conceived both as a counterweight and bridge to the ⇨ Common Market, it came into being after
the British failure (Dec. 1958) to negotiate a free trade area embracing
the whole of Western Europe. It succeeded in abolishing tariffs between
member states by 31 Dec. 1966, 18 months in advance of ⇨ EEC countries. The two organizations differ in their approach to external tariffs
(uniform in the case of EEC and nationally fixed by EFTA members) and
to agricultural products, exempted from tariffs within the EEC but not
within EFTA. While EFTA merely aimed at trade liberalization EEC's
ultimate goal was political integration. Both positions have been modified by the French insistence on an *Europe des patries* and abortive
British attempts at joining the Common Market (June 1961, May 1967)
followed in each instance by similar applications from the other EFTA
members. Organizationally EFTA is controlled by a council on which
each member is represented by one delegate, resolutions are carried by
simple majorities, but new obligations must be accepted unanimously.
The EFTA countries are inhabited by 98 million people whose internal
trade rose from $3,500 m. in 1959 to $7,488 m. in 1966. When Britain,
Denmark, Ireland and Norway applied for EEC membership, Austria,
Finland, Iceland, Portugal, Sweden, and Switzerland began to negotiate
their own bilateral trade agreements with the Common Market. Its
European Commission concluded a trade agreement in 1972 with the
EEC envisaging the creation of an industrial free trade zone between the
two communities.

Egghead. Unflattering description of intellectuals first used during
Adlai ⇨ Stevenson's 1952 campaign for the US presidency. A slighting
reference to Stevenson's alleged highbrowism, it may also have alluded
to his baldness.

Egypt. ⇨ United Arab Republic.

Eichmann, Adolf (1906–62). Head of the Nazi ⇨ ss' 'Jewish Department', responsible for the extermination of Jews in occupied Europe
(⇨ Holocaust). He was abducted from Argentina by the Israeli secret
service (May 1960), put on trial in Jerusalem (May–Oct. 1961), condemned to death and executed after the failure of his appeal.

Eire. ⇨ Ireland, Republic of.

Eisenhower, Dwight David (1890–1969). Thirty-fourth President of
the United States and Supreme Allied Commander in World War II.
He served as senior aide to General Douglas ⇨ MacArthur (1932–39)

and in 1941 was promoted to Brigadier-General. Commander of all American forces in Europe (1942), Supreme Commander of Allied Expeditionary Forces (1943) which launched the D-Day invasion of Europe (1944). On his return to the USA, he was made Chief of Staff (1945), but in 1948 left Washington to become President of Columbia University. Appointed Supreme Commander of ⇨NATO in 1950, he resigned two years later to enter the presidential race for the Republicans. He won a sweeping victory over his Democratic opponent, Adlai ⇨Stevenson, in 1952, and repeated the success in 1956 for his second term. The qualities that made 'Ike' a fine military leader were not always as useful to him as Chief Executive. Being politically inexperienced, he relied heavily on the advice of Sherman ⇨Adams in domestic affairs and John Foster ⇨ Dulles in foreign policy. Only when both advisers were lost to him did the President's leadership become personal in character. In the course of Eisenhower's two terms, domestic advances were made, notably in ⇨ Civil Rights, but an inflexible foreign policy inhibited moves towards rapprochement with the East.

Eisenhower Doctrine. A modified foreign-policy position of the USA towards the Middle East and adjacent areas, enunciated by President Dwight D. ⇨ Eisenhower in 1957, partly in response to the ⇨ Suez Crisis of 1956. The President pledged United States support for countries in the area seeking to maintain their integrity and independence against communist external aggression or internal subversion. With the authority of a Joint ⇨ Resolution of Congress, support could include the despatch of United States forces to the threatened country when requested by its government, as well as military and economic assistance under the ⇨ Mutual Security Program. In 1958, United States forces were sent to ⇨ Lebanon at the request of President Chamoun, and remained there from July to October. Within the framework of the 'doctrine', special commitments were made to Turkey, Iran and Pakistan by an ⇨ Executive Agreement in 1959. These supplemented US commitments through ⇨CENTO.

El Alamein. ⇨World War II.

ELAS. ⇨Greece.

ELDO. European Space Vehicle Launcher Development Organization – was founded in Paris (1964) to build and develop rocket launchers. Member countries are: Belgium, France, West Germany, Great Britain, Italy, Netherlands and Australia which has put the Woomera range at the organization's disposal.

Electoral College. In the USA, the body that formally elects the President and Vice-President. Each State has as many electoral votes as senators and representatives in ⇨ Congress, and the distribution is therefore roughly proportionate to population. The institution was intended to make election to the two highest national offices indirect, the final choice being made after due deliberation within each State. The intention has never been realized, however. The President is popularly elected, and he selects his own 'running-mate' who becomes Vice-President. This is achieved through the convention whereby electoral-college candidates pledge their support for one or other party 'ticket' in advance, and State law usually requires that they vote accordingly if elected. (In some States the names of electoral-college candidates do not even appear on the ballot.) By another convention, all the electoral votes of a State usually go to whatever ticket wins the majority of the popular vote, and this, also, is legally required. Hence, whilst the election of the President is not indirect it is still by States rather than by a single national constituency; and whilst the vote is popular, it is not proportionate. It is therefore possible for a presidential candidate, by losing some of the larger States only by narrow majorities, to receive a majority of the popular vote and yet fail to win a majority of electoral votes; and the latter are decisive. Minority candidates were elected in this way in 1876 and 1888, and the same nearly happened again in 1960 (⇨ Kennedy v. ⇨ Nixon) and 1968 (Nixon v. ⇨ Humphrey). For this reason there are frequent calls for the final abolition of the Electoral College. Should no candidate receive a clear majority of electoral votes and the Electoral College fail to make a choice, the election would be thrown to Congress, the House of Representatives choosing the President, and the Senate the Vice-President. A constitutional amendment to replace the Electoral College by popular election of the President was introduced in Congress in 1970, but action on it was delayed in the Senate after a ⇨ 'Filibuster.'

El Salvador. *Area* – 8,236 sq. miles. *Population* (1969 est.) – 3,390,000. *President* – Col. Arturo Armando Molina (1972–). *Constitution* (1962) – Unitary Republic with a President and uni-cameral Legislative Assembly. The constitution calls for the reconstruction of the Central American Republic. The smallest republic in Latin America, El Salvador has a history of continuous political instability. Vast social inequalities, now magnified by rapid population growth, have contributed to political unrest. In 1931, following the disastrous effects of the Depression on coffee prices, a communist-led insurrection was violently suppressed by General Hernandez Martinez, who ruled as a dictator until he was overthrown in 1944. Since then, attempts at democratic government and social reform were continually frustrated by the small wealthy oligarchy and military intervention, but in 1972 Col. Molina, the Official Party candidate was elected President.

EMA. European Monetary Agreement – ⇨EPU.

Enahoro, Chief Anthony (1923–). A former supporter of Chief ⇨Awolowo, he has had a chequered career in Nigerian politics. From detention (1962) which he broke, extradition from the UK, imprisonment in ⇨Nigeria and free pardon (1966), he became a chief negotiator for and proponent of the policies of the Federation of Nigeria in its conflict with secessionist ⇨Biafra.

Enosis. Movement in ⇨Cyprus for political union with Greece which had its origin in the nineteenth-century anti-Moslem movement against Turkish rule.

EOKA. *Ethniki Organosis Kyprion Agoniston* – the National Organization of Cypriot Fighters, a secret guerrilla organization led by General George ⇨Grivas which represented the extreme wing of the *Enosis* movement. It carried out terrorist activities in ⇨Cyprus between 1955 and 1959 and was disbanded when the island was granted independence.

EPU. European Payments Union – established under ⇨OEEC (July 1950) as a European clearing house to minimize hard currency shortages and trading imbalances between member countries. By channelling all trade through the EPU, member countries accumulated only residual credits or debits in EPU 'units of account'. In this way, credit could be extended to debtor countries enabling them to readjust their economies. When Europe's currencies became fully convertible in 1958, EPU was superseded by EMA, the *European Monetary Agreement* which, operating on the same basic principles, introduced new and tighter credit controls.

Épuration. The more or less legal French purge trials between 1944 and 1946 set up to punish traitors and to disqualify prominent collaborators and active supporters of ⇨Vichy from government and professional activity. Punishments – often unequal for near identical crimes – ranged from death sentences to a few years of 'national unworthiness'.

Equatorial Guinea. *Area* – 10,832 sq. miles. *Population* (1969 est.) – 286,000. *President* – Francisco Macias Nguema (1968–).

Equatorial Guinea (known as Spanish Guinea up to 1963) became the first independent Spanish-speaking state in Africa on 12 Oct. 1968. As a former Spanish province it had elected representatives to the Spanish *Cortes* (from 1960), but following a plebiscite (1963), was granted a degree of autonomy including its own Legislature. Following a plebiscite on the Independence Constitution (Aug. 1968) elections supervised by the UN were held in Sept. The state consists of Rio Muni (on the mainland) and the islands of Fernando Póo.

Erhard, Professor Ludwig (1897–). Chancellor of the German Federal Republic (1963–1966). Director of an economic research institute before the war and a ⇨CDU *Bundestag* member from 1949, Professor Erhard was Bavarian Minister of Industry (1945–1946) and head of the Anglo-American Bizone's Economic Executive Council (1948–1949), before, as Federal Minister of Economic Affairs (1949–1963) he became the architect of the 'German Economic Miracle'. Vice-Chancellor from 1957, he succeeded Dr ⇨Adenauer (Oct. 1963) but his short-lived and not very successful chancellorship was marked by a decline in Franco-German cooperation and economic recession. When the CDU–FDP coalition which provided his parliamentary majority split over proposed tax increases, he resigned (Nov. 1966) to be succeeded by his CDU colleague ⇨ Kiesinger who, by forming a 'Grand Coalition' with the Social Democrats, established a new and strong governmental majority.

Erlander, Tage (1901–). Swedish Prime Minister 1946–1969; joined Parliament as a member of the Socialist Party in 1933, and first held a government appointment as Under-Secretary in the Ministry of Social Affairs (1938/39). The longest-ruling Prime Minister in a democratic country, Erlander is one of the architects of Sweden's comprehensive system of social services.

Escalation. Raising the level or intensity of a conflict, in terms of verbal threats or military action. Derived from strategic studies, the term has been used in connection with the Vietnam conflict, referring to the increase in arms and men and step-up in the bombing of North Vietnam after 1964. (⇨Hawks.)

Eshkol, Levi (1895–1969). Prime Minister of ⇨ Israel (1963–69). Emigrated to ⇨Palestine (1914), served in the Jewish Legion (1918–20) before embarking on a long career of public service in agricultural settlements and Zionist organizations, including the directorship of agricultural settlement in the Palestine office in Berlin for three years during the Nazi period. A former executive member of *Mapai*, the *Histadrut* (National Workers' Federation) and the ⇨ Jewish Agency before becoming Director of the Ministry of State Security (1948–51) in the first Israel government, Minister of Agriculture (1951–52), Minister of Finance (1952–63) (a crucial decade in Israel's economic development) and subsequently Prime Minister (1963–69). His leadership was criticized (May 1967) when failures in public relations were, perhaps wrongly, thought to indicate a lack of determination. On 1 June 1967 he formed a Government of National Unity which included General ⇨Dayan as Minister of Defence. His Government of National Unity remained in office after his death (26.2.1969) and he has been succeeded as Premier by Golda ⇨Meir.

ESRO. European Space Research Organization – founded (1962) to promote joint launching programmes and to provide research facilities for member states. These are Belgium, Denmark, France, Germany, Great Britain, Italy, Netherlands, Spain, Sweden and Switzerland. Organizationally, it consists of the Council (Paris) made up of two delegates from each member state, which is assisted by a number of scientific and financial sub-committees.

Estonia. One of the 15 Federal Soviet republics constituting the USSR. *Capital* – Tallinn. (⇨ Baltic States.)

Ethiopia (formerly often referred to as Abyssinia). *Area* – 400,000 sq. miles. *Population* (approx.) – 23,000,000. *Head of State* – Emperor of Ethiopia ⇨ Haile Selassie I. *Prime Minister* – Aklilu Habtewold (1966–). *Constitution* (1955) – The Emperor is the final executive authority. The Government consists of a Prime Minister appointed by the Emperor and a Council of Ministers subject to his approval. There is a bi-cameral Parliament of an elected Chamber of Deputies and an appointed Senate.

The ancient Kingdom of Ethiopia – its hereditary rulers supposedly descended from King Solomon and the Queen of Sheba (Haile Selassie is titled King of Kings and Lion of Judah) – became the centre of international crisis following border clashes (Dec. 1934) and the subsequent Italian invasion of its territory (Oct. 1935). British and French attempts to 'appease' ⇨ Mussolini (⇨ Hoare–Laval Plan – Nov. 1935) shocked public opinion but failed to achieve a settlement, and the Italian army with the advantage of modern weapons and air power against poorly-equipped tribesmen was soon in control of most of the country. The Emperor Haile Selassie, in exile in Britain after the fall of Addis Ababa (May 1936), appealed for help to the ⇨ League of Nations. The failure of the League's sanctions policy (1935) and the permission granted to member states to recognize the Italian conquest (1938) was itself an important cause of the League's declining prestige. Following the successful British (Abyssinian) campaign in World War II, Haile Selassie was restored to the throne (June 1941) and Ethiopia's independence reestablished. The UN Trust Territory of Eritrea was federated to Ethiopia in 1952 and incorporated into the Kingdom ten years later. Despite sporadic unrest culminating in an attempted coup (Dec. 1960), after which the administration was reformed, Haile Selassie has continued to dominate Ethiopian politics. Border disputes with ⇨ Somalia, erupting into war (Feb. 1964), have led to defence agreements with ⇨ Kenya. Strictly neutral in foreign policy Ethiopia has increasingly co-operated with the newly independent African states; Addis Ababa is the headquarters of the ⇨ OAU.

EURATOM. European Atomic Energy Community – Brussels – was established under the ⇨ Rome Treaties to encourage development of nuclear industries and research within the Common Market. Its executive Commission responsible to the ⇨ European Parliament is entitled to inspect installations and control supplies which it has financed or provided to ensure their exclusive use for agreed peaceful purposes.

European Community. Denotes the functional interdependence of (the legally separate) ⇨ ECSC, ⇨ EEC and ⇨ EURATOM. These Common Market organizations already share the services of the European Parliament, the European Court of Justice and ancillary Community agencies such as the Committee of Governors of the Central Banks, European Investment Bank, European Social Fund, the Agricultural Guidance and Guarantee Fund, and similar commissions they have already set up or planned.

European Parliament. Originally an inter-state assembly for the supervision of the ⇨ ECSC, it assumed its present name and function when the ⇨ Common Market and ⇨ EURATOM were established. Its first 142 members appointed by national Parliaments (36 each by France, Germany, Italy; 14 each by Belgium, and Holland; 6 by Luxembourg) acted and voted as political rather than national groups. The main parties are Christian Democrats, Social Democrats and Liberals. The European Parliament convenes about ten times a year for its session in Strasbourg. Although a consultative body, it can by a two-thirds majority dismiss any executive of an EEC agency. It was greaty enlarged in 1973 when Great Britain, Ireland and Denmark joined the EEC.

European Recovery Programme. The programme for the economic recovery of European countries after World War II implemented by ⇨ OEEC in accordance with the ⇨ Marshall Plan with the aid of funds provided for the purpose by the USA between 1947 and 1951. The European countries that participated in the programme undertook to increase production and establish financial stability at home, cooperate with one another in economic matters, and, with the cooperation of the USA, increase exports to North America so as to overcome the problem of their dollar deficits. On the American side, the ⇨ ECA was established by ⇨ Congress in 1948 to administer 'Marshall Aid' which, by 1951, amounted to more than $13 billion.

The initiation of the European Recovery Programme coincided with the onset of the Cold War, so that in practice, though not in intention, it was confined to the non-communist countries of Europe. It was rejected by the Soviet Union and all the other communist-bloc countries, though ⇨ Czechoslovakia had at first reacted favourably to the idea. However, the Programme may well have contributed to the failure of communism to advance further in Europe by helping to minimize the economic distress of the post-war period in the countries participating in it and laying the basis for the rapid increase in prosperity they experienced after 1951.

Some aspects of the Programme were continued by the USA on a world-wide basis after 1951 in the ⇨ Mutual Security Program.

European Space Vehicle Launcher Development Organization. ⇨ ELDO.

Executive Agreement. In the USA, an instrument whereby the President can bring the United States into binding relations with foreign powers without the affirmative vote of two-thirds of the ⇨ Senate required for making treaties. An executive agreement may, but need not, have the backing of a Joint ⇨ Resolution of Congress. Increasingly, the power of the President to make such agreements is displacing the treaty-making power of Congress in the conduct of United States foreign relations. The ⇨ Bricker Amendment is intended partly to restrict this process.

Executive Office of the President (EXOP). The formal body embracing a number of agencies aiding the President of the USA in the performance of his executive duties, established by the Reorganization Act of 1939. It comprises the ⇨ White House Office, ⇨ Bureau of the Budget, ⇨ NSC, ⇨ NASA, Council of Economic Advisers (which prepares the annual ⇨ Economic Report of the President), Office of Emergency Preparedness, formerly Planning (which replaced the Office of Civil and Defense Mobilization in 1961), and other Offices established from time to time. It has offices in a building adjacent to the ⇨ White House.

Executive War. In the USA, military action initiated by the President as Commander-in-Chief without recourse to a declaration of war by ⇨ Congress. Both the Korean War and the Vietnam War were instances of this, though the latter was backed by the ⇨ Tonkin Gulf Resolution. During 1972 efforts were begun in both houses of Congress to define the war powers of President and Congress more precisely.

Export-Import Bank. A Federal agency in the USA established in 1934 to promote trade between the United States and other countries, originally as a means of combating the world-wide Depression and furthering the ⇨ Good Neighbour Policy, and later as a contribution to post-war recovery in Europe. It makes public loans and guarantees private loans for trade purposes.

F

Fabian Society (UK). Founded in 1884, largely an organization of middle-class intellectuals, advocates a peaceful and gradual transition to a socialist society. Its early members included Bernard Shaw and the Webbs and it has had an important influence on shaping Labour Party policies.

Faeroe Islands. *Area* – 540 sq. miles. *Population* – 32,000. Autonomous Danish overseas territory. (⇨ Denmark.)

Fair Deal. In the USA a twenty-one point programme put forward by President ⇨ Truman in 1949. Envisaged as a continuation of the ⇨ New Deal, it provided for the return to peace-time economy without large price and rent increases, or a rapid decrease of wage incomes and purchasing power. The programme was obstructed by a recalcitrant Republican majority in Congress.

Faisal, King (1905–). King of ⇨ Saudi Arabia since 1964. He was Prime Minister (1958–60, 1962–64) under his brother, King ⇨ Saud, with whom he disagreed over the modernization of the feudal state. Under his leadership, Saudi Arabia has emerged as a champion of conservatism opposed to the 'revolutionary' Arab policies of the ⇨ UAR. During the Arab-Israeli War of 1967 (⇨ Arab-Israeli Conflict), Faisal settled his differences with ⇨ Nasser, and after the war offered both the UAR and Jordan generous financial help to offset their losses.

Falange (Spain). The official political party of ⇨ Franco's corporate state. Fascist in ideology, it emphasizes national tradition, the superiority of the nation over classes and regional loyalties and obedience as the duty of the people, and exalts the leader to a semi-divine position. Founded in 1933 by José Antonio Primo de Rivera, it was the smallest of the right-wing parties until it merged with larger groups in 1937 to become the *Falange Espanola Tradicionalista*, the official and only permitted party in the nationalist state. It formed a National Council, but has never had the same position in the Spanish state as its pre-war counterparts in Italy and Germany. In recent years its importance has declined.

Falkland Islands. British colony in the South Atlantic, and the subject of dispute between the UK and Argentina, which claims sovereignty over them.

FAO. Food and Agricultural Organization – ▷UN.

Farm Bureau. American Farm Bureau Federation – largest of three major farmers' organizations in the USA, with one and a half million members, mainly larger operators from the prosperous areas of the Mid-West and South. The Farm Bureau maintains a strong ▷ Lobby in Washington which advocates reduced government intervention in agriculture and the economy generally, and gives evidence before ▷ Congressional Committees in favour of such policies. It is more conservative than either the ▷ Farmers Union or the ▷ National Grange.

Farmers Union. Farmers Educational and Cooperative Union, USA – smallest of three major farmers' organizations with about 300,000 members mainly from the difficult lands of the Great Plains States. It undertakes to ▷ Lobby for policies that are generally more radical or liberal than those advocated by either the ▷ Farm Bureau or the ▷ National Grange, often in alliance with AFL–CIO.

Farouk (1920–65). King of ▷ Egypt (1936–52). Either ill-advised or ill-equipped for high office, he rapidly squandered the goodwill of his countrymen which greeted his accession to the throne (1937) after the regency (1936–37). Like his father (Fuad), he was involved in a continuous struggle with the ▷*Wafd*. In 1942 he was forced by the British to accept a *Wafd* Premier. Marked by corruption, the prestige of the monarchy continued to decline, reaching its nadir after the 1948 Egyptian defeat by Israel. Following the officers' coup (1952), Farouk was deprived of his throne and exiled.

Fascism. Denotes both the movement which ▷Mussolini led to power in ▷ Italy (1922–45) and the doctrine inspiring it and similar parties abroad. Deliberately vague and pragmatic, Fascism, although influenced by it, did not aspire to the ideological coherence and dialectical rigidity of Marxism, to which it claimed to provide a valid alternative. Fascists regarded the destruction of communism as one of their main objectives but shared the socialists' hostility to the bourgeois establishment. Claiming to be genuine revolutionaries, Fascists scorned parliamentary democracy as pusillanimous, ineffectual and outdated. A decadent democracy was to be replaced by a system of government inspired by the principles of *Order, Obedience, Justice* rather than by *Liberté, Fraternité, Egalité*, the precepts of the French Revolution. Among the many intellectual influences which moulded Fascism, the most powerful were probably Sorel's syndicalism with its belief in the violent overthrow of the bourgeoisie, Hegel's glorification of the state, and Nietzsche's contempt for the ideals and assumptions of Western civilization.

Diverse but interrelated psychological, economic and political factors made these ideas relevant to Italy and other countries in which revolutionary right-wing movements prospered. Prominent among these factors was the 1919 peace, 'the mutilated victory' which, falling short of popular expectations, generated an atmosphere of national resentment, particularly among the returning soldiers whose re-integration into civilian society was in any case difficult. Moreover, the propertied classes as well as many of the ex-servicemen were alarmed by the increasing militancy of the working class which, encouraged by the Russian example, believed in the imminence of the revolution. This upsurge in the ideology of class struggle seemed to mock the war-time and front-line experience of comradeship and of a national solidarity transcending class. Much of the nationalist mystique, the glorification of the country and its past, was rooted in this war-time experience in which common efforts, sacrifices and exaltation seemed to have overcome the individual's sense of isolation within a society based on competitiveness and technological efficiency. Hence the Fascist rejection – more theoretical tha.1 real – of the industrial urban, free-enterprise, bourgeois society, and Fascism's somewhat paternalistic care for the proletariat as the neglected and estranged member of the national community.

Initially Fascism showed strong socialistic influences. Mussolini himself and some of his leading followers had been radical socialists until the party's neutralism in World War I offended their patriotism and resulted either in their expulsion or withdrawal from the party. The word Fascism itself reveals something of the movement's split personality. It is readily associated with the *fasces*, the bundle of rods with the projecting axe, symbolizing Roman state authority, and it also recalls the rebellion of the Sicilian peasant and workers' *fasci* at the turn of the century. Other factions (*fasci*) opposed the neutralism of the orthodox Italian socialists and syndicalists on the outbreak of World War I. Mussolini, after war-time service as a corporal, founded his Fascist movement in 1919 and, under the slogan 'Revolution and Fatherland', promised to gain for discontented ex-servicemen at home and for Italy abroad a status commensurate with their war-time sacrifices. His movement, which opposed both the liberal establishment and its Marxist opponents, was powerfully reinforced when it was joined by the National Syndicalists under Rossoni, who as Mussolini's Minister of Labour was to become the architect of the Corporate State. Mussolini's other supporters ranged from nationalists disillusioned with the meagre rewards of the Versailles peace treaty to politically-minded futurists eager to 'renew' Italy. When after their Naples party rally, coinciding with a government crisis and much social unrest, 40,000 Fascists marched on Rome, the intimidated King asked Mussolini to form a government (28.10.1922). Once in power, if only as the head of a minority government, Mussolini, by tampering with the electoral laws, by unleashing terror and by the murder of the Socialist leader Matteoti (June 1924), assured his ascendancy. He achieved absolute power no longer derived from or responsible to Parliament early in 1926, and as the *Duce* – the leader – promptly banned all other parties. A year later Rossoni's Charter of Labour established the Corporate State. Based on corporations, guild-like associations of employers and workers, it aimed under state direction at restoring industrial harmony without interfering with existing property relations. Strikes and lockouts became illegal and special labour courts were set up to investigate grievances and settle disputes. A *dopolavoro* organization was created to promote leisure-time activities and provide holiday facilities. The presidents and senior officials of the 22 corporations were appointed by the State, which was thus enabled to control and direct the national economy. In the last days of Fascism when the deposed *Duce* established his Social Republic in northern Italy under German tutelage, Mussolini reverted to his early socialism. He promised nationalization and workers' control. By then, however, Fascism had lost its credibility and following.

The State – according to Fascist dogma the ultimate goal and fulfilment of man's social existence – was entitled, indeed obliged to control and direct the lives of its subjects. Claiming total domination – hence totalitarianism – it took charge of the citizen from an early age. It enrolled the child in the *Balilla*, the adolescent in the *Avanguardia* and the adult in the party of the para-military *Milizia Volontare Sicurezza Nazionale*. Professional advancement in any occupation depended on party membership and loyalty. While all information media were censored and strictly controlled, a ubiquitous secret police, the OVRA tracked down dissenters. Mussolini's success in fusing heterogeneous political and social groups into a movement which achieved power and an apparent national renewal, gave rise to the emergence of Fascist parties in almost every European country. While some Fascist movements like the Austrian *Heimwehr*, the Croat *Ustasha*, Rumania's Iron Guard and Spain's *Falange* attained power at some time or another, others like Sir Oswald Mosley's ⇨ British Union of Fascists, notwithstanding their failure to enlist significant popular support, contributed by their militancy and calculated violence to the brutalization of politics in the thirties. However, of all the totalitarian right-wing movements which gained power after the advent of Fascism, German National

Socialism was by far the most important. Whether it represented a genuine Fascist movement remains open to argument. Although it shared the Fascist glorification of state and nation, it derived its deepest impulses, its sense of mission and its political activism from racial concepts which originally had no place in Fascist thought. Italian Fascism was free from antisemitism until Mussolini, already under Hitler's influence, introduced anti-Jewish legislation (1938). In the twenties and early thirties, politicians and intellectuals of considerable repute as well as, of course, reactionaries and opportunists, considered Fascism as a genuine third way between communist upheaval and democratic indecisiveness.

The communists and the radical Left regarded Fascism as nothing but a last-ditch defence of the doomed capitalist system, a cunning device to terrorize the working class and to keep it in a suitable state of subjugation. The communist refusal to recognize Fascism as a phenomenon *sui generis* with ideological and political objectives of its own, and the communist habit of branding opponents indiscriminately as 'Fascists' led to theoretical misinterpretations and practical blunders, which in the case of Germany facilitated the Nazi accession to power. For from the twenties to the mid-thirties Social Democrats and Labour parties figured in communist terminology as 'Social Fascists', and since these were considered a graver threat to the working class than 'open' Fascists, the communists refused to cooperate with the Social Democrats and the non-communist Left in their efforts to save democratic regimes from the rising tide of Fascism. Communist tactics changed only in 1935 when they participated in the establishment of the ⇨Popular Front.

Regimes with tendencies similar to those of Europe's inter-war Fascist states and movements have come to power in other parts of the world. However, even where Fascist influences are noticeable, the political context and economic and cultural background differ profoundly from those in inter-war Europe, and the use of the term probably obscures more than it explains. Thus ⇨Brazil under ⇨Vargas or ⇨Perón's ⇨Argentina, as well as contemporary Latin American dictatorships are probably better understood in terms of South American history and politics than by the attempt to superimpose European formulations.

After World War II traditional but inconsequential Fascist movements re-emerged in most European countries.

Fatah, Al. Movement for the Liberation of Palestine – the largest of several Arab guerrilla organizations engaged in activities against Israel. The letters of the name *Fatah* are the reverse of the abbreviation of its full Arab name, also meaning 'conquest' – an allusion to the Koranic verse, 'Assistance from God and imminent conquest'. The organization was founded by a group of Palestinian Arabs in West Germany in 1956. It was not until the mid-sixties, however, that *Fatah* began subversive activities inside Israel. Up until the Six Day War (⇨ Arab–Israeli Conflict), the organization's activities were opposed by all the Arab states, except Syria, who had supplied *Fatah* with weapons, training facilities and financial assistance in its early stages. Subversive action against Israel was condemned at Arab summit meetings and at the Arab Unified Command, and *Fatah* groups were arrested in the Lebanon and in Jordan. Until June 1967, *Fatah* was seen as a marginal group, operating as an auxiliary of the Syrian Intelligence and a political nuisance to the Arab States. Since the Six Day War, although *Fatah*'s operational successes have fallen short of its claims, it has grown into an independent factor in the Arab world. *Fatah*'s declared aim, while advocating a 'Palestinian revolution', is to change the whole structure of Arab society. Its ideology, with its emphasis on violence, has been influenced by Mao Tse-tung's theory of the successive stages of guerrilla warfare.

Faubus, Orval Eugene (1910–). The Arkansas, USA, Governor who used ⇨ National Guard troops to prevent the integration of a ⇨ Little Rock high school in 1957.

FBI. United States Federal Bureau of Investigation – an agency established within the Justice Department in 1909 with responsibility for investigating violations of Federal laws not specifically the concern of other Federal agencies. It became famous in the 1930s for its operations against the notorious gangsters, racketeers and kidnappers of the time, its agents being known as 'G-men'. Since World War II it has operated mainly in the area of internal security, though its function is to investigate, not to take action. In both periods the leading spirit of the FBI was its Director, J. Edgar ⇨ Hoover. It was criticized for its inadequate protection of the President by the ⇨ Warren Commission which investigated the assassination of John F. Kennedy in 1963, but Hoover rejected the criticisms.

FCC. United States Federal Communications Commission – an ⇨ Independent Regulatory Commission established in 1935 to regulate telecommunications within the United States in accordance with the ⇨ Commerce Clause. Its seven members are appointed for seven-year terms by the President with the consent of the Senate. The activities of the FCC in relation to radio and television have occasioned much controversy in recent years. Its sole power to grant broadcasting licences (renewable after three years) is said to encourage prior censorship, though this is specifically excluded by the Act creating it. On the other hand, it is sometimes accused of insufficient regulation and of condoning a variety of evils ranging from excessive sex and violence to 'payola' (bribes for promoting pop records) and rigged quizzes. Criticism has also arisen from the requirement imposed on the FCC to ensure 'equal time' for candidates of all parties at elections. This requirement was suspended by Congress in 1960 to permit the Kennedy-Nixon television debates.

FDA. United States Food and Drug Administration – a Federal agency within the Department of Health, Education and Welfare (HEW), which, together with the ⇨ FTC, administers the strict United States laws governing the sale and advertising of food, drugs, devices and cosmetics in inter-state and foreign commerce. The FDA was instrumental in preventing extensive distribution of the drug *thalidomide* in the USA. In 1969 the Agency instituted a ban on the use of cyclamates as from Aug. 1970. Since 1971, proposals have been canvassed in Congress for transferring the Agency's powers to a Consumer Protection Agency (CPA) and a Consumer Safety Agency (CSA) as part of a growing concern for consumer interests.

Federal Reserve System. The national banking system of the USA established by Congress in 1913. The system performs the functions of a central bank, including the regulation of credit and money supply and fixing the bank rate; but it is not centralized, and it is not fully controlled by the government. There is a Federal Reserve Bank in each of 12 districts to which all national banks in the district must, and approved State Banks may, belong. General policy for the whole system is made by a Board of Governors, the seven members of which are appointed for 14-year terms by the President with the consent of the Senate. Its independence sometimes makes it difficult for the President to pursue consistent economic policies, but this reflects the determination of the ⇨ Congress that established it to maintain the 'power of the purse' as a weapon against a too-powerful Executive.

Fédération de la Gauche Démocratique et Socialiste. Federation of the Democratic and Socialist Left – embracing the French Socialist Party (SFIO), the Radicals and the *Convention des Institutions Républicaines*, was established under ⇨ Mitterand (Sept. 1965) as an alternative to the ruling de Gaullist parties. It successfully contested the 1965 presidential election, obtaining 10·5 million votes (45% of the poll) and the General Election of April 1967 securing 121 seats. The Federation's detailed programme demands *inter alia* constitutional reforms at home, restriction of the President's powers and of presidential recourse to plebiscites; on the international level it calls for French adherence to the Test-Ban Treaty, the scrapping of the ⇨ *Force de Frappe*, ⇨ France's support for the UN's peace-keeping forces, her return to NATO and her cooperation in building a united '*Europe des peuples*'. An electoral alliance with the Communist Party (20.12.1966) stipulated that the left-wing candidate who polled most votes in the first ballot was to be jointly supported by both parties in the second ballot. A similar arrangement was concluded with ⇨ Mendès-France's PSU (Jan. 1967). A desire for closer inter-party cooperation led to a statement in which the *Fédération* and the Communist Party jointly defined the areas of agreement and disagreement between them (Feb. 1968). Although immediately de-nounced as a bid for totalitarian dictatorship, the declaration did not produce any extension of the already existing electoral arrangements in the June 1968 general elections. The PSU, however, under the extreme left-wing leadership of M. Michel Rocard, had severed its electoral alliance with the *Fédération*, which retained only 57 seats in the July 1968 Assembly.

Federation of Arab Emirates of the South. ⇨ South Yemen, People's Republic of.

Fifth Amendment of the US Constitution is one of the ten amend-ments making up the ⇨ Bill of Rights. It provides for indictment by grand jury, protection against double jeopardy and self-incrimination, and forbids the denial of life, liberty and property without due process of law. Its self-incrimination clause may be invoked not only in criminal proceedings but also in ⇨ Congressional Investigations. This allows a person to refrain from answering questions which might lead to his self-incrimination. Many witnesses before congressional committees on racketeering, internal subversion and un-American activities have there-fore 'pleaded the Fifth Amendment'. Although no legal action can be taken against them, loss of reputation and employment has often resulted, despite the original intention that no unfavourable inferences should be drawn from a refusal to testify.

Fifth Amendment Communism. In the USA, derogatory reference to the position of one who takes advantage of the ⇨ Fifth Amend-ment protection against self-incrimination in refusing to disclose his political affiliations to such a body as ⇨ HUAC. The imputation was typical of ⇨ McCarthyism and the doctrine of ⇨ Guilt by Association.

Fifth Republic. ⇨ France.

Figl, Leopold (1902–65). Chancellor of ⇨ Austria (1945–53) and co-founder of the Austrian People's Party, of which he was leader until 1951. He was later Foreign Minister (1953–59) when he negotiated the ⇨ Austrian State Treaty (1955). Before the war he was a leader of the Christian Social Party and supported the policy of ⇨ Schuschnigg to resist annexation by Nazi Germany; during the war he was imprisoned in concentration camps.

Fiji. *Area* – 7,055 sq. miles (more than 800 islands). *Population* (1966) – 524,598 of which 266,189 are Indians and 225,102 are Fijians. *Gov.-Gen.* – Sir Robert Stanley Foster. *Prime Minister* – Sir Kamisese Mara. A British colony from 1874 to 1970, when it became an independent state within the ⇨Commonwealth. The Constitution provides for a governor-general appointed by the Queen, an elected House of Representatives whose make-up guarantees representation of all races, and a Senate.

Filibuster. Device practised in the United States ⇨ Senate which permits a minority of Senators to block a Bill by 'talking it to death'. Custom and Senate rules allow unlimited debate on a motion before it can be brought to a vote; a filibuster is an abuse of this privilege by a group intending to talk until the pressure of other business forces the majority to make concessions or withdraw the Bill entirely. Closure, when two-thirds of the Senators voting support a petition limiting each Senator to a one-hour speech, enables a majority of Senators to break the filibuster. This technique was used for the first time in connexion with Civil Rights Legislation in 1964.

Finland, Republic. *Area* – 130,000 sq. miles. *Population* (1970) – 4.7 m. *Head of State* – President Urho Kekkonen. *Prime Minister* – Rafael Paasio (1972–). *Constitution* – Finland is a uni-cameral parliamentary democracy. Executive power is vested in the President elected by universal suffrage through an electoral college for a six-year term. He generally acts through his ministers but retains considerable independent powers over the appointment of senior officials, the dissolution of Parliament, etc. The President can initiate legislation, and bills passed by Parliament require his approval before they become law. The 200 member Parliament (*Eduskunta*), the source of all legislative power, is elected for a period of four years by direct, universal suffrage on a system of proportional representation. Parliament appoints an Ombudsman to investigate and prevent abuses of power.

Finland, in mediaeval times a Swedish and since the 18th century a Russian dependency, attained statehood after the 1917 Russian revolution. Frontiers, however, were not agreed until the Dorpat Peace Treaty (1920) ended the fighting between the two countries. Even so, relations with the USSR continued to overshadow Finnish domestic and foreign policies. In the twenties the activities of the Finnish Communist Party were regarded by the majority as a threat to national independence and led to repressive legislation. In foreign affairs, Finland, having signed a non-aggression pact with Russia (1932) aimed (like the other Scandinavian states) at maintaining her neutrality. This proved impossible when the ⇨ Hitler-Stalin Pact (Aug. 1939) assigned Finland to the Soviet sphere of influence. After the outbreak of World War II Russia requested the cession of strategically important territories (Oct.) and when, unlike the Baltic territories, Finland refused, the USSR repudiated the non-aggression pact and bombed Helsinki (Nov. 1939). Under Field Marshal Mannerheim, the Finns stubbornly defended themselves, but although they inflicted heavy losses on the Russian invaders, they eventually had to yield to the vastly superior force. The peace treaty (Moscow, March 1940) compelled them to cede the Karelian Isthmus, the western shores of Lake Ladoga, the Hangö naval base, altogether about a tenth of their territory. When Finland joined the Germans after their attack on the USSR (June 1941), Britain declared war on her (Dec. 1941). When after their initial successes, Russian counter-offensives (1943/44) forced the Finns to sue for an armistice (Sept. 1944), they had to accept the 1940 frontiers, and additionally to cede the Petsamo region as well as to lease the Porkkala base for a period of 50 years. An indemnity of $300 million payable within six years was also imposed.

By the closing stages of the war, the pro-Russian Communist Party had gained considerable influence and power. With 51 seats in the Parliament they held several government posts including the key Ministry for the Interior, but attempts at attaining power failed, after the Minister for the Interior was forced to resign on a vote of no-confidence (May 1948). The Party lost 13 seats in the general election (July 1948) and remained outside the government for almost two decades. Meanwhile Field Marshal Mannerheim, elected President in 1944, proved too ambiguous a figure for post-war Finland. He resigned (1946) to make way for Prime Minister Paasikivi, who had negotiated the armistice. The new President reorientated Finnish policy towards Russia, making good relations with her the cornerstone of his approach, which subsequent governments continued to regard as an essential condition for the maintenance of an internally free democratic government. He concluded a friendship treaty in 1948, which was extended in 1955 when Russia handed back the Porkkala base. Beset by economic crises, Finland frequently changed governments, often coalitions between the Social Democrats and the centre parties, since 1956 under the presidency of Kekkonen. In the 1966 general election the communist and left-wing socialists became the second largest party and supported a social democratic government in which they held some minor appointments (Ministry of Transport). In 1955 Finland became a member of the UN and the ⇨ Nordic Council and she became an associate member of ⇨ EFTA in 1961. At the January 1972 elections the main parties had gained the following number of seats in the Diet: Social Democrats 55, People's Democratic League (including Communists) 37, Centre Party 35, National Coalition Party (Conservatives) 34.

Finnish-Russian War. ⇨ Finland.

Fireside Chats. In the USA, familiar reference to broadcasts made by President Franklin D. ⇨ Roosevelt to put over his policies to the people when faced with opposition from powerful institutions and interests.

First Amendment. Added to the Constitution of the USA in 1791 as part of the ⇨ Bill of Rights. It establishes a strict separation of Church and State, and guarantees freedom of religion, speech, the Press, peaceful assembly and petition. Though originally binding only on the Federal Government, the application of most of its provisions has been extended to the States by ⇨ Supreme Court decisions based on the ⇨ Due Process of Law requirement. In other respects, the Court has vacillated between a liberal and a restricted construction of the First Amendment; and this has been particularly so with regard to freedom of speech as governed by the ⇨ 'Clear and Present Danger' doctrine.

Five Principles of Peaceful Co-existence. ⇨ Bandung Conference.

Flemings. ⇨ Belgium.

FLN. *Front de Libération Nationale* – was set up in Cairo (Nov. 1954) under the leadership of ⇨ Ben Bella to wrest independence for ⇨ Algeria from the French. The FLN opened its guerrilla campaign early in 1955 and waged war until ⇨ France conceded independence under the Evian Agreements (March 1962). Its armed forces, the ALN (*Armée de Libération Nationale*) were recruited both from secret supporters in Algeria itself and from Algerian refugees in Morocco and Tunis. When Ben Bella was arrested by the French (Oct. 1956), the FLN appointed a provisional government under F. ⇨ Abbas, Ben Khidder and Krim Belkassem. After the attainment of independence, the FLN became under the Algerian constitution (Sept. 1963) the only recognized legal party in the single party state. Ben Bella, who emerged victorious after a prolonged struggle for the leadership, was in turn deposed by Col. ⇨ Boumedienne (June 1964). A socialist party, the FLN instituted widespread nationalization and has supported plans for a united ⇨ Maghreb with Morocco and Tunisia as well as plans for Arab and Afro-Asian unity.

FLOSY. ⇨ South Yemen, People's Republic of.

FOA. United States Foreign Operations Administration – an agency established in 1953 to co-ordinate all foreign aid programmes and administer non-military aspects of the ⇨ Mutual Security Program, including the ⇨ Point Four Program previously administered by the Technical Cooperation Administration (TCA). It was replaced in 1955 by ⇨ ICA.

Foot, Hugh. ⇨ Caradon, Lord.

Foot, Michael (1913–). U K Labour politician and leader of the left wing in the Labour Party. Since 1960 he has held the seat of Ebbw Vale at one time the seat of Aneurin ⇨ Bevan of whom he was an ardent follower. Managing Director of the socialist weekly newspaper *Tribune* of which he was formerly editor.

Force de Frappe (also referred to as *force de dissuasion*). ⇨ France's nuclear strike force, developed after the successful explosion of a French atom bomb (Sahara, 13.2.1960), consisting of 62 *Mirage IV* bombers capable of delivering an 80–90 kiloton bomb each. By the late 1970s, 30 hardened sites in Southern France will house solid-fuel ballistic missiles of 2,000–2,500 miles range. A task force of three missile-carrying atomic submarines is also being built; the 9,000-ton *Redoutable* was launched at Cherbourg (29.3.1967), the *Terrible* is now on the stocks on which, immediately after her launching, the third vessel will be laid down.

Marginal by super-power standards (less than one per cent of the American capability) the *force de frappe* is conceived as a French nuclear trigger, bound when pulled in defence of France's inalienable interests, to engage potentially indifferent allies (America, ⇨ NATO).

Forced Labour Camps. Penal colonies in the USSR which, during the ⇨ Stalin era, developed into vast establishments of slave labour, nearly all of them situated in the Arctic Region and the Far East of the USSR. Among the largest and most dreaded of some 125 camps and clusters of camps identified in 1948 were Vorkuta, Kolyma and Karaganda. (⇨ USSR, ⇨ USSR State Security Service, ⇨ Yezhovsh-china.) With the spread of various forms of ⇨ dissent in the USSR, the detention of dissenters in forced labour camps (and/or mental institutions) has, from the mid-1960s, again become a widespread Soviet practice.

Formosa. ⇨ China, Republic of.

Formosa Resolution. In the USA, a 1955 Joint ⇨ Resolution of Congress authorizing the President (then Dwight D. Eisenhower) to take necessary action when required to defend the Chinese Nationalist island of Taiwan against attack from communist mainland China. An attempt at repeal in 1971, following the exclusion of the Nationalist Chinese delegation from UNO, did not succeed, but the Administration went on record as regarding the Resolution as not still operative.

Forrestal, James Vincent (1892–1949). American Secretary of Defense (1947–49). He was President of a New York banking firm before accepting an appointment to the newly created post of Under-Secretary of the Navy (1940). In 1944 Forrestal became Secretary, and devoted his efforts to increasing the nation's naval strength. Although his relations with President ⇨ Truman were not always smooth, he accepted the office of Secretary of Defense (1947), becoming the first to head the newly created ⇨ Defense Department. He worked at reorganizing and co-ordinating the Department, but was unsuccessful in winning the budget appropriations he believed necessary. He resigned in March 1949.

Four Freedoms. Formulated by US President Franklin D. ⇨ Roosevelt in his State of the Union Message of 6 Jan. 1941. They are: freedom of speech, freedom of worship, freedom from want, and freedom from fear.

Fourteenth Amendment of the US Constitution forbids States to deprive any person of life, liberty or property without ⇨ 'Due Process of Law' and extends to all citizens the 'equal protection of the laws'. In recent years the Federal courts' interpretation of this clause has undermined the practice of racial ⇨ Segregation and initiated the ⇨ Reapportionment of electoral districts by State Legislatures in a more uniform and equitable manner. While the due process clause has been used successfully by 'guilty' persons in appeals against their conviction on technical grounds, it has also been instrumental in guarding individual privacy.

Fourth International. A revolutionary international body founded by ⇨ Trotsky as a would-be alternative to both the ⇨ Second (Labour and Socialist) International and the (Third) ⇨ Communist International. The Fourth International never succeeded in gaining any influence.

Fourth Republic. The constitution under which ⇨ France was governed from 1946 to 1958. Although it differed somewhat from the provisions of the ⇨ Third Republic, particularly in the administration of the former colonial and now semi-independent territories of the ⇨ French Union, the Fourth Republic, like its predecessor, was marked by a succession of weak governments.

France. *Area* – 212,895 sq. miles. *Population* (1970 estimate) – 50,770,000. *President* – Georges ⇨ Pompidou (1969–). *Prime Minister* – Pierre Messmer (1972–). *Constitution* – The Fifth Republic, like its predecessors is a bi-cameral parliamentary democracy, but with considerable executive power vested in the President. Elected by popular vote (constitutional amendment 28.10.1962) to a seven-year term of office, the President appoints the Prime Minister and presides over the Council of Ministers. He can dissolve Parliament – but only once a year – and submit issues of national concern directly to a plebiscite. Though basically it remains responsible to Parliament, government has been strengthened and can rule by decree for a limited period. The National Assembly's power to defeat governments (one of the main factors of political instability in the Third and Fourth Republics – 20 governments between 1929–36, 25 between 1944–58) has been curtailed by a number of devices – e.g. shorter sessions – Parliament is not allowed to sit for more than roughly five months in a year; strict procedural rules, limiting the National Assembly's powers of control and investigation and a new system of voting on censure motions, which deems any vote not actively cast against the government, including abstentions and absences, as one cast in its favour. Deputies to the National Assembly are elected by universal suffrage for a five-year term of office, while members of the Senate, elected by an electoral college based on regional interests, serve nine years. The Senate is conceived as a *chambre de réflexion* with limited power to initiate or delay legislation.

France's inability to counter the threat of Nazi Germany resulted in her decline from military and diplomatic pre-eminence at the beginning of the thirties to total defeat in 1940. Protracted government crises culminating in riots by the semi-Fascist ⇨ *Croix de Feu* and ⇨ *Action Française* (Feb. 1934) prevented an early containment of Germany but led to the formation of a conservative government of 'National Unity'. Barthou, its Foreign Minister, strove to extend the French system of alliances to cover east and south-east Europe. Russia was persuaded to join the ⇨ League of Nations (Sept. 1934) and to conclude a mutual assistance pact with France (May 1935). After the murder of Barthou – assassinated with King Alexander of Yugoslavia by Croat irredentists (Marseilles, Oct. 1934) – ⇨ Laval endeavoured to improve Franco-Italian relations by major colonial concessions at the expense of Abyssinia (Rome agreements, Jan. 1935). When ⇨ Hitler, in breach of the Versailles treaty, introduced conscription (March 1935) Britain, France and Italy were still sufficiently united to protest vigorously (Stresa, April 1935).

Italy's invasion of Abyssinia (Oct. 1935) ended this tripartite unity. France supported the, albeit ineffectual, League of Nations sanctions while Italy now turned to Nazi Germany in her efforts to defeat them. How decisively Italy's switch of allegiances affected existing power relations became evident when Hitler, in contravention of the Locarno Treaty (Oct. 1925), remilitarized the Rhineland (March 1936). When France proved too weak to protect her own vital rights, the era of the Versailles security system under French hegemony came to an end.

The ⇨ Popular Front, after an overwhelming electoral victory (May 1936), was unable to re-establish French prestige. The Socialist Premier ⇨ Blum introduced a programme of social reforms (40-hour week, holidays with pay, nationalization of the Bank of France, partial liberation of colonies) against a background of devaluation, deflation and an unprecedented wave of sit-in strikes. Political dissensions ('rather Hitler than Blum') were intensified by the outbreak of the Spanish Civil War (July 1936) and the Popular Front disintegrated under the impact of Axis triumphs (annexation of ⇨Austria, March 1938), government re-shuffles, economic decline and the Senate's refusal to confirm the second Blum government (April 1938). ⇨ Daladier, the succeeding Prime Minister (April 1938–March 1940) lost Socialist support when in ⇨ Munich he sacrificed French treaty obligations and Czech in-dependence to the cause of ⇨Appeasement. After the Nazi occupation of Prague (March 1939), Franco-British policies were reversed but the guarantees extended to Poland, Rumania, Greece and Turkey failed to save the peace. When Hitler invaded Poland (1.9.1939) France reluc-tantly declared war on Nazi Germany (3.9.1939).

The Phoney War ended when German armoured columns executed the giant outflanking movement across Holland and Belgium (May 1940) which the Kaiser's armies had failed to achieve in 1914. Paris fell (14.6.1940) and, after ⇨Reynaud's failure to persuade the Cabinet to fight on from North Africa or accept Churchill's offer of union with Britain, Marshal ⇨Pétain took over and sued for peace (22.6.1940). Under the armistice Alsace-Lorraine was ceded, the French army in-terned, the French fleet disarmed and three-fifths of France occupied by the Germans. After the dissolution of the ⇨Third Republic (10.7.1940), Pétain established in the ⇨Vichy remnant of France his authoritarian *État Français* (*Travail, Famille, Patrie*) under the premiership of ⇨Laval, whose eager collaboration with the Nazis led to his replace-ment by Admiral Darlan (Dec. 1940). The regime's original popularity waned when, with receding prospects of victory, Germany's demands became increasingly oppressive. Laval had to be reinstated as Premier (April 1942) and encouraged the recruitment and transfer of French labour to Germany. The Pétain regime carried on even after Germany had occupied Vichy France in the wake of the Allied landings in North Africa (Nov. 1942).

France, however, had long since rallied to General ⇨ de Gaulle's Resistance movement. His London broadcasts immediately before and after the French surrender – 'France has lost a battle but not the war' – led to the establishment of the Free French (28.6.1940). Their first attempt to liberate an overseas territory failed (Dakar, Sept. 1940). Within a year, however, de Gaulle controlled most of French Africa and Syria. Claiming the status of a French government in exile, he set up a Provisional Committee (June 1940) which by inclusion of representa-tives from the French underground was transformed into a National

Committee (Aug. 1941). Anglo-American doubts regarding de Gaulle's popular following and their insistence that the Vichyist General Giraud should share with him the presidency of the Committee of National Liberation set up in Algiers after the North African landings, outraged de Gaulle. He adroitly ousted Giraud (Nov. 1943) and, after his triumphal entry into Paris (25.8.1944), his authority was formally recognized by the Allies.

In France, independently operating patriots had formed early in 1943 the National Resistance Council on which former parties, trade unions and civic organizations, etc. were represented. Its armed irregulars, the French Forces of the Interior (FFI) materially helped in the liberation after D-Day (6.6.1944). About 50,000 members of the Resistance are believed to have been killed, one-half fighting, the other executed by the Germans, while about 100–200,000 were deported to labour camps. Vengeance wreaked on collaborators was correspondingly savage; execution figures vary from 30–100,000.

De Gaulle, having set up a Provisional Government (Sept. 1944) was elected Prime Minister by the Constituent Assembly (Nov. 1945) but resigned (Jan. 1946) when it disregarded his wishes for a strong Executive in the constitution of the Fourth Republic. It emerged (Oct. 1946) after two referenda giving, like its predecessor, power to the Deputies rather than the government. From 1946 to 1951 France was ruled by left-wing coalitions of the Christian Democrat (MRP), Radicals, Socialists and Communists until the latter were deprived of their government posts (May 1947). After the 1951 elections, governments relied on right-of-centre coalitions including members of the de Gaullist ⇨RPF, which was thereupon dissolved by the General. Thanks to ⇨ OEEC aid and growing European integration (⇨ Schuman Plan), in the first post-war decade France experienced an economic boom unprecedented since the days of the Second Empire, achieving from 1953 onwards economic growth rates repeatedly in excess of 10%. Their full impact was, however, frustrated by costly wars marking France's retreat from empire. ⇨ Indochina revolted in 1946 and, in spite of steadily rising military commitment, had to be abandoned after the defeat at Dien Bien Phu (May 1954). Premier ⇨ Mendès-France, praised for ending the war (Geneva, July 1954), was nevertheless brought down (Feb. 1955) when he suggested similar renunciations in North Africa. Although independence was achieved by ⇨ Tunisia (Sept. 1955) and ⇨ Morocco (March 1956), the presence of more than a million French settlers complicated the issue of Algerian independence. When the native ⇨ FLN rebelled (Nov. 1954), the settlers' refusal to reconsider Algiers' status as an integral part of France involved the motherland in a protracted war.

which often decided the fate of governments, bringing the Fourth and de Gaulle's Fifth Republic to the brink of civil war.

When the allegedly anti-settler ⇨Pflimlin government took office, the Algerian settlers, supported by army generals, who had joined the newly formed Algerian Committee for Public Safety, rebelled (13.5.1958), while in France de Gaulle's supporters clamoured for the General's return. Under the threat of civil war, Pflimlin resigned (28.5.1958) and the National Assembly elected (329 votes to 224) the General as Prime Minister, empowering him to rule by decree for six months (1.6.1958). When the constitution of his Fifth Republic was accepted by a referendum (Sept. 1958) de Gaulle was elected its first President (Jan. 1959). Having re-established control over the army, his hints at the desirability of Algerian self-determination in Aug. 1958, and more unequivocally Sept. 1959, antagonized the forces that brought him to power. When a plebiscite (Jan. 1961) favoured an 'Algerian Algeria', the Army Command under Generals Jouhaud, Challe, Zeller and the retired ⇨Salan rebelled (April 1961) but their insurrection, lacking rank-and-file support, quickly collapsed. Hard core ⇨OAS fanatics continuing a campaign of terror in Algiers and France of indiscriminate murder and attempts on the President's life, failed to prevent the implementation of the referendum. At Evian (March 1962), the terms were negotiated under which Algeria achieved her independence (1.6.1962).

With peace returned, de Gaulle tried to put into effect his larger designs: the restoration of France as a leading power within a self-sufficient '*Europe des patries*', which eventually was to extend from the Atlantic to the Urals. To this end he created the nuclear ⇨*Force de Frappe*, concluded the Franco-German friendship treaty (Jan. 1963), withdrew from the military ⇨NATO commitments (June 1966), twice vetoed Britain's entry into the Common Market (Jan. 1963, Oct. 1967), intensified relations with the communist bloc – highlighted by visits to Russia (June 1966), Poland (Oct. 1967), Rumania (May 1968) – and courted the Third World by considerable development grants and presidential visits to Latin America (Sept. 1964) and Cambodia (Sept. 1966); while breaking off relations with Nationalist China (Feb. 1964) and South Vietnam (June 1965). In most international issues he opposed US and Western policies, e.g. Vietnam, the Congo, Israel, Biafra. Notwithstanding the absolute majority de Gaulle's supporters commanded in most of the Assemblies of the Fifth Republic, the satisfactory growth rates of the economy, and his enormous personal prestige, de Gaulle's own position and that of the state he created proved less invulnerable than anticipated. In Dec. 1965 he was re-elected by a far from impressive majority and in May 1968 student demonstrations escalating into near civil war and nation-wide strikes forced the government and nearly the President to resign. Even though subsequent general elections (June 1968) returned the biggest government majority (almost 75%) known in French Republican history, the franc crisis (Oct. 1968) revealed weaknesses and cleavages both economic and political which the seemingly stable Fifth Republic had by no means overcome. This became manifest when de Gaulle, elevating a referendum on regional and Senate reforms to a question of confidence, was defeated and immediately resigned the presidency (28.4.1969). Party representation in the 1968 National Assembly is: Union of Democrats for the Republic (UDR), (292), Independent Republicans (61), Progress and Modern Democracy (PDM), (33), Federation of the Left (57), Communists (34).

Under Pompidou's presidency, France's Gaullist stance was modified to admit Britain and her three ⟡ EFTA partners into the ⟡ EEC. A referendum on these accessions (April 1972) was carried by 62% of the vote which, however, represented only 36% of the electorate. Mainly left of centre abstentions amounted to 40% and Communist rejections to 17%. The Government's unpopularity and the approach of the 1973 general elections led Socialists and Communists (June 1972) to agree on a programme for an alternative Popular Front government, and the President to replace Prime Minister Chaban-Delmas by Pierre Messmer, a Gaullist of unimpeachable orthodoxy (July 1972.)

Franco, Bahamonde, Generalissimo Francisco (1892–). Head of State (*Caudillo*) and Prime Minister of ⟡ Spain since 1939. Franco has been virtual dictator since he came to power through military victory in the ⟡ Spanish Civil War. He established a corporate state and abolished all parties except the ⟡ Falange. In recent years, opposition has included elements of the Catholic Church, one of the main pillars of his dictatorship. Associated with the Fascist dictators of the 1930s who gave him military assistance in the Civil War, Franco, however, kept Spain out of World War II (a 'volunteer' Spanish division fought with the Germans on the Russian front). He remained in power after the defeat of the ⟡ Axis and in 1947 was declared *Caudillo* for life. After an initial rebuff by the former Allied Powers, Spain was admitted to several Western organizations, concluded a military agreement with the USA (1953) and became a member of the UN (1955). With Franco's advancing age, the main problem has been that of the succession and with it the question of the restoration of the monarchy. Franco was formerly a professional officer – he was successively Commander of the Spanish Foreign Legion (1923–27), head of the military academy at Saragossa (1927–31) and later Chief of the General Staff (1935) – and led the military revolt in Spanish Morocco (July 1936) which sparked off the Civil War. Franco rose rapidly to power and in addition to commanding the Nationalist forces, became head of the Nationalist Government (Oct. 1936).

Frei Montalva, Eduardo (1911–). President of ⇨ Chile (1964–70) has tried to develop his Chilean Christian Democratic Party (PDC) as a viable alternative to the radical left and the radical right. Hopes placed on the PDC have suffered a set-back through conflict between President and Congress. In 1967 the left-wing party coalition in the Senate refused Frei permission to visit the USA and this was followed by setbacks in municipal elections. He has been forced to take in outside allies to maintain his authority. His prestige in the OAS is considerable.

French Cameroon. ⇨ Cameroun.

French Committee of National Liberation. ⇨ de Gaulle.

French Community (*Communauté Française*). Successor to the ⇨ Fourth Republic's French Union, it offered ⇨ France's former overseas territories, in accordance with the principles of self-determination, a number of constitutional options within the new association or complete secession from it (constitutional referendum 28.9.1958). With the exception of French Guinea, the remaining overseas territories joined the Community. A constitutional amendment (June 1960) allowed member states to become fully independent without forfeiting their membership status. The Community finally emerged as a loose association on British ⇨ Commonwealth lines. Members recognize the French President as President of the Community, agree to participate in periodic conferences of Community heads of state, belong to the franc bloc, receive preferential French development grants and encourage inter-community activities. The French Community and its affiliated states is now composed of:

The French Republic – made up of Metropolitan Departments, the Overseas Departments (Martinique, Guadeloupe, Réunion, Guiana) and the Overseas Territories (French Polynesia, New Caledonia, French Somaliland, Comoro Archipelago, Saint Pierre and Miquelon).

Member States – Central African Republic, Republic of Congo, Republic of Gabon, Malagassy Republic, Republic of Senegal, Republic of Chad.

Affiliated States with 'special relations' – Republic of Ivory Coast, Republic of Dahomey, Republic of Upper Volta, Islamic Republic of Mauritania, Republic of Niger, Federal Republic of Cameroun.

The Member States and the Affiliated States, together with the Togo Republic, have jointly formed the *Organisation Commune Africaine et Malgache* (⇨ OCAM), while other regional organizations such as ⇨ UDEAC, the ⇨ *Conseil de l'Entente*, and monetary unions have emerged. France has concluded special agreements with the Republic of

⤳ Mali while her relations with ⤳ Algeria are governed by the Evian and subsequent agreements.

French Congo (Middle Congo). ⤳ Congo Republic (Brazzaville).

French Equatorial Africa. Former French colonies – the French Congo (⤳ Congo Republic), ⤳ Gabon, Oubangui-Chari (⤳ Central African Republic) and ⤳ Chad – which achieved independence in the same way as the colonies of ⤳ French West Africa. (⤳ OCAM.)

French Guiana. ⤳ French Overseas Departments.

French Overseas Departments. Comprise Guadeloupe (*area* – 583 sq. miles, *population* [approx.] – 320,000); French Guiana (*area* – 23,000 sq. miles, *population* [approx.] – 35,000) and Martinique (*area* – 420 sq. miles, *population* [approx.] – 340,000) in the Caribbean, all that remains of France's former Empire in the Western hemisphere; and in the Indian Ocean the island of Réunion (*area* – 968 sq. miles, *population* [approx.] – 418,000).

Since 1946 all the Overseas Departments have been administered as integral parts of France, and elect Deputies to the French National Assembly. Most of the French political parties have branches in the Overseas Departments. Though the policy of assimilation has brought economic benefits to the Departments, there have grown up, particularly in the Antilles and Guiana, left-wing independence movements. Since 1960 the Prefects have been empowered to suspend (without trial or appeal) any civil servant suspected of supporting independence.

French Overseas Territories (*Territoires d'Outre-Mer*). Comprise Comoro Islands, New Caledonia, French Polynesia, French Territory of the Afar and Issa Peoples (French Somaliland-Djibouti), Saint-Pierre et Miquelon, Wallis and Futuna Islands.

The Territories are administered as integral parts of the French Republic. Territorial Assemblies are elected by universal suffrage and send representatives to the French National Assembly and Senate.

The French Austral Lands (Adélie Land, the Kerguelen Archipelago) are not part of the *Territoires d'Outre-Mer*, and are governed under a special statute.

French Soudan. ⤳ Mali.

French Togoland. ⤳ Togo.

French Union. ⤳ French Community.

French West Africa. France's former West African colonies (now the independent states of ⤳ Dahomey, ⤳ Guinea, ⤳ Ivory Coast, ⤳ Mali, ⤳ Mauritania, ⤳ Niger) which, together with the former colonies of ⤳ French Equatorial Africa, covered a quarter of the continent. Although her colonies were conceived as an extension of France, in practice the problem of administering vast sparsely-populated areas required a large measure of ⇨ Indirect Rule. France had a common policy, and after the war, a common programme of independence for all her colonies. The ⇨ Brazzaville Conference (1944), the French Union, the *Loi Cadre* (1956) and the establishment of the ⇨ French Community (1958) were the stepping stones to independence which all the colonies had achieved by 1960. (⇨ *Conseil de l'Entente*.)

Frondizi, Arturo (1908–). President of ⇨ Argentina (1958–62). His attempt to maintain constitutional government, restore national unity and rebuild the economy was continually hampered by military opposition. Elected in 1958 with Peronist support, his removal of restrictions on their candidates in the 1962 elections (and their subsequent success) was too much for the military who deposed him and annulled the elections. Prevented from participating in the subsequent elections (1963), he took part in the 1965 elections when his new party *Movimiento de Integracion y Desarrollo* further eroded the strength of his former party – UCRI.

FTC. United States Federal Trade Commission – an ⇨ Independent Regulatory Commission established in 1915 to administer Federal Government operations under the ⇨ Commerce Clause and to enforce provisions of the ⇨ Sherman Antitrust Act and subsequent legislation. Its task has been to promote competition and discourage monopoly, restrictive and unfair trade practices, and false advertising in interstate and foreign commerce. It works largely through administrative direction and persuasion, though it can impose penalties in the last resort. In recent years the FTC has tended to look more favourably upon large corporations than previously. Its five members are appointed for seven years each by the President with the consent of the Senate.

Führer (Leader). The title favoured by Adolf ⇨ Hitler. It received formal sanction when, in succession to President ⇨ Hindenburg, Hitler as the new head of state, became the *Führer* and Chancellor of the German *Reich*. The term implies that supreme authority is vested not in popular majorities (democracy) or hereditary prerogatives (monarchy), but solely in the person of the leader. The *Führer* therefore stands above the law, in fact is the law, and can neither be challenged nor deposed. This glorification of the individual will, was basic to Nazi thinking which through the doctrine of the:

Führerprinzip (leadership principle) aimed at a hierarchically-structured society, where leaders issue orders and subordinates obey unquestioningly. Nazi Germany swarmed with major and minor leaders in every walk of life – factory owners were *Betriebsführer* (works leaders), editors were *Schriftführer* ('copy-leaders') etc. – at the very apex of which towered the *Führer*, Hitler.

Fujarah. ⇨ Trucial States.

Fulbright, James William (1905–). US Democratic politician, Rhodes scholar and university president, was elected to the House of Representatives (1943) and then as Senator from Arkansas (1945). As chairman of the Senate Foreign Relations Committee, Fulbright has strongly opposed US involvement in Vietnam and advocated a greater role for Congress in formulating foreign policy.

Full Faith and Credit Clause. A clause in the Constitution of the USA (Article IV, Section 1) requiring that 'Full faith and credit shall be given in each State to the public acts, records, and other judicial proceedings of every other State'. This provision applies specifically to civil judgements, and requires the mutual enforcement of these by the several States. It has been interpreted by the ⇨ Supreme Court as applying to the legal transactions of corporations, including contracts; but it has not been applied to all transactions between private persons, a notable example of this being divorce law. It does not require the enforcement by one State of the criminal law of another.

Fulton Speech. Speech made by ⇨ Churchill at Fulton, Missouri, on 5 March 1946, advocating an alliance of the USA and the Commonwealth nations against the growing threat from the Soviet Union.

G

Gabon. Area – 103,000 sq. miles. *Population* (1966 approx.) – 630,000. *Head of State and President of the Council of Ministers* – Albert Bongo. *Constitution* (1967) – Executive power is vested in an elected President and his appointed Council of Ministers. There is an elected uni-cameral National Assembly.

Gabon, a French possession from 1903, the smallest and richest territory of ⇨ French Equatorial Africa (from 1910), became self-governing in 1957, joined the ⇨ French Community in 1958 and achieved full independence in Aug. 1960, remaining in the Community. Gabon's wealth (timber, oil, iron ore) has attracted large foreign (French, EEC countries and American) investments with consequent economic rivalries. Despite states of emergency and a short-lived coup (1964), Léon M'ba continued in power from 1958 until his death (28.11.1967). Following M'ba's serious illness, Bongo was appointed his deputy (14.11.1966) and the National Assembly passed an amendment (15.2.1967) creating the post of Vice-President. In the last election (19.3.1967) M'ba was re-elected President and Bongo elected Vice-President – succeeding to the presidency on M'ba's death.

Gaitskell, Hugh (1906–63). Rose rapidly in ⇨ Attlee's Labour governments (1945–51) and to the leadership of the UK ⇨ Labour Party. He served at the Ministry of Economic Warfare before he entered Parliament in 1945, becoming Parliamentary Secretary to the Ministry of Fuel and Power (1946) and then Minister (1947). In March 1950 he became Minister of State for Economic Affairs and in Oct. succeeded ⇨ Cripps as Chancellor of the Exchequer. His imposition of National Health Service charges led to the resignations of ⇨ Bevan, ⇨ Wilson and Freeman and a rift which afflicted the party for some years. The 'Bevanites' feared a betrayal of Socialist principles resulting from Gaitskell's determination to modernize the party. Labour was defeated in the 1951 and 1955 elections and Gaitskell, opposed by Bevan, was elected Party Treasurer (1954 and 1955). In Dec. 1955 Gaitskell (with 157 votes, Bevan 70, ⇨ Morrison 40) succeeded Attlee as Leader of the

Labour Party. After Labour's 1959 electoral defeat, Gaitskell's attempt to re-write the Party constitution, including Clause IV on nationalization, was defeated. Again defeated by the left at the 1960 Party Conference which gave its support to a policy of unilateral nuclear disarmament, he pledged himself to 'fight, and fight, and fight again to save the party we love', and succeeded in reversing the policy at the next conference. He had earlier (166 votes to 81) defeated Wilson's challenge to his leadership. He died aged 56, the undisputed leader of a re-vitalized Labour Party.

Galanskov, Yuri (1939–). Soviet writer (⊳ Dissent – Eastern Europe).

Gambia. *Area* – 4,000 sq. miles. *Population* (1970 est.) – 374,000. *President* – Sir Dauda K. Jawara. The Gambia, a narrow tongue of land jutting into ⊳ Senegal – with whom she has mutual defence and external affairs arrangements – was formerly the oldest British colony in Africa with a Legislative Council dating back to 1888. Gambia became self-governing on 4 Oct. 1963 under a new constitution (1962). It attained full independence within the Commonwealth on 18 Feb. 1965, with a Governor-General who was the Queen's representative, and a Prime Minister and Cabinet drawn from and responsible to the House of Representatives. In a referendum (1970) it became a republic within the Commonwealth, with an executive President and a House of Representatives with a majority of elected members.

Gandhi, Mrs Indira (1917–). Prime Minister of ⊳ India since 1966 and leader of the ⊳ Congress Party. Daughter of Jawaharlal ⊳ Nehru, she was Minister for Information and Broadcasting (1964–66) during his premiership and became Prime Minister after ⊳ Shastri's sudden death in Jan. 1966. In office she has been mainly concerned with domestic problems, in particular those presented by mass poverty, the sharply rising birth rate and India's conflict with ⊳ Pakistan.

Gandhi, Mohandas (1869–1948). Leader of the nationalist movement for independence in ⊳ India. Although he organized mass support for the ⊳ Congress Party which came to rule India after independence, his main importance stemmed from his moral leadership in civil disobedience campaigns, and from his advocacy of *Satyagraha*, the doctrine of non-violence. He was imprisoned eight times, for a total of five and a half years, for his policy of non-cooperation. Gandhi, idolized by the peasant masses, whose dress he adopted, was given the name of *Mahatma* (great soul). One of his special concerns was to relieve the position of the 'untouchables', whom he called the *harijans* (children of God), and he sought to abolish the caste system. During the violence that followed the partition of India in 1947 Gandhi helped to reduce the tension by touring the disturbed areas and fasting. In Jan. 1948 he was assassinated by a Hindu fanatic, but his influence has survived especially in the American civil rights movement and the non-violent methods of Martin Luther ⇨ King.

GATT. See under United Nations.

Gdansk. ⇨ Danzig.

GDR. German Democratic Republic. ⇨ Germany.

General Assembly. ⇨ United Nations.

General Welfare Clause. A clause in the Constitution of the USA (Article 1, Section 8) giving ⇨ Congress the power to levy taxes to provide for the 'general welfare of the United States'. Broadly interpreted by the ⇨ Supreme Court in recent years, this Clause, together with the ⇨ Commerce Clause, has provided the basis for the extensive Federal Government involvement in economic management and social security that began with the ⇨ New Deal. A narrower interpretation is favoured by the advocates of ⇨ States' Rights.

Geneva Agreements. Following the conclusion of the armistice in ⇨ Korea (July 1953) the Foreign Ministers of Britain, France, the USA and the USSR met in Berlin (Feb. 1954) and agreed that a conference of all the interested parties should be held at Geneva to discuss (a) the issues left unresolved by the Korean armistice agreement and (b) the restoration of peace in Indochina. The first session of the Geneva Conference, devoted to Korea, opened on 25 April 1954. It failed to reach agreement on anything. The second session, devoted to Indochina, began on 8 May 1954. It took a number of decisions – the Geneva Agreements – on the cessation of hostilities in ⇨ Vietnam and on the future of ⇨ Laos and ⇨ Cambodia.

Geneva Convention. The body of international agreements protecting the victims of war whether battle casualties (Red Cross), prisoners-of-war or non-combatants. Dating back to 1864 when the first convention was signed and the Red Cross established, the various conventions, of which the one of 1949 signed by 61 governments is the latest, tried to keep pace with the increasing complexity of modern war and the growing involvement of civil populations. The 1949 additions deal specifically with the treatment and repatriation of war prisoners and the protection of civilians, problems which became particularly acute during ⇨ World War II.

Geneva Summit Conference (18–23 July 1955). Attended by the USA (Eisenhower), the USSR (Bulganin and Khrushchev), the UK (Eden) and France (Fauré), the conference discussed German reunification, European security, disarmament and East-West cultural and commercial intercourse. Although the conference was convened after both

sides had expressed their wish for a *détente* in the Cold War, no substantial agreements were reached. It was decided to continue the talks at
Foreign Minister level.

Georgia. One of the 15 Federal Soviet Republics constituting the
USSR. *Capital* – Tiflis (Tbilisi). Georgia is comprised of two autonomous Republics and one autonomous Province.

German Democratic Republic. ⇨ Germany.

German Federal Republic. ⇨ Germany.

Germany. Achieved nationhood when during the Franco-Prussian War
the King of Prussia accepted the Imperial Crown of Germany (Jan.
1871). The resulting *Deutsches Reich*, surviving defeat in World War I
and the abolition of the monarchy (Nov. 1918), continued in the Weimar
Republic. When Hitler came to power (30.1.1933), the Weimar Republic, although never formally dissolved, was replaced by what the
Nazis liked to call the Third Reich, which ceased to exist after its unconditional surrender in World War II (8.5.1945). The Allies, divided
by Cold War hostilities, bestowed sovereignty on their respective zones
of occupation, thus creating two successor states to the former German
Empire; out of the American, British and French trizone the German
Federal Republic (West Germany, April 1949), and out of the Russian
zone the German Democratic Republic (East Germany, Oct. 1949),
according a special status to the former capital ⇨ Berlin under the Four
Power Statute (not recognized by the Russians since Oct. 1962).

Weimar Republic (1918–1933)

The German Republic, which succeeded the *Kaiser's* Empire and was
itself succeeded by Hitler's Third Reich.

Third Reich (1933–1945)

On 30 Jan. 1933 the 86-year old President Hindenburg, unable or unwilling to counter the intrigues of his advisers, appointed ⇨ Hitler
(leader of the National Socialist Party – ⇨ NSDAP) Chancellor of
Germany. Through carefully organized mass support backed by storm-
troop violence, Hitler and the two other Nazi Ministers soon intimidated the conservative Cabinet designed to 'contain' them, and
out-manoeuvred it by dissolving the ⇨ *Reichstag* in which Nazi rule
remained dependent on conservative support. The *Reichstag* Fire (Feb.
1933) provided a pretext for gagging the Left on the eve of the crucial
elections (March 1933), in which a Nazi poll of 44% denied them the
majority needed for constitutional changes. By outlawing the communist deputies, the government nevertheless passed an Enabling Law
permitting it to rule by decree (24.3.1933), and to replace (in accordance

with ⟡ *Mein Kampf*) German democracy by a dictatorship, in which a suitably rearmed and indoctrinated German master-race was to conquer *Lebensraum* (living space) in the East and establish itself as a dominant world power. Legislation was introduced to abolish trade unions and collective bargaining (May 1933), dissolve parties other than the NSDAP (July 1933), and abrogate the autonomy of German *Länder* (Jan. 1934). Simultaneously, laws to deprive Jews of their civic rights were passed. The Civil Service Renewal Law (April 1933) barred Jews from national or local government employment, while administrative directives closed the arts and professions to them. Persecution of Jews (the embodiment of evil in Nazi mythology) was also an act of revenge on a resented industrialized, urban society without actually interfering with its workings. A gruesome propaganda and the official encouragement of ⟡ Antisemitism – the ⟡ Nuremberg Laws (Sept. 1935), the 1938 pogroms (⟡ Crystal Night), the burning of synagogues, the wholesale dispatch of able-bodied Jews to concentration camps and their total disenfranchisement and segregation – reached their climax with the massacre of European Jewry during the war (⟡ Holocaust). Posing as a 'bulwark against communism', the Third Reich concluded a ⟡ Concordat with the Holy See (July 1933). In Oct. 1933 Germany, demanding equality, left the Geneva disarmament conference and the ⟡ League of Nations. In a plebiscite-cum-elections referendum 92% of the nation endorsed this step and elected an all-Nazi *Reichstag* meant to serve purely ceremonial functions. Hitler's strategy of undermining the Versailles system of French-dominated alliances made further progress when Germany concluded a friendship and non-aggression treaty with ⟡ Poland, France's chief Eastern ally (Jan. 1934). It suffered a minor setback when, in an abortive attempt to seize power, Austrian Nazis killed Chancellor ⟡ Dollfuss, and ⟡ Italy moved troops to defend Austria's independence (July 1934).

Hitler's domestic position was greatly strengthened when, supported by ⟡ Goebbels, ⟡ Goering, ⟡ Himmler and the army, he brought the disaffected stormtroopers (SA) to heel by having their C.-in-C. Röhm and other leaders executed (June 1934). President Hindenburg's death (Aug. 1934) freed Hitler from the last constitutional restraints. As *Führer* and *Reichskanzler* to whom the armed forces were bound by a personal loyalty oath, Hitler now held absolute power. In a plebiscite 84% of the electorate approved of the summary 'Röhm purge' and the *Führer*'s new powers. A little later, 91% of the Saar population – since 1918 under French rule – voted for a return to Germany (Jan. 1935).

The European *status quo* was dealt another blow when, in breach of the Versailles Treaty, Germany introduced conscription (March 1935).

Although ⇨ Britain, ⇨ France and Italy agreed to oppose further uni-lateral treaty violations (Stresa Conference, April 1935), Britain never-theless permitted Germany in the Anglo-German naval agreement to rebuild her naval forces to 35% of the British strength. When Italy's invasion of ⇨ Abyssinia (Oct. 1935) and the sanctions imposed by the League of Nations ruptured the Stresa front, Hitler, in breach of the freely negotiated Locarno Treaty, marched into the demilitarized Rhine-land (March 1936). Encouraged by France's failure to counter this threat Germany, backed by the most modern army and airforce, pre-pared to embark on a policy of expansion. Italian-German military co-operation in support of General ⇨ Franco during the Spanish Civil War demonstrated the new alignment, known as the ⇨ Axis (Oct. 1936). In Nov. 1936 Germany signed the Anti-Comintern Pact with Japan.

Having notified the army (Hossback Protocols, Nov. 1937) of his intention to occupy Austria and Czechoslovakia, Hitler first purged the government of the last remnants of conservative influence. The Defence Minister (von Blomberg) and his army C.-in-C., General von Fritsch, were ousted. While personally taking over the Ministry of Defence, the *Führer* also replaced Foreign Minister von Neurath by the subservient party member von ⇨ Ribbentrop (Feb. 1938). Hitler then occupied Austria (March 1938), claiming that Chancellor ⇨ Schuschnigg had broken agreements concluded a month earlier. The ⇨ *Anschluss* was still regarded as a domestic German issue, but the demand for the cession of the Sudetenland containing the main Czech fortifications brought Europe to the brink of war. Three journeys to meet Hitler by Britain's Prime Minister Neville ⇨ Chamberlain left Europe tem-porarily at peace but at the price of British and French acquiescence in the dismemberment of ⇨ Czechoslovakia at ⇨ Munich (29.9.1938). Pledges to respect the integrity of the truncated state were soon broken. German forces occupied Prague, and Bohemia and Moravia became a German Protectorate (March 1939). With the return of the Memel territories from Lithuania a few days later, Hitler had gained the last of his 'bloodless' victories. British and French guarantees to Poland (March 1939) and Greece and Rumania (April 1939) indicated that further territorial demands would be resisted. Undeterred, Hitler in-sisted that Poland surrender her privileges in ⇨ Danzig. To strengthen her diplomatic position, Germany concluded the mutual defence Pact of Steel with Italy (May 1939). Then in Aug. 1939, in a startling reversal of previous attitudes, Germany and Russia signed a non-aggression and friendship treaty (⇨ Hitler-Stalin Pact). Now secure against the threat of a war on two fronts, Germany invaded Poland (1.9.1939). Britain and

France, honouring their guarantees to Poland, declared war on Germany (3.9.1939). (⇨ World War II.)

After the defeat of the Polish forces and Russia's occupation of the eastern part of the country (17.9.1939), Poland ceased to exist as an independent state, and the stage was set for the German conquest of western Europe.

The Japanese attack on ⇨ Pearl Harbor (7.12.1941) and Germany's subsequent declaration of war on the USA transformed a mainly European conflict into a global one. By 1942 Germany had reached the zenith of her power. Except for Britain and the Iberian peninsula, she practically controlled Europe and her 350 million inhabitants, and with her armies within sight of Alexandria, a major part of North Africa as well. The Battle of the Atlantic, with sinkings in 1942 topping seven million tons, seemed to go in Germany's favour. In Russia the German *Wehrmacht* approached the Volga at ⇨ Stalingrad (Volgograd) and an eventual link-up with Japan in India appeared strategically feasible. The vast Nazi empire was ruthlessly plundered, its 'racially inferior' population was exploited as slave labourers, more than seven and a half million of whom were deported to Germany. In the East particularly potential leaders of patriotic resistance were systematically persecuted and killed in the more than 2,000 concentration camps throughout Nazi-occupied Europe. Jews first segregated in ghettos, were from 1942 deported to special extermination camps, where an estimated six million of them perished, as did half a million gypsies.

Under the weight of Russian counter-attacks at Stalingrad (Nov. 1942–Feb. 1943), the Nazi Empire began to contract as quickly as it had expanded (⇨ World War II). D-Day landings on the Normandy beaches (June 1944) presaged the liberation of Western Europe. Although the war was lost and Germany's allies sued for peace (Rumania, Aug. 1944; Finland, Sept. 1944; Bulgaria, Oct. 1944), Hitler, vowing never to capitulate, fought on, regardless of the appalling destruction which German cities and industrial centres suffered under air bombardment. Hitler miraculously escaped an attempt on his life organized by a German resistance group of high-ranking officers (July 1944) and taking terrible revenge decimated Germany's military élite. Not before the Allied armies advancing from the East and the West had linked up in Germany and Hitler had committed suicide in beleaguered Berlin (30.4.1945), did the Third Reich collapse. Grand-Admiral ⇨ Doenitz, the Hitler-appointed new Chancellor, and his interim government, having authorized the unconditional surrender (7-9.5.1945), were deposed when the Allies (23.5.1945) assumed authority in their respective zones of occupation.

German Federal Republic (1949–)

Area – 95,263 sq. miles. *Population* (1971) – 61·5 m. *President* – Dr Gustav ⇨ Heinemann (1969–). *Federal Chancellor* – Willy ⇨ Brandt (1969–). *Constitution* – The Basic Law (*Grundgesetz*) of May 1949 established the *Bundesrepublik Deutschland* as a Federal Republic governed by a bi-cameral parliament. Ultimate power is vested in the ⇨ *Bundestag* (Parliament), elected for a four-year term by direct universal suffrage. At the beginning of each legislative period the *Bundestag* in a secret ballot elects the Federal Chancellor who cannot be deposed by a vote of censure unless and until Parliament has agreed on a successor. The second chamber, the 45-member *Bundesrat* to which each of the ten federal *Länder* sends representatives, can exercise a suspended veto on *Bundestag* legislation.

The President, a mainly ceremonial figure with little political influence other than his power to veto state appointments, is elected for a five-year term by a Federal Assembly of representatives drawn in equal number from the *Bundestag* and *Länder* parliaments and reflecting their respective party strengths.

A Supreme Constitutional Court decides on questions of constitutional legality and is the ultimate guardian over the civil liberties enshrined in the Basic Law; some so fundamental as to be unassailable by constitutional amendments, which require a two-thirds majority.

The *Grundgesetz* has in several respects tried to repair constitutional flaws held responsible for the collapse of the Weimar Republic. It curtailed the power of the President who is now unable to sustain governments unsupported by parliamentary majorities. It strengthened the position of the Federal Chancellor, who can no longer be defeated by purely obstructionist parliamentary alliances of otherwise mutually opposed parties. Finally, it modified the electoral provisions of ⇨ Proportional Representation so as to discourage the emergence of numerous small parties with limited sectional appeal and the unstable parliamentary majorities they produced.

The Federal Republic's immediate post-war developments were profoundly affected by her own and the world response to recent Nazi rule, and the varying tensions of the Cold War. The former impelled the Allies to take over the government of Germany and involved the Germans in efforts to 'overcome the past'; while the latter prevented the functioning of the Four Power Control Council set up by the ⇨ Potsdam Conference (July/Aug. 1945). Russia's refusal at the Moscow Foreign Ministers' Conference (March/April 1947) to let her zone participate in a process of integration that had produced the Anglo-American bi-zone (Jan. 1947), induced the Western Allies to proceed independently with overdue currency reforms (Jan. 1948) and plans for limited German self-government. These measures provoked Russia to impose the ⇨ Berlin Blockade ultimately rendered ineffectual by the Anglo-American airlift (June 1948–May 1949). The Federal Republic was formally set up (May 1949) when the Parliamentary Council which the London Six Power Conference (June 1948) had asked to prepare a constitution, accepted the Basic Law. In the subsequent General Elections the conservative Roman Catholic ⇨ CDU was returned as the largest party and its leader Dr ⇨ Adenauer became the first Federal Chancellor, an office he was to hold for the next 14 years. His determination to align the Federal Republic with the West was largely responsible for Germany's remarkable economic and political recovery. Step by step he regained international confidence; the Petersberger Agreements (Nov. 1949) modified the Occupation Statute to allow the Federal Republic the right to join international organizations, establish consulates abroad and rebuild her merchant navy. Revised again (March 1951) when Germany was granted the right to conduct her own foreign policy and exchange diplomatic missions with the rest of the world, it was finally scrapped when the Federal Republic on admission to ⇨NATO (May 1955) regained her full sovereignty. The Allies, however, retained special responsibilities for defence, the maintenance of West Berlin's special status and for German reunification.

As with every project of European integration, Dr Adenauer enthusiastically supported the ⇨ Schuman Plan and the American-inspired effort to set up a European defence force (EDC), notwithstanding considerable Social Democrat misgivings against Germany's remilitarization. The French National Assembly's refusal (Aug. 1954) to ratify the (May 1952) agreements for a unified European army led to Germany's admission to the West European Union and NATO. The Federal Republic undertook to put the 12 divisions she was to raise under NATO command and to refrain from the manufacture of ABC (atomic, biological, chemical) weapons. In the absence of a peace treaty the Western Allies had formally abandoned belligerency in July 1951 and the USSR followed suit in Jan. 1955.

With the establishment of the ⇨ Common Market (March 1957) and its subsidiary organizations, the Federal Republic, now prosperous, having worked an 'economic miracle', had once again become a leading European power. As a crowning achievement in this process of rehabilitation, Dr Adenauer concluded the Franco-German Friendship Treaty (Jan. 1963) which was to end the century-old feud between the two countries. However, when Dr Adenauer resigned (Oct. 1963) his successors, Professor ⇨Erhard (Oct. 1963–Nov. 1966) and Dr ⇨Kiesinger

(Dec. 1966–Sept. 1969), found the treaty somewhat irrelevant to Germany's needs, particularly since ⇨ de Gaulle's nationalist attitudes and his disregard of German interests in his wooing of the Eastern Bloc undermined the concept of European unity on which Germany's post-war policies were based.

Professor Erhard's attempts to re-activate the Anglo-American connection – visits to Germany by President Kennedy, June 1963, Queen Elizabeth II, May 1965 – although vastly popular, failed. The decision to establish diplomatic relations with Israel (May 1965), with whom Dr Adenauer had already concluded the DM 3·45 billion Luxembourg reparation agreement (Sept. 1952) caused the Arab states, except Libya, Morocco and Tunisia, to break off relations with Germany, since resumed by Jordan (Feb. 1967).

Willy Brandt, the Socialist Foreign Minister in Dr Kiesinger's 'grand coalition' government, made determined efforts to improve relations with the East, vitiated by the Russian insistence that the unrepresentative ⇨ German Democratic Republic (GDR) constitutes an independent German state and the Federal Republic's determination to sever diplomatic relations with countries other than Russia which so regard it (⇨ Hallstein Doctrine). The sincerity of Stalin's 1952 offer to permit the establishment of a unified, self-governing but unaligned and disarmed Germany was never tested by Dr Adenauer, whose Moscow visit (Sept. 1955) led to the USSR's recognition of the Federal Republic but little else. Brandt's attempts at a détente in disregard of the Hallstein Doctrine persuaded ⇨ Rumania (Jan. 1967) to establish diplomatic relations with the Federal Republic and incurred the wrath of Herr ⇨ Ulbricht whose resentment against any extension of West German influence in the East dissuaded Hungary from following Rumania's example. During the 1968 Czech crisis the denunciation of the Federal Republic as the chief instigator of the 'imperialist counter-revolution' further increased mutual suspicions.

Under the Federal Republic Germany has experienced a political stability and prosperity unknown since the Bismarck era. The conservative CDU has dominated the political scene (regularly polling more than 45% of the vote since the 1953 general elections, and gaining an absolute majority in 1957) with the Socialist SPD as the second largest party steadily gaining votes (lately about 37% of the poll) at the expense of the Free Democrats (FDP) and other small parties. This trend towards a two-party system of unassailable CDU–SPD 'grand coalition' may have been responsible for the rise of the allegedly neo-Nazi 'national democratic' ⇨ NPD, and the student-inspired 'extra-parliamentary opposition', which has made itself felt since the mid-sixties. Up to that time, political extremism had made no headway; the neo-Nazi

Sozialistische Reichspartei was banned in 1952 and the Communist Party in 1956; it was restarted (Sept. 1968) on a more democratic basis. The (October 1969) general elections increasing the SPD vote to 42·7% led to the break-up of the Grand Coalition and the formation of a SPD–FDP left of centre coalition with Willy Brandt as Chancellor. While maintaining the pro-Western orientation, actively supporting British entry into the EEC, his successful though controversial ⇨ *Ostpolitik* of accommodating the East resulted in the erosion of his majority and a premature election in which, however, he won an increased majority.

German Democratic Republic (1949–)

Area – 41,802 sq. miles. *Population* (1966) – 17,079,654. *Chairman, Council of State* – Walter Ulbricht. *Chairman, Council of Ministers* – Willy Stoph. *First Secretary, Socialist Unity Party* – Erich Honecker. The highest organ of state power is the People's Chamber, the unicameral Legislature elected by universal suffrage from a single list of candidates. Effective power rests with the leadership of the (communist) Socialist Unity Party (SED), headed until May 1971 by Walter Ulbricht and since then by Erich Honecker.

Proclaimed on 7 Oct. 1949 as an independent state – though not formally recognized as such by most non-communist states – the GDR was in effect established during the ⇨ Berlin Blockade of 1948/49 in the area of the Soviet zone of occupation. When the state was proclaimed, ⇨ Sovietization of the zone was already an accomplished fact. The middle-class parties licensed by the Soviet occupation forces had been placed under the leadership of communist nominees. The influential Social Democratic Party was compelled to merge with the communists in April 1946, thereafter called SED. Thanks to the massive presence and formal powers of the Soviet occupation forces, the imposition of total communist control proceeded more quickly and simply than in other East European countries. During the first period of its rule, the Ulbricht regime was committed to a programme of 'anti-fascist democracy' working for Germany's eventual reunification. These policies were abandoned in July 1952 when Ulbricht announced a new programme of socialist construction in conditions of 'intensified class war'. Conditions had been grim before as a result of the severe Soviet reparation policies and the wholesale dismantling of East German industries. The policies inaugurated in July 1952 made conditions even grimmer. They included the collectivization of agriculture, the sudden nationalization of small business enterprises and handicraft industries and increasingly harsh living and working conditions for industrial workers, all of them enforced by the Secret Police terror. This course was intensified after

⇨ Stalin's death with the decree, issued at the end of May 1953, increasing industrial working norms by a further 10%.

The explosion came in June, beginning with a protest strike of East Berlin building workers against the norm increase. On the following day (17 June) all East Germany was in the grip of a general strike accompanied by mass demonstrations against the communist regime, calling for free elections and tolerable living conditions. The rebellion was quelled, and the regime saved, by the massive intervention of Soviet tanks and troops. A brief interlude of relaxation following the June uprising was brought to an end in 1955, when the previous internal policies were resumed with little change. Their most notable effect was a long series of economic crises and a steadily swelling stream of people defecting from the GDR to the West. By August 1961, just before the erection of the ⇨ Berlin Wall, the grand total of GDR refugees registered in the West had risen to 3,700,000, about half of them people under 25 years of age. The erection of the Berlin Wall, which saved the GDR from collapse by depopulation, was followed by a few months of still further increased intimidation and police terror designed to forestall the expected outbreak of protests against the Wall. The first change for the better came in the summer of 1962. Reforms introduced into a number of different fields initiated a slow improvement in conditions, most pronounced and most successful in the area of economic reforms.

The GDR has remained wholly dependent on the USSR for its very survival and has retained its unchanged status as a Soviet satellite. Though Ulbricht remained the one first-generation Stalinist among the leaders of the ⇨ Warsaw Pact countries, he never had any choice but to adjust his policies, or at least his public pronouncements, to the changing requirements of Moscow's post-Stalin leadership. Ulbricht performed the required turns with conspicuous agility though he did so with considerably less display of enthusiasm in the case of ⇨ Tito's rehabilitation and of ⇨ Khrushchev's Destalinization campaigns than in Moscow's subsequent crusade against ⇨ Revisionism, its armed intervention in ⇨ Hungary in Oct. 1956, its stand in the ⇨ Sino-Soviet Conflict and its campaign of vengeance against ⇨ Albania. In the development of Moscow's later conflict with ⇨ Czechoslovakia, GDR propaganda and diplomacy played a leading part. The GDR participated in the armed intervention in Czechoslovakia in Aug. 1968. Ulbricht may however have been unwilling to make the concessions over Berlin required as a condition for the ratification of Bonn's Treaties with Moscow and Warsaw. He was replaced as the party's First Secretary, just prior to the crucial negotiations, by Erich Honecker (May 1971), retaining only the honorary post of the GDR's Head of State.

Gerö, E. (1898–). Former Hungarian Party leader. A communist since 1918, Gerö took part in Bela Kun's Soviet Republic of 1919. Imprisoned for a time after its collapse, he escaped to Vienna in 1925 and later went to the USSR where he remained until his return to Hungary in Nov. 1944. A rigid Stalinist and a member (with Farkas and Revai) of the ⇨ 'Muscovite quartet', Gerö was the most powerful communist leader after ⇨ Rakosi with special responsibility for economic reconstruction. When Rakosi was ousted (July 1956), Gerö became his successor as party leader, but proved incapable of coping with the situation which developed in the following Oct. He was replaced by ⇨ Kadar (25.10.1956), and has since lived in obscurity.

Gerrymandering (after Elbridge Gerry, Republican Governor of Massachusetts USA, 1812). In the USA, drawing electoral district boundaries so as to favour a particular party. Gerrymandering has been frequently practised by State Legislatures when drawing both Congressional and State legislative district lines. Its most frequent result is the over-representation of rural areas in Congress and State Legislatures. In 1964 the Supreme Court ruled that both congressional and State legislative districts must contain roughly equal populations. However, the practice of distributing some groups of voters throughout a number of electoral districts (thereby diluting their electoral power), while concentrating other groups in a single district (thereby insuring that their votes are translated into legislative representation) still persists.

Gestapo. Short for *Geheime Staatspolizei*, the Nazi secret police. Set up by ⇨ Goering (April 1933), subsequently taken over by ⇨ Himmler and merged with the ⇨ SS, it functioned as a completely self-contained organization. Subject to no outside control or judicial review it exercised unlimited power and was the main instrument of Nazi terror. The Nuremberg Allied Military Tribunal condemned it as a 'criminal organization' (⇨ Nuremberg War Crime Trials).

Ghana. *Area* – 92,100 sq. miles. *Population* (1970) – 8,559,300. *Head of State* – Colonel Ignatius Acheampong. *Constitution* (suspended) – The country was governed from 13 Jan., 1972 by a military National Redemption Council.

Ghana consists of the former Crown Colony of the Gold Coast, Ashanti, the Northern Protectorates and British Togoland (⇨ Togo). For nearly ten years, since it became the first British colony in Africa to attain independence (6.3.1957), Ghana's politics were dominated by Dr ⇨ Nkrumah and his CPP (Convention People's Party). Post-war discontent, not least among returning ex-servicemen, quickly turned to demands for independence. In 1947 the United Gold Coast Convention was formed with Nkrumah as General-Secretary. Impatient with its reformist character, he split the party to form the CPP (1949). Following civil disorders in 1948 and 1950 when Nkrumah was arrested, the CPP easily won the Feb. 1951 general election – the first to be held with an enlarged franchise. Nkrumah was released from prison to become Leader of Government Business. Though the CPP also won a majority at the next election (June 1954) the grievances of cocoa farmers and Ashanti dislike of the Accra government, resulting in the formation of Dr ⟡ Busia's National Liberation Movement, interrupted progress to independence. Only after further elections (July 1956) in which the CPP, though it lost all its seats in Ashanti, again won a substantial majority, was independence granted. Rapid economic development, including the extension of public services, went hand in hand with an increasing weight of repressive legislation. A Deportation Act (1957) was followed by the Preventive Detention Act (1958) which allowed for imprisonment without trial. Following a plebiscite (April 1960) Ghana became a Republic (1.7.1960) remaining in the Commonwealth, with Dr Nkrumah as its first President. Opposition to the policies (praised as 'socialist' in some quarters, condemned as 'totalitarian' in others) of the new Republic was reflected in strikes (1961) and attempts on Dr Nkrumah's life. Nkrumah responded by tightening his hold over his party and Parliament and assumed control of all the functions of the state. Two events were crucial in this process. First, the President dismissed his Chief Justice (Dec. 1963 – he had acquitted members of the Cabinet accused of treason). Secondly, a referendum (Jan. 1964 – by 2,773,920 votes to 2,452) empowered the President to dismiss judges of the High Court and created a one-party (CPP) state. (Opposition to Nkrumah became increasingly difficult and dangerous – Dr Danquah, founder of the UGCC and his opponent in the 1960 elections died in prison [1965].)

By placing himself in a position of supreme authority, surrounded only by his fervent admirers, Dr Nkrumah effectively isolated himself from public opinion; an isolation which made the military coup of 24 Feb. 1966 possible. The unsuspecting President was in Peking on a self-imposed peace-mission to Vietnam. From his exile in ⟡ Guinea he called on his countrymen to oppose the National Liberation Committee. In April 1967 an attempted *coup d'état* by a small section of the army was foiled. In 1967 a Commission was appointed to draft a new constitution for a return to civilian rule. The constitution, providing for an elected National Assembly, a non-executive President and an independent Judiciary took effect from Aug. 1969 and General ⟡ Ankrah's military rule gave way to Dr K. A. ⟡ Busia's elected government in Sept. Dr Busia's government was overthrown in a bloodless military coup in 1972.

Gheorghiev, K. ⊳Bulgaria.

Gheorghiu-Dej, Gheorghe (1901–65). Former Head of State of
⊳Rumania (1961–65). A militant in the inter-war Rumanian labour
movement, Gheorghiu-Dej joined the illegal Communist Party in 1929.
Jailed in 1933 after the organization of a big railway strike, he escaped
from prison (Aug. 1944) with the aid of Ion Gheorghe Maurer,
Rumania's present Prime Minister. A member of King Michael's
government in Nov. 1944 and, from Oct. 1945, General Secretary of the
Communist Party, he was at that time still overshadowed by the
Moscow-trained group of Ana Pauker which had been put in charge of
Rumania's ⊳Sovietization. Gheorghiu-Dej sided with Ana Pauker and
Vasili Luca against his potential rival Lucretiu Patrascanu, a founder
member of the Party who was imprisoned in 1948 for 'national deviations'. A ⊳Home Communist himself, Dej was particularly violent in
his denunciation of ⊳Tito and the victims of anti-Titoist persecutions
elsewhere. In 1952, at the time of Stalin's anti-Jewish campaign culminating in the Slansky trial in Czechoslovakia and the 'doctors' plot'
in the USSR, he in turn got rid of Ana Pauker (a Jewess) and her
group. His purges continued after Stalin's death. In 1954 he had the
imprisoned Patrascanu executed and in 1957 he removed his last potential rivals from the party leadership. After this final consolidation of his
power, he attempted a gradual changeover from the role of the dictator
to that of a national leader, emphasized by his assumption of the State
presidency in 1961 and by his increasing preoccupation with the defence
of Rumania's national interests until his death in 1965.

Ghetto. Originally denoted the strictly segregated living quarters of the
oppressed Jewish communities in the mediaeval town. The Nazis re-
established ghettos in the occupied East (Warsaw, Cracow, etc.). The
term with its connotations of racial discrimination, social injustice and
deprivation of opportunity is now increasingly used to describe the
anomalous position of Negroes and other minorities in the American
and European urban environment.

Giap, Vo Nguyen, General (1912–). Deputy Prime Minister and
Defence Minister of North ⊳Vietnam. The renowned victor of Dien
Bien Phu (1954) is regarded as one of the world's most outstanding
guerrilla leaders. A revolutionary nationalist since the 1920s and a communist party member since 1933, Giap participated in 1939 in fomenting
an insurrection and, after its failure, escaped to China. He returned in
1941 to organize underground rebel forces under the direction of ⊳Ho
Chi Minh. He played a prominent part in the Viet Minh seizure of
power and its proclamation of the Democratic Republic of Vietnam
(DRV) in August 1945. After a spell as Minister of the Interior in Ho

Chi Minh's Provisional Government, he was promoted to General in 1946 and Commander-in-Chief of the Viet Minh. He retained that post after the proclamation of North Vietnam as an independent State and became, in addition, Minister of Defence and Deputy Prime Minister. He is also one of the most influential members of the (communist) Lao Dong party's Politbureau.

Gibbs, Sir Humphrey Vicary (1902–). Governor of Southern Rhodesia whose authority has not been recognized by the Rhodesian Government since ⇨ UDI when he remained loyal to the Crown. He has played a mediatory role in talks between the UK and Rhodesian governments.

'GI Bill of Rights'. In the USA, popular name for legislation providing financial, educational and other benefits for veterans of World War II and later conflicts, administered by the ⇨ VA.

Gibraltar, British Crown Colony. *Area –* 2·5 sq. miles. *Population –* 25,200.

The 'Rock', dominating the passage into the Mediterranean from the Atlantic, has been British territory and a powerful naval base since England acquired it 'in perpetuity' under the terms of the Treaty of Utrecht (1713). Latterly Spain has claimed Gibraltar as an integral part of her territory, notwithstanding the fact that a plebiscite (1967) opted against incorporation into Spain by 12,138 votes to 44. A UN resolution (Dec. 1967) deplored this referendum. Spain's policy of cutting off Gibraltar from the mainland has exacerbated Anglo-Spanish relations. The UN General Assembly (Dec. 1968) again called on Britain to transfer sovereignty to Spain within a year.

Gierek, E. (1913–). First Secretary, Polish United Workers Party. An early convert to communism, Gierek spent most of the inter-war period in France where he joined the Communist Party. When World War II began, he was in Belgium where he organized an underground branch of the Soviet-sponsored Union of Polish Patriots. His Party career began soon after his return to Poland in 1948. A member of the Central Committee from 1954, he was promoted to the Party Secretariat in 1956 and the Politbureau in 1959. As First Secretary of the *Katowice Voivodship* Party committee, since 1957 he has been in effective charge of the important industrial region of Silesia. The Party's leading economic expert, Gierek became in the 1960s one of Poland's top leaders. He replaced ⇨ Gomulka as the party's First Secretary (Dec. 1970) after an outbreak of food riots in Poland's coastal cities.

Ginzburg, Alexander (1936–). Soviet journalist and editor of underground literature (⇨ Dissent – Eastern Europe).

Giri, Varahgiri (1894–). President of ⇨ India since May 1969. Vice-President since 1967, he formerly held regional offices including those of

Governor of Uttar Pradesh (1957–60), of Kerala 1961–65) and of Mysore (1965–67).

Gizenga, Antoine (1925). Deputy Prime Minister in the first ⇨ Congo (Kinshasa) government. Gizenga established a rival 'Lumumbist' government in Stanleyville after ⇨ Mobutu's first coup (14.9.1960). Back in Leopoldville a year later he served briefly as deputy Prime Minister in a new government (2.8.1961) which was soon split by differences of opinion over Katanga. Gizenga returned to Stanleyville, but his opposition 'government' (not to be confused with the later 1964 'People's Republic of the Congo') was defeated and he was arrested (Jan. 1962). Freed by ⇨ Tshombe (July 1964) he was subsequently re-arrested but was released after Mobutu's second coup (Nov. 1965). In Feb. 1966 he made his way to Brazzaville and from there to Moscow.

Glassboro. Town in New Jersey, USA, where a brief summit meeting between President ⇨ Johnson and Soviet Premier ⇨ Kosygin was held (23/25.7.1967). They discussed the Middle East and Vietnam; but though there was a lowering of international tension, no concrete proposals emerged.

Glubb, General J. B. (1897–). British commander of the Arab Legion of ⇨ Jordan (1939–56). Personal adviser to King ⇨ Abdullah, he was regarded by many Arabs as a symbol of British influence in the Middle East and in 1956, after popular pressure, was dismissed by King ⇨ Hussein.

Goa. Formerly Portuguese, occupied by the Indian Army (Dec. 1961), and incorporated in ⇨ India (1962). There had been pressure for incorporation since the foundation of the Republic of India (1950) but until the early 1960s this took non-violent forms, e.g. economic blockade, the severence of air and rail communications.

Goebbels, Dr Joseph (1897–1945). As Nazi Minister of 'Enlightenment and Propaganda' (1933) controlled all media of communication – radio, Press, film, theatre, book-publishing, etc. – exerting perhaps the most pervasive and lasting influence on the formation of opinion in the ⇨ Third Reich. He joined the party as a young philology graduate in 1922 and ⇨ Hitler, appreciating his genius for venomous political journalism and propaganda, made him *Gauleiter* of Berlin (1926) and head of party propaganda (1928). Goebbels founded his own paper *Der Angriff* which he edited from 1927–33. His virulent anti-semitism, his attacks on the existing order including incitement to street rioting, helped erode the authority of the ⇨ Weimar Republic. He belonged to the ⇨ NSDAP's left wing and on one occasion clashed with Hitler, who, however, had no difficulty in asserting his authority. Goebbels organized the ⇨ Crystal Night pogrom (Nov. 1938) and after the Stalingrad defeat clamoured for 'total war' (18.2.1943), a demand which brought him the appointment of Chief Commissioner for Total Mobilization (Aug. 1944). He remained in Berlin with Hitler, who made him *Reich* Chancellor in his testament, and he and his family committed suicide one day after the death of their leader.

Goering, Hermann (1893–1946). *Reichsmarshal*, C.-in-C. of the Nazi *Luftwaffe*, holder of innumerable high party and government appointments, and ⇨ Hitler's successor designate until stripped of all offices and expelled from the party for trying to form a government while Hitler was incapacitated in besieged Berlin (23.4.1945). Commander of the legendary *Richthofen* squadron in World War I, he joined Hitler in the early twenties, built up his para-military SA and participated in the abortive beer cellar *putsch* (8.11.1923). Among the first Nazi delegates elected to the *Reichstag*, he became its President in 1932. After Hitler's assumption of power (30.1.1933) he joined the Cabinet and as Prussian Minister of the Interior introduced concentration camps and organized the ⇨ Gestapo. With ⇨ Himmler's assistance he deposed the militarily ambitious SA Chief-of-Staff, Röhm (30.6.1934). Then, as Minister of Aviation, he secretly started to build the *Luftwaffe*, and as Commissioner for the Four-Year Plan supervised German rearmament (1936). In the war, the *Luftwaffe* spearheaded the early German victories, but its performance at Dunkirk (June 1940), the Battle of Britain (Aug./Sept. 1940) and its failure to keep Stalingrad supplied (Nov. 1942–Jan. 1943) revealed weaknesses. Goering's political influence declined in consequence. He surrendered to the Americans, was sentenced to death by the Nuremberg Military Tribunal (⇨ Nuremberg War Crime Trials) but succeeded in committing suicide on the eve of his execution.

Goldberg, Arthur Joseph (1908–). Former US ambassador to the UN and a successful labour lawyer, he played a significant part in the AFL–CIO merger of 1955. Appointed Secretary of Labour (1961) and then Associate Justice of the Supreme Court (1962), he was chosen by President ⇨ Johnson to fill the UN post (1965–68). Although Goldberg was known to oppose further escalation in Vietnam, his resignation in April 1968 was said not to be linked to his position on the war.

Gold Coast. ⇨ Ghana.

Goldwater, Barry Morris (1909–). US Senator (from Arizona 1953–65, 1969–) and unsuccessful Republican candidate for the presidency (1964). The leading spokesman for the conservative wing of his party, he advocated stiffer opposition to communism and a decrease in the power of the Federal Government. He and his running mate, William E. Miller, were heavily defeated by ⇨ Johnson and ⇨ Humphrey in an election in which moderate Republicans, alienated by Goldwater, ran independently of their national ticket, whilst Southern Democrats supported the conservative Republican candidate.

Gomez, General Juan Vicente, *Caudillo* of ⟡ Venezuela (1908–35).

Gomulka, W. (1905–). Polish communist. An active trade unionist and communist party member in the inter-war period, Gomulka was imprisoned between 1936 and the outbreak of World War II at the time when his Party was dissolved by the ⟡ Comintern and its most prominent leaders executed in the USSR. During the war, he played a leading part in the organization of the anti-German resistance inside Poland and joined the newly founded Polish Workers' Party, the successor to the CP. Elected to the Party's Central Committee (1942) he became its Secretary-General (1943) and retained that position after the merger of the Party with the ⟡ Muscovite communists who had meanwhile established the 'Lublin Committee'. In the early post-war years he became known as an opponent of compulsory collectivization and an advocate of a specifically 'Polish road to socialism'. He fell into disgrace in 1948 at the time of ⟡ Tito's break with ⟡ Stalin, and was accused of 'bourgeois nationalism' and appeasement of ⟡ Yugoslavia. Ousted from his Party positions, he was arrested in 1951 and kept in prison without trial until 1955. Rehabilitated by ⟡ Ochab (April 1956) as having been wrongfully imprisoned, but again attacked as a 'nationalist', Gomulka's popularity increased because of that very charge. After the Poznan Workers' riots (June 1956) he was re-admitted to the Party and, with the onset of the ⟡ Polish October, he remained the only communist with a chance of restoring the Party's rule. Threatened by a nation-wide revolt, the Party, at Ochab's suggestion, elected Gomulka as its new First Secretary – an office which he immediately used to dismiss a number of unpopular Soviet nominees from their posts, including the Defence Minister, the Soviet Marshal Rokossowski, in the teeth of threatened USSR armed intervention. Having persuaded ⟡ Khrushchev to respect Poland's internal autonomy, Gomulka removed the Stalinists from their leading positions, abolished Secret Police terror, ended compulsory collectivization, and established a *modus vivendi* with the Church. When these reforms were accomplished, Gomulka, from 1957 onwards, turned against 'revisionist' intellectuals and the more radical reformers in the Party. By the early 1960s, his conservatism had succeeded in blocking further reforms and innovations of every description and in involving Poland in a creeping economic and intellectual paralysis. After the Six Day War in the Middle East (June 1967), he initiated an 'anti-Zionist' campaign which, in the course of 1968, developed (possibly against his wish) into a general anti-Jewish campaign, linked with a vast new purge of 'revisionists' and liberal-minded reformers. Soon afterwards, a further deterioration in the economic situation led to a new upsurge of discontent, culminating, in Dec. 1970, in widespread food riots. In the aftermath, Gomulka was replaced as party leader by Edward ⇨ Gierek.

Good Neighbour Policy. Foreign policy stance of the USA towards Latin American countries during Franklin D. ⇨ Roosevelt's Administration. It was a reversal of Theodore Roosevelt's 'Big Stick' policy which emphasized American intervention. Originally introduced in Franklin Roosevelt's first inaugural address (Jan. 1933) its principal aims were diplomatic solidarity and a common defence of the Western hemisphere. It was implemented through informal governmental consultations, Reciprocal Trade Agreements, the ⇨ Export–Import Bank and military co-operation during World War II. After 1945 Latin America was again neglected by the United States until the Kennedy Administration revitalized Franklin Roosevelt's principles in the ⇨ Alliance for Progress.

GOP. 'Grand Old Party' – familiar name for the ⇨ Republican Party in the USA.

Gorbach, Alfons (1898–). Chancellor of ⇨ Austria (1961–64) and leader of the Austrian People's Party.

Gorton, John (1911–). Prime Minister of ⇨ Australia and leader of the Liberal Party from Jan. 1968 to March 1971. As a result of a Cabinet crisis he resigned and was replaced by William McMahon. Gorton served as Minister of Defence from March to Aug. 1971.

Gosplan. Soviet term, short for State Planning Commission.

Gottwald, K. (1896–1953). Former President of ⇨ Czechoslovakia. A founder-member of the Czechoslovak Communist Party in 1921 and, from 1927, its General Secretary, Gottwald was the Party's chief link with the Comintern in the inter-war years. After the ⇨ Munich Agreement of Sept. 1938, he went to live in the USSR and later became the main author of the political pact concluded with ⇨ Benes in April 1945. Deputy Premier in the first post-war coalition government, he became Prime Minister in June 1946 and, two years later, Benes's successor as President of the Republic, a post which he combined with the Party leadership until his death in 1953.

Goulart, Joao (1918). President of ⇨ Brazil (1961–64). A former ⇨ Vargas Minister of Labour; associated with the left (PTB), was Vice-President to ⇨ Kubitschek and again under Quadros, whom he succeeded. Distrusted by the army, he was forced to govern through a Prime Minister until his presidential authority was confirmed by plebiscite (1963). Harried by the left (some members of his own party) and the right, and frustrated by a hostile Congress, he attempted to appeal directly to the masses. Political confusion and continued inflation (a Kubitschek legacy) provided the army with a pretext for intervention (⇨ Costa E. Silva).

Gowon, Major General Yakubu (1934–). President of the Supreme Military Council of ⇨ Nigeria determined to end ⇨ Biafra's secession. His intervention in politics followed a distinguished army career, including service with the UN Peace-Keeping Force in the ⇨ Congo.

GPU. Russian abbreviation for State Political Directorate. (⇨ USSR State Security Service.)

Great Britain. ⇨ United Kingdom.

Great Leap Forward. ⇨ China.

Great Purge. ⇨ Moscow Trials, ⇨ Purges, ⇨ Yezhovshchina.

Great Society, The. Phrase used by US President Lyndon ⇨ Johnson to describe the broad goals of his domestic policy – 'abundance and liberty for all . . . an end to poverty and racial injustice' (1965). The achievement of the Great Society required plans for urban renewal, preservation of the natural environment, the ⇨ Anti-Poverty Program, far-reaching educational programmes; hence: the Job Corps, the Office of Economic Opportunity, the Teacher Corps, Operation Head Start, ⇨ VISTA, several ⇨ Civil Rights measures, the American 'Beautification Bill' and aid to Appalachia.

Greece. *Area* – 50,534 sq. miles (including the Greek mainland, Crete and other islands). *Population* (1971) – 8,768,641. *Prime Minister* – George ⇨ Papadopoulos (1967–). *Constitution* – A constitutional monarchy until the military coup of April 1967, Greece is now ruled by a military dictatorship. According to the 1968 constitution, which describes the country as a 'guided democracy', legislative power is exercised by the King and Parliament and executive power by the King and Government (as in the 1952 constitution), but the King is in exile and most of the provisions safeguarding rights are invalidated by the reservation that they must not violate 'the principles of the regime'.

Although Greece was a constitutional monarchy from the time of independence, her recent history has been marked by periods of revolution and counter-revolution. From 1924 until 1935 she was a Republic but the resulting strife led to the restoration of the monarchy under George II after a plebiscite (Nov. 1935). Parliamentary government did not last long. After he became Premier, General ⇨ Metaxas (1936–41) established, with the King's blessing, a form of government known as the 'Third Civilization', which had many Fascist characteristics: Parliament was dissolved, the Press censored and opponents exiled. Domestically it embarked on social reforms while its foreign policy concentrated on close cooperation with Yugoslavia, Rumania and Turkey (Balkan

Entente, 1934). At the beginning of ⇨World War II Greece succeeded in repulsing an Italian invasion (1940) but this led to Germany's intervention. After a whirlwind campaign (6 April–11 May 1941) Greece was occupied by the Axis powers. Resistance and guerrilla activities were carried out by two mutually opposed movements, the People's National Army of Liberation (ELAS), directed politically by the communist-dominated National Liberation Front (EAM), and the royalist Free Democratic Greek Army. After the Axis defeat this conflict erupted into the Civil War (1945–49), in which British attempts to mediate proved of no avail. EAM and ELAS, with a vast supply of arms and forces numbering 25,000 (1948), controlled the northern areas of the country. In 1947 they established their own government, but the support given them by Albania, Bulgaria and Yugoslavia increased international tension and led to controversy in the UN, with the Greek Government accusing the three northern states of violating her border, a charge supported by the UN enquiry commission in 1947. With the UK unable to continue financial and military support to the Greek Government, the USA stepped in with aid proclaiming the ⇨Truman Doctrine (March 1947). The Greek communists were dealt a further blow when ⇨Yugoslavia withdrew her support for ELAS because of her conflict with the USSR. The war left a legacy of political instability. Repeated changes in government – between 1947 and 1951 thirteen Cabinets held office – hindered Greece's economic recovery. In 1952 a new constitution was adopted replacing proportional representation with the majority system but the overwhelming election victory that same year of Field-Marshal Papagos' new right-wing Greek Rally underlined the difficulty of establishing a stable parliamentary system. After the death of Papagos (1955) the new Prime Minister, Constantine ⇨Karamanlis (1955–63), leader of the conservative National Radical Union (ERE), re-established parliamentary government. The moderate left split after holding office until 1952, but was re-united by George ⇨Papandreou, who in 1961 founded the Centre Union Party. This held power from 1963 (in 1964 it won a landslide victory) but a political crisis (summer and autumn 1965) over the investigation of a secret army organization (ASPIDA) led to differences with King ⇨Constantine XIII (who had succeeded King Paul, 1947–64). The constitutional crisis involved the future of the monarchy and the King's right to dismiss a Prime Minister who commanded a majority in Parliament. Papandreou resigned and the Centre Union Party split when 45 deputies left it to form the pro-King Liberal Democratic Centre Party. Papandreou was succeeded by three short-lived Centre Union governments which lacked Parliament's confidence. Demonstrations in favour of Papandreou and new elections on the issue of King v. People aroused old Civil War fears of a left-wing takeover. When elections were called, the army staged a coup (April 1967). Civil liberties were suspended, political opponents arrested and left-wing organizations banned, including the EDA (extreme left-wing successor to the Communist Party banned in 1947). Although the army remained in effective control, the new government under the civilian Kollias, contained only five military members out of nineteen. The power of the army came to the fore when Colonel Papadopoulos became Prime Minister (Dec. 1967) following an abortive counter-coup by the King, who then fled the country. In Sept. 1968 the new constitution was approved by a referendum (voting was compulsory) but confidence in promises to hold elections 'eventually' and to 'broaden' democracy has been weakened by allegations of police brutality and the Government's general intolerance (even to the extent of banning mini-skirts and beards). Furthermore, serious economic problems (only 15% of the land is productive) and persistent poverty remain and emphasize the contrast between rural and urban Greece. Notwithstanding the changes in domestic politics there have been no radical departures in foreign policy since World War II. The experience of the Civil War and geographical proximity to communist countries have been responsible for a pro-Western course – economically in joining the OEEC (1948) and the OECD (1961), militarily in joining ⇨NATO (1952), and politically in her ties with Western Europe (in 1949 Greece joined the Council of Europe and in 1962 became an associate member of the ⇨EEC). She also sought closer relations with her neighbours through the Balkan Treaty of Friendship and Cooperation with Yugoslavia and Turkey (1953), followed by the Balkan Pact (1954). Greece's relations with the UK and ⇨Turkey became strained when she supported the Cypriot movement for *Enosis* (i.e. union of ⇨Cyprus with Greece), which was strongly opposed by the island's Turkish community. Agreement on Cypriot independence was reached in 1959, but this did not prevent further clashes between the two communities and a consequent renewal of antagonism between Greece and Turkey.

Greenland. *Area* – 850,000 sq. miles of which 50,000 are ice-free. *Population* – 37,000.

Since 1953 an integral part of ⇨Denmark. In World War II the USA acquired several air-fields and weather-stations, three of which it was allowed to retain under ⇨NATO agreements. These were criticized when an American bomber carrying nuclear weapons crashed near Thule (Jan. 1968).

Grigorenko, Pyotr (1906). Former Soviet Major-General and lecturer at Moscow's Frunze Military Academy, sacked and demoted for his repeated outspoken protests against trials of writers, restraints on freedom, unconstitutional measures and the invasion of Czechoslovakia. In 1964, after one of his many protests, he was confined to a mental asylum for 14 months. He was re-arrested in 1969.

Grimond, Joseph (1913–). UK Liberal MP, former radical leader of the British ⟡ Liberal Party (1956–67).

Grivas, General George (1898–). Greek Cypriot officer who led the ⟡EOKA terrorist movement in ⟡Cyprus (1955–59) under the assumed name of Dighenis Akritas (a Greek folk hero who resisted Arab raiders). Later commanded the Greek Cypriot National Guard (1963–67) but refused to accept ⟡Makarios' abandonment of *Enosis* for sovereign independence. When his 'guerrillas' raided Turkish villages (Nov. 1967), starting a new round of civil violence in Cyprus, Grivas was recalled to Athens by the Greek Government. During World War II he fought in occupied Greece as a royalist guerrilla leader.

Gruber, Karl (1909–). Foreign Minister of ⟡ Austria (1946–53) who negotiated the ⟡ South Tyrol agreement with Italy (1946) and conducted preliminary negotiations for the ⟡Austrian State Treaty (1955).

Guadeloupe. ⟡ French Overseas Departments.

Guatemala. *Area* – 42,042 sq. miles. *Population* (1969 est.) – 5,014,000. *President* – Col. Carlos Araña Osorio (1970–). *Constitution* (1965) – Unitary Republic, provides for an elected President and uni-cameral Congress. Suffrage is compulsory for literate adults and optional for illiterate adults.

In 1931, in the wake of the Great Depression, and with US backing, General Jorge Ubico came to power in Guatemala. As with other Central American Republics, Guatemala's political development has been greatly affected by US pressure, increased in recent years through the cold war. In 1944, dissatisfaction with the government culminating in demonstrations (in which students were prominent) and a general strike led to Ubico's resignation. The subsequent military junta was equally unpopular. With the help of dissident officers, the government was overthrown (again students were prominent in the uprising) and replaced by an interim government pending a new constitution. Dr Juan José Arevalo was elected President (1945–51). Arevalo's democratic and reformist programme and in particular the freedom permitted to left wing including communist organizations exacerbated relations with the US. Under the next President, Colonel Jacobo Arbenz (1951–54), who depended on the support of the left and expedited economic and agrarian reform (including the expropriation of United Fruit Company property), strained relations with the US reached breaking point. With US connivance, the exiled Colonel Carlos Castillo Armas led a successful insurrection (1954). Support for Armas included many of the urban middle class made anxious by peasant militancy. Agrarian reforms were reversed and opposition suppressed. Increasingly unpopular, Armas was assassinated (1957). The next administration was not considered harsh enough by the military, who, fearing a return to power of the popular Arevalo in the elections, staged a coup (1963). When elections were held (1966) Mendez Montenegro (backed by his own party and also the followers of banned political parties) easily defeated his military opponents. In the early sixties Guatemala was used as a base for training anti-Castro forces. In recent years guerrilla activity and violence, both left and right wing, have increased. A state of emergency was proclaimed (Jan. 1968) followed by a state of siege (March 1968). Elections were held in 1970.

Guevara, Dr Ernesto (Che) (1928–67). Latin American revolutionary and guerrilla fighter of Argentinian origin.

As Fidel ⇔ Castro's right-hand man in the guerrilla campaign against the Batista regime, Guevara played an outstanding part in the revolution in ⇔ Cuba. After its victory in 1959, Guevara analysed the theory and practice of guerrilla warfare in a book *The Guerrilla War*, which introduced basic modifications into hitherto accepted Marxist-Leninist theories. He disappeared from Cuba in March 1965 in order to organize guerrilla wars in other Latin American countries. In Dec. 1966, he launched a guerrilla campaign in Bolivia where he lost his life when he was captured by Bolivian Government forces (Oct. 1967). Since his death, 'Che' has become the legendary hero of a growing cult among left-wing students and other young radicals in the Western World.

Guilt by Association. A critical expression for the doctrine that membership of an organization that is held to engage in or advocate unlawful activities, particularly of a political nature, itself constitutes a crime. In the USA it is applied to the offence, created by the ⇔ Smith Act, of knowingly organizing or being a member of any group having as its purpose the violent overthrow of the government. The phrase also refers to the tendency to condemn people for their supposed political (specifically communist) 'association', characteristic of ⇔ McCarthyism.

Guinea, Republic of. *Area* – 96,000 sq. miles. *Population* (1969 est.) – 3,890,000. *President* – Sékou ⇔ Touré (1961). *Constitution* (1958) – Elected President and uni-cameral National Assembly. Government policies are directed through the *Parti Démocratique de Guinée* (the only legal party) whose chairman is President Touré.

A part of ⇔ French West Africa from 1895; since independence (Oct. 1958), which badly damaged her relations with France, Guinea has emerged as the most radical of the former French Territories – committed to the 'total decolonization' of Africa and a leading member of the ⇨ OAU. The only colony to opt for independence outside the ⇨ French Community in 1958 (Sékou Touré – 'We prefer poverty in freedom to riches in slavery') all French aid was immediately withdrawn. Guinea's isolation led to the (still unrealized) ⇨ Guinea–Ghana Union (1958) and to trade links with the USSR. In 1961 the Soviet Ambassador was expelled (alleged complicity in an anti-government strike) and Guinean Marxism was remodelled to suit African conditions. Since then, Guinea has accepted aid from the West (the USA is the largest single donor) and the Communist Bloc. Guinea's relations with France, patched up in 1963, worsened in 1965 when France and the ⇨ Ivory Coast were accused of complicity in an anti-Touré plot. Though relations with Ghana were disrupted in 1963, Dr ⇨ Nkrumah was given refuge in Guinea (March 1966) and appointed co-President.

Guinea-Ghana Union (1958). Proposed when ⇨ Ghana offered ⇨ Guinea £10 m. (still not repaid) after the withdrawal of French aid from Guinea. ⇨ Mali joined in 1961 but the union remained ineffective and did not develop into the hoped-for larger federation. ⇨ Touré (believing Ghanaians to be implicated in the assassination of ⇨ Togo's President Olympio) announced its dissolution in 1963.

Gulag. Russian abbreviation for Main Administration for Corrective Labour Camps. (⇨ USSR State Security Service.)

Gursel, General Cemal (1895–1966). President of ⇨ Turkey (1961–66). Formerly Commander-in-Chief of the Turkish Land Forces (from 1958) he led the military coup in 1960 which overthrew ⇨ Menderes. From 1960 to 1961 he headed the military government which preceded the 1961 elections.

Guyana. *Area* – 83,000 sq. miles. *Population* (1970) – 714,230 (of whom about half are of East Indian and about one-third are of Negro descent). *President* – Arthur Chung (1970–). *Prime Minister* – Forbes ⇨ Burnham (1964–). In 1966 Guyana became a sovereign independent state within the ⇨ Commonwealth, with a governor-general representing the Queen. In 1970 it became a Cooperative Republic, still in the Commonwealth, with Arthur Chung elected President for a term of 6 years. The Prime Minister is responsible to a uni-cameral Legislature (National Assembly) of 53 members elected by secret ballot; the electoral system is proportional representation, each voter casting his vote for a party list of candidates.

Formerly the colony of British Guiana, Guyana's recent stormy history has been affected by 'cold war' politics and since independence (1966) its unity threatened by the continued rivalry between Dr Cheddi

⇨ Jagan's PPP (People's Progressive Party) and Forbes Burnham's PNC (People's National Congress). In 1947 a new constitution provided for an elected majority in the Legislature but only in 1953 (after ⇨ Jamaica – 1944 and ⇨ Trinidad – 1946) were elections held on a basis of universal suffrage. The 1953 constitution also introduced an Upper Chamber. Though the PPP controlled the National Assembly (1953 elections) Jagan's programme of reforms was blocked by the Upper Chamber. Frustrated in Parliament, the PPP leaders encouraged their followers to protest and take to the streets and the British governor suspended the constitution. In 1955 Burnham left the PPP to form the PNC which in the subsequent elections (1957) won three seats to the PPP's nine in a reformed uni-cameral Legislature. In the 1961 elections under a new constitution granting internal self-government, the PPP won 19, the PNC 11 and the newly-formed businessmen's party, Peter D'Aguiar's UF (United Force) won 4 seats. Suspected of communist sympathies, Jagan's authority was diminished by his inability to obtain economic aid from the UK and US, by economic crisis and outbreaks of violence and finally by the despatch of British troops to restore order (1962). (They remained by the provision of a 'State of Emergency' until 1965.) Political tensions threatened to explode into racial violence (the PPP's followers were largely East Indians and the PNC's Negroes). Promised independence was postponed and the political deadlock broken by the device of proportional representation – obviously aimed at Jagan's previously assured PPP majority. The immediate result (1964) was a PPP-led sugar-workers' strike and a serious outbreak of racial violence. The 1964 elections (in which the PNC won 40% of the votes and the UF 12%) resulted in a Burnham-led coalition administration. The PPP achieved 46% and Jagan, refusing to resign, was removed by a constitutional amendment. Guyana became independent in May 1966, since when Venezuela and Surinam have laid claims to areas of Guyanese territory. The economy has benefited from US and UK aid, but stability is threatened by politico-racial divisions. In the general elections (Dec. 1968) Burnham was returned to power, but there were charges of electoral manipulation.

H

Habsburg, Dr Otto von (1912–). Son of Emperor Charles (1916–18), the last reigning Habsburg. Lives in Bavaria and has been permitted to visit Austria, as a private citizen, only since 1966. Despite his disavowal, he is suspected (primarily by Socialists) of harbouring ambitions for a restoration of the monarchy.

Haganah. ⇨ Israel.

Haile Selassie (1891–). Emperor of ⇨ Ethiopia (crowned Nov. 1930). His plans for modernization and reform – he provided Ethiopia with a new constitution (1931) – were interrupted by the Italian invasion of his country (1935). A refugee in Britain from 1936, he twice appealed to the ⇨ League of Nations (1936 and 1938) and returned to lead his forces assembling in the Anglo-Egyptian Sudan (1940). In a rapidly changing continent, he has maintained his personal authority for over 40 years and played a leading part in establishing the ⇨ OAU.

Hailsham, Lord. ⇨ Hogg, Quintin.

Haiti. *Area* – 10,700 sq. miles. *Population* (1969) – 4,768,000. *President* – Jean-Claude Duvalier (1971–). *Constitution* (1964) – Executive power vested in the President for life. In 1961 the bi-cameral National Assembly was reformed into a uni-cameral Assembly. There is universal suffrage and deputies can be elected to serve for indefinite periods.

Haiti, populated largely by the descendants of Negro slaves, has a long history of violence and corruption, including strife with its neighbour on the island of Hispaniola – the ⇨ Dominican Republic. From 1915 to 1934, Haiti was occupied by US military forces. Stenio Vincent was elected President in 1930 and ruled as a dictator until 1941. In 1937, probably with Vincent's collusion, more than 10,000 Haitians were massacred by ⇨ Trujillo's Dominican Army. Growing Negro resentment of Mulatto domination (encouraged by the US) led to a successful revolution against Vincent's successor (1946). There was a brief period of responsible government and social reform during the presidency of Duvarsais Estime (1946–50) who was deposed by the army. Economic boom at the time of the Korean War was dissipated by corruption and later civil disorder which led to the fall of General Paul Magloire's junta (1950–56). Following a provisional government, Dr François Duvalier was elected President (1957) and subsequently dominated his country. Duvalier extended his term (1963) and (1964) nominated himself President for life. Known as 'Papa Doc' and claiming divine authority, Duvalier's power rested in a mixture of superstition (*Voodoo*), brutality and suppression of all opposition. His ignorant countrymen were terrorized by the activities of the '*Tonton Macoutes*' (literally – Bogey-men). His tyranny appears to have been even more disastrous for his country than was Trujillo's for the Dominican Republic. After Papa Doc's death in 1971, his son succeeded to the presidency and promised to continue his father's work 'with the same inexhaustible energy and the same inflexibility'.

Halifax, Earl of (Edward Wood) (1881–1959). UK Conservative MP, held ministerial posts from 1922 to 1926, then Viceroy of India (1926–31). Secretary for War (1935), Lord Privy Seal (1935–37), Lord President of the Council (1937–38), succeeded ⇨ Eden as Foreign Secretary (1938–40) and supported ⇨ Chamberlain's policy of ⇨ Appeasement. Served in ⇨ Churchill's Cabinet (1940) and was appointed Ambassador to the United States (1941–46).

Hallstein Doctrine. Formulated in 1955, enjoins the German Federal Republic not to enter into or maintain diplomatic relations with any country (except the USSR) which has extended diplomatic recognition to the ⇨ GDR. The doctrine is based on the claim that the democratic-ally constituted Federal Republic is the only authentic and legitimate representative of the German people, and its application has largely succeeded in limiting *de jure* recognition of the GDR to communist states. It compelled the Federal Republic, however, to break off diplomatic relations with Yugoslavia (1957) and Cuba (1963) and so stultified West German efforts to improve contacts with the East that it was quietly disregarded when diplomatic relations were established with Rumania (Jan. 1967) and re-established with Yugoslavia (Jan. 1968). The doctrine was further eroded, when in 1969 a number of ⇨ Third World countries (Cambodia, Iraq, Sudan, Syria) established diplomatic relations with the GDR, without provoking a retaliatory response from the German Federal Republic.

Hammarskjöld, Dag (1905–61). Swedish diplomat and UN Secretary-General. Professor of Economics at Stockholm University (1933), went into government service (1936) and entered the Cabinet as deputy Foreign Minister (1951). Elected UN Secretary-General in succession to Trygve ⇨ Lie (April 1953) and unanimously re-elected (Sept. 1957), his conduct of affairs particularly during and after the ⇨ Suez Crisis (Oct.

1956) and his championing of the rights of the smaller nations greatly increased the respect for and the influence of his office. His handling of the ⇨ Congo conflict brought him into a head-on collision with the Russian Prime Minister, N. ⇨ Khrushchev, who not only demanded his resignation but also the replacement of the Secretary-General's office by a (*troika*) three-man board representing the Western, communist and uncommitted countries, each armed with a veto. Hammarskjöld refused to resign or to agree to the curtailment of his powers. He was killed in a plane accident near Ndola, Northern Rhodesia (Zambia) while on a Congo peace mission, and was posthumously awarded the 1961 Nobel Peace Prize.

Harriman, William Averell (1891–). US statesman and Democratic politician; ambassador to the Soviet Union (1943–46) and to Great Britain (1946). During World War II he was present at every major international conference. He served as Secretary of Commerce (1946–48), and was appointed a special assistant to President ⇨ Truman (1950). He was elected Governor of New York (1954) but was defeated for re-election by Nelson A. ⇨ Rockefeller (1958). He has since served as Ambassador at Large (1961 and 1965), Assistant Secretary of State for Far Eastern Affairs (1961–63), and Under-Secretary of State for Political Affairs (1963–65). Harriman played a significant role in negotiating the neutralization of Laos (1962) and the agreement on a limited nuclear test-ban treaty (1963). In March 1968 he was named American representative to the Paris peace talks with North Vietnam.

Hatch Acts. In the USA, Acts of 1939 and 1940, successively amended, prohibiting party-political soliciting of, or activities by, Federal civil servants, and limiting private contributions to party funds in Federal elections. As a means of regulating political contributions, the Hatch Acts have been relatively ineffective, since contributions can be made through third persons, and to any number of party committees at various levels. The cost of election campaigns in the USA has steadily mounted in recent years, despite the legislation, and may have exceeded $150 m. in recent presidential elections. After the 1968 elections, a campaign was begun to limit election expenditures, and a Federal Election Campaign Act was passed by Congress to that effect in July 1972.

Havana Declarations. Two widely publicized statements by Fidel ⇨ Castro, the first made in Sept. 1960 and the second in Feb. 1962. In the first Havana Declaration Castro attacked the Organization of American States for upholding the Monroe Doctrine, which he described as a cloak for US imperialism; in the second he called for revolutionary guerrilla wars against the established governments all over the American continent.

Hawks. As opposed to Doves, a term most often used to describe American politicians who favour a successful military conclusion of the Vietnam War. Doves include those who believe that a military victory is not attainable in Vietnam and who would limit or even oppose U S military intervention in other countries. The terms have also been applied to other countries and situations (Middle East, Soviet Russia) where militants and moderates clash.

Haya de la Torre, Victor Raul (1895–). Peruvian political leader, a champion of the Indians (*indigenistas*) and advocate of radical political and economic change. (⇨Peru, ⇨APRA.) Though thrice an unsuccessful candidate for the presidency and forced to spend years in exile, his influence as a political leader – the exponent of nationalist revolutions in Latin America – extends far beyond Peru.

Healey, Denis Winston (1917–). British Labour Party MP, Minister of Defence (1964–70). Responsible for cuts in defence expenditure and proposed reduction of Britain's defence commitments ⇨ east of Suez.

Hearings. Formal proceedings, particularly public proceedings, of U S ⇨ Congressional Committees, involving the presentation of evidence and the examination of witnesses. Also, an alternative term for ⇨Congressional Investigations.

Heath, Edward (1916–). Prime Minister of the U K (1970–). Leader of the ⇨Conservative Party since 1965, he was the first to be so elected by the whole parliamentary party. (Heath – 150 votes, ⇨Maudling – 133 votes, ⇨Powell – 15 votes.) Chief Whip (1955–59), Minister of Labour (1959–60), Lord Privy Seal with special responsibility for foreign affairs (1960–63) and Secretary of State for Industry and President of the Board of Trade (1963–64), Heath was also Britain's chief negotiator for entry to the ⇨EEC (1961–63). As Prime Minister, Heath successfully re-opened negotiations for British entry to the ⇨EEC. MP for Bexley since 1950.

Heikal, Muhammad Hasanein (1924–). Editor of the UAR newspaper *Al Ahram*, one of the most influential journals in the Middle East, particularly as it is thought to reflect the official viewpoint.

Heinemann, Dr Gustav (1899–). President of the German Federal Republic since March 1969 and the first Social Democrat to hold this office since F. Ebert presided over the first German (⇨Weimar) Republic. A lawyer by profession, he was a prominent member of the anti-Nazi Confessional Church for which he printed clandestine pamphlets. One of the founding members of the ⇨CDU, he became Minister of Justice in Dr ⇨Adenauer's first Cabinet, but opposing German re-armament, resigned (Oct. 1950). Leaving the CDU in 1952, he founded the All German People's Party which by its pacifism and neutralism hoped to create the pre-condition for German reunification. The party failed to prosper and he joined the ⇔SPD (1957), where he made a name for himself as the party's legal expert – defending the news magazine *Der Spiegel* against Minister ⇔Strauss (1962). In Dec. 1966 he joined the ⇔Kiesinger coalition government as Minister of Justice.

Helou, Charles (1911–). President of the ⇔Lebanon (1964–70). He was formerly Minister of Justice and Health (1954–55) and Minister of Education (1964).

Hertzog, James Barry Munnik (1866–1942). Prime Minister of South Africa (1924–29 and 1933–39). A general in the Boer War and a minister in Botha's first Cabinet which he left in 1912. Opposed to South African participation in the war (1914) and even earlier to the Botha – ⇔Smuts policy of conciliation between Englishmen and Afrikaaners, he founded the ⇔National Party. A leading exponent of racial segregation he was Prime Minister of the Union from 1924 to 1929, first in coalition with the Labour Party and from 1933 in coalition with Smuts (⇔United Party). He was South Africa's delegate to the Imperial Conferences which led to the Statute of ⇔Westminster. Committed to neutrality, he resigned in 1939. Even in opposition, he was unable to reconcile his differences with Dr ⇔Malan, and with his remaining followers Hertzog founded the Afrikaaner Party.

Hess, Rudolf (April 1894–). ⇔Hitler's deputy (1933–41) to whom the *Führer* dictated ⇔*Mein Kampf* during his imprisonment. In May 1941, Hess flew to Scotland in an unofficial attempt to persuade the British Government to join in the Nazi attack on Russia. Sentenced to life imprisonment at the ⇔Nuremberg War Crime Trials, he is now the only surviving prisoner at the four-power-administered Spandau prison.

Heuss, Professor Theodor (1884–1963). First President of the German Federal Republic (1949–1959). Professor of Politics, who represented the German Democratic Party in the *Reichstag* (1930–33) and later suffered persecution under the Nazis. During his two terms as President he did much both at home and abroad to inspire confidence in the new Germany and its democratic constitution which he as a member of the Constituent Assembly (1948–49) had helped to draw up.

High Commission Territories. Formerly the territories of Bechuanaland, Basutoland and Swaziland which came under British protection in the late nineteenth century. Economically dependent on the Republic of South Africa (the last two situated within its borders), it was originally assumed that they would become part of South Africa. Their development neglected by the UK Government, they nevertheless preferred British guardianship to incorporation in South Africa. Following increased internal autonomy, ⇨ Botswana (Bechuanaland) became independent in Sept. 1966, ⇨ Lesotho (Basutoland) in Oct. 1966, and ⇨ Swaziland in Sept. 1968.

Himmler, Heinrich (1900–45). Nazi Germany's Chief of Police, Supreme Commander of the ss and Commandant of all ⇨ Concentration Camps. Minister of the Interior (Aug. 1943) and C.-in-C. of the Reserve Army (July 1944), he raised the last *Volkssturm* levies of ill-equipped boys and old men. An early ⇨ Hitler supporter, his meteoric career started when given command of Hitler's 280 strong bodyguard (1929). He had transformed this *Schutzstaffel* (ss) into a tightly organized force of 52,000 men, selected for physical fitness and racial purity, sworn to unquestioning obedience – a mould and model of the new master-race – by the time Hitler assumed power in Jan. 1933. He was made Chief of Police in Munich (1933) and by June 1936 he was in command of all German police forces. Meanwhile he had successfully conspired against the powerful sa to which his ss was still subordinate. The ss was responsible for the execution of the sa Chief of Staff Röhm, other sa leaders and sundry political opponents, on Hitler's orders (30.6.1934). During the war Himmler's ss and police were responsible for the extermination of gypsies and Jews. On learning of his peace-making efforts, Hitler expelled Himmler from the party, one day before he committed suicide (29.4.1945). Himmler was arrested by the British soon afterwards and committed suicide.

Hindenburg, Paul von (1847–1934). Second President of the ⇨ Weimar Republic (1925–33), Field-Marshal and war hero. Hindenburg's election to President was hailed as a triumph for the conservative right but he owed his re-election in 1932 to the support of the Weimar parties, and especially to the Social Democrats, against the opposition of the anti-Weimar forces under ⇨ Hitler. His position as President inevitably made him a key figure in the last critical years of the Republic, but through lack of political experience and growing senility he succumbed to the influence of a political clique under von Papen, a situation which led to his reluctant appointment of Hitler as Chancellor in 1933. Hindenburg personally disapproved of Hitler, but he appeared to acquiesce in the abolition of democratic government and, in his role as a symbol of the old Prussian order, gave an appearance of respectability to the establishment of the Nazi dictatorship.

Hirohito, Emperor (1901–). Emperor of ⇨ Japan since 1926. He has never exercised effective executive power although from the 1930s until the end of World War II he was the object of emperor worship. He renounced his divinity in Jan. 1946 and has since been only a ceremonial figure.

Hispaniola. ⇨ Dominican Republic and ⇨ Haiti.

Hiss, Alger (1904–). Former US State Department official and peace organization president who was convicted of perjury in Federal Court (1950) for denying before a Senate committee that he had passed secret documents to a Soviet agent.

Hitler, Adolf (1889–1945). Founder and leader of the National Socialist German Workers' Party (⇨ NSDAP), *Führer* and Chancellor of the German *Reich* (1933–45). The son of a minor Austrian customs official, his youth and adolescence at Brannau and Linz were soured by frustration. Intending to become a painter but unable to pass the entrance examination to the Vienna Academy, he eked out a miserable existence as a commercial artist and odd job man, living for a time in a hostel for the city's down-and-outs. An avid reader, the young Hitler eagerly absorbed the anti-semitic and racialist notions particularly prevalent in Austria, where the Germans ruling over the multi-national Habsburg empire welcomed theories asserting their innate superiority. From Vienna he moved on to Munich (1913) where he seemed to have lived by the sale of his paintings until he volunteered for service in a Bavarian regiment at the outbreak of World War I. He served in the front line and was promoted to the rank of corporal. After the war, as an army political agent in post-war Munich, he joined (party member number seven) the obscure, nationalist German Workers' Party.

Having taken over control of the party and renamed it the *National-sozialistische Deutsche Arbeiterpartei* Hitler, by the sheer extravagance of his revanchist anti-democratic and anti-semitic harangues and the hypnotic power of his oratory, soon commanded general attention and a growing following. The training of para-military strong arm squads – the brown-shirted stormtroops (SA) – gave the movement additional power and made it a force in Munich politics. When the *Reich* was at loggerheads with Bavaria, Hitler in the so-called 'beer cellar putsch' (Nov. 1923) forced the representatives of the Bavarian government at gun-point to pledge support for a Nazi 'march on Berlin'. This ended ingloriously when loyal government troops fired at and dispersed the rebellious stormtroops led by Hitler and his lieutenants. The *Führer*, notwithstanding his pledge to triumph or perish, was arrested, tried and sentenced to five years imprisonment of which, however, he had to serve only nine months of gentlemanly confinement in an army fortress (Landsberg).

These months were spent in dictating the first volume of *Mein Kampf*, the autobiography in which he explained his basic racial and political philosophy. All human progress, Hitler asserted, was the collective achievement of races of which the Aryans were the most creative.

Among the Aryans the Germans were by far the most gifted and dynamic ethnic group. Jews, because they completely lacked Aryan creativity, could and did only survive by exploiting and appropriating to themselves the fruits of Aryan toil; hence their unremitting efforts to corrupt and destroy the Germans. 'Miscegenation', the onset of World War I, Bolshevik revolution, capitalist exploitation, the corruption of artistic standards, were all part of a world-wide Jewish conspiracy. German survival depended on the re-establishment of their racial purity, and the rejection of Jew-inspired ideologies including Christianity, which imposed the ethos of slaves on a race destined to rule. Hence 'the nameless masses whose fate it is to serve, must again be granted the blessing of illiteracy', while the master race must learn 'to be cruel with good conscience'.

Released from prison, Hitler rebuilt the party (1925) which his abortive and melodramatic putsch had all but destroyed. The way to power, he now realized, was to acquire it legally by the ballot. In the 1928 elections, the movement, having gained only 12 seats in the *Reichstag*, remained an irrelevant, practically unknown, extremist splinter group. But the desolation wrought by the world economic crisis (more than six million German unemployed in 1932) provided the climate of fear and resentment in which Hitler could successfully appeal to the growing number of the embittered and bewildered. By 1930 the NSDAP had become the second largest German party. Now feared and courted by the respectable right, Hitler had formed with the conservatives and the para-military ex-servicemen's league *Stahlhelm* a 'national opposition' (Harzburg front, Oct. 1931), which tried to destroy the Weimar Republic by obstructing parliamentary government. In this they had the support of the communists who, together with the 'national opposition', commanded a majority in parliament. These wrecking tactics produced governmental instability which in turn benefited Hitler. In the April 1932 presidential elections which he lost to the incumbent ⊂> Hindenburg, he obtained 13·4 m. votes and three months later, polling 37% of the vote, the NSDAP became Germany's largest party. Hitler, the 'Bohemian corporal', of whom Field-Marshal von Hindenburg was extremely suspicious, repeatedly refused Cabinet appointments, and as the leader of the largest party, insisted on being given the chancellorship.

When he received it (⊂> Third Reich) Hitler acquired powers more complete and far-reaching than any German prince or Emperor had ever held before. In a series of diplomatic and military triumphs he also extended the frontiers of the *Reich* beyond its furthest historic boundaries. In the vast empire over which he briefly ruled barbaric repression was practised on a scale previously unknown. During the war, the *Führer*'s megalomania increased; he became the 'supreme war lord' and from Dec. 1941 onwards personally directed the operation of his field armies. Afflicted by an undiagnosed disease and kept alive by constant medication, he refused to acknowledge defeat when the tide of war turned against him. Neither the abortive attempt on his life (⇨ Twentieth July 1944) nor the mounting destruction of Germany could shake his determination to fight on. Besieged in his chancellory shelter amidst the burning ruins of Berlin, he committed suicide with his mistress Eva Braun whom he had married a few hours previously.

Hitler-Stalin Pact. On 23 Aug. 1939 Germany and the USSR concluded a ten-year Treaty of Non-Aggression. In a Secret Additional Protocol to the Treaty, the two sides agreed on a boundary between their respective spheres of influence in the event of territorial and political changes in ⇨ Poland, ⇨ Finland and the ⇨ Baltic States. The Secret Protocol also acknowledged the interest of the USSR in ⇨ Bessarabia. On 1 Sept. 1939, ⇨ World War II began with Germany's invasion of Western Poland. On 17 Sept., the USSR began its invasion of Eastern Poland. On 28 Sept., the USSR and Germany concluded a second 'German-Soviet Boundary and Friendship Treaty'. This second Treaty formally divided Poland between the two countries along a line described as definite. In a Secret Supplementary Protocol to the second Treaty, both sides undertook to suppress in their territories all Polish agitation affecting the territory of the other side and to inform each other concerning suitable measures for this purpose.

In Nov. 1940, after the conclusion of the military alliance between Germany, Italy and Japan, the Soviet Prime Minister and Foreign Minister, V. M. ⇨ Molotov, was invited to visit Hitler in Berlin to discuss a world-wide division of spheres of influence between the tripartite alliance and the USSR. During the visit the German Foreign Minister, von Ribbentrop, produced a draft agreement outlining these and other aims. On 25 Nov., Molotov informed the German Ambassador in Moscow that the Soviet Government agreed to accept the German draft agreement for a Four-Power Pact on the condition of its being supplemented by a number of agreements on specific points concerning the security and economic interests of the USSR in Europe and the Far East. The conditional Soviet acceptance of the German draft agreement remained unanswered. On 18 Dec. 1940 Hitler issued the directive for the 'Operation Barbarossa', designed to 'crush Soviet Russia in a quick campaign'.

Hoare-Laval Plan (Dec. 1935). Secret Franco-British proposals to 'appease' ⇨ Mussolini by Abyssinian territorial and political concessions to Italy. Its publication led to the resignation of both its authors. (⇨UK, ⇨Ethiopia.)

Ho Chi Minh (1890–1969). Former President of the Democratic Republic of Vietnam (VDR); Chairman of the Central Committee's Polit-bureau of the Vietnam Workers' Party.

Ho Chi Minh was the second adopted name of Nguyen That Than, born in Annam (in central Vietnam). An anti-colonialist from his early youth, the first pseudonym he chose for himself was Nguyen Ai Quoc, meaning Nguyen the Patriot. He travelled abroad (from 1911) and settled in France towards the end of World War I. A member of the French Socialist Party, he sided with the Left which, at the Tours Congress in 1920 split off in order to join the ⇨Communist International (Comintern). Nguyen thus became one of the founder-members of the French Communist Party though he was later to criticize it sharply for its lack of interest in the colonial question. In 1923 he went to Moscow to study at the Communist University of the Toilers of the East, set up in 1921 as a training centre for Asian communists, and he soon became a figure of importance in the Comintern. Two years later he returned to Asia entrusted with the task of promoting the cause of revolution in Indochina. The chief Soviet emissary in Asia at the time was Mikhail Borodin, acting as the official adviser to the ⇨Kuomintang in Canton. The multi-lingual Nguyen Ai Quoc acted as Borodin's translator but devoted most of his energies to the recruiting and training of young fellow-expatriates for the revolutionary anti-colonial war of the future. For this purpose he organized the Association of Revolutionary Annamite Youth – the forerunner of the Indochinese Communist Party, which he founded in 1930 and which, in turn, was the forerunner of the Vietnam Workers' Party, now ruling in North Vietnam. Between 1927, when Nguyen was forced to quit China, and 1940, when he once again sought refuge there, he seems to have been on the move most of the time, engaged in anti-colonialist propaganda and the organization of revolutionary groups in many parts of South-East Asia, including Malaya, Siam and the Dutch East Indies as well as Indochina. After the failure of an attempted uprising against the French in Indochina (1940), Nguyen escaped to South China where he soon afterwards founded the ⇨Viet Minh. From about that time onwards he called himself Ho Chi Minh and his personal history melted into the wider history of the struggle over ⇨Vietnam. The role he played in that struggle, allowing for the differences in their personalities and circumstances, is comparable to that played by ⇨Mao Tse-tung in ⇨China. Like Mao, Ho Chi Minh came to power not in the wake of the Soviet or other foreign armies but through the victory of the forces under his own leadership in a long drawn-out revolutionary war, the only anti-colonial war ever fought and won under communist leadership.

Hogg, Quintin (formerly Lord Hailsham) (1907–). Held ministerial rank in successive UK Conservative administrations from 1956 to 1964. He renounced his peerage to contest the Party leadership in 1963 having previously been Tory Leader in the House of Lords (1960–63). Known for his radical Toryism and fiery temperament, he has strongly opposed his political associates on the right in any attempt to use racialism to gain electoral support. Appointed Lord Chancellor (1970).

Holland. ⇨ Netherlands, Kingdom of.

Holocaust. Refers to the persecution, deportation and extermination of Jews in Nazi-occupied Europe. After the outbreak of World War II, Nazi Germany, implementing Hitler's repeated threats (*Reichstag* speech, 30.1.1939), set out to destroy the Jews in the growing number of countries under its control. They were all deported to the ghettos and work camps in Poland's Government General. When the death rate resulting from malnutrition, slave labour and sporadic mass-shootings proved too slow, a special meeting of high-ranking civil servants and SS officers (⇨ Eichmann) was convened (Wannsee Conference, Jan. 1942) to lay down guide-lines for the Final Solution, the physical destruction of Jews. Special extermination camps (Auschwitz, Belsen, Chelmno, Treblinka, etc.) were built, boasting technically perfected installations for mass-gassing and body disposal. Estimates of the numbers killed vary from 4·5–6 million.

Holt, Harold (1908–67). Prime Minister of ⇨ Australia and leader of the Liberal Party (1966–67). His short term of office was marked by stronger attachment to the American alliance and increased military commitment in the Vietnam War, on which issue he won an increased majority for his party in the general election of 1966.

Holyoake, Sir Keith (1904–) was ⇨ New Zealand Prime Minister and Minister for Foreign Affairs (1960–72), and leader of the National Party from 1957 to 1972. He was Deputy Prime Minister and Minister of Agriculture (1949–57), Prime Minister for a short time in 1957 and Leader of the Opposition (1957–60). He retired as Prime Minister in March 1972 in favour of John Marshall.

Home Communists. ⇨ Sovietization.

Honduras. *Area* – 43,227 sq. miles. *Population* (1969 est.) – 2,535,000. *President* – Dr Ramon Ernesto Cruz (1971–). *Constitution* (1965) – Unitary Republic, with an elected President and uni-cameral Congress.

The political development of Honduras has shown an attachment to the forms rather than the reality of constitutional government. The country is economically underdeveloped (half the population illiterate) and heavily dependent on US investment in its fruit plantations. Political development stagnated under Tiburcio Carias Andino (1933–49) who dispensed with elections for 16 years. Progress made under President Galvez (1949–54) was followed by manoeuvres (1954–57) to prevent the popular Ramon Villeda Morales from taking office. President under a new constitution, Villeda Morales (1957–63) put forward a programme of modernization and reform. On election day (1963), army chief Lopez Arellano staged a coup and ruled as provisional President till his (perhaps manipulated) election as President in 1965. In 1971 the Nationalist Party won the presidential election, having previously nominated Dr Cruz to head a coalition government.

Hong Kong. *Area* – 398 sq. miles. *Population* – 3,800,000. *Constitution* – British Crown Colony administered by the Governor through an Executive Council and a Legislative Council.

One of the principal *entrepôt* ports of the world and an important British military base, Hong Kong was conquered by the Japanese during ⇨ World War II but was returned to the UK after the cessation of hostilities. The colony suffered as a result of the embargo imposed on strategic goods to Communist China during the ⇨ Korean War (1951) but has since concentrated on developing industry (the products of which now comprise three-quarters of total exports). Economic success has helped to offset the disadvantages of her exposed position to the Chinese mainland, underlined during the communist-inspired riots of 1967 when the water supply was cut off. The absorption of more than one million refugees from the mainland since the communist assumption of power in 1949 has created enormous social and educational difficulties. These difficulties are only partly mitigated by intensive resettlement programmes, for the colony has the second highest birthrate in Asia (32.8 per 1,000) and a high density of population (8,600 per sq. mile). Hong Kong has been exempted from the British military withdrawal ⇨ East of Suez by 1971.

Hoover, Herbert Clark (1874–1964). Thirty-first President of the United States. Of Quaker parents, he amassed a fortune as a mining engineer. With the outbreak of World War I he became involved with the Committee for Relief in Belgium (1914) until he was appointed US Food Administrator (1917). Served as Secretary of Commerce under Presidents Harding and Coolidge (1921–28) and expanded and reorganized the Department. In 1928 Hoover received the Republican Party's nomination for the presidency and defeated Democrat Alfred W. Smith. After the Stock Market crash in 1929 Hoover failed to adjust adequately to new conditions. As foreign trade fell, banks failed and unemployment rose, he continued his opposition to direct government assistance to the unemployed, advocating the 'trickle down' theory of aid to big business instead. Although Hoover had anticipated some of the ⇨ New Deal measures and laid the foundation for the ⇨ Good Neighbour Policy towards Latin America, his loss of the presidential election to Franklin D. ⇨ Roosevelt in 1932 was considered a repudiation of his policies. He entered public life again after World War II, and was appointed chairman of two Commissions on the Organization of the Executive Branch of Government – the first and second ⇨ Hoover Commissions (1947–49, 1953–55). He was author of many books including his *Memoirs* (1951–52) and *The Ordeal of Woodrow Wilson* (1958).

Hoover, John Edgar (1895–1972). US lawyer and director of the ⇨ FBI. He entered the Justice Department as a special assistant to the Attorney General (1919–21) and became head of the FBI in 1924. Hoover was given responsibility for maintaining internal security in World War II and was criticized for his methods of investigation. Hoover died in office, having been head of the FBI for 48 years, serving eight Presidents. In his later years he was much criticized for his 'reactionary' views on ⇨ Civil Rights and dissent, but in Congress even his detractors were drawn into supporting congratulatory resolutions passed in his honour.

Hoover Commission. Refers to either of two Commissions on the Organization of the Executive Branch of the Government in the USA, both headed by former President Herbert ⇨ Hoover. The first was set up in 1947, and was composed of 12 members, 4 chosen by each House of Congress and the President. When it reported in 1949, Congress authorized the President to make proposals for reorganizing Federal agencies, based on its recommendations, which would take effect unless specifically rejected by both Houses. About three-quarters of the recommendations of the First Hoover Commission have since been acted on. The Second Hoover Commission, similarly composed, was established in 1953 and reported in 1955. Its terms of reference were widened to include questions of policy, and its recommendations were consequently more controversial, particularly those involving the return to private enterprise of activities taken on by public authorities. A number of States have set up similar bodies, often called 'little Hoover groups'.

Hopkins, Harry Lloyd (1890–1946). An adviser to President ⇨ Roosevelt during World War II, he entered public service as head of the Federal Emergency Relief Administration (1933). Appointed administrator for the Works Progress Administration (WPA) in 1935, he entered the ⇨ Cabinet three years later as Secretary of Commerce. Considered to be one of Roosevelt's most trusted advisers during the war years, he accompanied the President to several major conferences and acted as his personal emissary on special missions to London and Moscow. Hopkins resigned as special adviser to Truman in 1945.

Horthy, Admiral N. ⇨ Hungary.

'Hot Line'. A direct telecommunications link between the ⇨ White House and the Kremlin established by the USA–USSR Memorandum of Understanding signed in Geneva (20.6.1963). Its establishment was prompted by the ⇨ Cuban Missile Crisis of 1962.

Houphouët-Boigny, Félix (1905–). President of the ⇨ Ivory Coast since 1958. He was elected to the French Constituent Assembly (1945) and then to the French Assembly (1946) and was re-elected in 1951 and 1956. Through the RDA (*Rassemblement Démocratique Africain*), which he formed in 1947, Houphouët-Boigny played a major part in the political developments in ⇨ French West Africa which subsequently led to independence for its constituent territories. In 1958 he resigned a ministerial post in the French Government to become Prime Minister of the Ivory Coast. He was elected to the presidency in the same year and re-elected in 1965. With the independence of the former French territories and the different policies pursued by those territories, the RDA has rapidly declined in importance. However, Houphouët-Boigny's prestige remains high and he has continued to dominate his country's politics and to oversee her economic development. (⇨ Mali, Federation of.)

House of Commons. ⇨ UK Constitution.

House of Lords. ⇨ UK Constitution.

House of Representatives. The first and larger of the two houses of ⇨ Congress in the USA, the other being the ⇨ Senate. 'The House' is composed of 435 Congressmen elected from congressional districts that are distributed among the States in proportion to their population. This somewhat redresses the balance in the Senate in which all States are represented by two Senators each. The Constitution lays down that each State must have at least one representative; but the total membership was only finally fixed by Act of Congress in 1929. The seats are subject to reapportionment among the States after the census which takes place every ten years. After the 1970 census, seven States were assigned one seat each, and twenty-four had five or fewer. Nine States were between them given over half the total seats, the largest number (43) going to California, and the second largest (39) to New York. However, the distribution of seats within the States through the drawing of congressional district boundaries is left almost wholly to the State Legislatures. This has given rise to the widespread practice of ⇨ Gerrymandering, so that the population is by no means equally represented in the House. Reflecting the preponderance of rural representatives in State Legislatures, the rural population is overrepresented in the House (as well as, legitimately, in the Senate), and the urban and suburban population correspondingly underrepresented. This is said to have contributed to the neglect and decay of American cities. In 1964 the ⇨ Supreme Court, acting on the provision for 'equal protection of the law' contained in the ⇨ Fourteenth Amendment to the Constitution, declared that the value of votes in congressional elections should be as nearly as practicable equal. This may eventually result in substantial changes in the composition and character of the House.

Minimum qualifications for membership, as laid down in the Constitution, are that a member must be 25 years of age, seven years a citizen of the USA and, when elected, an inhabitant of the State for which he is chosen. The 'residence rule' is often interpreted quite strictly in the case of candidates for election to the House of Representatives; they are expected to be long-standing residents of the districts they seek to represent. This means that Congressmen are very much local representatives, in marked contrast to British MPs. Some States, however, have some or all of their representatives elected from the whole State, these being called 'congressmen-at-large'. The entire House, together with a third of the Senate, is elected every two years, and the short term of Congressmen further strengthens their local ties. At elections for the 92nd Congress held on 3 Nov. 1970, the state of the parties in the House was: ⇨ Democratic Party 255; ⇨ Republican Party, 180.

The presiding officer is the Speaker. He is the choice of the majority party, as are the other officers of the House. The Speaker is a very powerful political figure in Congress (sometimes the most powerful) and in the nation. He may even at times have a greater influence, certainly over legislation, than the nation's President. However, his ascendancy is based on his political influence with his party rather than his formal authority over the House, and the power of the office consequently varies with the man. Sam ⇨ Rayburn, who was Speaker for 17 years between 1940 and 1961, was particularly powerful.

The powers of the House are similar to those of the Senate, being those granted to Congress generally by the Constitution. Its principal powers are those concerned with legislation, though most of the legislative work is done by standing ⇨ Congressional Committees in both houses. The House has a special importance in relation to ⇨Appropriations inasmuch as revenue bills must originate there.

Partly because of the shorter term and (in most cases) smaller constituencies of Congressmen, the House is generally regarded as the more 'popular' of the two houses, with a more 'local' and less 'national' out-look than the Senate. It does not enjoy the same high esteem and authority among the public – perhaps because its larger membership leads to greater reliance on rules and, consequently, less open debate than in the Senate. It tends to be a more conservative body than the Senate, contrary to the expectations of the framers of the Constitution; but it is much more sensitive to changes in the public mood.

Hoveida, Amir Abbas (1919–). Prime Minister of ⇔Iran since 1965, he was formerly a diplomat (1942–58) and served as Minister of Finance (1964–65).

Hoxha, Enver (1908–). First Secretary, Albanian Workers' Party. While a student in France Hoxha became a Marxist and a member of the French Communist Party. He returned to ⇔Albania in 1936 and in 1941 became the leading founder member of the Albanian Communist Party and its Secretary-General, a post he has retained ever since under the changed title of First Secretary of the Albanian Workers' Party. The leader of the communist war-time Resistance, he was proclaimed Commander-in-Chief of the National Liberation Army (May 1944) and in Sept. 1944 he assumed the premiership in the newly created Pro-visional Government. A self-professed admirer of ⇔Stalin as well as of ⇔Mao Tse-tung, he has ruled Albania ever since as a dictator in the Stalinist tradition.

HUAC. United States House of Representatives Committee on Un-American activities, now the House Internal Security Committee (HISC) – an important ⇔Congressional Committee dealing with loyalty and security matters. It was originally concerned with the problem of persons who might be presumed to have sympathies with the Axis during World War II; but after the war, and especially after the onset of the Cold War, it became increasingly preoccupied with 'internal sub-version' by communists. During the period of ⇔McCarthyism, the Committee had considerable influence on popular opinion and public policy, participating in the 'witch hunts' that overtook America in the wake of the Korean War, and promoting Federal loyalty-and-security measures like the ⇔Subversive Activities Control Board and the ⇔Communist Control Act. HUAC continued its operations after the departure of Senator Joe McCarthy, becoming more prominent in the field than any comparable body in the Senate. Opposition to it began to grow towards the end of the 1950s, and in the 1960s it has been openly and vigorously denounced in many quarters. Championed by the ⇔New Right, it remains a particular *bête noire* of the American ⇔New Left. As HISC, it investigated the ⇔Black Panther Party over a two-year period beginning in 1969, but recommended no action to Congress. It has also attempted to revive action against Communists, but its recommendations have been largely ignored by the House.

Huggins. ⇨ Malvern, Lord.

Hull, Cordell (1871–1955). US Secretary of State (1933–44). He served in the Tennessee Legislature (1893–97), the US House of Representatives (1907–21, 1923–31) and as Senator from Tennessee (1931–33). Hull was an initiator of the ⇨ Good Neighbour Policy towards Latin America in the thirties, and later called for US aid to the Allies at the start of World War II. Famous as the 'father of the United Nations', he received the Nobel Prize (1945) for his part in building the world organization.

Humphrey, Hubert H. (1911–). US Democratic politician, Senator, and Vice-President of the USA (1965–69). He became Mayor of Minneapolis in 1945 and three years later was elected to the US Senate from Minnesota. During his 16 years in the Senate, Humphrey became known for his strongly liberal philosophy, and was especially effective in promoting farm and welfare programmes. In 1960 he announced his candidacy for the Democratic nomination for President, but was eliminated before the Convention after losing decisively in presidential ⇨ Primary Elections to John F. ⇨ Kennedy. In his remaining years in the Senate he served as Majority Whip (1961–64) and was largely responsible for guiding the Civil Rights Bill (1964) and the ⇨ Nuclear Test Ban Treaty through the Senate. In the 1964 presidential elections, Lyndon ⇨ Johnson chose Humphrey as his running-mate. As Vice-President he proved an asset to Johnson and vigorously supported the President's policy in Vietnam. After Johnson removed himself from the candidacy in 1968, the Vice-President entered the competition for the Democratic nomination along with Senators Robert F. ⇨ Kennedy and Eugene ⇨ McCarthy. Although he was successful in gaining his party's nomination, the turmoil at the Convention in Chicago, as well as his own inability to separate his position from that of the President, left the Democratic Party severely divided before the election, and handicapped his campaign. The Vice-President and his running-mate, Edmund Muskie, finally lost a close election to Republicans Richard ⇨ Nixon and Spiro Agnew.

A candidate for the Democratic nomination again in 1972, he was passed over by the Convention at Miami Beach in favour of Sen. George ⇨ McGovern.

Hundred Flowers Campaign. ⇨ China.

Hungary – Hungarian People's Republic. *Area* – 35,912 sq. miles. *Population* (1970 est.) – 10,334,000. *Chairman, Presidential Council* – Pal Losonczi. *Prime Minister* – Jeno Fock. *First Secretary, Hungarian*

Socialist Workers' Party - Janos ⇨ Kadar. The highest organ of state power is the National Assembly, the uni-cameral Legislature elected by universal suffrage from a single list of candidates. Effective power lies with the leadership of the (communist) Hungarian Socialist Workers' Party (HSWP), headed by Janos Kadar.

As a result of the Peace Treaty of Trianon (June 1920) Hungary lost its former status as a dominating European power and about two-thirds of its pre-war territory. Its principal foreign policy aim in the inter-war period was the recovery of at least part of these losses. Internally, the short-lived Soviet Republic of 1919 was followed by a period of White Terror and then by the emergence of a conservative regime of the extreme Right, which restored, with little change, the semi-feudal conditions of the past and was dominated by the Regent, Admiral Horthy. As a result of the ⇨ Munich Agreement (Sept. 1938), Hungary regained southern Slovakia and, after the Vienna Award of Aug. 1940, northern ⇨ Transylvania. In Nov. 1940, Hungary joined the ⇨ Tripartite Pact and, in 1941, Germany's invasion of, first, ⇨ Yugoslavia and then the USSR. In the spring of 1944, Germany occupied Hungary to counteract the increasing war-weariness of its people, and installed a new government which outlawed the hitherto semi-legal opposition parties and drove Hungary's surviving Jews into Hitler's death camps. On 15 Oct. 1944, Admiral Horthy, faced with the imminent approach of the Soviet armies, announced his intention to surrender. The reply was a German-backed *coup d'état* by Szalasi, the leader of the fascist Arrow Cross party, who imposed a reign of mounting terror and atrocities and continued the war.

Meanwhile, in the areas liberated by the Soviet armies, Hungarian communists returning from the USSR sponsored the formation of a coalition between their own party, the Smallholders, the Social Democrats and the (left-wing) National Peasant Party. In April 1945, this coalition became the new Provisional Government which inaugurated a radical land reform and a new electoral law. On the basis of this new law, free elections were held in Nov. 1945, which resulted in an absolute majority for the Smallholders (57%). They were nevertheless compelled by Soviet pressure to re-establish the old coalition and to instal a communist in the Ministry of the Interior, which went first to Imre ⇨ Nagy, the previous Minister of Agriculture, and, after a few months, to Laszlo ⇨ Rajk. The Communist Party, under the leadership of Matyas ⇨ Rakosi, then proceeded to liquidate its coalition partners one by one. This objective was achieved within three years. By a long series of denunciations, arrests, purges and other police interventions, first the Smallholders and then the National Peasant Party were rendered impotent by the replacement of their own leaders with communist nominees. The Social Democrats, under relentless pressure, eventually submitted to fusion with the communists, while the surviving independent peasant and socialist leaders escaped abroad. Bela Kovacs, the General Secretary of the Smallholders Party, was arrested by Soviet troops (Feb. 1947), while the simultaneous battle against the Church led to the arrest of Cardinal ⇨ Mindszenty (Dec. 1948). The formal adoption of a Soviet-type constitution in April 1949 marked the completion of ⇨ Sovietization.

By that time, the Communist Party (renamed Hungarian Workers' Party – HWP) had itself become engulfed in a purge, which began after ⇨ Tito's break with ⇨ Stalin and ended in the liquidation of the leading ⇨ Home Communists by the ⇨ Muscovites. The purge culminated in the ⇨ Show Trial and execution of Laszlo Rajk in Oct. 1949 but continued for a long time afterwards, accompanied by collectivization and the other facets of Sovietization. After Stalin's death, Rakosi tried to adapt himself to the new climate in Moscow by resigning from the premiership, which he had assumed in 1952 in addition to his post as the party's Secretary General. The new Premier appointed in July 1953 was Imre Nagy who became the chief spokesman of a 'New Course' of reform. His political and economic reforms, which included a halt in compulsory collectivization, the release of many political prisoners and far-reaching freedom in cultural activities, exceeded the limits which Rakosi was prepared to tolerate. In April 1955, Nagy was removed from the premiership and expelled from his party posts. Immediately afterwards Rakosi's own position became endangered as a result of ⇨ Tito's public rehabilitation by ⇨ Khrushchev and Khrushchev's subsequent denunciation of Stalin at the 20th CPSU Congress. Soviet orders transmitted by ⇨ Mikoyan combined with internal pressures to oust Rakosi from the HWP leadership. He resigned in July 1956 having made sure that he was succeeded by his fellow-Stalinist, Ernest ⇨ Gerö.

The internal opposition was led by intellectuals, outstanding among them the members of the ⇨ Petöfi Club and ex-victims of political persecution who had been freed by Nagy. There was widespread anger about the choice of Gerö as Rakosi's successor and, despite the rehabilitation of Nagy, Rajk and others, there was none of the renewal for which people had been hoping comparable to the changes which just then seemed to be occurring in ⇨ Poland. The Polish crisis in mid-October was the final spark. On 22 and 23 Oct., massive demonstrations of students and workers in Budapest and other centres called for a new government under Nagy and the withdrawal of Soviet troops. On 24 Oct., Nagy became the new Premier. Almost simultaneously Soviet tanks opened fire on unarmed demonstrators. It was this action which turned originally peaceful demonstrations into a national revolution in which Hungarian army units fought shoulder to shoulder with the country's students, workers and peasants against the Soviet occupation forces and their own Secret Police troops. Nagy then announced a new programme, including free elections, negotiations for the withdrawal of the Soviet forces, Hungary's withdrawal from the ⇨Warsaw Pact and a policy of permanent neutrality. Gerö was replaced as Party Secretary by Kadar who also joined Nagy's government. In the name of the party, renamed HSWP, Kadar supported the new programme, and, after negotiations with ⇨ Suslov and Mikoyan, the Soviet forces withdrew. On 3 Nov., Kadar went over to the Soviet side. The Soviet forces returned in strength and, in a second intervention, crushed the revolution after desperate resistance. Ever since then, communists have described the revolution as a 'counter-revolution'. Nagy and other resistance leaders were executed as traitors, and Kadar became the undisputed new leader. After a period of severe reprisals, he sought to achieve reconciliation by a programme of reforms and cautious liberalization. By the late 1960s the new policies had achieved notable successes and gained the regime a measure of public confidence. This confidence received a severe fresh jolt from Hungary's participation in the invasion of ⇨ Czechoslovakia in Aug. 1968, which the regime has been trying to live down ever since.

Husak, G. (1913–). First Secretary of the Czechoslovak Communist Party. A communist since the early 1930s, Husak was one of the chief organizers and leaders of the Slovak uprising of Aug. 1944. A champion of Slovak rights within the Czechoslovak Republic, he was accused of 'bourgeois–nationalist' deviations (1950) and tried and imprisoned on those charges (1954). Released in 1960, he was rehabilitated in slow stages and resumed full political activities only shortly before ⇨Dubček became Party First Secretary (Jan. 1968). A strong supporter of Dubček's reform programme, Husak became (April 1968) Deputy Premier in charge of the country's proposed federalization. After the Soviet and allied invasion (Aug. 1968), he was elected First Secretary of the Slovak Communist Party and emerged thereafter as the principal spokesman for a realistic acceptance of the facts of the occupation. In April 1969, he replaced Alexander Dubček as the Czechoslovak communist party's First Secretary.

Hussain, Zakir (1897–1969). President of ⇨ India (1967–69) and the first Moslem to hold that office. He was formerly Governor of Bihar (1957–62) and Vice-President (1962–67).

Hussein Ibn Talal, King (1935–). King of ⇨Jordan since 1952. While sharing the common Arab opposition to the State of Israel, he has generally tried to follow a more moderate line in Middle East conflicts and has opposed the pan-Arab ambitions of President ▷ Nasser, e.g. in 1958 he set up an Arab federation with Iraq in opposition to the newly-created UAR. He has been criticized by the ▷ Arab League for his pro-West policies, e.g. his acceptance of the ▷ Eisenhower Doctrine. Domestic pressures, particularly the presence of a large community of refugee Palestinian Arabs and the constant threat of subversion from neighbouring Arab states, have inevitably strongly influenced his decisions – his dismissal of General ▷ Glubb being a case in point. Although relations with the UAR had not been good and often bitter, Hussein suddenly signed a defence agreement with that country when he visited Cairo just before the Arab–Israeli War of 1967 (▷ Arab–Israeli Conflict). The loss of the West Bank and other results of the 1967 war have increased his difficulties.

I

Ibn Saud, King (*c.* 1880–1953). Founder of ⇨ Saudi Arabia and its first King (1932–53). In 1926 he became King of Najd and Hijaz, and after consolidating his power over most of the Arabian peninsula, changed the name of the kingdom to Saudi Arabia. His first years were spent in internal reconstruction, especially in forcing the rebellious nomadic tribes to settle on the land. The major event of his reign was the discovery (1932) and exploitation of oil, which transformed the economy and strategic importance of the country.

Ibos. ⇨ Nigeria.

ICA. United States International Cooperation Administration – an agency established within the ⇨ State Department in 1955 with responsibility for co-ordinating foreign aid programmes and administering non-military aspects of the ⇨ Mutual Security Program. Its main concern was with the provision of technical assistance and other aid directed towards the economic advancement of less-developed nations and, less directly, with maintaining their security and stability. It superseded ⇨ FOA and was itself replaced by ⇨ AID in 1961.

ICC. United States Interstate Commerce Commission – an ⇨ Independent Regulatory Commission established in 1887 to administer Federal transport regulations. At that time, the ⇨ Commerce Clause under which the regulations were made was narrowly construed by the Supreme Court; but the functions of the ICC have steadily expanded as new forms of transport have been introduced and greater Federal regulation of trade has been allowed, though much more is done by the newer ⇨ FTC. Following the Supreme Court ruling in ⇨ Brown v. Board of Education (1954) against ⇨ Segregation in the South, the ICC required passenger integration on all interstate transport under its jurisdiction from 1955. Its 11 members are appointed for seven years each by the President with the consent of the Senate.

Iceland, Republic of. *Area* – 39,750 sq. miles. *Population* – 196,000. *President* – K. Eldjarn (1968–). *Prime Minister* – O. Johanesson (1971–). *Constitution* – Formerly joined to ⇨ Denmark but since 1944 an independent Republic. Executive power is vested in the President, directly elected (for a four-year term) who acts through a Cabinet, responsible to the bi-cameral Parliament (*Althing*). Elected by universal suffrage, the *Althing* elects one-third of its own members to form the Upper Chamber.

The upheavals of World War II and the occupation of Denmark by Germany, and of Iceland by British (May 1940) and later American (July 1941) troops precipitated the attainment of independence. Allowing the Icelandic-Danish Treaty of Union to lapse, Iceland in a plebiscite (May 1944) voted overwhelmingly in favour of becoming an independent Republic. The war-time presence of about 80,000 Anglo-American troops and the influx of capital, although it caused inflation, had far-reaching results on the country's economy. Land-reclamation, electrification, road-building, etc. transformed a once poor and backward country into a prosperous one. After the war and the evacuation of Allied troops, the retention and manning of American bases became a hotly disputed domestic issue, even though Iceland had joined ⇨NATO (April 1949). At present the Americans are allowed to run Keflavik air-base. The Icelandic decision to extend her territorial waters from three to twelve miles from her coast led to the so-called 'cod war' (1958–64) with Britain, whose trawlers were most directly affected and, backed by naval protection, defied the new limits. The dispute was temporarily settled when Iceland imposed the new limits allowing British trawlers to fish within six miles of her coast for a transitional period expiring in 1964, but flared up again in 1972 when she attempted to extend the limits still further to 50 miles. Iceland joined the ⇨Council of Europe and is a founder member of the ⇨Nordic Council.

Ifni ⇨ Spanish Territories in Africa.

Ikeda, Hayato (1899–1965). Prime Minister of ⇨Japan (1960–64) and leader of the Liberal Democratic Party. His previous posts included Finance Minister (1956–58) and Minister for Foreign Trade and Industry (1959–60).

Imperialism. The extension of a state's territorial (⇨ Colonialism), economic or political dominion over other countries. It particularly refers to the nineteenth-century expansion of Europe overseas and the ensuing territorial rivalries of the metropolitan powers. Imperial policies were advocated and defended as a means of: extending the boundaries of civilization and the 'rule of law' (the White man's burden), stimulating trade and protecting vital national interests. For supporters of ⇨Marxism, following ⇨Lenin, these policies had to result in war, and imperialism, regarded as the last stage of 'monopoly capitalism', was inevitably doomed. With the rise of nationalism and the rapid post-1945 disintegration of the old colonial empires, the term is now most often used as a synonym for exploitation or the attempt of any government to impose its policies on others. Hence its applicability not only to Western but also to contemporary Russian and Chinese policies.

Inauguration. USA – the formal induction of a President or Governor. The inauguration of a President is normally a major ceremonial occasion, including a military parade, and the delivery by the President of an 'inaugural address' on being sworn in. The oath of office, customarily administered by the Chief Justice of the Supreme Court, is prescribed by the Constitution as follows:

'I do solemnly swear (or affirm) that I will faithfully execute the office of President of the United States, and will, to the best of my ability, preserve, protect, and defend the Constitution of the United States.'

Independent Agency. In the USA, an administrative agency of the Federal government not located within any of the 12 Departments whose heads are members of the President's ⇨ Cabinet. The head of such an agency is therefore directly responsible to the President, who appoints him with the consent of the Senate, and who can dismiss him at any time.

Independent Regulatory Commission. In the USA, an administrative agency established by Congress to exercise public authority in a specified field. These bodies are empowered to make and apply regulations having the force of law, thereby performing 'quasi-legislative' and 'quasi-judicial' functions as well as executive and administrative ones. Thus they do not conform to the theory of the ⇨ Separation of Powers that characterizes American government, and this is the essence of their 'independence'. Members of their boards are appointed by the President with the consent of the Senate in the usual manner; but the President cannot dismiss them except on grounds specified by law, and their appointments are often for very long terms (cf. the ⇨ Federal Reserve System). Their decisions are not subject to approval by the President or Congress, though they can sometimes be challenged in the courts. Generally, however, they work in close cooperation with the Administration. They represent an American method of dealing with the universal problems of delegated legislation and administrative autonomy.

India. *Area* – 1,127,345 sq. miles. *Population* – 550 m. (about 11% are Moslems). *President* – Varahgiri ⇨ Giri (1969–). *Prime Minister* – Mrs Indira ⇨ Gandhi (1966–). *Constitution* (1950) – The Union of India is an independent Federal Republic within the ⇨ Commonwealth. Executive power is vested in the President, elected for five years by the

Legislature, who acts on the advice of the Prime Minister and Cabinet, who are responsible to Parliament. Parliament consists of the *Rajya Sabha* (Council of States), whose members are elected by the state legislative assemblies, and the *Lok Sabha* (House of the People), elected by universal suffrage for five years. The Union comprises 17 self-governing states and eight centrally-administered territories.

Part of the British Empire until 1947, India is the largest non-communist parliamentary state in Asia and has played a major role in international politics as a leader of the non-aligned nations. The nationalist movement became an important political force after World War I, which stimulated Indian political consciousness. This found expression in indignation at the Amritsar massacre (1919) and dis-appointment with the Government of India Act (1919), granting some powers to elected officials in the provinces but retaining great powers in the appointed governors. Mahatma ⇨ Gandhi organized the Indian National Congress (founded 1885) into an effective mass organization and in 1919 he initiated the first of his many civil disobedience cam-paigns. In 1930 Congress adopted complete independence as its aim. The Imperial Round-Table Conferences (1930, 1931 and 1932) made no real progress but the Government of India Act (1935) established provincial elected legislatures and provided for a bi-cameral central Legislature of partly elected and partly appointed members. In the 1937 elections Congress was the only well-organized party and won absolute majorities in six of the eleven provinces and pluralities in three others. It formed ministries in the six provinces and in two more by 1938. Hindu-Moslem cooperation had broken down with Congress' growing agitation for independence and led to a more complicated situation with the aspirations of Congress conflicting with those of the ⇨ Moslem League under Mohammed Ali ⇨ Jinnah, which demanded the creation of a separate Moslem state. These divisions and Congress' dissatisfaction with British concessions explained India's lack of whole-hearted support for the U K during World War II. Congress was interested in cooperation only at the price of sweeping concessions. In 1942, hoping to take advantage of Britain's weakened position in south-east Asia, it rejected the officer of the ⇨ Cripps mission of autonomy for India after the war and again demanded full independence with an immediate British withdrawal. The real threat of a Japanese invasion boosted the recruitment of the Indian armed forces, although a group of anti-British dissidents led by Subhas Chandra Bose formed an 'Indian national army' and fought with the Japanese. Bose headed a Japanese-sponsored 'provisional government of India', which he set up in Singapore in 1943. Disturbances continued in India and Lord

Linlithgow (Viceroy, 1936–43) gaoled the leaders of the independence movement including Ghandi and Jawaharlal ⇨ Nehru and banned the Congress organization. These leaders were released at the end of the war. Political tensions, which had increased during the war, now reached breaking point. The new Labour Government in the UK proposed discussions of the offer made in 1942, but this was rejected by Congress. Jinnah's support among the Moslems was now assured, differences between the Hindu and Moslem leaders were sharper than before and there were frequent riots which combined with a food shortage to make conditions desperate. Elections early in 1946 gave large majorities to Congress in eight of the eleven provinces while the Moslem League took all seats reserved for Moslems. This only strengthened the determination of both sides. In March 1946 the British Government offered full independence to India but the ensuing negotiations over the future of India failed to break the deadlock between the Congress Party and the Moslem League. Jinnah decided on 'direct action' to achieve his aim of a separate state and boycotted the constituent assembly which met to discuss plans for independence. Communal violence increased and Gandhi's reliance on moral force (*Satyagraha*) seemed a less effective weapon than it had been in the 1930s. In Feb. 1947 the UK Government announced it would grant independence not later than June 1948 and appointed Viscount Mountbatten as Viceroy to work out the programme for the transfer of power. In June 1947 the British Government decided that the country should be partitioned and on 15 Aug. 1947 independence was granted to both India and ⇨ Pakistan. Nehru became Prime Minister of India and Jinnah Governor-General of Pakistan, but the occasion was marked by considerable bloodshed between Hindus and Moslems. Massacres in the Punjab cost about half a million lives, followed by large migrations of refugees from both countries totalling some six million people. In Jan. 1948 Gandhi was assassinated by a Hindu fanatic.

The immediate problem facing the new Indian Government was the need to assert its authority over the states. Most of them caused little trouble, including the 550 odd princely states, but force had to be used to quell opposition in Junagadh and Hyderabad. ⇨ Kashmir was a different problem because of its proximity to Pakistan and the fact that its population under a Hindu ruler was largely Moslem. War broke out and continued until a cease-fire in 1949, but Kashmir has continued to poison relations between the two countries ever since. In Jan. 1950 a new constitution made India a Republic and Rajendra ⇨ Prasad was elected President (1950–62; succeeded by Sir Sarvepalli Radhakrishnan 1962–67 and Zakir ⇨ Hussain 1967–69). In 1952 the first national elections gave an overwhelming majority to the Congress Party with 364 of the 489 seats. Nehru's principal aim in domestic politics was 'Indian socialism', which sought to achieve a secularization of social customs, the creation of social and economic equality and the modernization and industrialization of the economy. Faced with the problems of a backward agriculture (which still employs 70% of the working population), a rapidly-rising birth-rate, a consequent food shortage, great illiteracy and poverty and also the growing threat of communism in Asia, Nehru hoped to develop the economy through a succession of Five-Year Plans (1951–56, 1956–61 and 1961–66) which aimed at an increase in national income, self-sufficiency in food and the rapid expansion of industry. The success of these plans (during the second plan national income rose by 38%) has been qualified by the fact that the rise in population has far outdistanced the rise in food production (in the first 18 years the population went up by 140 million and there is now an annual increase of 15 million). The persistence of traditional religious and social attitudes has proved a barrier to modernization. The caste system has been slow to disappear, shown in the continuance of the castes of 'untouchables' (the lowly status of the depressed classes which comprise 20% of the population), although Gandhi worked for the abolition of 'untouchability' in the 1930s and it was outlawed in the Constitution. The Congress Party repeated its success in later elections – in 1962 it won 355 of the 500 seats with 126 million votes cast (India has an electorate of 175 million, the largest in the world). The dominant position of Congress has been both a strength and a weakness. It helped give the country the necessary stability during the first decade or two of independence, but it has also prevented the emergency of a real party system with an alternative government. The opposition is divided into several smaller parties, of which the most important are the Communist Parties, the Hindu extremist *Jan Sangh* and the *Swatantra* Party, which is anti-communist and pro-West. These parties are stronger in the provinces and in some cases have set up governments, e.g. the communists in ⇨ Kerala. This again has had a weakening effect on central power especially now with the Congress Party losing support since it was returned with a greatly reduced majority in the 1967 general elections – more than just a result of the departure of Nehru, who died in May 1964. His successors, Lal Bahadur ⇨ Shastri (1964–66) and since 1966 Mrs Gandhi, have been unable to avoid the consequences of the fact that a party in power for such a long uninterrupted period of office tends to stagnate, and that the problems of any national party are enormous in a country with six ethnic groups, seven religious communities and over 800 language groups. India's foreign policy has been preoccupied with relations with Pakistan and China as well as her part as international arbiter in the Cold War.

The Kashmir agreement of 1949 was only a temporary arrangement. India proceeded to integrate that part of the region occupied by its troops into the Union and good relations with Pakistan were marred. War broke out between the two countries in 1965 in the Rann of Kutch, a disputed border area. At a meeting in Tashkent in Jan. 1966 under Soviet chairmanship President Ayub ⇔ Khan and Shastri agreed to settle future differences by peaceful means and withdrew their troops to the positions they had held before the war. The secession of the Eastern state of Pakistan as Bangladesh in March 1971 led to the resumption of hostilities between India and Pakistan and full-scale war broke out between the two countries on 3 Dec. 1971. Indian troops with Bangladesh guerrillas defeated the Pakistan Army within a fortnight after heavy fighting on both fronts. On 3 July 1972 a formal peace treaty was signed between Mrs Gandhi and President Bhutto of Pakistan at Simla. Relations with China have become more complicated. Nehru at first sought to cultivate the friendship of the new communist government and in 1954 proclaimed the Five Principles of Peaceful Coexistence (*Panch Shila*), but the Chinese annexation of ⇔ Tibet occasioned much ill-feeling in India and the Chinese invasion of Indian territory in the north-east (Oct. 1962) led to a revision of Indian policy. Nehru dismissed ⇔ Krishna Menon as Defence Minister and requested US military aid to support Indian armed forces. India became more dependent on the West although she continued to receive aid from the USSR, signing a twenty year treaty of peace and cooperation in Aug. 1971, but her position as leader of the block-free states was not radically changed. She attempted to mediate in ⇔ Korea in 1950, joined the ⇔ Colombo Plan (1950) and helped organize the ⇔ Bandung Conference of non-aligned nations in 1955. Anti-colonialism has played an important part in foreign policy and the Indian annexation of the Portuguese enclave of ⇔ Goa in 1961 was consistent with this although it nevertheless opened India to charges of imperialism.

Indirect Rule. Refers specifically to Lord Lugard's policy in Britain's (former) African colonies of ruling through tribal authorities. Lack of finance and the tiny number of civil servants required to administer vast territories united policy with practice.

Indochina. ⇔ Vietnam, ⇔ Laos, ⇔ Cambodia.

Indonesia. *Area* – 1,905,000 sq. miles. *Population* – 97,000,000. *President* – Gen. T. N. J. ⇔ Suharto (1968–). *Constitution* (1945) – Republic with executive power vested in the President who is also Prime Minister. The President is elected by the Provisional People's

Consultative Congress (MPRS) which also determines the broad lines of national policy. The MPRS consists of members of the House of Representatives and delegates of the regional territories and of functional groups. Legislation is enacted by the President in concurrence with the House but the former has the right of veto. The House consists of nominated members, about one-half representing political parties and one-half representing functional groups.

Indonesia comprises a group of over 3,000 islands, of which the largest and most important are: Java and Madura (*area* 132,000 sq. miles, *population* 63 million), Sumatra (*area* 474,000 sq. miles, *population* 15·8 million), Kalimantan or Indonesian ⇨ Borneo (*area* 539,000 sq. miles, *population* 4·1 million), Sulawesi or Celebes (*area* 189,000 sq. miles, *population* 7 million), Bali and West Irian (formerly West ⇨ New Guinea). The large majority of the population are Malays and the main religion Islam.

Indonesia, formerly the ⇨ Netherlands East Indies, was ruled by the Dutch from the seventeenth century. A developing nationalist movement led in 1927 to the founding of the Indonesian Nationalist Party (PNI) with the aim of winning independence. During the 1930s the Dutch repressed all such revolutionary organizations and ⇨ Sukarno, the leader of the PNI, was arrested several times. The Japanese occupation in World War II (1942–45) precipitated the end of colonial rule. The Japanese released Sukarno and other nationalist leaders and, in the hope of gaining their support, permitted a degree of self-government and even created an Indonesian army. The nationalists used this opportunity to enlist mass support for their movement and, when the Japanese withdrew, proclaimed an independent republic with Sukarno as President. The Dutch refused recognition and sought to re-establish their dominion through force. Finally in 1949, at the Hague Conference, the Dutch agreed to recognize Indonesian independence but left the status of Western New Guinea undecided. The country was called the United States of Indonesia, which remained linked to the Dutch through the Netherlands-Indonesian Union under the Dutch Crown. In 1950 this federation was replaced by a unitary state. Since this favoured the Javanese more than the other Indonesian peoples, internal politics were marked by instability, aggravated by the lack of geographical unity. Political parties were also divided along communal lines – the PNI, the Communist Party (PKI) and the *Nahdatul Ulama* (Muslim Scholars) were predominantly Javanese, while the *Masjumi* (Islamic) party and the PSI (Socialists) represented the other Indonesians. Attempts at cooperation – coalitions between the PNI and the *Masjumi* – ended in failure. The next governments, which were Javanese, tried to cripple the

Masjumi by the use of patronage, and to follow Sukarno's plan of building up the PKI to offset the village-level support enjoyed by the *Masjumi*. The first elections (1955) resulted in a clear majority for the three Javanese parties. Resentment against the pro-Javanese policy of the government and growing poverty led to an autonomous movement and a military revolt in Sumatra in 1956 which spread to several of the other islands. The failure of parliamentary government to deal with the internal troubles – made worse by the dislocation of the economy through the conflict with the Netherlands over Western New Guinea – led Sukarno to proclaim a period of 'guided democracy', which gave the President broader powers. In 1959 the constitution of 1945 giving the President strong powers was reintroduced and the Constituent Assembly dissolved. A further step towards authoritarian government was taken in 1960 when a decree was passed enabling Sukarno to control the political parties and Parliament was reorganized to include only nominated members. In 1963 Sukarno declared himself President for life. His position now depended on two main centres of power, the army and the PKI, which was now the strongest communist party in Asia outside China and the third strongest in the world (in 1965 it had three and a half million members). The army's influence in political life had increased after its success in quelling the revolts in the late 1950s but it feared the growing power of the PKI and resented Sukarno's policy of NASAKOM (nationalism plus communism). A communist revolt in 1965 gave the army the opportunity of embarking on a wholesale slaughter of communists (about one million were killed within a year). The army was now more powerful and in 1967 Sukarno's executive powers were transferred to General ⊳Suharto while Sukarno remained nominal President (in 1968 Suharto also received the title of President). Foreign policy had long been concerned with the incorporation of Western New Guinea into Indonesia and in 1956 the Netherlands-Indonesian Union was abrogated. This was followed by the expropriation of Dutch property and the expulsion of Dutch citizens. The matter came to a head in 1962, when Indonesian forces clashed with Dutch. Agreement was reached that the UN should administer West New Guinea and hand it over to Indonesia in 1963. Settlement of this problem was followed by ⊳Confrontation with ⊳Malaysia (1963–66), the new federation which Indonesia refused to recognize. During the 1950s Sukarno had sought to establish himself as a leader of the Third World – he signed a Treaty of Friendship with India (1951) and in 1955 organized with India the Afro-Asian Conference at ⊳Bandung. Relations with the USA deteriorated in the early 1960s, when with the growing influence of the PKI, foreign policy became more anti-Western and Sukarno moved closer to the communist states, especially China. In 1961 a Treaty of Friendship was concluded with China and in 1963 an Agreement for Co-operation. Sukarno's aggressive foreign policy had distracted attention from domestic problems, especially the continuing poverty (in 1964 it was estimated that starvation threatened one million people), but also led to rampant inflation. After Sukarno's overthrow by the army led by Suharto, Indonesia adopted a less aggressive foreign policy. Action against Malaysia ceased and she rejoined the UN. The Suharto government claims to give priority to economic development and has adopted a five-year plan.

Inonu, Ismet (1884-). President of ⇨ Turkey (1938–50) and Prime Minister (1923–24, 1925–37). A professional officer, he was Chief of Staff and a close political associate of Mustapha ⇨ Kemal, whom he succeeded as President. As leader of the Republican People's Party he led the official opposition to ⇨ Menderes in the 1950s and became leader of the opposition again in 1965 after another period in office. He resigned the leadership of the Republican People's Party in 1972.

Integration. In the USA, the process of assimilating segregated groups into the rest of the community. Franklin D. ⇨ Roosevelt's 1941 executive order forbidding discrimination in defence industries and government offices, and ⇨ Truman's 1948 order ending ⇨ Segregation in the Armed Forces, as well as his directive that Federal jobs were to be awarded irrespective of race, were landmarks on the road to integration. A breakthrough came in 1954 when the ⇨ Supreme Court ruled that discrimination in public education was inherently discriminatory and hence unconstitutional (⇨ Brown v. Board of Education). Congress passed the Civil Rights Bill of 1957 which permitted the Federal Government to bring an action in the courts when a person was deprived of his civil rights, and created the ⇨ Civil Rights Commission. The Federal District Courts were given jurisdiction over proceedings involving civil rights; and the Civil Rights section of the Justice Department was expanded to a full division. Direct action by Negroes and Whites in the early 1960s, consisting of sit-ins, freedom rides and street demonstrations against the colour-bar in transport, housing, restaurants, etc. throughout the South also played a significant part. But whilst integration was the aim of the ⇨ Civil Rights Movement in its early stages, the rise of ⇨ Black Power movements has substituted more radical aims for it in recent years. Integration in schools by means of ⇨ 'Busing', though upheld by numerous Supreme Court decisions, became increasingly unpopular among White, and to some extent Black, parents, in the North as well as the South, from about 1968. President Nixon restricted Federal enforcement of the policy; attempts were made in Congress to institute a 'moratorium' on it; and it became an issue in the 1972 contest for the Democratic presidential nomination. Anti-busing provisions were included in the Higher Education Amendments legislation enacted in June, 1972, postponing court orders requiring busing till 1974.

Intelligentsia. Strictly refers to nineteenth-century Russian intellectuals who participated in revolutionary politics. In this sense there is no exact equivalent in the West where the intellectual élite was often part of the Establishment and the term is generally used to refer to writers, critics and academics. In Soviet Russia, the term has been used to differentiate the bureaucracy, writers and professional groups from other workers, although recent stirrings in Eastern Europe suggest that the older tradition of ⇨ Dissent is still alive. In the original sense, the term is perhaps applicable to the role of the educated élite in the Third World who led the demands for independence and are now often to be found in leading positions in the governments of their countries.

Internal Security Act, 1950. In the USA, the 'McCarran Act' which established the ⇨ Subversive Activities Control Board.

IRA. Irish Republican Army – Irish nationalist and terrorist organization. The IRA started as a protest movement against the partition of Ireland in 1922 and became notorious for its raids on barracks and bomb attacks (mainly in Northern Ireland although some occurred in England) which reached a climax in 1939 when 127 such incidents occurred in six months. During the 1930s it was shown some favour by ⇨ De Valera, who repealed the Public Safety Act, although it had been declared illegal. During World War II the IRA indulged in pro-German activities and many of its members were interned. Internment of suspected IRA members again followed the outbreak of violence in Northern Ireland in the early 1970s, in which the IRA played a major part. At that time, disagreement over tactics split the IRA into an 'official' and a 'provisional' wing.

Iran. *Area* – 636,000 sq. miles. *Population* – 25,781,090. *Head of State* – Mohammed Reza Shah ⇨ Pahlavi. *Prime Minister* – Amir Abbas ⇨ Hoveida. *Constitution* (1906, amended 1949) – Theoretically a constitutional monarchy. Executive authority is vested in the Shah, who appoints the Prime Minister with the approval of the National Consultative Assembly (*Majlis*), which may be dissolved by the Shah. Legislative power is vested in the Parliament consisting of the *Majlis*, elected by universal suffrage for four years, and the Senate (first convened 1950) whose members are partly appointed and partly elected for six years.

Iran (known as Persia until officially renamed in 1935) was an absolute monarchy until the early twentieth century, when a constitution was granted establishing a Parliament (see above). The power of the new Parliament was demonstrated in 1925 when the last of the Qajar Shahs, who had ruled the country since 1794, was deposed by the National Assembly, which elected as Shah Reza Khan Pahlavi (1925-41), an army officer who had become Prime Minister in 1923. The new Shah reorganized the army and government administration and encouraged the development of industry and education, but was forced to abdicate in favour of his son (Mohammed Reza Pahlavi) during World War II when the UK and the USSR protested at his close relations with the Germans and invaded the country (1941). The Allied Forces occupied Iran but guaranteed her independence by the Tripartite Treaty (1942), confirmed at the ▷ Teheran Conference (1943). At the end of the War the Russians refused to withdraw their troops from Iran and encouraged the establishment of an autonomous communist government in Azerbaijan (1945-46). The matter developed into an international crisis and was referred to the UN, but the Russians agreed to leave after a joint Soviet-Persian company had been formed to exploit the oil in the northern provinces. Oil, Iran's major industry (first discovered in 1901), has played an important part in its politics and was at the centre of a serious domestic crisis in the early 1950s. Political discontent arising from misgovernment but also from the unpopularity of the new Anglo-Iranian oil agreement of 1949 resulted in the rise to power of the National Front movement under Mohammed ▷ Mussadiq (Prime Minister 1951-53). Mussadiq persuaded Parliament to nationalize the oil industry (1951), which had serious international repercussions because of the UK's controlling interest. Internal unrest was compounded by a constitutional crisis when Mussadiq attempted to reduce the powers of the Shah, who fled the country but soon returned when monarchist elements forced Mussadiq from office. The oil dispute had led to a sharp deterioration in the economy (because of the British blockade) and in 1954 a new agreement was made. A succession of Prime Ministers restored order (the communist Tudeh Party was proscribed but continued to operate underground) and in 1957-58 political parties were formed: the opposition People's Party (*Mardom*) (1957) and the government National Party (*Melliyoun*) (1958). First elections were held in 1960 but the results were annulled after accusations of government rigging. New elections in 1961 were no more satisfactory and the electoral system was reformed in 1963. Elections in that year and 1967 resulted in overwhelming majorities for the Iran Novin (New Iran) Party founded in 1963. The major parties agreed on the need for land reform, and the initiative in this matter was taken by the Shah, who had since 1950 been dividing his estate among the peasants. The abolition of the rights of the feudal lords was the main domestic problem, for three-quarters of the population were employed in agriculture. In 1963 there were riots by landowners and priests following the Shah's broad programme for buying large estates and distributing them among the peasants, which was approved by a referendum (Jan. 1963). The programme also included a plan for social reforms (education and welfare) and the emancipation of women (they voted for the first time in the 1963 elections). But many of the abuses, which had forced these reforms, still remain. There is widespread poverty and illiteracy in the rural areas, corruption in government and persistent fear of communist subversion (fears which increased after an attempt on the Shah's life by left-wing students in 1965). Proximity to the Soviet Union has influenced the country's foreign policy just as Iran's strategical position plus her oil have determined the attitude towards her of other powers, e.g. the Allied occupation during the War. Tension resulting from the Soviet threat (1945–46) had relaxed but was renewed in 1955 when Iran joined the ⇨ Baghdad Pact (later ⇨ CENTO). Her ties with the West were strengthened by considerable military and economic aid from the USA, the ⇨ Eisenhower Doctrine (1957) and the bi-lateral defence agreement with the USA (1959). In 1963 a Commercial Treaty with the ⇨ EEC was signed and there has been 'regional cooperation for development' (chiefly economic and technical) with Turkey and Pakistan. Attempts were nevertheless made to improve relations with the Soviet Union and in 1965 the Shah visited Moscow (Russian aid was granted for the construction of a steel mill). Relations with the UK have improved since the oil crisis of the 1950s although there was friction over Iran's claim to sovereignty over the British-protected island of ⇨ Bahrein.

Iraq. *Area* – 169,240 sq. miles. *Population* (1970 est.) – 9,465,800. *President* – Major-General Ahmed ⇨ Bakr (1968–). *Constitution* (interim, 1964) – Independent Republic. Executive power is vested in the President, elected by the National Council of Revolutionary Command, who choose the Prime Minister and Government. Legislative power is vested in the National Assembly, elected by universal suffrage.

Formerly part of the Ottoman Empire, Iraq became a British mandate territory after World War I and in 1932 an independent state, as a constitutional monarchy with a bi-cameral Legislature (Faisal I 1921–33, Ghazi 1933–39 and Faisal II 1939–58). However, tribal animosities, the problem of minorities like the Kurds, and the pressing question of agrarian reform exposed the sharp tensions which have been a major obstacle to efficient government in the country, e.g. the Assyrian massacre (1933), the outbreak of tribal revolt (1935–36) and the consequent military *coup d'état* (1936). The discovery of oil in 1927 and its regular export from 1934 has made Iraq a major oil producer and explains the interest of major powers in her internal affairs. Close relations with the UK had been maintained in the Treaty of Alliance of 1930 establishing full consultation in foreign affairs and mutual aid in time of war, but there was an increase in anti-British feeling in the later 1930s (partly out of resentment over UK policy in Palestine). There was consequently a growth of German influence culminating in the military coup in 1941 under Rashid Ali al-Gaylani. The pro- ⇨ Axis Government was overthrown by British troops and in 1943 Iraq declared war on the side of the Allies. In 1945 Iraq joined the ⇨ Arab League and participated in the war against ⇨ Israel (1948). Defeat in that war combined with economic discontent led to riots in 1952 and the imposition of military law until 1953. There were frequent changes in government, any one government rarely lasting as long as a year, and this more often reflected personal and tribal rivalries than conflicting ideologies, for political power was largely confined to a small ruling class, e.g. Nuri as-Said was Prime Minister 14 times between 1930 and 1958. Generally this ensured a pro-Western foreign policy and in 1955 Iraq became the first Arab state to join the Western chain of alliances when she entered the ⇨ Baghdad Pact. The USA granted technical aid and after 1956 military assistance. The Iraqi Government also opposed the pan-Arab ambitions of the new ⇨ Nasser regime in Egypt and when the UAR was established in 1958 formed a rival Arab Federation with Jordan (the two countries had been in close cooperation since their Friendship Treaty of 1947). Meanwhile, anti-British feeling stimulated by the ⇨ Suez Crisis of 1956 (martial law was again declared 1956–57) paved the way for the military *coup d'état* of July 1958, which overthrew the monarchy and murdered the King, the Crown Prince and the Prime Minister. The new revolutionary government under Brigadier (later General) Abdul Karim ⇨ Kassem brought many radical changes in policy, such as the dissolution of the Arab Federation and a more anti-Western foreign policy, e.g. withdrawal from the Baghdad Pact, the establishment of diplomatic relations with the USSR and the Chinese People's Republic and trade agreements with several communist states. Although a defence pact was concluded with the UAR, antagonism persisted and increased after alleged Egyptian complicity in the unsuccessful military revolt against Kassem (1959) and the latter's collaboration with the communists against pro-Nasser groups in Iraq. Furthermore, the change of government did not cure the endemic political instability. Kassem's rule soon developed into a personal dictatorship and was marked by a struggle for power between him and the other leader of the revolution, Colonel Abdul Salam ⇨ Aref. The Kurdish problem also remained unsolved and in 1961 the government launched a large-scale campaign against the Kurds (about 16% of the population) who had revolted in the north and some of whom, under communist influence, demanded an autonomous state. In Feb. 1963 Kassem was assassinated after a coup led by Aref based on an alliance of army officers and the left-wing nationalist ⇨*Ba'ath* Party. The *Ba'ath* Party lasted only nine months in power (it fell mainly because of its loss of support among the army officers). The new government under Aref, now President, proclaimed that it would follow the 'true' aims of the 1958 revolution, but it quickly grew into another military dictatorship. A new constitution was promulgated (1964), the trade unions were dissolved and a new party, the Arab Socialist Union, was formed (1964) to replace all other parties (which had reappeared 1960 after being banned for six years). Agrarian reforms were carried out and about 75% of the country's industry (excluding oil) was nationalized. Aref changed the direction of foreign policy and favoured Arab unity. Plans for a federation were discussed with the UAR (1963), agreements were concluded for co-ordination of the economic and military policies of the two countries (1964) and in 1965 the Arab Common Market came into force. Iraq declined to take the further step of union with the UAR, and the abortive coup of the allegedly pro-Nasser Brigadier al-Razzaq (1965) was a reminder that Nasserism was often a cover for personal struggles for power in a country marked by political instability, and in the case of the Kurds, open revolt. In 1966 Aref was killed in an air accident and was succeeded as President by his brother, Abdul Rahman ⇨ Aref. The latter was deposed in July 1968 and replaced by Major-General Ahmed Bakr. The Arab defeat in the 1967 war led as before to increased domestic tension. Iraq has been a consistent opponent of the State of Israel. Alleged Israeli spies were publicly hanged in 1969. A Kurdish Settlement made in March 1970 put an uneasy halt to the fighting in Kurdistan and offered a degree of autonomy to the province. Iraqi relations with the USSR were strengthened by a Treaty of Friendship and Cooperation signed in April 1972.

Ireland. ⇨ Northern Ireland and ⇨ Ireland, Republic of.

Ireland, Republic of (Eire). *Area* – 26,600 sq. miles. *Population* – 2,971,230 (of whom 95% are Roman Catholic). *President* – Eamon ⇨ de Valera (1959–). *Prime Minister* – John Lynch (1966–). *Constitution* – The Irish Free State was established in 1922 following the 1921 treaty with the UK granting Ireland Dominion status within the ⇨ Commonwealth. The 1937 constitution provides for a President, elected for seven years, and a Parliament consisting of a Senate, elected on a vocational basis, and a House of Representatives (*Dail*) elected for five years by adult suffrage under a system of proportional representation. In 1949 Ireland became a Republic and left the Commonwealth.

Ireland's Catholic heritage and her bitter struggle with the UK to achieve independence have conditioned her political attitudes. In theory, the Republic does not accept the fact of partition, and still lays claim to ⇨ Northern Ireland. Since 1932 the Republic has been governed with short breaks (1948–51, 1954–7) by the *Fianna Fail*, the party of de Valera. His policy concentrated on removing the limitations imposed by the 1921 treaty with the UK – the powers of the Governor-General, the oath of allegiance to the English Crown and the law on citizenship which was changed to distinguish Irish from British nationality. De Valera's new constitution in 1937 declared Eire a sovereign state. Although she remained within the Commonwealth until 1949, Eire was the only dominion not to declare war against Germany during World War II, and the Republic's neutrality in foreign affairs has been continued since the war in her avoidance of defence alliances, e.g. she declined to join NATO. The partition of Ireland which followed independence continues to be a major source of friction in Irish politics. The civil disorder in Northern Ireland in the early 1970s increased tension between North and South and put a strain on the Irish government, especially in their relations with Britain. Strong economic ties have continued with Britain, which is still by far the greatest market for the Republic. In 1966 free trade was established between the two countries for all commodities except certain agricultural goods. In 1970 the Irish Republic applied for membership of the ⇨ EEC at the same time as Britain and, in Jan. 1973, became an official member.

Irish Free State. ⇨ Ireland, Republic of.

Iron Curtain. Symbolizes the physical obstacles and ideological divisions separating the 'communist' from the 'free' world. Although ⇨ Churchill is generally thought to have coined this term in his Fulton speech (5.3.1946), it probably originated in Germany where it was used by Dr ⇨ Goebbels, the Nazi Propaganda Minister, and anti-Bolshevik writers before him.

Iron Guards. ⇨ Rumania.

Isolationism. In the USA withdrawal and aloofness from international politics dating from Washington's Farewell Address warning against 'foreign entanglements'. Both America's self-interest and its self-image as being morally superior to the European practitioners of 'power politics' have dictated this posture. It was particularly popular in the nineteenth century and in the era of disillusionment after World War I. It took ⇨ Pearl Harbor to overcome the country's determination not to fight another World War for the benefit of the Europeans and 'the armament manufacturers'.

Israel. *Area* – 7,993 sq. miles (May 1967). *Population* (approx.) – 2,768,300 (including Eastern Jeursalem). *President* – Zalman Shazar (1963–). *Prime Minister* – Mrs Golda ▷ Meir (1969–). *Constitution* – Independent Republic, established 1948. Political authority is vested in the *Knesset* (a uni-cameral Parliament). The 120 *Knesset* members are elected for four years by universal adult suffrage, on a nation-wide system of proportional representation. (There are no constituencies and the electoral system seems to encourage a multiplicity of parties and the formation of coalition governments.) The Government – Prime Minister and Cabinet – is responsible to the *Knesset*. The Head of State is the President, elected by the *Knesset* for a five-year term. The *Knesset* has rejected proposals for a written constitution and has instead voted (1950) for the constitution to evolve through the incorporation of specific laws, e.g. The Law of Return (1950), The Election Law (1951), Equal Rights for Women (1951), The Basic Law (1958), etc.

On 14 May 1948, a day before the British Mandate in ▷ Palestine came to an end, and three decades after the ▷ Balfour Declaration, the State of Israel was proclaimed in Tel Aviv. The new state was born in conflict and chaos, its attitudes shaped by the antagonism of the Arab world, and the recent tragedy to European Jewry as well as by years of Zionist idealism and determination. In 1922, when the British Government assumed its Mandate from the ▷ League of Nations, the Jewish population of Palestine was about 80,000 (one tenth of the total). That by the onset of World War II it had risen to approximately 450,000 was the result not of events in Palestine or the policies of the mandatory power, but of Nazi persecution.

There had been Arab riots in 1921 and 1929, but after 1933 the competing demands of Jewish immigration and a rising Arab national-ism (particularly in the case of the Mufti of Jerusalem and his followers – influenced by Nazi propaganda) developed into an irreconcilable conflict. From 1936 to 1939 Arab opposition to Jewish immigration turned into rebellion. The British were forced to increase the size of their garrison and in an attempt to placate Arab nationalism they restricted Jewish immigration, thus provoking violent hostility, particularly at a time when European Jewish communities were threat-ened with extinction. During this period, in defence of their settlements, the Jewish defence organization *Haganah* gained the military experience which was of crucial importance after the war. The Jewish cooperative settlements – *kibbutzim* – spearheaded the Zionist Movement. This reflected the view that only by a return to the land – as opposed to the involvement in commerce of the Jews of the diaspora – could a Jewish nation emerge. As well as organizing their own defence, the Jewish population, through their *Vaad Leumi* (National Council) and the ⇨Jewish Agency, had created an embryonic government. The partition of Palestine, recommended by the 1937 Peel Commission, was rejected by both Jews and Arabs. The subsequent British White Paper (May 1939), especially in the context of the growing Nazi threat to European Jewry (and with most countries prepared to accept only small quotas of German refugees) was regarded by Zionists as the ultimate betrayal of the Balfour Declaration. Nor, though it severely restricted Jewish immigration (75,000 over the next five years and then no more) did it placate an increasingly intransigent Arab nationalism. Hostility to the White Paper was overshadowed by the outbreak of war. Many Jews volunteered for service with the British army. Arabs also served with the British forces, but for obvious reasons, Arab opinion was less committed to the Allied cause. The end of the war and the immediate post-war years saw a rapid increase in political activity and violence in the area. Throughout the Middle East the *status quo* was threatened by an increasingly militant Arab nationalism and Zionist determination stiffened by the catastrophe to European Jewry and the plight of the survivors. The application of the White Paper policy involved British forces in turning away boatloads of stateless Jews – remnants from the European ⇨ Holocaust. The UK government convened an Anglo-American Commission (1946), but rejected its recommendations for vastly increased Jewish immigration; and the atmosphere was further embittered by the emergence of Jewish terrorist organizations (the *Irgun Zvai Leumi* and the Stern Gang). The attitude of UK Foreign Secretary, Ernest ⇨ Bevin, who had insisted on his ability to solve the problem, changed from optimism to petulance as the situation deteriorated – Jews attacked the British, while Arabs attacked the Jews who increasingly depended on the *Haganah* for protection. In 1947 Britain announced her intention to end her Mandate in the following year, and the General Assembly of the UN established UNSCOP (United Nations Special Committee on Palestine). UNSCOP was boycotted by the Arabs, but the Jews largely agreed to its partition proposals, which were adopted by the UN (Nov. 1947) – against the wishes of the Arab states (the UK abstained from voting). Following the establishment of the State of Israel (May 1948) with ⇨Ben Gurion as its first Prime Minister, the ⇨Arab League states sent their armies into Palestine (though a state of war between Arab and Jew already existed). By the time of the armistice agreements (1949) Israel had secured and extended the area allotted to it. (⇨Arab-Israeli Conflict.)

Despite the drain on its resources and manpower, the War of Independence established the new state. The lessons of war (the need for constant military alertness) were thoroughly assimilated by its largely citizen defence forces. The tragic fate of the Palestine refugees (uprooted during the war, in some cases with the encouragement of the Arab states, and in others through the action of the Israeli army) have continued to bedevil a permanent settlement of the Arab-Israeli dispute.

The early years of the new state were dominated by the need to absorb a vast flow of immigrants and to consolidate a precarious economy. In the fifties Egyptian-sponsored *fedayeen* raids culminated in Israel's invasion of Sinai (⇨ Suez Crisis and ⇨ Arab-Israeli Conflict). The success of General ⇨ Dayan's army established Israel as a military power to be reckoned with in the area. Its military success was balanced by charges of collusion with Britain and France and increased Arab resentment. A decade later the smouldering Arab-Israeli Conflict again exploded into an Arab-Israeli war, which resulted in the rout of the Egyptian, Jordanian and Syrian military forces. Despite Israel's decisive victory and increased security, many of the problems that preceded the war still remain. Israel is still denied recognition by the Arab world and there is no formal peace treaty. The occupation of former Arab territory has created additional problems.

Twenty years of statehood have also resulted in a vast economic transformation of Israeli society. Arab resentment of Israel as an outpost of 'western imperialism' is not lessened by Israeli industrial and technological achievements nor by its maintenance of a stable and viable political democracy.

Since 1 June 1967, Israel has been led by a Government of National Unity. The most powerful party in the *Knesset* is the Israel Labour Party made up of *Mapai* (Israel Labour Party), *Rafi* (Ben Gurion's 1965 break-away Labour List) and *Achdut Ha-avoda-Poalei Zion* Party, which, by their merger (Jan. 1968) hold 59 of the 120 seats in the *Knesset*. *Mapam* (United Workers' Party) draws its strength from the *kibbutzim*, and recent events have narrowed the ideological differences between it and the Israel Labour Party. The *Herut* (Freedom) Party, also represented in the Government of National Unity, is on the right wing of the Israeli political spectrum and advocates a 'Greater Israel'.

Italy. *Area* – 116,280 sq. miles. *Population* – 53,000,000. *President* – Giovanni Leone (1971–). *Prime Minister* – Giulio Andreotti (1972–). *Constitution* (1948) – Executive power is vested in the President, who appoints the Prime Minister and is elected for a seven-year term by a bi-cameral Legislature, which consists of the Senate (elected for six years on a regional basis) and the Chamber of Deputies (elected by universal suffrage for five years).

Although Italy had been one of the victorious Allied Powers in World War I, the fact that Italy's gains by the Peace Treaty (South Tyrol, Trieste, Istria, etc.) fell short of promises made by other Allies during the war was a source of discontent. This discontent was manifested in the seizure of Fiume by a nationalist band under D'Annunzio (1919). Social unrest, parliamentary instability, fear of communism and the well-organized agitation of the Fascist Party led to ⇨ Mussolini's appointment as Prime Minister by the King after his 'march on Rome' (Oct. 1922). It was several years before Mussolini established a totalitarian state; the constitution remained in force, but he made use of royal decree, controlled elections (by new electoral laws 1923 and 1928) and crushed opposition groups. He survived the public shock over the murder by Fascists of the openly critical socialist Matteotti. He exercised control over the economic life of the country through the corporative state and in 1929 concluded the Lateran Treaties with the Pope which recognized the sovereignty and rights of the Vatican State and also granted a measure of 'respectable' approval to the Fascist Government. Although some projects were successful (e.g. the draining of the Pontine Marshes and 'the trains ran on time'), Mussolini's economic programme fell far short of its aims, largely because of the world Depression. During the 1930s Mussolini turned increasingly to an expansionist foreign policy. Mussolini had threatened to intervene after the independence of Austria was endangered following the assassination by Austrian Nazis of ⇨ Dollfuss (1934) and had joined in the (implicitly anti-German) Stresa Declaration in favour of European peace (April 1935). But his successful invasion of ⇨ Ethiopia (autumn 1935), which flouted the authority of the ⇨ League of Nations, and active participation (with Germany) in the ⇨ Spanish Civil War on the side of the Nationalists, led to the Rome-Berlin ⇨ Axis between Germany and Italy. This was initiated in the secret protocols (Oct. 1936) and confirmed by the Pact of Steel (May 1939). While Hitler annexed Austria and Czechoslovakia, Mussolini seized Albania (April 1939). Although Italy proclaimed her neutrality at the outset of ⇨ World War II, Hitler's swift military victories in Western Europe led to an Italian declaration of war against France and Britain (June 1940). Italy's armies failed in Greece and in North Africa until assisted by German reinforcements. The Allied victory there was followed by the invasion of Sicily (July 1943) and the resignation of Mussolini. The new government of Badoglio surrendered to the Allies (Sept. 1943) and later declared war on Germany (Oct. 1943). Mussolini had been rescued and made head of a German puppet government in Northern Italy but was captured by partisans and executed after the German defeat. Parliamentary government was re-established after the war. A referendum (1946) abolished the monarchy by 12¾ to 10¾ m. votes and a republican constitution came into force (Jan. 1948). In the new republic a most important factor was the emergence of the Christian Democratic Party (PDC) which owed its strength to the support of the Catholic Church, to American aid which helped Italy recover from the ravages of war, its adoption of social reform, the split of the left-wing vote between the two other main parties – the Socialists and the Communists (PCI) – and above all to the intensification of the Cold War. The major PDC victory of 1948 was won on the issue of communist control. Their leader, Alcide ⇨de Gasperi (Prime Minister 1945–53), was one of the chief promoters of European political and economic integration together with Count Sforza (Foreign Minister 1947–51). Italy joined the ⇨OEEC (1948), the ⇨Council of Europe (1949), the ⇨ECSC (1952) and in 1958 the ⇨EEC. In her foreign policy Italy was firmly pro-West. Having renounced all colonial claims and settled reparations (1947 Peace Treaty), she joined NATO (1949) and became a member of the UN in 1955. In 1953 the PDC lost its decisive majority, and although it continued to provide Prime Ministers, formed a series of coalitions usually with other centre and right-wing parties. In 1962 the first of the Centre-Left coalitions was formed under Amintore Fanfani. This 'opening to the Left' (*apertura a sinistra*) was continued by Aldo Moro (Prime Minister 1963–68) after the Christian Democrats lost their absolute majority in the elections of 1963, this time with the left-wing Socialists under Pietro ⇨ Nenni. After the elections of May 1968 the Socialists withdrew from the Government, but in Nov. of the same year a minority government was replaced by a new Centre-Left coalition under Mariano Rumor. The PCI, already the largest Communist Party in Western Europe and the second largest party in Italy, continued to grow and in 1968 won 26·9% of the vote. It had owed its strength in part to the stature of its leader, Palmiro ⇨Togliatti, and his policy of constitutionality, which was not changed by his death in 1964. Tensions inevitably arose within the party between this policy and its opposition to Italy's pro-Western foreign policy, but the PCI's independent attitude was shown when it criticized the Soviet invasion of ⇨ Czechoslovakia in 1968. Neo-Fascist groups have reappeared but at the moment do not pose any serious threat. In 1968 student riots erupted at many universities. In spite of the brief life of many governments and obvious discontent as evidenced by student protest, factors making for stability include Italy's remarkable post-war economic recovery, assisted by her

membership of the EEC, foreign aid and a programme of land reform –
between 1951 and 1961 the average annual increase in the GNP was 6%,
and between 1958 and 1963 industrial production increased by an
annual average of 14%. The May 1972 elections, producing a slight
shift to the right, persuaded Signor Andreotti to form a centre coalition
after more than a decade of centre-left-governments.

Ivory Coast. *Area* – 227,000 sq. miles. *Population* (1970 est.) –
5,100,000. *Head of State and President of the Council of Ministers* –
Félix ⇨ Houphouët-Boigny. *Constitution* (1960) – Executive power is
vested in an elected President. The Legislature, in a single-party system,
consists of the President and an elected National Assembly.

Formerly a province of ⇨ French West Africa, the Ivory Coast
became an independent Republic in the ⇨ French Community in 1958
and a fully independent Republic outside the Community on 7 Aug.
1960. Close links are maintained with ⇨ France through the ⇨ *Conseil
de l'Entente*, formed with neighbouring territories (1959), and as an
associate member of the EEC. Houphouët-Boigny played a leading part
in the movement for independence in French West Africa through his
RDA – *Rassemblement Démocratique Africain* – founded in 1946; however, since the late fifties, he has rejected pan-Africanism for *réalisation*
– i.e. rapid internal economic growth.

Izvestia. Soviet daily newspaper, published by the Presidium of the
USSR Supreme Soviet and expressing the official government point of
view.

J

Jagan, Dr Cheddi (1918–). First Prime Minister of British Guiana (⇨ Guyana), 1961–64. His policies incurred the distrust of the U K and U S A, heightened by fears that his P P P threatened East Indian domination of Guyana politics. However, U K and American enmity and the introduction of proportional representation, may have confirmed the P P P in its anti-Western attitudes.

Jamaica. *Area* – 4,244 sq. miles. *Population* (1969) – 1,972,130. *Prime Minister* – Michael Manley (1972–). *Constitution* (1962) – Independent Dominion within the ⇨ Commonwealth (the Queen is represented by the Governor-General). The Prime Minister is responsible to a bi-cameral Parliament of an appointed Senate and an elected House of Representatives. There is universal adult suffrage.

Formerly a British Crown Colony, Jamaica (a British possession since the seventeenth century) had a form of self-government from 1944. A Royal Commission (appointed in 1939 following rioting on sugar estates 1937–38) recommended a new constitution, based on universal adult suffrage, which came into force in that year. In the late thirties two leaders emerged. Alexander ⇨ Bustamante and Norman ⇨ Manley who at first cooperated, but whose later rivalry affected the political alignments and development of the country. In the first elections under universal suffrage (1944), Bustamante's newly-formed (1943) J L P (Jamaican Labour Party – despite its name a pragmatic and anti-socialist party) won a majority (22 out of 32 seats) in the House of Representatives. In the 1949 elections the J L P (though with a reduced majority) was again returned to power and in 1953 under a new constitution, granting Jamaica internal autonomy, Bustamante became Chief Minister (in effect Prime Minister). Manley (Chief Minister 1955–62), though one of the chief architects of the newly formed (1958) ⇨ West Indies Federation, agreed that opponents were entitled to express their dissent. Largely as a result of a referendum (Sept. 1961) in which the opponents of federation led by Bustamante were victorious (54% of the poll) the Federation was dissolved. After a further electoral victory (April 1962), Bustamante became the first Prime Minister of a fully independent Jamaica (Aug. 1962). In 1965, Donald Sangster replaced the ailing Bustamante as Premier, and led the JLP in a further electoral success (1967). Sangster, who died suddenly shortly afterwards, was succeeded by Hugh Shearer. Though Jamaica's economy has developed since independence, even the low standard of living of her predominantly Negro population is threatened by rapid population growth. It has always been necessary for many Jamaicans to seek employment away from home, and in this context the UK ⇨Commonwealth Immigration Acts have added to the island's economic difficulties.

Japan. *Area* – 142,726 sq. miles. *Population* (1970) – 103,720,000. *Head of State* – Emperor ⇨Hirohito (1926–). *Prime Minister* – Kakuei Tanaka (1972–). *Constitution* (1946) – Parliamentary monarchy. The Emperor has no executive power. Executive authority is vested in the Cabinet, responsible to the Legislature (the Diet), which consists of the House of Representatives and the House of Councillors, whose members are elected by universal suffrage, the former for four years and the latter for six.

The most highly industrialized nation in Asia, Japan underwent a process of Westernization from the Meiji Restoration of 1868. In spite of this she passed through a turbulent period between the two world wars partly because of a revival of traditional attitudes, which revealed that the outlook of a feudal society had not disappeared although its structure had been abolished. Japan emerged from World War 1 on the victorious side with the addition of former German colonial possessions to her Empire, which already included Formosa, Korea and enclaves in Manchuria. Although a formidable military power, she was prevented by Allied opposition from securing demands on China, which would have reduced that country to a subordinate position. She also lost her wartime economic advantages, both in trade and in the supply of munitions to the Allied Powers. A number of corruption scandals and enfranchisement struggles combined to discredit parliamentary government. The world economic depression, which ruined the country's vital silk trade, threatened an already depressed agriculture with further disaster and brought discontented military and nationalist groups to the fore. Agrarian distress prompted a radicalization of the army, most of whose recruits and junior officers were of rural origin. The social turmoil which resulted helped to bring about the increasing control of politics by the military, a process which began when the Kwantung Army took the initiative in conquering the whole of Manchuria (1931), establishing the Japanese-controlled state of Manchukuo. The Cabinet, which had no jurisdiction over the operations of the armed forces, was obliged to concur with a policy of aggression towards ⇨ China from 1932 leading to full-scale war from 1937. This nationalist policy was supported at home by the revival of old Japanese beliefs particularly state Shintoism with its belief in the divinity of the Emperor, whose authority was used to bypass the politicians. Formidable support also derived from state control of a rapidly expanding industry, big business (*zaibatsu*) with its armaments programme and increasing involvement in politics of the military. An endemic element of violence reappeared with the assassination of a number of public figures (1931–36) including two Prime Ministers. Japan claimed that she needed 'living space' for her dense and growing population (it in fact doubled in the 60 years up to 1935) and in pursuing an expansionist foreign policy she shared common aims with the ⇨ Axis Powers of Europe. In 1933 she withdrew from the League of Nations and in 1936 signed an anti-Comintern pact with Germany. After the outbreak of war in Europe she joined the ⇨ Tripartite Pact with Germany and Italy (Sept. 1940). Japan, jolted by Hitler's alliance with Soviet Russia (Aug. 1939), decided on an independent policy of conquest in south-east Asia (called the 'Greater East Asia Co-Prosperity Sphere'). The French and Dutch presence there had been greatly weakened by German victories in the summer of 1940. A Japanese puppet government had been set up in China (March 1940). Further Japanese aims, e.g. securing her oil needs from Dutch Borneo, conflicted with the interests of the USA. On 7 Dec. 1941 Japan launched her attack on the American fleet at Pearl Harbor extending the war to the Pacific (⇨ World War II). The Government, now directly in the hands of the military with General ⇨ Tojo as Prime Minister (1941–44), proceeded to overrun south-east Asia, the Philippines and the Dutch East Indies. In 1942 the tide began to turn with American naval victories and operations finally came to an end with the dropping of atomic bombs on Hiroshima (6.8.1945) and Nagasaki (9.8.1945), the first of these killing over 50,000 people. The Japanese surrender (formally on 2.9.1945) ushered in a new phase in Japanese history. The country was occupied by the Allied Powers (1945–51) although effective power was in the hands of General ⇨ MacArthur as Supreme Commander. He initiated a policy of 'democratization' whereby Japan would be purged of her imperialist past. The Emperor remained but only as a figurehead (he formally renounced his divinity in Jan. 1946) and the constitution of 1946 introduced parliamentary government and included a renunciation of war by the Japanese people. A series of decrees by MacArthur included far-reaching innovations such as the abolition of feudal land tenure and compulsory adherence to Shintoism, liberalization of the education curriculum, the restoration of civil liberties and universal suffrage. Cooperation with the Americans was firm Japanese policy under Yoshida (Prime Minister for the period 1948–54), but the priority of economic recovery and the advent of the ⊳ Korean War (1950) meant that the policy of dissolving the large industrial corporations was dropped (1948) and a measure of rearmament began in the creation of a National Police Reserve for defence purposes (1950). This was even before the Peace Treaty of San Francisco (8.9.1951) restored Japanese sovereignty as from 28 April 1952. Japan at the same time renounced her claims to colonial possessions. The key factor in her post-war history has continued to be her relationship with the USA. On 8 Sept. 1951 a Security Pact was signed with the USA, which retained its forces in the country and promised to come to Japan's defence. Japan signed reparations agreements with her former adversaries, joined the ⊳ Colombo Plan (1954), took part in the ⊳ Bandung Conference (1955) and was admitted to the UN (1956). The USSR and other communist states had refused to sign the Peace Treaty of 1951 but in 1956 diplomatic relations were resumed with Moscow. Relations with the ⊳ Chinese People's Republic have been complicated by Tokyo's recognition of the Nationalist Government as the legitimate government of China, although ideology presents no barrier to important trade links between the two countries since commercial relations were reopened in 1956. Although Japan became an integral part of the Western defence system during the Cold War, her attitude towards her connexion with the USA has been ambivalent, stemming from a strong pacifist element which draws its psychological force from the traumatic experience of Hiroshima. This appeared during the renegotiation of the Security Pact in 1960. Left-wing demonstrations resulted in the cancellation of President Eisenhower's visit and there were violent scenes in Parliament. Behind the unrest lurked the fear that the American air bases might attract Soviet missiles, for shortly after the ⊳ U-2 incident that year Khrushchev warned Japan that she would receive a 'shattering blow' should the bases be used for intelligence flights over Soviet territory. The most remarkable development since the war has been Japan's economic growth. Recovery was initially due to vast American aid, but the redirection of Japanese energies away from military adventures into economic channels has produced amazing results. Between 1946 and 1953 the national income more than doubled in real terms resulting in an increase of almost 90% in income per head. From 1953 to 1964 the gross national product grew at an average yearly rate of 10%; during the same period manufacturing production (the show-piece of the Japanese economy) increased fourfold. This has had a stabilizing effect, creating a stronger and more conscious middle-class in which bourgeois ideals have replaced military values. The main political effect has been the dominance of the conservative pro-American Liberal-Democratic Party, supported by both the business and the rural population. Since 1948 this party (formerly as the Liberal Party) has provided every Prime Minister (after Yoshida, Hatoyama 1954–56, Ishibashi 1956–57, ▷ Kishi 1957–60, ▷ Ikeda 1960–64, ▷ Sato 1964–72 and since then Tanaka. In the 1969 election it won 48% of the vote against 21% for the Socialist Party. Backed by the intellectuals, the trade unions and the younger urban voters, the latter has vented its political frustration in parliamentary obstruction and anti-Americanism and has been tempted by political violence. Japanese politics still retains its factional character – there are some 10,000 registered parties in the country. The assassination in 1960 of the Socialist Party Leader, Asanuma, by a right-wing extremist revealed an undercurrent of violence in Japanese political life. Violence reappeared in the late 1960s with student riots and their suppression, the revival of nationalist groups and rowdyism in Parliament.

Java. ▷ Indonesia.

JCS. United States Joint Chiefs of Staff – the highest body of military advisers to the President, the ▷ NSC, and the Secretary of Defense, operating within the ▷ Defense Department, and consisting of a Chairman (Chief of Staff to the Secretary of Defense), the Chiefs of Staff of the Army and Air Force, the Chief of Naval Operations, and (on matters affecting the Marines) the Commandant of the Marine Corps, all appointed for a two-year period by the President with the consent of the ▷ Senate. The JCS are responsible for planning military strategy, formulating joint supply, personnel, and training programmes, establishing unified commands, and providing US representation on the military commissions of ▷ UNO, ▷ NATO and ▷ SEATO. The members are also members of the ▷ Armed Forces Policy Council, and the Chairman, who is superior to all other military officers in the USA, is a member of NSC.

In line with the policy of unifying the defence forces of the USA, the purpose of JCS has been to achieve unity in the planning and execution of military policy. However, inter-service rivalries have persisted despite the efforts of JCS, though in recent years they have been mitigated, or at least obscured, by the management policies of Defense Secretary Robert ▷ McNamara.

Jenkins, Roy (1920–). UK Labour Party politician; a former Gaitskellite who has risen quickly in the Party and the Wilson government. Minister of Aviation (1964–65), Home Secretary (1965–67) and Chan-

cellor of the Exchequer (Nov. 1967–June 1970). The leader of the pro-
EEC faction of the Party, he resigned as the Party's deputy leader in
April 1972.

Jewish Agency. As envisaged in the ⇨ League of Nations Mandate
(1922) and finally constituted 1929, was formed to cooperate with the
British Administration in the development of a Jewish National Home
in ⇨ Palestine. Its functions were previously performed by the World
Zionist Organization, which charged it with the promotion of Jewish
settlement in Palestine. It collected and administered funds and provided
(with the *Vaad Leumi*) the nucleus of a Jewish administration – experience which proved invaluable when members of its executive, together
with executive members of the *Vaad Leumi*, formed the first ⇨ Israel
government (1948). Its 'executive' functions disappeared with the
emergence of the state, and it now serves to encourage immigration to
and investment in Israel.

Jim Crow Laws. Legislation in the Southern States of the USA
discriminating against the Negro. The term derives from a nineteenth-
century American song-and-dance act. A landmark decision by the
Supreme Court in ⇨ Brown v. Board of Education (1954) overturned
the ⇨ 'Separate but Equal' doctrine that permitted the separation of
races in school.

Jinnah, Mohammed Ali (1876–1948). Founder and first Governor-
General of ⇨ Pakistan (1947–1948). Disillusioned with the Hindu
majority in the Congress nationalist movement for Indian independence,
he led the ⇨ Moslem League from 1934 and pressed for a separate
Moslem state. He supported the UK during World War II and increased
support for his party among the Moslems. The League's victory among
the Moslem voters in 1946 strengthened his hand and he won British
support for the partition of ⇨ India.

John XXIII, Pope (1881–1963). Pope from 1958 to 1963, formerly
Cardinal Roncalli, a popular figure who followed the more austere
⇨ Pius XII and succeeded during his brief period in office in strongly
associating the Roman Catholic Church with the ecumenical movement. During his rule, the Second Vatican Council (1962–63) accepted
important Church reforms. He also broadened the Church's social
teachings (1961 encyclical *Mater et Magistra*) and emphasized the
importance of pastoral work through visits to prisons and schools for
the poor. He was previously Vatican diplomatic representative in
Bulgaria (from 1925) and in Turkey and Greece (from 1935), papal
nuncio in France (from 1944) and became Cardinal and Patriarch of
Venice in 1953.

John Birch Society. A political association in the USA belonging to the

American ⇨ New Right (or 'radical Right'). It was founded in 1958, and has been run as a semi-secret 'monolithic' organization by its founder, Robert Welch, a Boston candy manufacturer. The name of the Society commemorates the 'first American casualty of World War III', an American soldier and evangelist killed in China during the communist advance after World War II. In 1962, in his book *The Politician*, Welch accused President ⇨ Eisenhower of being a 'dedicated, conscious agent of the communist conspiracy', and in like vein called for the impeachment of Chief Justice Earl ⇨ Warren. Welch (but not the Society) was criticized for his extravagant accusations by, among others, Senator ⇨ Goldwater. Nevertheless, the Society continued to have a considerable influence on conservative politics in the United States during and after Goldwater's unsuccessful campaign for the presidency in 1964. Since then it has lost public attention; but it remains influential locally, especially in the West and South-West. Its organ, *American Opinion*, has provided a medium for ⇨ Anti-semitism and vilification of Black Americans, even though Welch, who edits it, repudiates such attitudes for himself and the Society.

Johnson, Lyndon B. (1908–73). Thirty-sixth President of the United States (1963–69) who succeeded to office on the assassination of John F. ⇨ Kennedy. Appointed Texas director of a ⇨ New Deal youth programme (1935), he was elected to Congress in a special election (1937–48), temporarily interrupting his duties for military service during World War II. While in the House of Representatives Johnson was a strong supporter of the New Deal and a personal friend and political ally of the powerful Speaker, Sam ⇨ Rayburn. Elected to the Senate (1949), he became Majority Whip (1951–53), ⇨ Minority Leader (1953–55), and ⇨ Majority Leader (1955–60). A consistent but moderate advocate of liberal causes, Johnson was often criticized for his pragmatic approach to politics – an approach that produced such significant legislative achievements as the Civil Rights Acts of 1957 and 1960. Unable to secure the Democratic Party's nomination for President in 1960, he was chosen by Kennedy as his running-mate and was elected Vice-President. When he became President following the assassination of Kennedy (22.11.1963), Johnson reassured the nation and proceeded with the former President's legislative programme with the addition of his own Poverty Program. Johnson enjoyed unusually harmonious relations with Congress, and secured the passage of important social legislation, such as the Civil Rights Act of 1964. Choosing Hubert H. ⇨ Humphrey as his running-mate in the 1964 election, Johnson swept to victory over his Republican opponent, Barry ⇨ Goldwater. In his first State of the Union Message (Jan. 1965) he put forward his ⇨ Great Society programme calling for large Federal expenditures on increased social welfare. In foreign policy, he met with opposition for his intervention in the ⇨ Dominican Republic (April 1965), and still more for his decision to commit large-scale American military force to the ⇨ Vietnam War. He pursued a middle course between domestic ⇨ Hawks and Doves, but the war alienated significant segments of the intellectual community and increased in unpopularity as the possibility of military victory receded. The President's decision to end most of the US bombing of North Vietnam (March 1968) eventually produced the peace negotiations of Paris but he declared that he would not seek another term as President. Lyndon Johnson left a record of controversy in foreign affairs but considerable achievements at home.

Jonas, Franz (1899–). President of Austria since 1965. Active in the inter-war Social Democrat movement, he was imprisoned in 1935 and after the war occupied elective municipal office in Vienna. He was Mayor of Vienna from 1951 to 1965.

Jordan. *Area –* 37,000 sq. miles. *Population* (1969 est.) – 2,300,000. *Head of State* – King ⇨ Hussein Ibn Talal (1952–). *Prime Minister* – Ahmad al-Lauzi. *Constitution* (1952) – The Hashemite Kingdom of Jordan is an independent monarchy. Executive power is vested in the King and legislative power in the Parliament consisting of the Senate (appointed by the King) and the House of Representatives (elected by universal suffrage for four years).

Jordan (then called Transjordan) was part of the Ottoman Empire until 1920, when it became a British mandate territory under the League of Nations. Transjordan became an autonomous state in 1923 and in 1928 was recognized as independent with the UK retaining military and some financial control. The same year a constitution was granted and in 1929 the Legislative Council met for the first time. In 1939 a regular Cabinet was formed. During World War II Transjordan troops (in particular the British-trained Arab Legion under General J. B. ⇨ Glubb) cooperated with the UK in the suppression of the Iraqi rebellion and the occupation of Syria (1941). Transjordan achieved full independence in 1946 when she became a kingdom under ⇨ Abdullah (who had been Emir since 1921). The traditionally close relations of the ruling Hashemite dynasty with the UK were maintained in a treaty of alliance and in 1948 a new treaty established a joint defence board. Apart from the continuing British connexion, the country's foreign politics have been dominated by her relations with other Arab states especially the ⇨ UAR and with ⇨ Israel. She became a member of the ⇨ Arab League (1945) and in the 1948 ⇨ Arab-Israeli Conflict made common cause with the other Arab states, but the aftermath of the war exposed her differences with her allies. Transjordan (renamed Jordan in 1949) was the only Arab state to acquire any considerable territory, the West Bank of the River Jordan, which she formally annexed in 1950. Even before 1948 Egypt had been suspicious of Abdullah's territorial ambitions. Jordan's acquisition of the West Bank (a major part of the Arab state envisaged by the UN partition plans of 1947), combined with her willingness to accept the new frontiers as permanent, increased Arab suspicions. Increasingly, Jordanian policy diverged from that of the other Arab League states. In 1951 Abdullah was assassinated and was succeeded by Talal, who was forced to abdicate the following year in favour of his son Hussein. A new constitution was promulgated in 1952 but generally governments have proved unstable and have been short-lived. Party groupings do exist, e.g. the Arab Constitutional Bloc (moderate conservative), the *Ba'ath* National Front (extreme national-ist) and the Moslem Brotherhood (nationalist) but they play no signifi-cant part in Jordanian politics and were banned from participation in the last two elections (1963 and 1967). In 1956 Hussein dismissed Glubb Pasha following anti-Western riots. After the ⇨ Suez Crisis the financial agreement with the UK was abrogated and the last British troops left the country. Hussein generally pursued a pro-Western foreign policy, e.g. he accepted the ⇨ Eisenhower Doctrine (1957), and this led to a breach with his pro-Soviet Prime Minister, Nabulsi. Hussein opposed the pan-Arab ambitions of President ⇨ Nasser and after the establishment of the UAR (1958) Jordan formed the short-lived Arab Federation with Iraq. Relations with the UAR further deteriorated after an attack on Hussein's aircraft by Egyptian planes (Nov. 1958), the assassination of Prime Minister Majali in 1960 (which Jordan attributed to the UAR) and the prompt recognition of Syria's independent status when she broke away from the UAR (1961). From 1961 to 1964 diplo-matic relations were again broken off between the two countries, though some differences were resolved at the Arab summit conference in Cairo (1964). UAR propaganda continued to urge the overthrow of Hussein and Nasser made abusive attacks on him until Hussein suddenly concluded a defence treaty with the UAR (30.5.1967). This provided for joint military operations in the event of an attack on either state and confirmed Israeli anxieties that Nasser was preparing for war, which broke out a few days later (⇨ Arab-Israeli Conflict). Jordan suffered heavy casualties and lost territory on the West Bank of the Jordan, which was occupied by Israel. The influx of more Arab refugees created further internal problems for Jordan. Although Hussein has usually shown a more conciliatory attitude than other Arab states towards Israel, domestic pressures have helped to produce a state of permanent crisis in home and foreign affairs, e.g. the presence of a large group of Palestinian Arab refugees (now about 700,000) whose allegiance to the Hashemite dynasty is doubtful. Frequent border clashes with Israel (Jordan has by far the longest frontier with that country – some 330 miles) have further increased tension.

Junta. An administrative council particularly in South America, Spain or Italy. Generally used to describe the government of a military clique which has come to power by a *coup d'état*.

K

Kadar, J. (1912–). First Secretary, Hungarian Socialist Workers' Party (HSWP), Kadar joined the underground Communist Party in 1932. Active in the communist Resistance during World War II, he became a member of the Central Committee in 1942 and of the party Secretariat in 1943. After the war, he was also promoted to the Politbureau, retaining both positions after the communist-socialist merger. In 1948, he became ▷Rajk's successor as Minister of the Interior, but was again transferred to party work in 1950. In April 1951, during a new purge of ▷ Home Communists, he was suddenly arrested and kept in prison until July 1954. Rehabilitated in 1956, after Rakosi's resignation, Kadar was re-instated in the party Secretariat and Politbureau and, in a number of statements, denounced Secret Police tortures of which he himself had been a victim. After the outbreak of the revolution, he replaced ▷ Gerö as First Party Secretary and became a member of ▷ Nagy's new government, whose programme he supported in a number of broadcasts. A few days later he changed over to the other side, supporting the second Soviet intervention and taking charge of the post-revolutionary regime. After a period of severe repression, Kadar launched in the early 1960s a new policy of national reconciliation and cautious liberalization. Under his leadership, Hungary participated in the invasion of ▷ Czechoslovakia in Aug. 1968, but Kadar has been notably more reticent than the other participants in condemning Czechoslovakia's reforms and justifying the intervention.

Kaganovich, L. M. (1893–). Soviet communist. A ▷Bolshevik since 1911, Kaganovich became one of ▷ Stalin's closest associates who played a prominent part in the routing of the various anti-Stalinist opposition groups and the subsequent purges. A member of the Party's Politbureau (later temporarily called Presidium) from 1930, he was the chief patron of ▷Khrushchev's party career and remained in the Party Presidium after Stalin's death until 1957, when he was expelled as a member of the ▷Anti-Party Group. He was subsequently denounced for the part he had played in the purges and repressions of the Stalin era and has since lived in obscurity.

Kamenev, L. B. (1883–1936). Russian communist. A ⇨Bolshevik from 1903, Kamenev was one of Lenin's close associates in exile before the revolution. Although he clashed with Lenin in 1917 over the seizure of power, he remained a member of the Party's Politbureau until Lenin's death. In the post-Lenin factional Party struggles, he was, with ⇨ Zinoviev, one of the leaders of the 'left' opposition to ⇨ Stalin. Together with Zinoviev he was arrested after ⇨ Kirov's murder (Dec. 1934) and, in a first (secret) trial (Jan. 1935), was sentenced to five years' imprisonment. In the following year he was, again with Zinoviev, one of the leading defendants in the first of the three public ⇨Moscow Trials and was convicted and executed as an enemy of the people.

Kang Sheng (1899–). Chinese Communist. Member of the Standing Committee of the Central Committee's Politbureau – a CCP member since 1925 and in the Party's Politbureau as an alternative member since 1945. Kang Sheng has since the onset of the Cultural Revolution been promoted to ⇨ Mao's new top hierarchy. Kang has frequently travelled abroad and attended many foreign and international communist gatherings and has maintained contact with the new 'Marxist-Leninist' communist parties and factions. According to Soviet sources, he described himself in the past as 'the ⇨ Beria of China'. The 9th party congress of April 1969 elected him to the Politbureau's 5-men Standing Committee.

Karaganda. ⇨ Forced Labour Camps.

Karamanlis, Constantine (1907–). Prime Minister of ⇨ Greece (1955–63). A member of various Cabinets (1946–55) at a time when governments lasted only a few months, his period in office was distinguished for its length. The conservative National Radical Union Party (ERE), which he founded, increased its majority in successive elections (1956, 1958 and 1961). His most notable achievement was the agreement with the UK and Turkey on independence for Cyprus (1959).

Karami, Rashid (1921–). Prime Minister of the ⇨Lebanon 1958–60, 1961–64, 1965–66, 1966–68 and 1969–70. He first became Prime Minister after leading Moslem rebels against the pro-Western policy of President ⇨Chamoun in the riots of 1958.

Kardelj, E. (1910–). Yugoslav communist since the 1920s and a partisan leader in World War II, during which he became one of ⇨ Tito's closest associates and emerged in the post-war period as the chief theoretician of the specifically 'Yugoslav road to socialism'. He has played a leading part in the formulation of his country's home and foreign policies and in polemics with Yugoslavia's communist critics.

Karelia. Autonomous Republic within the RFSFR. (⇨ Finland.)

Kasavubu, Joseph (1917–69). First President of the ⇨ Congo (Kinshasa) from June 1960 to Nov. 1965, with a brief period out of office during ⇨ Mobutu's first *coup* in Sept. 1960. After independence the compromise, by which he became President and ⇨ Lumumba Prime Minister, increased rather than diminished their rivalry. Following his dismissal of Lumumba (5.9.1960), Kasavubu himself was dismissed by Mobutu (14.9.1960) but quickly reinstated. When his attempt to bargain with ⇨ Tshombe failed (he was President when Lumumba was placed in Katangese hands) he included the 'Lumbumbist' ⇨ Gizenga in his new government (July 1961). He was later responsible for Tshombe's appointment to (10.7.1964) and dismissal from (Oct. 1965) the premiership of the Congo. He out-manoeuvred all his rivals till he himself was removed from office by Mobutu's second *coup*.

Kashmir. The State of Kashmir and Jammu with its population of 4,500,000 (of which 77% are Moslems) and an area of 86,000 sq. miles has been a source of dispute and tension between India and Pakistan since the partition of the Indian sub-continent which accompanied its independence in Aug. 1947. When British rule lapsed no special provision was made for the individual states except that their rulers should decide whether to join India or Pakistan or remain independent. The hereditary Hindu ruler of Kashmir, Sir Hari Singh, was reluctant to commit himself, unlike nearly all the other rulers. If he joined the Moslem state of Pakistan he would undoubtedly lose his throne, accession to India would provoke his Moslem subjects who resented his rule, while independence would leave him at their mercy. The matter came to a head with a Moslem revolt in Poonch (Aug. 1947), aided by guerrillas from Pakistan, which escalated into a war between the two countries after Singh had called on military assistance from India in return for signing an act of accession placing the state under the dominion of the Indian Union (Oct. 1947). The war lasted until the cease-fire under UN supervision (Jan. 1949) which set up a line of demarcation leaving smaller areas in Western Kashmir, Gilgit and Baltistan in the control of Pakistan, and the rest to India. Various attempts by the UN to demilitarise the region failed, as did its efforts to persuade India to agree to a plebiscite. While India has based her rights to Kashmir on the act of accession, Pakistan has maintained this is invalid because it is against the wishes of the majority of the population. Time has hardened attitudes on both sides. In the 1950s India proceeded to integrate the area occupied by her troops into the Union. In 1953 Sheikh Abdullah, the leader of the Kashmiri government, was imprisoned because of his opposition to this policy and in 1957 the state was incorporated. Further attempts at mediation by the UN failed as did direct negotiations between India and Pakistan. An effort by the UK to take advantage of the threat of a Chinese invasion of India in 1962 and to press for a solution collapsed when the Chinese threat diminished. Riots by Moslems in 1963–64, recalling the communal bloodshed that followed partition, led Nehru to seek an end to the problem but this was cut short by his death in May 1964. Hopes for a settlement were dashed when the new Shastri Government proclaimed the irrevocability of the integration of Kashmir in India (Dec. 1964). This led to a sharp deterioration in relations and after border incidents in the Rann of Kutch war broke out between India and Pakistan (Aug. 1965). In Sept. hostilities ceased after much international pressure on the contestants. In Jan. 1966 Shastri and President Ayub Khan met under the chairmanship of the Soviet Prime Minister at Tashkent and signed a declaration that they would in future settle their differences by peaceful means. But in the Indo-Pakistan War of Dec. 1971 heavy fighting again broke out along the border. The problem of Kashmir is still unsolved. Economic conditions favour a solution as Kashmir is an important communications centre, but questions of national and religious pride are involved.

Kassem, General Abdul Karim (1914–63). Prime Minister of ⇨ Iraq (1958–63), and leader of the 'revolution' of 1958, which overthrew the Iraqi monarchy. His irresolute handling of foreign and home affairs together with his strong opposition to President ⇨ Nasser of the ⇨ UAR led to his overthrow and assassination in 1963 by an alliance of army officers and members of the *Ba'athist* Party led by Colonel Abdul Salam ⇨ Aref.

Katanga. ⇨ Congo (Kinshasa).

Katyn Murders. In April 1943, the German Command announced the discovery of a mass grave of Polish officers in the forest of Katyn and alleged that these officers had been massacred by the Russians in 1940 while the area was under Soviet occupation. Ever since the conclusion of the Soviet-Polish Military Agreement of Aug. 1941, the Polish government-in-exile had been vainly trying to trace a large number of Polish officers who were known to have been captured by the Red Army in 1939 but who failed to re-appear when the Polish prisoners in the USSR were freed. With these missing officers in mind, the Polish Government asked the International Red Cross to investigate the German allegation on its behalf. This request served the USSR as a pretext to break off diplomatic relations with the Polish Government, accusing it of helping Nazi propaganda, and alleging that the Katyn murders – contrary to all available evidence – had been committed by the Germans.

Kaunda, Dr Kenneth (1924–). First President of ⇨ Zambia (1964). His leadership and organization of the UNIP (United Nationalist Independence Party) was a decisive factor in bringing the Federation of ⇨ Rhodesia and Nyasaland to an end and achieving independence for Zambia. An African nationalist and dedicated Christian opponent of racialism he has also opposed the persecution of white by black. His difficulties have been increased by the continued success of ⇨ Smith's regime in Rhodesia and the impatience of his own supporters.

Kazakhstan. One of the 15 Federal Soviet Republics constituting the USSR. *Capital* – Alma-Ata. Kazakhstan is sub-divided into 13 Provinces.

Keita, Modibo (1915–). President of Mali. Devout Moslem but socialist (Lenin Peace Prize) exponent of anti-colonialism and African unity through ⇨ Casablanca Group, the ⇨ Guinea-Ghana Union and now the ⇨ OAU. Deposed by a military *coup* (19.11.1968).

Kemal, Mustapha (1880–1938). Founder of modern ⇨ Turkey and first President of the Turkish Republic (1923–38), he brought about a political and social revolution in his country. The state was secularized, the legal system was overhauled and the process of Westernization included the abandonment of traditional dress. He adopted the name *Ataturk* (meaning 'Father of the Turks') in 1934 and ruled as virtual dictator, although he allowed a Parliament. In foreign policy he remained neutral and declined all foreign investment consistent with his policy of keeping Turkey free of foreign influence. He had risen to prominence as a military leader in World War I and afterwards as leader of the nationalist forces which drove the Greeks from Asia and led to a more favourable post-war settlement for Turkey.

Kennedy, Edward M. (1932–). US Democratic Senator and political heir to his assassinated brothers John and Robert. He managed John Kennedy's second campaign for the Senate (1958) and in 1962 won a special election to take his brother's vacated seat in the Senate (from Massachusetts). Elected to a full term two years later, 'Teddy' left the national spotlight to his brother Robert and concentrated on home-state matters, as well as certain special issues such as revision of the 'draft' (⇨ Selective Service System) and liberalization of the Immigration Laws. Frequently mentioned as a possible Democratic candidate for the Presidency, his prospects were set back in 1969 as a result of his involvement in a car accident at Chappaquiddick Island, off Martha's

Vineyard, Mass., in which Mary Jo Kopechne, a girl secretary was drowned. In 1971 he took up the cause of Northern Ireland Catholics, adopting a position generally hostile to the British Government. However, during Congressional Investigations into the question, initiated partly by him, he was strongly rebuked by the Prime Minister of the Irish Republic. In 1972 he declined Senator George ⇨ McGovern's invitation to become Democratic Vice-Presidential running-mate.

Kennedy, John Fitzgerald (1917–63). The thirty-fifth President of the United States, assassinated before the completion of his first term. A son of Joseph P. Kennedy, former U S ambassador to Great Britain (1937–40), and a Harvard graduate, he served with courage in the Pacific during the War, and in 1946 was elected to the House of Representatives as a Democrat from Massachusetts. Re-elected in 1948 and 1950, he entered the Senate in 1952 where he began to establish a national reputation. His political position varied while in Congress, though he was generally more liberal in domestic than in foreign affairs. Much to the chagrin of orthodox liberals, he took cautious stands on the issues of civil rights and ⇨ McCarthyism. He narrowly missed the vice-presidential nomination on the Democratic ticket in 1956, but returned to the Senate and an assignment to the Foreign Relations Committee (1957) aiming at the next presidential contest. Supported as always by a loyal, personal organization, he defeated Hubert H. ⇨ Humphrey in the 1960 presidential ⇨ Primary Elections and went on to win the Democratic nomination for President, taking his strongest rival, Lyndon B. ⇨ Johnson, as his running-mate. The November election was decided by the narrowest margin in American history when Kennedy defeated Vice-President Richard ⇨ Nixon to become the youngest President and the first Roman Catholic to hold the office. The new Chief Executive's foreign policy began inauspiciously when American-trained Cuban refugees failed in an attempted Cuban invasion at the ⇨ Bay of Pigs (1961). Other crises followed in Laos and Berlin until the climax of the ⇨ Cuban Missile Crisis (Oct. 1962) and a general relaxation of international tensions began. In June 1963 Kennedy called for an end to the Cold War and suggested mutual nuclear test restraints that eventually led to a limited ⇨ Nuclear Test Ban Treaty. The ⇨ Alliance for Progress, a massive programme for Latin American development, and the ⇨ Peace Corps, which aimed at aiding developing countries around the world, were both initiated in 1961. Kennedy was unsuccessful in getting his major domestic programmes through Congress, and some, such as a tax cut and major civil rights legislation, only passing after his death. He was assassinated in Nov. 1963 while riding in a motorcade through Dallas, Texas. John Kennedy's style, his recruitment of outstanding intellectuals to his team and his evocation of a New Frontier invigorated American politics, and when he died the sense of loss and grief extended far beyond the United States.

Kennedy, Robert Francis (1925–68). US Attorney General, Senator and brother of the late President John F. ⇨ Kennedy, he was assassinated while campaigning for the Democratic presidential nomination. A graduate of Harvard University, he entered public service as an attorney for the Criminal Division of the Department of Justice (1951). He left in 1952 to manage his brother's congressional campaign and was later named as counsel to the Senate Permanent Sub-committee on Investigations – the committee from which Senator Joseph ⇨McCarthy launched his notorious attacks. Resigning after six months, Kennedy rejoined the committee as Chief Counsel under a new chairman (1954) and began fruitful inquiries into labour racketeering. In 1959, with his brother, John, now seeking the presidential nomination, Robert again resigned and became his campaign manager, working tirelessly and successfully to strengthen party organization. Despite objections, the President-elect appointed his brother 'Bobby' US Attorney General. While he was effective in this post, particularly in the areas of civil rights, crime, and economic monopoly, Kennedy was most influential as one of the President's closest advisers in foreign and domestic affairs. Following the assassination of his brother, Robert Kennedy ran successfully for the Senate seat from New York. Long considered a presidential candidate for 1972, he announced his candidacy for the 1968 Democratic nomination after Senator Eugene ⇨ McCarthy had demonstrated the extent of dissatisfaction with ⇨Johnson's administration. Winning presidential ⇨Primary Elections in several States and strong support from the young and the under-privileged, Kennedy's campaign was ended suddenly when an assassin took his life in Los Angeles following a California primary victory. Robert Kennedy enjoyed wide national and international popularity, no doubt inspired partly by the 'Kennedy mystique', but also because he championed the cause of the Black and the poor American.

Kennedy Round. ⇨ United Nations.

Kenya. *Area* – 225,000 sq. miles. *Population* (1969) – 10,890,000 including 9,370,000 Africans, 188,000 Asians, 43,000 Europeans and 38,000 Arabs. *President* – Jomo Kenyatta (1964–). *Constitution* (1963 amended 1964) – Since 1967 provides for an executive of the President, Vice-President, and Cabinet and a Legislature of a one-party uni-cameral National Assembly.

Kenya formerly consisted of a British colony and a British Protectorate which were merged when it became self-governing (June 1963).

Its history was profoundly affected by white settlers and Asian immigration. From 1903 British (and South African) farmers were attracted to the 'White Highlands' – the outbreak of ⇨ Mau Mau terrorism (1952), which threatened to engulf the territory in civil war, was stimulated by Kikuyu land hunger and resentment of 'white' farmers. After the completion of the Mombassa-Uganda Railway (1920) Indian workers employed in its construction settled in the country, and they and their descendants played a crucial role in Kenya's economic development. Following constitutional changes (1954–60), Africans gained a majority of seats in the Legislative Council in the Feb. 1961 elections. In Aug. 1961 ⇨ Kenyatta (President of KANU – Kenya African National Union) became the Leader of the Opposition. With the KANU election victory (June 1963) he became Prime Minister and Kenya attained full independence (12.12.1963). In November 1964 the KADU (Kenya African Democratic Union) opposition dissolved itself and merged with KANU to form a single-party government and Kenya became a Republic in the ⇨ Commonwealth with Kenyatta as its first President (12.12.1964).

Kenyatta, Jomo (1891–). One of the pioneers of African nationalism and first President of ⇨ Kenya, he campaigned for land reform and African rights (Secretary of the Kikuyu Central Association 1928) before leaving for England (1929). In 1938 he published *Facing Mount Kenya* – a study of Kikuyu tribal life. He returned to Kenya in 1946 to become President of the Kenya African Union. Charged (despite his denial) with being one of the leaders of ⇨ Mau Mau he was sentenced to imprisonment (8.4.1953) and remained in detention till Aug. 1961, during which time he was elected President of the Kenya African National Union (March 1960). From 1961 he played a crucial role in the negotiations leading to independence. A founding member of ⇨ OAU he has advocated a neutralist foreign policy for Kenya.

Kerala. State of ⇨ India which elected the country's first communist provincial government (1957–59), prevented from holding office by the President. The Communist Party was again the strongest party in the 1965 elections and in 1967 formed a coalition government with other groups opposed to the ⇨ Congress Party.

KGB. Russian abbreviation for Committee for State Security. (⇨ USSR State Security Service.)

Khama, Sir Seretse (1921–). As Seretse Khama succeeded to the chieftainship of Bechuanaland's largest tribe in 1925, his uncle Tshekedi Khama was appointed Regent. In 1948 Seretse's marriage to an Englishwoman resulted in his banishment and six years in exile. Such treatment by a British (Labour) Government emphasized South Africa's influence on the internal affairs of her neighbours. Despite his renunciation of the chieftainship (a condition of his return), Sir Seretse Khama, first as the founder of the Bechuanaland Democratic Party and now as President of ⇨ Botswana, has achieved the undisputed leadership of his country. Committed to modernization and the ideals of a multi-racial democracy, his task is hampered by his country's poverty and the need to live in peace with powerful neighbours.

Khan, Field-Marshal Mohammed Ayub (1907–). President of ⇨ Pakistan (1958–69), who came to power after a military *coup*. He introduced a form of guided democracy and promoted land reforms and economic development. His main problem in foreign policy was the continuing dispute with India over ⇨ Kashmir and the 1965 war with that country combined with growing political discontent at home, which eventually brought about his downfall. Also President of the ⇨ Moslem League, Ayub Khan had formerly served as C.-in-C. of the Pakistan Army from 1951 and as Minister of Defence (1954–56).

Khan, General Yahya (1917–). President of ⇨ Pakistan from March 1969 to Dec. 1971, when he resigned after the loss of ⇨ Bangladesh, in favour of Zulfikar Ali ⇨ Bhutto. He had succeeded President Ayub ⇨ Khan after the latter's resignation. He was formerly C.-in-C. of the Pakistan Army from 1966.

Khrushchev, N. S. (1894–1971). Former First Secretary, CPSU Central Committee and Soviet Premier, Khrushchev became a communist during the 1917 revolution, fought in the civil war and joined the Party in 1918. His party career began in Moscow under the patronage of ⇨ Kaganovich. A member of the CPSU Central Committee from 1934 and of the Politbureau from 1939, he was First Secretary of the Moscow Regional Party Committee (1935–38) and the head of the Ukrainian Party organization (1938–49) as well as Ukrainian Premier (1944–47). Soon after his return to Moscow (1950) he was promoted to the CPSU Secretariat while being re-elected to the Party Presidium (later the Politbureau). Following Stalin's death (March 1953), Khrushchev emerged, after a brief period of uncertainty, as the Party's new First Secretary. During the next five years he gained ascendancy over all his rivals, achieving sole command in 1958, when he assumed the premiership in addition to his various party posts. During his years in power Khrushchev gained world fame as well as world notoriety for the new personal style which he introduced into the conduct of Soviet affairs at home and abroad. An action of lasting impact on both the USSR and ⇨ World Communism as a whole was his denunciation of Stalin's terror in his 'secret' speech at the 20th CPSU Congress (Feb. 1956) and his further public elaboration of the theme at the 22nd CPSU Congress (Oct. 1961), followed by the demonstrative removal of Stalin's body from the Lenin Mausoleum. Exactly three years later, in Oct. 1964, Khrushchev was overthrown in a bloodless *coup d'état* organized by his colleagues in the party leadership. Since then he lived in retirement until his death in 1971, while Soviet publications refrained from mentioning his name.

Kiesinger, Kurt Georg (1904–). Chancellor of the ⟡> German Federal Republic (1966–69). A lawyer and Nazi party member from 1933, during the war Kiesinger served in a junior capacity at the Foreign Ministry. Classified by a 1947 Denazification Court as 'innocuous', he entered the *Bundestag* as a ⟡> CDU member (1949) and headed its Foreign Affairs Committee (1954–58) until elected Prime Minister of Baden-Württemberg (Dec. 1958–Nov 1966). A senior member of his party, he managed by offering the ⟡> SPD key positions in his government to overcome the protracted leadership crisis which his predecessor ⟡> Erhard was unable to resolve. Backed by the new 'Grand Coalition' between the two major parties, the Kiesinger administration succeeded in arresting the slight recession responsible for Professor Erhard's downfall and in improving the somewhat strained relations with France. It failed, however, in its declared intention of bringing about a general *détente* with East Bloc countries, although it managed to establish diplomatic relations with Rumania (Jan. 1967) and Yugoslavia (Jan. 1968).

Kim Il-sung (1912–). Prime Minister of the Democratic People's Republic of ⟡> Korea; Chairman of the Korean Workers' Party.

The son of a Korean schoolteacher, Kim emigrated with his parents to China in 1925. An early convert to communism, he was active in China in anti-Japanese organizations among Korean refugees and was a founder-member of the Korean Independence Alliance. Later he went to the USSR where he underwent further political and military training at the Khabarovsk Communist Party School. Kim Il-sung returned to Korea in 1945 as a captain in the Soviet occupation forces. There were at that time three main communist factions in Korea, the Soviet-trained Stalinist faction, which took its cues from Moscow; the Chinese-trained 'Yenan' faction, under Maoist influence; and the 'home communists' who had worked underground in Korea during the Japanese occupation. Kim Il-sung quickly achieved ascendancy over all of them and ruthlessly eliminated all his actual or potential rivals and opponents. Effective leadership in the (communist) Korean Workers' Party is vested in the chairmanship, an office which Kim has occupied ever since 1945. After the establishment of the Democratic People's Republic in 1948, he also took over the premiership and, with the outbreak of the war in 1950, assumed in addition the office of Supreme Commander. Since that time, Kim Il-sung has become the centre of a growing 'personality cult' of his own, which remains, however, strictly confined to North Korea. After the open eruption of the ⇨ Sino-Soviet Conflict, Kim first tended to side with China against the Soviet Union, but later adopted an attitude of detached neutrality which enabled him to enjoy the advantages of Soviet economic and military aid without giving undue offence to his Chinese neighbour.

King, Martin Luther, Jr. (1929–68). Negro American Civil Rights leader and Nobel Peace Prize winner (1964) who gained world recognition in his non-violent crusade for social and legal equality. The son of a Baptist minister, and himself ordained, he accepted the pastorship of a Baptist church in Montgomery, Alabama (1954) and gained national attention by leading a successful boycott of city buses to end segregated seating in the city. Soon afterwards he helped form and became President of the Southern Christian Leadership Conference (⇨ SCLC) and continued to work for integration in the South and an end to *de facto* segregation in the North. He supported the 'freedom riders' (1961) in their attempts to win interstate bus desegregation. Led a mass non-violent protest in Birmingham, Alabama (1963) where local police brutality provoked Congress into passing stronger Civil Rights legislation. Believing in the civil disobedience teachings of Thoreau and Gandhi, King joined other Negro moderates in condemning city riots. In his last years he was caught between white racists and black militants who rejected his non-violent methods. In 1967 he added opposition to US involvement in Vietnam to his crusade for human dignity. He was assassinated in Memphis while there to lead a march in support of the city's garbage collectors. His murder caused country-wide rioting and a questioning of non-violent methods by many Negro leaders. He summarized his beliefs in *Why We Can't Wait* (1964).

King, William Lyon Mackenzie (1874–1950). One of the longest-serving Commonwealth Prime Ministers – Mackenzie King was Prime Minister of ⇨ Canada (1921–26, 1926–30 and 1935–48) and leader of the Liberal Party (1919–48). At home a supporter of *laissez-faire* economic policies; in foreign affairs he sought non-involvement, but developed closer relations with the USA and successfully led Canada through World War II.

Kirghizia. One of the 15 Federal Soviet Republics constituting the USSR. *Capital* – Frunze.

Kirilenko, A. P. (1906–). Member of the Politbureau and the Secretariat of the CPSU Central Committee. As a member of the two ruling bodies of the Soviet Communist Party, Kirilenko is one of the small group of men who determine USSR policy. A Party member since 1931, Kirilenko made his career, first in the Ukraine and then in the central Party apparatus, as a protégé of ⇨ Khrushchev. A member of the Central Committee since 1956, he became a member of the Presidium (later renamed Politbureau) in 1962 and, in 1966, he was in addition promoted to the Party Secretariat.

Kirov, S. M. (1886–1934). Leading Soviet communist. A ⇨ Bolshevik from 1905, Kirov succeeded ⇨ Zinoviev as head of the important Leningrad Communist Party organization (1926). A member of the Politbureau (1930–), his assassination (Dec. 1934) by a young communist became the signal for the start of the great Soviet ⇨ Purges culminating in the ⇨ Yezhovshchina and the ⇨ Moscow Trials. At the 20th CPSU Congress (1956) ⇨ Khrushchev hinted that Kirov's murder might have been organized from above. According to some sources, Kirov objected to ⇨ Stalin's ruthlessness and was beginning to gain too much popular support from the Communist Party membership for Stalin's liking.

Kishi, Nobusuke (1896–). Prime Minister of ⇨ Japan (1957–60) and leader of the Liberal Democratic Party. He was formerly Foreign Minister (1956–57) and held various ministerial posts during World War II.

Kissinger, Henry (1923–). Close adviser to President ⇨ Nixon. Born in Germany, he went to the USA in 1938 to escape ⇨ Hitler's persecution. He studied at Harvard University, and eventually became Professor of Government there (1962). Whilst at Harvard he acted as an adviser to Presidents ⇨ Eisenhower, ⇨ Kennedy, and ⇨ Johnson. He left Harvard in 1969 to become Assistant to the President for National Security Affairs under President Nixon, and has been the leading figure in most of the President's foreign-policy ventures, including his trips to Peking and Moscow in 1972, and the Vietnam cease-fire agreement announced in 1973. He was the first member of an American Administration to act on behalf of the President of the USA in Peking since the Communist Revolution.

Klaus, Josef (1910–). Chancellor of Austria 1964–1969. In the 1930s a Catholic trades union organizer, he was Provincial Commissioner of Salzburg (1949–61) and Minister of Finance (1961–63). As Chancellor, he discontinued the coalition with the Socialists in April 1966, after the People's Party obtained an overall majority in the elections.

KMT. ⇨ Kuomintang.

Knox, Frank (1874–1944). Unsuccessful US Republican vice-presidential candidate in 1936. He was President Roosevelt's Secretary of State for the Navy (1940–44).

Kolkhoz. Soviet term, short for Collective Farm.

Kolyma. ⇨ Forced Labour Camps.

Komsomol. Soviet term, short for All-Union Leninist Communist League of Youth.

Korea. Politically partitioned Asian peninsula to the east of China with an area of 85,250 square miles and a population of approximately 42,484,000.

Having derived the main elements of its civilization from China and having for long lived under Chinese suzerainty, the state of Korea regained nominal independence after the Sino-Japanese War of 1894/5. Russia's competition with Japan for dominant influence in Korea during the following decade was the principal cause of the Russo-Japanese War of 1904/5. After Russia's defeat in this war, Korea became first a Japanese Protectorate and, in 1910, was annexed by Japan. From that time onwards until Japan's surrender in World War II, the country remained part of the Japanese Empire. At the ⇨ Yalta Conference (Feb. 1945), Stalin endorsed the agreement previously made between Roosevelt and Churchill that Korea's independence should be restored after the defeat of Japan. In accordance with a subsequent inter-allied agreement, this was to be achieved after a temporary period of occupation by Soviet and American forces, with the USSR in charge of the zone north of the 38th parallel and the USA in charge of the southern half of the country. It was also agreed that a mixed Soviet-American Commission should set up a provisional Korean government, representing all 'democratic' parties and social organizations.

As in many parallel cases in Eastern and Central Europe, the American and Soviet authorities failed to agree on the practical meaning of the term 'democratic'. After Japan's surrender, a multitude of new parties and organizations, many of them led by returned exiles, had sprung up in Korea; but organizations and individuals acceptable to the Americans proved unacceptable to the Soviet authorities, and *vice versa*. As a result of this deadlock, the two zones of occupation developed along sharply different political lines, reinforced by the bitter mutual hatred between their respective Korean leaders. In the northern zone, communist rule was established under the leadership of ⇨ Kim Il-sung, while the South set up a provisional legislative assembly, dominated by the Representative Democratic Council – a right-wing nationalist coalition under the leadership of Dr Syngman Rhee. In a final attempt at securing the reunification of the country, the USA appealed in the autumn of 1947 to the United Nations Assembly. Against Soviet objections, the UN Assembly resolved that elections for a National Assembly should be held throughout Korea under the supervision of a temporary UN

Commission and that the thus elected Assembly should set up an all-Korean government. In the spring of 1948, when the UN Commission arrived in Korea, it was refused entry into the northern zone. Both zones subsequently held separate elections, which merely served to legalize the existing state of affairs. They resulted in the setting up of two rival governments, the proclamation of two rival constitutions and the formal establishment, soon afterwards, of the Republic of Korea in the South (capital – Seoul), under the leadership of Dr Syngman Rhee, and of the Democratic People's Republic of Korea in the North (capital – Pyongyang) under the leadership of Kim Il-sung.

By the autumn of 1948, Kim Il-sung had consolidated his rule sufficiently for the USSR to feel satisfied that he could be left in charge, and the Soviet occupation forces were withdrawn. In the South, on the other hand, a parallel US troop withdrawal was delayed by policy differences between Dr Syngman Rhee and his American advisers, by a chronic economic crisis and a state of political insecurity, exacerbated by the influx of communist guerrilla forces from the North. There was one other vital difference between the two zones. After the withdrawal of the Soviet forces, the USSR provided North Korea with a large amount of military equipment, including heavy artillery, tanks and combat aircraft, while the Americans, at that time, refused to supply the South with offensive weapons of any kind.

The American forces withdrew in the summer of 1949. Less than a year after their withdrawal, the Soviet-equipped armies of the North crossed the partition line and launched a massive assault on the South (25.6.1950). South Korea appealed for help both to Washington and the UN. President Truman immediately ordered US naval and air support for the South Korean forces, while the UN Security Council called for the cessation of hostilities and the withdrawal of the North Korean armed forces to the 38th parallel. This demand was ignored. The Security Council then – in the absence of the USSR, which was boycotting its proceedings – recommended in a second resolution that UN member states should assist the Republic of Korea to repel the attack and restore peace and security in its territory. In response to this resolution, 16 UN member nations sent contingents of various strengths to participate in the defence of South Korea under the newly created United Nations Command (UNC) headed by General ⇨ MacArthur.

Having gained an overwhelming initial success, the Northern armies were soon afterwards driven back. In Sept. the UNC was, moreover, authorized to cross the 38th parallel in pursuit of the retreating Northern armies. China had previously warned that it would enter the war if the

UNC moved northwards towards the Yalu river, the boundary between China and North Korea. This warning had not been taken seriously. General MacArthur launched a fresh and supposedly final offensive towards the Yalu (Nov. 1950). Immediately afterwards Chinese troops crossed the river into Korea and, in a massive counter-attack, drove the UNC armies into a headlong retreat. The Korean War dragged on until July 1953, when an armistice was concluded, repartitioning the country along a line close to the original boundary on the 38th Parallel.

In the communist-ruled North, Kim Il-sung has remained in power, and under his leadership, North Korea has preserved a form of independent neutrality vis-à-vis the ▷ Sino-Soviet Conflict. In the South, Dr Syngman Rhee stayed in office as President of the Republic until 1960, when mounting popular discontent and rioting forced him to resign and emigrate. His successor, the leader of the former main opposition party, was overthrown after ten months in office by a *coup d'état*. Power was then seized by the Supreme Council for National Reconstruction – a military junta under the leadership of General Pak Chung Hee. Having undertaken to restore civilian government by 1963, General Pak Chung Hee resigned from the army in that year and became a presidential candidate in a new election. He won the election with a small majority, but considerably increased his majority four years later, when he was re-elected for a second term of office. (▷ Geneva Agreements.) After over two decades of hostility, emissaries from North and South Korea held secret negotiations, which led to an agreement, in July 1972, to seek re-unification by peaceful means.

Kostov, T. (1900–49). A former Secretary-General of the Bulgarian Communist Party and a party member from 1920, Kostov was arrested in 1924, tortured and imprisoned for many years. After his release he again engaged in underground communist work and became the Party's Secretary-General (1940). Re-arrested (1942), he received a life sentence, but was freed when the Fatherland Front seized power (1944). Re-affirmed as Secretary-General and Deputy Premier under ▷ Dimitrov, he became, after Dimitrov's death, the victim of the ▷ Muscovite faction led by ▷ Chervenkov. Indicted in 1949 as an agent of ▷ Tito and an imperialist spy, Kostov was the only prominent communist who failed to conform to the routine of the ▷ Show Trial by withdrawing his confession to the Secret Police in open court and pleading 'not guilty' to the end. He was executed after his trial (Dec. 1949).

Kosygin, A. N. (1904–). Chairman of the Council of Ministers of the USSR; member of the CPSU Politbureau. Kosygin joined the CPSU in

1927, became a member of the Central Committee (1939), a candidate member of the Politbureau (1946) and a full member (1948). A graduate of the Leningrad Textile Institute, his main activites were in economic administration, a field in which he occupied a variety of increasingly important posts. Minister of Finance in 1948 and Minister of the Light and Textile Industries in 1949, after Stalin's death (1953) he became a Deputy Chairman of the Council of Ministers. In 1956, he was appointed First Deputy Chairman of the newly established State Economic Commission and, in 1959, Chairman of ⇨ GOSPLAN. In 1970, he became first Deputy Chairman of the Council of Ministers, a post he held until ⇨ Khrushchev's overthrow (Oct. 1964), when he succeeded Khrushchev as Chairman of the Council of Ministers. In that capacity he has ever since concentrated on problems of economic development and has become an advocate of cautious economic reforms.

Kovacs, B. ⇨ Hungary.

Krag, Jens Otto (1914–). Danish Prime Minister (1962–69; 1971–) and Chairman of the Social Democratic Party since 1962. A political scientist and author of books on economics and the cooperative movement, he became from 1947 onwards a dominating influence in Danish politics holding a variety of ministerial appointments.

Kreisky, Dr Bruno (1911–). Chancellor of ⇨ Austria (1970–) and leader of the Austrian Socialist Party (SPO). A socialist youth leader of Jewish parentage, he emigrated after the ⇨ *Anschluss* to Stockholm where he became associated with ⇨ Willy Brandt. After the War served as Ambassador to ⇨ Sweden (1946), Secretary of State in the Foreign Ministry (1953–59) and Foreign Minister (1959–66).

Kremlin. Castle overlooking Moscow, now the seat of the Soviet leadership.

Kremlinology. Semi-serious term applied to the interpretation, based on indirect evidence, of officially undisclosed policies and events in the USSR.

Krishna Menon, V. K. (1897–). Minister of Defence of ⇨ India (1957–62). A controversial figure both while in England (where he was borough councillor of St Pancras, 1934–47) and later, gaining a reputation as a supporter of Soviet Communist Party policies. He was formerly Indian High Commissioner to the UK (1947–52) and leader of his country's delegation to the UN (1953–62). ⇨ Nehru dismissed him from his post in 1962 following the Chinese invasion of Indian territory which demonstrated the weaknesses of the country's defences.

Kristall Nacht. ⇨ Crystal Night.

Kubitschek de Oliveira, Dr Juscelino (1902–). President of ⇨ Brazil (1955–60) and founder of Brasilia. Kubitschek believed that unlimited spending including public works, the encouragement of industry and investment was the panacea for all economic ills, but despite the boost to national pride there was inevitably increased unrest among those, especially in the cities, who did not benefit from the boom. During his presidency, reckless extravagance was combined with a second industrial revolution. Often cited as a most exciting phase in Brazil's recent history, it was marred by financial corruption and a soaring inflation that lowered urban living standards.

Kuchuk, Fazil (1906–). Vice-President of ⇨ Cyprus since 1960 and leader of the Turkish Cypriots. Also Chairman of the Cyprus Turkish National Union Party since 1943. When the Turkish Cypriots chose their own 'Transitional Administration' (Dec. 1967) Kuchuk was made its President. He was re-elected Vice-President of Cyprus by the Turkish community (Feb. 1968).

Ku Klux Klan. A secret society in the USA violently hostile to Negroes, Catholics, Jews and other 'aliens'. It was first organized in the South in the period of Reconstruction following the Civil War to resist and reverse the advance of the emancipated slaves.

Although it was officially disbanded in 1869, Congress found it necessary to pass legislation against it in the succeeding years, but its influence helped to perpetuate Lynch Law throughout the South. It was openly revived after World War I, its symbol of the 'fiery cross' appearing in many places even outside the South. The ⇨ FBI under its Director, J. Edgar ⇨ Hoover, played a significant part in containing it (or at least driving it underground). It was again revived following the decision against school ⇨ Segregation by the Supreme Court in ⇨ Brown v. Board of Education (1954); and it was prominent in the rise of the ⇨ White Citizens Councils in the following years. In the 1960s it not only intensified its intimidation of Negroes, but also terrorized White activists in the ⇨ Civil Rights Movement, resorting to murder in some cases. Its influence has become more widespread in recent years, with the extension of the ⇨ New Right. But it has also been weakened as a result of being openly challenged by ⇨ Black Power.

Kulak. Russian term (literally 'fist') for well-to-do peasants, extended by ⇨ Stalin during the period of compulsory collectivization of 1929/30 to virtually the entire peasantry under the slogan of 'extermination of the kulaks as a class'. (⇨ USSR.)

Kuomintang. KMT – National People's Party – national revolutionary party which played an important part in the overthrow of the Manchu dynasty (1911) and later became the governing party in China under ⇨ Chiang Kai-shek for two decades until the communists came to power in 1949. It was originally conceived by its first leader, Sun

Yat-sen, as a movement for establishing a Western-style democracy in China, an aim which it could not realize. The KMT's support was limited to the commercial middle class in Canton and Shanghai and in order to challenge the dominance of the war-lords, it created its own army under Chiang Kai-shek. Contact was made with the Soviet Government, which was regarded with more favour than the Western Powers by the Nationalists because of Soviet opposition to Japanese territorial claims on China. Russian political and military advisers were sent (1923) to train the Kuomintang Army at the new military academy at Whampoa. Sun Yat-sen also decided to cooperate with the communists, who were permitted to enrol individually as members of the KMT. This policy broke down after Sun Yat-sen's death (1925) and his replacement as leader of the KMT by Chiang Kai-shek. Matters came to a head when the latter marched north with his new army (1926) and won a series of easy victories over the war-lords and captured several cities (Hankow, Nanking). Chiang Kai-shek, alarmed at the growing influence of the communists in the KMT, purged them (1927) and so began the civil war between the two factions which lasted intermittently for over 20 years. The Nationalists, having captured Peking and defeated the war-lords, were recognized as the Government of China. Plans were made for the creation of an effective state administration to replace the anarchy of the previous decade, but these were interrupted by Japanese invasions of China. The loss of Manchuria (1931) deprived China of her most industrially developed area while the second war with Japan (1937–45) weakened her further. She was blockaded by sea and six of her seven largest cities were captured by the superior Japanese forces. The conflict with the communists continued and they were driven out from south and central China by the Nationalists (1934–35). In 1937, however, Chiang Kai-shek again reversed his policy and agreed to cooperate with the communists against the foreign invader. Japanese aggression was an important factor in the defeat of the KMT by the communists for the loss of the cities deprived the KMT of their urban base. Resistance had to come from the rural areas, where the communists with their mobilization of the peasants under Mao Tse-tung had a distinct advantage (⇨ Chinese People's Republic). Cooperation between the communists and the Nationalists continued only until 1940 when their civil strife was renewed. The KMT remained as the government of China (Chiang Kai-shek represented China at the Cairo Conference in 1943 and became one of the Big Five), but increasing criticism of his rule for corruption and inefficiency plus the devastation of the war and the resulting inflation weakened his position at home. In the civil war which followed (1945–49) the initial superiority in numbers of the

Nationalist troops (they were four times as large as the communist troops) was not sufficient to balance Mao Tse-tung's experience in guerrilla warfare, his exploitation of the unpopularity of the KMT government and the superior morale of the communist forces. When the communists seized power on the Chinese mainland (1949), the Nationalists withdrew to the island of Taiwan, where they have since continued to function as the Republic of ⇨China, still claiming that one day they will return to 'liberate' China from the communists.

Kuwait. *Area* – 5,800 sq. miles (excluding the Neutral Zone). *Population* (1969) – 733,000. *Head of State* – Sheikh Sabah as-Salim as ⇨ Sabah (1965–). *Prime Minister* – Jaber al-Ahmad al-Jaber (1965–). *Constitution* (1962) – Independent Arab Kingdom governed by a constitutional monarch. Executive power is vested in the Emir, exercised through a Council of Ministers. The Legislature is the National Assembly elected for four years by all native-born literate Kuwait males over 21 (half the population consists of foreigners, chiefly from neighbouring states).

Kuwait, one of the largest oil-producing countries in the Middle East, was a British Protectorate from 1899 to 1961, when she gained full independence. The production of oil, which began in 1946 and now comprises four-fifths of the country's revenues (oil exports in 1966 amounted to 926 million b.b.l.), has transformed Kuwait. Much of the profits has been used for the development of social services, in particular education and medicine (which are free), public works, and industrial and commercial development. The first elections in Kuwait's history were held in 1961 for a Constituent Assembly, which drafted a constitution (1962). The following year elections were held for the new National Assembly. There were further elections in 1967, but there are no political parties as such. Candidates stand as individuals, although there are various pan-Arab groups and also supporters of the Syrian *Ba'ath* Party. Largely because of her oil, Kuwait has assumed an importance in international affairs out of proportion to her size and geographical position. She joined the ⇨ Arab League (1961), which sent in troops the same year to guarantee Kuwait's independence after Iraq claimed sovereignty over her territory, but in 1963 Iraq recognized her independence and at the same time a commercial and economic agreement was concluded between the two states. Kuwait has tended to follow a neutral course in inter-Arab disputes, e.g. her attempts at mediation in the conflicts in the ⇨Yemen and South Arabia, but in the Arab-Israeli War of 1967 (⇨Arab-Israeli Conflict), she declared war on Israel and joined in the oil embargo on the USA and the UK. Relations with the UK have remained close since independence. Kuwait is the UK's most important source of oil, providing 23% of her requirements, and in 1961 the UK undertook to provide military assistance if requested. This defence pact ceased in 1971 with the virtual British withdrawal from the Persian Gulf. There is close economic cooperation with Saudi Arabia (1965 agreement) with whom Kuwait agreed (1963) to administer jointly the Neutral Zone.

L

Labor-Management Relations Act, 1947. In the USA, the ⇨ Taft-Hartley Act.

Labour and Socialist International. ⇨ Second International.

Labour Party. British political party which grew out of the Labour Representation Committee (1900) formed by working-class and socialist organizations. In 1906 it secured seats in the General Election and adopted its present name. In 1922 it became the official opposition in Parliament for the first time, ousting the ⇨ Liberal Party to become one of the UK's two main political parties. Following two short periods in office (1924, 1929–31) as a minority government its electoral strength was dealt a crushing blow when its leader and Prime Minister ⇨ Mac-Donald accepted the premiership of a National Government. Under ⇨ Attlee the Party was concerned to rebuild its electoral strength and offer a 'socialist' alternative to Conservative rule. Its leaders played a crucial part in supporting ⇨ Churchill (1940), and gained valuable administrative experience in his war-time government. The first post-war Labour Government (1945–50), after a decisive election victory, enacted a vast programme of domestic reform (nationalization, welfare policies) and colonial independence (⇨ India, ⇨ Burma), while maintaining the American alliance. 1951 ushered in a period of 13 years out of office with Party morale weakened by the loss of three successive general elections and continued internal strife. (⇨ Bevan, ⇨ Gaitskell, ⇨ Clause IV.) Unity was gradually restored as Gaitskell emerged as a national leader and in 1964 under ⇨ Wilson, the party was returned to office. Since its peak of popularity in 1966, the Labour Government's continued difficulties, particularly its handling of the balance of payments crisis, led to a sharp decline in popularity and its subsequent defeat in the 1970 General Election.

The British Labour Party has grown out of the Trades Union Movement and the political reforms of the last century. Committed to parliamentary democracy, the Labour Party has lacked the theoretical commitment of many European socialist parties. As much as the

⇨ Conservative Party, it represents a coalition of interests. Its dependence on trade union support, the need to maintain the support of the left without alienating the centre and right or the marginal voters whose support is necessary for electoral success, contribute to its difficulties in and out of office.

Leaders of the Labour Party from 1932:
1932–35 – George Lansbury
1935–55 – C. R. Attlee
1955–63 – Hugh Gaitskell
1963–   – Harold Wilson

Labour Party Election Results:

	MPs elected	Votes polled
1931	46	6,362,561
1935	154	8,325,260
1945	393	11,992,292
1950	315	13,265,610
1951	295	13,949,105
1955	277	12,405,246
1959	258	12,195,765
1964	317	12,205,581
1966	363	13,057,941
1970	287	12,141,676

LAFTA. Latin American Free Trade Association – was established by the Charter of Montevideo (18.2.1960). It aims at the eventual establishment of a South American Common Market. It works through regular meetings of a Council of Foreign Ministers and has a Permanent Executive Committee. Its progress has been hampered by vast differences in industrial development among its members, by inadequate transport systems and anxieties of national industries to maintain their protected status in their own countries. However, it benefited from a commission (suggested by Eduardo ⇨ Frei) to work out a detailed plan for a Common Market. At its 1967 session (Uruguay) it was agreed that the necessary steps be undertaken from 1970 to create a Common Market by 1985. Its members are: Argentina, Brazil, Chile, Colombia, Ecuador, Mexico, Paraguay, Peru, Uruguay, Venezuela.

Its example has been followed by Chile, Colombia, Ecuador, Peru and Venezuela, who have established the *Andean Development Corporation* (June 1967) for the purpose of cooperation in regional development including the establishment of a common external tariff for the whole region. Its aims received LAFTA support (Sept. 1967).

Lame Duck Amendment. Twentieth Amendment to the Constitution of the USA (ratified 1933) which reduced the period between the holding of presidential and congressional elections (Nov.) and the beginning of the successful candidates' terms (previously March, thereafter Jan.). In the intervening period the outgoing President or Congress was thought to be as capable of action as a 'lame duck'. Although considerably shorter, such a period still exists. It can still cause a dangerous hiatus in national affairs especially when the presidency changes hands, and still more when a party change is involved.

Land (*Länder*). Name for the semi-autonomous states constituting the Federal Republic of Germany.

Landrum-Griffin Act. The Labor-Management Reporting and Disclosure Act, passed by Congress in the USA in 1959 after a ⏵Congressional Investigation had revealed certain malpractices in trade unions. The Act defined the legal rights of members, especially with regard to elections, and prohibited certain persons holding office on the basis of their past records (criminal and political). It also strengthened provisions of the ⏵ Taft-Hartley Act against 'sympathy' action among unions.

Laos, Kingdom of. *Area* – 90,000 sq. miles. *Population* (1970) – 2,700,000. *King* – Sri Savang Vatthana. *Prime Minister* – Prince Souvanna Phouma.

Formerly an integral part of the French dependency of Indochina, Laos achieved autonomy within the French Union in 1949. As a result of the ⏵ Geneva Agreements of 1954, Laos was recognized as a fully independent state, committed to neutrality. By that time, however, three mutually hostile political groups were contending for ascendancy. They were (1) the neutralists, led by Prince Souvanna Phouma, (2) the pro-communists, led by his half-brother, Prince Souphanouvong, (3) right-wing pro-American nationalists, led by General Phoumi Novasan. From the late 1940s, Prince Souphanouvong had been in contact with the ⏵Viet Minh across the border. From 1953 onwards, the Viet Minh leaders helped Prince Souphanouvong in the establishment of a rival 'Free Laotian Government', the Pathet Lao, which recruited its own armed forces, first in Northern Laos and later in other parts of the country. The Geneva Conference of 1954 called for the re-integration of the areas under Pathet Lao rule into a unified Laos and for nationwide elections. Elections were duly held in Dec. 1955 in the areas under effective government authority, but not in the areas controlled by the Pathet Lao, which boycotted the elections. After a brief interval, Prince Souvanna Phouma became Prime Minister. In the following years he made repeated attempts at achieving a compromise with his brother,

Prince Souphanouvong and the Pathet Lao under his control. Agreement was eventually reached (Nov. 1957) to set up a coalition Government of National Unity under Prince Souvanna Phouma in which the Pathet Lao as well as the right-wing nationalists would serve together with the neutralists. This coalition has never been formally abandoned, but practical cooperation did not survive for long. From the early 1960s onwards, armed clashes between official government and Pathet Lao forces became more frequent and territories repeatedly changed hands, but the general outcome remained inconclusive. In between, General Phoumi Novasan attempted several unsuccessful *coups d'état*. In the spring of 1965, after his third unsuccessful *coup*, he escaped to Thailand.

Latvia. One of the 15 Federal Soviet Republics constituting the USSR. *Capital* – Riga. (⇨ Baltic States.)

Laval, Pierre (1883–1945). Progressed from poverty and left-wing radicalism, via Cabinet and Prime-Ministerial appointments in the twenties and thirties, to ⇨ Vichy's extreme right-wing premierships (1940, 1942–44) and execution as a traitor. He achieved notoriety when after ⇨ Italy's attack on ⇨ Abyssinia (3.10.1935) it became known that during his term as Foreign Minister (1934) and as Premier (June 1935–Jan. 1936) together with Sir Samuel Hoare, the British Foreign Secretary, he had secretly conceded Abyssinian territories to Italy. Although this was done to keep Italy in the French system of anti-German alliances, public indignation led to the resignation of both authors of the so-called ⇨ Hoare-Laval Plan. Laval re-emerged after the defeat of ⇨ France as Marshal ⇨ Pétain's deputy (June 1940), but was later arrested and dismissed on a charge of plotting (Dec. 1940). Released under German pressure, he was accepted back by the Marshal as his Premier (April 1942), and given near-dictatorial powers (Nov. 1942). He admitted into his Cabinet dedicated collaborators like Darnand (Feb. 1944), who had organized the establishment of a hated ⇨ ss-like French Militia and the deportation of French workers to Germany. Escaping shortly before the German collapse to Spain which refused him asylum, he surrendered to the Americans (July 1945) who turned him over to the French. Despite a transparently unfair trial and his own clever defence, he was found guilty of treason and shot at Fresne prison after an abortive suicide attempt.

League of Arab States. ⇨ Arab League.

League of Nations. Representing a major Allied war aim (as proposed in US President Wilson's Fourteen Points) – was the first attempt at establishing a world authority to prevent future wars and encourage international cooperation. Set up in Geneva (1920), its 42 nation membership did not include the USA as Congress refused to ratify the League Covenant. Pledged to collective security, the League was empowered to impose economic sanctions if attempts at arbitration failed.

The League consisted of the General Assembly, convened once a year, each member state having one vote, the co-equal Council made up of permanent and temporary members meeting more frequently, and the Secretariat, the organization's civil service. The Court of International Justice and the International Labour office (ILO) were permanently associated with the League while special commissions on minority rights, mandated colonial territories, etc., were set up as necessity arose.

Germany was admitted in 1926 after the signing of the Locarno Pact changing the League from an Allied into a more universal organization. From 1920 to 1932 the League enjoyed considerable authority, preventing or quickly terminating a number of local wars, e.g. the Polish-Lithuanian conflict over Vilna (1920), the Yugoslav invasion of Albania (1921), the Mosul conflict (1925). Respect for the League declined in the thirties when it failed to check the aggressions of powerful and increasingly totalitarian states. Japan, condemned by the Assembly for its attack on China and the setting-up of the puppet state Manchukuo (Manchuria), left the League in 1933 as did Nazi Germany when Versailles restrictions on her armaments were not lifted. In 1934 the USSR joined the League, but its waning authority finally collapsed when sanctions, but no oil embargo, imposed on Italy after her invasion of Abyssinia (Oct. 1935), proved ineffectual. Unable to protect Austria, Czechoslovakia, Albania, Spain or Poland from aggression, the League expelled Russia when she attacked Finland (Dec. 1939). Inoperative throughout the war, the League was reconvened (April 1946) merely to transfer its function and property to the ⇨ United Nations.

Lebanon. *Area* – 3,400 sq. miles. *Population* – 2,645,000 (50% of whom are Christians and 45% Moslems). *President* – Soliman Frangié (1970–). *Prime Minister* – Saeb Salam (1970–). *Constitution* (1926, frequently amended) – Independent Republic. Executive power is vested in the President (elected for six years, by convention a Christian) who chooses the Prime Minister (by convention a Moslem) and the Cabinet, who are responsible to Parliament (although they need not be members of it). Legislative power is vested in the Parliament consisting of the Chamber of Deputies, elected by universal suffrage for four years. Distribution of seats in the Chamber is made according to the strengths of the religious sects.

The Lebanon, part of the Ottoman Empire until World War I, came under French mandate in 1920 and in 1926 became a Republic (but still under French control), with a President and an elected Assembly.

Pressure for full independence continued (influenced by the nationalist movement in ⇨ Syria) but a treaty with France (1936) providing for constitutional reform was not ratified by the French Assembly. The real opportunity for independence came in World War II when the British and Free French forces, which had occupied the country, supported the declaration of Lebanese independence (Nov. 1941). Independence did not become an accomplished fact until 1946, when the last of the foreign troops were withdrawn. Post-war political and economic circumstances did not encourage stability. The failure of the Arab states (including the Lebanon) in the war with ⇨ Israel (1948–49) led to an unsuccessful attempt by disillusioned Arab nationalists to overthrow the government (1949). Growing unemployment, a high cost of living (the economy suffered from the loss of war-time trade, the French devaluation in 1948 and the severance of economic relations with Syria 1950–52) and charges of corruption resulted in the overthrow of President al-Khuri (1952). A new President (Camille ⇨ Chamoun, 1952–58) and government were elected with a promise of reform, i.e. of the electoral laws, the press laws and the organization of justice. Success here was not matched in the attempts to create national parties which might bridge tribal and religious divisions. Communal discontent among the Moslems (who felt dominated by the Christians and received moral, financial and military support from the UAR) led to rioting and a serious domestic crisis (1958). They objected to the pro-West foreign policy of the government; the Lebanon supported Egypt in the ⇨ Suez Crisis (1956) but did not break off diplomatic relations with the UK or France; she accepted the ⇨ Eisenhower Doctrine (1957) and declined to join the UAR (1958). In July 1958 against a background of widespread rioting and threatened civil war the government called for the assistance of US troops. The resulting international crisis was only solved when General ⇨ Chebab (supported by both communities) was elected President and Rashid Karami, the Moslem rebel leader, was chosen as Prime Minister. The Lebanon renounced the Eisenhower Doctrine and steered a course closer to the other Arab nations, e.g. the inter-Arab conference (1959) resulted in the settlement of various differences with Syria and improved relations with the UAR followed a meeting between Chebab and ⇨ Nasser (1959). She still tried to remain neutral in inter-Arab disputes, e.g. during friction between Syria and Jordan (1961) and in the Arab-Israeli War of 1967 she gave verbal support to the Arab states but did not participate in the campaign. This policy of non-involvement has sometimes been difficult to maintain. The Greater Syrian Party, which advocated union with Syria, continued its agitation and in 1967 attempted another *coup d'état*. Guerrilla bands operating from Lebanese soil (but without the blessing of the Lebanese Government) have not improved relations with neighbouring Israel. When tension arose between the two countries in 1965 after a series of border incidents, the Lebanon took measures to curb the activities of *Al* ⟴*Fatah*, the extremist Arab organization. In Dec. 1968 an attack on an Israeli aircraft at Athens by Arab guerrillas coming from the Lebanon resulted in Israeli reprisals on Beirut airport. Lebanon's position as a financial and commercial centre for the Arab world has had a major influence on her policy and has made her reluctant to become involved in adventurist foreign policies. These factors as well as her tourist trade make the Lebanon more reluctant than other Arab states to pursue anti-West policies. In 1965 she signed a commercial agreement with the EEC.

Lecanuet, Jean François (1920–). The French presidential contender who polled 3·77 m. votes in the first heat of the 1965 elections but failed to win a seat in the June 1968 elections. He fought in the Resistance, was an ⟴MRP Deputy (1951–55) and held a variety of high administrative appointments in the Fourth Republic. He headed the *Centre Démocrate* which combined with the PDM (Progress and Modern Democracy Party) gained 33 seats in the 1968 elections as against the *Centre Démocrate's* 27 seats in 1967.

Lee Kuan Yew (1923–). Prime Minister of ⟴Singapore since 1959 and leader of the People's Action Party of which he was one of the founders. He negotiated Singapore's membership of the Federation of ⟴Malaysia (1963) but secession followed two years later after this proved unworkable. He is concerned about the future of Singapore in view of the withdrawal of British forces ⟴East of Suez. In spite of his country's small size, Lee Kuan Yew has been an influential figure at ⟴Commonwealth meetings.

Left & Right. Since these terms were first used during the French Revolution, each has undergone so many shifts of meaning and been used to include so many, often contradictory political tendencies that no precise definition is possible. Popularly the Left has favoured rapid social change (revolution or reform), greater social equality, state intervention in the economy and colonial independence. The label has been applied to a whole range of 'Socialists' from Attlee to Trotsky, and to parties as diverse as the ⟴SPD and Chairman ⟴Mao's Communists. The Right, accepting class differences as part of a natural order, has favoured patriotism, tradition (the Church), strong government and a minimum of state intervention in the economy. The description has included a range of attitudes from moderate Conservatism to Fascism. During the thirties, Left was associated with opposition to Fascism and support for the Soviet Union, although internal disagreements were acute and made more so by the Soviet Purges and later by the Nazi-Soviet Pact. Post-war developments (e.g. the ⇨ Sino-Soviet conflict, recent changes in Eastern Europe, the emergence of a ⇨ 'New Left', student militancy in the West and East) have led to further shifts of meaning, though the terms Left, Right (and Centre) are still helpful in describing internal party divisions (e.g. within the British Labour Party).

Lend-Lease. Arrangement for the supply of war materials made by the USA, initially with the UK (11.3.1941) and later with other countries, to overcome the problem of payment. Ownership of supplies remained nominally in the USA, and payment for them was deferred until after hostilities or discounted in return for long-term leases of military bases to the United States. After the United States entered World War II the arrangement was supplemented by mutual aid agreements with the Allies. The programme continued until August 1945, by which time aid amounting to over $43 b. had been furnished by the USA, including $30 b. to the British Commonwealth and above $10 b. to the USSR. The British Commonwealth provided £1·6 b. ($7·6 b.) in reciprocal aid to the USA. Lend-lease enabled Britain to finance her war effort without having to maintain exports and despite the depletion of her monetary reserves.

Lenin, V. I. (1870–1924). Founder and leader of the ⇨ Bolshevik Party, architect of its seizure of power in Oct. 1917 and founder and leader of the Soviet state emerging from the October revolution. (⇨ Bolshevism.)

Leningrad Case. A large-scale political purge in the USSR, beginning in 1949, of former associates of A. A. ⇨ Zdhanov, leading to the execution of nearly all communist party leaders in the Leningrad region and of other top-ranking communists formerly connected with Leningrad, among them N. A. Voznesensky, the President of ⇨ Gosplan and a member of the Politbureau. In 1956, ⇨ Khrushchev named ⇨ Beria as the chief culprit in organizing the Leningrad purge on the basis of trumped-up charges. Five years later, several speakers at the 22nd CPSU Congress attributed the main guilt for the Leningrad purge to G. M. ⇨ Malenkov who had been Zdhanov's chief rival and who, after Zdhanov's sudden death in 1948 and the subsequent extermination of his supporters, succeeded to Zdhanov's erstwhile role as ⇨ Stalin's heir-apparent.

Leninism. ⇨ Bolshevism.

Leninist Norms. A term frequently used by the post-Stalin leadership of the USSR to circumscribe the approved departures from Stalinist practices as well as the limits set to reforms by the guidelines allegedly laid down by Lenin.

Lenin's Testament. Notes dictated by Lenin during his last fatal illness on the political future of the Soviet Communist Party, including critical personal appreciations of ⇨ Stalin, ⇨ Trotsky, ⇨ Bukharin and other Bolshevik leaders. Concerned that the clash between Trotsky and Stalin, the two principal leaders, might produce a split, Lenin appealed in a postscript to the notes, added in 1923, to his colleagues in the Party leadership to remove Stalin from his powerful post as the Party's General Secretary. Though published in the West in the mid-1920s, the 'testament' was suppressed in the USSR during Stalin's lifetime. It was first made public there in 1956, during the 20th CPSU Congress, when copies of the 'testament' were distributed to the Congress delegates.

Leoni, Raul (1905–). President of ⇨ Venezuela (1964–68) and Minister of Labour (1945–48). A founder member of AD (*Accion Democratica*) 1937 and one of the leaders of the *coup* (1945). In exile from 1939 to 1941 and from 1948 to 1958. His army clashed with guerrillas – claimed by the government to be Castro-sponsored and opposed by Venezuelans.

Lesotho. *Area* – 11,716 sq. miles. *Population* (approx.) – 970,000 (of which 3,000 are Europeans). *Prime Minister* – Chief Leabua Jonathan. *Constitution* – A constitutional monarchy with a bi-cameral Parliament made up of a Senate (Chiefs and King's nominees) and a National Assembly elected by universal adult suffrage. Executive power is vested in a Prime Minister and Cabinet responsible to the Assembly. The Government cannot restrict civil liberties without recourse to the courts.

Formerly the ⇨ High Commission Territory of Basutoland, Lesotho was only granted representative government in 1959. Following the general election (April 1965) the present constitution, agreed at the London Conference (May 1964), came into force. Lesotho achieved independence within the ⇨ Commonwealth on 4 Oct. 1966. Extremely poor, surrounded by and economically dependent on ⇨ South Africa, Lesotho is faced with the same sort of problems as ⇨ Botswana. South African currency is used, and the wages of the 200,000 Basuto, who yearly migrate to the Johannesburg gold mines, contribute significantly to the economy. Lacking the political stability of Botswana, dislike of the ⇨ Apartheid policies of her powerful neighbour is a potent source of unrest and fuel for pan-African political movements. In Dec. 1966, the King, Moshoeshoe II, was arrested for plotting the overthrow of the government but was released the following month on his agreement to abide by the constitution. With no easy solution to its economic problems and chronic dissatisfaction with government policies, political stability will not be easily achieved.

Lewis, John L. (1880–1969). US labour leader, President of the United Mine Workers (UMW) (1919–60) which he made into one of the most powerful unions in the country. Setting out to organize workers on an industry-wide basis, he helped form the Committee for Industrial Organization and became its first President (1935). It became the ⇨CIO after its expulsion from the ⇨AFL in 1936. Six years later Lewis led the mineworkers out of the CIO (1942) and eventually back into the AFL (1946). A strong supporter of Franklin D. ⇨ Roosevelt in 1936, he shifted his position in 1940 and led many strikes during World War II that resulted in government seizure as well as better conditions for miners. Although Lewis had a strong anti-communist record, he refused to sign the required non-communist oath of the ⇨Taft-Hartley Act and led his UMW out of the AFL (1947). Though often at odds with the government and courts, Lewis was one of America's most successful union leaders.

Liberal Party. British reformist political party whose power slumped dramatically with the rise of the ⇨ Labour Party after World War I, though it continues to return a handful of MPs to Westminster. Under Jo ⇨ Grimond (1956–67) and his successor Jeremy ⇨ Thorpe (Jan. 1967–) it has attempted to present itself as a radical left-wing alternative to Labour.

Liberalism. Fundamentally a belief in the rights of individuals to base their religious and political convictions on the dictates of conscience, and the Rule of Law. Usually favours national self-determination and the ballot-box, and is opposed to the restriction of individual freedom through arbitrary government, state interference or economic monopoly. In Britain, liberal also refers to membership of the ⇨ Liberal Party. In its wider usage, liberalism is associated with the protection of individual rights – in the twentieth century particularly with rights of racial and religious minorities – and with attempts to defend and enlarge the freedom of individuals.

Liberia, Republic of. *Area* – 43,000 sq. miles. *Population* (1971 est.) – 1,500,000. *President* – William Richard Tolbert (1971–). *Constitution* – Copied from the USA with an elected President assisted by a Cabinet and a bi-cameral Legislature, Senate and House of Representatives elected by universal suffrage.

Founded by Negro immigrants from the USA and the West Indies, helped by American philanthropists and established as an independent Republic (the first in Africa) on 26 July 1847, Liberia has an enviable record of political stability. The True Whig Party has been continuously in power for over ninety years. In its early years the country was dominated by its immigrants who have since merged with the indigenous population. Reforms in 1964 gave the interior regions the same constitutional status as the coastal immigrant counties. In 1930 the scandal of a continuing slave trade led to a League of Nations investigation and a change of government. Since 1943, under the dominating personality of President Tubman, Liberian economic development, with the help of large-scale foreign, particularly American, investment (the US dollar is an official unit of currency) has been rapid. Tubman was at the Accra Conference of 1958 and sponsored the Monrovia Conference of 1961 and since Addis Ababa two years later has attended every OAU conference. In 1966 he was granted special powers for twelve months to deal with labour unrest. Following Tubman's death (July 1971), the Vice-President William Tolbert became President.

Libya. *Area* – 810,000 sq. miles. *Population* (1969 est.) – 1,869,000. *Prime Minister* – Col. Moamer al Kadhafi (1970–). *Constitution* – The United Kingdom of Libya, consisting of the three provinces of Cyrenaica, Tripolitania and Fezzan, was formed as a Federal State in 1951. Constitutional amendments (1963) renamed Libya the Kingdom of Libya, and abolished the federal system. The new constitution also enfranchised women. Libya was a hereditary constitutional monarchy until Sept. 1969 when a military *coup* deposed King Idris and declared Libya a republic. In Sept. 1971 Libya formed the Federation of Arab Republics with Egypt and Syria.

Libya was formerly an Italian colony, though the colonizers had to wage long campaigns (1912–19, 1923–33) to enforce their rule. With a view to encouraging Italian peasant settlement, rapid economic development, only marginally affecting local inhabitants, was undertaken from 1930 onwards. During World War II the country became a main battle-ground of the North African campaigns. With the Allied occupation (1942), Cyrenaica and Tripolitania were administered by Britain, and Fezzan by the French, and then under the UN which (1949) voted for Libyan independence which was achieved in 1951. Combined political rivalries with economic inefficiency paved the way for the replacement of federal government by a unitary one based on ten administrative districts (1963). In 1953 Libya joined the ⇨Arab League and the development of her oil industry (exporting started in 1961) is likely to increase her importance in the Arab world. Since the Suez Canal closure, the importance of Libyan oil to Europe has increased. During the Six Day War (⇨Arab-Israeli Conflict) there were violent anti-Israel, anti-US and anti-UK demonstrations, the government demanded that UK and US troops be withdrawn, and their military installations (agreed by previous treaties) be closed down. The Republican government nationalized British oil interests in Libya in February 1972.

Lidice. A Czech mining village which, since World War II, has become a byword for Nazi terror. In June 1942, the German occupation forces destroyed the whole village, executed all its male adults and deported its women and children to concentration camps in retaliation for the assassination of the German 'Protector', Reinhold Heydrich, Himmler's assistant as Head of the Nazi Security Police.

Lie, Trygve (1896–1968). Norwegian Socialist politician, and from 1935 to 1946 a member of all Norwegian governments, including the one exiled in London during the war. He became the UN's first Secretary-General (1946–1953).

Liechtenstein. *Area* – 61 sq. miles. *Population* (1969) – 22,000. *Head of State* – Prince Francis Josef II. A hereditary principality (independent since 1719) on the upper Rhine. Under the 1923 treaty with Switzerland, it uses Swiss currency as well as her postal and customs services.

Lindsay, John V. (1922–). Mayor of New York City, USA (1965–). Graduated from Yale College and Yale Law School, he served in the US Justice Department (1955–57), and in the ⊏> House of Representatives (1957–63). Although a ⊏> Republican, he was of markedly liberal persuasion, and frequently voted against the majority of his own party. Elected Mayor of New York as a Republican in 1965, he failed to secure his party's nomination for re-election in 1969, but nevertheless won a second term as an independent. In 1971 he finally broke with the Republicans and registered as a ⊏> Democrat. He declared himself a contender for the Democratic presidential nomination in 1972, but failed to secure any significant popular support in ⊏> Primary Elections.

Lin Piao, Marshal (1908?–). Chinese communist and soldier. A CCP member since 1925 and participant in the Comintern-sponsored communist uprisings of 1927, Lin joined Mao after the defeat of the risings in the Kiangsi Soviet area. Appointed Commander of the First Red Army in 1932, he won special distinction during the Long March and later proved an outstandingly successful military commander in the war against Japan and the civil war. After the proclamation of the CPR in 1949, Lin steadily advanced in China's Party and government hierarchy. Created a Marshal and promoted to the Politbureau (1955), he became a member of its Standing Committee (Mao's innermost top circle) (1958), and in 1959 he became Minister of Defence and the effective Head of the Party's powerful Military Affairs Committee. Emerging in the early 1960s as Mao's most ardent supporter and the tireless propagandist of the study of 'Mao's Thought', Lin Piao played the leading part in the organization of the Cultural Revolution. By Aug. 1966, he had replaced ⊏> Liu Shao-chi as Mao's second-in-command. The Party's new Statutes, adopted by the 9th Party Congress of April 1969 named Lin

Piao as 'Mao Tse-tung's successor'. Just over two years later, Lin vanished in mysterious circumstances. He was unofficially reported to have perished in an air accident, while trying to escape to the USSR after an unsuccessful *coup* against Mao.

Literacy Tests. Tests of ability to read, write or comprehend, applied as a qualification for voting. In the USA, literacy tests have been used to restrict voting especially by Negroes in the South. The Voting Rights Act of 1965 prohibited the use of any such 'test or device' in States and districts where less than half the voting-age population was registered, and provided for the appointment of Federal registrars where this was deemed necessary by the ⇨ Attorney General. The passage of the Act was a major event in the ⇨ Civil Rights Movement.

Lithuania. One of the 15 Federal Soviet Republics constituting the USSR. *Capital* – Vilna. (⇨ Baltic States.)

Little Entente. Alliance established in 1920, with the encouragement of ⇨ France, between ⇨ Czechoslovakia, ⇨ Yugoslavia and ⇨ Rumania, chiefly directed against ⇨ Hungary's claims to formerly Hungarian territories incorporated in these countries since World War I.

Little Rock. Town in Arkansas, USA, where in 1957 resistance to the abolition of ⇨ Segregation in schools in accordance with the 1954 Supreme Court decision in ⇨ Brown v. Board of Education reached such a pitch that President Eisenhower had to send Federal troops to protect Negro children going to the previously all-White Central High School. It was a turning-point in the enforcement of ⇨ Integration.

Litvinov, Maxim (1876–1952). Soviet Foreign Minister (1930–39). A ⇨ Bolshevik from his early youth, Litvinov succeeded Chicherin as Soviet Commissar for Foreign Affairs (1930). In the 1930s, Litvinov was the main Soviet spokesman for a policy of collective security, of a rapprochement with the West and of Soviet support for the League of Nations. He was dismissed in May 1939 and replaced by ⇨ Molotov so as to facilitate the rapprochement with Germany then favoured by ⇨ Stalin.

Litvinov, Pavel (1937–). Soviet physicist (⇨ Dissent – Eastern Europe).

Liu Shao-chi (1898–). Chinese communist and former Head of State. In 1919 Liu went as a student to Moscow where he joined the CCP on its foundation (1921). Back in China, he became the Party's foremost labour organizer, first in Shanghai, then in Canton and later in Manchuria. A member of the Central Committee since 1927 and of the Politbureau since 1931, he thereafter escaped to the Kiangsi Soviet area and participated in the Long March as a Political Commissar. During the Yenan period he became one of the Party's leading theoreticians and organizers, second only to ⇨ Mao. He was confirmed in that position after the foundation of the CPR (Oct. 1949), when he was appointed Vice-Chairman to all important party and state institutions and the Honorary Chairman of the Chinese trade unions. In April 1959, Liu succeeded Mao as Chairman of the CPR, while retaining his position as the Party's First Vice-Chairman and Mao's heir-apparent. The first sign of his disgrace came in Aug. 1966, when in an official listing he dropped from his traditional second to eighth place in rank. He last appeared in public in Nov. 1966. Thereafter the target of an ever-mounting (though, for two years, formally 'anonymous') campaign of vilification, he was first denounced by name as an allegedly life-long 'scab, traitor and renegade' at the enlarged CCP Central Committee meeting of Oct. 1968, which officially stripped him of all his Party and state offices.

Lleras Restrepo, Carlos (1908–). President of ⟡ Colombia (1966–).

Lloyd, John Selwyn Brooke (1904–). UK Conservative politician, served as Minister of State (1951–54) representing the UK at the UN, Minister of Supply (1954–55) and Minister of Defence (1955). As Foreign Secretary (1955–60), he actively supported Lord ⟡ Avon's (then Sir Anthony Eden) military intervention in ⟡ Suez. Chancellor of the Exchequer (1960–62), and Lord Privy Seal and Leader of the House of Commons (1963–64). In Jan. 1971 he was elected Speaker of the House of Commons in succession to Dr Horace King.

Lloyd George, David (1863–1945). British Prime Minister (1916–22), war-time leader, leader of the Liberal Party, social reformer and brilliant orator. His political influence declined rapidly after his fall from power and the collapse of the ⟡ Liberal Party.

Lobby. Interested persons making representations to a legislature or other department of government in order to influence public policy in favour of themselves or a wider group. Lobbying has been an accepted practice in Western (and especially English-speaking) countries for a long time; but in recent times, with the growth of ⟡ Pluralism, it has become more systematic and professional, and has provoked some opposition. In the USA, where it is exceptionally developed, attempts have been made to regulate the activities of organized lobbies and professional lobbyists. The 1946 Federal Regulation of Lobbying Act required the registration of organizations and individuals engaging in this activity, and the publication of their sponsorship and finances. No attempt has been made to prohibit them, however, and many millions of dollars are spent by lobbies in Washington each year.

Lodge, Henry Cabot (1902–). US statesman and unsuccessful Republican Vice-Presidential candidate. He served in the Massachusetts House of Representatives (1932–36) and as US Senator from Massachusetts (1936–44), resigning in his second term to begin active military service.

Re-elected to the Senate in 1946, he was defeated in 1952 largely because his efforts to secure General ⇨ Eisenhower the Republican presidential nomination alienated conservatives in his home state. As US ambassador to the UN (1953–60) Lodge gained a national reputation. In Richard ⇨ Nixon's 1960 bid for the presidency, Lodge was again defeated as vice-presidential candidate. Appointed US ambassador to South Vietnam (1963–64), he was replaced by General Maxwell D. Taylor, whom he relieved again in 1965. Two years later Lodge was appointed ambassador-at-large.

'Long Hot Summer'. The anticipated annual period of disturbances, particularly among Negroes, in the slum areas of cities and towns in the USA.

Long March. ⇨ Chinese People's Republic.

Loyalty Oaths. Were first demanded from Americans at the time of the Revolution. They have been exacted in successive crises – Civil War, World War I and also during the 'Red scare' of the twenties, and since World War II (especially during the McCarthy era) they have become a matter of course for government employees. In its modern form the oath requires a declaration from the individual that he does not advocate the violent overthrow of the government, such advocacy being prohibited by the ⇨ Smith Act, and that he is not a member of a subversive organization.

Lübke, Heinrich (1894–1972). President of the German Federal Republic until March 1969. He succeeded Professor ⇨ Heuss in 1959 and was re-elected in July 1964. Lubke started his political career as a deputy of the Roman Catholic Centre Party in the Weimar Republic's Prussian Diet (1931–33). Several times arrested by the Nazis, he founded the Westphalian branch of the ⇨ CDU and served as Minister of Food first for North-Rhine Westphalia (1947–52) and then for the Federal Republic (1953–59).

Lublin Committee. ⇨ Poland.

Lublin Government. ⇨ Poland.

Luca, V. (1898–1960?). A Transylvanian of Hungarian origin, Luca served his political apprenticeship as a supporter of Bela Kun's Hungarian Soviet Republic of 1919. A member of the Rumanian Communist Party from 1922, he spent many years in prison in the inter-war period. Released by the Soviet armies on their occupation of North Bukovina (1940), he went to live in the USSR until his return to Rumania in 1944 together with Ana ⇨ Pauker. As a member of the party's Secretariat and Politbureau and as Minister of Finance and later Vice-Premier, he belonged in the early post-war years (together with A. Pauker and ⇨ Gheorghiu-Dej) to Rumania's ruling triumvirate.

Suddenly disgraced and arrested in 1952, he was tried two years later and given a death sentence commuted to life imprisonment. Believed to have died in 1960, in Sept. 1968 Luca was rehabilitated as the victim of unjustified persecution.

Lulchev, K. ⇨ Bulgaria.

Lumumba, Patrice (1925–61). Founder of the MNC (*Mouvement National Congolais*) (1957) whose electoral strength secured him the first premiership (July–Sept. 1960) of an independent ⇨ Congo (Kinshasa). The bitter controversies – inflamed by the 'Cold War' – which marked his brief political ascendancy still threatened to destroy the new republic after his murder (Jan. 1961) ordered by the Katanga Cabinet. Lumumba had antagonized the UN representatives (whose intervention he had sought in July 1960), and increasingly relied on the support of the USSR, Ghana (he met ⇨ Nkrumah in 1958 at the Accra pan-African Conference) and the UAR, thereby strengthening ⇨ Kasa-vubu's position. Kasavubu's dismissal of his Premier (Lumumba) (5.9.1960) followed by Lumumba's dismissal of the President (Kasavubu) paved the way for ⇨ Mobutu's first coup (14.9.1960). On his way to ⇨ Gizenga in Stanleyville Lumumba was captured (Dec. 1960) by Mobutu's troops and later handed over to the Katangese. His ill-treatment and murder shocked world opinion. It further diminished the prestige of the Congolese and Katangese governments and led to the UN resolution (21.1.1961) authorizing the use of force by UN troops to prevent civil war. Lumumba's name is still a source of controversy – victim of the chaos he contributed to? or martyr of the struggle against colonialism? (In 1960 the 'Patrice Lumumba – Peoples Friendship University' was established in Moscow.)

Luns, Joseph M. A. (1911–). Dutch Foreign Minister (1956–71), a supporter of greater European integration, he has pressed strongly for Britain's admission to the Common Market. From 1952 to 1956 he was a junior Minister Without Portfolio.

Luthuli, Chief Albert John (1898–1967). Former President of the banned ⇨ African National Congress and a continual embarrassment to the government – even more so after he was awarded the Nobel Peace Prize for 1960 for his leadership of the non-violent campaign against racial discrimination in ⇨ South Africa – which reacted during the 1950s by imposing, lifting and re-imposing restrictions on his movements. Deprived of his chieftainship in 1952, he was arrested in 1956 (released a year later) on a charge of treason (⇨ Treason Trials). He was finally banished to his farm in 1959 under the Suppression of Communism Act and the Riotous Assemblies Act (⇨ *Apartheid*). In March 1960 he publicly burned his pass and called for a day of mourning in protest against the ⇨ Sharpeville shootings, and was later detained when a state of emergency was declared on 30 March (⇨ Verwoerd). Attacked by more militant Africans, frustrated by the failure of passive resistance, his personal integrity and dignity nevertheless made him a symbol of African protest against racism.

Luxembourg, Grand Duchy of. *Area* – 999 sq. miles. *Population* (1970) – 339,848. *Head of State* – Prince Jean. *Prime Minister* – Pierre Werner. *Constitution* – The Grand Duchy is a constitutional monarchy with executive power vested in the sovereign who appoints his ministers. Legislative power is exercised by the uni-cameral, 56-member Chamber of Deputies which is elected for a period of five years. In addition to the Cabinet there is a Council of State whose 21 members are appointed by the monarch.

In 1921 Luxembourg established an economic union with Belgium. During World War II it was overrun by Nazi Germany (May 1940) which declared it an integral part of the *Reich*. The induction of Luxembourgians into the Nazi army sparked off a violent revolt (Aug. 1942) which was ruthlessly suppressed; more than 16,000 people were imprisoned or sent to concentration camps. Luxembourg joined ⇨ Belgium and ⇨ Holland in the ⇨ BENELUX Customs Union (Jan. 1948) and has since become a member of all the major European organizations: EEC, OECD, NATO, WEU, etc. After 45 years of rule, the Grand Duchess Charlotte abdicated (Nov. 1964) in favour of her son Prince Jean. In spite of its smallness the country's iron and steel industry contributes significantly to Western Europe's economy.

M

Macao. ⇨ Portuguese Overseas Provinces.

MacArthur, Douglas (1880–1964). The American Commander of Allied Forces in the Pacific during World War II and early commander of UN troops in ⇨ Korea. He led the US 42nd Division in France in 1918, and by 1930 had risen to be US Army Chief of Staff. He was recalled from retirement in 1941 to command army forces in the Far East, and in 1942 made a courageous but unsuccessful defence of the Philippines against the Japanese. Launching a counter-offensive from Australia, he recaptured the islands and went on to accept the Japanese surrender in 1945. MacArthur supervised the occupation and reconstruction of ⇨ Japan, establishing a liberal government and instituting sweeping reform. After the outbreak of the Korean War (1950–53) he was given command of UN forces and executed a brilliant counter-attack at Inchon. He then pushed the war far into North Korea, miscalculating Chinese intentions, and was forced to retreat. When President ⇨ Truman would not agree to his plan for an attack upon Communist China, MacArthur made his opinions public and Truman responded by relieving the General of his command. Although MacArthur was a superior military leader, his action represented a challenge to civilian authority which the President did not hesitate to meet.

MacDonald, James Ramsay (1866–1937). Founder member and leader of the UK ⇨ Labour Party in the Commons from 1911 until his continued opposition to the war caused him to resign (1914). Prime Minister of the first Labour Government (Jan.–Nov. 1924). His failure to pursue socialist policies as Labour Premier (1929–31) and his alliance with conservatives as Prime Minister of the ⇨ National Government (1931–35) permanently discredited him in the eyes of his own party. Defeated in the elections (1935), a safe seat was found for him and he served in ⇨ Baldwin's government as Lord President of the Council (1935–37).

Macedonia. A ⇨ Balkan territory which, after centuries of Turkish rule, was divided between ⇨ Yugoslavia ('Vardar Macedonia'),

⇨ Bulgaria ('Pirin Macedonia') and ⇨ Greece ('Aegean Macedonia'). After World War II, the communist leaders of Yugoslavia and Bulgaria for a time championed the idea of uniting the three parts in an autonomous Macedonian state within the framework of a Balkan Federation. These plans were opposed by Greek communists, who wanted to retain Aegean Macedonia as an integral part of Greece, and finally abandoned as the result of ⇨ Stalin's opposition to the project of a Balkan Federation. The largest part of the area now forms the Socialist Republic of Macedonia, one of the six constituent Republics of the Socialist Federal Republic of Yugoslavia with the constitutional right to its own independent nationhood and national language. In the Bulgarian part of the territory, the Pirin Macedonians are, by contrast, not regarded as a separate nationality with a language of their own, but as Bulgarians speaking a Bulgarian dialect. These differences over the question of a separate Macedonian nationality and language reflect the ancient rival claims to the whole of Macedonia and have been at the root of repeated conflicts between Yugoslavia and Bulgaria with mutual charges of allegedly annexationist designs. In Aegean Macedonia, as a result of migrations and resettlements, Greeks now account for the majority of the population.

Macleod, Iain (1913–70). UK Conservative politician, Shadow Chancellor of the Exchequer. Colonial Secretary (1959–61), Leader of the House of Commons and Chairman of the Conservative Party Organization (1961–63), he declined to serve under ⇨ Douglas-Home (1963).

Macmillan, Harold (1894–). British Prime Minister and Leader of the ⇨ Conservative Party (Jan. 1957–Oct. 1963). He restored confidence in his Party after the Suez withdrawal and the resignation of ⇨ Eden as Prime Minister. Increasing prosperity in the later fifties ('You never had it so good') led to the general election triumph of Oct. 1959 when the Conservatives were returned with an increased majority of 100. In foreign policy Macmillan sought to strengthen the 'special relationship' with the USA which was helped by his war-time association with President ⇨ Eisenhower. He also tried to act as mediator between Moscow and Washington, visiting the Soviet Union (Feb./March 1959), but the hoped-for summit conference was abandoned – the meeting between ⇨ Khrushchev and Eisenhower in Paris in 1960 was called off after the U-2 affair. Macmillan's cooperation with ⇨ Kennedy helped towards the signing of the Test Ban Treaty (July 1963). Foreign policy in the early sixties was marked by the rapid emergence of independent states in Africa (⇨ Wind of Change); and Macmillan's initiative in seeking British entry into the ⇨ EEC (1961–63) – frustrated by ⇨ de Gaulle's veto (Jan. 1963). In home affairs the

Conservatives adopted more economic planning, e.g. National Economic Development Council (NEDC), but the earlier phase of rapid economic growth and relatively stable prices was followed by one of slow growth and rising prices. Rising unemployment, the balance of payments crises together with the fundamental problem of incomes rising more rapidly than productivity increased Government unpopularity. Confidence in the Government was further diminished by Macmillan's dismissal of seven Cabinet ministers (July 1962) and subsequently by a public scandal (⟡Profumo Affair). Macmillan first entered Parliament in 1924. In the 1930s, although a Conservative, he favoured economic planning and was later an opponent of Chamberlain's ⟡ Appeasement policy. His previous Cabinet posts included Minister of Housing (1951–54), Foreign Secretary (1955) and Chancellor of the Exchequer (1955–57).

Madagascar. ⟡ Malagasy Republic.

Maghreb (in Arabic – the West). Collective term for the states of North-west Africa – ⟡Morocco, ⟡Algeria, ⟡Tunisia and ⟡Libya.

Maghreb Permanent Consultative Committee (est. 1964). Aims at increasing economic co-ordination (particularly in the fields of transport, tourism, utilization of natural gas, electricity and oil) between its member states which are ⟡ Algeria, ⟡ Libya, ⟡ Morocco and ⟡Tunisia.

Majority Leader. In the USA, the official spokesman in each House of Congress of the party holding the majority of seats. He is chosen by the party ⟡ Caucus. In the ⟡ Senate, the Majority Leader is often the single most powerful member, though his power is based on his personal influence and is consequently variable. In the ⟡House of Representatives, the equivalent figure is the Speaker, the Majority Leader being the party's second-in-command. The corresponding official in the opposition party is the ⟡Minority Leader.

Makarios III, Archbishop (1913–). President of ⟡Cyprus since 1960. Elected Archbishop of Cyprus in 1950 and effective leader of the *Enosis* movement, in which the Greek Orthodox Church played a key role. For his involvement with EOKA the British government exiled Makarios to the Seychelles (1956–57). He abandoned *Enosis* in favour of independence for Cyprus but his period of office has not seen any marked improvement in relations between the Greek and Turkish communities and there has been renewed violence. In 1963 his plan for constitutional changes led to one such outbreak. In Feb. 1968 Makarios was re-elected President by an overwhelming majority of Greek Cypriots.

Makkawi, Abdul. ⟡South Yemen, People's Republic of.

Malagasy Republic. *Area* – 227,900 sq. miles. *Population* (1965) – 6,335,000. *President* – P. Tsiranana. *Constitution* (1959) – Executive power is vested in an elected President. A bi-cameral Legislature is made up of a Senate of appointed and elected members and a National Assembly elected by universal suffrage.

Formerly the colony of Madagascar (annexed by France in 1896) the country became a self-governing republic within the ⇨ French Community on 14 Oct. 1958 and achieved full independence on 26 June 1960. On the way to independence nationalist uprisings were sternly repressed by the French in 1947. Since independence, Malagasy has retained close links with France and is a member of the French Community and also of the ⇨ OAU, and ⇨ OCAM. The President is a founder member of the Social Democratic Party and unlike some mainland African states, opposition parties are legally recognized.

Malan, Daniel François (1874–1959). Prime Minister of ⇨ South Africa (1948–55), Dr Malan was representative of a generation of Afrikaner political leaders whose attitudes were permanently shaped by the Boer War. Minister of Labour in ⇨ Hertzog's Government (1924–33) he sought the repatriation of South Africa's Indian population. Leaving the ⇨ Smuts-Hertzog ⇨ United Party coalition in 1935 he founded the reformed ⇨ National Party aimed at the eventual establishment of a Republic. He opposed South Africa's participation in the war (1939–45) in which many of his followers openly favoured Nazi Germany. Propaganda exposing the threat to 'white civilization' had its effect in the nationalist election victory of 1948. Although the National Party secured a minority of votes, it was favoured by the delimitation of constituencies. As Prime Minister of the new government, Malan set out to implement his policy of ⇨ *Apartheid*. Successive South African Premiers have followed his example in repressing opposition and extending the range of discriminatory legislation. He was succeeded in 1955 by J. G. ⇨ Strijdom, an even more extreme advocate of White supremacy.

Malawi. *Area* – 36,897 sq. miles. *Population* (1970 est.) – 4,000,000 (including approx. 7,000 Europeans). *President* (1966) – Dr Hastings Banda. *Constitution* (1966) – Independent Republic within the Commonwealth. Malawi is a one-party state with an Executive President and a uni-cameral National Assembly.

Formerly the British Protectorate of Nyasaland, Malawi after attaining independence (July 1964) later became a Republic (July 1966) within the Commonwealth. Underdeveloped, primarily agricultural, the smallest in area but the most densely populated of the territories of the former Federation of ⇨ Rhodesia and Nyasaland (1953–63), many of Malawi's people are forced to seek work in neighbouring countries. However, afraid of jeopardizing their protected rights, the people, supported by chiefs and missionaries strongly opposed union with neighbouring states. By 1950 Dr Hastings Banda (who has since dominated Malawi's politics), then living in London, led the opposition to the Federation, which, despite protest, was established in Aug. 1953. In 1956, a new constitution (for the first time) established an elected majority (five Africans, six Europeans) on the Legislative Council. Distrust of the Federation continued, and opposition was strengthened by Dr Banda's return (1958). After rioting (1959) a state of emergency was declared, and, with the intervention of Federal forces, Banda and many of his followers were arrested. The Devlin Commission (1959), exonerating Banda on charges of plotting large-scale massacre, was not at first accepted by the UK and Banda was only released in 1960, following ⇨ Macleod's appointment as UK Colonial Secretary. A new constitution (1960), enlarging the Legislative Council, resulted in a decisive victory for Dr Banda's Malawi Congress Party. Backed by his electoral victory, Dr Banda got the UK government to consider the question of secession from the Federation (1962) and to accept the principle (1963). Under a new constitution (agreed 1962) Dr Banda became the first Prime Minister of a self-governing Nyasaland (1963). Shortly after independence (July 1964) Dr Banda dismissed Cabinet colleagues (who have since fled the country) on charges of conspiracy, and subsequently introduced a Preventive Detention Act. It is not only the dictatorial nature of his regime in Malawi, increasingly so since the country became a Republic under his presidency, that has made Dr Banda a controversial figure in African politics. Despite membership of the ⇨ OAU, Malawi has recognized South Africa (diplomatic relations were announced by Dr Banda in Sept. 1967 and implemented in Jan. 1968), signed trade agreements with that country and Rhodesia and has scoffed at OAU ideas (after ⇨ UDI) of deposing Ian ⇨ Smith. He has defended his stance on the grounds of economic and geo-political realities. Malawi's economy is still subsidized by the UK and Banda has also accepted financial help from South Africa.

Malaya. *Area* – 50,700 sq. miles. *Population* – 8,415,000 (of which 4,221,000 are Malays, 3,076,000 are Chinese and 932,000 are Indians). *Constitution* – The former Federation of Malaya has since 1963 formed part of the Federation of ⇨ Malaysia.

Malaya was formerly a British colony, the Straits Settlements. Prized as the world's leading producer of natural rubber and tin, she was occupied by the Japanese during World War II (1942–45). The Japanese left behind a strong nationalist movement in Malaya, which was further influenced by the growth of Indonesian nationalism. In 1946 the colony was dissolved and replaced by the Union of Malaya subject to British jurisdiction, but this aroused Malay opposition leading to the formation of the United Malays' National Organization (UMNO). In 1948 the Federation of Malaya was established consisting of the nine states of the Malay peninsula and the two settlements of Penang and Malacca. This was less centralized than the Union, with the states retaining important powers. Chinese disappointment with the Federation (which was dominated by the Malays), their experience of guerrilla activity against the Japanese and post-war economic circumstances (inflation and food shortage) led to a Chinese insurrection, and for a decade Malaya was the scene of guerrilla warfare. The guerrillas were gradually overcome with British help after their supplies had been cut off through the planned resettlement of some half a million Chinese. The constitution of 1955 granted a ministerial system of government and in the elections of that year an overwhelming victory was won by the Alliance Party led by Tunku Abdul Rahman and composed of an alliance of communal groups – the UMNO, the Malayan Chinese Association and the Malayan Indian Congress. This has dominated Malayan politics ever since and there has been no really effective opposition. Pressure for independence increased and in 1957 Malaya became a sovereign state in the ⊳Commonwealth (for constitution ⊳Malaysia) with Tunku Abdul Rahman as Prime Minister. In the same year Malaysia signed a treaty of defence and mutual assistance with the UK and in 1961 joined Thailand and the Philippines in the Association of South-East Asia (⊳ASA) to promote closer economic and cultural relations. With the establishment of Malaysia in 1963 Malaya ceased to be a separate independent state in the Commonwealth.

Malaysia. *Area* – 128,570 sq. miles. *Population* (1970) – 10,434,034 (of which 4,400,000 are Malays, 3,400,000 are Chinese and 1,000,000 are Indians). *Prime Minister* – Tun Abdul Razak (1970–). *Constitution* (1963) – Federal; an independent state in the ⊳Commonwealth, consisting of the Federation of ⊳Malaya, and the former British colonies of Sarawak (*area* – 48,342 sq. miles, *population* – 887,000), and North Borneo, now renamed Sabah (*area* – 29,388 sq. miles, *population* – 578,000). ⊳Singapore left the Federation in 1965 to become an independent Republic. The constitution is based on that of the former Federation of Malaya with the head of state (Supreme Head) and Prime Minister of Malaysia the same as those of Malaya. The Supreme Head is elected for five years by the rulers of the nine Malay states from among themselves. The Federal Parliament consists of the Senate, partly elected for five years, but there are safeguards for Sabah and Sarawak which have their own rulers, legislatures and constitutions.

Malaysia enjoys one of the highest living standards in Asia based on her two main industries of tin and natural rubber of which she is the world's largest producer. The Federation was formed, with UK backing, to achieve greater political stability in the area. To counterbalance Singapore's mainly Chinese population, Malaysia insisted on the inclusion of the smaller territories on the island of ⇨ Borneo. Despite this compromise and the fact that the ruling party, the Alliance Party, is a combination of three racial groups, the racial problem has hindered progress in the Federation. Malays have insisted on special privileges, e.g. in the civil service (they predominate in the diplomatic service and the army) and in business (four Malays must be employed for every non-Malay). Malay is the only official language and Islam the official religion (most Chinese follow Buddhism, Confucianism or Taoism). This attitude of the Malays, perhaps influenced by memories of Chinese insurgency in Malaya in the 1950s, and also the under-representation of Singapore in the Federal Parliament led to Singapore's secession from the Federation in 1965. Malaysia also faced a serious external threat in the hostility of ⇨ Indonesia, which pursued a policy of ⇨ Confrontation (1963–66) encouraging subversion in and even making raids on the Federation. Although this has ceased, the ⇨ Philippines, the other Malay state, have continued to claim sovereignty over Sabah and in the summer of 1968 confirmed this by passing a law defining their claim. Relations with Indonesia have improved considerably since ⇨ Sukarno's fall (diplomatic relations were reestablished in 1967) but the problems posed by the UK's withdrawal ⇨ East of Suez and the continuing racial question, of which the communal riots in west Malaysia following the devaluation of sterling (1967) were a reminder, suggest that the situation in Malaysia remains unsettled.

Malcolm X (Malcolm Little) (1925–65). Black Nationalist leader in the USA. He was second-in-command of the ⇨ Black Muslims until he broke with the organization to start a more militantly political movement in 1964. In that year he made a pilgrimage to Mecca (adopting the name Al Hajj Malik Shabazz), and on returning declared his renunciation of Black racism. He was assassinated by a member of a rival organization (Feb. 1965).

Malenkov, G. M. (1902–). Former Soviet Prime Minister. Communist Party member from 1920, Malenkov rose to prominence in the mid-1930s. By 1939, he had become a member of the Party Secretariat and head of the Orgbureau's Department in Charge of Party Personnel. An able organizer and administrator, he was for a time during the war a member of the State Defence Committee, ⇨ Stalin's 'war Cabinet'. In 1946 he became a member of the Politbureau and a Deputy Chairman of the Council of Ministers. In 1947, he attended the foundation meeting of the ⊳ Comintern together with ⊳ Zhdanov and, after Zhdanov's death in 1948, his status in the Soviet hierarchy was second only to that of Stalin's. As Prime Minister after Stalin's death in 1953 and, briefly, also First Party Secretary, he became a spokesman for the expansion of the hitherto neglected consumer goods industries of the USSR. He was gradually edged out by ⊳ Khrushchev who succeeded him (1953) as First Party Secretary. In 1955, Malenkov lost the premiership to ⊳ Bulganin and in June 1957, after an abortive conspiracy with ⊳ Molotov, ⊳ Kaganovich and others to oust Khrushchev, he and his fellow-conspirators were denounced as members of the ⊳ Anti-Party Group and were deprived of all their party and other official positions. Malenkov was subsequently charged with responsibility for the ⊳ Leningrad Case and for wholesale purges in other parts of the USSR, including Armenia and Belorussia. Having worked for a time thereafter as an engineer at a local power station, in 1968 Malenkov was reported to be living in Moscow as an old age pensioner.

Maleter, General P. ⊳ Nagy, I.

Mali. *Area* – 500,000 sq. miles. *Population* (1969 est.) – 4,929,000. *Head of State* – Lt. Moussa Traore (1969–). *Constitution* (1960 – suspended 1968) – Executive power vested in a President who appoints a Council of Ministers. There is a uni-cameral National Assembly elected on a single-party basis.

Formerly the French Soudan (est. 1899) which achieved self-government within the ⊳ French Community as the Republic of Soudan in 1958 joining the short-lived Federation of ⊳ Mali in 1959. It became the Republic of Mali, outside the Community, in June 1960. A member of the former ⊳ Casablanca Group and now of the ⊳ OAU, Mali is militantly anti-colonialist and socialist. This and President ⊳ Keita's belief in strong central government was a cause of a three-year dispute with ⊳ Senegal. Mali's cool relations with France were improved in 1967 with the negotiation of trade agreements. Maintaining close links with communist countries, Mali has also accepted aid from the USA, West Germany and Israel. In Nov. 1968, Keita was deposed by a military coup.

Mali, Federation of. As French West African states achieved independence, the attempted formation of a Federation floundered on the opposition of M. ⊳ Houphouët-Boigny (⊳ Ivory Coast) who later formed the ⊳ *Conseil de l'Entente* with ⊳ Dahomey and ⊳ Upper Volta leaving only the Republic of the Soudan (⊳ Mali) and ⊳ Senegal in the Federation which attained independence in June 1960 and broke up in August. Mali's radical leadership and ⊳ Senghor's gradualist pro-French approach were irreconcilable. The ensuing bitterness forced Mali – at greater cost – to find an alternative (to Dakar in Senegal) rail link to the coast. In 1963, in Addis Ababa at the foundation of the ⇨ OAU, the quarrel was patched up and in 1966 ⇨ Keita went on a state visit to Senegal.

Malraux, André (1901–). From 1958 to 1969 the ⇨ Fifth Republic's Minister of Cultural Affairs; a distinguished writer (Prix Goncourt 1933) and man of action – organizer of the Spanish Republican Air Force – during World War II he twice escaped German imprisonment. After the Resistance he was ⇨ de Gaulle's Minister of Information (1945).

Malta. Monarchy under the British Crown. *Area* – 122 sq. miles. *Population* – 319,164. *Prime Minister* – Dominic Mintoff (1971–). *Constitution* (1964) – Independent state within the Commonwealth, with the British sovereign represented by a Governor-General. Executive power is vested in the Prime Minister and Cabinet responsible to a 50-member uni-cameral Parliament elected for a five-year term by universal suffrage on a system of proportional representation.

Malta, as Britain's principal naval base in the central Mediterranean during World War II, had to withstand heavy and prolonged aerial bombardment and the island was awarded the George Cross. The island gained internal self-government in 1947, but when it failed to achieve either complete independence or total integration with the UK, the Mintoff Labour Government resigned (April 1958) and the Governor assumed direct control. A new constitution was adopted (1961) (modified May 1964) to give Malta complete independence within the British Commonwealth. The island's economy suffered heavily from cut-backs in British naval expenditure, and threats to withhold facilities from British Forces induced Britain (1967) to spread these reductions over a period of five years. After long negotiations a new defence and financial agreement was signed by Britain and Malta in March 1972. At the July 1971 elections the Labour Party gained 28 and the Nationalist Party 27 seats.

Malvern, Lord (1883–). Formerly Sir Godfrey Huggins, Prime Minister of Southern ⇨ Rhodesia (1933–53) and of the Federation of ⇨ Rhodesia and Nyasaland (1953–58), long dominated Rhodesian politics. Opposed ⇨ UDI and played a leading part with Roy ⇨ Welensky in advocating the Federation of Rhodesia and Nyasaland.

Mandela, Nelson. ⇨ Treason Trials (South Africa).

Manhattan Project. Code name for the Atomic Bomb Development Program in the USA. Between 1941 and 1945 Congress voted ⇨ Appropriations of about $2,000 m. for the project knowing only that it concerned a secret weapon.

Manley, Norman Washington (1893–). Chief Minister of ⇨ Jamaica (1955–62) and founder of the democratic socialist People's National Party (1938). An ardent supporter of the ⇨ West Indies Federation (1958), his political prospects were damaged by its subsequent failure.

Mao Tse-tung (1893–). Chairman, CCP Politbureau (⇨ Chinese People's Republic). A revolutionary nationalist from an early age, Mao participated in the rebellion which overthrew the dynasty (1911) and in the revolutionary student 'May 4th' movement (1919). By 1920, according to his own account, he had become a Marxist, and in 1921 he participated in the foundation congress of the CCP. During the time of the CCP's collaboration with the ⇨ KMT, Mao worked in the KMT propaganda department concerned, among other things, with the training of peasant organizers. After the break between the two parties, the CCP ordered Mao to organize the Autumn Harvest Uprising (1927) which, however, was defeated, and Mao escaped with a remnant of his forces to the mountains where he was later joined by ⇨ Chu Teh. In 1929, Mao and Chu moved their forces to Kiangsi where they organized their first communist base area for guerrilla war which (Nov. 1931) was proclaimed the Chinese Soviet Republic. Mao became its chairman, although he was out of favour with the top party leaders who had just before arrived there from Shanghai and who disapproved of his guerrilla tactics and neglect of urban centres. For a time he lost most of his political power to ⇨ Chou En-lai and only gained his ascendancy over the party during the Long March, when the Politbureau elected him its Chairman (Tsunyi, Jan. 1935). Between the end of the Long March (Oct. 1935) and March 1947, Mao directed the communist movement from his headquarters at Yenan in the province of Shensi, writing numerous essays on strategic, political and social problems which, with a few subsequent additions, constituted the essence of *The Thought of Mao Tse-tung*. After the proclamation of the CPR (Oct. 1949), Mao took over the chairmanship of the Republic and of the National Defence Council in addition to the party leadership. He remained the principal initiator of all subsequent policies up to and including 'the Great Leap Forward' launched in the spring of 1958. In Dec. 1958, Mao announced his intention to retire from the chairmanship of the Republic in order to devote himself fully to party and ideological work. He relinquished the state chairmanship in April 1959, when ⇨ Liu Shao-chi succeeded him as Head of State. Though continuing thereafter to be honoured as the supreme leader and, since the early 1960s, the centre of an evergrowing personality cult, Mao apparently lost effective control of affairs after the failure of 'the Great Leap Forward'. He made his come-back in 1965/66 with the onset of the Cultural Revolution, which he prepared with a small group of followers, headed by ⇨ Lin Piao, and, after a period of prolonged strife and chaos, successfully re-asserted his authority in the autumn of 1968, when his principal adversary, Liu Shao-chi, was publicly ousted and Lin Piao formally named as his successor. Three years later, Lin Piao, too, had fallen into disgrace. Since then Mao relied, for the practical conduct of affairs, almost exclusively on Chou En-lai.

Mapai. ⇨ Israel.

Mapam. ⇨ Israel.

Maphilindo. Name for the proposed federation of Malaysia, the Philippines and Indonesia which was not realized because of the Indonesian-Malaysian ⇨ Confrontation and the Filipino claim to Sabah.

Maquis. Originally French workers during World War II who had taken to the countryside in order to avoid compulsory labour transfers to Germany. Their main strongpoints were the mountainous regions in Southern France where they were joined by other Resistance fighters. From 1944 onwards the *maquisards* became part of the French Forces of the Interior (FFI).

Marcos, Ferdinand (1917–). President of the ⇨ Philippines since 1965 and leader of the *Nacionalista* Party since 1964. He was a Liberal member of Congress from 1949 but changed parties in 1964.

Marshall, George Catlett (1880–1959). US General and Secretary of State who won the Nobel Peace Prize (1953) for his proposal of the European Recovery Programme. After serving as a staff officer during World War I, he rose to General and Army Chief of Staff (1939) where he worked effectively to increase American preparedness for the military engagements he foresaw. During the war Marshall was the chief military strategist for the Allied powers in both war theatres and was numbered among the President's advisers on the development of the atomic bomb. In 1945 he was sent to China to resolve the differences between Nationalists and communists but only succeeded in gaining a temporary cease-fire. Secretary of State (1945), he proposed the successful ⇨ Marshall Plan aimed at rebuilding Western Europe to reduce its vulnerability to communist expansion. Marshall served briefly as Secretary of Defence (1950–51) during the Korean War.

Marshall, Thurgood (1908–). The first Negro to be appointed to the US Supreme Court (1967). A former counsel for the National Association for the Advancement of Colored People (⇨ NAACP), he argued many cases before the Court including ⇨ Brown v. Board of Education (1954), the historic school desegregation case.

Marshall Plan. Proposals put forward in 1947 by George C. ⇨ Marshall, US Secretary of State, for promoting the economic recovery of Europe after World War II. Marshall suggested that the nations of Europe (including the Soviet Union) should draw up a programme for recovery with the aid and later support of the USA. The British, French and Soviet Foreign Ministers met to discuss the Plan; but whilst Britain, France and fourteen other countries accepted it, the Soviet Union and other communist countries did not. Those who accepted met in Paris for a Conference on European Economic Co-operation (July 1947), and drew up the ⇨ European Recovery Programme for the years 1947–51.

Martinique. ⇨ French Overseas Departments.

Marxism. Karl Marx (1818–83), in collaboration with Friedrich Engels (1820–95), developed his critique of bourgeois society under the cumulative influence of three main strands of thought – Hegelian philosophy, socialist theories developed in France under the impact of the French Revolution, and Ricardian economics. Marx's synthesis of these influences with his own original thought has been variously described as Historical Materialism, Dialectical Materialism and Scientific Socialism.

History, according to Marx, is the process of man's self-transformation through his labour. The structure of each historical epoch is in the last analysis determined by the prevailing modes and relations of production, each having given rise so far to a specific form of private property and specific constellations of antagonistic social classes. The motor of social change has been the struggle between these classes – the exploiters and the exploited, the rulers and the oppressed. All past forms of private property have hampered the development of human potentialities. Capitalism has given a powerful impetus to an unparalleled development of productive forces on a world-wide scale. But it has also given birth to a new class, the ⇨ Proletariat, which is being de-humanized by the (economic) compulsion to sell its labour potential – the essential human characteristic – and to transform it into an alienated market commodity. With this development, according to Marx, history has reached a qualitatively new stage. All past revolutions and social transformations resulted in the replacement of one ruling class by a new ruling class. The proletariat, having not even a potential sectional stake in society, cannot emancipate itself without emancipating mankind as a whole, once and for all, from all forms of exploitation and class distinction. With the transformation of the means of production into common property, 'prehistory' will have come to an end; history proper will begin.

The inner dynamics of bourgeois society, as Marx set out to demonstrate in *Das Kapital* and elsewhere, produce the conditions for its ultimate destruction and create, in the proletariat, its own 'grave-diggers'. Scientific insight into this process of conflicts enables men to make themselves the instruments of revolutionary change. Socialist ideals without scientific analysis of actual trends must remain utopian. Scientific analysis and philosophical contemplation without the will to change remain barren. In order to realize its proper aim of human freedom, philosophy must become practical. Only in the union of theory and practice will socialists, according to Marx, eventually be able to usher in the classless society in which man can at last unfold his full human potential.

The combination of Marx's prophetic vision with his political invective and passion for scientific truth and learning acted as an explosive force on socialists and communists all over the world. To this day, both revolutionaries and reformers try to lay claim to the Marxian heritage. Marx's own view on the issue of revolution versus evolution changed with the changing social and political circumstances of his own lifetime. In the *Communist Manifesto*, written under the impact of the gathering revolutionary upheavals of 1848, Marx and Engels expressed their conviction that, at least in Germany, the coming bourgeois-democratic revolution would 'be but the prelude to the immediately following proletarian revolution'. Once these expectations had been disappointed and the revolutionary tide had passed, Marx increasingly thought of the eventual revolution as the consummation of a long-term process of continuing change. In 1859 he insisted that no social order ever founders before all the productive forces which it is capable of developing are developed and that no higher form of society appears until its material conditions of existence have fully matured in the womb of the old society. At a yet later stage, when the modern democratic labour movement had begun to develop in Western Europe, Marx came round to the view that the full development of this movement belonged itself to the essential conditions of the eventual emergence of a socialist society. That was the attitude to which he adhered from 1864, when he wrote the *Inaugural Address* for the Working Men's International Association (the First International) and which he expressed in the opening passage of the *Inaugural Address* itself with the words that the emancipation of the working class must be the work of the working class itself. (⇨ Bolshevism.)

Marxism-Leninism. A term, claimed to embrace the theory and practice of ⇨ Marxism as developed and applied by Lenin, which was first coined in the USSR after Lenin's death in polemics against ⇨ Stalin's opponents. In the post-Stalin period, the epithet 'Marxist-Leninist' has increasingly been used as a weapon in the rivalry between different communist parties (notably those of the USSR and ⇨ China) over the authority to interpret the common dogma and as an alleged distinguishing mark between ideological truth and heretical deviations. (⇨ Bolshevism.)

Masaryk, Jan (1886–1948). Former Czechoslovak Foreign Minister. The son of Czechoslovakia's Founder-President and a close associate of ⇨ Benes, Masaryk was a career diplomat serving at various foreign posts from 1919 onwards. Ambassador in London from 1925, he resigned after the ⇨ Munich Agreement of Sept. 1938. In 1940, he became Benes' Deputy Premier and Foreign Minister in the London based Czechoslovak government-in-exile and continued as Foreign Minister in the post-war coalition government until after the communist coup of Feb. 1948. A few days later, he fell to his death from a window in the Prague Foreign Ministry in circumstances which have never been fully cleared up.

Massive Retaliation. Policy advocated in 1954 by US Republican Secretary of State, John Foster ⇨ Dulles who favoured a 'harder' foreign policy than that pursued by Democratic Secretary of State, Dean ⇨ Acheson. The 'massive retaliation' doctrine threatened to unleash the full nuclear capabilities of the United States in retaliation for acts of communist aggression anywhere in the world. It was thought that the United States should not meet communist aggression locally but rather 'by means and at places of our own choosing'. The doctrine was formulated to satisfy demands for a 'hard line' vis-à-vis the East; to reduce defence expenditures by relying on nuclear rather than conventional weapons (a 'bigger bang for the buck'); and to discourage future communist aggression by raising the cost to an unacceptably high level.

Matsu and Quemoy. Two small Chinese off-shore islands under the control of the Nationalist government of Formosa but, like Formosa itself, claimed by the mainland government as an integral part of China. The two islands have suffered repeated artillery bombardment from the mainland.

Maudling, Reginald (1917–). Deputy Leader of the UK ⇨ Conservative Party since 1965 when he stood unsuccessfully for the party leadership (⇨ Heath – 150 votes, Maudling – 133, ⇨ Powell – 15). Member of the ⇨ Macmillan and ⇨ Douglas-Home Cabinets – President of the Board of Trade (1959–61), Colonial Secretary (1961–62) and Chancellor of the Exchequer (1962–64). Home Secretary 1970–72.

Mau Mau. A Kikuyu secret society which aimed at driving the 'white man' out of ⇨ Kenya. The uprising began with the assassination of a Kikuyu chief (Oct. 1952) and attacks on European farmers, though the majority of Mau Mau victims were African tribesmen. By 1956, government forces, including large detachments of British troops, had forced the Mau Mau to seek refuge in the mountain forests, but the state of emergency proclaimed in 1952 lasted until 1959. Though defeated (and condemned for its brutality) the Mau Mau rebellion was followed by a phase of rapid constitutional change in Kenya and East Africa.

Mauritania, The Islamic Republic of. *Area* – 418,000 sq. miles. *Population* (approx.) – 1,000,000 (approx. 800,000 Moors and 200,000 Negroes). *President and Prime Minister* – Moktar Ould Daddah. *Constitution* (1961) – Executive power vested in an elected President. There is an uni-cameral National Assembly. Islam is the official religion though freedom of conscience is guaranteed. Mauritania is a one-party state.

A French Protectorate from 1903 and a colony from 1920 when French control was complete, Mauritania became a self-governing member of the ⇨ French Community (from 1958) and achieved full independence in Nov. 1960. Heavily dependent on French aid, Mauritania has also established close ties with communist countries, while territorial disputes with ⇨ Morocco have helped to forge close links with ⇨ Algeria. Internally there has been friction between the Moors (largely nomadic) and the settled Negro population who advanced more rapidly under French rule. A member of ⇨ OAU, Mauritania withdrew from ⇨ OCAM in 1965.

Mauritius. *Area* (including the island dependency of Rodriques) – 805 sq. miles. *Population* (approx.) – 773,000 made up of 395,000 Hindus, 126,000 Moslems, classified as Indo-Mauritians, i.e. of Indian descent; 210,000 Creoles (mixed African and French descent); 25,000 Chinese and an elite of 14,000 Europeans of French descent. *Prime Minister* – Sir Seewoosagur Ramgoolam. *Constitution* (1967) – The sovereign is represented by the Governor-General who appoints as Prime Minister the member of the Legislative Assembly most likely to command a majority in the House. The Prime Minister and Cabinet are responsible to an elected uni-cameral Legislative Assembly.

A British possession (from 1810), Mauritius became an independent state within the Commonwealth on 12 March 1968. A degree of internal autonomy was achieved (1948) by the replacement of the Council of Government by an enlarged Legislative Assembly with a majority of elected members. Independence was advanced through discussions with the UK government (1955 and 1965) and by constitutional reforms preceding the 1963 general election. Communal rioting between Creoles and Moslems (Jan. 1968) necessitated the dispatch of British troops and the declaration of a state of emergency still in force at the date of independence. (Because of anxiety about the riots, the UK was represented by a Cabinet Minister (Anthony Greenwood) instead of Princess

Alexandra as originally intended.) Mauritian political stability is affected by its economic dependence on a single crop – sugar, and (already densely populated) by its rapid population growth. Ethnic and religious rivalries, reflected in its political parties, dominate the island's politics. Mauritius is a member of the ⇨ OAU and the UN and has diplomatic relations with the USSR and Communist China.

Maurras, Charles (1868–1952). The most brilliant intellectual among the anti-republican, anti-German, anti-semitic activists of the extreme right-wing ⇨ *Action Française* whose 1938 election to the *Académie Française* caused consternation among liberal intellectuals. A dedicated collaborator after the fall of ⇨ France (1940), he was found guilty of treason (Jan. 1945), and received a life sentence, but was released shortly before his death.

Mboya, Tom (1930–69). Minister for Economic Planning and Development in the ⇨ Kenya government and Secretary-General of KANU (Kenya African National Union). Assassinated July 1969.

McCarran Act. In the USA, the Internal Security Act of 1950 which established the ⇨ Subversive Activities Control Board.

McCarthy, Eugene E. (1916–). US Senator and contender for Democratic presidential nomination in 1968. He served in the House of Representatives (1948–58) until elected to the Senate from Minnesota in 1958. McCarthy gained a position on the Senate Foreign Relations Committee and developed a reputation as an articulate liberal spokesman. Finding himself in opposition to the Administration's ⇨ Vietnam War policy, he announced his candidacy for the Democratic presidential nomination (Nov. 1967) and attracted national attention with his success in ⇨ Primary Elections. Although unsuccessful in his bid for the nomination, McCarthy demonstrated the extent of anti-war sentiment, mobilized large segments of the nation's youth, and brought about important reforms in ⇨ National Convention procedure.

McCarthy, Joseph Raymond (1907–57). The US Senator who led the investigations into alleged 'internal subversion' that branded the early fifties as the 'McCarthy Era'. He was elected to the Senate as a Wisconsin Republican (1946), and began his crusade in 1950 by accusing the State Department of employing over two hundred communists, and making personal attacks on the Secretaries of State and of the Army, as well as broadly denouncing the Roosevelt and Truman Administrations. By the use of unsupported allegations and ambiguous suggestions the Senator ruined men's careers and aroused fear and suspicion in the nation, while himself protected from retaliatory action by senatorial immunity. Re-elected to the Senate (1953) and made Chairman of the Permanent Sub-Committee on Investigations, he initiated a confrontation with the US Army which was viewed across the country on television (1953). Partly as a result of the Army hearing and after a condemnation by President Eisenhower, a Senate committee brought charges against him for his conduct (1954) and a vote of condemnation marked the eclipse of his political influence. Although McCarthy had (and still has) many supporters who saw him as a great patriot, most now recognize in the phenomenon of ⇨ 'McCarthyism' an exaggerated fear of communism heightened by political opportunism.

McCarthyism. Political ideas and practices of the kind associated with the efforts of Senator Joseph ⇨ McCarthy to uncover communist subversion in the USA in the early 1950s. Sanctioned by public fears of a communist threat to the security of the United States during the Cold War – fears that were increased by the Senator's own activities – McCarthyites used the powers of ⇨ Congressional Investigations to make general charges against public officials and private citizens, often with little or no substantiation, whilst protected by congressional immunity. McCarthyism was characterized by the extensive use of ⇨ Loyalty Oaths, security tests, and 'black lists' of persons suspected of communist sympathies, and had many of the features of an old-time witch-hunt. It fostered widespread suspicion and anxiety in government and academic circles, and ruined many careers. Its appeal lay partly in its combining the opportunity to attack the 'Eastern Establishment' and to demonstrate '100 per cent Americanism'.

McGovern, George (1923–). US Senator from South Dakota, Democratic presidential candidate, 1972. Son of a Methodist preacher, and a Professor of History and Political Science, he served, and was wounded, as a bomber pilot in the US Air Force during World War II. In 1956 he was elected to the US ⇨ House of Representatives, the first ⇨ Democrat to be elected from South Dakota for twenty years. He was re-elected in 1958, and in 1962 he became the first Democratic Senator from the State for twenty-six years, having served in the interim as President ⇨ Kennedy's first Food-for-Peace director. In the ⇨ Senate he became a leading liberal figure, and was re-elected in 1968. From the start of his career in the Senate, he was an advocate of United States withdrawal from ⇨ Vietnam, and of Federal aid to adapt the American economy to peacetime full employment. He was a contender for the Democratic presidential nomination in 1968, receiving the backing of supporters of Sen. Robert ⇨ Kennedy after the latter's assassination, but he lost to Sen. Hubert ⇨ Humphrey. He began his campaign for nomination for the next presidential election in mid-1970, and became an official contender at the beginning of 1971, an almost unprecedentedly early start. He conducted an effective campaign in the ⇨ Primary

Elections and by other means, and was nominated as Democratic presidential candidate on the first ballot at the ⇨ National Convention in Miami Beach, July 1972. He chose as his Vice-Presidential running-mate, first, Sen. ⇨ Eagleton, and then Sargent Shriver. However, he lost when Nixon was re-elected President by a large majority.

McNamara, Robert Strange (1916–). US Secretary of Defense (1960–67). A successful business executive, he resigned as President of the Ford Motor Company to accept the post of Secretary of Defense, offered to him by the incoming President ⇨ Kennedy. McNamara acted quickly and firmly in modernizing the Department's procedures and in modifying defence policy. By increasing the strength of conventional forces he provided greater flexibility in military response as a means of combating guerrilla warfare. He opposed further building of heavy bombers, resisted the deployment of anti-ballistic missiles, and maintained that America should accept nuclear parity with the Soviet Union instead of striving for superiority. A close and trusted adviser of Presidents Kennedy and ⇨ Johnson, he was often at odds with the Joint Chiefs of Staff and Congress over defence policy or programmes. Resigning in 1967, McNamara became President of the World Bank and was succeeded as Secretary by Clark ⇨ Clifford.

Meany, George (1894–). Labour leader in the USA. A plumber by trade, Meany became President of the New York State Federation of Labor (1934–39). From 1940 to 1952, he was Secretary-Treasurer of the ⇨ AFL, and in 1952 he became its head. When the AFL and ⇨ CIO re-merged in 1955, Meany became President of the combined body, which then had 16 m. members. The AFL had always tended to be more to the Right than the CIO, and both before and after they came together again Meany strongly reflected that tendency in his own policies, particularly as regards opposition to ⇨ Communism. He has come into conflict with Administrations of all complexions in his pursuit of the interests of Labour as he sees them. In 1971 he strongly opposed president ⇨ Nixon's 'new economic policy', especially the wage-freeze part of it, and in Mar. 1972 he resigned with other labour representatives from the President's Pay Board, a body he had himself proposed. He also expressed opposition to Nixon's visits to Peking and Moscow in early 1972. At the same time, he came into conflict with some of the leading contenders for the ⇨ Democratic Party's presidential nomination, particularly the more liberal of them, and when Sen. George ⇨ McGovern was chosen at the Miami Beach convention in July 1972, he refused to endorse him on behalf of the AFL-CIO.

Medicare. In the USA, a limited programme of medical benefits for the aged provided by the Federal Government. It was strongly advocated by President ⇨ Kennedy, and finally enacted by Congress under the leadership of President ⇨ Johnson in 1965.

Mein Kampf (*My Struggle*). Adolf ⇨ Hitler's autobiography and political programme. It sold over ten million copies in the ⇨ Third Reich (⇨ Germany), and acquired scriptural status as the ultimate authority on Nazi doctrine. The first volume was completed while Hitler served his prison sentence (1924) for instigating the abortive 1923 Nazi uprising. It revealed all his ambitions (incorporation of Austria, subjugation of France, conquest of living-space in the East, extermination of Jews, etc.), and provided a detailed – if woolly – exposition of his views on racialism, communism, religion, government, propaganda (only the big lie succeeds), education, etc. Although published early in his career (*F. Eher Verlag*, Munich 1925) Hitler never retracted anything written in *Mein Kampf*, which translated into every major language, could have provided statesmen and politicians with a guide to his thought and actions. Put off by the work's repetitiveness and dullness of style, opponents at home and abroad failed to read it, or if they did, to take it seriously. After the war, the Bavarian state acquired the copyright and prohibited reprints. Pirated editions continue to appear, particularly in Spain, Latin America and the Middle East.

Meir, Mrs Golda (1898–). Prime Minister of ⇨ Israel (March 1969–). Born in Russia but emigrated to the USA as a child. She was prominent in American Zionist activities – delegate to the World Jewish Congress (1921) – before emigrating to ⇨ Palestine (1921). Active in the *Histadrut* she became head of the Political Department of the Federation of Labour (1939) and subsequently head of the Political Department of the ⇨ Jewish Agency (1946–48). After the establishment of the State of Israel she was its Minister to the USSR (1948–49), then Minister of Social Insurance (1949–52), Minister of Labour (1952–56) and Foreign Minister (1956–66) Secretary-General of *Mapai* (1966–) and noted for the strength of her party loyalty, she opposed General ⇨ Dayan's appointment as Minister of Defence (1967), preferring General ⇨ Allon. Her emergence from retirement to accept the premiership has been interpreted as an attempt to maintain party and government unity.

Menderes, Adnan (1899–1961). Prime Minister of ⇨ Turkey (1950–60) and leader of the Democratic Party of which he was a founder. During his premiership, Turkey's system of alliances with the West was strengthened and she joined ⇨ NATO (1952) and the ⇨ Baghdad Pact (1955). His domestic policies failed and economic difficulties, allied with resentment of his dictatorial rule, led to his overthrow and execution by a military coup.

Mendès-France, Pierre (1907–). French Prime Minister (1954–55) who brought the eight-year-old Indochinese War to an end (22.7.1954, Geneva Treaty). He strongly supported European integration and signed the Paris agreements (23.10.1954) which admitted the ⇨German Federal Republic to ⇨NATO. His government was brought down when he tried to apply to North Africa the principles of disengagement which had brought peace to Vietnam. He served in Mollet's government as deputy Prime Minister (Feb. 1956–May 1957), but disagreement over the Algerian pacification issue led to his resignation. A committed left-wing Radical Socialist, he started his political career as a Treasury Under-Secretary of State in ⇨ Blum's 1938 government, joined de Gaulle in North Africa (1942), served in his Committee of National Liberation and became Minister of Economic Affairs in the Provisional Government (Sept. 1944–June 1945). He resigned when his drastic anti-inflationary measures were rejected. Mendès-France, a prominent member of the Radical Socialist Party (its Vice-President May 1955–May 1957) was expelled from the party when he opposed the liquidation of the Fourth Republic, and de Gaulle's accession to power; and founded his own Unified Socialist Party (USP). Not elected to the 1962 National Assembly, he won the Grenoble seat in the 1967 elections, but lost it in the elections of June 1968.

Mensheviks. ⇨Bolsheviks.

Menzies, Sir Robert (1894–). One of the longest-serving ⇨Commonwealth Prime Ministers and a dominant figure in Australian politics for 30 years. He was Prime Minister of ⇨Australia (1939–41 and 1949–66), Leader of the Opposition (1943–49) and leader of the Liberal Party and formerly of the United Australia Party. His period of office was marked by his advocacy of Commonwealth interests and links with the UK, his conclusion of defence alliances, e.g. ⇨ANZUS Treaty and ⇨SEATO, and industrial expansion. In 1956 he was appointed by 18 nations to head a mission to persuade President ⇨Nasser to agree to the proposal that the Suez Canal should be internationalized but was unsuccessful. In recognition of his services as a Commonwealth elder statesman Menzies was made Warden of the *Cinque Ports* in 1965.

Messmer, Pierre (1916–). French Prime Minister (July 1972), an orthodox Gaullist of the first hour (London 1940). Passing the years of ⇨ de Gaulle's interregnum (1946–58) in the Colonial Service, he became his Minister of Defence (1960–69). President ⇨Pompidou first omitting him from his ministerial team made him Minister of the Overseas Department in February 1971.

Metaxas, Joannis (1871–1941). Prime Minister of ⇨Greece (1936–41) who dissolved Parliament and established a dictatorship (in 1938 he was named Prime Minister for life). A strong royalist, he helped secure the restoration of the monarchy after the fall of the Republic in 1935. His rule was repressive but he also introduced social reforms and strengthened the country's defences. Although known as pro-German (he had opposed Greece's entry on the Allied side in World War I) he resisted Axis aggression in World War II. His forces defeated the Italian invasion but he died before the German invasion took place.

Mexico. *Area* – 761,530 sq. miles. *Population* (1970) – 48,313,000. *President* – Luis Echeverria Alvarez (1970–). *Constitution* (1917) – Federal Republic (The United States of Mexico). Executive power is vested in a President elected by direct popular vote. A bi-cameral Legislature – Congress made up of a Senate and Chamber of Deputies – is also elected by direct popular vote. Voting is by universal adult suffrage (women were enfranchised in 1953).

Mexican politics in the twenties and early thirties were dominated by Plutarco Elias Calles. President (1924–28), he became the undisputed leader (*Jefe Maximo*) of Mexico and continued to govern the country up to 1934, through the President he nominated. Through his PNR (*Partido Nacional Revolucionario* – founded 1929), he succeeded in institutionalizing the revolution. The present PRI (*Partido Revolucionario Institucional* (1946)) developed out of the PNR. The power of the *callistas* was broken by President ⇨ Cardenas (1934–40), himself a Calles nominee. Cardenas instituted a programme of land redistribution and socialization based on the 1917 constitution. Under the next two Presidents, Avila Camacho (1940–46) and Miguel Aleman (1946–52), social reform was neglected but industry, stimulated by war, developed rapidly. (Mexico declared war on the Axis in May 1942.) As a result of the war and increasing American investment in Mexican industry, relations between the two countries (frequently strained in the past) were much improved. A split between the right led by Aleman and the left grouped round Cardenas, threatening the unity of the PRI, led to the adoption of a compromise candidate for the presidency – Adolfo Ruiz Cortines (1952–58). Though government participation in the economy increased, the administration was handicapped by inflation and industrial conflict already strongly evident during Aleman's presidency. President Adolfo Lopez Mateos (1958–64) promised Mexico a dynamic socialist administration but found his freedom of action limited by a number of factors. Right wing pressure forced him to modify his policies and he was also opposed by the extreme left. (Though the 'right to successful revolution' is specifically denied by the constitution – the aims of the Mexican revolution being officially served by the PRI – 'Marxist' parties have continued to grow in strength.) Though Mateos opposed the expulsion of Cuba from the ⇨OAS, Mexico later supported the US blockade of Cuba and inevitably opportunities for an independent foreign policy are affected by American political and economic pressure. Gustavo Diaz Ordaz was elected President in July 1964. Despite Mexico's record of political stability, compared to the recent history of most of Latin America, on both the right and left of the administration there is growing discontent with Mexico's present economic and political structure and the official means of altering it. With world attention focused on Mexico through the Olympic Games (1968) the army and police intervened forcefully against the developing student protest. Though other political parties have been officially permitted (since 1954), the PRI (with its various factions) has maintained its monopoly of political power. Close economic ties with the United States (tourism is of growing importance in the Mexican economy and more than 60% of Mexico's foreign trade is with the US) remains a crucial factor in Mexico's political development.

MGB. Russian abbreviation for Ministry for State Security. (⇨USSR State Security Service.)

Michael, King. ⇨Rumania.

Middle Congo. ⇨Congo, Republic of (Brazzaville).

Mihailovic, D. ⇨Yugoslavia.

Mikolajczyk, S. (1900–). Polish Peasant Leader and Premier 1943/44 who, in the inter-war years, devoted himself to the Polish peasants and their party, the People's Party, becoming its President in 1937. After the outbreak of World War II, he joined the Polish government-in-exile. As deputy Premier and Minister of the Interior, he was in charge of the government's contacts with the underground resistance in Poland. After General ⇨Sikorski's death (June 1943) Mikolajczyk succeeded him as Premier. Having vainly attempted to influence and alter the agreements between Stalin, Roosevelt and Churchill on Poland's future, he resigned the premiership in Nov. 1944. Despite strong misgivings, he joined the new government set up by the Soviet-sponsored 'Lublin Committee' as Vice-Premier and Minister of Agriculture. As a result of Mikolajczyk's attempt to preserve the independence of the peasant party, both he and his Party became the victims of an ever increasing communist campaign of vilification and terror. Warned of his imminent arrest, he secretly left Poland in the autumn of 1947 and has since then lived in the USA.

Mikoyan, A. I. (1895–). Member of the CPSU Central Committee, Mikoyan is one of that tiny group of old ⇨Bolsheviks who succeeded in surviving all his country's changing political fortunes. A Bolshevik since 1915, he played a prominent part in establishing Soviet rule in the Caucasus. A member of the party's Central Committee since 1923, he became ⇨People's Commissar (1926) first of internal and later of external trade. From then until his retirement in 1965, he had control of all the foreign economic relations of the USSR and in addition has been repeatedly used as a troubleshooter in times of crisis between the USSR and its allies. A loyal supporter of ⇨ Stalin in all his factional struggles against the various opposition groups within the CPSU, Mikoyan was the first to attack Stalin's ⇨ Personality Cult publicly at the 20th Congress of the CPSU (1956). In the 1950s and 1960s Mikoyan travelled extensively in Europe, Asia, Africa and, especially, North and Latin America until his appointment in 1964 as ⇨ Brezhnev's successor as Head of State of the USSR, a post from which he retired in Dec. 1965 on grounds of old age.

Mindszenty, Cardinal J. (1892–). Primate of Hungary. Ordained in 1915, Mindszenty became Papal Prelate in 1937, Bishop of Veszprem in 1944, and the Prince Primate of Hungary in Sept. 1945. A strong opponent of the communist take-over, he was arrested in Dec. 1948. At his trial (Feb. 1949), he was charged with treason and currency offences. His sentence to life imprisonment was commuted to house arrest in July 1955, and he was freed and returned to Budapest in Oct. 1956. His broadcast address on 3 Nov. led his communist opponents to accuse him of seeking to restore the old order. On 4 Nov. he took refuge in the US Legation in Budapest where he remained until Sept. 1971, when he left for Rome, following an agreement between the Hungarian government and the Holy See.

Minority Leader. In the USA, the official spokesman in each House of Congress of the minority party, chosen by the party ⇨ Caucus. His importance depends on his influence with his own congressional party, and on his relations with the ⇨ Majority Leader. The Minority Leader in the ⇨ House of Representatives usually becomes Speaker if his party wins a majority.

Mitterrand, François (1916–). Became a national figure when, after having held several ministerial appointments in the Fourth Republic, he opposed ⇨ de Gaulle in the 1965 presidential elections and polled 44% of the vote. As the leader of the ⇨ *Fédération de la Gauche Démocratique et Socialiste*, he is the Prime Minister of the Federation's shadow government (*Contre-Gouvernement*), which won 121 seats in the 1967 parliamentary elections. His offer to stand for the presidency at the height of the May 1968 riots failed, however, to elicit a favourable response. His FGDS like other left-wing parties lost heavily in the June 1968 elections (57 seats retained), and he resigned the presidency of the FGDS (Nov. 1968) after disagreement with the Socialists.

MLF. Multilateral Force – unsuccessful American proposal for the establishment of a nuclear ⇨ NATO force, manned and operated by multi-national crews drawn from member states. The plan originally conceived by General Norstad (1960) envisaged NATO with a fleet of about 25 ▷ Polaris-carrying submarines as a fourth atomic power. It was meant to allay European doubts as to the American willingness to use the nuclear deterrent in defence of European interests in the face of the USA's growing vulnerability to Russian nuclear missiles. While allowing NATO members a real share in the control and operation of the alliance's nuclear deterrent, the MLF would, it was hoped, obviate the hankering after independent, national atomic armaments. For this reason it was resolutely opposed by France, intent on building up her nuclear ▷ Force de Frappe. The plan, backed by the Kennedy and Johnson administrations, was violently resented by the USSR on the grounds that it would give the German Federal Republic access to nuclear armaments – a view shared by the British Labour Government, which suggested the ▷ ANF (Atlantic Nuclear Force) alternative.

MNR. *Movimiento Nacional Revolucionario.* ▷ Bolivia.

Mobutu, General Joseph (1930–). Head of State and Prime Minister of Zaire, the ▷ Congo (Kinshasa). An ex-NCO turned journalist who joined the MNC, Mobutu accompanied ▷ Lumumba to the Brussels Round Table Conference (Jan. 1960). The first Chief of Staff of the new Republic, he gradually asserted his authority over the mutinous *Force Publique* (later the ANC). With his army in control of Leopoldville, Mobutu held the key to political power. After his first coup (14.9.1960) Mobutu attempted to govern through a ▷ College of Commissioners but soon reinstated ▷ Kasavubu. The occasion for his second coup (25.11.1965) was provided by the rivalry of Kasavubu and ▷ Tshombe. He declared his intention of governing for five years, assumed the presidency and restricted the power of Parliament, and in Oct. 1966 he also assumed the premiership. In 1972 he changed his name to Mobuto Sese Soko.

Moczar, General M. (1913–). Leader of the Polish 'Partisan' organization. A pre-war member of the Polish Communist Party, Moczar distinguished himself in the Polish communist war-time resistance against the Germans. A member of the Party's Central Committee since 1945 and active in Secret Police work, he suffered an eclipse in 1948, but made a come-back in 1956 when he was again elected to the Central Committee and appointed deputy Minister of Internal Affairs. He became prominent in 1964, when he was appointed Minister of the Interior (and Chief of the Security Forces) and was elected Chairman of the ZBoWiD ('Fighters for Freedom and Democracy') – the nationalistic powerful 'partisan' organization of former resistance fighters, which played a conspicuous part in the anti-Jewish campaign beginning in the spring of 1968. Moczar ceased to be Minister of the Interior in July

1968, when he became a member of the Party Secretariat and an alternative member of its Politbureau. After ⇨ Gomulka's replacement by ⇨ Gierek (Dec. 1970) Moczar was dropped from the Party Politbureau and Secretariat.

Mohieddin, Zakaria (1918–). Prime Minister of the UAR (1965–66), deputy Prime Minister (1964–65 and again since 1967). Nasser, announcing his resignation, put forward Mohieddin as his successor, but Mohieddin indicated that he wished to continue serving under Nasser's leadership. In 1968, however, Mohieddin, along with many of Nasser's oldest associates, was ousted from the leadership, a probable result of Nasser's increasing reliance on the Soviet Union.

Moldavia. One of the 15 Federal Soviet Republics constituting the USSR. *Capital* – Kishinev. (⇨ Bessarabia.)

Mollet, Guy (1905–). Leader of the French Socialists and prominent politician in the Fourth Republic. He held office under Blum, Pleven, Queuille; became Prime Minister (1956–57) and Vice-Premier in ⇨ Pflimlin's ill-fated government, and under ⇨ de Gaulle in the Fifth Republic's first administration. A devoted European, he presided over the Consultative Assembly of the Council of Europe (1954–56), was a signatory of the Rome Agreements (25.3.1957), establishing the ⇨ Common Market. His failure to stand up to the Algerian settlers led to his own downfall and that of the Fourth Republic, but his support for de Gaulle greatly assisted the peaceful transfer of power.

Molotov, V. M. (1890–). Former Premier and Foreign Minister of the USSR. A ⇨ Bolshevik since 1906, Molotov carved a career in the CPSU and Soviet Government as one of ⇨ Stalin's earliest and most loyal supporters. A member of the party Politbureau from 1926 and Chairman of the Council of People's Commissars from 1930 to 1941 (when Stalin assumed the premiership), Molotov also replaced ⇨ Litvinov as Foreign Minister in 1939 at the time of the rapprochement with Germany. He was Ribbentrop's co-signatory of the ⇨ Hitler-Stalin Pact and he acted as Stalin's chief plenipotentiary in all subsequent Soviet negotiations with the Germans and, later, the Western Allies. After the war, he also acted as the co-signatory of Stalin's letters to the Yugoslav communists preceding their expulsion from the ⇨ Cominform in 1948. In 1949, he was replaced as Foreign Minister by ⇨ Vyshinsky but continued to play a prominent part in international affairs. Reappointed Foreign Minister after Stalin's death, he opposed ⇨ Khrushchev's reconciliation with ⇨ Tito and was ousted from the Foreign Ministry in June 1956 on the eve of Tito's state visit to the USSR. Expelled from his party offices in June 1957 as a member of the ⇨ Anti-Party Group, he suffered his final eclipse after the 22nd CPSU

Congress in 1961, when he was denounced for the part he had played in Stalin's repression and purges.

Molotov-Ribbentrop Pact. ⇨ Hitler-Stalin Pact.

Monaco, Principality of. Constitutional monarchy. *Area* – 1 sq. mile. *Population* (1970) – 24,000. *Head of State* – Prince Rainier III. The principality has a customs union with France. Friction arose over the tax status of French companies registered in Monaco. After the French set up customs barriers (1962), Monaco introduced a new constitution under which these companies came under France's fiscal laws.

Mongolian People's Republic (Outer Mongolia). *Area* – 604,095 sq. miles. *Population* (1969) – 1,240,000. *Chairman of the Council of Ministers* – Yu. Tsedenbal. *Constitution* – Legislative power is formally vested in the Great People's Khural, a nominatively elected assembly modelled on the USSR Supreme Soviet. Effective leadership rests exclusively with the leadership of the (communist) Mongolian People's Revolutionary Party, headed by the First Secretary of its Central Committee, Yu. Tsedenbal.

For over two centuries a province of the Chinese Empire, Outer Mongolia achieved autonomy in the wake of the Chinese revolution of 1911, but became soon afterwards – *de facto* if not *de jure* – a Russian Protectorate. After a period of turmoil, following the Russian revolution of 1917, this old relationship was restored in a new form. In 1921, Outer Mongolia was transformed into the Mongolian People's Republic. It applied for Soviet aid and protection, which was promptly given and has continued ever since. The Mongolian communist leaders, in turn, have given Moscow automatic support on every issue of controversy, including especially the ⇨ Sino-Soviet Conflict. As a result of this stand, Chinese aid for Mongolia – mainly in the form of labour teams for construction projects in this greatly underpopulated country – was terminated in the early 1960s. Nevertheless, China concluded a border treaty with Mongolia in 1962, settling hitherto disputed questions. In Jan. 1966, the Soviet Union, in turn, signed a new Treaty of Friendship and Mutual Assistance with Mongolia. Mongolia is the only non-European country which, since 1962, has been a member of the ⇨ Council for Mutual Economic Assistance.

Monnet, Jean (1888–). Architect and first President of the ⇨ ECSC (1952–55), started his career as an economist at the Versailles Peace Conference and with the ⇨ League of Nations. Chairman of the Franco-British Economic Co-ordination Committee (1939) he planned the details of Churchill's abortive 1940 proposal for Anglo-French union. A member of the British Supply Council in Washington (1940–43), he transferred to Algiers to effect cooperation between Generals

▷ de Gaulle and Giraud. He became Commissioner for Armaments, Supplies and Reconstruction in Algiers (1943–44) and later head of the official French Modernization Plan (1947). Frowned on by de Gaulle as the champion of 'supranational monstrosities', he publicly supported the candidature of ▷ Lecanuet in the 1965 presidential elections.

Monopoly Capitalism. Term used mainly (but not exclusively) by Marxists for the transformation, enforced by technical progress, of the earlier capitalism of freely competing small *entrepreneurs* into a stage of capitalism distinguished by the concentration of capital in comparatively few giant enterprises and financially inter-dependent large-scale corporations and trusts.

Montgomery, Alabama. Capital of Alabama, USA, where in 1955 the Negro community, led by the Rev. Martin Luther ▷ King, boycotted the city's buses in protest against continued ▷ Segregation in them. The boycott lasted for 381 days, and is estimated to have cost the city $1,000,000. Its success accelerated desegregation throughout the South, and established Dr King's pre-eminence in the Negro ▷ Civil Rights Movement.

Montini. ▷ Paul VI (Pope).

Moral Rearmament (MRA). International evangelist movement stressing the values of honesty, purity, love and unselfishness, founded by Frank Buchman in 1938. It claimed to be concerned with the spiritual revival of nations – Buchman advocated a 'new social order under the dictatorship of God's spirit'. After World War II it began to organize annual world assemblies as part of a crusade against communism and atheism. Its claim to moral leadership was not helped by its reluctance to disclose the sources of its plentiful funds.

Morocco. *Area* – 111,370 sq. miles. *Population* (1970.) – 15,525,000. *Head of State* – King Hassan II (1962–). *Constitution* – Under a state of emergency (June 1965) the King assumed full legislative and executive authority, pending the introduction of a revised constitution. Under the former constitution (1962) the King appointed the Cabinet and presided over its meetings. There was a bi-cameral Legislature of a House of Representatives and a House of Councillors.

From the turn of the century, Morocco's strategic importance to the European powers and French and Spanish opposition to German attempts to gain a foothold in the area precipitated a series of international crises. From 1912 (following the Treaty of Fez) until 1956, Morocco was divided into French and Spanish Protectorates and (from 1923) the free port of Tangier. (General Franco's successful revolt was launched from Morocco.) One reaction to France's successful conquest of their territory by the early 1930s (including assistance to Spain) was the emergence of a nationalist movement which developed rapidly after World War II. Loyal to ⇨ Vichy, after the fall of France, Morocco was quickly occupied by the Allies (Nov. 1942) – (⇨ World War II). By 1943, *Istiqlal* – a newly formed nationalist party – was demanding full independence. During the next decade, the struggle for independence led by Sultan Muhammed Yusuf and *Istiqlal* was complicated by the clash of interests between conservative Berber tribesmen and the Sultan's urban followers. The Sultan was forced into exile (1953) but after continual unrest he was reinstated (1955) and when, after independence, Morocco changed from a Sultanate to a Kingdom, he became King Muhammed V (1957). Following a joint Franco-Moroccan declaration (March 1956) and subsequent Spanish agreements (April), Morocco achieved full independence and membership of the UN (Nov. 1956). Tangier lost its special status (1959) but became a free port again (1962) by royal decree. Morocco has been involved in territorial disputes with Spain over Spanish Morocco and ⇨ Ifni and with ⇨ Mauritania. In 1963 a territorial dispute with ⇨ Algeria resulted in open warfare and Moroccan troops advanced southwards into the disputed territories. The conflict was settled through an ⇨ OAU Armistice Commission (1964) (President ⇨ Keita of Mali earlier mediated a truce). The ⇨ UAR, which had supported Algeria, resumed diplomatic relations with Morocco (severed 1963). In 1962, King Hassan succeeded to the throne on the death of his father Muhammed V. Elections were held for the House of Representatives in 1963, but governmental changes failed to heal political rivalries, and in 1965 (June) after continued appeals for national unity, King Hassan announced a state of emergency and assumed executive and legislative authority. Since 1964 Morocco has established closer links with her North African neighbours through the ⇨ Maghreb Permanent Consultative Committee. Though the Government gave its vocal support to the Arabs in the 1967 Arab-Israeli War, it opposed the unofficial trading boycott of its Jewish community, whose numbers have declined greatly since 1956. Soviet penetration in the area and especially the supply of arms to Algeria has been viewed with alarm by King Hassan who has called for a UN disarmament commission. Relations with France, which have since improved, were badly affected by the ⇨ Ben Barka affair.

Morrison, Herbert S. (1888–1965). Pragmatic UK ⇨ Labour Party politician who thrice failed to be elected Leader of the Party (1935, 1945, 1956). As Secretary of the London Labour Party, he transformed it into an election-winning organization, capable of administering the affairs of the capital. It dominated the London County Council for a number of decades. As Minister of Transport (1929–31), Leader of

London County Council (1934–40), Minister of Supply (1940) and Home Secretary and Minister for Home Security (1940–45), he proved himself an able administrator, and as Lord President of the Council and deputy Prime Minister (1945–51) he played an important part in carrying through the Labour Government's post-war nationalization measures. Foreign Secretary (1951), he was made a Life Peer (1959).

Moscow Declaration (1957). ⇨ World Communism.

Moscow Statement (1960). ⇨ World Communism.

Moscow Trials. Collective description of three political show trials of former leading ⇨ Bolsheviks, the first held 19–24 Aug. 1936, the second, 23–30 Jan. 1937, the third, 2–13 March 1938, with A. Y. ⇨ Vyshinsky acting as Prosecutor in all three. The defendants in the three trials, 54 in all, were accused and found guilty of terrorist murder plots, sabotage, espionage, wrecking and conspiracies to dismember the USSR in the interest of Germany and Japan. Seven of them were sentenced to long terms of imprisonment from which they never again emerged; the remaining 47 were executed immediately after the trials. The victims had been, without exception, lifelong revolutionaries, and they included Lenin's closest personal associates in the Bolshevik leadership, among them ⇨ Zinoviev, ⇨ Kamenev, ⇨ Pyatakov, ⇨ Radek, ⇨ Bukharin and ⇨ Rykov. Other leading Bolsheviks escaped execution at the time only by committing suicide, among them Tomsky and (according to ⇨ Khrushchev) Ordzhonikidze. A few of the defendants, including Bukharin, denied some of the specific accusations made during the trials, but they all publicly confessed to having committed intrinsically incredible crimes. In his 'secret speech' at the 20th CPSU Congress (1956), Khrushchev – like many non-communists before him – attributed the public confessions of guilt in these and similar trials to 'cruel and inhuman torture' and other forms of Secret Police pressures.

Linked with the public Moscow trials was the secret trial in June 1937 of Marshal Tukhachevsky, the Commander-in-Chief, and seven other top-ranking military leaders. According to subsequent Soviet press reports, they had been involved in the conspiracies exposed in the public trials and were similarly found guilty of high treason and executed. Only the alleged chief instigator of all the conspiracies, the exiled ⇨ Trotsky, escaped the net spread by ⇨ Stalin's police. They caught up with him in 1940, when one of their agents murdered him in Mexico. (⇨ Yezhovshchina, ⇨ USSR, ⇨ USSR State Security Service, ⇨ Show Trials.)

Moslem Brotherhood. Egyptian extremist right-wing religious organization, founded by Hassan al Banna' in 1929. It gained increasing support in the thirties and by the mid-forties had a membership of over two million. It was banned in 1948 and its leaders arrested. In the subsequent reprisals, the Egyptian Prime Minister, Mahmud Nukrashi and Hassan al Banna' were assassinated. Dissolved in 1954, the Brotherhood went underground and has continued to be active behind the scenes.

Moslem League. Led the movement for the creation of the independent state of ⇨ Pakistan. Founded in 1906 as a religious organization to protect the interests of the Moslem population in British ⇨ India, it became a political movement under Mohammed Ali ⇨ Jinnah after Moslems left the ⇨ Congress Party in 1935 because of the latter's predominantly Hindu character. The break between the two organizations widened with Congress successes in state elections in 1937. In World War II the League supported the British war effort, unlike Congress whose leaders were imprisoned. Jinnah advocated a separate Moslem state and in the 1946 elections won the overwhelming support of the Moslems in India. The UK Government, and eventually Congress, accepted the partition of India. The League became the major political party in the new state of Pakistan, but the death of Jinnah (1948) and internal divisions seriously weakened it. Since the mid-1950s it has not played an effective part in Pakistani politics – Ayub ⇨ Khan's assumption of power (1958) inaugurated 'controlled democracy', although political parties, including the League, were permitted again in 1962.

Mosley, Sir Oswald (1896–). Founder (1932) and leader of the ⇨ British Union of Fascists (BUF). His movement aimed at establishing a corporate state in Britain and was influenced at first by the Italian model but later increasingly by German political developments. He organized marches through the East End of London, especially the Jewish areas, and accusations of antisemitism and brutality at his meetings won his movement increasing notoriety. The Union failed to attract a widespread following and declined rapidly after the Public Order Act of 1936 banned political uniforms and political processions. The decline in the BUF's fortunes also reflected the British public's growing suspicion and dislike of Nazi foreign policy in Europe. Mosley had been a member of ⇨ MacDonald's Labour Cabinet until 1930, when he resigned over economic policy. Disillusioned with parliamentary democracy, he resigned (1931) from the Labour Party and founded his 'New Party'. Until his conversion to Fascism he had a distinguished parliamentary career. He was imprisoned under wartime regulation 18b from 1940 to 1943.

Mourir pour Danzig? Defeatist slogan coined by ⇨ Déat shortly before the outbreak of World War II, suggesting that it was absurd for the French to go to war in defence of obscure Polish privileges in Danzig.

Mozambique. ⇨ Portuguese Overseas Provinces.

MRP. *Mouvement Républicain Populaire* – officially constituted in Nov. 1944 (Lyons), this Christian party differed from the other Continental Christian-Democratic movements in its more radical commitment, and formed with the communists and socialists the coalition which ruled ⇔France from 1945 to 1947. In the first general election it polled 4·75 m. votes, almost as many as the communists, a success partly due to the disappearance of the traditional parties of the right, whose conservative voters regarded the MRP as a 'bulwark' against the radical left. With the emergence of ⇔ de Gaulle's RPF (*Rassemblement du Peuple Français*) and other right-wing parties, support for the MRP declined in the fifties to about 12% of the electorate, half of its previous strength. The Algerian war added to the tensions between the right and the left within a party leadership somewhat slow to dissociate itself from the views of G. ⇔Bidault, its former President, and subsequently an outlawed leader of the terrorist ⇔OAS. Under the leadership of Jean ⇔ Lecanuet, the pro-European presidential candidate, who in the first heat of the 1965 election polled 3·8 m. votes, it formed the *Centre Démocrate* with various centre and centre-left groups, notably the CNI (*Centre National des Indépendents et Paysans*). In the general elections (March 1967) this alliance obtained 1·23 m. votes – 41 seats. After this election the MRP decided to 'efface itself' and it played no role as a national party in the June 1968 general elections.

Multilateral Force. ⇔MLF.

Munich Agreement. Concluded 29 Sept. 1938 by ⇔ Chamberlain, ⇔ Daladier, ⇔ Hitler and ⇔ Mussolini on behalf of Britain, France, Germany and Italy, it compelled ⇔Czechoslovakia to cede its fortified Sudeten German border districts to the ⇔Third Reich (⇔Germany), and to cede territory to Hungary and Poland at a later conference. The integrity of the truncated state, guaranteed by the Agreement, was violated when the German army marched into Prague. The name 'Munich' has since acquired a symbolic significance as an equivalent for short-sighted and dishonourable appeasement.

Munoz Marin, Luis (1898–). Puerto Rican Senator from 1932, founder of the PPD (*Partido Popular Democratico*) 1938, President of the Senate 1941–48, Governor 1949–64. He has been responsible for Puerto Rico's modern constitutional and political development, especially since co-operation with the US, dating from Roosevelt's presidency.

Muscat and Oman. *Area* – 82,000 sq. miles. *Population* – 750,000. *Head of State* – Sultan Qabus bin Said (1970–), following the deposition of Sultan Said bin Taimur (1932–). An independent state under the absolute rule of the Sultan. The country has had a close relationship with the UK for over 150 years – Treaties of Friendship and

Commerce were concluded in 1891, 1939 and 1951 – and in 1957 British forces were used to crush a revolt in Oman. The 'question of Oman' continued to be a subject of Arab propaganda which charged the Sultan with oppression despite the contrary findings of a UN Commission of Inquiry (1963). In 1967 oil production began in Oman.

Muscovites. ⟿ Sovietization.

Muskie, Edmund S. (1914–). US Senator from Maine, Democratic Vice-Presidential candidate in 1968, and unsuccessful contender for the ⟿ Democratic presidential nomination in 1972. Of Polish-American parentage, he graduated from Bates College and Cornell University, and after practising law for a time, he saw active service in the US Navy during World War II. He served in the Maine State legislature (1946–50), and was elected Governor of the State in 1954, the first Democrat to win the office for twenty years. In 1958 he became the first Democrat to be popularly elected to the US ⟿ Senate from Maine, and he was re-elected in 1964 and 1970. In the Senate he chaired a number of important sub-committees. Named as running-mate to Hubert H. ⟿ Humphrey in 1968, he was defeated when ⟿ Republican President Richard M. ⟿ Nixon and Vice-President Spiro T. ⟿ Agnew were elected. He was long considered front-runner for the Democratic presidential nomination in 1972, and advanced his claim by trips to the Soviet Union, Israel and Egypt, and the German Federal Republic in 1971. However, his campaign for the nomination suffered decisive setbacks in the early ⟿ Primary Elections, and he soon withdrew from the race, lacking funds to continue.

Mussadiq, Mohammed (1881–1967). Prime Minister of ⟿ Iran (1951–53) who nationalized the British-controlled oil industry and so precipitated an international crisis. Royalist forces resisted Mussadiq's attack on the powers of the Shah and he was deposed and arrested. He had come to power at the head of the militantly nationalist National Front movement and had earlier held several ministerial posts.

Mussolini, Benito (1883–1945). Founder of ⟿ Fascism, Italian Prime Minister then dictator of ⟿ Italy (1922–45). The son of a blacksmith (who had suffered imprisonment for his socialist beliefs), Mussolini grew up in the atmosphere of revolutionary politics. He started work as a teacher at the age of 18, but soon emigrated to Switzerland where he came under the influence of Georges Sorel, who prophesied a brilliant future for him – 'Mussolini is not an ordinary socialist'. He returned to Italy (1904), and was imprisoned for socialist agitation (1908). After his release he joined the editorial staff of the Trento socialist paper *Avvenire* (1909), but was again imprisoned when in 1911 he denounced the Italian-Turkish war, culminating in Italy's occupation of Libya, as an immoral imperialist adventure. However, his 'martyrdom' and his insistence on militant action won him a national reputation, which in turn gained him the editorship of *Avanti*, the party's official paper. At the outbreak of World War I he publicly disagreed with the party's neutralist stand (1914) and campaigned in the *Popolo d'Italia*, a paper he had meanwhile founded, for Italian participation on the side of the Allies. Mussolini maintained that Italy could only come into her own as a great European power if she played a part in the struggle which would decide who was to rule the continent in the years to come. Although expelled from the party and denounced as a French agent, Mussolini's views were widely shared, particularly by radical syndicalists like Rossoni who organized the patriotic dissenters into a national syndicalist movement. After Italy's entry into the war (May 1915) Mussolini joined the elite Bersaglieri Regiment. Serving as a corporal, he was wounded and invalided out of the army (1917), returned to the *Popolo d'Italia* and became the spokesman for the discontented ex-servicemen and others who were dissatisfied with Italy's small share of the spoils of victory. With the foundation of his first *Fascio di combattimento* (Milan, March 1919), Mussolini introduced Fascism as a new political concept and movement. He quickly gained middle-class and right-wing support when he pitted his black-shirt Fascist bands against the militant workers who were competing with the Fascists for control of the state. Despite beatings, castor oil cures and occasional murders with which Mussolini terrorized his political opponents, the ruling Liberals acquiesced in this display of deliberate violence. They allowed him to secure the premiership after the king had been successfully intimidated by his legion's 'March on Rome' (Oct. 1922). In power, and as the leader of what was soon to become the only legal party, he displayed considerable political acumen both in home and foreign affairs. However, in the early thirties, stimulated by Japan's and then Nazi Germany's territorial ambitions and fired by his philosophy of activism, Mussolini embarked on an expansionist foreign policy which ultimately led to his own undoing. He invaded ⇨ Ethiopia (1935), assisted ⇨ Franco in Spain (1936–39) and annexed ⇨ Albania (1939). Although he gloried in these easy conquests, as a martial dictator he was increasingly overshadowed by ⇨ Hitler. In ⇨ World War II Mussolini only declared war on the Allies after the collapse of France made a German victory seem inevitable. His armies invaded ⇨ Greece (Oct. 1941) but soon suffered defeats both in Africa and in the Balkans. After the loss of Sicily, even the Fascist '*Grand Council*' turned against him. He resigned (July 1943) and was arrested by the succeeding Badoglio government. Liberated by German parachutists (Sept. 1943), the dispirited *Duce* established his short-lived

Social Republic in German-occupied Italy. In the closing stages of the war he tried to escape in the wake of the retreating Germans to Switzerland, but was caught and executed by Italian partisans (28.4.1945).

Mutual Security Program. General term for United States assistance to foreign countries of the kind administered by the Mutual Security Agency between 1951 and 1953. Under the 1951 Mutual Security Act, two kinds of foreign aid were provided – military aid, and economic and technical aid. Both kinds of aid could be extended to all friendly countries, so that the scope of the Program was wider than that of the ⇨ECA, which the Agency replaced. General responsibility for mutual security programmes was transferred in 1953 to ⇨FOA. Since the 1957 Mutual Security Act a feature of the Program has been the provision of investment capital through the ⇨ Development Loan Fund. In 1961 administration of non-military aspects of the Program became the responsibility of ⇨AID.

MVD. Russian abbreviation for Ministry for Internal Affairs. (⇨USSR State Security Service.)

N

NAACP. National Association for the Advancement of Colored People – a non-racial association in the USA, founded in 1909 to press for improvements in the conditions of Negroes, largely through action in the courts supported by its Legal Defense Fund. It has played an important part in the Negro ▷ Civil Rights Movement, working in close association with ▷ CORE, ▷ SCLC and ▷ SNCC, and maintaining a strong ▷ Lobby in Washington. In the 1950s it met strong opposition, sometimes violent, from ▷ White Citizens Councils seeking to maintain ▷ Segregation in the South. It has also been attacked by more militant Negro groups, such as the ▷ Black Muslims, as being composed of ▷ 'Uncle Toms'. It continues to favour racial ▷ Integration and constitutional methods.

Nagy, I. (1896–1958). Hungarian communist and former Premier. A prisoner-of-war in Russia at the time of the revolution, Nagy became a communist before his return to Hungary in 1921. After some years of political underground work, he escaped to Austria (1928). In 1930, he went to the USSR where he engaged in research and practical work in agriculture. On his return (Nov. 1944) he became Hungary's first postwar Minister of Agriculture, responsible for the radical land reform instituted in 1945. After a few months as Minister of the Interior, he alternated between full-time party work and various ministerial appointments until he was made Prime Minister in July 1953. In that capacity, he became the chief spokesman of Hungary's 'new course', ending compulsory collectivization, giving priority to the provision of consumer goods, freeing many political prisoners and providing writers and other intellectuals with considerable freedom of expression. Having just gained substantial popularity as a result of these innovations, in April 1955 he was dismissed from all his government and party positions for 'right-wing deviations'. The demand for his return figured prominently in the mass demonstrations in Oct. 1956. He resumed the premiership on 24 Oct. and thereafter made himself the chief spokesman of the popular clamour for national independence and radical internal reforms.

After the start of the massive second Soviet intervention, Nagy and some of his close communist associates, including General Pal Maleter – the chief military organizer of the national resistance against the Soviet intervention – were given asylum in the Yugoslav Embassy in Budapest. They left, after a Soviet promise of safe conduct, and were arrested in Rumania. On 17 June 1958, it was announced that Nagy, Maleter and two of their associates had been executed for treason after a secret trial at which they had pleaded 'Not Guilty'.

Nahas Pasha. ⟜> UAR and ⟜> *Wafd*.

NASA. United States National Aeronautics and Space Administration – an ⟜> Independent Agency established in 1958 to co-ordinate the civil aspects of the United States space programme. It is responsible for launcher development, meteorological and communications satellites, and the space flights of American astronauts. Its Manned Spacecraft Center, at Houston, Texas, has become a world-famous location in connexion with American Moon missions. The Administrator is appointed by the President with the consent of the Senate, and there is a ⟜> Congressional Committee in the Senate to oversee its conduct. The President must personally settle any 'demarcation' disputes between NASA and the ⟜> Defense Department. Its activities have been considerably curtailed in recent years, precipitating a recession in the American aerospace industry.

Nassau Agreement, 1962. Agreement between John ⟜> Kennedy and Harold ⟜> Macmillan for the USA to provide Britain with Polaris missiles. Shortly afterwards ⟜> de Gaulle vetoed the UK's EEC application.

Nasser, Gamal Abdel (1918–70). President of Egypt (1956–58) and of the ⟜> United Arab Republic (1958–70). During the thirties he was associated with the Egyptian Fascist 'Green Shirts'. A serving officer, Nasser founded the Society of Free Officers (1942) which was to be his spring-board to power a decade later. The humiliation caused by defeat in the Arab-Israeli War (1948–49), in which Nasser served as a Major, confirmed the view of the younger officers that a radical change in Egyptian politics was needed. The dominating figure in the 1952 Officers' Coup, Nasser ousted the more conservative Neguib (1954), becoming Prime Minister and Military Governor of Egypt, and two years later President. An insight into Nasser's attitudes and ambitions was provided in his *Egypt's Liberation – The Philosophy of the Revolution* (1955). His determination to increase Egypt's prestige, his position as the leading spokesman of Arab nationalism, his opposition to the West and his diplomatic initiatives in the neutralist bloc made Nasser the most powerful and popular leader in the Arab world. His claims to leadership of the 'Arab Revolution' also provoked the hostility of ⇨ Saudi Arabia, ⇨ Tunisia and ⇨ Jordan. Nasser's prestige reached new heights following the nationalization of the Suez Canal and the Anglo-French-Israeli military attack on Egypt (⇨ Suez Crisis). Although the Egyptian army was routed by the Israelis in Sinai, Egypt secured a great diplomatic victory, making Nasser the hero of the Arab world. One effect of his enhanced prestige was the short-lived union with ⇨ Syria (1958). With Syria's departure from the UAR, Egypt's military involvement in the Yemen, the emergence of Saudi Arabia under Feisal, and the debacle of the Six Day War, to some extent weakened Nasser's position. For a long time after 1956 Nasser advocated caution in the conflict with Israel, claiming that the Arabs should first be thoroughly prepared before risking war, but, perhaps provoked by Syrian militancy, changed his mind suddenly in precipitating the 1967 crisis (⇨ Arab-Israeli Conflict). Though Nasser's resignation after defeat (possibly stage-managed) was not accepted, the army trials, the student and workers' unrest and the economic effects of the war increased his difficulties. His own freedom of action may also have suffered through his increasing dependence on Soviet military aid. Nasser's predicament in 1967 high-lighted the gap between the scale of his ambitions and the actual resources of his country.

National Communism. Term applied by non-communists to those communist states, parties or factions which emphasize their right to full national autonomy and to complete independence from the USSR or other international centres of control. The term, which is often used as a synonym for ⇨ Titoism, was first applied to ⇨ Yugoslavia after Tito's break with Stalin (1948), but was later enlarged to include parallel trends in other communist countries and parties. The term 'national communists' is sometimes also applied to the so-called 'home communists' who were members of the anti-Nazi Resistance in their own countries during World War II in contrast to the 'Muscovites' who during the war lived in the USSR.

National Convention. In the USA, a four-yearly delegate assembly of a political party which nominates the party's candidates for President and Vice-President. In both the Democratic and Republican Parties, State delegations are roughly proportionate to population, but additional delegates are assigned to States that supported the party's candidates in the previous congressional and/or presidential elections. The method of choosing delegates is regulated by State law and varies considerably across the nation, presidential ⇨ Primary Elections being the most notable method. Nomination campaigns begin long before the national conventions meet, the contestants competing for the advance support of

State delegations and trying to convince delegates generally of their ability to win. There is an increasing tendency for one contestant to emerge as the likely nominee by the time the convention meets, and for the nomination to be made on the first ballot of delegates. This was the case with both presidential candidates – Democrat Hubert ⇔Humphrey and Republican Richard ⇔ Nixon – in the 1968 conventions, and of Democrat George ⇔ McGovern in 1972. Sometimes, however, the choice is finally made only after much manoeuvring and many ballots at the convention. Thus, Franklin D. Roosevelt took four ballots to secure the Democratic nomination in 1932; but at that time the Democrats operated a two-thirds-majority system which they thereafter abandoned. In any case, conventions are conducted in an atmosphere of frenzied activity and wild enthusiasm, though much of the real business is done in 'smoke-filled rooms' away from the public spectacle.

In addition to nominating a presidential and vice-presidential candidate (the latter usually being the choice of the former), the national convention sets out the party's 'platform' for the elections. However, candidates are not bound by its 'planks', before or after election, and the alternative platforms have little impact on the campaign. The convention also nominates a National Committee to act for it during the ensuing four years. It, too, has little real authority. Its chairman is in practice nominated by the presidential candidate and acts as his campaign manager. After the campaign his role is much reduced, especially if his party's candidate is the winner (in which case he is apt to be appointed ⇔Attorney General); though he will probably preside at the opening of the next convention. The general weakness of the national party organs in the United States, especially as contrasted with their State and local counterparts, reflects the decentralized character of American politics generally.

National Government (UK). Coalition government formed (Aug. 1931) after the failure of ⇔ MacDonald's Labour Government to deal successfully with the financial crisis and growing unemployment. MacDonald's decision to serve as Prime Minister of the coalition split the Labour Party and dealt a crippling blow to its morale and electoral strength. At the general election in Oct. 1931 the National Government (predominantly the Conservatives with National Labour and National Liberal) won over 60% of the vote, and the Labour Party won two million votes less than in 1929. The Government was dominated by the Conservatives and included ⇔ Baldwin who led it from 1935 to 1937 and ⇔ Chamberlain who led it from 1937 to 1940. A National Government was returned to power in the 1935 general election in a landslide victory. There was no further election for ten years; in 1940 the National Government was replaced by ⇨ Churchill's wartime coalition.

National Grange (USA). Oldest and second largest of three major farmers' organizations, with about 800,000 members, mainly from the North-Eastern States. It maintains a strong ⇨ Lobby in Washington and gives evidence before ⇨ Congressional Committees, taking a position on agricultural and economic policies between that of the ⇨ Farm Bureau and the ⇨ Farmers Union, and a moderate or conservative position on other questions.

National Guard. In the USA, the militia of the States, organized (in accordance with the Constitution) as provided by Act of Congress. National Guard units in each State are available to the Governor for maintaining law and order, but can be called into the service of the United States by the President to enforce Federal law in time of war or internal emergency. By acting thus, the President can deny to the authorities of a State important means of compelling citizens of the State to comply with their demands. This can be an important protection for minorities such as the Negroes in the South.

National Labor Relations Act. In the USA, the ⇨ Wagner Act.

National Party (South Africa). The ruling political party of ⇨ South Africa. Under the successive premierships of ⇨ Malan, ⇨ Strijdom, ⇨ Verwoerd and ⇨ Vorster, it has governed continuously since 1948. Its history, to date, can be divided into three phases. It was founded by General ⇨ Hertzog in opposition to the Botha ⇨ Smuts South African Party. It governed, in coalition with the Labour Party, from 1924 to 1933 and implemented South Africa's industrial colour-bar. The second phase of its history began with Hertzog's 'desertion'. Rejecting his ⇨ United Party coalition with Smuts, Dr Malan established the Reformed National Party in 1935. Anti-British, neutral (many of its members even pro-German) in 1939, committed to an Afrikaaner Republic, elevating the concept of 'white supremacy' into a religious mission, the party used the war years to overhaul its organization and increase its appeal to the electorate. The success of ⇨ *Apartheid* as a vote-catcher and Malan's 1948 election victory heralded a new phase in its history. Successive electoral victories with increased majorities, combined with disenfranchisement of the majority of the population, have, up to the time of writing, virtually eliminated opposition. Repressive legislation and its endorsement by the courts, has made genuine opposition to government policies both difficult and dangerous. The party sees itself as the champion of Afrikaaners' political aspirations and the guardian of the '*Volk*'. In the same way its progenitor and ally, the Dutch Reformed Church, is regarded as the source of moral authority and the guardian of Afrikaans culture. It is impossible to understand the attitudes of Afrikaans nationalism without reference to the Dutch Reformed Church.

Premier Vorster's attempts to establish diplomatic links with Black African states and his effort to encourage a common 'White' South African loyalty as opposed to narrow Calvinist Afrikaaner loyalties have exacerbated the conflict between moderates and extremists in the party. Both groups are committed to *Apartheid* but the *Verligtes* (enlightened ones) as opposed to the *Verkramptes* (constricted ones) are anxious about South Africa's image abroad and apparently favour a relaxation of the rules of 'petty *Apartheid*' (⇨ *Apartheid*). National Party domination of South African politics seems assured for the near future at least.

National Socialism. Ideology inspiring the National-Socialist German Workers' Party (NSDAP) which evolved from the German Workers' Party after ⇨ Hitler had joined it in 1919 as its seventh member. The economic radicalism of the 'unalterable' 25-point party programme (Feb. 1920), insisting on the 'abolition of unearned income', 'the elimination of middle men', 'the nationalisation of trusts and holding companies', 'support for the independent businessman and closure of chain and department stores', was ignored once the party achieved power, while its racialist and anti-semitic demands – 'only Germans of German stock qualify for citizenship; Jews are excluded', were more formally elaborated in ⇨ *Mein Kampf* which replaced the party programme as the fountainhead of doctrine.

After Hitler's release from prison, the re-established NSDAP (Feb. 1925) made a spectacular recovery. Membership grew rapidly: 1925 – 27,000 members; 1929 – 176,000; 1931 – 806,000; and close to two million when Hitler came to power. By 1945 party membership – a valuable career asset and pre-condition for many senior appointments – had passed the six million mark. The party's rapidly increasing political influence was also reflected in the growing strength of its parliamentary representation: 12 seats in the 1928 *Reichstag*; 107 in 1930, 230 in 1932 (by then the largest party) and 288 in the March 1933 elections which were already over-shadowed by terror and Press censorship.

The party, created by Hitler to embody the nation's political will, took – as in communist countries – precedence over government, 'the party rules over the state'. It headed a proliferating number of 'affiliated organisations' of which the SA, ⇨ SS, the Hitler Youth and the Labour Front (trade union substitute) were the best known. Its elaborate system of regional subdivision from the *Gauleiter* down to the leader of street-blocks ensured that party directives were rigidly enforced. In this way the party became the main instrument of totalitarian rule.

After Germany's defeat it was dissolved and its resuscitation became an offence under the constitution of the German Federal Republic. At the ⇨ Nuremberg War Crime Trials the NSDAP's Leadership Corps and the SS were declared 'criminal organizations'. Former party members were screened by de-Nazification courts. More than 6,000,000 cases were investigated, about 175,000 persons were punished as having been directly responsible for instigating or executing reprehensible policies, about one million were held to have been 'innocuous camp followers', while a further million defendants were acquitted. The rest of the cases were either not proceeded with or fell under various amnesties.

NATO. North Atlantic Treaty Organization – established on American initiative in response to growing cold war pressures (Czech coup, Feb. 1948, ⇨ Berlin Blockade, June 1948) by Belgium, Canada, Denmark, France, Great Britain, Iceland, Italy, Luxembourg, the Netherlands, Norway, and the USA in Washington (April 1949). Greece, Turkey and Portugal were admitted (Feb. 1952) and West Germany (Oct. 1954). Members pledged themselves to maintain peace, uphold the ⇨ UN Charter, promote 'conditions of stability and well-being' by 'economic collaboration', and to regard 'an attack on one of them as an attack on all'.

The alliance's highest policy-making body is the North Atlantic Council composed of the Prime Ministers or departmental ministers (Transport, Finance, Foreign Affairs, etc.) of member countries according to the issues under discussion. Under the chairmanship of the Secretary-General it generally meets twice a year. Persuasive rather than executive, it can recommend but not enforce. The Council's day-to-day work is carried out by the permanent delegates of ambassadorial rank who meet weekly under the chairmanship of the Secretary-General (up to March 1967 in Paris, since then in Brussels).

The Council is assisted by the International Secretariat, whose Secretary-General is NATO's administrative head and ex officio Vice-President and Chairman of the North Atlantic Council. The Secretariat convenes the Council, prepares its agenda, transmits its resolutions and controls a number of subordinate, technical committees. Its Secretaries-General were Lord Ismay (1952–57), H. ⇨ Spaak (until 1961), D. ⇨ Stikker (until 1964) and since then M. ⇨ Brosio. Military matters are under the direction of the Military Committee, consisting of the C.-in-C.s of member states. It meets twice yearly to submit recommendations to the Council and implement its decisions. Representatives of the member states' Chiefs of Staff form the Military Representative Committee (Washington) which provides the link between NATO and the national military establishments. A smaller Standing Group

(Washington) formulates defence policies and supervises the operational planning.

There are three NATO Commands: SHAPE, Supreme Headquarters Allied Powers Europe (formerly Paris, from 1967 Casteaux, Belgium), CHANCOM, Channel Command (Portsmouth) and SALLANT, Supreme Allied Command Atlantic (Norfolk, Virginia). CUSRPG, Canada United States Regional Planning Group is responsible for the defence of the North American Continent. SHAPE under SACEUR, Supreme Allied Command Europe, is NATO's most important Command and controls four regional Commands: AFCENT, Allied Forces Central Europe (HQ formerly Fontainbleau, since 1967 Maastricht), AFNORTH, Allied Forces Northern Europe (HQ Kalsaas, nr. Oslo), AFSOUTH, Allied Forces Southern Europe (HQ Naples), and AFMED, Allied Forces Mediterranean (HQ Malta). With the US making the largest financial contributions to NATO and providing it with its nuclear capability, all Supreme Commanders have been American: ⇨Eisenhower (1950–52), Ridgeway (until 1953), Gruenther (until 1956), Norstad (until 1962), Lemnitzer (until 1969) and since then Goodpaster. The actual forces at NATO's disposal vary according to the military exigencies of member states. At the beginning of 1966, SHAPE's 'shield' force comprised about 60 divisions, of which Turkey's 14 divisions and the NATO-integrated West German *Bundeswehr* (12 divisions) constituted the largest national contingents; the USA contributed six divisions, Britain three, France two (since withdrawn). To the total cost including the construction and up-keep of an elaborate infra-structure (communication systems, aero-dromes, radar installations, pipe-lines, etc.) the major contributions came from the USA – 31%, West Germany – 20%, France – 12%, Great Britain – 10·5% (1964 figures).

During the first decade of its existence NATO, with the cold war at its height, gave Western Europe a sense of security. Since then NATO influence and popularity among its members have considerably declined. When Russian missiles exposed the US from 1959 onwards to nuclear counter-attacks, NATO members feared that America, in exclusive control of the alliance's nuclear armoury, would sanction its use only under threat to her own, rather than her allies' security. This led to the demand for a share in the control and deployment of NATO's atomic weapons, particularly from West Germany which had assigned its entire defence force to NATO and shared, moreover, a long frontier with Eastern Bloc countries. The USA suggested the formation of a Multi-lateral Force (⇨MLF) of ⇨Polaris-carrying submarines under direct NATO command and manned by multi-national crews. Although welcomed by West Germany, the scheme was not enthusiastically received by other members, notably Britain, which produced as a modified version (Dec. 1964) the plan of an Atlantic Nuclear Force (⇨ ANF) which was to assign part of the national American, British and French nuclear forces to NATO. Both plans have been abandoned for the time being. Undoubtedly the most serious blow to NATO was ⇨ France's withdrawal from the military part of the alliance (she remains a member adhering to the non-military clauses), which, taking formal effect on 1 July 1966 deprived NATO not only of the French manpower and financial contributions but also of its French installations, headquarters, port facilities, etc. which had to be evacuated by March 1967. This together with the USA's increasing preoccupation with and commitment in Vietnam has for the time being reduced NATO to a state of suspended animation. However, the invasion of Czechoslovakia by Russia and her satellites (Aug. 1968) re-emphasized the importance of NATO. To keep Malta within the Western orbit, NATO agreed to contribute towards the cost of maintaining and using the island's military facilities (March 1972).

Natolin Group. Name given to a communist faction in Poland which in 1956 attempted to preserve the power of the old Stalinists within the Party leadership and to resist all attempts to change and reform. The name is derived from a place just outside Warsaw where the faction held its meetings.

Nazi. ⇨ National Socialism.

Nazi–Soviet Pact. ⇨ Hitler-Stalin Pact.

NEFA. North-Eastern Frontier Agency – territory of ⇨ India administered by the Governor of Assam. Populated by Naga Tribes, the NEFA is the most vulnerable part of India's border. Part of it was occupied by China in 1960 and in 1962 China launched a full-scale attack on it but later withdrew.

Neguib, General Mohamed (1901–). Became Prime Minister and President of ⇨ Egypt (1953–54) after leading the Free Officers' Movement which staged the *coup d'état* deposing King ⇨ Farouk (1952). Neguib's military rank and his presidency of the Free Officers' Club lent authority to the junta, but he was probably never more than a figurehead with policy increasingly determined by younger officers led by ⇨ Nasser. Conflict between Neguib and Nasser was intensified by the latter's suppression of the ⇨ Moslem Brotherhood. Neguib was removed from the premiership (Feb. 1954), reinstated (March), again removed first from the premiership (April) then from the presidency and placed under house arrest (Nov.).

Nehru, Jawaharlal (1889–1964). First Prime Minister of independent ⇨ India (1947–64) and international statesman. Of a Brahmin family, he was educated in England and returned to India to practise law. After the massacre at Amritsar (1919) he became involved in the nationalist movement and he was soon one of its prominent leaders and a close associate of ⇨ Gandhi. He was first elected President of the ⇨ Congress Party in 1929 and was imprisoned many times with Gandhi – in 1921, 1922, 1931–32, 1932, 1934–35 and from 1942 to 1945 because he opposed Indian aid to Britain in World War II unless independence was granted immediately. As Prime Minister he advocated 'Indian socialism' and attempted to solve the problem of mass poverty by a series of five-year economic plans, accompanied by efforts to secularize the state and eliminate restrictions imposed by Hindu social customs through equality of education. Rapid population growth nullified the effects of his economic policies. Nehru's foreign policy was based on non-alignment with either the Eastern or Western blocs. As his own Foreign Minister he had direct control over external affairs and won considerable prestige abroad both for himself and for India. He played a prominent part in the ⇨ Bandung Conference (1955) and became an acknowledged leader of the uncommitted Afro-Asian nations. He was an outspoken opponent of Anglo-French action in the ⇨ Suez Crisis (1956) but less so of the concurrent Soviet invasion of ⇨ Hungary. He maintained connections with the ⇨ Commonwealth, but also cultivated friendly relations with the USSR and Communist China and opposed the latter's diplomatic isolation. In 1954 he enunciated with ⇨ Chou En-lai the Five Principles of Peaceful Coexistence. Indian hopes for good relations with China received a setback when the Chinese annexed ⇨ Tibet and later invaded Indian territory (1962). A persistent problem has been the dispute with Pakistan over the possession of ⇨ Kashmir. An ardent anti-colonialist and critic of the use of force, Nehru's own reputation suffered from his decision to use force to annex ⇨ Goa in 1961. Nehru's domination of Indian politics made it difficult to choose a successor after his death and difficult for alternative leaders to emerge during his lifetime.

Nenni, Pietro (1891–). Leader of the Socialist Party (PSI) of ⇨ Italy. He was its Secretary-General (1944–63) and participated in post-war governments as deputy Prime Minister (1945–46) and Foreign Minister (1946–47). Although earlier he had favoured cooperation with the communists, Nenni joined the coalition with the Christian Democrats as deputy Prime Minister (1963–68).

Neo-Destour. Re-named (1964) *Parti Socialiste Destourien* (PSD), the nationalist party of ⇨ Tunisia formed by Habib ⇨ Bourguiba as a breakaway from the Destour (Constitution) Party. Disbanded in 1938 after the war and Bourguiba's forced exile (1945), it was reorganized and led by Salah Ben Youssef. Its call for independence (1946) was met by the inclusion of Ben Youssef and others in the Chenik government (1950), but the resumption of violence led to the arrest of most of the Neo-Destour leaders (1952). Neither Ben Youssef's rejection of the Franco-Tunisian Convention (2.6.1955) followed by his dismissal, nor terrorist activities weakened the party, and the first government (20.3.1956) was totally Neo-Destour, including leaders of the powerful *Union Générale des Travailleurs Tunisiens* (UGTT).

NEP. Russian abbreviation for New Economic Policy, introduced by Lenin in March 1921 and abandoned by ⇔ Stalin in 1929 against the opposition of the 'Right', led by ⇔ Bukharin.

Nepal. *Area* – 54,362 sq. miles. *Population* – 9,412,996. *Head of State* – King Birendra (1972–). *Constitution* (1962) – Independent Kingdom with executive power vested in the constitutional monarch, who appoints a Council of Ministers from the National *Panchayat*. The *Panchayat* is chosen from members of the local *panchayats* or councils.

Until 1951 Nepal was a feudal state ruled by the Rana family, who from 1846 had supplied all the Prime Ministers, the King being virtually powerless. In 1951 the King proclaimed a constitutional monarchy, an Advisory Assembly was formed and elections were called. The country was not prepared for democratic government – there was no national consciousness to replace tribal loyalties, little administrative machinery and poor communications – and political instability followed leading to the formation of as many as 29 political parties. In 1955 Mahendra, the new King, dismissed the Cabinet, dissolved the Assembly and introduced direct rule. He was forced by the parties to hold new elections in 1959, when the Nepali Congress Party won a majority. The country's first constitution was adopted establishing the constitutional monarchy. The short government of Koirala was not a success and in 1960 the King, tired of the bickering, corruption and maladministration, again introduced direct rule, dissolving Parliament and banning political parties. In 1962 a new constitution introduced the *panchayat* system. The largest of the three border hill states (⇔ Bhutan and ⇔ Sikkim), Nepal's foreign policy is dominated by her relations with India and China. In 1950 she signed a Treaty of Commerce and Friendship with India, which has continued to provide her with substantial economic aid. During the 1950s tension increased between Nepal and India and in 1956 Nepal settled her differences with China by treaty. Nepal thereafter received economic aid from China (as well as from the USSR and the USA) but this rapprochement with China cooled after the Chinese invasion of India in 1962.

Netherlands, Kingdom of the. *European territory* – 12,908 sq. miles. *Population* (1969 est.) – 13,259,000. *Overseas territories*: ⇔ Surinam

⇨ Netherlands Antilles. *Head of State* – Queen Juliana (1948–). *Prime Minister* – Barend W. Biesheuvel (1971–). *Constitution* – Constitutional monarchy, executive power vested in the Sovereign acting through a Council of Ministers responsible to Parliament. Legislative powers are exercised conjointly by the Crown and bi-cameral Parliament (States-General) made up of a 150-member Lower House elected by direct, universal suffrage for four years, and a 75-member Upper House elected by the provincial estates for six years, one half of the House retiring every three years. In matters concerning the whole of the Kingdom (defence), the ministers plenipotentiary from the Overseas Territories must be consulted and have an advisory vote.

After the Napoleonic wars the Netherlands, determined not to become involved in any European big-power conflict, preserved its neutrality until attacked by Nazi Germany (May 1940). This long period of unbroken peace, great commercial flair, a thriving empire (Dutch East Indies) and a prosperous peasantry, made Holland one of Europe's wealthiest countries. Nevertheless, the great Depression of the early thirties, aggravated by the deflationary policies of the ruling Conservative coalition hit the country hard and caused widespread discontent. When Anton Mussert, the leader of the Dutch Nazi Party, polled 8% of the vote (1935), the Socialists, hitherto adamantly opposed to any cooperation with bourgeois administrations, began to support the government and joined it in Aug. 1939. The German attack took the Dutch by surprise, Rotterdam was destroyed and within five days military resistance collapsed. The Queen and the government fled to London to continue the struggle. In Holland the Nazi *Reichskommissar*, Seyss-Inquart (executed Oct. 1946), found the Dutch, whom the Germans regarded as fellow Nordics, resentful and resisting. They organized strikes against the deportation of Jews (Feb. 1941) and the failure to release Dutch prisoners-of-war (May 1943), and during the Battle of Arnhem (Sept. 1944) the railway men refused to work until final liberation. About 200,000 Dutch workers were compelled to work in Germany and more than 2,000 Resistance fighters were executed or perished in concentration camps. Holland became a battle area (winter 1944/45) when, in order to defend the Shelde estuary, the Germans flooded the country which suffered appalling food and fuel shortages. After ⇨ Pearl Harbor (Dec. 1941) the Dutch lost their East Indian navy in the Battle of the Java Sea (Feb. 1942) and were unable to prevent the Japanese occupation of their colonies. Post-war Dutch governments in which the Socialists continued to participate, tried to maintain the Indonesian empire and, nearer home, to integrate Holland into a broader European framework. The unsuccessful effort to regain ⇨ Indonesia (in which the Japanese had established an independent government under ⇨ Sukarno – March 1943) and the subsequent colonial war (1947–49) led to the establishment of a Netherland–Indonesian Union (Hague Round Table Conference, Nov. 1949). The Union, which proved unworkable, was dissolved by Sukarno (Feb. 1956). West Irian (Dutch New Guinea) remained an autonomous Dutch dependency until 1962 when, after the Dutch–Indonesian conflict over the country's sovereignty and sporadic fighting, the Netherlands left the island under UN administration which then handed the territory over to Indonesia (May 1963). Declaring it an integral part of the Republic, Indonesia refused to allow a West Irian plebiscite on independence (April 1965).

The Netherlands government, while still in exile, set up the ⇨ Benelux economic union (Sept. 1944) and has since joined all the organizations aimed at European and North Atlantic integration, such as the ⇨ EEC, ⇨ NATO, ⇨ WEU, ⇨ OEEC, etc. Queen Wilhelmina abdicated (Sept. 1948) in favour of her daughter, Queen Juliana. The marriage of the Crown Princess Beatrix to the German diplomat, Claus von Amsberg (1965) strained loyalty to the royal family. The bridegroom had been a member of the Nazi Youth Movement. Dutch domestic politics are complicated by religious tensions between the well-organized Catholic People's Party and the smaller Calvinist Party, the Christian Historical Union and the Anti-Revolutionary Party. The General Election of April 1971 shifted the political balance towards the left, replacing de Jong's government by another coalition under Barend Biesheuvel (July 1971), in which Norbert Schmelzer succeeded the popular Dr ⇨ Luns as Foreign Minister.

Netherlands Antilles and Surinam. Netherlands Antilles: *Total area* (of the six islands) – 394 sq. miles. *Total population* (approx.) – 210,000 (made up of many different ethnic groups).

Surinam: *Area* – 62,500 sq. miles. *Population* (approx.) – 324,000 – includes over 100,000 Creoles, over 100,000 East Indians (Hindus) and about 50,000 Indonesians.

Constitution – By Charter of the Kingdom of the Netherlands (1954) the Netherlands, Surinam and the Netherlands Antilles form a single realm. Surinam and the Netherlands Antilles have complete internal autonomy, and each is represented by its own Minister Plenipotentiary appointed to safeguard their interests in Holland. Universal suffrage was introduced in 1949. Each country has a Governor – representing the Queen of the Netherlands – and Council of Ministers responsible to an elected Legislature (the *Staten*). The *Staten* (with seats proportioned among the Islands) of the Netherlands Antilles is in Curaçao.

In Surinam political parties tend to form along ethnic lines. There is also a movement (influenced partly by events in Guyana with whom Surinam has a boundary dispute) for national independence and also support for the idea of a 'greater Guiana'.

Neurath, Baron Konstantin von (1873–1956). German Foreign Minister from 1932, remained in office under ⇨ Hitler until 1938. Neurath had been a popular ambassador in London and he wished to improve Anglo-German relations, but his influence counted for little with Hitler who ran his own foreign policy and often by-passed the Foreign Office. Neurath was *Reich* Protector in Bohemia and Moravia from 1939, but later resigned. He was sentenced to 15 years at the ⇨ Nuremberg War Crime Trials, released in 1954.

Neutrality Acts. A series of Acts of Congress in the USA (1935, 1937, 1939) having the object of preventing the involvement of the United States in the armed conflicts of the period leading up to the outbreak of World War II. They authorized the President to impose embargoes on arms sales to belligerent powers, to place the sale of other strategic materials on a 'cash and carry' basis, to prohibit the arming of US merchantmen, and to restrict travel by US citizens to war zones or in the vessels of belligerents. They were never fully enforced, and from 1939 they were systematically evaded by President ⇨ Roosevelt (by such devices as ⇨ Lend-Lease) in the interests of national defence and security. They reflected the return to ⇨ Isolationism after US involvement in World War I, and belated attempts by ⇨ Congress to recover some power over US foreign policy. Though moderated by the Act of 1939, some measures remained in force until the USA had entered the war.

New Deal. Was launched to rescue the USA from the Great Depression. The phrase was used by Franklin ⇨ Roosevelt in his speech accepting the Democratic nomination for President in July 1932 when he promised 'a new deal for the American people'. Its welfare–economic policies softened some of the effects of depression and helped promote but failed to achieve complete recovery until in 1940 the economy was put on a war-time basis. The New Deal's range of legislation is evidenced in the following summary: measures aimed at meeting the immediate economic and financial crisis; aid to large economic groups such as industry, farmers and labour; aid to the unemployed and the hardest stricken; increased social and economic security for most citizens during periods of illness and old age; Federal-sponsored work projects, ranging from soil conservation to the arts; measures to allow threatened house-owners to re-finance their mortgages at low interest rates.

Newfoundland. Became a province of ⇨ Canada (1949) following a referendum (1948). Formerly a ⇨ Dominion (1917) she again became a Crown Colony (1933) owing to a severe financial crisis. During World

War II, Newfoundland was an important Allied military base.

New Frontier. Evoked in the USA by J. F. ⇨ Kennedy in his speech accepting the Democratic presidential nomination in 1960. It was used to refer to the relatively youthful personnel, the new policies and the vigorous image presented by the Kennedy Administration.

New Guinea. The second largest island in the world (312,000 sq. miles), consists of West Irian (formerly Netherlands New Guinea and since 1963 an Indonesian territory) and the Australian external territories of New Guinea Territory and Papua. New Guinea Territory became an Australian Mandate Territory under the League of Nations in 1921 and has been administered by Australia as a UN Trust Territory since the war. In 1949 she formed an administrative union with Papua, which had been administrated by Australia since 1906. During World War II New Guinea was the scene of bitter fighting between Japanese and Allied troops.

Ne Win, General (1911-). Prime Minister and Minister of Defence of ⇨ Burma (1958-60 and since 1962) and Chairman of the Revolutionary Council since 1965. He has also been Chief of the General Staff since 1960. He has continued Burma's neutralist foreign policy and in internal affairs adopted policies of nationalization and centralization.

New Left. In America, a broad grouping of political tendencies and organizations embracing many varieties of neo-Marxism, socialism, syndicalism, anarchism, pacifism and more personal forms of opposition to established society. Important bodies within it include ⇨ SDS, ⇨ SNCC and the ⇨ Black Panther party, and its main strands are ⇨ Black Power, 'student power' and opposition to the Vietnam War and the 'draft' (⇨ Selective Service System). It is largely a movement of the under-thirty-year-olds, heavily concentrated in academic institutions, which began in the early 1960s in conjunction with the Negro ⇨ Civil Rights Movement, and became broader in scope and more militant in action with the escalation of the war in Vietnam after 1964. It is distinguished from the 'Old Left' (socialism, communism, Marxism, etc.) in being more concerned with action and less with ideology, and from the 'liberals' in being more radical and favouring 'direct action', including violence where it is thought necessary. The American New Left has both influenced and been influenced by similar movements elsewhere. (⇨ New Right.)

New Right. In America, a broad grouping of political tendencies, organizations and individual publicists, united primarily in their common opposition to international communism and the internal 'communist conspiracy'. Most prominent is the ⇨ John Birch Society, but there are many others in different parts of the country – some, like the

Minutemen, favouring violent action, and others, like the Christian Crusade of Dr Billy James Hargis and the Christian Anti-Communist Campaign of Dr Fred C. Schwartz, engaged primarily in instructional activities. The 'Radical Right' differs from the older extreme Right of Nazism and Fascism in being strongly anti-statist and (officially) anti-racist, though it is heavily infiltrated by anti-semitic and anti-Negro extremists of the kind traditionally associated with the ⇨ Ku Klux Klan. It also has affinities with ⇨McCarthyism, which it has both continued and replaced. It is sometimes distinguished from the 'Conservatives', as represented by Senator ⇨ Goldwater, and from 'extreme (or ultra-) Conservatives' like William F. Buckley, editor of the *National Review*. Here the difference is one of degree and of relative realism and rationality. The two positions are characterized by a number of common themes – anti-communism, anti-statism and anti-collectivism generally, and also such things as 'balanced budgets' and ⇨ States' Rights. (⇨ New Left.)

New Zealand. *Area* 103,740 sq. miles. *Population* (1971) – 2,869,187. *Prime Minister* – John Marshall (1972–). *Constitution* (1917) – The constitution is basically the same as in the UK with the Prime Minister responsible to Parliament and the Queen represented by the Governor-General, who is advised by the Executive Council of Ministers. The uni-cameral Legislature – the House of Representatives – is elected for three years by universal adult suffrage. (The Upper House was abolished in 1951.)

New Zealand, a Commonwealth Dominion since 1907, its sovereign status formally recognized by the Statute of ⇨Westminster (1931), has a predominantly agricultural economy and a largely white population, 90% of which consists of emigrants from the UK and their descendants. There are two main parties: the National Party, a combination of Conservatives and Liberals, which governed from 1949 to 1957 (first under Holland and later ⇨Holyoake) and again since 1960 (under Holyoake and Marshall); and the Labour Party which ruled from 1935 to 1949 (under Savage and then Fraser) and again from 1957 to 1960 (under Walter Nash). It has been led by Norman Kirk since 1965. The earlier Labour governments introduced important social legislation, including a comprehensive social security law in 1938 and a programme of broad socialized medicine in 1941. At the last general election (1969) the National Party won 45 seats and the Labour Party 39. The Maori population of 200,000 is represented by four designated seats in Parliament. New Zealand has strong trade links with the UK – in 1966 44% of all her exports went to the UK. The negotiations following Britain's two applications for entry into the EEC, when special priority was given

to New Zealand's economic interests, emphasized her continued economic dependence on the UK but also showed the need for more regional
cooperation – in 1965 a free trade agreement was concluded with
Australia. The country recognizes South-East Asia as her strategic
centre – she has been a member of ⇨ SEATO since 1954 – but during
the 1960s she had to meet the problems arising from Britain's changed
position in the world. Britain's ⇨ East of Suez policy marked a decline
in the defence cooperation between the two countries (New Zealanders
are proud of the record of their troops in two world wars). Her membership of the ⇨ ANZUS Treaty (1951) already foreshadowed a greater
dependence with Australia on the USA. This cooperation was confirmed by the military support from the two Australasian nations for the
USA in the Vietnam War. Under the ⇨ Colombo Plan New Zealand
has contributed to the development of Asian countries. She was responsible for the trusteeship territory of Western Samoa, until it achieved
full independence in 1962.

Nguyen Ai Quoc. ⇨ Ho Chi Minh.

Nicaragua. *Area –* 57,143 sq. miles. *Population* (1970 est.) – 1,984,000.
President – General Anastasio Somoza Debayle (1967–). *Constitution*
(1950) – Unitary Republic – with an elected President and bi-cameral
Congress.

For over 30 years Nicaragua has been ruled by a (Somoza) family
oligarchy (despite formally democratic constitutions) – a fact which may
account for its slow social and economic development. For 20 years
(1936–56, excepting a brief period in 1947) until he was assassinated,
Anastasio Somoza Garcia ruled Nicaragua as his private domain. He
was succeeded by his son Luis, then by a family nominee (to conform
with the constitution) and since 1967 by another son Anastasio Somoza
Debayle. Opposition to Somoza domination, sometimes violent, has so
far been to no avail.

Niger. *Area –* 484,000 sq. miles. *Population* (1970 est.) – 4,016,000. *Head
of State and President of the Council of Ministers –* Hamani Diori (1960).
Constitution – Republican – similar to the other members of the ⇨ *Conseil de l'Entente –* with an elected President and uni-cameral National
Assembly.

Niger has a turbulent history of warring chiefs, whose descendants
still oppose social change. A province of ⇨ French West Africa from
1904, French authority was not completely secured until 1922. Niger
became self-governing within the ⇨ French Community in 1958. The
left wing *Sawaba* party (its leader now in exile), victorious in the 1957
elections, opposed the 1958 constitution and was heavily defeated. In
Aug. 1960 Niger achieved full independence outside the Community. It

is a semi-desert area, still afflicted by tribal rivalries, with a subsistence economy. In 1963 an army mutiny failed as did an attempt on the President's life in 1965.

Nigeria. *Area* – 356,669 sq. miles. *Population* (1970 est.) – 66,174,000. *President* (of Supreme Military Council) – Major-General Yakubu ⇨ Gowon (1966–). *Constitution* – The former Federal constitution of Nigeria ceased to function in Jan. 1966. Legislative and executive power is vested in the Supreme Military Council (by decree March 1967). The Government has adopted proposals (May 1967) to create a 12-state Federation in place of the former four-state Federation.

The Federation of Nigeria (formerly a British Crown Colony and Protectorate (from 1914)), Africa's most populous state, includes a number of tribal groups of whom the largest are the Hausa (who are Moslem) in the north, the Ibo in the east, and the Yoruba in the west. Thus, like many African states, the Nigerian political entity was delimited by the policies and ambitions of the former metropolitan power rather than by actual regional and tribal boundaries. Tribal rivalries have contributed to recent tragedy and civil war, a tragedy heightened by the hopes placed in Nigeria's future and the fact that Nigeria appeared to be (until recent events) a most successful example of national loyalties overriding tribal interests. (Until the recent emergency numerous representatives of the various tribes were found in regions other than their own.) After World War II, as in ⇨ Ghana, there was a quickening demand for independence in which the Ibo leader, Dr Nnamdi ⇨ Azikiwe, the Yoruba Chief Obafemi ⇨ Awolowo, and from the north Sir Abubakar Tafawa ⇨ Balewa were prominent. Reforms followed the establishment of a federal structure composed of Northern, Eastern and Western Regions (1946). Only then was a Legislative Council for the whole of Nigeria set up. The constitution of 1951, modified (1954) in favour of greater regional autonomy, led to regional self-government for the East and West Regions in 1957 and the Northern Region in 1959. Nigeria became an independent Federation within the ⇨ Commonwealth on 1 Oct. 1960, with Dr Azikiwe as Governor-General and Tafawa Balewa as its first Prime Minister, and later a Republic within the Commonwealth (Oct. 1963). Following a plebiscite (1961) the UN trust Territory of the former British Cameroons opted to join Nigeria.

A referendum (1963) led to the creation of a Mid-Western Region. Post-independence politics were dominated by the regions' suspiciousness and distrust of each other. In the Western Region, Chief Awolowo became increasingly critical of the Federal Government which he saw as too dominated by northern and eastern interests. Disputes in the

Western Region Assembly resulted in a Declaration of Emergency by the Federal Government (1962). (The Coker Commission (1963) claimed that public funds had been appropriated by Chief Awolowo's 'Action Group'.) In Sept. 1962 Awolowo and his leading supporters had been arrested. The extradition of one of his supporters, Chief Anthony ⇨ Enahoro from London to appear in a treason trial aroused strong feelings in the UK. Despite the lifting of the emergency in the Western Region, unrest continued and there was a general strike (1964). In the 1965 elections, after considerable manoeuvring, Dr Azikiwe eventually called on Tafawa Balewa to form a broad-based government. Despite its internal difficulties, Nigeria played a prominent part in African politics and Nigerian forces helped to restore order in the Congo. In Jan. 1966, the premiers of the Northern and Western Regions as well as the Federal Prime Minister, Balewa, were assassinated in an Eastern Region-inspired military coup. The rebellion was suppressed by the army commander, General Ironsi – an Ibo who later (May 1966) introduced a unitary form of government in place of the Federation, which increased Northern suspicions with tragic consequences for the Ibo. Ibos living in the North were massacred by the thousand and the remainder forced to flee to the South. (This blood-bath has had an important affect on Nigerian attitudes, explaining the continued Biafran resistance and their fears of genocide.) In July 1966, Ironsi was killed in a Northern-led army mutiny and was succeeded by Colonel Gowon. Relations between Gowon and the Military Governor of the Eastern Region, Col. ⇨ Ojukwu deteriorated rapidly. In April 1967 Ojukwu's Eastern government made itself responsible for all Federal institutions in its region including tax collection. Lagos in turn imposed financial sanctions. Each government was anxious to claim the Eastern Region's rich oil revenues for itself. When the Federal Government (May 1967) proposed a new constitution which would *inter alia* have split the Eastern Region into three states, incidentally depriving the Ibos of the oil-rich coast, Ojukwu proclaimed Biafra an independent Republic (30 May 1967).

Biafra–Nigeria Conflict – Civil war broke out in July (1967) with the advance of the Federal armies. Despite initial Biafran successes, the better-equipped and larger Federal forces gradually extended their control right up to the Ibo heartland. The capture of Port Harcourt (May 1968) swung the war decisively in Nigeria's favour. (Enugu, the Biafran capital had fallen in Sept. 1967.) By Oct. 1968 Biafran-held territory had been reduced to 8–9,000 square miles. During the course of the war each side accused the other of employing foreign mercenaries. There appear to be French mercenaries in Biafra, and

British, South African and Egyptian pilots have operated with the Federal forces. Despite Nigerian claims (going back to 1967) that the war would soon be over, Biafran resistance stiffened (late 1968), perhaps due to receiving French equipment supplied via ⇨ Gabon. The Nigerians were supplied by the USSR and especially by the UK. (The British Government claimed that it had to fulfil obligations to a member state of the Commonwealth.) Biafra was recognized by Tanzania (April 1968) and by ⇨ Gabon, ⇨ Ivory Coast and ⇨ Zambia (May 1968). At the end of July 1968 French government sources announced France's support for Biafra, claiming that through its continued survival Biafra had demonstrated its right to exist as a separate state. Initial peace initiatives (including moves by the Vatican and the World Council of Churches, Dec. 1967) by the Commonwealth Secretariat and the ⇨ OAU failed. The Fifth OAU Assembly (Kinshasa, Sept. 1967) condemned Biafran secession and sent a special mission to General Gowon. Following further Commonwealth and OAU moves, peace negotiations were held in Kampala (May 1968) but soon broke down. Again (July 1968) preliminary meetings (Niger) were followed in August by formal negotiations under OAU auspices and the chairmanship of Haile Selassie at Addis Ababa. Chief Enahoro rejected the Biafran terms as unrealistic, but some agreement was reached on methods of transportation for relief measures. In Sept. 1968 the Sixth OAU Assembly (Algiers) again adopted a resolution (approved by Awolowo of the Nigerian Government, but without any Biafran representation) re-affirming its condemnation of Biafra's secession. World opinion was horrified by the desperate plight of civilians in the civil war particularly children of whom frightening numbers have died of starvation and by the failure of the Federal Government and Biafra to give priority to the relief of civilians. While some claimed, including UK government sources, that the best hope for reducing loss of life lay in a quick Nigerian victory, Biafrans claimed to be threatened with genocide, which the Nigerians hotly disputed. In the UK Press and parliament (June 1968) there was increasing dissatisfaction with the UK government's role in supplying arms to Nigeria. The reputation of the OAU as well as the powers supplying arms to the contestants was affected by the outcome of the war. The Eastern Region (re-named Biafra by the secessionists) had a population (1963) of 12,400,000 in an area of 29,484 sq. miles. It is believed that over a million Ibo (refugees from other Regions, particularly the North) have returned to the Eastern Region since 1966. Biafran resistance finally collapsed in January 1970. Col. Ojukwu was granted asylum in the Ivory Coast.

Nixon, Richard M. (1913–). Thirty-seventh President of the United States (1969–), and former Vice-President (1953–61). Immediately after war service, he won a seat in Congress from his home state of California (1946, re-elected 1948), and in 1950 won a bitterly contested election for the Senate, defeating the Democratic incumbent. While in Congress Nixon gained a conservative reputation, working for the passage of the ⇨ Taft–Hartley Act and co-authoring the Mundt–Nixon Bill on control of communists. He was a member of the House Committee on Un-American Activities (⇨ HUAC) and became nationally known for his persistence in the investigation of Alger ⇨ Hiss. Chosen by Gen. ⇨ Eisenhower as his running-mate on the Republican ticket, he was elected Vice-President in 1952 and again in 1956. Nixon was an active Vice-President, travelling extensively and often presiding at Cabinet and other executive meetings during the President's illnesses. In 1960 he was unanimously chosen by the Republicans as their nominee for President, but lost the election by a narrow margin to the Democratic candidate, John F. ⇨ Kennedy. Two years later Nixon was unsuccessful in an attempt to win the governorship of California. In 1968 he sought and won the Republican nomination for President and chose as his running-mate the relatively unknown Governor of Maryland, Spiro ⇨ Agnew. Campaigning continuously and benefiting from the Administration's unpopularity, Nixon defeated his Democratic opponent, Vice-President Hubert H. ⇨ Humphrey, by a narrow margin. As President, particularly after the mid-term elections of 1970, Nixon made a number of new departures in American policy. At home, most notable was his 'new economic policy', introduced in 1971, which was designed to contain inflation, reduce unemployment, and correct the American balance of payments deficit, and which entailed the use of Keynesian measures previously eschewed by the Republican President. The policy showed some success during 1972 in containing inflation, though not in reducing the balance of payments deficit. Abroad, the continuing policy of the President from the outset was the reduction of US involvement on the ground in Vietnam, and in excessive foreign entanglements generally – the 'Nixon doctrine'. By 1972, American ground forces had been reduced to comparatively small numbers after the massive escalations of President ⇨ Johnson. Despite the renewal of air strikes against the North in Apr. 1972, a cease-fire agreement was announced in Jan. 1973. The de-escalation of the war was in part intended to contribute to another Nixon initiative, the normalization of relations with the ⇨ Chinese Peoples Republic. After sending his aide, Henry ⇨ Kissinger to prepare the way, Nixon visited Peking in Feb. 1972, thus reversing the long-standing American policy of non-recognition of the Communist regime. This visit was followed by a presidential visit to Moscow in May 1972, where, in addition to promoting his new China policy, Nixon signed a Strategic Arms Limitation agreement. There was less success for the President's initiative for peace in the Middle East, the particular concern of Secretary of State ⇨ Rogers. Though Nixon was often able to act effectively and decisively, he had to contend with considerable opposition to his legislative programme and his nominations from a Democratic Congress. Only 20 per cent of his legislative proposals for 1971 were enacted, the poorest record since Eisenhower's in 1954; and in 1969 and 1970 two of the President's nominees for the ⇨ Supreme Court were turned down by the Senate, an unprecedented rebuff. In Nov. 1972 he was reelected in a landslide victory.

NKGB. Russian abbreviation for People's Commissariat for State Security. (⇨ USSR State Security Service.)

Nkomo. ⇨ ZAPU.

Nkrumah, Dr Kwame (1909–72). First Prime Minister and then President of ⇨ Ghana (1957–66). As the founder and dynamic leader of the CPP he played a crucial role in the Gold Coast's struggle for independence. After independence Nkrumah used the CPP to achieve and maintain his political dominance – he was referred to as '*Osagyefo*' – 'The Redeemer'. After General ⇨ Ankrah's coup, he lived in exile in ⇨ Guinea, nominally as its co-president. (Earlier he had come to Sékou ⇨ Touré's aid – (⇨ Guinea–Ghana Union).) Through his support of the ⇨ OAU and early concern for African Unity (viz. proposed Guinea Union, Accra Conference (1958), ⇨ Casablanca Group, etc.) Nkrumah has been regarded as a champion of Pan-Africanism despite Ghana's frequent friction with neighbouring states (even including Guinea) and his opposition to larger groupings (particularly of Francophone Africa) in which he was not a key figure.

NKVD. Russian abbreviation for People's Commissariat for Internal Affairs. (⇨ USSR State Security Service.)

NLRB. United States National Labor Relations Board – an ⇨ Independent Regulatory Commission created by the ⇨ Wagner Act in 1935 to enforce the provisions against 'unfair labor practices' by employers, and to settle disputes between unions. These were then rife, due to the Depression and the ⇨ AFL–CIO split. Its original pro-union character was modified by the ⇨ Taft-Hartley Act which declared certain union practices 'unfair'. Its five members are appointed for five years each by the President with the consent of the Senate.

Nordic Council. Set up in Stockholm (Feb. 1953) to promote economic, social, legal and cultural cooperation and to 'create uniform rules in the Nordic countries in as many respects as possible'.

Members are: Denmark, Iceland, Norway, Sweden and (since 1956) Finland.

The Council consists of delegates elected by the national Parliaments (5 from Iceland and 16 from each of the other countries) and of (non-voting) government representatives. Resolutions in the form of recommendations are submitted to the governments, which must report back to the Council on the action taken.

Standing committees made up of Council members work out the recommendations submitted by the Council. It meets annually in one of the Nordic capitals. The Nordic Council represents an area of 1,275,000 sq. kms. and a population of 21,227,000 people.

North-Eastern Frontier Agency. ⇨NEFA.

Northern Ireland. *Area* – 5,206 sq. miles. *Population* – 1,527,593. *Governor* – Sir Ralph Grey (1968–). *Secretary of State for Northern Ireland* – William Whitelaw (1972–). *Constitution* – Under the Government of Ireland Act (1920), as amended by the Irish Free State Act (1922), Northern Ireland had limited self-government exercised by a Parliament consisting of a Senate and a House of Commons. Certain legislative matters, e.g. defence and foreign affairs and fiscal powers, were reserved to the UK Government – Northern Ireland returns 12 members to the House of Commons in London (1970 election – 8 Unionist (Conservative)). In March 1972, the UK Government transferred power to Westminster and prorogued the Northern Ireland Parliament. Northern Ireland is often known as Ulster but really consists of only six of the original nine Ulster counties.

Northern Ireland was governed from 1921–72 by the pro-British Unionist Party – its present strength in the House of Commons is 35 seats out of 52 (1969 election) – and its dominance helps to explain the continuing strong connection with Britain. This has been reinforced by strong economic links with Britain, which is Northern Ireland's main market and forms a fiscal unit with her. During World War II Northern Ireland served as a military base and was a principal centre of war industry. In contrast to the Republic of ⇨Ireland, Northern Ireland has a Protestant character – nearly two-thirds of the population are Protestants – but the Catholic minority is growing steadily. Raids across the border by the ⇨IRA in the past, the demagogy of the militant ⇨Paisley, and riots involving the 'civil rights' movement in Londonderry in the autumn of 1968 – with its complaints of discrimination against Catholics in education, housing and voting (there is a property qualification) – had grown by the early 1970's into a state of near civil war in the cities of Belfast and Londonderry. Barricades were thrown up in the Catholic districts and later in the Protestant ones too, and bomb attacks and sniper fire became daily occurrences. The Protestant majority has its fears and the Catholic minority its grievances, the chief of which has been the voting system in local government, which is loaded against the Catholics. These growing problems led to serious divisions within the Unionist Party and to challenges to O'Neill's leadership, both from within his party (several Cabinet ministers resigned) and from the extreme Protestants under Paisley. In April 1969 O'Neill resigned office and was succeeded as Prime Minister by James Chichester-Clark, who was replaced in turn by Brian Faulkner in March 1971.

In August 1969 the British army took over control of the province's security, but polarization of the two communities continued and was evidenced by the appearance of para-military partisan troops on both sides and by an increasing number of sectarian civilian murders. In August 1971 the army introduced the internment without trial of suspected members of the IRA, and in March 1972 the British government imposed direct rule from Westminster.

Northern Rhodesia. ⇨ Zambia and ⇨ Rhodesia and Nyasaland, Federation of.

North Korea. ⇨ Korea.

North Vietnam. ⇨ Vietnam.

Norway, Kingdom of. *Area* – 125,000 sq. miles. *Population* – 3·8 m. *Head of State* – King Olav v. *Prime Minister* – Trygve Bratteli (March 1971–). *Constitution* – Constitutional monarchy. Executive authority is vested in the King acting through a Cabinet (*Statsrad*) responsible to Parliament (*Storting*). Quadrennially elected by universal suffrage, the 150-member *Storting* cannot be dissolved either by the King or of its own accord. Each new *Storting* elects a quarter of its members to form the Second Chamber, the *Lagting*, while the rest make up the *Oledsting*.

An independent Kingdom from 1905 (when its union with Sweden was dissolved), Norway was not involved in European power politics for more than 30 years. Even though a strongly neutralist Labour Party (in office from 1935) had refused France and Britain transit facilities to support the Finns in the Finnish-Russian War (1939–40), Norway was nevertheless invaded by Germany (9.4.1940) in her attack on the West. Supported by Anglo-French landings (15–19.4.1940), Norwegians resisted determinedly until the link-up of German troops (Dombas, 30.4.1940), bisecting the country, led to the capitulation of the Norwegians and the evacuation of the bulk of the Allied forces. The King and the Government (in exile) went with them and arrived in England (5.5.1940). They supported, as did the Norwegian navy (the third largest in the world), the continued resistance of the Norwegian underground. In 1942 the Nazi Vidkun ⇨ Quisling, who had assisted the invading forces, became Prime Minister of occupied Norway. After the war (and following her failure to secure a credible Scandinavian neutrality pact) Norway, now sharing a frontier with the USSR, joined ⇨NATO (April 1949). In 1947 Russia questioned Norway's ownership of Spitzbergen and demanded the right to instal a base on the island, which Norway refused.

Norway is a member of the ⇨Nordic Council and ⇨EFTA and since the 1965 general election has, for the first time in 30 years, been governed by a non-Labour coalition. Although the Labour party gained 74 out of the 150 *Storting* seats (Sept. 1969) Per Borton's centre coalition stayed in office until March 1971. It was replaced by a Labour government under T. Bratelli, which upholding Norway's decision to join the ⇨EEC, signed the Brussels Treaty of Accession (Jan. 1972), but as the result of a referendum Norway decided not to join.

Novotny, A. (1904–). Former President of ⇨ Czechoslovakia. A founder-member of the Communist Party in 1921, Novotny became prominent at the time of the disgrace of the Party's former First Secretary, Rudolf Slansky, and his associates. For many years active in local and regional party work, Novotny was promoted to the Party Secretariat (Sept. 1951) and, three months later, after the arrest of Slansky, also to the Party's Politbureau. Publicly praised for his contribution to the preparation of Slansky's ⇨ Show Trial in 1952, Novotny became the Party's First Secretary (1953). In 1957, after the death of President ⇨Zapotocky, he assumed in addition the presidency of the Republic. Incapable of coping with the gradually mounting crisis within the Party and the country at large, he lost his position as the Party's First Secretary to Alexander ⇨Dubček (Jan. 1968). Under steadily rising pressure, he also resigned from the presidency and from all his remaining Party functions (March 1968).

NPD. *Nationaldemokratische Partei Deutschlands* – an extremist, West German, right-wing party founded in Nov. 1964 to unite and give parliamentary representation to the Federal Republic's 'homeless Right'. It emerged under the guidance of Adolf von ⇨Thadden from the equally extremist but unsuccessful *Deutsche Reichspartei* (DRP), which he had hitherto led. Chauvinistic and reactionary, the NPD was denounced both in Germany and abroad as 'neo-Nazi'; a charge strenuously denied by supporters in spite of resemblances in the party programmes, persistent efforts to white-wash the Nazi era and the fact that 12 out of 30 members on the NPD Executive had been members of the Nazi Party. After polling 2% of the vote in the 1965 general election, the NPD caused a national and international sensation, when between 1966 and 1968 it consistently polled in *Land* parliament elections from

6 to 10% of the vote. However, in the 1969 elections it was unable to win the necessary 5% of the poll to be represented in the *Bundestag*. Subsequently it declined and by 1972 was no longer represented in any *Land* parliament.

NSC. United States National Security Council – an agency established by the National Security Act of 1947, and one of the group of agencies forming the ⇨ Executive Office of the President. Its members are the President, who usually presides at meetings, the Vice-President, ⇨ Secretary of State, Secretary of Defense, and Director of the Office of Emergency Preparedness. In addition, it has as advisers the Chairman of the ⇨ JCS and Director of the ⇨ CIA and, occasionally, the Secretary of the Treasury, director of the ⇨ Bureau of the Budget, ⇨ Attorney General, and Director of ⇨ USIA. It directs the work of the CIA and assists the President in co-ordinating all areas of policy affecting the security of the USA in the widest sense. Members of this 'super-Cabinet' are supposed to act as a unit, not as representatives of their respective agencies.

The NSC was of major importance under Presidents Truman and Eisenhower but President Kennedy made much less use of it, relying more on the direct advice of his Special Assistant for National Security Affairs, McGeorge Bundy; and this policy was continued by President Johnson. The change reflected criticisms of NSC made by members of the armed forces and Congress that too much time was wasted preparing annual Basic National Security Policy documents which could mean 'all things to all men' and gave no clear guide to the ⇨ Defense Department or JCS. NSC continues to bring forward broad issues of security policy for decision by the President in consultation with his closest advisers.

NSDAP. ⇨ National Socialism.

Nu, U. (1907–). First Prime Minister of ⇨ Burma, he held office 1948–56, 1957–58 and 1960–62. A leader of the nationalist movement, U Nu was Foreign Minister in the government set up by the Japanese during their occupation but also organized an anti-Japanese guerrilla force. After the war he became leader of the Anti-Fascist People's Freedom League (AFPFL). While in office he followed neutralist policies abroad and socialist policies at home. A devout Buddhist, he sought, against opposition, to promote Buddhism as a political force and established it as Burma's official religion.

Nuclear Test Ban Treaty. Treaty between the USA, USSR and Great Britain (5.8.1963) prohibiting the testing of nuclear weapons in the atmosphere, outer space and under water, but permitting continued underground testing. The treaty was adopted after extended negotiations (beginning 1958) and a voluntary suspension of tests by the nuclear powers (1958–61). France and the Chinese People's Republic alone refused to adhere to it. A Nuclear Non-Proliferation Treaty was negotiated between the USA and USSR under United Nations auspices during 1968, but acceptance of it by other powers has proceeded more slowly. A treaty excluding nuclear weapons from South America was signed by 21 States at Mexico City (14.2.1967).

Nuremberg Laws. Anti-semitic legislation promulgated at the Nuremberg ⇨ Nazi Party Rally (Sept. 1935), defining who, in legal terms, was a Jew. Under the complementary 'Law for the Protection of German Blood and Honour' it became a criminal offence for Jews to have sexual relations with Germans or to marry them. The Nuremberg Laws, reducing Jews to the status of second-class citizens, were the first step towards their complete isolation and ultimate murder.

Nuremberg War Crime Trials (Nov. 1945–Oct. 1946). Prosecution and punishment of Nazi leaders accused of 'crimes against peace', the planning and waging of aggressive war; 'war crimes', ill treatment of prisoners and civilians; and 'crimes against humanity', the persecution, repression and extermination of racial minorities and political opponents, by a specially constituted international military tribunal of American, British, French and Russian judges. The accused (sentence in brackets) were: M. Bormann (death, *in absentia*), Admiral K. Doenitz (10 years), H. Frank (death), W. Frick (death), H. Fritzsche (acquitted), W. Funk (life), H. Goering (death), R. Hess (life), General A. Jodel (death), General W. Keitel (death), E. Kaltenbrunner (death), C. von Neurath (15 years), F. von Papen (acquitted), Admiral E. Raeder (life), J. von Ribbentrop (death), A. Rosenberg (death), E. Saukel (death), H. Schacht (acquitted), B. von Schirach (20 years), A. Seyss-Inquart (death), A. Speer (20 years), J. Streicher (death).

Subsequently 12 American courts tried more subordinate persons and organizations, i.e. the ⇨ SS extermination squads, the doctors responsible for experiments on human beings, the industrial concerns – Krupp, I. G. Farben, etc. responsible for exploiting slave labour and the Nazi Foreign Office for planning aggression and subversion. Of the 177 indicted in these trials, 25 were sentenced to death, 20 to life imprisonment, 97 to lesser prison sentences and 35 were acquitted.

Sometimes denounced as biased and one-sided, the Nuremburg trials, by assembling a vast amount of incontestible evidence, did much to reveal the scope and brutality of Nazi rule.

Nyasaland. ⇨ Rhodesia and Nyasaland, Federation of, and ⇨ Malawi.

Nyerere, Julius Kambarage (1922–). President of ⇨ Tanzania and referred to as *Mwalimu* (teacher), by his countrymen. A month after leading Tanganyika to independence (9.12.1961) he amazingly resigned the premiership to concentrate on reorganizing the Tanganyika African National Union. His subsequent presidency has provided further proof of his originality and acumen. He has attempted to build a Christian and socialist political system attuned to the needs of Africa. In a one-party system candidates have to compete for office at constituency level. Nyerere is a leading member of ⟡ OAU and a keen exponent of Pan-Africanism. The 'African Liberation Committee' has its headquarters at Dar es Salaam. Union with Zanzibar has strengthened Nyerere's links with the communist world but he has attempted to maintain an independent foreign policy though the pressures of competing ideologies, nationalism and resentment of 'white'-dominated Rhodesia and South Africa allow little room for manoeuvre. He was an early advocate of East African Unity.

O

OAS. Organization of American States – established at the Ninth International Congress of American States (Bogota 1948). Its aims include the peaceful settlement of disputes, the strengthening of continental security and the promotion of economic development. Its policies are organized through:

- the Inter-American Conference which meets every five years;
- meetings of foreign ministers and a Council of the Organization (coas) on which every member nation is represented.

It has a Permanent Secretariat – the Pan-American Union. It also includes a number of specialized committees and agencies, amongst which is the ⇨Alliance for Progress. Cuba was expelled in 1962 by 14 votes to 1 (Cuba) with 6 abstentions (Argentina, Bolivia, Brazil, Chile, Ecuador, Mexico). It is opposed to communist penetration in Latin America (1954 – Declaration of Solidarity for the Preservation of the Political Integrity of the American States against the Intervention of International Communism; 1962 – oas unanimously supported US blockade of Cuba). It has intervened in a number of inter-American disputes, most recently (Oct. 1968), the US invoked oas provisions concerning military take-overs when announcing its severance of relations with Peru.

Its members are: Argentina, Barbados, Bolivia, Brazil, Chile, Colombia, Costa Rica, Dominican Republic, Ecuador, El Salvador, Guatemala, Haiti, Honduras, Mexico, Nicaragua, Panama, Paraguay, Peru, Trinidad and Tobago, USA, Uruguay, Venezuela.

OAS. *Organisation de l'Armée Secrète* – was set up after the abortive army revolt (21.4.1961) to preserve settler privilege in an *Algérie Française* and to prevent the establishment of an independent Algeria. Backed by generals ⇨Salan and Jouhaud and Gaullist ex-Ministers ⇨Soustelle and ⇨Bidault (head of the settler *Conseil National de la Résistance* (CNR)), the oas was supported by the settlers, the officer corps, long-service and élite-formation soldiers (parachutists) and right-wing extremists in France. Its attempts to attain its ends by violence seriously threatened the survival of the ⇨ Fifth Republic. It produced the lawless chaos which led to the unexpected mass exodus of French settlers, whose security, status and possessions in an independent Algeria were carefully safeguarded by the Evian agreements (18.3.1962). After the loss of Algeria, the OAS terror continued in France, culminating in numerous attempts on ⇨ de Gaulle's life, the most daring of which was the machine-gunning of his car at Petit Chamart (22.8.1962). With the capture of its leaders (General Jouhaud, 25.3.1962; General Salan, 20.4.1962; Colonel Argoud, Feb. 1963), or their flight (Bidault to Brazil, April 1963) and the integration of the settlers into the mainstream of French life, the OAS ceased to pose a serious threat.

OAU. Organisation of African Unity – was established at Addis Ababa (May 1963). Its aims include the promotion of unity among African states, raising African living standards and the eradication of colonialism in Africa. The chief obstacles to its achievement of the last-mentioned aim are the Portuguese colonies, Rhodesia (especially since ⇨UDI) and the Republic of ⇨ South Africa. Further, despite aid given by the OAU and member states to anti-colonial liberation movements, the Organisation as a whole lacks the economic and military resources as well as the degree of unity necessary to achieve the fulfilment of its aims in the near future. However, in its short history, the OAU has been successful in advancing cooperation among member states and settling inter-African disputes (Algeria ⇨ Morocco border dispute). But, with most African states unwilling to accept the right of regional or ethnic secession from sovereign states, the OAU was unable to find a solution for the ⇨ Nigeria-Biafra Conflict. The attempt to foster African unity predates the establishment of the OAU and goes back to pre-independence struggles and organizations like the Pan-African Congress formed by African exiles in England. Its post-independence history begins with the Accra Conference (1958), attended by Egypt, Ethiopia, Ghana, Liberia, Morocco, Sudan and Tunisia, and with observers from other countries (⇨Lumumba). ⇨Nkrumah emerged as a champion of African unity and as an example to those political leaders whose countries had not yet achieved independence. Differences of opinion between Francophone and 'British' African states and between 'revolutionary' and gradualist interpretations of African unity hampered cooperation (⇨Guinea-Ghana Union, ⇨ OCAM). The radical wing, consisting of Egypt, Ghana, Guinea, Mali, Algeria, Libya and Morocco, met in Casablanca in 1961 to formulate their conditions for African unity. A summit conference held in Monrovia failed to unite the various blocs. A further meeting in

Lagos in 1962 was boycotted by the Casablanca Group. Finally, at a third meeting in Addis Ababa in 1963, held on the initiative of Haile Selassie, the OAU was founded.

Its members are: Algeria, Botswana, Burundi, Cameroun, Central African Republic, Chad, Congo (Brazzaville), Congo (Kinshasa), Dahomey, Ethiopia, Gabon, Gambia, Ghana, Guinea, Ivory Coast, Kenya, Lesotho, Liberia, Libya, Malagasy, Malawi, Mali, Mauritania, Morocco, Niger, Nigeria, Rwanda, Senegal, Sierra Leone, Somalia, Sudan, Swaziland, Tanzania, Togo, Tunisia, Uganda, United Arab Republic, Upper Volta, Zambia. The Heads of State meet annually and its Council of Ministers bi-annually. It has three Specialized Commissions - the Economic and Social Commission, the Educational, Cultural, Scientific and Health Commission, and the Defence Commission. It also sponsors the Scientific, Technical and Research Commission (STRC).

Obote, Dr Milton (1924–). President of ⇨ Uganda (1966–71). Prominent in negotiations leading to Ugandan independence he later ousted the *Kabaka* and, declaring the need for revolution, promised governmental reform to alter the political structure of his country. Deposed by army coup headed by Gen. ⇨Amin while out of the country attending Commonwealth conference.

OCAM. *Organisation Commune Africaine et Malgache* – political and economic association of African states (former French and Belgian colonies) within the ⇨ OAU. At a 1959 conference called by M. ⇨ Houphouët-Boigny a number of states (⇨ Brazzaville Group) met to discuss attitudes to the ⇨ FLN (refusing unconditional support) and later formed the UAM (1961) which, beset by tribal jealousies and disagreements with the OAU, dissolved itself (March 1964) but was reconstituted (Feb. 1965) as OCAM.

Its members are: Cameroun, Central African Republic, Chad, Congo (Brazzaville), Congo (Kinshasa), Dahomey, Gabon, Ivory Coast, Malagasy Republic, Niger, Rwanda, Senegal, Togo, Upper Volta, and Mauritania who withdrew (July 1965).

Ochab, E. (1906–). Former Head of State of ⇨ Poland (1964–68). A communist since 1929, Ochab spent many years in prison in the interwar period. Released on the outbreak of World War II, he escaped to the USSR where he helped in the organization of the Soviet-sponsored Union of Polish Patriots. On his return to Poland he held various government posts until he was promoted to the Party Secretariat (1950) and devoted himself to full-time party work as one of ⇨Bierut's main lieutenants. A full member of the Politbureau (1954) he became First Party Secretary after Bierut's death (March 1956). His assumption of office coincided with Poland's mounting crisis, as a result of which Ochab resigned (Oct. 1956) in favour of ⇨ Gomulka, but remained an influential member of the top party leadership. Soon after relinquishing the post of Poland's Head of State (April 1968), he also ceased to be a member of the Party's Politbureau and Central Committee.

Oder–Neisse Line. A demarcation line along the rivers Oder (Odra) and the western Neisse, which became Poland's new frontier with Germany after World War II. At the ⇨ Yalta Conference, Roosevelt and Churchill agreed in principle to Stalin's proposal that Poland should be compensated for its territorial losses to the USSR by the addition of formerly German territories in the west. At the ⇨ Potsdam Conference the Oder-Neisse Line was recognized *de facto* as Poland's new western frontier. *De jure* recognition was held over for a future peace treaty. East Germany (German Democratic Republic), like other communist states, has meanwhile given *de jure* recognition to the new frontier.

OECD. Organization of Economic Cooperation and Development (headquarters Paris) – replaced ⇨ OEEC (Dec. 1960) when the USA and Canada joined the 18 West European members of that organization, followed by Japan (April 1964). The new organization's objectives are to achieve economic growth and financial stability, to contribute to the expansion of world trade and to provide development aid to the emergent countries. Its internal structure was taken over from its predecessor with minor alterations. Work is mainly carried out through specialized agencies, sometimes independently constituted, of which the best known is DAC, the Development Assistance Committee whose members dispense about 90% of the aid to developing countries. A Technical Cooperation Committee attends mainly to assistance programmes to economically less-advanced member countries like Greece, Iceland, Portugal and Turkey. While other Committees tackle tariff, exchange and investment problems, OECD, representing the world's most highly industrialized nations, is increasingly preoccupied with providing, harmonizing and dispensing development aid.

OEEC. Organization for European Economic Cooperation – was set up to maximize the productive use of ⇨ Marshall Aid, promised (5.6.1947) on condition that the recipient countries would collectively tackle the economic problems of a war-shattered Europe. After a preparatory Committee for Economic Cooperation had reported on the state of the European economy and suggested the economic measures and the institutional structures needed for its improvement, OEEC was formally established (16.4.1948). It included all the countries of Western Europe with the exception of Finland; and succeeded in rebuilding Europe's industry and agriculture, in liberalizing trade, stimulating production and initiating an unprecedented 'economic miracle' which continued long after the end of Marshall Aid (1952). In the 13 years of OEEC's existence, production in member countries more than doubled. Its aims and organization provided both a sound economic base and an institutional framework from which ⇨EEC and ⇨EFTA developed. Ironically, the widening gulf between EEC and EFTA approaches to European integration threatened to wreck OEEC, which on American initiative assumed broader, global responsibilities, and was reconstituted in its Paris headquarters as ⇨OECD (Dec. 1960).

Oginga Odinga (1912–). Vice-President of ⇨Kenya who resigned in April 1966. Though an early supporter of ⇨Kenyatta, he accused the government of supporting capitalism and neglecting African interests. Through his Kenya People's Union he has advocated 'leftist' policies and attempted to organize the opposition to Kenyatta.

OGPU. Russian abbreviation for United State Political Directorate. (⇨USSR State Security Service.)

Ojukwu, Lt.-Col. Chukwuemeka Odumegwa (1933–). Military governor of the Eastern Region of ⇨Nigeria (1966). Fled to ⇨Ivory Coast (Jan. 1970) when Biafran resistance collapsed.

OLAS. Abbreviation for Latin American Solidarity Organisation, a movement inspired by ⇨Castro and aiming at the revolutionary transformation of all Latin America on the model of ⇨Cuba.

Oman. ⇨Muscat and Oman.

O'Neill, Captain Terence (1914–). Prime Minister of ⇨Northern Ireland and Leader of the Unionist Party (1963–69). Regarded as a moderate on the question of civil rights for the Catholic minority population, his leadership was challenged by more extreme (Protestant) elements in his party and outside by supporters of Ian ⇨Paisley. He called an election in Feb. 1969 but failed to receive the popular mandate he had hoped for and after pressure from within his party resigned two months later.

Ongania, General Juan Carlos (1914–). President of ⇨Argentina (1966–70) following a military coup. He assumed legislative authority, dissolved Congress, revised the constitution and banned political parties. Deposed by an army coup, June 1970.

Open Primary. Form of ⇨Primary Election in the USA.

Organisation Commune Africaine et Malgache. ⇨OCAM.

Organisation de l'Armée Secrète. ⇨OAS.

Organisation of African Unity. ⇨OAU.

Orgbureau. ⇨USSR.

Ostpolitik. The ⇨German Federal Republic's attempt to improve relations with the Communist East. Inaugurated by the ⊳ Brandt Government and culminating in treaties with Poland and Russia (May 1972), it gives *de facto* recognition to the ⊳ Oder–Neisse frontier and the ⊳ GDR. A new departure in East–West relations, it is expected to facilitate a détente between the ⊳ NATO and ⊳ Warsaw Pact powers.

Oubangui-Chari. ⊳ Central African Republic.

P

PAC. Pan-African Congress (⇨ South Africa) – formed in 1959 when young African militants seceded from the ⇨ ANC to undertake more positive action against the Pass Laws and other discriminatory measures against Africans. It was banned in 1960 since when its leader, Robert Sobukwe, has been in continuous imprisonment.

Pacelli, Cardinal. Pope ⇨ Pius XII.

Pahlavi, Mohammed Reza Shah (1919–). As Shah of ⇨ Iran (1941–) he has initiated social and agrarian reforms, e.g. six-point programme of 1962 which pressed for the abolition of feudal estates and advocated an improved education and welfare system. The Shah refused coronation on his accession in 1941 because he wished to improve the economic and social condition of his people before formally taking the crown, which he finally did in 1967. In 1953 an unsuccessful attempt was made by ⇨ Mussadiq to reduce his powers.

Paisley, Rev. Ian (1927–). Leader of the extreme Protestants in ⇨ Northern Ireland. As a street orator, he was a prominent opponent of civil rights for the Catholic minority population in the crisis of autumn 1968. In the elections of Feb. 1969 some of his followers stood as separate candidates against the Unionist Party (Protestant Unionists). Paisley himself stood in ⇨ O'Neill's constituency and won a large vote.

Pakistan. *Area* – 310,000 sq. miles. *Population* – 60 m. *President* – Zulfikar Ali ⇨ Bhutto (Dec. 1971). *Constitution* – suspended in 1971 until a new one had been drawn up. Executive power is vested in the President, who is indirectly elected for five years by the Basic Democracies consisting of electors who are in turn elected by universal suffrage. Legislative power is vested in the National Assembly, elected by the same method for five years. Until the formation of Bangladesh in 1972, East and West Pakistan each had a Governor representing the President, a provincial Government and a provincial Assembly.

Pakistan was formerly part of British India until the sub-continent was partitioned on 15 Aug. 1947, the day on which both ⇨ India and Pakistan achieved independence. The country owed its separate existence largely to the agitation of the ⇨ Moslem League (founded in 1906) and its President Mohammed Ali ⇨ Jinnah. Fearful of Hindu dominance in an independent Indian state, the League began to press for a separate Moslem state especially after the Congress Party confirmed its control over the nationalist movement in its election successes of 1937. In 1940 Jinnah publicly demanded the establishment of a Moslem state in those north-east and north-west areas of India where the Moslems were in the majority (the name 'Pakistan' is coined from the initial letters of the north-west areas of *P*unjab, *A*fghan Frontier, *K*ashmir, *S*ind and Baluchis*tan*). During World War II Jinnah supported the UK while Congress was divided on the matter, and support for the League increased among Moslems. This was confirmed when it won almost the whole Moslem vote in the 1946 elections. The British Government accepted partition as did ⇨ Nehru for the Congress Party. The transfer of power was marked by communal bloodshed and the loss of a million lives. Jinnah became the first Governor-General but his early death in 1948 deprived the country of a strong figure at a time when political stability was further threatened by the outbreak of war with India over ⇨ Kashmir. This issue has continued to poison relations between the two countries, and while it has served as a focus for Pakistani nationalist feelings, the Kashmir problem has had an unsettling effect on internal politics (about 11% of Pakistan's total population is Hindu). For a decade Pakistan attempted to follow a constitutional path in difficult times. There were frequent government crises, Prime Minister Ali Khan was assassinated (1951), corruption was rife and little progress was made in the drafting of a constitution. In 1954 the seven-year old Constituent Assembly was dissolved on the grounds that it was no longer representative. Economic conditions were precarious with famine an ever-present threat. Pakistan profited temporarily from the Korean War with a sudden demand for her raw materials, but she is a predominantly agricultural country (90% of the population depend directly on agriculture) and while there was an annual growth rate in agriculture of 1.3% the rise in the population was 2.5% per year. Pakistan has benefited from massive economic aid especially from the USA, but the major internal problem was really structural, namely the separation of East and West Pakistan. Although the two populations have a common religion, they speak different languages (the West Urdu and the East Bengali) and their cultures are unalike in many other ways, e.g. the Western section has closer affinities with the Middle East. The East is far more densely populated, has a larger Hindu minority population and is undeveloped. Resentment against administration from the West (the capital was first in Karachi, later in Rawalpindi) led to charges that the

Government favoured the West in economic development and that the East did not enjoy fair political representation (in spite of the difference in population, the two provinces have an equal number of seats in the national Legislature). The East also resented the privileges enjoyed by Punjabis in the civil and armed services. In 1954 the East Bengalis elected an opposition party to the Moslem League but a few months later the chief minister was dismissed and troops sent to restore order. A constitution at last came into force in 1956 and Pakistan became a Republic with Iskander Mirza as President (1956–58). Parliamentary government had broken down and in Oct. 1958 General Mohammed Ayub ⇨Khan became President after the military had assumed control. In an attempt to put an end to the instability that had plagued the country since Jinnah's death, Ayub Khan introduced a form of guided democracy in 1959 called Basic Democracies – the political structure from local government upwards was pyramidal with the President exercising control at the pinnacle. Ayub Khan kept the army in the background and in 1962 a new constitution ended martial law and re-introduced legislative assemblies. Parties resumed their existence but the Moslem League was the dominating party – in 1965 it won 126 of the 155 seats in the National Assembly. In the same year Ayub Khan was re-elected by a two-thirds majority against the opposition of Miss Jinnah, sister of the founder of the state. The Government passed land reforms, adopted five-year economic plans and met grievances of the Bengalis, but its reputation for efficiency and relative tolerance suffered with accusations that Ayub Khan's political stability was really political suffocation, which received much credence with growing disaffection in the Eastern province. The opposition was encouraged by the President's failure to benefit from the 1965 war with India over the Rann of Kutch and by the public disapproval of the peace declarations at Tashkent (1966). Kashmir had continued to be the central issue in foreign affairs and the quarrel with India was a major reason for Pakistan's seeking close relations with Peking. This policy received encouragement from Z. A. ⇨Bhutto, Foreign Minister 1963–66, who signed commercial and cultural agreements with the People's Republic and also a provisional border treaty (1963). Bhutto, a hard liner on India and Kashmir, left office some months after Tashkent and late in 1967 formed the People's Party to combat Ayub Khan. The latter responded to the revival of opposition with oppression (Bhutto was imprisoned), but in the autumn of 1968 the situation escalated with increased student riots and demonstrations in the Eastern province. After promising not to stand again for the presidency, Ayub Khan was forced to resign in March 1969 and was replaced by General Yahya Khan, who took office as President and proclaimed martial law. The differences between East and West Pakistan finally came to a head after the Dec. 1970 General Election in which the East Pakistan Secessionist Awami League led by Sheikh Mujibar Rahman won an absolute majority. Deadlock between Sheikh Mujibar and Z. A. Bhutto, the leading Western Pakistan politician gave way in March 1971 to East Pakistan's declaration of independence and the outbreak of civil war. The new Republic of Bangladesh (literally free Bengal) was quickly and bloodily defeated and millions of Bengalis streamed over the border to India. Tension between Pakistan and India built up until in Dec. 1971 war between the two countries broke out. Within a fortnight Pakistan's army was defeated, half its navy was sunk and it had irrevocably lost the Eastern state now recognized as an independent republic ⇨ Bangladesh. President Yahya Khan resigned in favour of Mr Bhutto and sweeping reforms were initiated. A formal peace treaty was signed between President Bhutto and India's Mrs Gandhi at Simla in July 1972.

Palestine. Until the end of the First World War, part of the Ottoman Empire. Following the ⇨ Balfour Declaration (1917), Palestine was administered by Britain under a ⇨ League of Nations Mandate (1922–48). The period of the Mandate was marked by increasing conflict between Arab and Jew, and especially in its last years by bitter hostility between Zionists and the British administration (⇨ Israel). After the UK (announcing its intention to terminate the Mandate) referred the matter to the UN, the ⇨ Arab League states rejected the UN partition proposals and invaded Israel (which had proclaimed its independence (May 1948)). In the subsequent war (1948–49), Israel increased the area of Palestine allotted to it by the UN (Nov. 1947). Jordan (then Trans-Jordan) annexed areas on the West Bank of the river, and Egypt occupied the Gaza Strip. (⇨ Arab–Israeli Conflict.)

Palestine Liberation Organization. One of the Arab groups engaged in guerrilla warfare against Israel. Established during the early fifties, it operated mainly from the Egyptian-occupied Gaza Strip and maintained offices in all major Arab centres. Led by Ahmed Shukairy, the PLO gained notoriety by threatening to exterminate the Israeli population after an Arab victory. Early in 1968, Shukairy was replaced by the more moderate Yahia Hammuda. Although the PLO claims to have 7,000 of its members under arms with the Egyptian forces, its guerrilla activities after the Six Day War were overshadowed by *Al* ⇨ *Fatah.*

Pan-African Congress. ⇨ PAC.

Panama. *Area* – 29,200 sq. miles including the ⇨ Panama Canal Zone. *Population* (1970) – 1,428,082. *Constitution* (1946) – Executive

President and uni-cameral Legislature elected by universal suffrage – suspended Oct. 1968.

Panama – an independent Republic since 1903 when it granted the USA the right to build and operate a canal with perpetual sovereignty over the Canal Zone – has been decisively affected by its strategic importance to the USA. Panama has no army (except a National Guard) as under the treaty the USA accepts responsibility for Panamanian defence. These developments made Panama attractive to American business investment and for many years made the government less subject (than other Central American governments) to military coups, but they have also stimulated anti-American sentiment (⇨ Panama Canal Zone). Panamanian politics have been dominated by a few wealthy families of Spanish origin; the mass of the population of mixed Spanish–Indian–Negro descent living at subsistence level. In 1941 President Arnulfo Arias was overthrown. Again President (1949) he was again deposed (1951). The succeeding President, José Remon, was assassinated (1955). His successor, President Ernesto de la Guardia, put down a revolt led by Roberto Arias (1959). After Robert Chiari (1960–64), Marco Robles (1964–68) was elected President. Arnulfo Arias claimed the election was fraudulent. In 1968 President Robles was impeached (on charges relating to the forthcoming election), but the charge was rejected by the Supreme Court. Arias was elected President (May 1968), but was overthrown by a military coup a few days after taking office (Oct. 1968). In 1969 the army members of the government were replaced by civilians.

Panama Canal Zone (*area* – 647 sq. miles). US administered territory extending five miles on either side of the Canal. Following serious rioting and loss of life (1964) US President Johnson and President Robles agreed to put forward a new treaty (1965) for the Canal Zone, recognizing Panamanian sovereignty in the Zone, and discussions were started in 1966.

Pan-American Union. Forerunner of the ⇨ OAS, established 1890. It continued to function as the secretariat of the OAS after the latter was established in 1948. It prepares regular and special Inter-American Conferences. Its offices are in Washington, DC.

Papacy. ⇨ Vatican City State and Popes ⇨ Pius XII, ⇨ John XXIII and ⇨ Paul VI.

Papadopoulos, George (1918–). Prime Minister and Minister of Defence of ⇨ Greece since Dec. 1967. Colonel Papadopoulos became a member of the Cabinet formed after the military coup in April 1967 as Minister to the Prime Minister's Office but emerged as the strong man in the military government after his assumption of the overall direction of government policy in the autumn of 1967.

Papandreou, Andreas (1919-). Greek politician and son of the former Prime Minister of ⇨ Greece, George ⇨ Papandreou. He held Cabinet posts under his father, including that of Minister to the Prime Minister (1964-65) and Minister of Economic Co-ordination (1965).

Papandreou, George (1888-1968). Prime Minister of ⇨ Greece (1944, 1963, 1964-65) – a talented and popular orator whose last premiership came to grief over a conflict with the King which led to his resignation and eventually to the military coup in 1967. Papandreou had been a minister in various governments from 1923 and leader of the Socialist Democratic Party from 1935. An opponent of the Axis occupation, he was arrested in 1942 but after his flight to Cairo became head of an exiled government, which returned to Greece in 1944. Between 1946 and 1952 he was a member of several Cabinets. In 1961 he succeeded in uniting the moderate left-wing groups in the new Centre Union Party, which formed the basis for his return to power.

Paraguay. *Area* – 157,042 sq. miles. *Population* (est. 1967) – 2,500,000 (of predominantly Indian stock). *President* – General Alfredo ⇨ Stroessner (1954-). *Constitution* – Unitary Republic with executive power vested in the President. The new constitution (superseding 1940 constitution) came into force in Aug. 1967, and provides for a bi-cameral Legislature, and stipulates that a two-thirds majority of both houses can overrule executive decisions.

Paraguay's geographical position, land-locked in the centre of a vast continent, has conditioned her history. The necessity of maintaining good relations with her neighbours (or at least, of not antagonising more than one at a time) was emphasized by a catastrophic war (1865-70) against Argentina, Brazil and Uruguay. Her population was decimated and her slender resources exhausted. Disaster again threatened in the ⇨ Chaco War (1932-35) against ⇨ Bolivia. Though Paraguay was victorious, the war dislocated its economy and disrupted its politics – it ended the long Liberal Party ascendancy and resulted in (still continuing) Colorado (Conservative) Party and military dominance. From the war's end till the virtual dictatorship of General Higinio Morinigo (1940-47) there were frequent changes of government. Economic reconstruction under Morinigo benefited from the provision of a military base for the United States, made anxious by Argentina's pro-Axis attitudes. From 1948 to 1954, the country was rent by political feuds, but its politics have since been dominated by one man – General Alfredo Stroessner. The only presidential candidate in 1954 he was re-elected in 1963 and 1968. A believer in strong government, he has encouraged economic development, but at the cost of civil liberties. As under

Morinigo, many Paraguayans, especially liberals and intellectuals, live in enforced or chosen exile.

Paris Peace Talks. Talks between the belligerents in the Vietnam War convened in Paris (13.5.1968) with a view to finding a political solution to the War. The talks continued, though without results, until Mar. 1972, when they were broken off by the USA following a fresh invasion of the South by North Vietnamese troops, and shortly before the resumption of US bombing of the North. Both sides maintained objections to returning to the conference table for some months, but eventually did so in July 1972. In Jan. 1973 a cease-fire agreement was announced.

Paris Treaty (18.4.1951). Established the ⇨ECSC (European Coal and Steel Community) between Belgium, France, the German Federal Republic, Italy, Luxembourg and the Netherlands. After its ratification by the various national governments (25.7.1952), the community's High Authority became operative in Aug. 1952.

Park Chung Hee, General. ⇨Korea.

Parliament Act, 1949. A sequel to the UK Parliament Act of 1911, it reduced from three sessions to two the time by which the British House of Lords could delay legislation already passed by the House of Commons.

Parti Républicain Radical et Radical Socialiste. Neither radical nor socialist, this famous left of centre and fervently republican party over which Clemenceau presided in its early years, was under Herriot and ⇨Daladier a major force in the ⇨France of the thirties. It emerged greatly weakened after the war, but quickly regaining influence, gave seven Prime Ministers to the Fourth Republic, of whom ⇨Mendès-France was the most prominent. Torn by internal dissensions, the party split several times; in 1956 the right wing under Queuille established an independent splinter group, and in 1959 ⇨Mendès-France and his followers veered off to the left. The Radicals – as they are commonly known – had 25 seats (7·8% of the poll) in the 1962 Assembly where the process of fragmentation continued with a group under Fauré attaching itself to the ⇨MRP, while another allied itself with the Socialists.

Patrascanu, L. (1900–54). A Rumanian communist party member from 1921 and a lawyer by profession. In the inter-war years Patrascanu specialized in the defence of left-wingers indicted for political offences. A leader of the communist Resistance in ⇨Rumania during the war, he became Minister of Justice in the coalition government set up in 1944. Regarded by ⇨Gheorghiu-Dej as a serious rival in view of his relative popularity as a ⇨Home Communist with comparatively liberal views, Patrascanu became the victim of a temporary alliance between Gheorghiu-Dej and the ⇨Muscovite faction of Ana ⇨Pauker and

⇨ Luca. He was arrested in 1948 on charges of 'nationalist' deviations and, after six years in prison, he was summarily tried and executed (May 1954). In April 1968, he was formally rehabilitated as an innocent victim of political repression.

Pauker, Ana (1893–1960). A member of the Rumanian Communist Party since 1921. In the inter-war years Ana Pauker divided her time between underground work in ⇨ Rumania and repeated stays in Moscow (where her husband, Marcel Pauker, was executed in 1938 as an alleged Trotskyite). She herself was arrested in Rumania in 1935 and given a ten-year sentence, but was released in 1940 under an exchange-of-prisoners scheme with the USSR where she then went to live. A protégé of Stalin, she returned to Rumania with the Red Army in 1944 to take charge of her country's ⇨ Sovietization. A member (with ⇨ Luca and ⇨ Gheorghiu-Dej) of Rumania's ruling triumvirate as well as Foreign Minister during the early post-war years, she was ousted by Gheorghiu-Dej (1952) for various 'deviations' and stripped of all her party and government posts at a time when the Slansky trial in Czecho-slovakia and the 'Doctors' Plot' in the USSR set the pace for purges of communists of Jewish origin like herself. Nothing further was heard of her until June 1960 when her death was unofficially reported.

Paul VI, Pope (1897–). Pope since 1963, Paul VI (formerly Cardinal Montini) has continued the policy of his predecessor, ⇨ John XXIII, of encouraging the ecumenical movement, e.g. the establishment of a joint Roman Catholic-Anglican Preparatory Theological Commission (1966) and a joint declaration of Christian unity with the Greek Orthodox Church (1967). He has attempted to mediate in international conflicts, e.g. he has appealed for peace in Vietnam and has made cautious approaches to communist countries including an audience with President ⇨ Podgorny of the Soviet Union (1967). He issued an encyclical (1967) on combating world poverty, a theme he further elaborated during his visit to Latin America (1968). However, Pope Paul's stress on traditional doctrine in his encyclical on birth control (*Humanae Vitae*, 1968), has crystallized the divisions between progressives and conservatives in the Church. Montini was in the Vatican Secretariat of State from 1924, became Pro-Secretary of State (1952), Archbishop of Milan (1954), and was made Cardinal in 1958.

Paz Estenssoro, Victor (1907–). President of ⇨ Bolivia (1952–56 and 1960–64), founder of the MNR and key figure and Treasury Minister in the Villarroel government (1943–46). Like ⇨ Peron, whom he admired, his appeal depended on a mixture of socialist reform and authoritarian-ism. Under fire from the left and forced to accept ⇨ Barrientos as his Vice-President to placate the right, Paz was deposed in 1964. But his

MNR-led revolution (1952) had radically altered Bolivia's economic and political power structure.

Peace Ballot (UK) 1935. Referendum in which a large majority (over 10 million out of 11½ million) voted for disarmament, collective security and continued membership of the League of Nations. This put popular pressure on the British Government to support League of Nations sanctions against Italy after the invasion of ⇨ Ethiopia.

Peace Corps. A Federal organization in the USA, established by President ⇨ Kennedy in 1961, and subsequently approved by Congress, which sends volunteers from the United States to developing countries, where their training and skills can temporarily make good local deficiencies. Peace Corps Volunteers (PCVs) live and work among the people they are serving for two years. In 1964, the Director of the Peace Corps, Sargent Shriver, organized ⇨ VISTA to operate a similar programme within the United States.

Peaceful Co-Existence. A communist slogan referring to the long-term co-existence of capitalist and socialist states without war between them, the interpretation of which has been the subject of repeated disputes between various communist parties, notably those of China and the USSR. (⇨ Khrushchev, ⇨ Bandung Conference).

Pearl Harbor. US naval base in Hawaii which was attacked by Japanese air and naval forces on 7 Dec. 1941 when many vessels of the American fleet at the base were destroyed. The attack was made without declaration of war, or any threat or warning of hostilities, and at a time when peace messages were being exchanged. On the following day a Joint ⇨ Resolution of Congress was adopted declaring that a state of war existed by act of Japan, and similar resolutions were passed on 11 Dec. with reference to Germany and Italy which had meanwhile declared war on the United States. Thus the United States entered World War II. Pearl Harbor has since become a byword for a devastating surprise attack on the one hand, and a disastrous state of military unpreparedness on the other.

Pearson, Lester (1897–1972). Prime Minister of ⇨ Canada (1963–68) and leader of the Liberal Party (1958–63). His premiership was marked by support for UN peace-keeping abroad and the growing problems of nationality at home -- in 1967 a Royal Commission on Nationalities was appointed. A Secretary of State for External Affairs (1948–57), after 20 years as a diplomat, he received the Nobel Peace Prize (1957) for his work for the United Nations. President of the UN General Assembly (1952–53).

Pentagon. A five-sided public building near Washington DC that houses the ⇨ Defense Department and gives its name to the military establishment of the USA.

People's Commissar. Term for (government) Minister, used in the USSR until 1946.

People's Communes. ⇨ China.

People's Democracy. ⇨ Democracy.

Perez Jimenez, Colonel Marcos (1914–). Leader of army *coup d'état* and President of ⇨ Venezuela (1952–58). His financially corrupt and autocratic rule came to an end in a popular uprising and he was forced to flee to the USA. Extradited and imprisoned (1963); brought to trial and sentenced (to over four years' imprisonment) in 1968 but immediately released in view of term already spent in prison, and exiled to Madrid.

Permanent Revolution. A concept derived from the ideas developed by ⇨ Trotsky in 1906 stipulating the interdependence both of Russia's own bourgeois and proletarian revolution and of the Russian and the European revolution. In Russia, according to Trotsky, only the proletarian minority could bring about a successful revolution. This revolution, Trotsky argued, could and would pass in an uninterrupted process from its bourgeois-democratic to its proletarian stage with the initially willing support of the peasantry. But in order to maintain and consolidate its power and to overcome the anticipated peasant resistance to its policies of collectivism and internationalism, the Russian proletarian minority would have to rely on the support of victorious proletarian revolutions in Europe to be set in motion by its own example. These concepts, which envisaged both Russia's own and the European revolutions as a single continuous process, anticipated the strategy which Lenin adopted at a much later stage for the ⇨ Bolshevik seizure of power in 1917 and the subsequent foundation of the ⇨ Communist International. They were irreconcilable, on the other hand, with the still later attempt to build 'socialism in one country', and they subsequently served ⇨ Stalin as ammunition in his struggle for Trotsky's liquidation.

Perón, Juan Domingo (1895–). President of ⇨ Argentina (1946–55), who although a soldier, broke with *Caudillo* tradition when he achieved power by organizing the urban proletariat. He won their support by raising living standards (wages, holidays with pay, urban reconstruction) and introducing welfare legislation. Péron's doctrine of *Justicialismo*, an Argentinian adaptation of Fascist and socialist theory, claimed to reconcile conflicting social forces. It appealed for national greatness and social justice without challenging the basic social structure. Hence Péron's support from an unlikely coalition of Labour, Church, conservative Fascist and army interests. He was aided by the persuasive Eva Duarte (d. 1952) whom he married after his success was assured by her organization of the *descamisados* (shirtless ones) in the crisis of Oct. 1945. In a one-party state the regime became increasingly totalitarian, Péron and Eva (even after her death) were idolized, opposition suppressed and the press muzzled (*La Prensa* seized 1951). Economic crises, popular resentment and Church antagonism weakened the Péronist coalition. Resentful of Church interference in labour matters, Péron threatened legislation (1954) to disestablish the Church, legalize prostitution and divorce. In Sept. 1955, Péron was forced to flee. He returned in 1972 but left again soon after.

Persia. ⇨ Iran.

Persian Gulf States. ⇨ Bahrein, ⇨ Qatar and the ⇨ Trucial States.

Personality Cult. Term used in the USSR and other communist countries both as a (disapproving) description of the adulation accorded to ⇨ Stalin (and other individual communist leaders) and as a euphemism for the Stalinist tyranny in general and the bloodbath of the great purges in particular.

Peru. *Area* – 496,093 sq. miles. *Population* (1970 est.) – 13,600,000 of whom 40% are Indian. *President* – General Juan Velasco (1968–). *Constitution* – Unitary Republic – Executive President and bi-cameral Legislature suspended (Oct. 1968).

As with so many South American countries, Peru's economy was shattered by the Great Depression. It stimulated popular discontent with President Leguia's long-serving but autocratic administration, which was overthrown by a military *coup* led by Sanchez Cerro (1930). More important, it unleashed new social forces which, though frequently suppressed, have profoundly affected Peru's political development. In 1924 the exiled populist leader Victor Raul ⇨ Haya de la Torre had founded the ⇨ APRA (*Alianza Popular Revolucionaria Americana*). Haya de la Torre failed to beat Cerro in the elections (1931), subsequently attempted to organize an uprising and was again exiled and the APRA outlawed. Cerro, assassinated by an *Aprista*, was succeeded by General Benavides (1933). Benavides quashed the 1936 elections (the winning candidate had APRA support) and continued in power until 1939, when he was succeeded (in a manipulated election) by Manuel Prado, a moderate conservative. Prado's presidency (1939–45) benefited from the war-time economic boom and also from a successful military campaign against Ecuador. A pact between moderate conservatives and *Apristas*, aimed at achieving social reforms, peaceably, secured the electoral victory of Bustamante y Rivero (1945). However, Bustamante's administration was paralysed by the opposition of APRA factions still committed to revolution. An attempted uprising (Callao 1948) was followed by military intervention and the assumption of the presidency by General

Odria (1948–56). APRA was again banned and Haya de la Torre forced to seek asylum in the Colombian Embassy. At first Odria's government benefited from a fantastic economic boom (engendered by the Korean War) but was finally threatened by spiralling inflation and its own economic mismanagement and corruption. As a result of carefully ordered elections, Manuel Prado was recalled for a second term (1956–62). The 1962 elections resulted in a stalemate with none of the candidates achieving the required one-third of the votes cast (Haya de la Torre – 557,000; Fernando ⊳ Belaunde Terry (AP – *Accion Popular*) – 544,000; Odria (*Union Nacional Odriaista*) – 520,000). The deadlock resulted in a surprising *Odriaista-Aprista* pact and provided (together with charges of *Aprista* election frauds) a pretext for military seizure of power. The junta governed for a year (US severed relations with Peru and cut off economic aid) before holding elections. On this occasion, against the same opponents, Belaunde gained the necessary majority. He initiated a programme of reform, much of it directed to benefit the Indians, but he was faced with a hostile *Aprista* and *Odriaista*-dominated Congress. As in other Latin American states, the role played by the army is of decisive importance and in 1968 Belaunde was deposed by a military *coup*. The junta led by General Juan Velasco invoked the 'necessity of ending economic chaos, administrative immorality and the surrender of natural resources of wealth to foreign interests'. The United States, in keeping with provisions of OAS, has severed relations.

Pétain, Henri Philippe (1856–1951). Marshal of France, was hailed as the 'saviour of Verdun' in 1916 and convicted as a traitor in 1945. He held all the top military appointments in the twenties and served in Doumergue's right-wing government as Minister of War (Feb.–Nov. 1934). An outspoken opponent of the ⊳ Popular Front, he was appointed ambassador to Franco's Spain (March 1939). Made Vice-Premier at the moment of supreme crisis (18.5.1940), Pétain succeeded ⊳ Reynaud whose Cabinet refused to continue the war (June 1940). After the armistice, Pétain was granted full power (by 569 to 80 votes) from a National Assembly which thereupon dissolved itself (Clermont-Ferrand, July 1940). Assuming the title 'Chief of State' the Marshal then proclaimed his autocratic *État Français* for which he promised but never presented a constitution. Pétain tried to steer a more independent course than his Premier, ⊳ Laval, whom he subsequently dismissed (Dec. 1940). Although avoiding a French commitment to side with Germany at his Montoire meeting with ⊳ Hitler (24.10.1940), his regime, imitating the Nazis, enacted anti-semitic legislation (July 1941). After reinstating Laval on German insistence (April 1942), it collaborated in the 'transfer' of nearly 750,000 workers to Germany. With the

German occupation of ⇨ Vichy France, Pétain's government (now obviously only a puppet government) was removed to Sigmaringen after D-Day. Having escaped to Switzerland towards the end of the war, Pétain voluntarily returned to France to face treason charges. Found guilty by a Paris court (Aug. 1945), his death sentence was commuted by de Gaulle to life imprisonment on the Ile d'Yeu. Released a month before his death, he died at the age of ninety-five.

Peter, King. ⇨ Yugoslavia.

Petkov, N. ⇨ Bulgaria.

Petöfi Club. A group of libertarian Hungarian intellectuals whose demonstrations in June 1956 against ⇨ Rakosi precipitated his downfall. The club took its name from the revolutionary poet Petöfi who became a national hero during the 1848/9 Hungarian rising against the Austrian Empire.

Pflimlin, Pierre (1907–). Last Prime Minister of the ⇨ Fourth Republic (14–31.5.1958). Having failed to assert the authority of his government and unable to suppress the military insurrection in Algiers (13.5.1958) rather than risk civil war, he allowed General ⇨ de Gaulle to assume power and legally to dismantle the Fourth Republic. He served in the General's first Cabinet (June 1958–Jan. 1959) and fleetingly under ⇨ Pompidou's premiership (April–May 1962). President of the ⇨ MRP (*Mouvement Républicain Populaire*), he has been mayor of Strasbourg since 1959.

Philippines. *Area* – 115,600 sq. miles. *Population* (1972) – 39,102,000. *President* – Ferdinand ⇨ Marcos. *Constitution* – Republic since 1946 (similar to the US) – with executive power vested in the President, who is elected by direct vote for four years but may not serve more than eight consecutive years. There is a bi-cameral Legislature – Congress, composed of the Senate and House of Representatives. Both houses are elected by universal (literate) adult suffrage.

The Philippines archipelago consists of some 7,100 islands and islets, of which the two largest and most important are Luzon (40,800 sq. miles) and Mindanao (36,900 sq. miles). A Spanish colony for three centuries, then ruled by the USA from 1898, the Philippines became a Commonwealth in 1935 with an elected President (Manuel Quezon), a considerable measure of local autonomy and the promise of independence. Important strategically, the islands were occupied during World War II by the Japanese (1942–45). When liberated by the Americans in 1945 the re-established Commonwealth became an independent Republic (1946). Since then the Philippines have been ruled by two parties, which are not typically Asian in that they do not reflect communal differences and do not show any radical distinction in policy. They were both formed when the *Partido Nacionalista* Party split in 1946 into the Liberal Party (the centre-liberal wing), which ruled from 1946 to 1953 (under Manuel Roxas, 1946–48 and Elpidio Quirino, 1948–53) and from 1961 to 1965 (under Diosdado Macapagal); and the *Nacionalista* Party (the right-wing of the old *Partido Nacionalista*) which ruled from 1953 to 1961 (under Ramon Magsaysay, 1953–57, and Carlos Garcia, 1957–61) and has been in office again since 1965 under Ferdinand Marcos. The war left a legacy of economic dislocation, which encouraged unrest and violence leading to the guerrilla activity of the *Huks* who had originated as a movement of partisans during the Japanese occupation and now demanded land reform. Based in Luzon and led by Luis Taruc, the *Huks* became identified with the Communist Party (later banned) and continued to harass the Government until the mid 1950s, when President Magsaysay introduced a programme of social and economic reform. After independence relations with the USA remained close. America granted the Philippines financial aid and eight years of free trade with the USA which was followed by graduated tariff increases. In 1951 a mutual defence treaty was signed. Friction arose over the military and naval bases which the USA retained after independence, but Filipino sovereignty over these was recognized in 1956 and in 1959 the 99-year lease was shortened to 25. The Philippines is still very dependent economically on the USA, particularly for the high price which the latter pays for the entire sugar crop. In foreign policy generally the country has taken a firm anti-communist line – she joined ⇨SEATO in 1954 and has sent troops to support the Americans in the Vietnam War. She has also joined the non-communist regional associations of ASA (1961), ASPAC (1966) and ASEAN (1967). Relations with her neighbours have been marred by her continued claim to Sabah, which became part of the Federation of ⇨Malaysia in 1963, although after a survey the UN was satisfied that the people of Sabah wanted to join. The Philippines has persisted in her claim and in 1968 passed a law making Sabah part of her territory. In a two-party system, with no problem of racial or religious minorities (83% of the population are Roman Catholics) the chief threat to political stability lies in the extremes of wealth and poverty. Since 1965 there has been a revival of *Huk* activity.

Pibul Songgram (1892–*c.* 1958). Prime Minister of ⇨Thailand (1938–44, 1947–57). A leader of the 1932 revolt which abolished the absolute monarchy, Pibul came to power with the support of the army. He followed a pro-Japanese policy leading to an alliance with Japan in World War II. He returned to power after leading a successful military coup. During his years as military dictator, he followed a pro-Western foreign policy, receiving substantial aid from the USA and joining ⇨SEATO.

Pius XII (1876–1958). Pope from 1939 to 1958. As Cardinal Pacelli, he negotiated the ⇨ Concordat of July 1933 with Nazi Germany. During World War II, concerned with the position of Catholics in the belligerent countries, he sponsored relief programmes for civilians and for prisoners-of-war. His papacy has since been criticized for the Church's failure to speak out more loudly against Nazi persecution, especially the extermination of the Jews. After the war Pius XII criticized the political persecution of Catholics in communist states and in 1953 excommunicated Hungary, Rumania and Poland. In his 1947 encyclical ('*Optatissima pax*') he advocated social reforms. During the Palestine crisis (1946) he called for the international guardianship of the Holy Places. Pacelli was formerly Papal Nuncio in Germany (Munich 1917–19, Berlin 1919–29), was made Cardinal in 1929 and became Papal Secretary of State in 1930.

PLA. People's Liberation Army – collective name for all Chinese armed forces.

Pluralism. The conception of society as made up of many heterogeneous associations with differing legitimate interests. This proliferation of associations, with both political and non-political objectives, is thought to protect society against centralized governmental power, while the interplay of their interests as nearly as possible produces a 'fair distribution' of government-generated costs and benefits. Thus, economic and political power and public goods come to be widely distributed without any single interest dominating. The doctrine has gained currency, especially in America, since the beginning of the present century, although ever since Alexis de Tocqueville first wrote about the active group life of Americans in the first half of the nineteenth century, the United States has served as the prime example of such a society. Pluralism is most strongly supported by liberals and is rejected by both the ⇨ New Left and the ⇨ New Right.

Podgorny, N. V. (1903–). President of the Presidium of the Supreme Soviet USSR (Head of State), member of the CPSU Politbureau. Podgorny made his career in the party and government apparatus of the Ukraine as ⇨ Khrushchev's protégé. After some years in the ⇨ Komsomol, he joined the CPSU in 1930. An engineer by training, he held a number of administrative posts in the Ukraine and Moscow until 1946 when he became a full-time official first in the government and then in the party apparatus of the Ukraine, at that time led by Khrushchev as the Ukrainian CP's First Secretary. Under Khrushchev's patronage, Podgorny made a rapid career first in the Ukrainian and then in the central party leadership. A member of the Central Committee in 1956, two years later he became a candidate member of the Presidium (now the Politbureau) and a full member in 1960. He is believed to have opposed Khrushchev's overthrow in Oct. 1964. In Dec. 1965 he became ⇨ Mikoyan's successor as the mainly honorary Head of State of the USSR.

Point Four Program. From US President ⇨Truman's 1949 Inaugural Address, the fourth point of which suggested that the wealthier nations had a moral and self-interested responsibility to help the poorer countries. At the time, the American programme stressed only technical assistance, and it was not until 1950 that Congress appropriated the additional funds required. Since then, the United States ⇨ Mutual Security Program has grown to include outright financial aid, loans and commodity gifts.

Poland. ⇨Polish People's Republic.

Polaris Submarine. A United States-developed, nuclear-powered, underwater vessel capable of launching Polaris intermediate-range ballistic missiles (IBMs) while submerged. The missile first became operational in 1961 and was the result of simultaneous advances in solid-propellants and compact high yield warheads (1956–57). Because of its relative invulnerability, the Polaris submarine was made a major component in British and American deterrent forces, giving them a credible retaliatory strike capability. (⇨Balance of Terror.) In 1968, advances in military technology claimed by the Soviet Union put its future in doubt.

Polish October. Name given to the ferment in Poland (Oct. 1956) leading to the election of ⇨ Gomulka to the Communist Party leadership. (⇨ Polish People's Republic, ⇨ Revisionism, ⇨ World Communism.)

Polish People's Republic. *Area* – 120,359 sq. miles. *Population* (1970) – 32,589,000. *Chairman of the Council of State* – Henryk Jablonski (1972–). *Chairman, Council of Ministers* – Piotr Jaroszewicz (1970–). *First Secretary, Polish United Workers' Party* – Edward Gierek (1970–).

The highest organ of state power is the *Sejm*, a one-chamber Legislature, elected by universal suffrage from a single list of candidates. Effective power is exercised by the (communist) Polish United Workers' Party under the leadership of its First Secretary.

Between the wars, Poland was governed by a succession of dictatorial right-wing regimes. Polish foreign policy aimed at striking a balance between Germany and the Western Allies. The conclusion of a non-aggression pact with Germany in 1934 was followed by a deterioration in Polish–German relations after Hitler occupied Czechoslovakia. Britain formally guaranteed Poland's security (March 1939). Hitler's invasion of Poland (Sept. 1939) was followed shortly afterwards – as envisaged in the ⇨Hitler–Stalin Pact – by the Soviet occupation of Eastern Poland. After Germany's invasion of the USSR in June 1941, Poland and the

USSR became allies and Stalin recognized the broadly democratic Polish emigré government in London (first led by General ⇨ Sikorski and, after his death in 1943, by the Peasant Party leader, W. ⇨ Mikolajczyk), which directed the anti-German resistance of the underground Home Army in Poland. Resistance in Poland grew with the mounting Nazi atrocities against the Polish population committed simultaneously with the systematic extermination of nearly $3\frac{1}{2}$ million Polish Jews in the ghettoes and death camps. The resistance of the Home Army reached its climax with the Warsaw rising of Aug. 1944 which, after 63 heroic days, finally collapsed, with the Soviet armies just outside the capital refusing to help.

By that time relations between Moscow and the Polish emigré government had already been broken off and the nucleus of a Soviet-sponsored communist counter-government had been created in the form of the 'Lublin Committee'. The Lublin Committee was set up in July 1944 by a merger of two separate communist centres: the Polish Workers' Party (PPR) under the leadership of W. Gomulka, which since Jan. 1942, had organized its own anti-German partisans in occupied Poland, and the Union of Polish Patriots (UPP), set up by the surviving Polish communists in the USSR, who returned to Poland with the Soviet armies and occupied the key positions of power in the Lublin Committee. On 31 Dec. 1944 the Lublin Committee declared itself the provisional government of Poland, and was immediately recognized by the USSR.

At the ⇨ Teheran, ⇨ Yalta and ⇨ Potsdam Conferences, the USA and Britain yielded to Stalin's demands for Poland's new boundaries between the ⇨ Curzon Line in the east and the ⇨ Oder–Neisse Line in the west. They reached an apparent agreement that Poland's political future was to be determined by 'free elections'. In July 1945 the Western powers recognized the provisional government. Nominally a five-party coalition, which Mikolajczyk joined as Vice-Premier, it was from the outset dominated by the (Muscovite) communists who controlled all police and security forces as well as the army. ⇨ Sovietization proceeded in the stereotyped manner, beginning with mass persecutions of the highly popular Peasant Party, the execution or flight of its independent leaders, elections staged in an atmosphere of terror and resulting in fake returns, followed finally by the enforced fusion of the socialists and communists in the new United Workers' Party (Dec. 1948).

The fusion was preceded by a purge of 'nationalists' and 'pro-Titoists' in the Communist Party itself. The chief victim of this purge was Gomulka. First ousted from all his party and government posts, he was jailed (1951) and released only at the time of ⇨ Tito's rehabilitation.

Shortly afterwards ⟳ Khrushchev's anti-Stalin speech at the 20th CPSU Congress (Feb. 1956) produced a burst of free discussion in Poland which, after the Poznan workers' riots in June, led to that upsurge of patriotism and calls for freedom which has since become known as the 'Polish October'. In that situation most Polish communists regarded Gomulka as the only man capable of enlisting sufficient popular support to ensure the survival of communist party rule. In the teeth of threatened Soviet military intervention, but morally supported by the Chinese communists, Gomulka was re-elected as the Party's First Secretary and Poland's new effective leader. Later Gomulka succeeded in gaining Khrushchev's consent for a considerable degree of internal Polish autonomy as a *quid pro quo* for Poland's unconditional support of Moscow's foreign policies.

The new policies initiated by Gomulka after Oct. 1956 included the abolition of secret police terror, the guarantee of private peasant ownership, a *modus vivendi* with the Roman Catholic Church and, initially also, the toleration of comparative freedom in cultural activities. From 1957 onwards and more markedly since 1962, toleration of cultural and intellectual freedom gradually made way for a return to conservative intolerance, accompanied by purges of liberal-minded 'revisionists' and the shelving of economic and other reforms. This retrogression reached its climax after the Six Day War in the Middle East (1967), when many Poles vented their anti-Russian feelings by welcoming the defeat of the Soviet-supported Arab states. Gomulka's counter-move – the 'anti-Zionist' campaign – turned into a violently anti-Jewish campaign and a mass purge of Jews from their Party, governmental and professional posts at all levels after large-scale student demonstrations (March 1968). In August 1968 Poland participated in the invasion of ⟳ Czechoslovakia. Soon afterwards, a further deterioration in the economic situation led to a new upsurge of popular discontent, specially among industrial workers, culminating, in Dec. 1970, in large-scale protest riots in the coastal cities. In the aftermath, Gomulka resigned as party leader. His successor, E. ⟳ Gierek, later removed most of Gomulka's close associates from the party and state leadership, replacing them by mainly young men, most of whom began their political career after World War II.

Politbureau. ⟳ USSR.

Polycentrism. Term first applied by ⟳ Togliatti to the communist world movement after the 20th CPSU congress of Feb. 1956. In an interview with *Nuovi Argomenti* in June 1956, Togliatti concluded from ⟳ Khrushchev's revelations about ⟳ Stalin that the Soviet model should cease to be obligatory for other communist parties; instead of relying on a single guiding centre as in the past, he said, the communist world movement was in fact becoming polycentric. (⟿ World Communism.)

Pompidou, Georges (1911–). President of France (June 1969), French Prime Minister (1962–68). A schoolmaster by profession, he came into politics as a friend of de Gaulle whose secretariat he joined after the liberation. During the General's retirement (1946–58) he became a director of the Rothschild bank in Paris, and upon de Gaulle's return to power (May 1958) was appointed head of the Cabinet Office, a post he relinquished when de Gaulle became President (Jan. 1959). He returned to the bank but was made Prime Minister when de Gaulle accepted the resignation of M. ⟿ Debré. Pompidou's skilful handling of the May 1968 crisis is believed to have saved the Gaullist regime and to have won the Gaullists the biggest election victory in their history. Not reappointed by de Gaulle, Pompidou announced his intention to contest the presidency long before the General launched his unsuccessful referendum on constitutional reforms which led to his resignation. Pompidou, gaining 56% of the vote in a second ballot, from which the communists abstained, became the second President of the Fifth Republic in June 1969.

Popular Front. Movement aimed at uniting the Left in an effort to stem the advance of Nazism, Fascism and other right-wing totalitarian systems. Launched in 1935 after the ⟿ Comintern, which had earlier anathematized other left-wing parties and particularly the Social-Democrats as 'social Fascists', changed its tactics and began to encourage cooperation and electoral pacts between communists, social-democrats, radicals and liberals. As a result of these alliances, Popular Front governments had come to power in ⟿ Spain and ⟿ France by 1936 while in ⟿ Chile it took over in 1938. In Spain, the Popular Front victory under President Azana led to immediate clashes between right and left groups. Strikes, land seizures, anti-clerical excesses, violence and counter-violence culminated in the outbreak of the ⟿ Spanish Civil War (July 1936). In France the Popular Front's electoral triumph put Léon ⟿ Blum – the first socialist Prime Minister in the history of the Third Republic – in power. His government, tolerated, although not actively supported by the communists, enacted an ambitious programme of social reform and secured solid wage benefits for the industrial workers (Matignon Agreements, June 1936). The government, constantly attacked from the right, was also harassed by left-wing radicals; dissensions which led to the break-up of the coalition under ⟿ Daladier (April 1938). The Popular Front lasted longest in Chile, where it attained power under President Pedro Aguirre Cerda (1938–41), under whose aegis it adopted a comprehensive social welfare programme. It also backed the radical President Gonzalez Videla (1946–52). However, in 1947, the communists withdrew from the coalition and were banned (Sept. 1947) prior to the severing of diplomatic relations with the USSR (Oct. 1947).

Population Explosion. Refers to the growth of population following the Industrial Revolution and especially to the rapid post-war increase in world population. It has been suggested that if the rate of increase is not checked, the world-wide economic and political consequences could be disastrous. It is estimated that the world population will have doubled by the year 2005. In Latin America and Asia, population pressure threatens already depressed living standards, and a number of countries have embarked on birth-control programmes. The Catholic Church has been under pressure to revise its attitudes towards birth control, but Pope Paul's encyclical *Humanae Vitae* (29.7.1968) pronounced against a revision of the Church's teaching on the subject of birth control.

Portugal. *Area* – 35,000 sq. miles. *Population* – 9,200,000. *President* – Admiral Americo Thomaz (1958–). *Prime Minister* – Marcelo ⇨ Caetano (1968–). *Constitution* (1933, frequently revised) – A corporative state. Executive power is vested in the President, who is elected for seven years by the Legislature, which consists of the National Assembly (elected for four years by all literate males) and the Corporative Chamber (consisting of representatives of the professions). The Prime Minister and the Council of Ministers are chosen by the President and are responsible to him alone.

Formerly an imperial power and until 1910 a monarchy (virtually absolute, although it underwent some liberalization in the nineteenth century), Portugal experienced little stability with the change to republican government – there were 24 revolutions or coups between 1910 and 1926. In that year a military coup installed General Carmona, who was elected President in 1928. Recurring economic troubles, magnified by the world depression, led to the appointment of Antonio de Oliveira ⇨ Salazar as Minister of Finance (April 1928) with extraordinary powers. Salazar's stringent solutions provided the basis for his domination of Portuguese politics over a period of 40 years. He became Prime Minister (1932) and introduced a new constitution (1933) establishing the *Estado Novo* which was approved by a referendum in the same year. The only party permitted by the government was the National Union, a Fascist-type party founded in 1930. In spite of his pro ⇨ Franco sympathies Salazar avoided direct involvement in the ⇨ Spanish Civil War, and similarly in World War II he remained neutral although he did grant air and naval bases to the Allies (1943). The defeat of the ⇨ Axis powers led to increasing pressure for more political freedom at home and Salazar allowed the formation of opposition parties (Oct. 1945), removed censorship (soon restored) and granted a political amnesty. At the same time a tight check was kept on opposition activities, reinforced by the *Pide* (secret police), so that the opposition parties boycotted the elections. Opposition increased and in the presidential elections of 1958 Salazar's opponent, General Humberto Delgado, polled 23% of the vote. As a result of this a constitutional amendment (1959) abolished the popular election of the President and replaced it by an electoral college consisting of members of the Legislature. The opposition continued to grow but was weakened by its differing elements (which included monarchists, liberals, socialists and communists). In 1961 Portuguese exiles under Captain Galvao seized a Portuguese cruise ship, the *Santa Maria*, with the aim of attracting international attention to the suppression of the opposition. Various attempts to overthrow the government by communists (1959) and military groups (1961) were not successful. Opponents of the regime recently received additional publicity through student riots. Unlike Spain, Portugal was not politically ostracized after the war and soon became integrated in the Western system of alliances – ⊳NATO (1949), ⊳OEEC (1948), the ⊳UN (1955 – previous attempts had been blocked by the Soviet veto) and ⊳EFTA (1960). Portugal has maintained her traditional alliance with the UK (the 'oldest in the world', dating back to the treaty of 1373) and also kept close relations with Spain (Friendship and Non-Aggression Pact renewed 1948, agreement on political and military defence against 'Soviet aggression' 1952, and Salazar–Franco conference at Merida 1963) and with her former colony of Brazil (Treaty on 'Luso-Brazilian Community' 1955). During the 1960s and 1970s the overriding problem in external relations was Portugal's retention of her last colonies (re-styled ⊳Portuguese Overseas Provinces 1951) in spite of the granting of independence to emergent African states by the other colonial powers. An insurrection was crushed in Angola in 1961 but in the same year the Portuguese enclave of ⊳Goa was annexed by India. Portugal's resistance to change has been strengthened by her economic ties with her African territories and her alliance with South Africa and Rhodesia. Her defiance of oil sanctions against the latter strained relations with the UK. In Sept. 1968 Dr Salazar resigned as Prime Minister following a serious illness and was succeeded by Professor Caetano.

Portuguese Guinea. ⊳Portuguese Overseas Provinces.

Portuguese Overseas Provinces. Comprise Angola*, Mozambique†,

* Angola – *area* – 481,352 sq. miles, *population* (approx.) – 5,200,000.
† Mozambique – *area* – 297,731 sq. miles, *population* (approx.) – 6,600,000.

Portuguese Guinea,* the Cape Verde Islands (*area* – 1,557 sq. miles, *population* – 222,000), and the Sao Tome and Principe Islands (*area* – 400 sq. miles, *population* – 560,000) in Africa and in the Far East, Macao (*area* – 6 sq. miles, *population* – 280,000) and Portuguese Timor (*area* – 7,383 sq. miles, *population* – 560,000). Though each of the provinces has a degree of financial and administrative autonomy (Organic Law for Overseas Provinces – 1963), they are regarded as integral parts of ⇨Portugal and executive and political control is vested in the Portuguese Government. Since 1930 Portugal has repeatedly emphasized that the provinces are and will remain inseparably linked to the metropolis. There is no provision, nor is any intended, for ultimate independence. Further, the economic contribution of the African provinces, particularly Angola and Mozambique, has become increasingly significant for Portugal's own development.

Dr ⇨ Salazar frequently proclaimed Portugal's civilising mission, based on a theory of assimilation. In practice, poverty, lack of educational provision, a system of Contract (i.e. forced) Labour meant that very few Africans could become *assimilados* (by 1960 probably less than 1% of the population of the above territories). To qualify, *assimilados* had to satisfy certain educational and professional or financial provisions. Under pressure of violent unrest (Angola 1961) the Organic Law (1961), which came into force (1963) for the first time, granted the rights of full Portuguese citizenship to all Africans. However, this removal of legal sanctions still affects only a tiny proportion of the indigenous population, and in practice the opportunities for an African to advance beyond the lowest rungs of the socio-economic ladder are remote. (For the Africans of Angola and Mozambique, rising Portuguese (white) immigration and Portugal's alliance with Southern ⇨Rhodesia and ⇨ South Africa, further inhibit radical advance in this direction.) Since World War II, two developments have profoundly affected Portuguese thinking – they are: (following years of stagnation) a very rapid economic transformation, particularly in Angola and Mozambique, and the emergence of a militant African nationalism. The pace of Angolan economic development is reflected in the rapid rise of the white settler population (also a reflection since 1961 of Portugal's determination to maintain her grip on the province) which rose from 44,000 in 1940 to 78,000 ten years later, and from upwards of 170,000 in 1960 to perhaps nearly 500,000 in 1968. Mozambique's white population, 27,000 in 1940, more than tripled in the next twenty years. For many years the Portuguese Contract Labour system ('officially' abolished in 1961),

* Portuguese Guinea – *area* – 13,944 sq. miles, *population* (approx.) – 523,000.

combined with a largely subsistence economy in the rural areas, resulted in many Angolans living in temporary or permanent exile in neighbouring states. Portuguese administrative methods were subjected to criticism in the UN. In March 1961, Roberto Holden's UPA (*União das Populações de Angola*) embarked on a course of violence and civil war which in turn was ruthlessly suppressed by the Portuguese. Since 1964, the Portuguese have been involved in a campaign in Northern Mozambique against guerrillas (with bases in Tanzania and organized by Dr Eduardo Mondilane's *Frente de Libertacão de Mocambique* (FRELIMO). Mozambique has strong ties with Rhodesia, for whom her ports are of vital importance. Like South Africa, she has helped Rhodesia to survive the imposition of economic sanctions. (In March 1966 Beira was blockaded by a U K naval force.) Portugal appears determined to maintain her position in Africa despite the recent British and French withdrawals. The outcome is likely to depend on the balance between economic benefit and the cost of military operations, and whether material benefits that may accrue to the indigenous population can offset the appeal (despite internal divisions) of African national movements. Since 1963, Portugal has been engaged in increasingly expensive operations against guerrilla forces in Portuguese Guinea.

Portuguese Timor. ⇨ Portuguese Overseas Provinces.

Potsdam Conference. Meeting held after Germany's surrender (July/Aug. 1945) between Attlee (replacing Churchill after the British election in the middle of the conference), Stalin and Truman to settle the shape of Europe's post-war future. The conference took a number of detailed decisions on the administration of Germany by the Allied occupation forces; on Germany's de-Nazification; the trial of war criminals; reparation payments; the dismantling of industries; and the transfer of certain German territories to Poland and the USSR. Many of these agreements, like those reached at the ⇨ Yalta Conference, later became the subject of opposite interpretations and mutual charges of bad faith.

Powell, Adam Clayton (1908–72). US Negro politician and cleric. He was elected to Congress as a Democrat from Harlem in 1945, and was Chairman of the House of Representatives Committee on Education and Labour until being unseated on charges of financial and legal irregularities in March 1967. He claimed that racial prejudice and the ⇨ White Backlash underlay his expulsion. He was reinstated after being re-elected to Congress in 1968.

Powell, John Enoch (1912–). Ardent advocate of free enterprise and contestant for the U K Conservative Party Leadership in 1965, winning 15 votes. (Edward Heath – 150 votes, Reginald Maudling – 133 votes.)

He was Shadow Minister of Defence until forced to resign by Mr ⇨ Heath (21.4.1968) as a rcsult of his speeeh (notable for the violence of its language) in Birmingham (20.4.1968) suggesting repatriation of coloured immigrants.

Poznan Riots. ⇨ Poland.

Prasad, Rajendra (1884–1963). First President of ⇨ India (1950–62). An early supporter of the civil disobedience campaign led by ⇨ Gandhi, of whom he was a close colleague, he was imprisoned during World War II. He became Minister of Food in the interim Indian Government (1946–47) and President of the Constituent Assembly which drafted the Indian Constitution (1946–49). In 1952 and 1957 he was overwhelmingly re-elected Head of State.

Pravda. Soviet daily newspaper, published by the CPSU Central Committee and expressing the official party point of view.

Presidential Primary. A ⇨ Primary Election for presidential candidates in the USA.

Presidential Veto. Power of the President of the USA under the Constitution to prevent bills and other instruments of ⇨ Congress becoming law by refusing to sign them. The President must indicate his objections to Congress within ten days of receiving a measure if the veto is to apply – otherwise it becomes law automatically. An exception is when Congress adjourns within the ten days, when the President may veto the measure simply by 'pocketing' it – omitting to sign it – which is called the 'pocket veto'. Congress can use this procedure to shift blame for a failure to satisfy a popular demand from itself to the President. If the 'regular' veto is used, however, and Congress is still in session, it can be overridden by a two-thirds vote in both houses. President ⇨ Truman's veto of the ⇨ Taft-Hartley Act was overridden in this way. The President, unlike most State Governors, does not have an 'item veto', but must accept or reject a bill as a whole, including any 'riders' that Congress may have added to restrict or extend its operation in ways not favoured by the Administration. It is common for foreign-aid legislation to contain riders excluding countries thought to be unfriendly to the USA, and the President is obliged to accept them if he is to get any aid voted at all. The use of the veto by recent Presidents has somewhat declined after reaching a peak under Franklin D. ⇨ Roosevelt who used it 631 times (371 'regular', 260 'pocket', 9 overridden).

Prices and Incomes Policy (UK). Policy of restraint coordinating rises in prices and incomes with an increase in productivity. Legislation passed by the ⇨ Wilson administration (1966, 1968) granted the Government delaying powers in respect of price and pay increases and powers to require price reductions. The policy called for voluntary cooperation from both sides of industry and disputes were referred to the Prices and Incomes Board created in 1965.

Primary Election. In the USA, a legally-instituted election held to choose official party candidates to stand at a subsequent election for public office. The 'direct primary' system has been adopted in varying completeness by all the States, beginning with Wisconsin in 1903 and ending with Connecticut in 1955. It was intended to overcome the lack of 'democracy' in other methods of choosing candidates, such as nomination by a ⇨ Caucus or convention, though these methods are still used alongside primaries in some States. A *non-partisan* primary is one in which candidates are chosen without regard to their party affiliations, the final election being held to choose between the two leading candidates only when none secures an absolute majority in the primary. It is used mainly where it is thought that party membership should not be a consideration, as in elections for judicial office. *Partisan* primaries are of two main types. A *closed* primary is one in which only members of a party may participate in the vote for its candidates. The voter must declare his party affiliation, either at the ⇨ Registration of Voters or at the time of the primary, and in some cases he must prove previous support for the party. This method was formerly used in the South to exclude Negroes from primaries, and consequently (since Democratic candidates almost invariably all won in the final election) from effective participation in general elections. The 'white primary' was finally invalidated by the ⇨ Supreme Court in 1944. One-party domination in the South has also led to the institution of the *runoff* primary, which is a second primary held to choose between the leading candidates in the first primary when, due to a large number seeking the Democratic label, none has been able to win a clear majority. A runoff primary can virtually take the place of the formal election to office. In an *open* primary, the voter is not required to indicate his party affiliation, but may participate in choosing candidates of any one (or, rarely, all) of the parties. *Presidential* primaries are held in a number of States to choose ⇨ National Convention delegates, thus giving voters an indirect choice (they sometimes have a direct choice) among the contenders for the parties' presidential nominations. In recent years, the number of States holding presidential primaries has decreased from above a half to under a third, though they remain important in campaigns for nomination. In 1960, John F. ⇨ Kennedy did well enough in the primaries to be virtually assured of the Democratic nomination by the time the National Convention met. Senator ⇨ Goldwater's bid for the Republican nomination in 1964 was also advanced by this means, as was that of Sen. ⇨ McGovern for the Democratic nomination in 1972. In 1964 and 1968,

Governor George ▷ Wallace was enabled by his performance in the presidential primaries to project himself as a national candidate whose support was not confined to the South. However, whilst primary elections have complicated and prolonged the electoral process in the United States, it may be doubted whether they have 'democratized' the choice of candidates.

Privy Council. ▷ UK Constitution.

Profumo Affair. Mr John Profumo, UK Conservative Secretary of State for War (1960–63) resigned (5.6.1963) after admitting to having lied to the House of Commons (22.3.1963) regarding his relationship with Miss Christine Keeler. The discovery of his involvement with people of dubious character aroused fears of security leaks. The publication of the Denning Report (Sept. 1963) dissipated these fears, but the affair led to a further decline in the popularity of the Conservative Government.

Progressive Moderation. Description of the policies of the ▷ Eisenhower Administration used by its supporters, suggesting a successful combination of liberal aims and conservative methods. It was meant as an answer to criticisms of the Administration coming from liberals (mainly, but not exclusively, Democrats) on the one hand, and from disappointed conservatives of the rising ▷ New Right on the other.

Prohibition. The Eighteenth Amendment to the Constitution of the USA (ratified Jan. 1919) prohibited the sale of intoxicating beverages in the United States. This led to widespread breaking of the law by otherwise respectable citizens and to a serious breakdown of law and order in the big cities. Prohibition encouraged the rise of racketeers and gangsters who gained influence over city officials and police, the 'bootleggers' using bribery to protect their illegal manufacture and sale of alcoholic drinks. In 1933 the Amendment was repealed by the Twenty-first Amendment. The prohibition amendment is generally considered a last effort by rural and small-town Americans to combat what they saw as the degeneration of American morals led by the cities.

Proletariat. Term applied by communists and socialists to the industrial working class in derivation from the Latin *proletarius* – the class of people which served the Roman state with their offspring (*proles*) for want of property. In its modern sense, the term was first used and explained in the *Kommunistische Zeitschrift*, published in London in Sept. 1847, and it gained world-wide currency after the publication of the *Communist Manifesto* by Karl Marx and Friedrich Engels (Feb. 1848).

Proportional Representation (PR). System of voting designed to secure legislative representation proportional to the actual party strength at the level – municipal, state, general – at which elections are held, by allocating seats on the total poll rather than on the outcome of straight constituency contests (plurality voting). In proportional representation votes cast for unsuccessful candidates are not disregarded, so correcting the anomaly which permits the attainment of power and a parliamentary majority on a minority vote. However, proportional representation encourages the growth of numerous small parties and concomitantly the emergence of unstable coalition governments, which in turn frequently accord minuscule groupings political influence totally out of proportion to their electoral support.

Protocols of the Elders of Zion. ⇨ Anti-semitism.

Puerto Rico. *Area* (including off-shore islands) – 3,423 sq. miles. *Population* (approx.) – 2,700,000. *Governor* – Luis A. Ferré, leader of the New Progressive Party, was elected Governor in Nov. 1968. *Constitution* (1952) – Commonwealth associated with the US (*Estado Libre Asociado*) with internal self-government. Modelled on the US – an executive Governor directly elected for a four-year term and a bi-cameral Legislature (Congress) of a Senate and House of Representatives. There is universal adult suffrage. Puerto Ricans are citizens of the US but do not vote in Federal elections, and Puerto Rico is exempt from US Federal tax laws.

Puerto Rico, formerly Spanish, was ceded to the US (1898). Puerto Ricans have been US citizens since 1917 with their own elected bi-cameral Congress, but the US exercised certain veto rights. Puerto Rico's outstanding politician has been Luis ⇨ Munoz Marin, first elected to the Senate in 1932. Expelled from his own party and unpopular with the US for supporting nationalist agitation, he formed the PPD (*Partido Popular Democratico*) in 1938 which won the 1940 general elections. Puerto Rican-US relations were improved by Roosevelt's sympathy for Puerto Rican aspirations and the appointment of Governor Tugwell. The series of reforms from 1947 resulted in the present constitutional status (1952). Vast US aid programmes since 1940 have more than trebled real incomes. However, Munoz's policy of economic and political development in association with the US has produced (though in a minority) strong splinter groups demanding complete independence and a radical break with the US. Puerto Ricans attempted to assassinate President Truman (1950) and in 1954, four Puerto Rican nationalists shot at US Congressmen from the visitors' gallery of the (US) House of Representatives. Attitudes to Puerto Rican statehood have been affected by Latin American developments – e.g. Cuba and US intervention in the Dominican Republic – and by questions at the UN. The Puerto Rican/US Commission (1964) recommended a plebiscite in which

Puerto Ricans could vote for independence or a continuation of their association with the US, and at the referendum (1967) 60% voted for the Commonwealth. In the 1964 elections, Munoz Marin refused to stand for a fifth term, but his PPD lieutenant, Roberto Sanchez-Vilella was elected Governor. Despite US aid, Puerto Rican standards of living are threatened by rapid population growth. Under-employment resulted in large-scale emigration to the US from 1950, but since the mid-sixties many emigrants have returned.

Purges. In communist usage a procedure originally designed to maintain the purity of the Communist Party by cleansing its ranks of corrupt or politically unreliable elements. The practice of systematic purges, involving a close scrutiny of the conduct and political views of each individual party member (in Russian: *chistka*), was first sanctioned by the 10th Congress of the Russian Communist Party in March 1921 and has since then become a regular procedure in all communist parties. During the Stalin era, 'purges' became an instrument of police terror leading to the physical liquidation of opposition leaders and other Party members deemed undesirable. (▷ Moscow Trials, ▷ Show Trials, ▷ USSR, ▷ USSR State Security Service, ▷ Yezhovshchina).

Pyatakov, G. L. (1890–1937). Soviet communist. An anarchist in his early youth, Pyatakov became a ▷ Bolshevik in 1910. A member of the Party's Central Committee, after the revolution he occupied leading positions in economic administration. Described in ▷ Lenin's Testament as one of the ablest of the younger generation of Bolsheviks, Pyatakov, in the post-Lenin factional party struggles, was a follower of ▷ Trotsky and was expelled from the Party (1927). Like many other members of the various opposition groups, he was later re-admitted after a public recantation. He also shared their fate. Accused, in the second of the ▷ Moscow Trials, of treason, espionage and terrorist activities, he was convicted and executed.

Q

Qatar, Emirate of. *Area* – 4,000 sq. miles. *Population* – 60,000. *Ruler* – Sheikh Khalifa bin Hamad al-Thani (1972). An independent Arab state, it was under British protection until 1971. Its principal source of income is revenue from oil (production began in 1949).

Quemoy. ⇨ Matsu and Quemoy.

Quisling, Vidkun (1887–1945). Founded the Norwegian Nazi Party *Nasjonal Samling* (1933). He helped the Germans prepare for and assisted their invasion of Norway (April 1940) and later ruled the country under the aegis of their army. He started his career as an army officer and, transferring to the diplomatic service, helped Nansen's relief efforts during the Russian famine in the early 1920s. Shot as a collaborator, his name has become a synonym for betrayal to and collaboration with an alien tyranny.

R

Raab, Julius (1891–1964). Chancellor of Austria (1953–61), Christian Social Deputy (1927–34), Transport Minister in pre- ⇨ *Anschluss* Cabinet (1938), post-war co-founder of Austrian People's Party and its parliamentary leader until 1953. As Chancellor he played a key part in negotiating the Austrian State Treaty (1955).

Race Relations Acts (UK). Passed by Premier ⇨ Wilson's Labour Government – aimed at preventing racial discrimination. The 1965 Act covered discrimination in public accommodation and the 1968 Act in employment and housing. Neither act instituted subpoena powers. Cases of discrimination may be referred to the Race Relations Board and subsequently, if necessary, to the Attorney General.

Radek, K. B. (1885–1939). Soviet communist. Born in Poland, an early convert to ⇨ Bolshevism and for several years before World War I active in the revolutionary wing of the German Social Democratic Party, Radek was a cosmopolitan revolutionary. He returned to Russia together with Lenin after the February Revolution of 1917 and, following the ⇨ Bolshevik seizure of power, was in charge of the Department for International Propaganda attached to the Commissariat for Foreign Affairs under ⇨ Trotsky. He participated in the foundation congress of the German Communist Party (Dec. 1918) and later became a leading functionary of the ⇨ Communist International, frequently intervening on its behalf in the affairs of the German and other communist parties. In 1925 he became President of the newly established Moscow Sun Yat-sen University of the Toilers of the East. An active member of the Trotskyite opposition to ⇨ Stalin, he was expelled from the Party in 1927. Reinstated in 1930 after a public recantation, he was arrested in Sept. 1936 and became one of the leading defendants in the second ⇨ Moscow Trial (Jan. 1937). Among the few whose life was then spared, he was sentenced to ten years imprisonment and was later reported to have perished in a Forced Labour Camp in 1939.

Radical Socialists (France). ⇨ *Parti Républicain Radical et Radical Socialiste.*

Rajk, L. (1909–49). A member of the Hungarian underground Communist Party from 1931, Rajk went to Spain (1936), where he joined the International Brigade and became the Party Secretary of the Hungarian 'Rakosi Battalion'. Wounded in 1938, he sought refuge in France where he was interned until after the outbreak of World War II, when he secretly returned to Hungary. After a period of internment there, he became the leader of the communist Resistance in Hungary until his re-arrest (1944). Following his release (1945), he became the Secretary-General of the Budapest party organization and, in Feb. 1946, he succeeded ⇨ Nagy as Minister of the Interior. He lost this post in Aug. 1948, soon after ⇨ Tito's expulsion from the ⇨ Cominform, and after a short spell as Foreign Minister, was arrested in May 1949 on charges of having plotted with Tito on behalf of Western intelligence agencies and of having been since early youth in the service of Horthy's police. At his ⇨ Show Trial (Sept. 1949) he pleaded guilty to all charges and was executed. He was rehabilitated in March 1956 and solemnly re-interred in a public ceremony in Sept. 1956.

Rakosi, M. (1892–1971). Hungarian communist. A prisoner-of-war in Russia at the time of the revolution, Rakosi had become a ⇨ Bolshevik before he returned to Hungary in 1918. A founder-member of the Hungarian Communist Party and a junior Commissar in Bela Kun's Soviet Republic of 1919, he escaped, after its collapse, to the USSR, where he became a roving emissary for the ⇨ Comintern. Back in Hungary in 1924 to reorganize the underground party, he was arrested and spent the next 15 years in prison. Following a Soviet-Hungarian exchange deal, he was released in 1940 and returned to the USSR. He headed the team of ⇨ Muscovites who went back to Hungary in 1944 to take charge of their country's ⇨ Sovietization, a task Rakosi performed with ruthless skill. His reputation as an unrepentant Stalinist induced the post-Stalin Soviet leadership to remove him as too much of a liability. In July 1956, he was compelled to resign as First Party Secretary in favour of his second-in-command, E. ⇨ Gerö. Shortly afterwards, he left for his third period of asylum in the USSR.

Rankonvic, Aleksandar (1903–). Yugoslav communist and former Secret Police Chief, Rankovic joined the illegal Yugoslav Communist Party in 1928. Having spent long years in prison and suffered police torture in the pre-war period, he became a Partisan leader during the war and, after the war, the new government's Minister of the Interior. Appointed Vice-President of the Republic in 1953, he was generally regarded as ⇨ Tito's heir-apparent until his sudden fall from power in 1966, when he was accused of responsibility for illegal secret police activities and the obstruction of economic and democratic reforms.

Rapacki Plan. Proposal for the establishment of a nuclear-free zone in Central Europe – to include both Western and Eastern Germany, Poland and Czechoslovakia – made by the former Polish Foreign Minister, Adam Rapacki, in a speech to the United Nations General Assembly (2.10.1957).

Ras Al Khamah. ⇨ Trucial States.

Rassemblement du Peuple Français. ⇨ RPF.

Rayburn, Samuel T. (1882–1961). American Democratic politician, Speaker of the US House of Representatives (1940–46, 1950–61). He served in the Texas State Legislature (1906–12) until being elected from that State to the House of Representatives where he remained for 48 years (1913–61). Although not a liberal New Dealer, he aided in the formulation and passage of important government regulatory legislation. As ⇨ Majority Leader (1937–43) and, still more, as Speaker of the House, Rayburn exercised considerable influence and leadership.

Reactionary. Commonly used with reference to anyone of the right who reacts against a particular ideology or political system. In this sense a reactionary might oppose reforms which endanger traditions which claim his loyalty or might wish to re-establish a political system which has disappeared through revolution or reform. In popular usage an opponent of change – most often in a derogatory sense in which anyone on the right of the political spectrum (from conservative to fascist) is so described. In Marxist-Leninist terminology reactionaries can include liberals and social democrats as well as Conservatives.

Reagan, Ronald W. (1911–). Former US movie actor who entered politics in 1966 when he was elected Governor of California after having actively supported Barry ⇨ Goldwater in 1964. A conservative Republican, Reagan was considered a possible candidate for the presidency in 1968 and is expected to remain a prominent Republican hopeful in the future. He has adopted a 'hard line' in dealing with student unrest in California.

Reapportionment. In the USA the redrawing of voting district boundaries in many States ordered by the Supreme Court (1962, 1964) to prevent the ⇨ Gerrymandering which had given disproportionate representation to rural over urban voters. Each State was to submit a plan for reapportionment, but there has been slow compliance by legislative majorities whose power depends on the continuation of present electoral boundaries. Opposition from many States was so strong that in 1967 there were lacking the votes of only two of their number for the two-thirds required to call a Constitutional Convention on the issue, something that had never previously occurred.

Recognition. Lacking a generally agreed definition, political expediency rather than legal principle or precedent is the crucial factor determining the degree of international recognition accorded to a new state or government. This is clearly so in many cases, (eg, ⇨China, ⇨German Democratic Republic, ⇨Israel). Where prior constitutional provision is made for the emergence of a new state (eg, ⇨Zambia, ⇨Botswana) no problem exists and recognition is automatic.

De Facto Recognition accepts that the government concerned is in effective control of its country and provides a formula for business and low-level (non ambassadorial) political transactions without thereby implying –

De Jure Recognition, ie, complete legal and diplomatic recognition usually followed by membership of the UN and exchange of ambassadors with other states.

Red Guards. Name first adopted by the armed Russian workers' contingents which were instrumental in the ⇨ Bolshevik seizure of power (Oct. 1917) and which later became the nucleus of the Red Army. Outside the USSR, the name Red Guards has been used by various militant communist detachments. The name was revived in ⇨China in 1966, when the country's students were encouraged by ⇨Lin Piao and his associates to organize themselves as Red Guards dedicated to the promotion of the Cultural Revolution, the defence of ⇨Mao Tse-tung's 'thought' and the defeat of Mao's enemies. For well over a year, from the autumn of 1966 onwards, the youngsters of the Chinese Red Guards were encouraged to 'make revolution' according to their own lights and were flattered by all means of publicity as 'Mao's little generals'. Their ever-mounting excesses and factional struggles were gradually subdued in the course of 1967/68. Publicity for the Red Guards has since almost entirely ceased, and their members were once again subjected to the discipline of their elders. From 1968 onwards, increasing numbers of Red Guards have been removed from the cities and sent to rural and frontier areas with orders to engage in agricultural and construction work.

Registration of Voters. In the USA, the procedure whereby the citizen must himself establish his qualification to vote to the satisfaction of State officials. This is required once only in some States, but before each election or ⇨Primary Election in many, which partly accounts for the relatively low level of voting in the United States. The registration of Negroes has been discouraged in some States, particularly in the South. Recent action to overcome this has included: the establishment of the ⇨ Civil Rights Commission in 1957; ratification of the Twenty-fourth

Amendment to the Constitution prohibiting poll-tax qualifications in 1964; and passage of the Voting Rights Act restricting the use of ⇨ Literacy Tests in 1965.

Reichstag. The pre-1945 German Parliament in Berlin. The building itself was burnt down in an act of arson (Feb. 1933) by a young Dutch communist (van der Lubbe) soon after Hitler came to power. The *Reichstag* Fire provided the Nazis with so welcome a pretext to pass repressive legislation that they have long been suspected of complicity in the fire-raising. Latest evidence tends to acquit them of this particular crime. (⇨ Germany, Third Reich.)

Renner, Karl (1870–1950). President of ⇨ Austria (1945–50) and Austrian Social Democratic leader. He was Chancellor (1918–20), President of the National Council (1931–33) and advocated the ⇨ *Anschluss* with Germany. He took no active part in politics during the war but became head of the provisional post-war government in 1945.

Republican Party. One of the two major political parties of the USA, the other being the ⇨ Democratic Party. It was organized in 1854 at a time when a realignment of political forces was taking place over slavery; but it had a 'pre-history' in a succession of older parties – Federalists, National Republicans, Whigs. The new party advanced rapidly, and in 1860, in the second presidential election after its foundation, its candidate, Abraham Lincoln, became President, winning the support of a minority of voters, but of all the States outside the South. Lincoln's election precipitated the Civil War, one result of which was that the Democrats were discredited and the Republicans gained almost unbroken control of the ⇨ White House and a preponderance in ⇨ Congress that lasted until the Great Depression of the 1930s. In its period of ascendancy, despite being the newer party, it came to be known as the 'Grand Old Party' or GOP. With the defeat of Republican President Herbert ⇨ Hoover by Democrat Franklin D. ⇨ Roosevelt in 1932, the Republican Party suffered eclipse, but recently it has recovered its former ascendancy. Since World War II, it has been as successful as its rival in presidential elections, the Republicans winning in 1952 and 1956 (Dwight D. ⇨ Eisenhower) and in 1968 and 1972 (Richard M. ⇨ Nixon), and the Democrats in 1948, 1960 and 1964. But in the biennial elections for Congress the Republicans have, since 1932, secured majorities in the ⇨ Senate and ⇨ House of Representatives only twice, in 1946 and 1952. President Eisenhower, though personally very popular, was able to achieve only a short-lived improvement in his party's fortunes, and they reached a low ebb in 1964 when Senator Barry ⇨ Goldwater was defeated in the presidential contest. Because the Republicans are usually in the minority in Congress,

Republican Presidents have to rely on the support of some Democrats to make legislative headway. Such support is often forthcoming, however, as party lines are not rigidly drawn in Congress – though for the same reason a Republican President cannot count on the support of all congressional members of his own party. This state of affairs reflects the conditions in which both American parties operate; and these being basically the same for both parties, the Republican Party is basically similar in organization to the Democratic Party. Like the Democratic Party, it has its four-yearly ⇨ National Convention and its National Committee, and innumerable committees at all levels. Like the Democratic Party, the Republican Party is essentially a national electoral alliance of local, State and regional interests concerned primarily with fighting presidential elections. But the combination of interests it represents is different from the one represented by its rival, and it is in this that the difference between Republicans and Democrats chiefly lies.

The Republican Party has retained the support of the bulk of the business and professional community through all its vicissitudes, and it gets the votes of the majority among the higher-income, higher-educated and older-established groups throughout the nation. Its chief centres of strength are small towns and suburbs across the country and the rural areas of the Midwest and North-East. Probably reflecting the preferences of most of its supporters, the Republican Party is in a general sense more conservative than the Democratic Party, though it has a sizeable liberal wing, and its conservatism is not typically of the kind called 'Goldwaterism', or, indeed, ⇨ McCarthyism. Republican Presidents tend to favour private enterprise, national interest, balanced budgets, and personal saving; but they are also apt to support ⇨ Civil Rights more than ⇨ States' Rights. There has been considerable historical continuity with regard to the sort of interests that are aligned with the Republican Party and the principles Republicans profess. At present, these interests are in the minority (it is estimated that there are about as many independent voters as committed Republicans) and this seems likely to continue unless the party can give itself a broader appeal. But Republican candidates may well continue to be relatively successful in presidential contests.

Resolution of Congress. In the USA, an instrument of either or both Houses of ⇨ Congress, usually relating to some specific issue or occasion. Each house provides for its own business by *Simple Resolution*, and the two provide for their common business by *Concurrent Resolution*. A concurrent resolution may also be used to express the opinion of Congress on a matter not falling directly within its jurisdiction. Most important is a *Joint Resolution*, which, when passed by both houses and

signed by the President, has the force of law. An important ⇨Executive
Agreement may well be backed by a Joint Resolution of Congress.
Constitutional amendments are proposed by joint resolutions approved
by two-thirds of both houses.

Réunion. ⇨ French Overseas Departments.

Reuther, Walter Philip (1907–70). US union leader. He became
President of the American Auto Workers' Union in 1946, 13 years after
being discharged from Ford Motor Company for union activities, and
President of the ⇨CIO in 1952. Reuther has fought for 'wage increases
without price increases', an annual guaranteed wage, and the elimina-
tion of racketeering and communist influence in labour organizations.
He was instrumental in bringing about the reunion of the CIO with the
⇨AFL in 1955. He was killed in an air accident.

Revanchism. A term used by East German, Soviet, Polish and Bulgarian communist propagandists to describe alleged West German intentions to change forcibly the European *status quo* established after World
War II.

Revisionism (i) – term applied in the inter-war period to the aspirations of certain European countries (notably Germany, Hungary and
Bulgaria) to regain some or all of the territories which they had lost as a
result of the peace treaties following World War I.

Revisionism (ii) – term widely used in the ideological controversies
between communist countries and parties. The term first came into use
after the publication, in the 1890s, of a series of articles by the German
social democrat, Eduard Bernstein, setting out to revise orthodox
Marxist theories in the light of actual developments. In its contemporary
usage, the term was first widely applied to the practices and ideas
gaining currency in ⇨Yugoslavia after ⇨Tito's break with ⇨Stalin.
The meaning of the term was later enlarged to embrace all communist
reform movements aiming at a radical departure from the Stalinist past
and emphasizing the humanist aspects of the Marxian heritage with a
special stress on cultural freedom and democratic practices. With the
escalation of inter-communist party polemics, 'revisionism' has at the
same time become a general term of abuse, freely exchanged so as to
distinguish innovations regarded as unacceptable by one particular
country or party from others which are actively promoted and, in
contradistinction, described as 'a creative development of Marxism-
Leninism'.

Reynaud, Paul (1878–1966). The ⇨ Third Republic's last Prime
Minister, replacing ⇨ Daladier (March 1940) under whom he had
served as Minister of Finance. After the German break-through he
appointed ⇨Pétain as his deputy (May 1940) but strongly opposed the

Assembly's decision to sue for peace, make the Marshal Head of State and dissolve the Third Republic (17.6.1940). Imprisoned by the ⇦Vichy authorities on a war guilt charge, he spent the years 1943–45 in German concentration camps. Returning to politics, he served the short-lived Marie administration (Aug. 1948) as Finance Minister and the Laniel Government as deputy Prime Minister (1953–54). An outspoken and active supporter of European integration, he was a Deputy in the first Assembly of the Fifth Republic (1959–62).

Rhee, Dr Syngman. ⇦Korea.

Rhodesia (Southern). *Area* – 150,820 sq. miles. *Population* (1969 est.) – 5,190,000 of whom approx. 234,000 are Europeans. *Constitution* – The constitutional position of Rhodesia has been complicated by ⇦ U D I (1965). Although negotiations have taken place at various times between Her Majesty's Government and the Rhodesian Government, the Rhodesian Government is theoretically still in a state of rebellion against the Crown. In Nov. 1968 the Government was given *de facto* recognition from the Rhodesian High Court but it has not been recognized by any other governments.

Rhodesia was formerly administered by the British South Africa Company from 1893 until 1923 when it became a self-governing colony. This granting of responsible government (in effect to the white minority) but without ⇦ Dominion status, created an anomalous position. The U K government retained control over external affairs and the right to veto legislation related specifically to the African population. Many of the difficulties which have since arisen between Rhodesia and the U K and Rhodesia and her northern African neighbours (e.g. during Federation and since U D I) are a result of this anomalous position by which, contrary to its usual procedures, the British government granted internal autonomy to a minority within the country. Two main (and apparently irreconcilable) contradictions arise from this state of affairs:

(1) Southern Rhodesian Africans who include in their ranks more literate and more professionally qualified people than the former British territories to the north which are now independent, are considered not ready for independence;

(2) The Rhodesian white population, in effect self-governing for more than 40 years without assistance from the U K, is unwilling to accept a limitation of its power today.

Sir Godfrey Huggins (Lord ⇦ Malvern) was Prime Minister of Rhodesia for 20 years (1933–53) and the first Prime Minister (1953–56) of the Federation of ⇨ Rhodesia and Nyasaland (1953–63). His long tenure of office, although the party he led underwent changes of name, reflected the strength of a business and industry-dominated establishment. Its politics were mildly liberal and paternalistic, while no serious African challenge to the status quo appeared likely. The main opposition was from the extreme right which was denied the fruits of office and found even the Rhodesian establishment too liberal for its liking. Parallel to developments in South Africa during and since Federation, a predominantly white electorate has moved increasingly rightwards, as indicated by its choice of Prime Ministers since Garfield ⇨ Todd's period of office (1953–58) – Sir Edgar ⇨ Whitehead (1958–62), Winston Field (1962–64), Ian ⇨ Smith (1964–). In each case the Premier's freedom of movement appears to have been increasingly limited by the demands of a predominantly white electorate. After the war, the idea of a federation, propagated by Roy Welensky and Huggins, with the prospect of the economy being stimulated by the vast resources of the Northern Rhodesia copper belt, became increasingly attractive, and following a referendum the Federation was formed (Aug. 1953). The Federation period witnessed some relaxation in traditional discriminatory attitudes. However, growing African nationalism inevitably came into conflict with the governments of the day, and nationalist leaders and parties (⇨ZANU, ⇨ZAPU) have been successively banned or prevented from participating in elections (1957, 1961, 1962, 1963, 1964). Before the war, franchise qualifications limited the number of African electors. Since the war, Rhodesian constitutions have been complicated by differently weighted electoral rolls designed not to frighten the white electorate yet offer representation to Africans. (The first Africans were only elected to the Legislature in 1962. African nationalist tactics of boycotting elections under constitutions which they do not like may yet prove to have been a tactical error.) The hopes of partnership and multi-racialism were dealt a crushing blow by the right-wing Rhodesian Front victory in the 1962 elections, and the political ascendancy of the Rhodesian Front was again demonstrated by a nearly clean sweep in the 1965 elections. As the attitudes of the UK and most of the Commonwealth countries and that of the Rhodesian Front to the political role of the African majority in Rhodesia drew wider apart, Ian Smith announced Rhodesia's Unilateral Declaration of Independence (Nov. 1965). The Governor, Sir Humphrey ⇨ Gibbs, remained loyal to the UK; but his position became increasingly difficult. The UK responded to UDI by imposing economic sanctions supported by the UN (Security Council resolution, April 1966) and Britain was empowered to use any means to prevent oil deliveries to Rhodesia via Beira in Mozambique. (In March 1966, Beira was blockaded by a UK naval force.)

So far, talks between the two governments have failed to produce agreement. The UK government has insisted that the Six Principles on which independence can be given are ones which it shared with previous UK governments; they include an end to racial discrimination, the need to be satisfied that independence is acceptable to all the people of Rhodesia and assurance that there would be no oppression of racial groups. Talks held on board HMS *Tiger* (Dec. 1966) failed to get the support of Mr Smith's Cabinet, the details of a return to legality posing a stumbling block. In Dec. 1966, the UN Security Council adopted a British resolution calling on member countries to boycott Rhodesian products and implement sanctions against Rhodesia. Further talks between Mr Wilson and Mr Smith (on board HMS *Fearless*, Oct. 1968) also ended in failure, as did further soundings by the UK Commonwealth Secretary, George Thomson. The chief obstacle to agreement appears to be the blocking mechanism designed to ensure that rights of Africans cannot be whittled away by future governments, and the limitation of Rhodesian sovereignty through recourse to the Privy Council. Recent South African experience where clauses entrenched in the constitution failed to protect African rights suggests that constitutional devices without either a limitation of sovereignty or sufficient African representation are unlikely to prevent future governments from reversing established policies. In years of economic difficulty, failure to solve Rhodesia's crises was an additional burden for the UK Labour Government. Mr Wilson's freedom of action was limited by the threat of left-wing revolt and accusations of sorting out difficulties with the Commonwealth on how far he could go to meet Mr Smith. In the *Tiger* and *Fearless* talks, the NIBMAR proposals (no independence before majority rule) put forward at Commonwealth Prime Ministers' conferences, appear to have been sacrificed in an attempt to reach an agreement with Mr Smith. Mr Smith, however, seems unable or unwilling to make concessions which the UK government could present as acceptable to Parliament. The South African Government on whose good-will and sanctions-breaking activities the Rhodesian Government has relied, appears anxious for a settlement. Successive British governments have insisted that a settlement can only take place within the limits of the five principles (first laid down in October 1965) – 1. unimpeded progress to majority rule, 2. no retrogressive amendment of the constitution, 3. immediate improvement in the political status of Africans, 4. progress towards ending racial discrimination, 5. independence must be acceptable to the people of

Rhodesia as a whole. Following negotiations between the two governments, Sir Alec Douglas-Home announced in the Commons, November 1971, that a draft agreement had been signed on proposals ('within the five principles') for a new constitution for Rhodesia. The Pearce Commission, set up to test the acceptability of the proposals, published its conclusion (May 23, 1972) 'that the people of Rhodesia as a whole did not regard the proposals as an acceptable basis for independence'.

Rhodesia and Nyasaland, Federation of (1953–63) (also known as the Central African Federation). Comprised the self-governing colony of Southern ⇨ Rhodesia, and the Protectorates of Northern Rhodesia (now ⇨ Zambia) and Nyasaland (now ⇨ Malawi). Despite its obvious economic advantages, the Federation was beset by political difficulties throughout its brief existence. Its formation was opposed by African nationalists and many Africans in Northern Rhodesia and Nyasaland regarded it as a device to restrain their progress to independence. The right-wing Southern Rhodesian parties (first the Dominion Party, then the Rhodesian Front) adopted an equivocal attitude to the Federation, while even pro-Federal Southern Rhodesian politicians became increasingly anxious about the effects on their own position of later U K concessions to the two northern territories. Despite some relaxation of Southern Rhodesia's traditionally segregatory policies (during the Federal period) to conform with provisions of the Federal constitution, the difficulty of reconciling the conflicting aspirations of the European minority with African nationalism was manifested in civil disorder (e.g. Nyasaland 1959) and violence in Southern Rhodesia. The Report (Oct. 1960) of the Monckton Commission (set up to review and advise on the constitution) recommended that African representation in the Assembly be increased, discriminatory legislation (particularly applicable to Southern Rhodesia) be removed and that the individual territories should have the right to secede. Despite attempts at conciliation by the U K (still as the colonial power the ultimate political authority) through a Constitutional Conference (1961), the gulf between the territories as well as internal divisions widened. The right (indeed the likelihood) of secession was implicit in developments in Nyasaland and Northern Rhodesia from 1962.

The U K government soon explicitly recognized (March 1963) that the Federation could not be held together against the wishes of member territories and it was officially dissolved (Dec. 1963).

Rhodesian Front. Governing political party of ⇨ Rhodesia since 1962.

Ribbentrop, Joachim von (1893–1946). ⇨ Hitler's principal adviser on foreign affairs, he was successively head of the 'Ribbentrop Bureau', ambassador in London (1936–38) and German Foreign Minister (1938–

45). Responsible for the ⇨ Hitler-Stalin Pact with the Soviet Union (23.8.1939) and the Tripartite Pact with Italy and Japan (27.9.1940), which secured Germany's position at the beginning of World War II, he was sentenced to death for war crimes at the ⇨ Nuremberg War Crime Trials.

Right. ⇨ Left and Right.

Right-to-Work Laws. In the U S A, laws in several States restricting the actions of Trade Unions, particularly regarding the 'closed shop', ostensibly to protect the rights of non-members, but often with the intention of weakening the unions.

Rio Treaty. 21-nation Inter-American Treaty of Reciprocal Assistance signed at Rio de Janeiro, Brazil (2.9.1947) binding the signatories to support any American State subject to aggression. The precise conditions for activating the Treaty obligations were not specified. Provision was also made for calling special Inter-American Conferences to deal with emergency situations, and permanent arrangements for dealing with matters covered by the Treaty were made when ⇨ O A S was established (1948). The Rio Treaty was invoked by Costa Rica when that country was invaded from Nicaragua by some of its own nationals in exile (11.1.1955). The U S A met a Costa Rican request for aircraft to deal with the emergency, which was finally settled through the O A S.

Riom Trials. Proceedings initiated Sept. 1940 against the political and military leaders whom the ⇨ Vichy authorities deemed responsible for the outbreak of war and the fall of ⇨ France. Among the accused were former Prime Ministers ⇨ Blum, ⇨ Daladier, ⇨ Reynaud and the French C.-in-C. General Gamelin. A demand for further evidence led early in 1942 first to an adjournment and then to a *sine die* postponement of the trial. The defendants, however, remained in custody and most of them were later handed over to Germany and interned in concentration camps.

Rivonia Trial. ⇨ Treason Trials (South Africa).

Rochet, Waldeck (1905–). Succeeded Maurice ⇨ Thorez as Secretary-General of the French Communist Party in 1964. A Moscow-trained functionary – he attended the Lenin School for three years – Waldeck Rochet first gained a seat in Parliament after the 1936 Popular Front victory. As a member of the proscribed Communist Party (Sept. 1939) which, after the signing of the ⇨ Hitler-Stalin Pact, actively opposed France's war effort, he was sentenced to five years' imprisonment. After the liberation, he was elected to the provisional Consultative Assembly and later became leader of the communist parliamentary party. In 1961 he was appointed deputy Secretary-General. More flexible than his predecessor, he concluded election pacts with the ⇨ *Fédération de la*

Gauche and is known to favour popular front alignments, without sacrificing party identity.

Rockefeller, Nelson A. (1908–). U S statesman. Governor of New York (1958–). Holder of many government posts, including co-ordinator of inter-American affairs (1940–44), Assistant Secretary of State (1940–44) and special assistant to the President for foreign affairs (1954–55), Rockefeller has three times been elected Governor of New York State (1958, 1962, 1966). Losing to Richard ⇨ Nixon in his attempt to gain the Republican Presidential nomination in 1960, he failed a second time four years later when Barry ⇨ Goldwater captured the nomination. Rockefeller led the liberal wing again in 1968 when he actively, but belatedly, sought his party's nomination for the third time. In spite of significant popular support, he failed to gain delegate support and again lost to Nixon.

Rogers, William Pierce (1913–). U S Secretary of State (1969–). A prominent lawyer, Rogers served as assistant District Attorney in New York (1938–42, 1946–47), and as counsel to a number of congressional investigating committees (1957–60). He was appointed U S Attorney General by President ⇨ Eisenhower (1957) after serving as deputy Attorney General (1950–53), and played an important part in the passage of the 1957 Civil Rights Act and the establishment of the Civil Rights Division in the Justice Department. It was whilst serving in the Eisenhower Administration that he established his close working association with Richard M. ⇨ Nixon, then Vice-President, and the latter nominated him as his Secretary of State immediately after winning the presidential election (1968). He was a member of the United States delegation to UNO and served on the organization's *ad hoc* Committee on South-West Africa (1967). He initiated the 'Rogers Peace Plan' for the Middle East, but this met with as little success as other peace plans for the area. As Secretary of State he was greatly overshadowed by presidential aide, Henry ⇨ Kissinger, upon whom Nixon tended to rely far more for diplomatic advice and action.

Röhm, Ernst (1887–1934). As 'Chief-of-Staff' of ⇨ Hitler's para-military storm-troops (SA), Röhm represented the militant, proletarian element within the Nazi movement. Invaluable in the days of street fighting, Röhm and his unruly storm-troopers became an embarrassment to Hitler after he had attained power. The SA's ambition to merge with the *Reichswehr*, the Weimar Republic's army of 100,000 professional soldiers, was opposed and resented by a Hitler now anxious to win the confidence of the army and its generals. To resolve the smouldering conflict, Hitler, under the pretext of preventing an SA uprising, the so-called 'Röhm Putsch', had Röhm and other SA leaders shot out of hand (June 1934). This event marked an important stage in consolidating Hitler's dictatorship.

Rollback. U S Secretary of State ⇨ Dulles' demand (1954) for action to liberate certain areas from communist domination, if necessary by force, particularly China and Eastern Europe. However, government policy has been one of ⇨ Containment, preventing further advances of communism, rather than rollback. This became evident during the 1956 Hungarian uprising when the United States failed to help the rebels.

Roman Catholic Church. ⇨ Vatican City State and Popes ⇨ Pius XII, ⇨ John XXIII and ⇨ Paul VI.

Rome Treaties (25.3.1957). Established the ⇨ EEC and ⇨ EURATOM, and laid down their institutional framework. Under it the Common Market members were to eliminate internal tariffs and all barriers to the movement of people, capital, goods and services in three four-year stages. External tariffs were to be adjusted until uniform throughout the area.

Roosevelt, Anna Eleanor (1884–1962). Wife of US President Franklin D. ⇨ Roosevelt. Several times a US delegate to the UN General Assembly, she was also Chairman of the UN Committee on Human Rights (1947). She was an active campaigner for ⇨ Civil Rights and for the social betterment of the American poor.

Roosevelt, Franklin D. (1882–1945). Thirty-second President of the United States, who led the nation through the ⇨ New Deal era and World War II. Elected as a Democrat to the New York State Senate (1910) he actively supported Woodrow Wilson for the presidency (1912), and was appointed Assistant Secretary of the Navy (1913–20). In office, Roosevelt began to formulate some of his political and economic ideas concerning the role of government and restricted competition, along with a conception of the presidency as a position of dynamic leadership. In 1920 he gained national prominence when he ran unsuccessfully for the vice-presidency with James Cox. Stricken the following year with poliomyelitis, Roosevelt demonstrated his great personal courage by his determination to remain in public life, and in 1928 was elected Governor of New York, though still partially paralysed. During his two terms as Governor (1928–32) he promoted conservation and social welfare programmes, enunciating his belief in the responsibility of the Federal Government in national problems. In accepting the Democratic nomination for the presidency in 1932, Roosevelt promised a 'New Deal' for victims of the Great Depression and was swept into office by voters grown tired of the Republicans. Taking advantage of the popular desire for action, he quickly initiated many progressive legislative programmes and secured their passage through Congress in his early months in office. During his first term, Roosevelt made use of the Press conference and radio to establish a unique relationship with the people – one that brought him a landslide re-election victory by 528 to 8 votes in the ⇨ Electoral College (1936). Somewhat restrained by the ⇨ Supreme Court in his second term, the President's programme did not produce the expected economic recovery which eventually came about only as a result of stimulation from the war in Europe. The war presented a problem for Roosevelt, who proved more capable of establishing good relations with Latin America than of convincing the American public of the necessity of aiding the Allies. After running successfully for an unprecedented third term as President (1940), Roosevelt gained greater freedom of action in foreign affairs and was able, for example, to evade the ⇨ Neutrality Acts. But war came when Japan launched a surprise attack on ⇨ Pearl Harbor (7.12.1941). Leading America in a war on two fronts, the President prevailed in the crucial decision to launch the major Allied offensive across the English Channel (1944) rather than through the Balkan route favoured by the British. Roosevelt represented the United States at several major conferences during the war years. His last, the ⇨ Yalta Conference (1945), proved to be a significant determinant of post-war European alignments. Re-elected for a fourth term as President (1944), Roosevelt died of a cerebral haemorrhage on 12 April 1945. He was succeeded by Vice-President Harry ⇨ Truman.

During his lifetime and after, Roosevelt always evoked strong feelings, both of admiration and criticism. A master political strategist, his technique as an administrator was never orderly but almost always effective. Having successfully led his nation through an extended period of crisis, he is considered one of the greatest American Presidents.

Rosenberg, Alfred (1893–1946). Chief ideologist of the Nazi Party during ⇨ Hitler's rise to power. After 1933 his influence declined. In the Third Reich he was *Reichsleiter* and head of the NSDAP's Foreign Policy Bureau (1933), supervisor of Party education (1934) and from 1941 Minister for the Occupied Territories of Eastern Europe. Was sentenced to death at ⇨ Nuremberg as one of the chief promoters of Nazi racialism.

Royal Commission (UK). A special committee of investigation appointed by the Crown on the initiative of Parliament. It is intended to be non-partisan – members may include MPs, government officials or private individuals – and is appointed to gather evidence both from experts and from the general public. A Royal Commission can have several purposes: it may provide background information for major reforms and it may also be a result of public pressure on a controversial issue and a means of postponing a decision. It provides a substitute for specialist parliamentary committees and differs from an ordinary commission of enquiry in that it enjoys more prestige and its enquiries may last several years. The Royal Commission may make legislative proposals but the Government has no obligation to accept them.

RPF. *Rassemblement du Peuple Français* (Rally of the French People) – founded (7.4.1947) to promote ⇨ de Gaulle's return to power after his resignation and refusal to govern within the planned framework of the ⇨ Fourth Republic (20.1.1946). Opposed to 'party rule', inviting the 'vast French masses' to forsake sectional interests and to bring about 'a fundamental reform of the state', the movement's authoritarian approach appealed to the conservatives and produced the 'de Gaulle miracle' when it polled 40% of the vote in the municipal elections of Oct. 1947. The RPF's anti-parliamentarian, anti-European, anti-American, anti-communist stance led to its rapid decline. It polled 30% of the vote in the Senate Elections (Nov. 1948), 21% in the general elections (June 1951) and a bare 10% in the municipal elections (April 1953). De Gaulle dissociated himself from the movement (April 1953), which no longer formally acknowledged by him continued from 1954 as the *Union Républicaine et d'Action Sociale*.

RSFSR. Abbreviation for Russian Socialist Federal Soviet Republic, the largest of the 15 Federal Republics constituting the USSR. *Capital* – Moscow. The RSFSR is sub-divided into 16 autonomous Republics, 6 Regions (which, in turn, contain 5 autonomous Provinces) and 49 Provinces.

Ruanda-Urundi. ⇨ Burundi and ⇨ Rwanda.

Rules Committee. A standing committee of the US ⇨ House of Representatives that regulates its legislative programme. All proposed legislation must be referred to this committee, and the 'rule' that it gives the proposal may determine whether it will be considered by the House at all and, if so, with what urgency, and whether or not amendments to it will be allowed. Consequently, the Rules Committee is one of the most powerful of all ⇨ Congressional Committees. The committee was long dominated by conservative members of the ⇨ Democratic Party and the ⇨ Republican Party acting together, especially before 1961. In that year its membership was increased from 12 to 15 in an attempt to make it a more liberal body, but this had only a limited effect. In 1965 the House took steps to reduce the power of the committee by amending the rules governing its control over the legislative programme. Under the amended rules, the Speaker of the House of Representatives could 'recognize' the chairman or authorized spokesman of a legislative committee seeking to bring forward a measure for consideration by the

House if the Rules Committee had failed to report favourably on it within 21 days. However, the committee has retained a great measure of its influence over legislation.

Rumania, Socialist Republic of. *Area* – 91,671 sq. miles. *Population* (1970 est.) – 20,250,000. *President of the State Council* – Nicolae ⇨ Ceausescu (1967–). *President, Council of Ministers* – Ion Gheorghe Maurer (1961–). *General Secretary, Communist Party* – Nicolae Ceausescu (1965–). The highest organ of state power is the Grand National Assembly, a one-chamber Legislature, elected by universal suffrage from a single list of candidates. Effective power is exercised by the Communist Party under the leadership of its General Secretary, Nicolae Ceausescu.

Inter-war Rumania was for long dominated by King Carol II who, after his restoration in 1930, skilfully split and weakened the traditional political parties until he established his own royal dictatorship (Jan. 1938). During the same period the Fascist Iron Guards grew in power. King Carol tried to curb them by having some of their leaders arrested and shot, but he was unable to stand up to their German patrons. Forced by combined German-Soviet pressure to relinquish ⇨ Bessarabia and North Bukovina to the USSR, North ⇨ Transylvania to Hungary and South ⇨ Dobrudja to Bulgaria, he had to abdicate in favour of his son Michael (Sept. 1940). Effective power then passed to the pro-German General Antonescu who headed a government composed first of both members of the Iron Guards and representatives of the old ruling classes. After mounting Iron Guard atrocities and massacres of Gentiles as well as Jews, Antonescu repressed the Iron Guards with German consent. In June 1941, Rumania joined Hitler's invasion of the USSR, recovering Bessarabia and North Bukovina and annexing a large chunk of Soviet territory. Inside the country heavy casualties and German arrogance produced increasing war weariness. On 23 Aug. 1944 King Michael took the initiative in having Antonescu arrested, ending the war with the Allies, declaring war on Germany and installing a new government composed of anti-Axis generals and the leaders of the National Peasant, Liberal, Communist and Socialist parties. The USSR recovered its former territories and the Red Army arrived in Rumania.

⇨ Sovietization began with the arrival of the Soviet Deputy Foreign Minister, A. ⇨ Vyshinsky (Feb. 1945), who ordered King Michael to appoint a new government of the 'National Democratic Front'. The new Premier was Petru Groza, leader of the Ploughmen's Front, a left-wing peasant group under communist influence, while the vital Ministries of the Interior, Justice and the National Economy were immediately taken over by communists. Elections held (Nov. 1946) in an atmosphere of intimidation and resulting, in many places, in faked returns, gave the government Front a huge majority. Terror increased in 1947 when most opposition leaders were arrested and the socialists came under growing pressure to merge with the Communist Party. In Dec. 1947, King Michael was forced to abdicate. Soon afterwards fusion between socialists and communists was imposed. The opposition socialists and all other non-communist parties were outlawed. Sovietization was completed early in 1948 when Rumania was proclaimed a People's Republic (later renamed Socialist Republic).

Before their seizure of power, the communists had been singularly uninfluential. Until the late 1950s, when they began to attract a measure of popular support, they were forced to rely exclusively on police terror and Soviet protection which they repaid by unconditional subservience to ⮞ Stalin. Their self-assertion began during the ⮞ Khrushchev era. In 1956, Moscow dissolved the last of the joint Soviet-Rumanian companies, till then a source of blatant Soviet economic exploitation. In 1957, the Communist Party Leader, ⮞ Gheorghiu-Dej, after a series of purges of all his potential rivals, had made his own power unassailable. In 1958, the Soviet troops hitherto stationed in Rumania were withdrawn. Thereafter Rumania embarked on an ambitious economic development programme which its leaders refused to abandon for the supra-national ⮞ CMEA plans favoured by the USSR. Rumanian defiance of Moscow in these and other matters was facilitated by the aggravation of the ⮞ Sino-Soviet Conflict which gave Gheorghiu-Dej more room for manoeuvre. From 1963 onwards Bucharest's attitudes to ⮞ China began to diverge openly from those of Moscow. At the same time, patently anti-Russian, nationalist gestures multiplied and gained the regime increasing popularity. The new trend towards national self-assertion became still more pronounced after Gheorghiu-Dej's death and the ascent to power of Nicolae Ceausescu in March 1965. Insisting on each country's inalienable right to determine its own foreign and domestic policy, Bucharest has since then defied Moscow and its other ⮞ Warsaw Pact allies on a large number of vital issues. Rumania has established increasingly fruitful economic and cultural relations with many Western countries. Against strong East German opposition, it has established diplomatic relations with the Federal German Republic. It refused to take sides in the Middle East war of 1967 and to follow the example of the other Warsaw Pact countries in breaking off diplomatic relations with Israel. It has normalized relations with ⮞ Albania and established close ties with ⮞ Yugoslavia. It refused to participate in the invasion of ⮞ Czechoslovakia and immediately afterwards sharply condemned it. Some weeks later official reactions became more restrained in an evident effort to avoid giving Moscow a pretext for intervention in Rumania. The Rumanian leaders have, however, upheld their basic attitudes, and they have, in the course of 1968, made a simultaneous successful bid for broader popular support by seeking to create a bond of national unity between the national minorities and the Rumanian peoples, by the rehabilitation of a large number of victims of past political persecutions (including Gheorghiu-Dej's victims) and by a number of measures designed to strengthen the effective rule of law and a degree of popular participation in decision making.

Rumor, Mariano (1915–). Prime Minister of ⇨ Italy (Nov. 1960–July 1970), as head of a Christian Democratic coalition with the Socialists. He was formerly Minister of Agriculture (1959–63) and secretary of the Christian Democratic Party (from 1964).

Runoff Primary. Type of ⇨ Primary Election in the USA.

Rusk, David Dean (1909–). US Secretary of State under Presidents ⇨ Kennedy and ⇨ Johnson. He was director of the Office of UN Affairs (1947–49) and deputy Under-Secretary of State (1949–50). As Assistant Secretary of State for Far Eastern Affairs (1950–51) he was a strong supporter of President ⇨ Truman's policies in Korea. After serving for eight years as President of the Rockefeller Foundation, he was appointed by President-elect Kennedy as his Secretary of State (1960). Often overshadowed because of the President's keen interest in foreign affairs, Rusk was active throughout the many international crises of the early sixties. He remained Secretary of State until the inauguration of President ⇨ Nixon (Jan. 1969), and was throughout a staunch defender of the policies of the Johnson Administration.

Russo-Finnish War. ⇨ Finland.

Rwanda. *Area* – 10,000 sq. miles. *Population* (1969 est.) – 3,500,000. *President* – Grégoire Kayibanda. *Constitution* (1962) – Republic with a President and uni-cameral National Assembly.

Formerly part of the Belgian-administered Trust Territory of Ruanda-Urundi, Rwanda became independent on 1 July 1962. Its recent history has been marked by bitter tribal conflict including large-scale massacres (Dec. 1963). The monarchy was abolished through a referendum held at the same time as the first (UN-supervised) general election (Oct. 1961).

Rykov, A. I. (1881–1938). Soviet communist. An early ⇨ Bolshevik, Rykov was one of the 'conciliators' who favoured healing the split with the Menshevik wing of the Russian Social Democratic Party. Despite repeated differences with Lenin, he occupied leading positions after the victory of the Oct. revolution. From 1918 to 1920 and again from 1923 to 1924 he was Chairman of the Supreme Council of the National Economy and, from 1921 to 1924, Deputy Chairman of the Council of People's Commissars. In 1924 (after Lenin's death) he succeeded Lenin as Chairman of the Council of People's Commissars. A member of the Party's Politbureau from 1922, Rykov sided with ⇨ Bukharin in opposing ⇨ Stalin's turn towards compulsory collectivization. He was expelled in 1930, and in 1938 was one of Bukharin's leading co-defendants in the last of the three ⇨ Moscow Trials. He was convicted and executed as a traitor.

S

Saar. *Area* – 991 sq. miles. *Population* (1965) – 1,200,000.

The Saar is part of the German Rhineland on the left bank of the river. Because of its great mineral wealth (1954 production: coal 168 m. tons; steel 2·8 m. tons) the Versailles peace-makers handed the territory over to the French who under a ⇨ League of Nations administration were to work the mines for 15 years at the end of which a plebiscite was to decide the territory's national status. In Feb. 1935 more than 90% of the people opted for union with Germany. After ⇨ World War II, France dropped outright annexation schemes in favour of an economic union and local autonomy. This solution was endorsed by the Saarlanders in the Oct. 1947 elections. However, the precarious autonomy, thinly veiling French rule, lost its local appeal when Germany's economic recovery outstripped that of France. Efforts to disenfranchise the pro-German vote (1952) and to 'Europeanize' the territory under ⇨ WEU auspices failed (1953–54) when the Saar Diet (*Landtag*) refused to ratify Franco-German agreements regarding the territory's status. The Saar rejoined the German Federal Republic (Jan. 1957) conceding France special mineral extraction rights and other economic privileges. In Oct. 1959 it was, by agreement with France whose extraction concession was to run until 1981, economically integrated into the Federal Republic.

Sabah, Sheikh Sabah As-Salim As- (1913–). Emir of ⇨ Kuwait since 1965, he was previously deputy Prime Minister and Minister of Foreign Affairs (1962–63), and Prime Minister (1963–65).

Salan, Raoul, General (1899–). Former French Army C.-in-C., who, after his retirement, joined the abortive Algiers revolt (22.4.1961) against President ⇨ de Gaulle and the ⇨ Fifth Republic. Condemned to death *in absentia* as the military leader of the terrorist ⇨ OAS, this sentence was commuted to life imprisonment after his arrest in Algiers (20.4.1962) and retrial in ⇨ France. He was released from prison (June 1968) when de Gaulle pardoned former OAS leaders after the May 1968 riots.

Salazar, Dr Antonio de Oliveira (1889–1970). Prime Minister of ⇨ Portugal (1932–68), the longest-serving Prime Minister in recent history. A professor of economics, he became Minister of Finance (1928), restored financial stability and thereafter became virtual dictator. As well as being Prime Minister he was also Minister of War (1936–44) and Minister of Foreign Affairs (1936–47). He established a corporative state (1933 constitution) but although his rule had many affinities with European Fascist dictatorships of the period, Salazar maintained Portugal's neutrality both in the Spanish Civil War and in World War II. After the war Portugal became a member of several Western alliances, but Salazar was an opponent of both liberalization at home and independence for the colonies. He retired in Sept. 1968 following a serious operation, having dominated Portugal's politics for 40 years.

Sallal, Abdullah (1917–). President of the ⇨ Yemen 1962–67 and concurrently Prime Minister (1962–64, 1966–67) and Foreign Minister (1963–64). He led the revolution against the rule of the Imams in 1962. He established closer relations with the U A R and the communist states but his efforts to create a new republican state were hindered by civil war with the royalists and by opposition from other republicans. He was overthrown in Nov. 1967.

Samoa. ⇨ Western Samoa and ⇨ American Samoa.

Sanchez-Vilella, Roberto (1913–). Elected Governor of Puerto Rico in 1964, succeeding ⇨ Munoz Marin.

Sandys, Duncan (1908–). U K Conservative politician; Minister of Defence (1957–59), Secretary of State for Commonwealth Relations (1960–64) and also for the Colonies (1962–64) and member of the Shadow Cabinet (1965–66). He was chairman of the War Cabinet Committee for defence against German 'V' weapons (1943–45) and in 1947 founded the European Movement. Since his time as Colonial Secretary, Sandys has moved to the right on questions like Commonwealth immigration and has advocated acceptance of the Smith regime in ⇨ Rhodesia.

Sao Tome and Principe Islands. ⇨ Portuguese Overseas Provinces.

Saragat, Giuseppe (1898–). President of ⇨ Italy since 1964. The country's first Social Democratic Head of State, he was formerly deputy Prime Minister (1947–49, 1954–57) and Minister of Foreign Affairs (1963–64).

Sarawak. ⇨ Malaysia.

Sarit Thanarat, Field-Marshal (1908–63). Prime Minister of ⇨ Thailand (1959–63) after, as C.-in-C. of the army, leading a successful military coup which overthrew ⇨ Pibul Songgram. Although he established a military dictatorship, his years in office were marked by increased attention to economic development, an alliance with the West and growing communist insurgency.

Satellite. Term frequently used in the West for the states under the domination of the USSR. (⇨ Sovietization.)

Sato, Eisaku (1901–). Prime Minister of ⇨ Japan (1964–72) and leader of the Liberal Democratic Party. His previous posts included Minister of Finance (1958–60) and Minister of Internal Trade and Industry (1961–62). He resigned in 1972 and was succeeded by Kakuei Tanaka.

Saud, King (1901–). King of ⇨ Saudi Arabia (1953–64), son of King ⇨ Ibn Saud (1932–53). He was also his own Prime Minister (1953–58, 1960–62) but disagreed over policy with his brother ⇨ Faisal, who was Prime Minister in the intervening years. In 1964 he was deposed and replaced by Faisal.

Saudi Arabia. *Area* – 850,000 sq. miles. *Population* (1969 est.) – 7,200,000. *Head of State* – King ⇨ Faisal (1964–). *Constitution* – Independent Islamic Kingdom. The King is virtually an absolute monarch; he is both Prime Minister and Foreign Minister, but is advised by a Council of Ministers.

Saudi Arabia was formed in 1932 after the union of the provinces of Najd and Hijaz and other territories. King ⇨ Ibn Saud (1932–53) concentrated on unifying and developing the country – communications were modernized, land settlements established and the nomadic Bedouins were encouraged to abandon their tribal vendettas. The country suffered economically during World War II but the discovery of oil in 1936 and its exploitation from the war period onwards transformed the economy. These oil reserves are among the richest in the world – production increased from 26 million metric tons in 1950 to 75 million in 1962. Otherwise the country is still undeveloped and the modernization of a feudal society is a slow process – slavery was abolished officially as late as 1963. During the 1950s ministerial government began to develop. The office of Prime Minister was created in 1953 but this was occupied by the King himself (King ⇨ Saud 1953–64, King Faisal since 1964) except for intervals when it was occupied by the Crown Prince (1953, 1958–60, 1962–64). Saudi Arabia has played a loyal but minor part as a member of the ⇨ Arab League, which she helped to found in 1945 – in 1948 she contributed a small force in the war against ⇨ Israel. Her cautious attitude in inter-Arab affairs has accounted in part for her changing relations with the ⇨ United Arab Republic. She concluded mutual defence pacts with Egypt and Syria (1955) but refused to join either the UAR or the rival Arab Federation. Relations with the UAR worsened in 1958 with charges that each side had tried to assassinate the other's Head of State. Saud visited Cairo (1959) but relations deteriorated again after Saudi Arabia supported Syria in her break with the UAR (1961) and with the civil war in the ⇨Yemen (1962–65), when Saudi Arabia assisted the monarchists while the UAR supported the republicans. Diplomatic relations were severed from 1962 until 1964. In the Arab-Israeli War of June 1967 (⇨Arab-Israeli Conflict) Saudi Arabia gave moral support to the Arab cause but did not take up arms. After the war she gave financial aid to Jordan and the UAR to help restore their economic strength. Arab guerrillas also depend on Saudi Arabian financial support. Since 1945 Saudi Arabia has received economic and military aid from the USA.

Schuman, R. (1886–1963). Member of the ⇨MRP (1945–62), Prime Minister (Nov. 1947–July 1948), Foreign Secretary (July 1948–Jan. 1953), one of the most prominent politicians of the ⇨Fourth Republic and a chief architect of European integration. The so-called Schuman Plan, prepared by the French planning authority under ⇨Monnet (9.5.1950), led to the setting up of the ⇨ECSC (18.4.1951). He resigned as Foreign Secretary when the Assembly opposed his efforts to create a genuine European Defence Force, and although he held further Cabinet posts, his main impact on French political thought remained his advocacy of European integration. President of the Strasbourg European Parliament, he retired from political life in 1962.

Schuschnigg, Kurt von (1897–). Chancellor of ⇨Austria (1934–38) who unsuccessfully resisted the annexation of his country by Nazi Germany. Minister of Justice and Education (1932–34), he was a close collaborator of Chancellor ⇨Dollfuss, whom he succeeded when the latter was assassinated by Austrian Nazis. He continued Dollfuss' policies – the corporative state at home and the reliance on support from Italy against the German threat. When after the formation of the Rome-Berlin ⇨Axis Italian support ceased, Schuschnigg sought to defend his now much weakened position by appeasing ⇨Hitler. Hitler's demands on Austria became more persistent and in Feb. 1938 he treated Schuschnigg to a humiliating interview at Berchtesgaden. Schuschnigg failed, however, to prevent the forced ⇨*Anschluss* with Germany and resigned. During the war he was imprisoned by the Nazis and emigrated to the USA in 1947.

SCLC. Southern Christian Leadership Conference – an association in the USA, mainly of Negro Southern Baptists, organized by the Rev. Martin Luther ⇨King in 1955 (initially in connexion with the bus-boycott in ⇨Montgomery, Alabama) to fight against ⇨Segregation in the South by non-violent means. It gave immediate support to the ⇨Sit-ins beginning in 1960, and played a leading role in the formation of ⇨ SNCC. Under the leadership of Dr King it maintained its non-violent stance in the face of taunts by more militant groups that its members were ⇨'Uncle Toms'.

SDS. Students for a Democratic Society – in the USA, a political association within the ⇨ New Left. Formed in 1962, it rapidly became the largest of the many New Left student organizations, working closely with ⇨ SNCC in the Negro ⇨ Civil Rights Movement, and leading student opposition to the Vietnam War and the ⇨ Draft. In the context of the German New Left, SDS stands for *Sozialistischer Deutscher Studentenbund*. It is the most important radical students' organization and it resembles its American namesake in outlook and militancy.

SEATO. South-East Asia Treaty Organization – collective defence treaty signed in 1954 in Manila by Australia, France, New Zealand, Pakistan, the Philippines, Thailand, the UK and the USA, following the defeat of the French in Indochina. The signatories agreed to take collective action to resist armed attacks on themselves and Laos, Cambodia and South Vietnam, to counter subversion of their governments and to cooperate in economic matters. The Treaty Organization, with its headquarters in Bangkok, includes the Secretariat-General and a military planning office. The SEATO Council, consisting of the Foreign Ministers of the member countries, decides general policies and usually meets once a year. SEATO has no standing force nor any integrated command structure but relies on the forces of the member nations, especially the USA. France, because of her disagreement with American policy in Vietnam, no longer cooperates with SEATO.

Second Bandung Conference. ⇨ Bandung Conference.

Second International. Founded in 1889 as a successor to the First International, the 'International Working-men's Association' (1864–76), the Second International was in its early period dominated by socialists under the influence of Marxist ideas. Committed to joint international action for the prevention of war, most of its member parties nevertheless supported their respective governments at the outbreak of World War 1. After the foundation of the (Third) ⇨ Communist International, which was supposed to take its place, the Second International was reconstituted in the 1920s as the Labour and Socialist International – a loose association of labour and social democratic parties, in which form it has continued ever since.

Secretary of State. In the USA, senior member of the President's ⇨ Cabinet and head of the ⇨ State Department. He is appointed by the President with the consent of the Senate (in this case, usually a formality) and may be dismissed by the President at any time. As departmental head he has extensive administrative responsibilities, especially in connexion with the foreign service; but in recent times these have tended to be delegated to subordinate officials, leaving the Secretary free to deal with major foreign policy questions. Primary responsibility for United States foreign policy rests with the President, however, and it is now usual for him to make many minor decisions as well as all major ones. He does so, moreover, in consultation with many advisers besides the Secretary of State, sometimes informally, and sometimes through such agencies as ⇨ NSC. But should the President choose to limit his involvement in foreign affairs, great power and influence may pass to his Secretary of State, as happened in the case of John Foster ⇨ Dulles under President ⇨ Eisenhower (though afterwards it was the Vice-President, Richard M. ⇨ Nixon, who rose to prominence in foreign affairs). In any case, the office is often filled by men of great eminence. Apart from Dulles, notable recent Secretaries include George ⇨ Marshall and Dean ⇨ Acheson (both under President ⇨ Truman).

Security Council. ⇨ United Nations.

Segregation. In the USA, the separation of one racial group from another, in public and private institutions and facilities. The tradition of legal segregation was sanctioned by the Supreme Court decision in Plessy v. Ferguson (1896) which upheld such 'Jim Crow' laws on the condition that 'separate but equal' facilities be provided. In 1954 the Court reversed its ruling in a landmark decision on school segregation (Brown v. Board of Education) maintaining that segregation deprived Negroes of their constitutionally guaranteed equality. This encouraged demands for ⇨ Integration, culminating in the ⇨ Sit-Ins of the early 1960s. ⇨ White Citizens Councils were formed to resist desegregation, opposition to which reached a peak at Little Rock, Arkansas, in 1957, necessitating the despatch of Federal troops to maintain order.

Selective Service System. In the USA, the Federal organization dealing with military conscription. The selection of conscripts is the responsibility of local 'draft boards' who grant exemptions and defer-ments on grounds laid down by Federal law. Appeals against their decisions can be made to special judicial-district boards. The 'draft' tended in the past to bypass students, especially in graduate schools; but with the escalation of the Vietnam War this ceased to be so. One consequence of the change was an increase in student resistance to both the War and the draft, led by ⇨ SDS and symbolized by the burning of 'draft cards'. Black militants have pointed to the disproportionate number of Negroes selected, and have called for desertion, especially in Vietnam. After the 1968 elections, various proposals were canvassed for modifying or abolishing the draft. In 1970, a ⇨ Senate sub-committee, headed by Senator Edward ⇨ Kennedy, criticized the operation of the

System, and made proposals for eliminating some anomalies, which were accepted. In 1971, the draft was extended for a period of two years, but only after the previous extension had already expired; and in 1972 consideration began of proposals to end the draft altogether and change to all-volunteer forces.

Senanayake, Dudley (1911–). Prime Minister of ⇨Ceylon since 1965 and leader of the United National Party. Son of D. S. Senanayake who founded the party, he was formerly Prime Minister from 1952 to 1953 and in 1960. From 1961 to 1965 he was Leader of the Opposition.

Senate. The second and smaller of the two houses of ⇨Congress in the USA, the other being the ⇨House of Representatives. The Senate is composed of two elected Senators from every State, irrespective of the size of its population. The full membership is currently 100. Minimum qualifications for membership as laid down in the Constitution are that a member must be 30 years of age, nine years a citizen of the USA and, when elected, an inhabitant of the State for which he is chosen. Senators serve for a six-year term, a third retiring every two years, when they may stand for re-election. By the terms of the Seventeenth Amendment to the Constitution (ratified 1913) Senators are elected by the people of their States. Previously, they were elected by the State Legislatures. As a result of the elections held on 3 Nov. 1970, the state of the parties in the Senate was: ⇨ Democratic Party, 55; ⇨ Republican Party, 43; others, 2. Any casual vacancy in the Senate is usually filled by temporary appointment by the Governor of the State concerned.

The President of the Senate is the Vice-President of the USA *ex officio*, or, in his absence (which is frequent), a President *pro tempore*, who is a member of the majority party. When the Vice-President presides he may not speak in debate and he may vote only in the event of the Senators dividing equally. The office of President *pro tempore* of the Senate has not acquired the importance of that of the Speaker of the House of Representatives.

The powers of the Senate are similar to those of the House, with some relatively minor differences. The principal business of the Senate, as of the House is legislation, though measures for raising revenue must originate in the House. Much of the legislative work is done in standing ⇨ Congressional Committees in both houses. One very important special power of the Senate is that of consenting to presidential appointments, which gives its members a measure of control over political patronage, regulated by the custom of ⇨ Senatorial Courtesy. In 1968 the Senate refused its consent to President Johnson's appointment of Abe Fortas as Chief Justice of the Supreme Court. Also important is the requirement that the Senate must give its consent, by a two-thirds majority of those present, for the ratification of any treaty between the USA and a foreign power. This, together with the requirement for senatorial approval of foreign-service appointments, has given the Senate a considerable voice in foreign affairs. Most treaties proposed by the President are in fact ratified by the Senate, but there have been some notable exceptions – for example, the Treaty of Versailles (involving membership of the USA in the League of Nations), and the protocol for participation of the USA in the World Court at the Hague. Though not strictly required, leading Senators can be brought into treaty negotiations so as to increase the likelihood that the Senate will ratify a treaty; but equally, the possibility of rejection by the Senate can inhibit the President in negotiations with foreign leaders. In recent times, because of the difficulties inherent in this power of the Senate, there has been increasing resort to instruments other than formal treaties. The ⇨European Recovery Programme, ⇨Point Four, and the ⇨Formosa Resolution were adopted by ordinary legislative procedures (involving the House as much as the Senate), whilst the most frequently employed instrument is the ⇨Executive Agreement. For such reasons the differences between the two houses in foreign affairs are becoming less important. The ⇨ Bricker Amendment has been proposed to reverse this trend. One further difference is that the Senate has the sole power to try cases of impeachment, but this is of little practical importance nowadays.

The rules and procedures of the Senate are less stringent than those of the House. The rules governing its debates are particularly lax, and the procedure for closing debate is so difficult to apply that it is always possible for a small number of Senators to conduct a ⇨ Filibuster to delay or prevent legislation they dislike.

Partly because of the longer terms of Senators, and partly because of their smaller numbers, the Senate has been able to maintain a higher standard of public debate than the House; and its relaxed way of conducting business increases rather than diminishes public esteem for it. The Senate is generally more liberal than the House, and not more conservative as its founders expected. However, the House of Representatives is in many ways closer to the people, and reflects popular feeling more accurately and more quickly than the Senate.

Senatorial Courtesy. Custom of the US ⇨Senate whereby consent to presidential appointments affecting a particular State is conditional on the approval of the majority-party Senator(s) from that State. Its application is particularly important with regard to the appointment of Federal law officers within the States.

Senegal. *Area* – 76,000 sq. miles. *Population* (1970 est.) – 3,800,000.

Head of State and President of the Council – President Léopold-Sédar ⇨ Senghor. *Constitution* (1963) – Executive power vested in an elected President who (in an emergency) can rule by decree. All seats in the National Assembly go to the party polling a majority of votes in the elections.

Senegal, an independent Republic in the ⇨ French Community, was the oldest French colony in Africa (represented in the French Parliament from 1848 and Dakar was the administrative capital of ⇨ French West Africa) with the result that it has a significant and long-established French-educated professional and technical middle-class. In 1958 Senegal became a self-governing republic within the Community. As part of the ⇨ Mali Federation formed with ⇨ French Soudan (1959) it achieved full independence in June 1960. When the Federation was dissolved in Aug. 1960, Senegal rejoined the Community as an independent republic. Senegal's failure (1957–58 and 1959) to form larger federal groupings has left it without the population and natural resources for rapid economic development despite its educated élite and its former political pre-eminence in French West Africa. The Prime Minister, M. Mamadou Dia was arrested in 1962 when his attempted coup against President Senghor failed. Under the new constitution, the President incorporates the functions of the Prime Minister and appoints the Council of Ministers. Senegal is a member of ⇨ OCAM and of the ⇨ Senegal River States Organization. The Senegalese are anxious for closer ties with the ⇨ Gambia which forms an enclave in their Republic, and in April 1967 a Treaty of Association was signed by the two countries, providing for closer cooperation.

Senegal River States Organization. Comprises ⇨ Guinea, ⇨ Mali, ⇨ Mauritania, ⇨ Senegal and aims at joint regional economic development.

Senghor, Léopold-Sédar (1906–). Poet and author (considered for the Nobel Prize for Literature in 1962) President of ⇨ Senegal. Despite involvement in French affairs (a former Deputy and French delegate to UNESCO) and insistence on close ties with France, Senghor is also an exponent of *négritude*. Senghor is the dominating influence in Senegal politics especially since the 1963 constitution which gives the President a near monopoly of executive power. (⇨ Mali, Federation of.)

Seniority Rule. Custom of US Congress whereby committee chairmanships are awarded to members of the majority party with the longest service on a committee. The system has been criticized for holding back able men while steadily advancing mediocre ones, and filling most key positions with conservatives of both parties who tend to come from 'safe' districts.

'Separate but Equal'. A legal doctrine in the USA formerly sanctioned by the ⇨ Supreme Court which ruled (in 1896) that ⇨ Segregation was constitutional provided separate facilities for the two races were equal. This ruling upheld ⇨ Jim Crow Laws previously and subsequently enacted in the Southern States. In 1954, the Court finally reversed the ruling by its decision in ⇨ Brown v. Board of Education.

Separation of Powers. Constitutional doctrine that for the avoidance of tyranny the several powers or functions of government should be exercised by separate persons or institutions. Though the doctrine can be traced back to Aristotle, its modern version was developed by European political philosophers of the seventeenth and eighteenth centuries, notably Locke in England and Montesquieu in France, and is based on their observations of the British Constitution during the period of transition from royal to parliamentary government. The 'powers' are those of making, executing, and administering laws – legislative, executive and judicial. It is to be noted that the reference in each case is to law, not 'policy'. This has always raised problems regarding the application of the doctrine, and it does so more than ever at the present time. Where the doctrine is not applied there is said to be a 'fusion' or 'conjunction' of powers, as in Great Britain. The most important example of the doctrine in operation is found in the USA, where the Federal Constitution vests the legislative, executive and judicial powers in ⇨ Congress, the President, and the ⇨ Supreme Court respectively. However, though the institutions are strictly separate as regards personnel (membership in any one is incompatible with membership in any other), their powers are partly conjoint. Thus, appointments to the Supreme Court are made by the President with the consent of the Senate. For this reason, the separation of powers in the USA is best regarded as one aspect of the system of ⇨ Checks and Balances rather than a strict application of the doctrine. However, the USA does illustrate the difficulties of applying the doctrine in modern conditions, when urgent considerations of policy claim more attention than settled processes of law. The executive acquires 'quasi-legislative' and 'quasi-judicial' powers of its own, and the distinctions on which the doctrine is based break down. This is especially true in the fields of foreign and economic policy where speed, flexibility and secrecy are necessary for successful action. The growing powers of the President in these fields are illustrated by the increasing recourse to ⇨ Executive Agreements, ⇨ Executive War; and such instruments of 'delegated legislation' as the ⇨ Trade Expansion Act (1962). Welfare programmes create similar needs, and in addition entail the establishment of large administrative agencies which normally come under the control of the Executive and thus strengthen it. The ⇨ Independent Regulatory Commission was intended to retain for Congress some control over administrative operations, and the ⇨ Bricker Amendment was intended to reverse the trend towards executive domination in foreign relations. But the separation of powers continues to be undermined to the advantage of the Executive. In other countries the process has gone even further. In ⇨ France, in particular, the Constitution of the Fifth Republic specifically restricts the legislative powers of Parliament and reserves others to the Executive, thus formally reversing the assumptions on which the doctrine of separation is based.

Serbia. ⇨ Yugoslavia.

Seyss-Inquart, Arthur (1892–1946). Austrian Nazi leader co-opted in Feb. 1938 (on Hitler's insistence) into Cabinet of ⇨ Schuschnigg whom he replaced as Chancellor on 11 March. He called in German troops to prevent 'disorders' and proclaimed the ⇨ *Anschluss*. Wartime governor of Holland from 1940, he was tried at ⇨ Nuremberg in 1946 on charges of ordering mass deportations of Jews to death camps and other war crimes; convicted and hanged.

Shadow Cabinet (UK Parliament). Consists of senior members of the Opposition who are the Party spokesmen on specific topics (e.g. Foreign affairs, Defence, etc.). Only the Leader of the Opposition holds an official position (since 1937) and as he chooses its members, he can use the Shadow Cabinet to increase his popularity or authority through the promotion or demotion of party members.

Sharjah. ⇨ Trucial States.

Sharpeville (⇨ South Africa). On 21 March 1960, following the lead of the ⇨ Pan-African Congress, Africans gathered in the township of Sharpeville (near Vereeniging) to demonstrate against the Pass Laws. Police, equipped with automatic weapons, opened fire on the demonstrators. It was estimated that over 80 Africans were killed and more than 360 injured. African leaders claimed that the demonstration was peaceful and the massacre an example of South African police brutality. The police claimed that the crowd was in a dangerous mood threatening violence. Sharpeville was followed by police raids on African townships throughout South Africa. A state of emergency was declared followed by a wave of arrests and the ⇨ PAC and ⇨ ANC were banned. There was a brief decline in confidence in the South African economy and South Africa was attacked in international organizations. Like the ⇨ Treason Trials, Sharpeville was not a happy advertisement for the benefits of ⇨ *Apartheid*. In the same year South Africa left the Commonwealth.

Shastri, Lal Bahadur (1904–66). Succeeded ⇨ Nehru as Prime Minister of ⇨ India (1964–66). He was active in the Congress Movement from 1921 and held the posts of Minister of Railways (1952–56), Minister of Transport (1957–58), Minister of Commerce (1958–61) and Minister of Internal Affairs (1961–63). The main event during his short period as Prime Minister was the outbreak of war with Pakistan in 1965 over the Rann of Kutch. Shastri met President Ayub ⇨ Khan the following January to agree on the peaceful solution of future differences between the two countries, but died at the end of the conference.

Sherman Antitrust Act. In USA, a measure to promote competition and prevent monopolies, adopted in 1890 in accordance with the ⇨ Commerce Clause. It was supplemented in 1914 by the Clayton Act, the ⇨ FTC being established in the following year to enforce certain of its provisions. Various exemptions were specifically made under subsequent legislation. The extent of enforcement of the legislation, which is the responsibility of a Division of the Department of Justice, has varied from era to era, as has the interpretation of its terms by the ⇨ Supreme Court. During the ⇨ New Deal period the antitrust policy was more vigorously pursued, and this has been true in the postwar period, also.

Show Trials. Sham legal procedures, repeatedly used in the USSR and other communist countries during the ⇨ Stalin era, designed to dramatize specific political campaigns and/or eliminate prominent individuals. Conviction in show trials is exclusively based on a combination of public confession and the mutual incrimination of various co-defendants, without any kind of independent evidence. In all cases public confession followed extensive periods of preliminary interrogation and 'investigation' by the Secret Police. All the defendants ever appearing at a show trial had previously provided the Secret Police with signed confessions of guilt. In a few exceptional cases, defendants later attempted to retract their confessions in open Court, but such retractions had no influence on the pre-arranged verdicts.

In the first show trials in the USSR (the Shakhty Trial of March 1928, the 'Industrial Party' trial of Nov./Dec. 1930, the trial of former Mensheviks of March 1931, and the Metro-Vickers Trial of April 1933) the defendants were non-communists. The techniques used in these first show trials were similar to those later employed in the ⇨ Moscow Trials of old ⇨ Bolsheviks, but they had not yet been fully developed and were later further refined.

After World War II, the techniques of the show trials were exported from the USSR to Eastern Europe. Employed first against prominent non-communists in the countries under Soviet domination, they were later used against top-ranking communist leaders, among them Koci Xoxe of Albania (executed June 1949), Laszlo Rajk of Hungary (executed Oct. 1949), Traicho Kostov of Bulgaria (executed Dec. 1949) and Rudolf Slansky of Czechoslovakia (executed Nov. 1952).

Sierra Leone. *Area* – 27,699 sq. miles. *Population* (approx.) – 2,180,000. *Prime Minister* – Mr Siaka Stevens. *Constitution* (1961) – Independent state within the Commonwealth, with a Governor-General (representing the Queen), a Prime Minister and a House of Representatives, elected by universal suffrage except for ten chiefs. In 1971 it became a republic.

From 1896 until its first elected House of Representatives (1937), Sierra Leone was governed as a British Crown Colony and Protectorate. Its first political party – Sierra Leone's People's Party – was formed by Dr (Sir) Milton Margai who became its first Prime Minister (1958). Party political dissension was overcome in order to form a united front to press for independence in an April 1960 conference. Sierra Leone became an independent state within the Commonwealth on 27 April 1961. Sir Milton Margai, again successful in the 1962 elections, was succeeded, not without political conflict, by Sir Albert Margai. Following disputed elections (March 1967), the army under Colonel Juxon-Smith, took control of the country. However, a further revolt (April 1968) restored civilian government and returned the elected Prime Minister (1967) Mr Siaka Stevens to power. Despite promised reforms, political unrest continued; a state of emergency was declared in 1968, and 1971 saw an attempted coup by the Army Commander.

Sikkim. *Area* – 2,828 sq. miles. *Population* – 161,080. *Head of State* – King Palden Thondup Namgyal. Sikkim is a Protectorate of ⟡ India, with whom relations are governed by the treaty of 1950. This granted Sikkim full internal autonomy but gave India responsibility for foreign affairs, defence and communications. Sikkim receives considerable aid from India, with no restriction on trade between the two countries. Sikkim is ruled by a hereditary monarchy through an Executive Council and a Legislature. Until 1947 she was a British Protectorate.

Sikorski, General W. (1881–1943). A distinguished professional soldier and an opponent of the Pilsudski dictatorship in inter-war Poland, Sikorski escaped after the outbreak of World War II and became Prime Minister of the Polish government-in-exile, set up first in France and then in Britain, and Commander-in-Chief of the Polish Home Army. Diplomatic relations established between his government and the USSR in July 1941 were again broken off by Moscow after General Sikorski's request for a Red Cross investigation of the ⟡ Katyn Murders. He died in an air accident in 1943.

Singapore. *Area* 225 sq. miles. *Population* (1970) – 2,074,500 (75% of which are Chinese). *Prime Minister* – ⟡ Lee Kuan Yew (1959–). *Constitution* (1965) – Independent Republic in the ⟡ Commonwealth. A uni-cameral Parliament, the Legislature, to which the Prime Minister is responsible, is elected by universal adult suffrage. (After her secession from the Federation of ⇔Malaysia in 1965 she became a Republic.)

Originally part of the British Straits Settlements, the island of Singapore's politics have been affected by its importance as a commercial port and British naval base. Singapore was occupied during World War II by the Japanese (1942–45), but after the war became a separate colony (1946) and in 1955 a new constitution introduced a large measure of self-government. Full self-government followed in 1959 with the UK retaining responsibility for defence and external affairs. Singapore's politics have been dominated by the People's Action Party (PAP), which is moderately left-wing (socialist and anti-colonialist but non-communist) and is led by Lee Kuan Yew. At the last general election (1968) the PAP won all seats unopposed because the only real opposition party, the Barisan Socialists, boycotted Parliament after refusing to accept independence. Singapore joined the Federation of Malaysia when it was formed in 1963 but seceded in 1965 claiming political discrimination by the Malays against the Chinese. She then became a separate and independent state but continued to cooperate with Malaysia on defence matters. This was confirmed at the Conference on Far East Defence (Kuala Lumpur, June 1968), called to discuss the problems arising from the UK's withdrawal ⇔East of Suez which will particularly affect Singapore, as the British military presence accounts for 20% of the Gross National Product. Unemployment is already a growing problem with over half the population under 21 years of age, but the UK Government has promised economic aid to offset the effects of the withdrawal.

Siniavsky, Andrei (1925–). Soviet writer (⇔Dissent – Eastern Europe).

Sino-Japanese War. ⇔Chinese-Japanese War.

Sino-Soviet Conflict. The Chinese Communist Party (CCP) traces its differences with the Soviet Communist Party (CPSU) back to the 20th CPSU Congress of 1956, when Khrushchev suddenly denounced Stalin without prior consultation with other communist parties. With this complaint about lack of prior consultations, the CCP raised its claim to an equal share in Soviet decision-making on all matters of common interest. This claim was expressed in numerous Sino-Soviet clashes over communist ideology, over conflicting national interests, over domestic as well as foreign and defence policies and over mutual economic relations.

The conflict escalated in three stages. The first differences arose over Soviet relations with other socialist states in Eastern Europe. In 1958 tension between the two countries began to mount over Mao Tse-tung's policies of 'the Great Leap Forward' and the revival of China's campaign against Taiwan (Formosa). In the course of 1959, tension turned into outright hostility. According to the CCP, Khrushchev then encouraged Chinese visitors to Eastern Europe to oppose 'the Great Leap Forward'. In June 1959, according to the CCP (later indirectly confirmed by the CPSU), the USSR cancelled an earlier undertaking to supply China with a sample of a nuclear bomb and the technical data concerning its manufacture. In Sept., the USSR publicly deplored the flare-up of the Sino-Indian border conflict with the impartiality of a non-ally. A still worse Chinese grievance was the simultaneous Soviet search for a détente with the USA, obtainable only at the expense of China's national interests, especially its claim to Formosa. The point of no return seems to have been reached during Khrushchev's visit to Peking immediately after his tour of the USA (Sept. 1959) and his Camp David meeting with President Eisenhower. Contrary to normal practice, his visit to Peking even failed to produce a joint communiqué.

In the second phase, the conflict was brought into the open by public polemics designed to mobilize support from other communist parties. Though unmistakable, the targets of these polemics were then not yet identified by name. The polemics began in April 1960 with the Chinese article *Long Live Leninism*. Two months later, at a conference in Bucharest, Soviet and Chinese delegates clashed angrily for the first time in front of delegates from other communist parties. On that occasion only ⇨ Albania supported the Chinese position. At the Moscow conference of 81 communist parties (Nov. 1960) the conflict continued with increased bitterness and before a much larger communist audience. In between, the USSR withdrew all its technical specialists from China (Aug.). Towards the end of the year the first of many subsequent frontier incidents broke out on the Sino-Soviet border.

At the Moscow conference of Nov. 1960, the assembled communist parties had to take sides. The great majority sided with Moscow; but, except for the Indians and Mongolians, all the Asian communist parties leaned towards the Chinese point of view, while Albania again supported China unreservedly. Thereafter Moscow used Albania as a substitute target for attacks on China, just as Peking had even earlier used Yugoslavia as a substitute target for attacks on the USSR. During the next two years mutual attacks broadened in scope and became increasingly bitter. Mediation attempts by the Vietnamese and other communist parties ended in failure. More frontier incidents followed after which public polemics became even more abusive than before. The ⇨ Cuban Missile Crisis (Oct. 1962) coincided with the almost simultaneous outbreak of a large-scale new Chinese offensive against India.

For a few days Peking and Moscow supported one another in these confrontations. After the settlement of the Cuban crisis, China denounced the withdrawal of the Soviet missiles as an act of shameful capitulation, while the USSR reverted to its previous stance of formal neutrality on the Sino-Indian war and continued to supply India with arms.

The prelude to the third and last phase of the conflict came in the winter of 1962/3, when the two sides and their respective communist supporters began to denounce one another by name. A new and more critical confrontation began in the summer of 1963 when the distribution of Chinese documents in the USSR led to the expulsion of some Chinese diplomats and students from the Soviet Union. The conclusion of the Nuclear Test Ban Treaty immediately afterwards became the occasion for raising the conflict between the CCP and CPSU to the level of government hostility. From then on, a large number of documents were published revealing the hitherto confidential details of earlier exchanges over Soviet economic, technical and military aid for China, over specific foreign policy issues and over alleged mutual interference in domestic affairs. At the same time, Peking began to organize its own factions in communist parties loyal to Moscow or 'Marxist-Leninist' communist rival parties. Simultaneously, the conflict was extended to a number of neutralist and other officially non-communist international organizations. At the same time, Moscow also started its campaign for another communist world conference designed to excommunicate the CCP. Opposition from other communists compelled Moscow to modify both the avowed purpose and timing of the conference.

In the winter of 1964/5, Khrushchev's successors made a determined attempt at winning China's most important international supporters over to their side, in the first place North Vietnam and North Korea. The attempt was partially successful. Most of the Asian communist parties, which had previously tended to side with China, gradually changed over to a position of neutrality between Moscow and Peking, seeking to maintain good relations with both. The onset of China's Cultural Revolution was accompanied by a further deterioration in Sino-Soviet relations, a large number of serious diplomatic incidents, hostile mass demonstrations and new charges in their mutual polemics. Having first accused one another of a variety of 'revisionist', 'dogmatic' and other anti-Leninist heresies, Moscow and Peking, from the mid-1960s onwards, denounced one another for alleged direct collusion with Washington over the Vietnam war and other issues and for attitudes and views variously described as 'outright imperialist', 'racialist' and 'savagely Fascist'. (⇨ World Communism, ⇨ Bandung Conference.)

A certain improvement in the formal relations between the two countries on the state (if not on the party) level came with the renewed exchange, after a gap of 3 years, of Ambassadors and the start of desultory talks on the unsettled border problems (1970).

Sithole. ⇨ZANU.

Sit-Ins. Demonstrations aimed at ending racial ⇨ Segregation that occurred in the early 1960s in luncheonettes and restaurants in the Southern States of the USA. Negro ⇨ Civil Rights workers, whose non-violence was sometimes met by the violence of onlookers and restaurant-owners, would ask to be served in a non-integrated restaurant and when refused, stay until removed by the police. They caused and threatened financial loss. ⇨SNCC was formed to coordinate them.

Slansky, Rudolf (1901–52). Secretary-General of the Czech Communist Party who, by organizing armed demonstrations of the Workers' Militia, assisted the communist take-over in ⇨ Czechoslovakia under the aegis of Prime Minister Clement ⇨ Gottwald (17–28.2.1948). Dismissed and arrested three years later, Slansky together with 12 other leading communists (including Clementis, the Foreign Minister) were accused of Trotskyite, Titoist and Zionist deviations and executed. During the trial (Slansky and nine other defendants were Jews) anti-semitism was used to whip up popular resentment against the accused.

Slave Labour. ⇨ Forced Labour Camps, ⇨ Concentration Camps, ⇨Holocaust.

Smethwick. Once the constituency of Sir Oswald Mosley (1926–31), it achieved notoriety when Patrick Gordon Walker, its Labour MP for 13 years, lost his seat to a Conservative, Peter Griffiths (referred to by the Prime Minister as a 'Parliamentary leper') in the general election (Oct. 1964). Griffiths was accused of basing his electoral campaign on resentment of coloured immigrants. In the subsequent general election (1966), the seat was won back by Labour.

Smith, Ian Douglas (1919–). Leader of the Rhodesian Front political party, Prime Minister (1962–) whose government announced ⇨UDI (Nov. 1965). Controversial political leader who has been accused by his opponents of inconsistency for claiming to be conciliatory towards the UK Government while at home his own party follows a policy little different from the South African doctrines of separate development. The determination of his regime to go ahead with executing sentences on condemned African nationalists after some years of imprisonment resulted in a degree of international disapprobation. He has been regarded by some UK politicians as the victim of his own Rhodesian Front caucus but by others as using the caucus to implement his own policies. His leadership has been challenged by both the Rhodesians within his own party (key members of his party have resigned) and by constitutionalists, but despite challenges to his leadership, all election results so far indicate the continued support of the White electorate. (⇨ Rhodesia.)

Smith Act. The 1940 Alien Registration Act in the USA which made it an offence to advocate the overthrow of the government by force with intent to bring it about. It prohibits the distribution 'with disloyal intent' of material promoting such a course of action. The Act makes it a crime knowingly to organize or be a member of any group having such a purpose, and is said therefore to have introduced into the criminal law of the United States the concept of 'guilt by association'. Decisions of the ⇨ Supreme Court relating to the Act have not been altogether consistent, and this has led to inconsistencies in the application of the ⇨ 'Clear and Present Danger' doctrine. The provisions of the Smith Act were extended and strengthened by the Act establishing the ⇨ Subversive Activities Control Board in 1950.

Smrkovsky, J. (1910–). Czechoslovak communist since his early youth, Smrkovsky was active in the anti-German resistance during the war and played a leading part in the Prague uprising of 1945. As one of the organizers of the workers' 'action committees', Smrkovsky also played an important part in the communist coup of Feb. 1948 but, like other ⇨ Home Communists, soon after fell into disgrace and was imprisoned (1951). Rehabilitated in 1965, he became prominent after Jan. 1968 as the earliest and most outspoken communist champion of radical libertarian reforms. One of the most popular communist leaders in ⇨ Czechoslovakia, Smrkovsky became one of the chief targets of a Soviet and allied campaign of personal vilification, as a result of which he was step by step ousted from all the important state and party posts to which he had been elected.

Smuts, Jan Christiaan (1870–1950). Former Prime Minister of ⇨ South Africa, scholar and international statesman. After serving as a General with the Boers, he helped General Botha negotiate the Peace of Vereeniging which led to the Act of Union. He held Cabinet office under Botha and helped to bring South Africa into the 1914–18 war on the Allied side. After military service in South West Africa and the command of Allied troops in East Africa, he became a member of the Imperial War Cabinet in 1917. He participated in the Paris Peace conference and the formation of the League of Nations as two decades later he was to help in the formation of the UN. After Botha's death in 1919 he became Prime Minister of South Africa. However, the violent suppression of an African religious sect, similar treatment of a Hottentot protest against new taxation, and in particular armed intervention against a strike of White miners on the Rand ensured the defeat of Smuts' South Africa party in the general election of 1924. In 1933 he returned to Cabinet office under General ⇨ Hertzog with whom he formed the United Party in 1934. Again in 1939, Smuts played a crucial role in bring South Africa into the war as Britain's ally. The Governor-General invited him to form a government and the dissident members of the United Party joined Dr ⇨ Malan's Nationalist Party opposition. In 1946 Smuts' government again used force to break a miners' strike, although this time, indicative of the growing unrest of the submerged African population, the strikers were Black. In 1948 Smuts' United Party was defeated by Dr Malan's Nationalists. This defeat also threatened the traditional bond between Britain and South Africa which for so long had been the basis of Smuts' foreign policy.

In a career spanning more than 50 years, Smuts dominated South African politics. As the elder statesman of the Commonwealth, war leader and philosopher, he was admired abroad and respected as the representative of a liberal tradition. The truth was more complicated. In South Africa, for the part he played in the act of Union and for his later pro-British attitudes, he was regarded as a traitor by Afrikaans Nationalists; while many Africans, opponents of the colour-bar, and politicians of the left, detested him, as the chief architect of South Africa's system of segregation. To the end of his life he remained a firm believer in segregation. On the key issue of White supremacy the main difference between his followers and those of Dr Malan was one of method rather than aim.

SNCC. Student Non-violent Co-ordinating Committee (SNICK) – a political association of predominantly Negro students in the USA, formed in 1960 in connexion with the ⇨ Sit-Ins then going on at lunch-counters in the South. It worked in close collaboration with ⇨ CORE, ⇨ SCLC, and ⇨ NAACP in the Negro ⇨ Civil Rights Movement, with the aim of ending ⇨ Segregation and achieving ⇨ Integration. However, since about 1966, when Stokeley ⇨ Carmichael, 'prime minister' of the ⇨ Black Panther Party, became its chairman, SNCC has been closely identified with the ⇨ Black Power movement and the American ⇨ New Left.

Socialist Legality. Term used in the USSR and other communist countries for the rule of law as limited by the claim of the ruling communist party to a permanently 'leading role' in society.

Solzhenitsyn, Alexander (1918–). Soviet novelist who, between 1945 and 1953, was confined to a forced labour camp and thereafter exiled until his rehabilitation as 'innocently convicted' (1956). The author of the first novel published in the USSR on the theme of forced labour camps (*One Day in the Life of Ivan Denisovich*), Solzhenitsyn was prevented from the legal publication in the USSR of most of his other work, including his major novels, *The First Circle, Cancer Ward, August 1914*, which were published abroad but appeared in the USSR only in the form of surreptitiously distributed typescripts. A fearless champion of human rights, Solzhenitsyn has for years been subjected to an official campaign of denunciations and victimization. In 1970, he was awarded the Nobel Prize for Literature, but the Soviet authorities blocked the attempts of the Swedish Academy at formally presenting the recipient with the Nobel Prize insignia.

Somalia (also referred to as the **Somali Republic**). *Area* – 246,135 sq. miles. *Population* (1969 est.) – 2,730,000. *Chairman of Revolutionary Council* – General Mohammed Siyad Barreh (1969–). *Constitution* (1960) – After a military coup in Oct. 1969 the Constitution was suspended and the National Assembly was replaced by a Revolutionary Council. Legislative authority is vested in a uni-cameral National Assembly elected by universal suffrage.

The new Republic came into being when the former territory of British Somaliland and the Italian Trust Territory of Somalia (formerly Italian Somaliland) were united (July 1960). Somalia's short history (it is a poor and underdeveloped country many of whose people live a semi-nomadic life) has been marked by border disputes with neighbouring territories. Many Somalis live in Ethiopia, Northern Kenya and French Somaliland (Djibouti). There was fighting along the Ethiopian border (1964). There has been a long dispute with Kenya (including border skirmishes) though agreement was reached in 1967, and Somalia established diplomatic relations with Kenya and resumed them with Britain (severed 1963) in 1968.

Soustelle, Jacques (1912–). An early follower of General ⇨ de Gaulle until his unqualified support for an *Algérie française* drove him into the ⇨ OAS opposition, and exile. A leader of the *Ligue des Intellectuels Antifascistes*, he joined de Gaulle in 1940, headed his information departments (1942), held administrative offices in Algiers (1943) becoming Minister of Information (1945). He organized the Gaullist ⇨ RPF and served as its General Secretary (1947–52). As Governor-General of ⇨ Algeria (1955–56) he championed the views of the settlers and his recall gave rise to demonstrations. A vociferous campaigner for de Gaulle's return in 1958, he became Minister of Information in his first Cabinet (1958). His views increasingly diverging from those of the President, he was given the inconsequential post of Minister attached to the Prime Minister for the Sahara and Atomic Questions (1959–60). Dismissed from the government after the 'Bloody Sunday' riots in

Algiers (Jan. 1960), he became a member of the OAS executive (May 1962). Exiled (Sept. 1962), he found asylum in Mexico and returned to France (Oct. 1968) after de Gaulle pardoned former OAS leaders following the May 1968 riots.

South Africa, Republic of (*Republiek van Suid Afrika*). *Area* – 471,445 sq. miles. *Population* (1966 approx.) – 18,298,000 classified into four main groups:

> White (European) – 3,481,000
> African (Bantu) – 12,465,000
> Asiatic – 547,000
> Coloured (mixed descent) – 1,805,000

State President – J. J. Fouche. *Prime Minister* – B. J. ⇨ Vorster. *Minister of Foreign Affairs* – Dr H. Muller. *Constitution* – The Republic established on 31 May 1961, following South African tradition, limits franchise rights, legislative and executive power to people of European descent, (i.e., the White minority) and provides for an Executive of the State President acting on the advice of the Prime Minister and Cabinet; a Senate of elected and appointed members; an elected House of Assembly including four European members elected by Coloured voters on a separate roll. Legislation (1968) extended the term of office of these four European members elected by Coloured males over 21 resident in the Cape Province until 1971 when this representation will be abolished.

Racial and cultural conflict, the continuing theme of South African history, can be traced backwards from today's ⇨ *Apartheid* legislation, based on the segregatory laws of the inter-war ⇨ Smuts -⇨ Hertzog era, through the Boer War, the discovery of diamonds and gold and the consequent emergence of a voteless Black proletariat, to the extension of European settlement inland from the Cape Peninsula. South Africa's independence dating from the Act of Union (1910) – with its entrenched clauses – was confirmed by the Statute of ⇨ Westminster (1931). Internally, four events between 1910 and 1939 were of crucial importance:

– the Mines and Works Act (1911 amended in 1926) which, by denying Africans the right to skilled employment, protected the privileged position of White workers;
– the Land Act (1913) which prohibited Africans from owning land except in the 'Native' Reserves;
– the merger of Premier Hertzog's Nationalist Party with Smuts'

South African Party to form the ⇨ United Party (1934), with ⇨ Malan deserting the coalition to establish his reformed ⇨ National Party;
- the Representation of Natives Act (1936) which excluded African voters in the Cape Province from the common roll.

In 1939 Smuts became leader of the United Party (Hertzog resigned on the war issue) and managed to bring South Africa into the war on Britain's side. Many leading members of Dr Malan's National Party, including future Cabinet members and Prime Ministers (⇨ Strijdom, ⇨ Verwoerd, Vorster), made no secret of their pro-Nazi sympathies. While South African forces were engaged in North Africa and Smuts again emerged as a senior allied statesman, Fascist and pro-Nazi organizations mushroomed at home. Despite her participation in the war and although a founding member of the UN, the South African government was not a signatory to the UN Declaration of Human Rights. During the war and the immediate post-war years, the National Party in opposition, through its press, the ⇨ Broederbond, 'cultural organizations' and a propaganda which harped on the 'threats to White civilization', prepared itself for power. Malan's 1948 election victory heralded the decline of the United Party, the end of Smuts' 30 years of political dominance and the weakening of ties with Great Britain despite alliance in two world wars. In 1948 the Nationalists still formed a minority of the White electorate. However, the weighting of rural constituencies, the increasing number of Afrikaans workers in the towns, political converts, the removal of non-European voters from the common roll, the extension of police power (the Suppression of Communism Act, the Ninety Day Law, etc.), new *Apartheid* legislation and the lack of parliamentary opposition have ensured the continuing electoral success of the party. Under successive Prime Ministers, Malan (1948–54), Strijdom (1954–58), Verwoerd (1958–66) and Vorster since 1966, South Africa has come into conflict with world opinion over her internal policies – culminating in the outcry over the ⇨ Treason Trials and ⇨ Sharpeville – and her policy of incorporating ⇨ South West Africa. By a slight majority (52% to 48%) in a referendum in Oct. 1960, the White electorate voted in favour of a Republic which was established outside the ⇨ Commonwealth on 31 May 1961. Under Verwoerd the concept of *Bantustans* was offered as a future alternative to a multi-racial society. While government policy increasingly regulates the social life of the citizen (where he may live, whom he may marry or choose as friends), the economic facts of life and the growing number of Africans living and working in the towns result in a daily contact between people of different races at all levels contradicting the official aim of complete separation of races.

South Arabian Federation. ⇨ South Yemen, People's Republic of.

South-East Asia Treaty Organization. ⇨ SEATO.

Southern Rhodesia. ⇨ Rhodesia.

South Korea. ⇨ Korea.

South Tyrol. *Population* – 380,000 of which 232,000 are German-speaking, and 130,000 Italian-speaking.

The region, a subject of dispute between Austria and Italy, belonged to the Austro-Hungarian Empire until 1919 (Treaty of Saint Germain) when it was given to Italy. Mussolini's government followed a policy of intensive Italianization making Italian the only official language, and arousing bitter opposition. The Hitler-Mussolini agreement (1939) provided for the transfer of South Tyroleans to Germany, but the war interrupted large-scale resettlement. In 1946 the Italian and Austrian governments signed an agreement and the Italian constitution of 1948 granted South Tyrol the status of an autonomous region with protection of minority rights. Both German and Italian were made official languages and German schools were permitted in the German-speaking Alto Adige (or Bolzano) province. The Austrian Government has since claimed that Italy has not fully implemented the agreement, that preference is given to Italians in the public service, that the Italians encourage the immigration of their own people and that the Italian majority in the province of Trentino is generally favoured. The Italian Government denies this but there have been a series of negotiations between the two countries since 1958, all to no avail. The German-speaking population is represented by the South Tyrolean People's Party (SVP).

South Vietnam. ⇨ Vietnam.

South West Africa. *Area* – 317,827 sq. miles. *Population* (approx.) – 610,000 (approx. 485,000 Africans, 96,000 Whites, 29,000 Coloureds).

Formerly a German colony occupied by South African forces in World War I, and since administered by ⇨ South Africa under a ⇨ League of Nations Mandate (1920). Since World War II South African governments, despite UN protests and the opposition of the African majority in the territory, have steadily moved towards complete incorporation of South West Africa. By a South African Act of Parliament (1949) the White electorate of the territory is represented in the South African House of Assembly and Senate. South West Africa also has its own elected House of Assembly (its members and those who elect them have to be of European descent). A complaint from Ethiopia and Liberia alleging South African contravention of its Mandate was rejected by the International Court of Justice (18.7.1966). In a report (1964) the South African Government had indicated its intention of dividing the territory into White and African Areas (*Bantustans*) in accordance with the Republic's ⇨ *Apartheid* system. As in the Republic, discriminatory legislation has increasingly made open opposition to government policies illegal.

South Yemen, People's Democratic Republic of. *Area* – 112,000 sq. miles. *Population* – 1,500,000. *Chairman of Presidential Council* – Salem Ali Rubayyi (1969–). *Prime Minister* – Ali Nasser Hassaniya (1971–). *Constitution* – When independence was proclaimed (Nov. 1967) the National Liberation Front (NLF) took over the government. As-Shaabi, Prime Minister as well as President, announced that the NLF High Command would act as Legislature until a constitution had been drafted. The constitution was completed in Nov. 1970 and legislative power was transferred to an elected People's Supreme Council in May 1971. There is a three-man Presidential Council.

The Republic of South Yemen consists of the former South Arabian Federation, including the former British colony of Aden, and the three states of the Eastern Aden Protectorate. The 21 states of Aden's hinterland had long-standing treaty and protective arrangements with the UK. In 1959 six of the seventeen territories in the then Western Aden Protectorate formed the Federation of the Arab Emirates of the South. By 1963 all the territories of the two former Protectorates (except for a small group which retained the collective title of Eastern Aden Protectorate) had joined the Federation, which in 1962 changed its name to South Arabian Federation (also known as the Aden Federation). This also included the colony of Aden, which became the Aden State within the Federation. Aden, a British military base and important port on the trade route to the East, had been a British possession since 1839 and was administered as part of British India until 1937, when it became a Crown Colony ruled by a governor and a Cabinet responsible to a partly-elected Legislature. The UK retained control over external relations, defence and internal security in Aden when she was incorporated into the Federation in 1963. There was strong opposition to incorporation in Aden from the Trades Union Congress, the People's Constitutional Congress Party and the People's Socialist Party. In Dec. 1963 following a bomb attack on the British High Commissioner, a state of emergency was declared. This marked the beginning of a terrorist campaign which continued until independence (over 500 military and civilian casualties between 1964 and 1967 in South Arabia) and in 1965 the National Front for the Liberation of Occupied South Yemen, an extremist group operating from the Yemen with Egyptian support, was outlawed. The High Commissioner was given wide powers to enforce order, but violence increased. Chiefly responsible was the Front for the Liberation of Occupied South Yemen (FLOSY), a nationalist movement uniting various extremist groups in which Abdul Makkawi, Chief Minister in Aden since 1965 played a prominent part. Negotiations dragged on but made no progress because of the diverging interests of the UK, the Federation and Aden. In 1964 the London Constitutional Conference agreed on independence for South Arabia by 1968 but the conference called in 1965 to establish a unified regime was postponed. A constitutional commission (1965) failed (it was refused admission to Aden) as did further discussions in London, the UK differing with Makkawi over the immediate lifting of all security restrictions and an early withdrawal of British forces from the Aden base. This resulted in a further increase in terrorism, and the suspension of the Aden regime, which in turn led to serious rioting (Sept. 1965). Further attempts to bring the sides together were not helped by the feuds between FLOSY and the more moderate FLN (formed 1963) nor by the conflict in neighbouring ⇨ Yemen. The nationalist organizations refused all cooperation with the British and federal authorities and a UN mission to South Arabia (1967) met with no more success than previous efforts in mediation. Finally the UK government announced its proposals for independence, which were speeded up, including financial and military aid and plans for eventual elections. The departure of British forces (Nov. 1967) in effect marked the end of a UK military presence in the Middle East.

Soviet. Russian for council, a term which first acquired political significance in the Russian revolution of 1905, when strike committees grew spontaneously into workers' councils. The revolution of Feb. 1917 led to the election of new workers' and soldiers' councils, which, in turn, elected their own All-Russian Congress. The Congress of Workers' and Soldiers' Councils became the instrument through which the ⇨ Bolsheviks, with their slogan 'All Power to the Soviets', finally seized power. After their victory, the new communist state was formally based on a pyramid of elected Soviets on all administrative levels. In theory, the Soviets became the Legislatures and, according to the (still valid) 1936 Constitution, they are elected 'by equal, universal suffrage and by direct and secret ballot'. In practice, voters in Soviet elections have never been offered a choice but have invariably been presented with a single candidate for a merely formalized endorsement. (⇨USSR.)

Soviet Constitution. ⇨USSR, ⇨Soviet.

Sovietization. The imposition on foreign countries of communist regimes through the direct or indirect intervention of the USSR. In the endphase and aftermath of World War II, satellite communist regimes of this type were imposed on ⇨ Bulgaria, ⇨ Czechoslovakia, ⇨ East Germany, ⇨ Hungary, ⇨ Poland and ⇨ Rumania. Despite slight local variations, the pattern of Sovietization in all these countries was remarkably similar. After the arrival of the Red Army, accompanied by native communists who had been trained in the USSR (known as 'the Muscovites'), the first step everywhere was the establishment of broad coalition governments of various left-wing and centre parties, in which communists rarely predominated. Invariably, however, the communists immediately took control of the Ministry of the Interior, the Security Police, the Army General Staff and the publicity machine. During the second stage, the coalition parties, with a mass following (generally peasant parties), were driven into opposition by active persecution and replaced by parties under covert communist control. This stage ended with the arrest and execution or flight of popular non-communist leaders. The third stage began with the liquidation of the social democratic parties through enforced fusion with the communists. As with the peasant parties, those who resisted were liquidated or driven into exile. During the fourth stage, which began at the time of ⇨ Tito's conflict with ⇨ Stalin, the communist parties themselves were purged of leading 'home communists' who, in contrast to the 'the Muscovites', had spent the war in their own countries, fighting the Nazis and Fascists. Suspected of reluctance to act as simple Soviet agents, they were accused of 'nationalist' and 'Titoist' deviations and some of the most prominent among them, including the Hungarian, Laszlo Rajk, and the Bulgarian, Traicho Kostov, were executed after sensational ⇨ Show Trials.

Soviet Russia. ⇨ USSR.

Soviet Union. ⇨ USSR.

Sovkhoz. Soviet term, short for State Farm.

Spaak, Paul Henri (1899–1972). Belgian statesman who worked for the establishment of a unified Europe. He presided over the UN's first General Assembly (1946), the ⇨ Council of Europe's Consultative Assembly (1949–51) and succeeded Lord Ismay as ⇨ NATO General Secretary (1957–61). Spaak held several Belgian cabinet posts in the thirties and served with minor interruptions as Foreign Minister from 1936 to 1949. He spent the war years in London, was several times his country's Prime Minister (1938/39, March 1946, 1947–49) and from 1961 was the leader of the Belgian Socialist Party.

Spain. *Area* – 194,900 sq. miles. *Population* (1970) – 34 m. *Head of State and Prime Minister* – Generalissimo Francisco ⇨ Franco Bahamonde (1939–). *Constitution* (1937) – Corporative state. Absolute authority is vested in the *Caudillo*. As Head of State he is responsible to God and the Nation (Organic Law, 1966). He is also Prime Minister and Commander-in-Chief of the Armed Forces. He initiates legislation through the Council of Ministers, of which he is chairman, and this is discussed by the Parliament (*Cortes*) which is a corporative body consisting of partly nominated and partly elected representatives of permitted organizations. Spain is officially a monarchy – the Law of Succession (1947) states that Franco will be succeeded by a King.

The effects of World War I on neutral Spain had extended beyond purely economic dislocation. Allied victory helped place the issues of democracy and national self-determination – which in the Spanish context meant Catalan and Basque autonomy – squarely in the centre of political debate. Primo de Rivera's military dictatorship (1923–30) came to an end in a welter of army revolts, student riots and strikes. After an overwhelming victory for the Republicans in the municipal elections (April 1931) King Alfonso XIII abdicated. The new republic, under the presidency of Alcala Zamora, instituted radical reforms, e.g. land reform, autonomy for Catalonia, disestablishment of the Church, dissolution of the Jesuit Order and the secularization of education. Inevitably there was a right-wing reaction but the reforms also failed to satisfy the demands of the extreme left. While right-wing parties generally gained in elections (1933), the Government was forced to suppress a separatist uprising in Catalonia (1934) and a miners' revolt in the Asturias, where a communist government had been installed. The victory of the Popular Front in the Feb. 1936 elections was followed by a military revolt. (⇨ Spanish Civil War.) The victory in the war of the Nationalists over the Republicans resulted in the establishment of a corporative state under Franco's dictatorship (1939), although in fact he had already assumed power in the territory conquered since 1936. The ⇨ Falange was the only party permitted, Catalan (and Basque) auton-omy was denied and the Church reclaimed its property and its privileged position in the state. In spite of military support from the ⇨ Axis Powers in the Civil War, Franco remained neutral during World War II although he had joined the anti-Comintern Pact (April 1939). The Hitler-Franco meeting at Hendaye (Oct. 1940) did not produce the expected Spanish entry into the war. The experience of the Civil War was as much as anything a deterrent, for Franco needed a period of peace to establish his regime. After the war the Franco regime remained in power in the face of internal and external pressure – there was opposition from socialist, liberal and monarchist groups (Don Juan, the Bourbon claimant, called for Franco's resignation and the restora-tion of the monarchy), while abroad Spain for a time was treated as an international pariah. In 1942 Franco had restored the *Cortes* but reconstructed on corporative lines. In 1945 he announced a Bill of Civil Rights (finally ratified by the *Cortes* in 1960) but his primary concern was to heal the scars remaining after the Civil War. This was complicated by increasing agitation by the monarchists – Franco's law of succession (1947) was rejected by Don Juan while in 1948 the exiled monarchists and republicans (except the communists) issued a 'statement of accord'. The problem of the succession has persisted since the 1950s. Franco had refused to make any public commitment to one of the rival pretenders (as well as Don Juan, there is his son Don Juan Carlos), but in 1969 he nominated Don Juan Carlos to succeed him. In 1959 liberal and right-wing opponents collaborated in forming the Spanish Union and the same year another party, the Christian Democratic Left Party, was started by a liberal Catholic group. From the early 1960s the Church, which had previously not voiced any opinion, began to show signs of discontent particularly among younger priests, e.g. in June 1960, 342 Basque priests in a letter to their bishops protested against police brutality to political prisoners. This was accompanied by a number of serious strikes beginning with one in the Asturias coal industry in 1962. The 1966 Fundamental Law, approved by referendum, introduced various constitutional changes including the diversification of the *Cortes* by the inclusion of members elected (for the first time since the Civil War) by the heads of families. After the war Spain was excluded from membership of the UN by the Allied Powers and in Dec. 1946 the UN called on its members to break off diplomatic relations with her. The intensifying Cold War gradually lessened Spain's international isolation – the UN rescinded its 'ostracism' resolution (1950) and in 1955 Spain was admitted to the UN. In Sept. 1953 a treaty granted the USA the right to establish naval and air bases on its territory in return for military and economic aid (this ceased in 1964 because of Spain's trading with Cuba). Spain also became a member of the ▷ OECD (1959), ▷ GATT see under United Nations (1960) and since 1962 has sought entry to the ▷ EEC. Spain has granted more autonomy to her overseas possessions (▷Spanish Territories in Africa). Relations with the UK have been marred in recent years by Spain's agitation against British rule in ▷ Gibraltar. Still economically backward by European standards, the Spanish economy has benefited initially from the American bases and more recently from a vast tourist industry. Economic advance, accompanied by large-scale rural migration to the cities, has also coincided with increasing political agitation.

Spanish Civil War (1936–39). Political stability in the new Republic of ▷ Spain was threatened not only by right-wing opposition (monarchists, the Church and the Army), but also by the dissatisfaction of the extreme left. In a country without a stable middle class, conflicts over such issues as the position of the Church in the state, land reform and regional autonomy (as in the Catalan and Basque provinces) demonstrated the irreconcilable differences between the Government and its traditionalist opponents. Following the Popular Front's victory in the elections of Feb. 1936, General ⇨ Franco led a military revolt in Spanish Morocco (July 1936) which resulted in the outbreak of war. The revolt spread quickly to the mainland, where the Nationalists seized control of many of the garrisons and by the end of 1936 held over half of the country, mainly the south and west, which included the vital supply line along the Portuguese frontier. The Republicans retained the cities of Madrid, Barcelona and Valencia. During 1937 the Nationalists attempted to encircle Madrid and divide the Republican territory into two. The Nationalists had important political and military advantages. Their supporters were less divided than those of the Republicans. The latter's military effectiveness was crippled by internal conflicts, particularly between communists and anarchists (who hoped to achieve a genuine social revolution), and by Catalan and Basque separatist movements (an autonomous Basque government was set up in Oct. 1936). The Nationalists enjoyed strong military aid from Italy (whose forces eventually numbered 50,000) and Germany (who contributed 10,000 men as well as vital air power). The Republicans only received equipment and military advisers from the USSR. The British and French policy of 'non-intervention' not only failed (a pact was signed by 27 powers, including Germany, Italy and the USSR, in Aug. 1936) but its one-sided implementation by the UK and France (e.g. the neutrality patrol off the coast of Spain) strengthened Franco's position. The Republicans were deprived of possible assistance through the closing of the French frontier across the Pyrenees. The Nationalists captured Bilbao (June 1937) and cut off Republican territory in Castille from Catalonia after a series of attacks (March–June 1938). They finally captured Barcelona (Jan. 1939) and Madrid (March 1939). The war aroused the idealism of intellectuals outside Spain, who favoured the Republican cause and International Brigades (dominated by communists) were made up of volunteers from other countries. Although the war was often represented as a struggle between the forces of Fascism and democracy, this was an oversimplification. In fact the communists, the chief opponents of Franco, also waged an internecine war against other factions in the Republican coalition. German and Italian military involvement (which provided them with the opportunity to test new weapons) embarrassed the League of Nations and contributed to its decline. The Republican Government came increasingly under Soviet influence after Juan Negrin replaced Largo Caballero as Prime Minister in May 1937. The conflict resulted in about one million casualties with widespread devastation and all the horrors of twentieth-century war. After the German bombing of Guernica, the name of the Basque village has lived on as a symbol of innocent suffering in total war.

Spanish Guinea. ⇨ Equatorial Guinea.

Spanish Sahara. ⇨ Spanish Territories in Africa.

Spanish Territories in Africa. Include the North African ports of Ceuta and Melilla, and the province of the Spanish Sahara. (The former Spanish province of ⇨ Equatorial Guinea became independent in 1968, while Ifni was incorporated into Morocco in 1969.

Ifni. *Area* – 580 sq. miles. *Population* (approx.) – 51,000. Administered by ⇨ Spain since 1934, and as an Overseas Province since 1958, electing its own representatives to the Spanish *Cortes*, Ifni has been granted an increasing measure of local autonomy (1963). Changes in Spanish policy have been affected by political developments in North Africa, including pressure from Morocco. In 1956–57 Spain had to reinforce its troops in Ifni to suppress a revolt and in 1969 it was incorporated into Morocco.

Spanish Sahara. *Area* – 102,703 sq. miles. *Population* (approx.) – 19,000. Spanish Sahara, administered as a Province since 1958, with its own representatives in the Spanish *Cortes*, since 1963, has had an elected Council, and further autonomy is promised.

SPD. *Sozialdemokratische Partei Deutschlands* – the ⇨ German Federal Republic's second largest party whose roots can be traced back to the Social-Democratic Workers' Party (1868). Founded and guided by the disciples of Marx, A. Bebel and W. Liebknecht, it became, after merging with other Marxist movements, the largest and most powerful socialist party in the pre-1914 world. As the largest German party it took over after the 1918 collapse of the monarchy and established the Weimar Republic for whose short and inglorious existence it is often, if unfairly, blamed. The only party to refuse Hitler special powers (Enabling Bill, March 1933), its members were persecuted during the ⇨ Third Reich era. Reconstituted after the war (Wenningsen Conference, Oct. 1945), it had to confine its activities to West Germany, when the Russian zone Socialist Unity Party (SED) was established (April 1946) forcing the SPD to merge with the smaller Communist Party. In the Federal Republic the SPD steadily gained ground (general election 1949, 29·2%; 1965, 39·3% of the poll) and in Dec. 1966 joined the leading CDU in a 'grand coalition' government. Now a broadly-based mass party appealing to the liberal and progressive voter as well as to the working class, its *Godesberger Programm* (Nov. 1959) abandoned basic Marxist tenets (dictatorship of the proletariat, nationalization of the means of production) and accepted the democratic welfare state based on a market economy geared to consumer demand. In the Sept. 1969 elections, the party gaining 42·7% of the vote, formed with the Liberals (FDP) a coalition government with its leader Willy ⇨ Brandt as chancellor.

Spychalski, Marshal M. (1906–). Polish former Head of State, Spychalski played a leading part in the communist war-time resistance to the Germans in Poland. Rapidly promoted in the immediate post-war period, he suffered an eclipse in 1949 as one of ⇨ Gomulka's closest associates and spent six years in prison without trial. Rehabilitated in 1956, he became Minister of Defence in 1957 and has been a member of the Polish United Workers' Party's Politbureau since 1959. Created Marshal of Poland in 1963, he succeeded ⇨ Ochab as Chairman of the Council of State (1968), a post he lost again in Dec. 1970, when ⇨ Gierek replaced Gomulka.

Sri Lanka. ⇨ Ceylon.

SS. *Schutzstaffel* – originally (1925) ⇨ Hitler's bodyguard. When ⇨ Himmler took over command (1929), he transformed the black-uniformed troopers into a militarily trained and ideologically indoctrinated party élite. It was used to suppress the rival and larger SA during the 1934 Röhm purge (⇨ Third Reich). SS power was further extended when Himmler, put in charge of the German police (1936), incorporated it into the SS structure. An omnipresent security force, the SS, with its élite mystique of racial purity, ruthlessness and unquestioning obedience to the *Führer*, soon became the most feared and powerful organization in Nazi Germany. A state within the state with its own settlements, schools, hospitals, industrial enterprises, it controlled the concentration camps and during the war was responsible for the terror and mass murder in occupied Europe. Between 1939 and 1945, the SS military branch, the *Waffen SS*, an élite formation under army command, was greatly expanded. Towards the end of the war about 900,000 men served in the force, which included divisions of volunteering Nazi sympathizers from almost every occupied country. At the ⇨ Nuremberg War Crime Trials, the SS was proscribed as a 'criminal organization'.

Stakhanovism. A movement initiated in the USSR to promote maximum industrial output, named after the Soviet worker Alexei Stakhanov who, in one shift on 30 Aug. 1935, was reported to have hewn 102 tons of coal instead of the then normal 7 tons per shift.

Stalin, J. V. (1879–1953). Of Georgian descent, Stalin became a revolutionary during his studies at a theological seminary in Tiflis and joined his first clandestine Socialist circle in 1898. A ⇨Bolshevik from 1904, he spent most of the period before the 1917 revolution in underground work inside Russia, interrupted by repeated terms of prison and exile. Co-opted on to the Bolshevik Central Committee (1912), Stalin belonged to the party's top leadership at the time of the 1917 revolution, but was both then and during the subsequent civil war hardly known outside the leading party circles and was wholly eclipsed by ⇨Trotsky. Appointed People's Commissar of Nationalities (1917), Stalin between 1919 and 1922 acquired control over most of the principal levers of power in the party and state apparatus. In 1919 he was simultaneously promoted to the newly established Politbureau and Orgbureau of the Party's Central Committee and to the Commissariat of Workers' and Peasants' Inspection (*Rabkrin*). Though created as a counterweight to bureaucracy and corruption in other state institutions, *Rabkrin* developed under Stalin's leadership into a supervisory organ over all other Commissariats and state institutions until, in 1923, its functions were taken over by the Party's control commission which, by then, was also dominated by Stalin. In April 1922, Stalin had become the Central Committee's first Secretary General – a post which he retained until his death despite the warnings expressed in ⇨ Lenin's Testament. Though in full control of the party apparatus even before Lenin's death (Jan. 1924), Stalin's role as Lenin's successor became clear only after the piecemeal elimination of his many actual and potential rivals. In 1923/24, he relied on a temporary alliance with ⇨Zinoviev and ⇨Kamenev to discredit and isolate his most formidable rival, Trotsky. Having achieved this objective, he relied, in 1925/26 on the party's right wing led by ⇨ Bukharin, ⇨ Rykov and Tomsky, to discredit and isolate Zinoviev and Kamenev. In 1926, when the defeated left opposition groups combined to challenge his leadership with a programme of accelerated industrialization, Stalin resorted to administrative measures against them culminating in their expulsion from the party in 1927. With the Left opposition groups out of the way, Stalin, in 1928, suddenly adopted their programme, applying it with a ruthlessness far beyond anything ever contemplated by them, and used the switch of policy as a means of ridding himself of his erstwhile right-wing allies. By the end of 1929, he had succeeded in finally breaking them and having them expelled from their various party offices. After his triumph over Bukharin, Stalin's personal dictatorship became absolute. His subsequent assumption of new offices and titles – Chairman, Council of People's Commissars (May 1941) and, after the German invasion in June 1941, Chairman of the State Defence Committee and Generalissimo – merely added to the outward trappings, not to the substance, of his power. Between 1930 and his death in March 1953, no decision of consequence in either domestic or foreign affairs was taken in the Soviet Union without Stalin's personal initiative or consent. His own biography during that period became the history of the USSR.

Stalingrad. Soviet city on the lower Volga famous for the ferocious five-month battle fought there from Sept. 1942 onwards. The Soviet victory under General ⇨Zhukov in the Battle of Stalingrad constituted the decisive turning point in the war against Germany. Formerly called Tsaritsyn, Stalingrad was renamed Volgograd after ⇨ Khrushchev's denunciation of ⇨ Stalin at the 20th CPSU Congress (1956), but in recent years has frequently been called Stalingrad again.

Stalinism. ⇨Destalinization, ⇨Personality Cult, ⇨Stalin, ⇨USSR.

State Department (United States Department of State). Senior department of the Federal Government established in 1789 to assume responsibility for the administration of foreign policy under the newly adopted Constitution. It remained relatively small throughout the long period of American ⇨Isolationism, and became really large only after World War II with the more extensive and sustained involvement of the United States in world affairs. It has always been an important department, however, and its head, the ⇨ Secretary of State, has occupied a leading position among the President's advisers in most administrations. But whilst the Secretary derives influence from his standing in the Administration and the nation as the senior member of the President's Cabinet, the Department, having few domestic responsibilities, must depend for its influence on the relative importance attached to foreign relations at the time. Even in this sphere, the State Department is often rivalled, and sometimes over-shadowed, by the ⇨Defense Department or the ⇨CIA, since the greater involvement of the USA in world affairs is in so large a measure subservient to the goal of national security.

State of the Union Message. Annual message of the President of the USA to ⇨Congress, delivered to a joint session of the two houses, as required by the Constitution. It sets out the general views and detailed requests of the Administration regarding congressional action for the session.

State of the World Message. In the USA, recent term for an annual message of the President to ⇨Congress, delivered in Feb., in which he reviews international affairs, as distinct from national affairs, which are the subject of his annual ⇨ State of the Union Message.

States' Rights. In the USA, the political doctrine that the several States should enjoy exclusive exercise of powers not specifically granted to the Federal Government in the Constitution, in accordance with the Tenth

Amendment, the final clause of the ⇨ Bill of Rights. The scope of Federal jurisdiction has been progressively extended, by constitutional amendment, ⇨ Supreme Court interpretations (or 'misinterpretations') and by usage (or 'usurpation'). This whole tendency is opposed as undesirable and unconstitutional by the advocates of States' Rights, particularly in the South where the doctrine has had great appeal since before the Civil War in the face of external attacks on the 'peculiar institution' of slavery and later ⇨ Segregation. Southern States have frequently supported presidential candidates known or thought to favour States' Rights, including the ⇨ 'Dixiecrat' Senator J. Strom Thurmond (1948), Senator Barry ⇨ Goldwater (1964) and Governor George ⇨ Wallace (1968). The States' Rights doctrine is also supported by the ⇨ New Right, and is associated with strong attacks on the Supreme Court.

Stettinius, Edward Reilly, Jr (1900–49). US Secretary of State under President Franklin D. Roosevelt (1944–45). An industrialist and financier, he was a close adviser to the President from 1932, first on industrial reorganization and later on defence. He was appointed head of the War Resources Board in 1939, and was Under-Secretary of State from 1943 until he succeeded Cordell ⇨ Hull as Secretary the following year. As Secretary of State he accompanied the President to the 1945 ⇨ Yalta Conference. In 1944 he took the chair at the ⇨ Dumbarton Oaks Conversations on International Security, and he headed the US delegation to the Inter-American Conference on the Problems of War and Peace at Mexico City the same year. He also headed the US delegation to the San Francisco Conference of the UN in 1945, and he resigned as Secretary of State to become the first permanent representative of the United States at the United Nations (1945–46).

Stevenson, Adlai Ewing (1900–65). US political leader, UN ambassador, and unsuccessful presidential candidate. A lawyer until his appointment as special assistant to the Secretary of the Navy (1941–44), he subsequently served as an assistant to the Secretary of State (1945) and as chief of the US delegation to the Preparatory Commission of the UN. Elected Governor of Illinois in 1948, he effected reforms in education, welfare and civil rights. In 1952 he received the presidential nomination at the Democratic ⇨ National Convention. A vigorous campaigner, Stevenson succeeded in raising the level of political debate, but was defeated by General ⇨ Eisenhower's personal popularity and national dissatisfaction with the Democratic administration's foreign policy. He was again defeated by Eisenhower in 1956, and in 1960 refused to seek the nomination a third time. Appointed US ambassador to the UN by President-elect Kennedy (1960), Stevenson brought greater autonomy to the post, and eloquently and effectively represented his country until his death in 1965.

Stewart, Michael (1906–). U K Labour politician and senior member of the Wilson Cabinet – Foreign Secretary (1965–66) and again 1968–70 after an interval as First Secretary of State and Minister for Economic Affairs.

Stikker, Dirk (1897–). Liberal Dutch politician and Foreign Minister (1948–52), he served as ambassador in London (1952–58) and to ⇨ NATO (1958–61) before becoming NATO Secretary-General (April 1961–July 1964), a position which ill-health forced him to resign.

Stimson, Henry Lewis (1867–1950). American statesman who served in the Cabinets of four presidents and enunciated the doctrine of non-recognition which bears his name. He was Secretary of War to President Taft (1911–13), Secretary of State to President Hoover (1929–33) and Governor-General of the Philippines (1927–29), before President Roosevelt made him Secretary of War in July 1940. Stimson had been an early advocate of aid to Great Britain and compulsory military training, and proved to be an able Secretary during his five years of service. Resigning after the Japanese surrender, he warned of the necessity of maintaining military strength to preserve American influence.

'Stop-Go' (U K). Economic policy combining short periods of restrictions ('stop') with short periods of inflation ('go'). The term was used in the early 1960s to criticize the ⇨ Macmillan government for a lack of long-term economic planning.

Strasbourg Parliament. ⇨ Council of Europe.

Strauss, Franz Joseph (1915–). West German politician and leader of the CSU, the Bavarian counterpart of the ⇨ CDU. As the Federal Republic's Defence Minister (1956–62) and architect of its new army, the *Bundeswehr*, Strauss gained a national and international reputation. Abuse of his official position (*Spiegel* affair) outraged public opinion and led to his resignation. Right of centre, he returned to power as Finance Minister (Dec. 1966) in Dr ⇨ Kiesinger's 'grand coalition' government.

Strijdom, Johannes Gerhardus (1893–1958). Prime Minister of ⇨ South Africa (1954–58). From 1934 he was leader of the extremist Transvaal section of the ⇨ National Party. During his premiership, following ⇨ Malan's retirement in 1954, further ⇨ *Apartheid* legislation was passed and those laws already in effect were more strictly enforced. Coloured voters in the Cape were removed from the common roll. The Separate University Education Bill challenged the liberal traditions of the multi-racial universities. In Dec. 1956, 156 people were arrested on charges of treason. Opposition to government policies was to become increasingly hazardous. Foreign criticism of *Apartheid* policies led to a head-on collision at the UN and South African delegates were temporarily withdrawn. Less subtle in his approach than his predecessor and than subsequent apologists of *Apartheid*, Strijdom's name was associated with the concept of *Baaskap*. On his death in Aug. 1958 he was succeeded by Dr ⇨ Verwoerd.

Stroessner, General Alfredo (1912–). President of ⇨ Paraguay since 1954, and a former Commander-in-Chief of the Paraguayan army. His dictatorial regime has allowed some opposition in recent years. Paraguay has become notorious as a haven for Nazi war criminals.

Subversive Activities Control Board. In the USA, an ⇨ Independent Agency established by the Internal Security Act of 1950 (the McCarran Act), partly as a reaction to the outbreak of the Korean War, to enforce measures aimed at bringing communist activities into the open and, generally, preventing the establishment of a 'totalitarian dictatorship' in the United States. It remedied what was regarded as a serious deficiency in the ⇨ Smith Act. At the request of the ⇨ Attorney General, the Board determines whether a suspect organization is a 'communist-action', 'communist-front' or 'communist-infiltrated' organization; and if its determination is positive, the organization concerned is required to register full details of its membership and accounts with the Justice Department. Members of 'action' and 'front' organizations are subject to serious disabilities, especially with regard to employment; and this is sometimes held to establish ⇨ Guilt by Association and to infringe the ⇨ 'Clear and Present Danger' doctrine. The registration requirement was upheld against the Communist Party by the ⇨ Supreme Court in a decision of 1961. Still more severe restrictions were introduced by the ⇨ Communist Control Act of 1954. From time to time, proposals for curtailing the activities of the Board or abolishing it altogether have been introduced in Congress. There have also been attempts to strengthen it, as in 1972, when it was proposed that it be replaced by a Federal Internal Security Board that would exercise its powers and the relevant powers of the Attorney General besides. The Attorney General has not for some years exercised his powers respecting registration, or maintained his 'list' of subversive organizations, which makes it virtually impossible for the Board to act, lacking the initiative as it does.

Sudan. *Area* – 967,500 sq. miles. *Population* (1970 est.) – 15,312,000. *President and Prime Minister* – General Jaafer al-Nemery (1969–). *Constitution* – A transitional constitution (1955) vested authority in a Supreme Commission responsible for appointing the Prime Minister and Cabinet from Members of Parliament. This constitution was suspended (1958) but re-invoked 1964, pending a permanent constitution (promised since 1967). Again in suspension following military *coup d'état* (May 1969).

Political attitudes in the towns (along the Nile) differ markedly from those of the remote and undeveloped countryside. In particular, ethnic and religious loyalties are often stronger than loyalty to the state, and political stability has been threatened by the clash of interests between the more developed Arab and Muslim North and the Negro South whose people have strong tribal links with the Congo and Uganda.

The Sudan was ruled by a British-Egyptian condominium (1899–1956) and was known as the Anglo-Egyptian Sudan. From 1924–36 it was, in effect, ruled by Britain in a similar manner (⇨ Indirect Rule) to other British territories in Africa. Italian ambitions in Africa and international realignments paved the way for the Anglo-Egyptian Treaty (1936) and the restoration of Egyptian influence in the Sudan. Nationalist and pro-Egyptian sentiment, previously discouraged by the British, developed rapidly, and was further stimulated by the war in which Sudan fought on the British side. In 1944 an Advisory Council for Northern Sudan was set up, followed (1948) by a Legislative Assembly for the whole of the Sudan. After the Anglo-Egyptian Agreement (1953) a Sudanese Parliament was elected and a Sudanese Government with internal autonomy established (1954), and the country became a Sovereign Independent State on 1 Jan. 1956. This rapid development was stimulated by the Egyptian military coup (1952), and civil unrest provoked by ethnic and religious rivalries. Two main political parties had emerged in the North – the *Umma* (*Mahdist*) Party (Sudan for the Sudanese) and the NUP (Nationalist Unity Party) which first favoured unity with Egypt and formed the Government (1954) under Premier Ismail el-Azhari. However, in response to changed circumstances, especially after violent Umma inspired demonstrations, the NUP led the country to independence. While independence prevented an outbreak of civil war in the North, prior to its achievement there was an attempted violent revolution in the South (1955). A split in the NUP and the formation of a new party, the PDP (People's Democratic Party), resulted in an uneasy PDP-*Umma* coalition confirmed in the 1958 elections (Feb.). In the same year (Nov.), through a *coup*, General Ibrahim Abboud (subsequently President) established his military regime (1958–64) until a popular revolution re-established civilian government. In the South (since 1955) a number of leaders-in-exile of SANU (Sudanese African National Union) favoured the outright secession of the three southern provinces. In 1963 a terrorist movement developed in the South which was ruthlessly suppressed. Christian missionaries were expelled (1964) and the army acted not only against the terrorist society

(*Anya Nya*) but also against villages accused of sheltering its members. It has been estimated that over 100,000 southern Sudanese sought refuge in neighbouring territories. The 1965 elections resulted in a coalition government with Sayed Mahgoub as Premier. He was replaced (1966) by Sayed Sadik el Mahdi, but again became Premier (1967). In subsequent elections (May 1968) Mahgoub retained the premiership and Ismail el-Azhari retained the presidency. Despite an amnesty promised in the South (Jan. 1968) the elections (May 1968) were accompanied by loss of life and William Deng, leader of SANU was killed in an ambush. President el-Azhari and Prime Minister Mahgoub were overthrown in a bloodless coup in May 1969. A Revolutionary Council, led by Col. al-Nemery, assumed power. A left-wing coup temporarily deposed Nemery from 19–22 July 1971 and was followed by a series of summary trials and executions. The USSR's implication in the failed coup led to a radical change in Sudan's foreign policy with a renewal of diplomatic contact with West Germany and the signing of an economic agreement with China in Dec. 1971. In March 1972, a peace treaty was signed between the Sudanese government and the Southern Sudanese rebels, granting the South regional autonomy.

Sudeten Germans. The German minority inhabiting Sudetenland, the mountainous border regions between ⇨ Czechoslovakia, Germany and Austria. Because of their strategic importance the Versailles peacemakers awarded these territories to the newly independent Czechoslovakia. Friction between Czechs and Sudeten Germans was greatly exacerbated by the rise of Nazism. It led to the Sudeten German demand first for autonomy and then for reunification with Germany which was finally achieved under the ⇨ Munich Agreement. Czech reoccupation (May 1945) led to the expulsion of the three and a half million Sudeten Germans.

Suez Crisis, 1956. Following Nasser's assertion of Egyptian independence and Anglo-French anxieties that their interests in the area were threatened, came to a head when the ⇨ UK, ⇨ France and ⇨ Israel invaded Egypt (Oct./Nov. 1956) after the latter had nationalized the Suez Canal Company (July 1956). The UK had already withdrawn her forces from the Canal Zone in accordance with the Anglo-Egyptian Treaty of 1954, but the Company's shares were held by Britain and France. The Egyptian action was partly in retaliation for the American and British withdrawal of financial aid, for Nasser argued that he needed the Canal dues for financing the Aswan Dam. For Egypt, Britain and France, national prestige played a crucial role in the dispute. Israel's primary concern was to halt Egyptian-sponsored *fedayeen* raids on her borders. Several attempts at negotiation failed: three conferences held in

London (Aug., Sept. and Oct.) discussed various compromise plans but were boycotted by Egypt. Following secret agreements with the UK and France, Israel invaded the Sinai Peninsula (29. Oct). Nasser rejected an Anglo-French ultimatum demanding the cessation of hostilities by both sides, and Anglo-French air operations began against Egypt on 31 Oct., followed (5 Nov.) by paratroop landings. Under pressure of public opinion, expressed at the UN with both the USA and the USSR voicing their criticisms, ⇨ Eden suddenly announced a cease-fire and Anglo-French forces were withdrawn (6 Nov.). The UN then set up an emergency peacekeeping force. The crisis had important international effects. The UK lost considerable prestige through claiming to have acted under provocation and by her ineffective execution of the campaign. Eden, with his memories of betrayal at Munich, likened Nasser to the Fascist dictators of the 1930s. 'Suez' came to symbolize Britain's post-war decline as a major power. It also led to serious political divisions in the UK and to Eden's resignation as Prime Minister a few months later. Israel achieved her aims of re-opening the Straits of Tiran for her shipping and of halting Egyptian border attacks. Israel's victory in Sinai increased Arab resentment and as a result of her collusion with Britain and France, she was accused of being a 'tool of Western imperialism'. Although Egypt's forces had been beaten in the field, Nasser's defiance of the Western powers strengthened his claim to the leadership of Arab nationalism at a time when he faced much resistance from other Arab states as well as serious domestic problems. The union of Syria with Egypt in the ⇨ United Arab Republic was one direct consequence. These events increased Egyptian dependence on Soviet financial and military aid, thus assisting the USSR in its penetration of the Middle East. The crisis also strained relations between the USA and the UK.

Suharto, General T. N. J. (1925–). President of ⇨ Indonesia since March 1968. Previously deputy Chief (1960–65) and Chief (1965–66) of the Army Staff and deputy Prime Minister and Minister of Defence (1966–67), he became acting President in 1967 when ⇨ Sukarno was shorn of his powers. Under his direction Indonesia has adopted a more moderate foreign policy and is concentrating at home on economic development.

Sukarno, Achmed (1901–70). First President of ⇨ Indonesia (1945–68). He was leader of the movement for independence (PNI), formed in 1927, and as such was imprisoned several times by the Dutch. Released by the Japanese when they occupied the Dutch East Indies, he continued the agitation for independence and at the end of the war proclaimed an independent republic, of which he became President. He remained in this office when Indonesian sovereignty was recognized by the Dutch (1949). Sukarno's later years as President were marked by a growing authoritarianism (he adopted the title of 'Great Leader of the Revolution') and in 1967, after the army had strengthened its position by suppressing a communist revolt, he was deprived of his executive powers and in 1968 of the title of President.

Sumatra. ⇨ Indonesia.

Sunay, Cevdet (1900–). President of ⇨ Turkey since 1966. A professional officer, he was formerly Chief of Staff (1960–66).

Supreme Court. The highest Federal court of law in the USA, located at Washington DC. The Constitution (Article III) vests the 'judicial power of the United States . . . in one Supreme Court, and such inferior courts as the Congress shall from time to time ordain and establish'. Though the Court has original jurisdiction in some cases, notably ones in which a State is a party, its greatest importance is as the final court of appeal, in which capacity it determines for itself what cases it will hear. The Supreme Court early acquired the power of Judicial Review whereby it can decide on the constitutionality, and hence the legal validity, of Acts of ⇨ Congress, treaties, actions of the President and his agents, and actions of the States. Thus it has come to be regarded as the 'guardian of the Constitution' and protector of the ⇨ Civil Liberties and ⇨ Civil Rights of the people as set forth in the ⇨ Bill of Rights. The Supreme Court has great authority and importance in American public life, and its reasoned decisions can have an influence even outside the USA. In the course of adjudicating constitutional issues it sometimes makes decisions of the greatest political consequence. It played a significant part, for example, in stimulating the Negro ⇨ Civil Rights Movement when, in 1954, in the case of ⇨ Brown v. Board of Education, it reversed an earlier Supreme Court decision and declared that ⇨ 'Separate but Equal' facilities for the races were unconstitutional, and thus removed the legal basis for ⇨ Segregation and ⇨ Jim Crow Laws in the South. Similarly, the Court made what may prove to have been a major contribution to political evolution when in 1964, in relation to the ⇨ Reapportionment of seats in State Legislatures, it ruled that votes in congressional elections should be of equal value, so striking a blow against ⇨ Gerrymandering and the rural preponderance in the ⇨ House of Representatives. Because of such decisions the Supreme Court is sometimes accused of encroaching upon the powers of the other branches of the Federal Government and of the States, especially by strong advocates of ⇨ States' Rights. During the early days of the ⇨ New Deal similar criticisms of the Court were made from the opposite standpoint when it declared several measures for social and economic reform unconstitutional. However, after 1937, under pressure from the President and Congress, the Court relented, and reversed its position on this kind of legislation. In this change, Justices Louis D. ⇨Brandeis and, later William O. ⇨Douglas played a major part. The Court is, in fact – in the broadest sense, at least – 'political'; and it is consequently open to some political pressure.

The composition of the Supreme Court is determined by Act of Congress. Since 1869, its membership has remained at nine Justices, though in an attempt to overcome the Court's opposition to his New Deal measures President ⇨Roosevelt proposed that the number be increased to a maximum of fifteen, and was accused of trying to 'pack the Court'. Opposition to the proposal in Congress, and the timely reversal by the Court of its position on the President's programme, ensured that the number remained at nine. These are the Chief Justice, who is the presiding officer, and eight Associate Justices. They are appointed for life by the President with the consent of the ⇨Senate, and hold office 'during good behaviour'. Their removal requires impeachment, although they may, if they wish, retire at full pay on attaining 70 years. These provisions help to ensure the independence of the Court from executive and legislative interference. The Chief Justice, in addition to acting as President of the Court, performs some special duties – for example, it is his duty, by custom, to administer the oath of office at the ⇨Inauguration of a President. Chief Justice Earl ⇨Warren headed a commission of inquiry, the ⇨Warren Commission, into the assassination of President Kennedy in 1963. However, the authority of the Chief Justice in deciding cases is no greater than that of any other member of the Court; and each member is free to pursue his own methods of work. Earl Warren who was appointed Chief Justice by President Eisenhower in 1953 played a leading role. He has played a leading role in the Court's stand for civil liberties in recent times, supported by Justices William O. Douglas and Hugo L. Black (both Roosevelt appointments), and, after 1962, Arthur ⇨ Goldberg (a Kennedy appointment). A more cautious position on this issue was taken by a number of members led by Justice Felix Frankfurter and, after his retirement in 1962, by Justice John M. Harlan (appointed by President Eisenhower in 1955). In 1968, President Johnson nominated Abe Fortas to succeed Earl Warren as Chief Justice, but the Senate refused its consent to the appointment. President Johnson's nomination of Thurgood ⇨Marshall, who became the first Negro Associate Justice in 1967, received Senate consent only after much debate. Such cases were, till then, exceptional; it was considered normal for the Senate to confirm the President's nominations, although the possibility of conflict between

President and Congress in this area has always served to highlight the limited application of the doctrine of the ⇨Separation of Powers to the judiciary in America. Conflict seemed to become normal for a time, however, after Republican Richard ⇨ Nixon became President and confronted a Democratic majority in the Senate. Two of his nominees – Clement F. Haynesworth, Jr, in 1969, and G. Harrold Carswell in 1970 – were refused confirmation by the Senate. Both were Southerners, which appeared to count against them, and the Senate finally accepted a nominee from the North, Harry A. Blackmun, who joined the Court in 1970.

Prior to this, President Nixon had appointed Blackmun's close associate, Warren L. ⇨ Burger, to be Chief Justice following the resignation of Earl Warren in 1969. His appointment, which secured easy Senate acceptance, marked the passing of the 'Warren Court', and it became something of a 'Nixon Court' when, in 1971, Justices Harlan and Black departed, and were replaced by two more Nixon nominees, Lewis F. Powell, Jr, and William H. Rehnquist. These changes make it much more likely that the Court will in future adopt a more strict construction of the Constitution. However, on the issue of ⇨ 'Busing' the Court has tended to continue roughly along the lines of the Warren Court.

Supreme Soviet. Name of the official bi-cameral Legislature in the USSR, consisting of the Soviet of Union and the Soviet of Nationalities. (⇨Soviet, ⇨ USSR.)

Surinam. ⇨Netherlands Antilles.

Suslov, M. A. (1902–). Member of the Politbureau and the Secretariat of the CPSU Central Committee. As a member of the two ruling bodies of the Soviet Communist Party, Suslov is one of the select group of men who determine USSR policy. A party member since 1921, Suslov's party career began in the mid-1930s. A member of the CPSU Secretariat since 1947 and a specialist in ideological orthodoxy, he was one of the three Soviet delegates who signed the declaration expelling ⇨Tito from the ⇨Cominform. After a spell as Chief Editor of ⇨*Pravda* (1949/50), he specialized increasingly in defending the CPSU's own version of 'Marxism-Leninism' against sceptics at home and its communist critics abroad. He has played a prominent part in the controversies arising from the ⇨ Sino-Soviet Conflict and in the Soviet pursuit of another communist world conference. Since 1955 he has been, in addition to a member of the Secretariat, a full member of the Party Presidium (later re-named Politbureau).

Svoboda, General L. (1895–). President of ⇨ Czechoslovakia. A professional soldier in the first Czechoslovak Republic, Svoboda escaped after the German invasion of 1939 first to Poland and then to the USSR where he helped to form the first Czechoslovak Army Corps. As Minister of Defence in the post-war coalition government, he was responsible for keeping the army neutral during the communist coup of Feb. 1948. He resigned from the Ministry of Defence in 1950 and for a time disappeared from public life. From the mid-1950s he worked at the Military History Institute and emerged as an active member of the Czechoslovak-Soviet Friendship Society and of the Union of Anti-Fascist Fighters. On his 70th birthday in 1965 his own government awarded him the title 'Hero of the Republic' while the USSR made him a 'Hero of the Soviet Union'. He was elected ⟡Novotny's successor as President of the Republic (March 1968).

Swaziland. *Area* – 6,704 sq. miles. *Population* (1971 est.) – 465,000 (of which 10,000 are Europeans). *Prime Minister* – Prince Makhosini Dlamini.

The smallest and the least constitutionally advanced of the former ⟡High Commission Territories, Swaziland faces difficulties similar to those of ⟡Botswana and ⟡Lesotho, with the advantage of a more prosperous economy. Tribal leadership combined with White settler interests have inhibited the growth of popular political movements. In 1963 British troops from Kenya suppressed civil disorders. A constitutional monarchy – internal self-government since April 1967 with an elected House of Assembly and a Senate (elected and nominated members) – the London Conference (Feb. 1968) made Sept. 1968 the date for full independence despite continuing disagreement on land resettlement. With Swaziland's independence, Rhodesia is Britain's sole remaining constitutional responsibility in Africa. (Swaziland became an independent member of the Commonwealth on 6 Sept. 1968.)

Sweden, Kingdom of. *Area* – 173,400 sq. miles. *Population* (1970) – 8,013,700. *Head of State* – King Gustaf VI. *Prime Minister* – Olaf Palme (1969–). *Constitution* (1809) – Sweden is a constitutional monarchy. Executive power is vested in the King who acts through the Cabinet (*Statsrad*), and elects as Prime Minister the party leader who commands a majority in the Parliament (*Riksdag*). Legislative powers are vested in the bi-cameral *Riksdag*. The 151-member Upper Chamber (*Första Kammaren*) is elected for a period of eight years – one-eighth being replaced every year – by regional bodies, while the 233-member Lower Chamber (*Andra Kammaren*) is elected quadrennially by universal suffrage based on proportional representation. Legislation must be approved by both chambers but can be initiated by either. A *Justitieombudsman* defending the citizen against abuse of the civil powers has his counterpart in the *Militieombudsman*. Proposals for a new 350-member uni-cameral *Riksdag* to be elected for a period of three years have been agreed upon by all major parties and may be enacted in the present (1968–72) legislative period.

The Social Democrats emerged from the twenties onwards, as the dominant power in Sweden's social and economic transformation. The party's sustained popularity – but for an all-party coalition during the war it has been uninterruptedly in power since 1932, even increasing its lead after the Sept. 1968 elections – is based on achievements which gave Swedes the highest living standards in Europe. Though hard hit by the depression in the thirties, the Social Democrats, in coalition with the farmers, passed expansionist legislation which eventually overcame economic stagnation, improved labour relations and broadened the country's industrial base. In foreign policy, Sweden, departing some-what from her traditional neutrality, supported the League of Nations until the League's sanctions policy failed (Ethiopia 1935/36). In May 1939 – Stockholm meeting of Nordic Foreign Ministers – Sweden, ⇨ Norway and ⇨ Finland reaffirmed their neutrality and rejected a proffered German non-aggression pact. The outbreak of the Russo-Finnish war (1939/40) led to the formation of an all-party government, which short of actual military involvement gave all-out aid to Finland, although it refused Britain and France transit rights for a projected military operation. After the invasion of Denmark and Norway (April 1940), her encirclement as well as her military weakness compelled Sweden to grant Germany certain transit rights across her northern territories. This elicited sharp Allied protests, but by summer 1943 with the decline of German power and the growth of her own, Sweden stopped this traffic as well as the export of strategic raw materials to Germany. Throughout the war she provided refuge for an estimated 200,000 Balts, Danes, Finns, Jews, Norwegians, etc.

With the return of peace, the Social Democrats resumed govern-mental responsibility and after overcoming post-war shortages and balance of payment difficulties, initiated an era of rapid economic growth and expansion of the social services. In 1950, 92 year-old King Gustaf v died; as *Landsfather* he had presided over the country's advance from a rural backwater to a leading industrial nation. Although like Finland, Sweden chose absolute, bloc-free neutrality – now backed by formidable military forces – she actively supports all international cooperative efforts. A member of UN, ⇨OEEC, ⇨OECD, the ⇨Council of Europe, the ⇨ Nordic Council, ⇨EFTA, etc., her soldiers played a prominent part in UN peace-keeping actions and two of her diplomats Count Folke Bernadotte and Dag ⇨Hammarskjöld were killed on UN service. Apart from devoting about one third of state expenditure to the social services, Sweden also enacted advanced labour and trade union legislation.

Her main parties (Sept. 1968 elections) are: Social Democrats – 113 seats, Centre Party – 36, Liberals – 43, Conservatives – 33, Communist – 8. Unwilling to become a full EEC member, Sweden in her negotiations with the Common Market (1971/72) was prepared to accept its common agricultural policy, competition rules and the free movement of labour.

Switzerland. *Area* – 15,941 sq. miles. *Population* (1970) – 6 million. *Head of State* (one-year term of office) – President of the Confederation – Dr Nello Celio (1972/73). *Constitution* (1874) – Federal trilingual Republic, with a bi-cameral Parliament (Federal Assembly) of two co-equal chambers – National Council and the Council of States – formed by the 22 cantons. The cantons enjoy considerable autonomy and four of them – Vaud, Neuchâtel, Geneva and Basle – have given votes to women. The 200-member National Council is elected quadrenially by male suffrage (a referendum in Feb. 1959 denied women the vote). A joint session of the Federal Assembly elects the Federal Council, which acts as the Confederation's government and elects from among its members, a President and Vice-President, who serve for one year. The constitution can only be amended by a referendum which can also decide on other laws.

Switzerland's 'permanent neutrality' has deep roots in her history going back to the early middle ages. It has made the country the home of countless international organizations, best known among them the International Red Cross and the ⇨ League of Nations. For a time, Swiss membership of the League was not considered incompatible with neutrality; she severed trade relations with Italy (1935) when sanctions were imposed. After the League's failure to enforce its demands, Switzerland gave notice (1938) that it would no longer participate in any collective action, and has therefore refused to join the UN, although she is a member of ⇨ EFTA and ⇨ OECD. Democratic and politically conservative (the Social-Democrats and a diminutive Communist Party rarely exceed 28% of the vote), Switzerland has often been called a 'moral Big Power' in recognition of its peace policy and the exemplary way in which it rules a multilingual and ethnically diverse populace. Like other ⇨ EFTA countries unwilling to join the ⇨ EEC, Switzerland negotiated (1971/72) bilateral trade agreements with the EEC which will have to be ratified by a national referendum.

Syria. *Area* – 71,210 sq. miles. *Population* (1970) – 6,294,000. *President* – General Hafez al Assad (1971–). *Constitution* (1966, provisional) – Independent Republic. Executive power is vested in the President and the Council of Ministers, who are elected by the Provisional Regional Command of the ⇨ *Ba'ath* Party, which exercises legislative power. Effective power is in the hands of the army.

Syria, a part of the Ottoman Empire until 1920, became with the Lebanon a French mandate territory under the League of Nations. To combat the emergent Arab nationalism which occasionally erupted into open revolt (1925–26) the French granted certain measures of representative government without, however, relaxing their control. A constituent Assembly was duly elected in 1928 but the constitution it drafted was rejected by the High Commissioner. In 1936 the Popular Front Government in France appeared more sympathetic to nationalist demands and it signed a Franco-Syrian treaty which recognized the principle of Syrian independence, but the French Assembly refused to ratify this. During World War II the Allies invaded Syria to forestall the threat of ⇨ Axis control through the Vichy Government (1941) and the country's independence was formally recognized. Syria did not in effect achieve full sovereignty until after the War, when the Allied forces finally departed (1946). From the beginning, Syria's politics were marked by chronic instability resulting from the lack of secure political institutions. The one constant controlling factor has been military groups. Syrian politics are characterized by personal and group rivalries, disputes with other Arab states, and resentment against foreign control and interference (this has more often than not taken on an anti-Western character, although it has lain at the root of Syria's apparently vacillating policy towards the UAR). She is also the most extreme opponent of the State of ⇨ Israel. As a member of the ⇨ Arab League Syria took part in the war against Israel (1948), but the Arab defeat and loss of Palestine had important repercussions in Syrian politics. There followed in 1949 the first three of the coups which have since become commonplace (between 1949 and 1966 there were 18 coups). These led to the rule of various military juntas and then to a dictatorship under Colonel Adib Shishakli (1951–54), who banned political parties, dissolved parliament and was elected President under a new constitution. He was overthrown by an alliance of political opponents, who had formed the Front of National Opposition, but the new attempt at constitutional government was hardly successful – the elections of 1954 produced no clear-cut results and serious conflict arose between those who wanted closer relations with Iraq (this included the advocates of a Greater Syria, i.e. union with Jordan and Iraq under one of their Hashemite rulers) and those who preferred Egypt as a partner. At the same time Soviet influence increased. The Communist Party in the country was the only one allowed in any Arab state and it was well-organized and spread intensive propaganda. In foreign policy Syria was drawing closer to the communist bloc. There were trade agreements with the USSR, Bulgaria, Hungary and Albania, Syrian recognition of the People's Republic of China and the delivery of large amounts of Soviet arms. Russian influence increased, especially in the army, and fears of a communist coup led the *Ba'ath* Party to join with conservative and nationalist groups to seek union with Egypt. The two countries had drawn closer after making a military agreement in opposition to the ⇨ Baghdad Pact (1955) while the ⇨ Suez Crisis of 1956 had increased pan-Arab feelings. The result was the ⇨ United Arab Republic, which came into force in Feb. 1958. Syria was very much the junior partner in the new system – political parties in Syria were dissolved and although two of the original four Vice-Presidents were Syrians, real executive and legislative power rested with President ⇨ Nasser. The latter's personal dictatorship and the callous behaviour of Egyptian administrators in Syria produced disillusionment among those groups which had originally supported the union, notably the Ba'athists and the armed forces. Further Egyptian measures to reduce the country's autonomy sparked off a military coup (Sept. 1961) when Syria seceded from the UAR and reverted to her independent status. The new government was no more secure than any previous one; it was overthrown by yet another military *coup* (1962) and for a time a new and modified union with Egypt was considered. The re-opening of this question only created greater divisions within the country. In March 1963 the *Ba'ath* Party came to power after a military coup. It was opposed to Egyptian dominance in any proposed union and proceeded to purge the army and the civil service of pro-Nasser elements. The *Ba'ath* Party itself was split between the moderates (the old party leaders who favoured some accommodation with Egypt) and the extremists (the 'left wing' of the party consisting of younger and more radical groups who demanded a more activist policy against Israel, independence from the UAR and closer ties with the communist bloc). The latter gained the upper hand and in Feb. 1966 seized power by a military coup. The new government under Noureddine el Atassi as President and Yusef Zuayen as Prime Minister – who were the civilian cover for the military which controlled the bureaucracy of the new *Ba'ath* Party – followed a pro-communist foreign policy, e.g. Zuayen's first official visit was to Moscow and financial aid was received from the USSR and China. It also pursued a more militant line towards Israel and during the winter 1966–67 armed attacks on the border between the two states were a regular occurrence. The Syrian Government, by its aggressive posture – it gave its active support to the guerrilla activities of *Al Fatah* – may have hoped to distract attention from its weak domestic position. In spite of its previous anti-Nasser stand it concluded a defence agreement with the UAR (Nov. 1966) with Russian mediation. Its continuous hostility towards Israel and border attacks as well as accusations of weakness and vacillation against Nasser were an important factor in provoking the crisis which led to the Arab-Israeli War of June 1967. As a result of the war, Syria lost the strategically important Golan Heights overlooking Israeli settlements. Despite her intransigence towards Israel and verbal denunciations of her Arab rivals there still remains a large gap between Syria's military and 'socialist' claims and her ability to carry them out. In Sept. 1971 Syria formed the Federation of Arab Republics with Egypt and Libya.

Szalasi, F. ⇨ Hungary.

T

Tadjikistan. One of the 15 Federal Soviet Republics constituting the USSR. *Capital* – Dushanbe. Tadjikistan comprises one Autonomous Province and one Province.

Taft, Robert A. (1889–1953). A leading conservative Republican legislator in the USA and son of President William H. Taft. He entered national politics with his election to the US Senate from Ohio (1932), after serving in the State Legislature (1921–26, 1931–32). He was a strong opponent of ⇨ New Deal programmes and American involvement in Europe, and co-sponsored the ⇨ Taft-Hartley Act (1947). Unsuccessful candidate for the Republican presidential nomination (1940, 1948, 1952), Taft became the Senate ⇨ Majority Leader (1953). He was a constant critic of the Administration's Korean policy.

Taft-Hartley Act. In the USA, the Labor-Management Relations Act of 1947. It redressed the pro-union tendency of the ⇨ Wagner Act and the ⇨ NLRB, declaring certain kinds of union action illegal or 'unfair'. It prohibited the 'closed shop' and permitted the States to go even further in passing ⇨ Right-to-Work Laws (Section 14b); it outlawed strikes or boycotts conducted by Federal employees, or between unions, or in sympathy with other strikers; and it restricted political expenditures by unions. The Act also established machinery for dealing with disputes where a major stoppage threatens national health or safety. This included a possible 80-day court injunction against a strike, the appointment of a presidential board of inquiry, and a secret vote among employees on the employers' last offer conducted by the NLRB. The Taft-Hartley Act was passed by the first Congress since 1932 with a Republican majority in both Houses. It was declared by President Truman to be 'unworkable' and likely to cause 'serious harm', and incurred the ⇨ Presidential Veto – only to be given the necessary two-thirds majority of both Houses to become law. Despite continuing union opposition to it (especially '14b'), it has remained in force, and its machinery has been used, with variable success, by successive Presidents. Some of its provisions were strengthened by the ⇨ Landrum-Griffin Act of 1959.

Taiwan. ⇨ China, Republic of.

Talhouni, Bahjat (1905–). Prime Minister of ⇨ Jordan (1960–62, 1964–65 and 1967–70). Minister of Foreign Affairs (1961–62).

Tanganyika. ⇨ Tanzania.

Tanzania. *Area* (including Zanzibar and Pemba) – 363,000 sq. miles. *Population* (1967) – 12,311,991. *President* – Dr Julius ⇨ Nyerere. *Constitution* – A one-party state under an interim Constitution (1964). Executive authority is vested in the President elected by universal suffrage. There is a uni-cameral Parliament – the National Assembly.

A Republic within the ⇨ Commonwealth, Tanzania (so named 29.10.1964) was formed by the union of Tanganyika and Zanzibar (27.4.1964).

Prior to independence (9.12.1961) Tanganyika was administered by Britain, first under League of Nations Mandate and then under UN Trusteeship. A combination of factors including the leadership of Dr Nyerere, the effectiveness of his party TANU (Tanganyika African National Union), a Governor sympathetic to African claims and the avoidance of racial strife allowed Tanganyika to achieve independence rapidly and without violence from 1945 when Africans were first appointed to the Legislative Council. Dr Nyerere was appointed Chief Minister, following TANU's pre-independence electoral victory – 70 of the 71 seats in the National Assembly. In 1962 Tanganyika became a Republic with Nyerere as its first President (Nov.). In Jan. 1964 an army mutiny and an attempted coup were only overcome with the aid of British, Nigerian and Ethiopian troops.

A British Protectorate from 1890 Zanzibar prior to 1964 was in many ways more closely linked to the Arab world than to the East African mainland. The government of Zanzibar (an independent constitutional monarchy within the Commonwealth from 9 Dec. 1963) was overthrown in Jan. 1964. The leaders of the revolution – the Afro-Shirazi Party – like TANU favoured a union of Zanzibar and Tanganyika and the two parties agreed to establish a United Republic (April 1964). The new union was faced with internal and external difficulties – e.g. Zanzibar recognized East Germany but Tanganyika recognized West Germany. The effect of the Union has been to confirm Tanzanian opposition to colonialism and to strengthen trading and political links with Communist countries. Tanzania was the first country to recognize Biafra officially (April 1968) (⇨Nigeria), and in July 1968 she resumed diplomatic relations with the UK, severed as a criticism of UK policies with regard to ⇨UDI by Rhodesia.

Tchad. ⇨ Chad.

Teheran Conference. Meeting between Churchill, Roosevelt and Stalin (Dec. 1943) which reached agreement on the early establishment of a second front against Germany in Western Europe and on certain broad outlines of a post-war settlement, as later determined in greater detail at the ⇨ Yalta Conference.

Tertz, Abram. Pseudonym of Andrei ⇨ Siniavsky.

Thadden, Adolf von (1921–). Leader of the German right-wing ⇨ NPD. Although without a political Nazi past, von Thadden joined the radical, right-wing *Deutsche Rechtspartei* (German Right Party) in 1947 and from 1949 onwards represented it in the first Federal Parliament. The party did not prosper and von Thadden lost his seat at the next elections. He renamed the party *Deutsche Reichspartei* and under this masthead succeeded in achieving party representation in the Rhineland-Palatinate Diet. Since it failed in successive general elections to enter the Federal Parliament, von Thadden founded the NPD (Nov. 1964) which tried to appeal to a wider conservative public. This the NPD did; from 1966 onward it gained representation in most *Land* diets, notwithstanding some internecine struggle for the party leadership, from which von Thadden emerged as the undisputed leader. He resigned (Nov. 1971) after the party's repeated defeats in *Land* and Federal elections.

Thailand. *Area* – 198,250 sq. miles. *Population* – 34,205,000. *Prime Minister* – Field-Marshal ⇨ Thanom Kittikachorn. *Constitution* – Constitutional monarchy with executive power vested in the Prime Minister and Council of Ministers. The Constituent Assembly, which is appointed by the King (since 1946, Bhumibol Adulyadej), is only advisory and has no checks on the Prime Minister. The country is divided into 71 provinces, each under a governor. In Nov. 1971 a bloodless military *coup* led by the Prime Minister dissolved the Cabinet and Constituent Assembly, suspended the Constitution and established martial law.

Until 1932 an absolute monarchy, Thailand (called Siam until 1948) was the only country in south-east Asia not subjected to colonial rule. There has consequently been no nationalist movement or development of political parties and in place of parliamentary government the country has been ruled in the last three decades largely by a succession of military regimes. The revolt in 1932 was led by a group of young civilians and officers and during the 1930s the army increased its political control and in 1938 Field-Marshal Pibul Songgram became Prime Minister. His admiration for Japanese militarism led him to establish a dictatorship and in 1941 to form an alliance with Japan, on whose side Thailand entered the war (1942). With Japanese help Thailand received territory in Cambodia, Laos, Burma and Malaya but had to return this to the British and the French in 1945. Pibul was replaced by Pridi Panomyong, who had organized a resistance movement with Allied help. His attempt to establish parliamentary government was discredited by inflation, corruption and the mysterious death of King Ananda (1935–46), and in 1947 he was overthrown by Pibul, who ruled as dictator until 1957 when he in turn was ousted by a military coup this time led by Field-Marshal Sarit Thanarat. There was a brief interlude with elections but in 1958 the constitution was abrogated, parliament dismissed, parties abolished and martial law declared. In 1959 Sarit became Prime Minister with extended powers. One of his main aims was to combat communism (there is a Chinese population of three million). Growing communist pressure in ⇨ Laos resulted in the despatch of American, British and Australian troops to ensure that Thailand was not invaded. Sarit's regime was also marked by impressive economic development including large-scale irrigation and hydro-electric projects and in 1961 a six-year development plan. On his death in 1963 he was succeeded by Thanom Kittikachorn, who has continued his predecessor's policy of encouraging economic progress but has moved away from arbitrary rule. There has been a new constitution and new elections but as with previous elections the low voting record (20–40%) has reflected a popular indifference to politics. Communist insurgency, previously restricted to the poor areas in the north-east (populated largely by Laotians), spread during 1967 with the encouragement of the 'Thailand Patriotic Front', a Peking-sponsored guerrilla movement. In foreign relations Thailand has sought security in commitments with the West. She joined ⇨ SEATO (the headquarters of which are in the capital Bangkok) and the UN (sending supporting troops to the Korean War) and has maintained close relations with the USA from whom she receives substantial economic and military aid (1950 agreement). American military bases in Thailand have been used to bomb North Vietnam and since early 1967 Thailand has sent troops to assist American forces in the Vietnam War. With the communist threat in mind, she signed a common defence agreement with Malaysia (1965) and also joined non-communist regional organizations, e.g. ⇨ ASA, ⇨ ASPAC and ⇨ ASEAN. Amicable relations with her neighbours have been marred by a series of border disputes with Cambodia. However, Thailand's foreign policy is dominated by her fear of her powerful neighbour, Communist China.

Thanom Kittikachorn, Field-Marshal (1911–). Prime Minister of ⇨ Thailand since 1963, he was previously Prime Minister and Minister of Defence (1958) and Deputy Prime Minister and Minister of Defence (1959–63).

Thaw. Term applied to the post-Stalin atmosphere of relaxation in the USSR, derived from the title of a novel by Ilya Ehrenburg.

Thieu, General Nguyen Van. ⇨ Vietnam.

Third International. ⇨ Communist International.

Third Reich. ⇨ Germany.

Third Republic. The constitution under which ⇨ France was governed from 1871 to 1940. The government was responsible to a bi-cameral Parliament consisting of the Senate and the Chamber of Deputies, of which the former was indirectly, the latter directly elected by universal suffrage. Deep-rooted suspicion of authoritarian, anti-republican rule resulted in a constitution favouring weak and unstable governments. During the seventy years the Third Republic existed more than a hundred Cabinets succeeded each other with an average life of a little under eight months.

Third World. As opposed to the power 'blocs' of the Western and Communist Worlds – a generic term for the countries of Latin America and the more recently independent states of Africa and Asia. Three traits are shared by most of the countries of the 'Third World':

(1) A colonial past and resentment of the former colonial power and of imperialism. (In South America these resentments are now directed against the US. In Afro-Asian countries long dominated by Europe a growing nationalism was stimulated by a sense of racial grievance.)

(2) 'Underdeveloped' economies – compared to the advanced industrial economies of Europe, the USA or Japan. In Asia and Latin America the ⇨ Population Explosion continually threatens living standards and the gap between the 'rich' countries and the Third World has widened.

(3) As a consequence of (1) and (2) mass illiteracy is common and political life tends to be dominated by a small (often Western) educated élite.

Many Third World countries (⇨ India) have favoured a neutralist foreign policy. This has not prevented different interpretations of such a policy, internal dissensions or political re-alignments. Since the emergence of the Afro-Asian Bloc (⇨ Bandung 1955) and later conferences (⇨ Belgrade 1961, Algiers 1965) unity has been more often proclaimed than achieved. The Third World accounts for about one-third of UN membership.

Thomaz, Admiral Americo (1894–). President of ⇨ Portugal since 1958 and former Minister of the Navy (1944–58).

Thorez, Maurice (1900–64). Founding member (1920) and Secretary-General of the French Communist Party (1936–64). An unquestioning executant of ⇨ Comintern policies, he voted first against the defence budgets and then, after the Franco-Soviet Pact, for them (1935), attacking the Socialists and then joining them in the ⇨ Popular Front. Conscripted but opposed to fighting an 'imperialist war' (the ⇨ Nazi-Soviet Pact 1939–41 was still operative), he deserted to Russia and returned after the liberation. Vice-President in ⇨ Bidault's 1946/47 government. An unyielding dogmatist in the Stalin tradition, he was succeeded after his death by Waldeck ⇨ Rochet.

Thorpe, Jeremy (1929–). Succeeded Mr Joseph Grimond as Leader of the British ⇨ Liberal Party (18.1.1967).

Tibet. Autonomous Region in the ⇨ Chinese People's Republic (CPR). A Buddhist priest-state under the spiritual leadership of the Dalai Lama, Tibet's claim to political independence repeatedly clashed with China's claim to a right of suzerainty long before the communist victory in 1949. After the proclamation of the CPR, the arrival of Chinese settlers and troops, the imposition of taxes and other CPR interventions led, from the mid-1950s onwards, to mounting revolts by the East Tibetan Kham tribes. In tune with its temporarily 'liberal' attitude of the time, the CPR tried, early in 1957, to calm the situation by concessions. It closed down some of the Chinese garrisons, withdrew many settlers, appointed the Dalai Lama Chairman of the Tibetan Autonomous Region, allowed him to visit Nehru in India and promised to abstain for another six years from introducing changes into the feudal social structure. These policies induced the Dalai Lama to cooperate with the CPR up to a point, but he refused help in the suppression of the Kham revolt. The CPR then increasingly resorted to repressive measures, with the result that the Kham revolt expanded into a nationwide rebellion spreading from Eastern Tibet to Lhasa the capital. The rebellion reached its climax in March 1959, when the rebels attacked the Chinese garrison in Lhasa. They were eventually subdued after bitter fighting. The Dalai Lama fled to India where he was granted asylum, while the Tibetans staying behind were 'pacified' by the Chinese army.

Tito, Josip Broz (1892–). President of ⇨ Yugoslavia. Born in Croatia, Tito served with the Austrian army in World War I and became a prisoner-of-war in Russia. On the outbreak of the revolution there, he joined the International Red Guard and, on his return to Yugoslavia in 1920, the newly-founded Communist Party which was outlawed soon afterwards. After some years of underground work and a spell in prison, he went in 1934 to Moscow where he worked for the ⇨ Comintern and later travelled widely to help with the organization of the International

Brigades for the Spanish Civil War. During the great Soviet purges, the entire Yugoslav communist leadership then in Russia was liquidated (most of them posthumously rehabilitated by Tito in 1959), and in 1937 Tito was appointed as the Party's new Secretary General. He returned to Yugoslavia in 1938 and, after the German invasion of the country, became the Supreme Commander of the Partisan army with the rank of Marshal. As President of the Liberation Committee set up Nov. 1943, he headed the provisional government. After the war, he first headed the new Federal Government and since 1953 he has been President of the Republic. He remained the Secretary General of the League of Communists until Oct. 1966, when this post was abolished and he became the League's President. His defiance of ⇨ Stalin in 1948 and the subsequent course of reform under his leadership has given rise to the term 'Titoism' as a synonym for ⇨ Revisionism and 'national communism'.

Titoism. A term which came into use after ⇨ Yugoslavia's break with Stalin (1948) and which is applied both to the specific domestic and foreign policies evolved in Yugoslavia since that time and to the policies of other communist parties embodying a similar combination of ⇨ National Communism and ⇨ Revisionism.

Todd, Garfield (1908–). Prime Minister of Southern ⇨ Rhodesia (1953–58), has since declared his support for ⇨ ZAPU. A strong opponent of ⇨ Smith, he was restricted to his ranch after ⇨ UDI.

Togliatti, P. (1892–1964). Italian communist and a socialist since his student days, Togliatti sided with the minority which, on orders from the ⇨ Communist International, split the Italian Socialist Party at its Leghorn Congress of 1921 and reconstituted itself as the Communist Party. After Mussolini's advent to power, Togliatti escaped to the USSR where he worked for the Comintern as a member of its Executive until his return to Italy in 1944. Under his leadership, the Italian Communist Party participated in the post-war coalition government up to 1947 and subsequently developed into the largest and most influential non-ruling communist party in Europe. Togliatti's international influence grew after his enunciation of the thesis of ⇨ Polycentrism which he developed following ⇨ Khrushchev's denunciation of ⇨ Stalin at the 20th CPSU Congress of 1956. Between 1956 and his death in 1964, Togliatti emerged as one of the leading advocates of the reformers and 'revisionists' within the realm of ⇨ World Communism, upholding the right of full national autonomy for each communist party, championing the strivings for democratic, individual and cultural freedom and criticizing the survivals of Stalinism within the communist-ruled countries. He incorporated most of these and related views into the 'Yalta memorandum' which he wrote just before his death as the basis of an intended discussion with Khrushchev. The Memorandum was published posthumously (5.9.1964) in *Rinascita* and has since been treated both as Togliatti's political testament and the authoritative guideline for Italian communist policies.

Togo. *Area* – 21,000 sq. miles. *Population* (1970 est.) – 1,857,000. *President* – Général Etienne Eyadema. *Constitution* (1963) – Providing for an elected President and uni-cameral National Assembly, was suspended in Jan. 1967.

A German colony from 1894; after the first World War under League of Nations Mandate and following World War II under UN Trusteeship, Togo was administered by Britain and France. In 1956 (under UN supervision) British Togoland opted for union with the Gold Coast (⇨ Ghana). French Togoland became an autonomous republic in the ⇨ French Union (1956), attained full independence in 1960 and joined the ⇨ *Conseil de l'Entente* in 1965. Poorer than her neighbours (relations with Ghana strained since 1956) and one of the smallest African states, Togo has suffered from political instability. Sylvanus Olympio came to power in the 1958 elections (under UN supervision), dominating Togo politics till his assassination in Jan. 1963. A second military *coup d'état* took place in Jan. 1967 and the following April, its leader, Lt.-Col. Eyadema, assumed the presidency.

Tojo, General Hideki (1884–1948). Prime Minister and war leader of ⇨ Japan (1941–44). Formerly Chief of Staff of the Kwantung Army (1938–40) and Minister of War (1940), his accession to office (Oct. 1941) marked the final control of the military over the political affairs of the country and was followed soon after by the attack on the American fleet at Pearl Harbor (Dec. 1941), leading to the outbreak of war in the Pacific. He resigned in July 1944 after the American victory in Saipan and was later executed as a war criminal.

Tonga. *Area* – 270 sq. miles. *Population* (1970 est.) – 87,000. An independent Kingdom under British protection. Relations with the UK are governed by the Treaty of Friendship (1897), which was revised in 1958 granting more local autonomy. Tonga is a constitutional monarchy with a Prime Minister, Cabinet and Legislative Assembly (elected for three years by universal suffrage).

Tonkin Gulf Resolution. A joint ⇨ Resolution of Congress in the USA adopted (7.8.1964) after incidents in the Gulf of Tonkin in which US warships were attacked by North Vietnamese torpedo boats and the US airforce retaliated by attacking torpedo-boat bases and oil refineries in North Vietnam (2–5.8.1964). The Resolution, similar to the ⇨ Formosa Resolution, approved the retaliation and authorised the President to 'take all necessary steps, including the use of armed forces' to assist

⇨SEATO members in the defence of their freedom. With its authority, President ⇨ Johnson progressively increased United States military involvement in Vietnam, making what amounted to ⇨ Executive War. After the 1968 elections several attempts were made in Congress to repeal or modify the Resolution, and although these were generally not formally successful, they did encourage the reduction of American involvement in Vietnam and other parts of Indo-China.

Tory. Popular term applied to the UK ⇨Conservative Party. It was the name of that party's predecessor (late 17th–early 19th century).

Totalitarianism. Term coined to cover the common features of communist and Fascist states, notably the role of the ruling party and/or state leadership as the sole source of authority and the sole initiator of change endowed with sufficient military and/or police power to subject all sectional interests and all social, political, cultural and religious institutions to its own arbitrary purposes. Among the characteristic differences between older forms of tyranny and the modern totalitarian state or party is the latter's reliance on uninterrupted mass mobilization by a combination of propaganda and terroristic pressure designed to enforce popular participation irrespective of individual or group consent.

Touré, Sékou (1922–). Moslem and socialist President of ⇨ Guinea. First involved in politics as a trade-unionist (organizer of the ⇨CGT in West Africa) and through the RDA. A former mayor of Conakry and deputy to the French Assembly he is a leading opponent of neo-colonialism and champion of pan-Africanism. (⇨ Guinea-Ghana Union, ⇨Casablanca Group, ⇨OAU.)

Trade Expansion Act, 1962. Act of Congress in the USA authorising the 'Kennedy round' of tariff-reduction negotiations. The measure was supported by the ⇨AFL–CIO and the ⇨ Farm Bureau in combination with the US Chamber of Commerce, but was strongly opposed by a wide range of special-interest groups and by bodies hostile to any extension of presidential power. Supplementary measures were introduced at the same time to mitigate any resulting social dislocation; and while these allayed the fears of some, they provoked the opposition of others. Negotiations involving the ⇨EEC and Great Britain (1964–67) resulted in agreement on substantial tariff reductions, but not of the order originally envisaged by President Kennedy.

Trades Union Congress. ⇨TUC.

Trans-Jordan. ⇨Jordan.

Transport House. Headquarters (London) of the British Labour Party and of the Transport and General Workers' Union.

Transylvania. An area inhabited by a majority of Rumanians and a substantial minority of Hungarians now forming part of the Socialist

Republic of ⇨ Rumania. Transylvania belonged to ⇨ Hungary until the end of World War I, but became Rumanian as a result of the Peace Treaty of Trianon. Hungary upheld its claim to Transylvania throughout the inter-war period. In 1940, the ⇨Axis Powers, anxious for both Hungarian and Rumanian support, divided the territory between the two countries by the Vienna Award of 30 Aug., which restored Northern Transylvania to Hungary. After the end of World War II, Northern Transylvania reverted to Rumania as a result of the 1947 Peace Treaty of Paris.

Treason Trials (⇨South Africa). The preliminary hearings of the long drawn-out Treason Trial began in 1956. In the previous year, non-White and anti ⇨ *Apartheid* organizations had gathered to protest against repressive government legislation and had called for a 'Freedom Charter' – equal rights for all citizens irrespective of colour, and universal suffrage. In the wave of arrests that followed, 156 people were charged with treason. The prosecution case included more than 10,000 documents and the court had to adjourn in 1957 to allow defence counsel time to prepare their case. At the end of the preliminary hearings (Dec. 1956–Jan. 1958) charges against 65 of the accused were dropped (including Albert ⇨Luthuli). The remaining 91 were charged with high treason. (The prosecution was led by Oswald Pirow (d. 1959), a former minister in ⇨Hertzog's pre-war governments, and vociferous opponent of South Africa's declaration of war against Germany. His political doctrines ('New Order') hardly differed from Nazi theories.) The 91 appeared before a specially convened court of three judges (Pretoria – 1 Aug. 1958). The charges were later withdrawn (13.10.1958) and the accused divided into two categories and re-indicted. The new charges against 61 of the accused were later quashed (April 1959). The remaining 30 (24 Africans, 3 Indians, 2 Whites, 1 Coloured) were charged (Jan. 1959) (as members of the ⇨ ANC and ⇨ PAC) with conspiring to 'overthrow the state by violence . . .' After more than four years (March 1961) the accused were acquitted with the charges not proven that the ANC was a communist organization and that it advocated violence.

The Treason Trial was unique in South African history both for its length and the mass of evidence produced. Ending with an acquittal it was, however, only a temporary set-back for the government. Political trials continued. Additional legislation and amendments and increases in ministerial power (⇨*Apartheid*, ⇨Verwoerd, ⇨Vorster) reduced the independence of the courts. In political trials and matters relating to discriminatory legislation the South African Judiciary (formerly distinguished for its independent judgements) was increasingly forced to give 'legal' endorsement to government policies.

In the Rivonia Trial (Oct. 1963–June 1964) eight people (6 Africans, 1 White, 1 Indian) (including Nelson Mandela and Walter Sisulu, former Secretary-Generals of the ANC) were accused of sabotage and charged under the 'Suppression of Communism Act' and the 'General Law Amendment Act'. Seven of the accused, including Mandela, were sentenced to life imprisonment. Defence counsel claimed that 156 of the alleged 199 acts of sabotage occurred while Mandela was in prison. In 1966 Abraham Fischer, defence counsel in the Rivonia trial, was sentenced to life imprisonment.

Trinidad and Tobago. *Area* – Trinidad, 1,864 sq. miles; Tobago, 116 sq. miles. *Population* (approx.) – 1,000,000 of whom Negroes (about 47%) and East Indians (35%) predominate. *Prime Minister* – Rt. Hon. Dr Eric ⇨ Williams (1961–). *Constitution* (1962) – Independent Dominion within the ⇨Commonwealth – (the Queen is represented by the Governor-General). The Prime Minister is responsible to a bicameral Parliament of an appointed Senate and a House of Representatives elected by universal adult suffrage.

Trinidad and Tobago was formerly a British Crown Colony. As with ⇨Jamaica, there was serious political unrest in the thirties, and after the war, the constitution was altered (1945) to provide for elections (1946) under universal suffrage. Trinidad's political development, complicated by the continual emergence of splinter groups, based on ethnic divisions, was slower than Jamaica's. A national political party only emerged in 1956 with Dr Eric Williams' PNM (People's National Movement). The appeal of Trinidadian, as opposed to ethnic, loyalties, was emphasized by the PNM's electoral victory (1956) and subsequent election successes (1961 and 1966). Granted internal self-government (1959), following the dissolution of the ⇨West Indies Federation, Trinidad became fully independent (1962). Premier Williams has recognized the need to strengthen Trinidad's economy. A representative was dispatched to Brussels to report on Britain's Common Market negotiations and, nearer home, Trinidad and Tobago became the first Commonwealth country to join the ⇨OAS.

Tripartite Pact. Concluded in Sept. 1940 between Germany, Italy and Japan as the military successor to the ⇨Anti-Comintern Pact. The signatories pledged mutual assistance should they find themselves at war with another major power. Hungary, Slovakia and Rumania joined the pact in 1940, Bulgaria and Yugoslavia in March 1941. The rejection of the pact by a Yugoslav government which overthrew its pro-German predecessor, led to the German invasion (⇨World War II) of Yugoslavia (April 1941).

Troika. Russian term (literally a three-horse vehicle) for a team of three men exercising combined political leadership or domination.

Trotsky, L. D. (1879–1940). Former Russian Commissar for Foreign Affairs and Commissar for War. A revolutionary from the age of 18, Trotsky became a Marxist during several years of prison and exile at the turn of the century. In 1902 he escaped from Siberia and made his way to London where he first met Lenin and Martov and became a contributor to the leading socialist party paper, *Iskra*. When the party split in 1903, Trotsky sided with Martov against the ▷ Bolsheviks, accusing Lenin of carrying the principle of centralism to excess and of seeking to establish a dictatorship over the proletariat. Back in Russia in 1905, Trotsky played an outstanding part in the revolutionary upheaval of that year, becoming the Chairman of the St Petersburg ▷ Soviet. Banished to Siberia after the defeat of the Soviet, he again escaped to London in time for the Party's 5th Congress (May 1907) where he kept aloof from both the Bolshevik and Menshevik factions. During the next ten years he argued in vain for a reconciliation between the two factions. During World War I, Trotsky, jointly with Martov, published a Russian anti-war newspaper in Paris until he was expelled from France and went to the USA. After the outbreak of the February revolution, he made his way back to Russia, arriving in May 1917. By then nothing was left of the differences between Lenin and Trotsky. The two men had adopted similar attitudes to the war and they were in full agreement on the current situation in Russia. In the early summer of 1917, Trotsky joined the Bolshevik party. He was immediately co-opted onto its Central Committee, became a member of the Politbureau on its creation in 1919 and Lenin's closest associate. Elected President of the Petrograd Soviet (Sept. 1917) and Chairman of its Military Revolutionary Committee, Trotsky became the chief organizer of the Bolshevik seizure of power in the capital. As Commissar for Foreign Affairs in Lenin's new government, he conducted the peace negotiations at Brest-Litovsk but, being opposed to the acceptance of the German surrender terms, he resigned from this post early in 1918. As Commissar for War and President of the Supreme War Council from March 1918, Trotsky gained unrivalled prestige as the creator of the Red Army and the chief organizer of its victories in the civil war. Regarded by the outside world as an equal of Lenin in the leadership of revolutionary Russia, and treated as such by Lenin himself despite a number of policy differences, Trotsky neither tried nor succeeded in overcoming the profound distrust of the rest of the old Bolshevik leaders. Lenin's death in Jan. 1924 exposed his almost complete isolation in the party leadership. Despite his former pre-eminence, his enemies, led by ▷ Stalin, ▷ Zinoviev and ▷ Kamenev quickly succeeded in discrediting him first in the Bolshevik party and then in the ▷ Communist International. A belated attempt, after

Zinoviev's and Kamenev's own disgrace, at combining with them against Stalin only hastened Trotsky's final defeat. Ousted first from the Politbureau, he was expelled from the Party (Nov. 1927), deported to Alma Ata (Jan. 1928) and exiled from the USSR (Jan. 1929). Deserted by almost all his former followers and associates (who tried to make their peace with Stalin), Trotsky sought refuge first in Turkey, then in Norway and finally, from 1936 onwards, in Mexico. During the great ⇨ Moscow Trials of 1936, 1937 and 1938, he was chosen to play the part of the chief defendant *in absentia*. On 20 Aug. 1940, he was battered to death in his Mexican home by one of Stalin's agents. A prolific and brilliant writer, Trotsky wrote his most famous book, *The History of the Russian Revolution*, during his exile in Turkey. The practical impact of his ceaseless activities during his years of exile, including his attempt at creating a revolutionary alternative to the Comintern (the Fourth International), remained negligible, though small scattered groups of Trotsky's followers exist to this day in many countries of the world.

Trucial States, renamed United Arab Emirates (1971). *Total area* – 32,000 sq. miles (of which Abu Dhabi comprises 25,000 sq. miles). *Total population* – 240,000 (70,000 in Dubai and 85,000 in Abu Dhabi). They consist of the following seven sheikdoms: Abu Dhabi, Dubai, Sharjah, Ajman, Umm al Quwain, Ras al Khaimah and Fujairah. *President* – Sheik Zaid (of Abu Dhabi).

The Trucial States was so called because their relations with the UK were governed by truces (1820, 1853 and 1892). The Trucial Council was set up in 1952 to induce the rulers to adopt a common policy in administrative matters. Following the decision of the UK government to withdraw from the Persian Gulf by 1971, the Trucial States formed the United Arab Emirates and became independent in Dec. 1971. Oil production in Abu Dhabi (and to a lesser extent in Dubai) is the most crucial factor in its economy.

Trudeau, Pierre (1919–). Prime Minister of ⇨ Canada and leader of the Liberal Party since April 1968. A French Canadian, he won a strong victory for his party in the general election of June 1968 after a rapid rise in politics – he only entered Parliament in 1965 and the Cabinet in 1967 as Minister of Justice.

Trujillo, Rafael (1891–1961). Officially President (1930–38) and (1942–52), but in fact the absolute ruler (1930–61) of the ⇨ Dominican Republic. Even by twentieth-century standards his regime had an unenviable, but justified, reputation for terrorism, corruption and the efficient suppression of all opposition. He was responsible for some material progress (including public works) though it hardly touched the lives of the mass

of Dominican poor. His regime appeared to be devoid of any real programme except increasing the wealth of the Trujillo family and maintaining his personal power. In 1937 his army was responsible (with the
probable connivance of the President of ⇨ Haiti) for the massacre of
more than 10,000 Haitians. He had the capital re-named Ciudad
Trujillo (it reverted to Santo Domingo after his death). There is strong
evidence that his agents kidnapped the poet and critic of his regime,
Jesus de Galindez, in New York (1956) and that de Galindez was
subsequently murdered in the Dominican Republic. Trujillo's involvement in the affairs of other Latin American countries was, in the
case of Venezuela, a factor in his downfall. He was assassinated in
1961.

Truman, Harry S. (1884–1972). Thirty-third President of the United
States and Vice-President to Franklin D. ⇨ Roosevelt. Raised on a
farm in Independence, Missouri, he entered national politics with his
election to the US Senate (1934) from his home State. During his first
term, Truman gained an appreciation of the role of government in
regulating the economy, although it was only after his re-election (1940)
that he enjoyed national prominence as chairman of a committee investigating war-time expenditures. Designated vice-presidential candidate by the Democrats in 1944, he succeeded to the presidency after the
death of Roosevelt the following year (April 1945). Since he had not
taken part in decision-making as Vice-President, Truman came to the
office of Chief Executive relatively uninformed and surrounded by
advisers not of his own choosing. At the outset he continued to implement his predecessor's policies and was an early advocate of the creation
of the United Nations. He decided in favour of using the atom bomb to
bring the war with Japan to an end (July 1945). Gradually restaffing his
⇨ Cabinet, Truman proceeded to institute new policies to meet post-
war problems. In order to check the immediate threat of Soviet expansion the ⇨ Truman Doctrine (1947) was enunciated and ⇨ NATO
established (1949), while the ⇨ Marshall Plan for European recovery
(1947) and the ⇨ Point Four Program for underdeveloped countries
(1949) were intended as long-range programmes to strengthen friendly
nations. Truman was re-elected President in an unexpected victory over
Republican Thomas E. ⇨ Dewey (1948), but was unable to implement
his ⇨ 'Fair Deal' domestic policies over the opposition of conservative
Republicans and Southern Democrats in Congress. At the outbreak of
the Korean conflict (1950), Truman ordered American troops, with
subsequent UN approval, to aid the South Koreans. Always acting forcefully, the President found it necessary to remove General Douglas
⇨ MacArthur as commander in the Far East (1951) and later to seize

the American steel mills to prevent a damaging strike (1952) – an action that was later declared unconstitutional by the ⇨Supreme Court. Often criticized for his failures in domestic matters, Truman nevertheless provided the strong leadership necessary during the post-war period in which the United States acquired a new role of responsibility in world affairs. He declined to run for re-election, and retired to private life in 1952.

Truman Doctrine. Enunciated in 1947 by President Harry S. ⇨Truman, pledged American support to any country of 'free peoples who are resisting attempted subjugation by armed minorities or by outside pressures'. The immediate impetus for this policy was the crises in Greece and Turkey and Britain's inability to assist these countries. To help avoid a communist takeover in these two countries, President Truman asked Congress to appropriate $400 m. in economic and military aid.

Trust Busting. In USA, popular term for action taken under the ⇨Sherman Antitrust Act and similar legislation.

Tshombe, Moise (1919–69). President of Katanga (1960–63) and probably the ⇨Congo's (Kinshasa's) most controversial politician. At the Brussels Round Table Conference (Jan. 1960) Tshombe, favouring a loose tribal federation, unsuccessfully opposed ⇨Lumumba's plans for a unitary state. Backed by the *Union Minière* he declared Katanga independent (11.7.1960). For his refusal to end Katanga's secession, his involvement in Lumumba's murder and his employment of 'white' mercenaries, he was denounced as a traitor. In exile from June 1963 he returned to the Congo to become Prime Minister (July 1964). With the defeat of the Stanleyville 'government' (again mercenaries were employed) Tshombe increasingly challenged ⇨Kasavubu's leadership, but returned to exile after ⇨Mobutu's second coup (Nov. 1965). In Kinshasa on 6 March 1966 Tshombe was tried *in absentia* and sentenced to death for treason (13.3.1966). Kidnapped on board an aeroplane (30.1.1967), he was held prisoner in Algiers. The Congo applied for his extradition (2.7.1967), but he died in captivity in July 1969.

Tubman, William V. S. (1895–1971). President of ⇨Liberia.

TUC. Trades Union Congress – the central organization of British trade unions. Established in 1868, it is now an association of 185 unions with an affiliated membership of about 8,900,000. It is primarily a co-ordinating body, for member unions remain autonomous and conduct their own wage negotiations. Its policy is formulated by the General Council, which is represented on the National Council of Labour together with the Labour Party and the Cooperative Union, and it takes a major part in industrial consultations. The TUC has a close connection with the ⇨ Labour Party, which it helped to found, and after the latter's split in the early 1930s came under Ernest ⇨ Bevin to have a more decisive influence on party policy. It has continued to be a mainstay of the Party both in office and in opposition especially as a source of funds. This relationship entered a critical phase with the Wilson Government's proposals for trade union reform (*In Place of Strife*, 1969). It has opposed with determination the Heath Government's Industrial Relations Act.

Tukhachevsky Trial. ⇨ Moscow Trials.

Tunisia. *Area* – 63,078 sq. miles. *Population* (1971) – 5,194,000. *President* – Habib ⇨ Bourguiba (1957–). *Constitution* (1.6.1959) – The President is the head of the Executive and legislative power is exercised by an elected uni-cameral National Assembly.

Tunisia had close links with Europe even before the French invasion of 1881. Though there was a nationalist party from 1920 (the *Destour*), a popular nationalist movement only emerged in 1934 with Habib Bour-guiba's breakaway ⇨ Neo-*Destour* party. The failure of the ⇨ Popular Front (1936) to introduce reforms encouraged the Neo-*Destour*'s growth, but a successful general strike (1938) and unrest led to Bour-guiba's arrest and the dissolution of the party. The Free French administration which followed war-time Vichy (1940–42) and German (1942–43) rule, by refusing moderate reforms provoked the Tunisian 'National Congress' to demand total independence (1946). On the return of Bourguiba (1949) internal autonomy was promised and the Chenik ministry (17.8.1950) even included Neo-*Destour* members. Settler hostility, however, and French government procrastination pro-voked *fellagha* (terrorist) hostilities, which were aggravated by the arrest of Neo-*Destour* leaders (Feb. 1952). When, finally, the Bey (monarch with titular authority) was forced by threat of deposition to accept empty reform proposals (Dec. 1952), an outbreak of civil war was only prevented by the Mendès-France proposals (31.7.1954). The agreement that followed (2.6.1955), granting internal autonomy to Tunisia, in-curred the opposition and dismissal of Salah ben Youssef, the Secretary-General of the Neo-*Destour*. *Fellagha* and Youssefist terrorists, the French involvement in the war in ⇨ Algeria and the example of the recent independence of ⇨ Morocco finally forced France into granting independence (20.5.1956). The monarchy, never very popular, was soon abolished and Bourguiba established as President. Tunisia's sympathy with Algeria exacerbated the major problem of French bases in Tunisia, but the French bombing of the border town of Sakhiet (25.2.1958) forced French agreement (17.6.1959) to the evacuation of all but their Bizerta base. Bourguiba's demand for the evacuation of this base prompted clashes (July 1961) between the French and Tunisians (800

Tunisians died), but after long negotiations it was handed over to Tunisia (30.6.1962). The Bizerta crisis, though it improved Tunisian relations with the ⇨ UAR and ⇨ Arab League, did not stop Bourguiba from making considerable financial and trade agreements with France (2.3.1963), though the appropriation of all remaining French lands (11.5.1964) temporarily halted this. In foreign affairs Bourguiba has moved Tunisia towards a united ⇨ Maghreb with Morocco and Algeria, and notably attempted to mediate (as he did in Algeria) over the Palestine problem (1965). At home, the re-named (1964) *Parti Socialiste Destourien* (PSD) has maintained its popularity and reputation for moderation in its collectivization of agriculture and its socialist policies.

Turkey. *Area* – 301,302 sq. miles. *Population* (1970) – 35 m. *President* – Cevdet Sunay (1966–). *Prime Minister* – Ferit Melen (1972–). *Constitution* (1961) – Independent Republic. Executive power is vested in the President, who is elected for seven years by the Legislature. He appoints the Prime Minister, who is responsible to the Legislature (Grand National Assembly), which consists of the Senate, and the National Assembly, both elected by universal suffrage.

Following the collapse of the Ottoman Empire after World War I, Turkey (reduced mainly to Asia Minor) underwent a political and social revolution under Mustapha ⇨ Kemal (Ataturk) who was first President (1923–38) of the Republic which was proclaimed in 1923, the Sultanate having been abolished the year before. Acknowledged as the founder of modern Turkey, Kemal passed measures which changed the face of his country, including the secularization of the state (Islam ceased to be the state religion in 1928), introduced new civil, criminal and commercial law codes based on Western European models, and abolished many traditional customs, e.g. the Arabic script, polygamy and the wearing of the fez. In accordance with his policy of Westernization the constitution provided for a Parliament elected by universal suffrage (extended to women in 1934) and a Cabinet, but in fact Kemal was virtual dictator. Turkey won new prestige abroad – an alliance was established with Soviet Russia and in 1936 the Montreux Convention returned the Dardanelles to Turkish control. Consistent with his nationalist programme Kemal rejected foreign loans, but in the absence of domestic capital this slowed down industrialization and necessitated state ownership. Turkey remained neutral for most of World War II, although Ismet ⇨ Inonu (President 1938–50) made little secret of his sympathy for the Allied cause. The possibility of a German invasion persuaded Turkey to conclude a non-aggression pact with Germany (July 1941). However, at a later stage (Feb. 1945) Turkey declared war on Germany.

In March 1945 the USSR demanded a revision of the Montreux Agreement and territorial concessions. Turkey rejected these demands. Fear of Soviet expansion in the area led to Turkey's post-war alliance with the West. By the ⇨ Truman Doctrine (1947) she received military and economic aid from the USA, sent troops to assist the UN in the Korean War (1950), joined ⇨ NATO (1952) and the ⇨ Baghdad Pact (1955), signed a security treaty with the USA (1959) permitting US missile bases on her soil, and became an associate member of the ⇨ EEC (1964). Until 1946 Turkish politics were dominated by the Republican People's Party founded by Ataturk, but in that year pressure forced the government to allow the establishment of the Democratic Party under Celal Bayar and Adnan ⇨ Menderes which followed a more conservative line. The electoral system was reformed and in 1950 the new party won an absolute majority, making Bayar President (1950–60) and Menderes Prime Minister (1950–60). Menderes' most notable achievement was his negotiation of Turkish membership of Western alliances to resist communist pressure (see above) but his domestic policy failed to live up to his aim of extending the modern revolution. He concentrated on developing the economy with the help of foreign aid and investment but rapid industrialization produced tensions which he attempted to solve by suppression. His rule became more dictatorial after the elections of 1954 returned his party to power. Apart from the worsening economic situation, resulting partly from his inflationary policies, discontent grew following restrictions on the press and with the belief that Menderes was encouraging an Islamic revival. This won him the hostility of the intelligentsia, who were ardent followers of Ataturk's secular reforms, and in April 1960 student riots were followed by a military coup (May) under General ⇨ Gursel, who set up a military junta called the Turkish National Union Committee. Menderes and other leaders of the Democratic Party (banned Sept. 1960) were tried on charges of 'violating the Constitution' and corruption and were executed (1961). With a new constitution elections were held (Oct. 1961) and Gursel became President (1961–66). The Republican People's Party regained power under Inonu as Prime Minister (1961–65). The new government was preoccupied with the economic troubles left by Menderes and the problem of what to do with his former supporters (a military coup failed in 1962) but the overriding problem was that of ⇨ Cyprus. Turkey's defence of the Turkish minority population on the island led to a deterioration in relations with ⇨ Greece and to demonstrations at home from the middle 1950s, but the situation became no better after Cypriot independence (1959) and the possibility of armed conflict has arisen several times since. In 1965 the Justice Party (successor to the

Democratic Party) came to power with Demirel as Prime Minister. Riots, students and left-wing unrest brought Demirel's government down in 1971 and his successors were forced to institute martial law.

Turkmenistan. One of the 15 Federal Soviet Republics constituting the USSR. *Capital* – Ashkhabad.

TVA. Tennessee Valley Authority – in the USA, a Federal Government corporation established in 1933 to operate a number of related projects for the improvement of the 40,000 square miles of the Tennessee River basin. Dams have been built to provide for flood control, hydroelectric power and inland navigation; and extensive reafforestation and land reclamation have been carried out. The productivity and amenities of the whole area have been greatly increased. The TVA, one of President Franklin D. ⇨ Roosevelt's major programmes, is often held up as a model of what the Federal Government should do elsewhere, but it is sometimes condemned as 'socialistic'.

Twentieth July 1944. Date of abortive attempt on ⇨ Hitler's life by high-ranking army officers, prominent civilians and disillusioned party members in an effort to end the war and achieve a negotiated peace. The conspiracy collapsed when the Reserve Army failed to occupy government, party and communication centres in Berlin after it became known that the bomb exploded by Colonel Stauffenberg at the *Führer*'s HQ had merely injured Hitler. Striking back quickly, loyal officers had the rebellious generals shot the same day, while prolonged and relentless ⇨ Gestapo investigations uncovered a widespread anti-Nazi conspiracy of Field Marshals, diplomats, priests, teachers and conservative as well as socialist activists. Of the more than 7,000 arrested persons an estimated 5,000 were executed, some after show-trials in the Nazi People's Court like Field Marshal von Witzleben and Generals Hase and Stieff, while others like Field-Marshals von Kluge and Rommel were compelled to commit suicide.

Twentieth Party Congress. ⇨ Destalinization, ⇨ Khrushchev, ⇨ Personality Cult, ⇨ World Communism.

Two Chinas Policy. In 1949, after the communists won control of mainland China and the Nationalists retreated to ⇨ Taiwan, the United States continued to recognize the Nationalist Government of Chiang Kai-shek as the only Chinese government. If the United States were to recognize Communist China and/or Communist China were to be admitted to the United Nations, the problem would arise of determining Nationalist China's diplomatic status. Hence the 'two Chinas policy' has been suggested, whereby the United States would extend diplomatic recognition to both regimes, thus presumably allowing Communist China to replace Nationalist China as one of the five permanent members of the UN Security Council. When, in 1971, this happened, however, the U S Administration showed some hostility to those friendly governments that had voted for the exclusion of the Nationalists. With the visit of U S President, Richard M. ⇨Nixon, to Peking in Feb. 1972, the American position became increasingly unclear, but seems still to lean towards a two-Chinas standpoint.

U

U-2 Incident. Occurred (May 1960) when a specially designed American high-altitude reconnaissance aircraft was brought down over the Soviet Union near Sverdlovsk. A summit conference (May 1960), held to settle the question of the status of West Berlin, subsequently collapsed when President ⇨ Eisenhower refused to accede to Premier ⇨ Khrushchev's demand that the USA apologize for the overflight. The U-2 photographic flights over the Soviet Union, which had been carried on for three years before the incident, were terminated and the American pilot, Francis Gary Powers, was eventually returned in exchange for the convicted Soviet spy, Colonel Rudolf I. Abel (Feb. 1962).

UAM. *Union Africaine et Malgache* (1961–64) – now superseded by ⇨ OCAM.

UAR. ⇨ United Arab Republic.

UD-Ve République. ⇨ UDR

UDEAC. Customs union of ⇨ Chad, ⇨ Central African Republic, ⇨ Congo Republic, ⇨ Gabon and ⇨ Cameroun.

UDI. Unilateral Declaration of Independence by the Rhodesian Government (Nov. 1965). (⇨ Rhodesia, Ian ⇨ Smith.)

UDR. *Union pour la défence de la République* – French party under which the Gaullists contested the June 1968 elections. It emerged from other Gaullist groupings in the Fifth Republic of which the UNR (*Union pour la nouvelle République*, established Sept. 1958) was the first. In 1962 it joined the more broadly-based UDT (*Union démocratique du Travail*) to fight the 1962 and 1967 elections under the UNR-UDT label. After the party lost 40 seats in 1967 (244 seats as against 284 seats in 1962), the Lille Party Congress (Nov. 1967), trying to appeal to the Gaullist left, renamed it *UD-Ve République* (*Union des Démocrates pour la Cinquième République*). Endeavouring to secure the broadest possible backing for the crucial June elections after the May 1968 uprisings, Premier ⇨ Pompidou established the UDR, a loose grouping answering de Gaulle's call for 'a union for peace and freedom'. It gained 292 of the 487 Assembly seats. The Gaullist Independent Republicans, with whom the UDR maintained a second ballot alliance, won another 61 seats.

Together the Gaullist alliance commanded almost a three-quarter majority, the biggest in French republican history.

UDT. ⇨ UDR.

Uganda. *Area* – 91,076 sq. miles. *Population* (1970 est.) – 9,764,000. *President* – Gen. Idi Amin (1971–). *Constitution* (Sept. 1967) – Republic whose supreme legislature is Parliament, consisting of a National Assembly of 82 elected members and executive President who is Head of State and Leader of Government. Former regional governments have been divided into 18 Administrative Districts.

A British Protectorate from 1894 Uganda attained full independence within the ⇨ Commonwealth (9.10.1962). Africans were first appointed to the Legislative Council in 1945 and by 1961 they formed a directly elected majority on the Council. The anxiety of the Kingdom of Buganda (its claimed independence (31.12.1966) was not recognized) that its privileges would be eroded in an independent Uganda were catered for (London Conference, Oct. 1961) by allowing it a special federal relationship with the central government and a greater degree of autonomy than the other three kingdoms. As a result, political stability came to depend on the relationship between the Prime Minister and the *Kabaka* (King) of Buganda. The Governor-General was replaced by an elected President in 1963. In April 1966 Dr ⇨ Obote promulgated a new constitution abolishing Buganda's special status and strengthening the central government, and in May (following army action) the *Kabaka* was forced into exile and Dr Obote assumed the presidency, now the executive arm of the government. He was deposed in a military coup by Gen. Amin, who then pursued a policy of expelling non-Ugandan nationals.

UK. ⇨ United Kingdom.

Ukraine. One of the 15 Federal Soviet Republics constituting the USSR. *Capital* – Kiev.

Ulbricht, W. (1893–). Chairman, Council of State, ⇨ German Democratic Republic. Ulbricht joined the German Social Democratic Party during World War I and the Communist Party (KPD) on its foundation in 1918. A Party official in the inter-war years, he played an important part in the ⇨ Bolshevization of the KPD. He emigrated after Hitler came to power and from 1938 to the end of the war lived in the USSR. An unfailingly loyal Stalinist, he became the effective head of the illegal KPD and was put in charge of the preparations for the post-war take-over. He returned to Germany with the Soviet armies in April 1945 to supervise the reorganization of the party. Under various titles he remained, until 1971, the head of the newly established Socialist Unity Party and East Germany's virtual dictator. In May 1971, he retired from the party leadership, retaining only the honorary post of Chairman of the State Council, which he had inherited in 1960 from the late Wilhelm Pieck, the GDR's first Head of State.

Ulster. ⇨ Northern Ireland.

Umm Al Quwain. ⇨ Trucial States.

UN. ⇨ United Nations.

Uncle Tom. A term currently used by Black militants to describe Negroes who, in their opinion, do not question the structure of 'White' politics and society, especially in the USA. It is a contemptuous allusion to the hero of Harriet Beecher Stowe's pre-Civil War novel, *Uncle Tom's Cabin*, implying that Negroes today who attempt to work within 'the System' are as weak and ineffectual as the nineteenth-century slaves who accepted the Southern social structure.

Union of Soviet Socialist Republics. ⇨ USSR.

Union Pour la Nouvelle République. ⇨ UNR.

United Arab Republic. *Area* – 386,198 sq. miles. *Population* (1971 est.) – 34,000,000. *President* – Anwar Sadat (1970–). *Constitution* (1971) – Provided for a democratic socialist state, with Islam the official religion and the Egyptian people part of the Arab nation. Executive power is vested in the President and an Executive Council. There is an elected People's Assembly.

Contemporary Egyptian attitudes have been shaped by a number of factors: its strategic importance (linking Africa and Asia); its Islamic heritage; the struggle to escape British hegemony; its claims to leadership of the Arab world, especially in the context of the Arab-Israeli conflict; and its attempt at social revolution. These attitudes and the policies they determine are decisively affected by continuing mass poverty exacerbated by a population explosion. (The population has more than doubled in the last 50 years.) The British, while retaining the right to maintain troops on Egyptian territory, formally abolished (1922) the Protectorate they had established at the outbreak of World War I. Under a new constitution Egypt became a kingdom, the Sultan was proclaimed King Fuad (1922–36) and a Parliament was established. The new arrangement was partly an attempt to frustrate the growing popularity of the ⇨ *Wafd* party, which led the demand for complete independence. Rivalry between the palace and the *Wafd*, with Britain supporting one or other contestant in accordance with its own interests, hindered the growth of parliamentary government. In 1936 King ⇨ Farouk succeeded to the throne. But the palace, locked in struggle with the *Wafd*, was increasingly isolated from the masses by its dependence on British support. (From 1930–35 the constitution was suspended and government was by decree.)

Egyptian demands for independence were frustrated by Britain's and Egypt's failure to agree on the status of the ⇨ Sudan and on the presence of British troops on Egyptian territory. These questions were partly resolved by the Anglo-Egyptian treaty of 1936, under which Egypt and Britain became allies and eventual withdrawal of British troops stationed in Egypt for the defence of the Canal was promised. In 1937 the ending of extraterritorial rights on Egyptian territory was agreed and Egypt joined the League of Nations. With the onset of World War II Egypt became a vital base for British armies in North Africa, though Egypt itself did not declare war until 1945. Fascist movements had already made their appearance in Egypt, and Farouk appeared to be an unreliable ally for the British. In 1942, with the British army in North Africa in a critical position, the British Ambassador (supported by troops) forced Farouk to recall Nahas Pasha, the *Wafd* leader, to the premiership. After the war the *Wafd*, compromised by their war-time cooperation with Britain, failed to match the growing mood of nationalism – a nationalism stimulated by disagreements over the Sudan (on which Egypt appealed to the UN), the British garrison on the Suez Canal and by opposition to Jewish settlement in ⇨Palestine. Violently opposed to the UN partition of Palestine (1948), Egypt, in company with other ⇨Arab League states, sent forces to the area. Their defeat by smaller Israeli forces increased popular resentment against the corruption and inefficiency of the Egyptian Government. With large-scale rioting (partly the result of British action in the Canal Zone), the threat of anarchy and the *Wafd* unable to control events, General ⇨ Neguib of the Free Officers' Movement staged his *coup d'état*. Farouk abdicated in favour of his infant son, but the monarchy was abolished and Neguib assumed the presidency of a military regime. Though land reform destroyed the power of the feudal (*pasha*) class, Neguib failed to match the increasingly radical mood of his followers and was ousted by ⇨Nasser, the strong man behind the scenes (1954). Elected President for a six-year term under a new constitution (Nov. 1954), Nasser established Egypt as the dominant Arab state to which the younger intellectual and radical elements in the Arab countries looked for leadership. Nasser's government initiated actions aimed at increasing Egyptian influence not only in its own region but in the world at large. Negotiations with the British resulted in the agreement to complete evacuation of the Canal Zone by June 1956 (⇨ Suez). Following the ⇨ Bandung Conference and especially through the establishment of close ties with Marshal ⇨Tito and ⇨Nehru Egypt became with India and Yugoslavia an influential member of the Neutralist Bloc. Nasser's prestige in his own country was enhanced by his confirmation as

President with increased powers under a new constitution (June 1956). Meanwhile, Egyptian support for *fedayeen* raids into Israeli territory increased tension between the two countries. In 1955, Nasser had negotiated an arms deal with Czechoslovakia. His foreign policies inevitably antagonized the West and the UK and USA withdrew their promised financial aid for the proposed Aswan High Dam. Nasser then nationalized the Suez Canal (July 1956). On 29 Oct., acting in collusion with France and Britain, Israel invaded the Sinai peninsula (⇨ Suez Crisis), and a couple of days later British and French forces invaded Egypt. Within a week, world opinion forced the UK, France and Israel to withdraw and the Canal Zone was occupied by UN forces (Dec. 1956). Though the Egyptian armies in Sinai were defeated and suffered severe losses, and the Egyptian economy was placed in a precarious position, the effect of the Suez Crisis was to give Nasser a resounding diplomatic victory and enhance his prestige, especially in the Arab world. A further effect of the crisis was to increase Egyptian dependency on Soviet financial and military aid. Reflecting Nasser's ambition to create a greater Arab nation under his leadership, Egypt and Syria were formally linked in the UAR (Feb. 1958) followed by Yemen's association with the UAR to form the United Arab States (March 1958). However, despite common Arab opposition to Israel, external and internal rivalries continued to frustrate attempts at greater unity. In 1961, Syria withdrew from the UAR and Egypt became involved in civil war in the Yemen. At a national congress (1962), Nasser stressed the need for a genuine socialist revolution and for greater unity of Arab states. The Arab Socialist Union was formed and a national charter for its guidance was ratified by the National Congress (June 1962). The visit of Khrushchev to Cairo (1964) confirmed the strengthening of relations between Egypt and Russia and Egypt's hostility towards the West which she accused of supporting Israel. Egypt initiated attempts at closer Arab unity under UAR leadership through a succession of Arab summit conferences and efforts to embrace Iraq, Syria and Egypt in a unified Arab High Command as well as in a closer general union. Increased tension between Israel and Syria (May 1967) resulted in an abrupt reversal of Egyptian policy towards Israel. For some years up to then, Nasser, while strongly opposed to Israel, had advocated the need for caution and greater preparation so that an Arab victory would be assured before precipitating a conflict. Following unconfirmed Russian reports of an Israeli military build-up on the Syrian border, Egypt mobilised its armies in Sinai (17.5.1967), demanded the withdrawal of the UN emergency forces (19.5.1967), reoccupied Sharm Al Shaikh and blockaded the Straits of Tiran (23/24.5.1967). Israel replied with air attacks on Arab bases (5 June) effectively destroying the Arab air forces and paving the way for the rapid defeat of the Egyptian and Jordanian forces (⇨ Arab-Israeli Conflict). With Israeli troops on the Suez Canal, Egypt agreed to a cease-fire (10 June). In a nation-wide broadcast, Nasser accepted responsibility for the disaster and offered his resignation (11 June), but after large-scale demonstrations the following day he agreed to remain in office. However, the repercussions of the war continued to be felt. In Egypt, blame for the debacle was shifted from Nasser to the military leaders who were replaced and many put on trial. The arrest of Field Marshal Abdel Hakim ⇨ Amer was announced (4 Sept.) and his subsequent suicide (15 Sept.). The announcement of the sentences (15 years in one case, 10 in another and 2 acquittals) imposed by a military court on senior air-force officers, led to serious demonstrations and rioting in Cairo (Feb. 1968). The demonstrators complained of the leniency of the sentences and President Nasser promised a re-trial (March). Nasser died in Sept. 1970 and was succeeded by Vice-President Sadat.

Attempts to close the Arab ranks have continued. Following the Khartoum conference (Aug. 1967) it was announced that UAR forces were to withdraw from the ⇨ Yemen. Up to the June War relations with ⇨ Saudi Arabia had deteriorated, especially with reports of Egyptian use of poison gas in the Yemen (Jan. 1967), followed by the closing of Egyptian banks in Saudi Arabia (Feb.) and the UAR's denunciation of ⇨ Jordan and Saudi Arabia as reactionary puppets of Western imperialism. Saudi Arabia, ⇨ Kuwait and ⇨ Libya agreed to provide Egypt with £95 m. annually to offset losses incurred by the war and the closure of the Suez Canal. In Aug. 1971, Egypt formed a Federation of Arab Republics with Libya and Syria and reverted to its former name of Egypt. The USSR's importance as a military ally was strengthened by a 15-year Treaty of Friendship and Cooperation between Egypt and the USSR, signed in May 1971.

United Kingdom of Great Britain and Northern Ireland. The island of Great Britain consists of England, Wales and Scotland. ⇨ Northern Ireland has been a part of the United Kingdom since 1920. The UK formerly included the whole of Ireland. Though represented in the UK Parliament, Northern Ireland also has its own Parliament. Scotland has a separate Judiciary and legal system.

Area	– England and Wales –	58,348 sq. miles
	Scotland –	30,411 sq. miles
	Northern Ireland –	5,206 sq. miles
Population	– England and Wales –	48,594,000
(1971)	Scotland –	5,228,000
	Northern Ireland –	1,525,000

Head of State – Queen Elizabeth II (1952–). *Prime Minister* – Edward
⇨ Heath (1970–). *Secretary of State for Foreign Affairs* – Sir Alec
⇨ Douglas-Home. *Chancellor of the Exchequer* – Anthony ⇨ Barber.
Constitution – The UK is a constitutional monarchy. Its 'unwritten'
constitution has evolved over the centuries through precedent and con-
vention, including Acts of Parliament and judicial decisions.

Though as Head of State the Sovereign's formal assent is required
before a parliamentary bill becomes law, she acts on the advice of her
ministers. Consequently, executive authority is vested in the Prime
Minister and his Cabinet who are responsible to Parliament. Legislative
authority is vested in a bi-cameral Parliament consisting of the House of
Commons and the House of Lords.

The *House of Commons* is elected by adult universal suffrage for a five-
year term. It has 630 members each representing a single constituency.

The power of the *House of Lords* has been curtailed over the years. It
cannot prevent the passage of legislation nor delay its enactment (Parliament Act 1949) for more than one year. Membership of the House of
Lords includes hereditary peers and (since 1958) life peers and peer-
esses.

With the growth of Cabinet power the importance of the *Privy
Council* (formerly the Sovereign's close advisers) has declined. Its
judicial functions (which included hearing appeals from the Dominions
and Colonies), already diminished by the Statute of ⇨ Westminster
(1931) have been further diminished by the number of Colonies that
have achieved independence since World War II.

The Prime Minister (appointed by the Sovereign) is the leader of the
party which gains a majority of seats at a General Election. The development of a strong two-party system and especially in recent years
the amount of government legislation enacted in each parliamentary
session, has tended to increase the power of the Prime Minister and
Cabinet at the expense of the Commons.

From 1933 to 1938 Britain slowly and unevenly recovered from the
ravages of the Great Depression, while a succession of ⇨ Conservative-
dominated ⇨ National Governments (⇨ MacDonald, ⇨ Baldwin,
⇨ Chamberlain) failed to contain or divert German and Italian aggression abroad. Those who voted for Baldwin's National Government in
the General Election (Nov. 1935) in the belief that they were also voting
for support of the ⇨ League of Nations and collective security were to
feel cruelly cheated when the proposals of the ⇨ Hoare-Laval Plan became known a month later. The public outcry led to the appointment of
⇨ Eden in place of Hoare as Foreign Secretary. After Baldwin, whose
reputation was restored by his handling of the ⇨ Abdication Crisis,

resigned (27.5.1937) Neville ⇨Chamberlain formed a new government. The British and French policy of non-intervention in the ⇨Spanish Civil War dealt a further blow to the declining prestige of the League. Chamberlain's policy of ⇨Appeasement was dramatically reversed after the ⇨Munich Agreement when Germany swallowed most of what was left of ⇨Czechoslovakia (March 1939). In the following months the British Government gave pledges of support to ⇨Poland, ⇨Greece, ⇨Rumania and ⇨Turkey. After the German invasion of Poland (1.9.1939), Britain and France declared war on Germany (3.9.1939) (⇨World War II).

For the people of Britain, the Phoney War came to an end with the German victories in ⇨Denmark and ⇨Norway. Under the impact of military reverses Chamberlain at last acceded to the demands for his resignation – (L. S. Amery in the House of Commons (7.5.1940) quoting Cromwell – 'Depart, I say, and let us have done with you. In the name of God, go!' – voiced the feelings of the majority of his countrymen). On May 10 with the German armies already sweeping through ⇨Holland and ⇨Belgium, Winston ⇨Churchill became Prime Minister and under his leadership the nation achieved a new sense of unity and purpose. With the fall of France, Britain alone in Europe stood out against Nazi Germany. The evacuation of ⇨Dunkirk not only rescued a beleaguered army but salvaged hope and pride out of military defeat, and for the first time, in the Battle of Britain, a serious defeat was inflicted on the German war machine.

Through the difficulties and defeats that still lay ahead (⇨World War II) the British war effort was sustained by belief in ultimate victory – much less in doubt once the USSR and the USA were drawn into the conflict. The war hastened Britain's decline as a great world power (the USA assumed Britain's role as the leading maritime and trading nation). Internally the measures needed for an all-out war effort and the determination to avoid the squalor and misery that followed the First World War paved the way for ⇨Attlee's Labour Government and the ⇨Welfare State. The record of the Labour administration has to be measured in terms of its aims – maintenance of full employment and social security, nationalization of basic industries, colonial independence – against a background of financial difficulties heightened by the war and a continuing adverse balance of payments.

The new social concern reflected in welfare measures included raising the school-leaving age (1947), National Insurance Act (1946), Housing Acts (1946, 1949) and the National Health Service Act (1946). The programme of nationalization began in 1946 with the Bank of England Act and the Coal Industry Nationalization Act, and was followed in 1947 by the Electricity Act, the Transport Act, the Gas Act, and most controversially in 1949 the Iron and Steel Act. (Steel was later de-nationalized by a Conservative Government (July 1953) and has since been re-nationalized (July 1967).)

UK GENERAL ELECTION RESULTS:

	Seats		Votes polled	
1935	Conservatives	387	For National Govt.	11,791,461
	Liberal National	33	Opposition	9,992,710
	Labour	154	Unopposed votes	1,884,754
1945	Labour	398	Labour	11,992,292
	Conservative	189	Conservative	9,988,306
	Nat. Lib.	13		
	Liberal	12		
1950	Labour	315	Labour	13,265,610
	Conservative	298	Conservative	11,166,026
	Liberal	9	Liberal	2,621,489
1951	Conservative	321	Conservative	13,718,069
	Labour	295	Labour	13,949,105
	Liberal	6	Liberal	730,552
1955	Conservative	344	Conservative	13,311,938
	Labour	278	Labour	12,405,246
	Liberal	6	Liberal	722,395
1959	Conservative	365	Conservative	13,750,965
	Labour	258	Labour	12,195,765
	Liberal	6	Liberal	1,661,261
1964	Labour	317	Labour	12,205,581
	Conservative	303	Conservative	11,980,783
	Liberal	9	Liberal	3,101,103
1966	Labour	363	Labour	13,057,941
	Conservative	253	Conservative	11,418,433
	Liberal	12	Liberal	2,327,533
1970	Conservative	330	Conservative	13,064,965
	Labour	287	Labour	12,141,676
	Liberal	6	Liberal	2,109,218

The pattern of future ⇨Commonwealth developments was set by the Indian Independence Act (1947) (⇨India, ⇨Pakistan) followed by independence for ⇨Ceylon and ⇨Burma, and in Africa by steps leading to Gold Coast self-government (⇨Ghana). The ⇨Palestine mandate was relinquished in 1948 (⇨Bevin, ⇨Israel).

The Conservative Party, promising relief from austerity, returned to power in 1951. During a period of increasing affluence the ⇨Labour

Party was afflicted by internal divisions (⇨ Gaitskell, ⇨ Bevan, ⇨ Clause IV). The Conservatives, despite ⇨ Suez – which emphasized Britain's declining status as a great power – and leadership rivalries, remained in office for 13 years. Decolonization, including criticism from the left and right over the manner of its implementation (⇨ Cyprus, ⇨ Kenya, ⇨ Guyana, etc.) was continued. A chronic balance of payments crisis (⇨ 'Stop–Go') plagued successive administrations. Retrospectively the first post-war Labour administrations appear less as a new departure than as an interlude in habitual conservative rule. The popularity of Wilson's Labour administrations from 1964 (at first high in reaction to '*You've never had it so good*') slumped dramatically with measures (including wage-freeze and devaluation) taken to deal with economic crises. Policies on entry into the ⇨ Common Market, ⇨ Rhodesia, ⇨ Race-Relations, ⇨ Vietnam have at different times alienated left- and right-wing support; all of them issues which had also divided opinion among the parliamentary opposition. The Conservatives were elected to office in June 1970. In Jan. 1972 the United Kingdom signed the Treaty of Accession to the ⇨ EEC.

United Nations. Term coined by President Roosevelt and first used officially in the Washington (Jan. 1942) pledge of the 26 nations fighting the Axis not to conclude a separate peace and to abide by the principles of the ⇨ Atlantic Charter. The structure of a supra-national authority to succeed the ⇨ League of Nations was debated at the Moscow Foreign Ministers' Conference (Oct. 1943). Its Charter, worked out by the Big Four – Britain, China, USA, USSR – at Dumbarton Oaks (Aug./Oct. 1944), was only approved by the ⇨ Yalta Conference (Feb. 1945) after the Russians had inserted the controversial veto, which allowed a dissenting permanent member of the Security Council to defeat majority decisions. The UN was formally established on 24 Oct. 1945, when the 51 states had ratified the Charter which they approved at the founding conference (San Francisco, June 1945). The aim of the UN, according to its preamble, is 'to save succeeding generations from the scourge of war . . . reaffirm faith in the fundamental human rights . . . promote social progress'. While the Charter prohibits intervention 'in matters which are essentially within the domestic jurisdiction of any state' rendering human rights etc. unenforceable, 'threats to peace' are explicitly exempted from these provisions. To safeguard peace the UN can impose economic sanctions, or intervene militarily with forces made available by member states. Apart from a host of specialized agencies and *ad hoc* committees, the UN operates through its six main organs: the *General Assembly*, the *Security Council*, the *Secretariat*, the *Economic and Social Council*, the *Trusteeship Council* and the *International Court*.

The *General Assembly* – all member nations have one voice and one vote. It may enquire into and submit recommendations about any issue dealt with by, or brought to the notice of any UN organ or agency, except matters under Security Council consideration. Decisions are made by simple majority vote unless they touch 'substantive' issues which require a two-thirds majority. Such issues are the election of the Security Council's non-permanent members, Charter amendments, the admission of new or the expulsion of recalcitrant members, or any matter deemed 'substantive' by the majority. While the Assembly, by passing the budget, exercises some power over the executive (Security Council) and the administrative (Secretariat) branches, its main function was meant to be deliberative. However, in view of the veto-bound Security Council's inability to act, the Assembly in its Uniting for Peace resolution (Nov. 1950) asserted its right to recommend collective action and the use of force in the defence of peace. There is doubt whether such recommendations are constitutionally binding.

The *Security Council* – was conceived as the UN's executive organ, able to deal with threats to peace, and therefore has the power to enforce its decisions, which under the charter are binding on members. Unlike the Assembly, the Security Council remains in continuous session and can convene at any time. Of its 15 members (1965 Amendment; previously 11 members whose affirmative majority was 7), the Big Five – the Republic of China, France, Great Britain, the USA, the USSR – are permanent. The remaining ten serve for a period of two years. Geographical criteria are a determining factor in their election, allowing the various regions (Africa, Arabia, Latin America, etc.) to be equitably represented in the Council. Decisions on routine matters are carried by nine votes; on 'substantive' issues these votes must include those of the permanent members. The veto power derives from this rule. Abstention of a permanent vote is generally not regarded as negating a decision, although certain matters, i.e. issues affecting membership (admission, suspension, expulsion), Charter amendments, etc., explicitly demand affirmative unanimity among the permanent members. Although the veto has been widely resented as stultifying and contrary to the principle of sovereign equality, it acknowledges the need for cooperation between those who yield effective power and may be called upon to use it. Such cooperation has been tenuous and infrequent. During the Korean crisis, UN action in support of the victim of aggression was only possible by the USSR's boycott of and absence from the Security Council at the critical moment. Threats to peace are regarded by the Council under two aspects: 'disputes', which may develop into conflicts and in which it may try to arbitrate and make 'recommendations'; or actual breaches of the peace which can be dealt with by sanctions and, if necessary, by military action which, if called for by the Council, is mandatory on members. The Charter allows member states to enter into regional arrangements for the defence of peace (⇨NATO, ⇨Warsaw Pact, etc.).

Secretariat (New York City) – provides the administrative civil service for the UN. But its head, the Secretary-General, as the UN's chief official, enjoys a status far transcending that of a chief administrator. Although the Secretary-General has no vote, he can attend Security Council meetings; he is empowered, indeed obliged, to bring contentious issues to the notice of the appropriate UN organs and to act as their chief mediator. He presents to the General Assembly the annual report on UN activities and problems. As the organization's chief executive he will 'perform such functions' as UN organs have entrusted to him. He is supported in his various tasks by a staff of approximately 4,500 internationally recruited members. The Secretary-General is appointed by the General Assembly on the recommendation of the Security Council; his term of office, left indefinite by the Charter, runs by usage for five years but can be extended. The first Secretary-General, Trygve ⇨ Lie (1945–52) incurred the wrath of the USSR over his handling of the Korea conflict. His successor, Dag ⇨ Hammarskjöld, although re-elected (1957) was again attacked by the Russians who proposed that his office be replaced by a ⇨ *Troika* of Western, East-Bloc and Bloc-free representatives. Flying home from a Congo peace mission, Hammarskjöld was killed in an air crash (Sept. 1961). He was succeeded by ⇨U Thant, replaced after two terms of office by Dr Kurt ⇨Waldheim of Austria (Jan. 1972).

Economic and Social Council – was set up to encourage and co-ordinate the UN's cultural, social, economic and humanitarian activities. Its 27 members (1963 Amendment, previously 18 members) are elected by the General Assembly for a three-year term, and can and are re-elected if their participation is considered of particular value to the Council's work. The Council initiates studies within its jurisdiction, makes recommendations to the General Assembly, member nations or special UN agencies. It is assisted by regional (Europe, Asia, Africa, Latin-America) and functional Commissions on Statistics, Population, Social Developments, Human Rights, Status of Women, Narcotics. The Council meets at least twice a year.

Trusteeship Council (New York City) – originally set up to administer the League of Nations mandated territories and other non-self-governing territories. Due to decolonization it now has only the Australian-administered part of New Guinea and the USA-administered Trust Territory of the Pacific Islands under its jurisdiction. These comprise the Marshalls, Marianas and Carolines with a total population of approximately 75,000 inhabitants. The Council meets once a year and is made up of administering and non-administering countries.

International Court of Justice (The Hague) – taken over from the League of Nations Court of International Justice, is the principal judicial organ of the UN. Only sovereign states can ask the Court to adjudicate and in so doing undertake to abide by its ruling, against which there is no appeal. Failure to comply with Court decisions may result in action by the Security Council to enforce them. The Court is composed of 15 judges of different nationalities, regions and legal systems. They are appointed by governments, but to be elected need an absolute majority both in the General Assembly and the Security Council. They serve for a term of nine years and can be re-elected. The Court elects its own President and Vice-President who serve a term of three years.

UN OPERATIONS:

1946 – Sponsors arrangements for the withdrawal of Soviet troops from ⇨ Iran.

1946/47 – Council vetoes, General Assembly condemns Albanian, Bulgarian and Yugoslav intervention in Greek civil war (⇨ Greece).

1947 – ⇨ Palestine partition plan.

1948 – Attempts at settling ⇨ Kashmir conflict.

1949 – Mediation between the Dutch and the emerging government of ⇨ Indonesia.

1950–53 – Intervention in the ⇨ Korea conflict.

1956 – Intervention in the ⇨ Suez Crisis.

1956 – Abortive attempt to persuade USSR to desist from military intervention in ⇨ Hungary.

1958 – Protection of ⇨ Lebanon against UAR subversion.

1960–64 – Deployment of UN forces in the ⇨ Congo.

1962 – Mediation in and settlement of the West Irian dispute between Indonesia and the Netherlands.

1963 – Failure to mediate in the ⇨ Malaysia/Indonesia confrontation resulting in Indonesia's withdrawal from the UN.

1964 – Installation of peace-keeping force in ⇨ Cyprus.

1965 – Cease-fire demand for the ⇨ Dominican Republic.

1967 – Cease-fire arrangements in the Arab-Israeli Six Day War (⇨ Arab-Israeli Conflict) and passing of the (Nov.) peace formula.

1971 – Admission of ⇨ Chinese People's Republic to UN and expulsion of the ⇨ Republic of China (Taiwan).

1972 – Disarmament Convention on Prohibition and Destruction of Bacteriological Weapons signed by UK, US and USSR.

Of the 15 *Specialized Agencies* the best known are: IAEA (International Atomic Energy Agency) (Vienna) – established in 1957 to promote the development of the peaceful uses of atomic power. 1968 budget – approx. US $12·5 m.

ILO (International Labour Organization) (Geneva) – dating back to League of Nations days, it aims at improving work conditions, labour relations, social benefits, etc., by international agreements and conventions. 1968 budget – US $25·7 m.

IBRD (International Bank for Reconstruction and Development) (World Bank) (Washington DC) – set up (1944) to further economic development of member nations by granting loans to governments or government-guaranteed enterprises. The Bank's capital is made up by share subscriptions of member states based on their respective wealth. Total capital subscribed amounts to approximately US $23,000 m. of which about 10% has been called up. Total loans between 1947 and 1967 amounted to US $10,500 m. and are rising.

IDA (International Development Association) (Washington DC) – affiliated to the World Bank, it aims at helping the emerging countries with capital projects on particularly flexible terms. Founded in 1960, between 1960 and 1967 it backed 109 projects in 38 countries, advancing approximately US $1,700 m. Capital is subscribed by member states.

IFC (International Finance Corporation) (Washington DC) – an affiliate of the World Bank, it was set up in 1956 to assist productive private enterprise not backed by government guarantees. Its main field of activity is in the emerging countries. Up to June 1967 the IFC invested US $221 m. in 138 projects in 36 countries.

IMF (International Monetary Fund) (Washington DC) – set up (1944) to promote the growth of international trade and to support currency stability. It plays an important role in keeping exchange rates stable and defending currencies under pressure.

GATT (General Agreement on Tariffs and Trade) (Geneva) – founded 1948, aims at liberalizing tariff levels. The Kennedy Round Trade Agreements (1964–67), negotiated under its auspices, resulted in across-the-board tariff cuts of industrial goods affecting a trade of about US $40,000 m.

UNESCO (United Nations Educational, Scientific and Cultural Organization) (Paris) – established in 1945 'to advance through the educational and scientific and cultural relations of the people of the world the objectives of international peace and the common welfare ...'. To this end UNESCO endeavours to raise educational standards, advance adult education, improve communication between libraries, archives, etc., encourage artistic cooperation, preserve the cultural heritage of mankind, expand channels of communication through press, radio, television, etc. These objectives are furthered by sponsoring relevant programmes initiating studies, arranging conferences, etc. Numerous regional and functional offices support work for which in 1968 a budget of US $118·5 m. was available.

WHO (World Health Organization) (Geneva) – set up in 1948 as the directing and co-ordinating authority on international health. It assists governments in strengthening health services, stimulates research into the eradication of epidemics, tries to improve nutritional standards, sanitation, etc. in cooperation with other agencies, encourages co-operation among scientific and professional groups; in short, promotes every factor making for physical, mental and social well-being. 1968 budget – US $56·1 m.

FAO (Food and Agricultural Organization) (Rome) – founded 1946, aims at providing and spreading knowledge on food production and related subjects (fisheries, forestry, nutrition, etc.). It gives technical advice, initiates research projects, runs pilot schemes and with the UN administers the food stocks collected from member nations for distribution in an emergency. The two-yearly budget amounts to US $50 m.

Among the *Temporary Agencies*, originally set up to deal with particular problems as they arose, such as the provision of peace-keeping forces (Congo, Cyprus, Middle East, etc.), the best known are:

UNICEF (United Nations Children's Fund) (New York City) – established in 1946 to aid mothers and children in war-ravaged countries. Having served its original purpose, UNICEF has, since 1950, increasingly assisted the development of maternal and child health services in the developing countries, and supported their educational and vocational training schemes. Financed by voluntary contributions from governments and individuals, its 1967 allocations amounted to approximately US $50 m.

UNRWA (United Nations Relief and Works Agency for Palestine Refugees in the Near East) (Beirut) – was set up by the General Assembly in May 1950. It aims at providing relief services for Arab refugees who lived in Palestine for a minimum period of two years before the 1948 conflict and assisting them to become self-supporting. Including the post-1967 refugees, UNRWA now looks after 1,750,000 displaced Arabs. Current expenditure runs to an estimated annual amount of US $42·5 m., of which about 36% is spent on food, 34% on education, and 10% on medical aid.

United Nations Command (UNC). ⇨ Korea.

United Party (⇨ South Africa). Founded in 1934 with the coalition of

⇨ Hertzog's ⇨ National Party and ⇨ Smuts' South African Party, it continued in power until 1948. On Hertzog's defection in 1939, Smuts became Prime Minister. The United Party based its appeal on Afrikaans-English reconciliation, racial segregation and the maintenance of strong ties with Britain. The party of business, industrial and particularly mining interests, its supporters ranged from moderate Afrikaaners (certainly up to 1939) to white liberals. The latter, unhappy about some of its domestic policies, preferred it to ⇨ Malan's National Party. In opposition from 1948 (and after Smuts' death in 1950 without an effective leader), it appealed to the constitution embodied in the Act of Union, hence its opposition to the removal of Coloured voters from the common roll. However, its own record when in office (in 1936 African voters in the Cape were removed from the common roll) and its acceptance of the basic tenets of white supremacy have inhibited it as an opposition and hastened its decline.

United States Agency for International Development. ⇨ AID.

United States of America. ⇨ USA.

United States Atomic Energy Commission. ⇨ AEC.

United States Joint Chiefs of Staff. ⇨ JCS.

UNR. ⇨ UDR.

Upper Volta. *Area* – 105,800 sq. miles. *Population* (1970 est.) – 5,330,000. *President* – Gen. Sangoulé Lamizana (1966–). *Prime Minister* – Gérard Ouedraogo (1971–). *Constitution* (1970) – elected president and uni-cameral National Assembly.

Established as a French colony in 1919, Upper Volta ceased to exist in 1932 when its territory was divided between the ⇨ Ivory Coast, Soudan (⇨ Mali) and ⇨ Niger, but was re-established in Sept. 1947. Upper Volta attained self-government within the ⇨ French Community in 1958, full independence outside the Community in 1960 and is a member of the ⇨ *Conseil de l'Entente*. Economically undeveloped, many of its people work in the Ivory Coast with whom Upper Volta has strong economic and political links. On 4 Jan. 1966, Sangoulé Lamizana deposed the President and made himself Head of State. Governed by military decree for the next four years, a new constitution was drawn up and free elections took place in 1970.

Uruguay. *Area* – 72,172 sq. miles. *Population* (approx.) – 2,750,000. *President* – Bordaberry, Juan Maria (1972–). *Constitution* – Democratic Republic – the people's sovereignty guaranteed by elections and if necessary by referendum. The unwieldy collegiate system (National Council) in force from 1951 was abandoned when the country voted (plebiscite 27.11.1966) for a return to the presidential system. The new constitution provides for an Executive of an elected President (and

Vice-President) and Council of Ministers. There is a bi-cameral General Assembly of a Senate and Chamber of Representatives.

The history of twentieth-century Uruguay, with its attachment to democratic institutions and its advanced social legislation, contrasts uniquely with the experience of other Latin American Republics. A small homogeneous population (mostly of Spanish and Italian descent) and a relative absence of extreme social inequalities contributed to these developments. They also owe a great deal to the inspiration and leadership of one man – José ⇨Batlle y Ordonez (1856–1929). By 1920 social-democratic legislation, including old-age pensions, an eight-hour working day, holidays with pay and the nationalization of basic industries and public services, had turned Uruguay into a welfare state. The Church was disestablished, religious instruction in schools abolished and divorce legalized. Orderly progress was threatened by economic depression and there was a short period of dictatorial rule during Gabriel Terra's presidency (1931–38). Terra added to the socialist legislation started by Batlle. A brief coup (1942) was rapidly followed by constitutional government. Uruguay's political stability may be threatened by a continuing unfavourable trade balance. Advanced social legislation has not precluded social unrest in the sixties. (In 1961 the Soviet and Cuban ambassadors were expelled.) Nor has Uruguay been spared violent demonstrations including clashes between students and police (1968). The (liberal) *Partido Colorado* dominated the administration for over 90 years up to 1958 when the (conservative) *Partido Nacional* (*Blancos*) formed the government. The *Colorados* returned to power in 1967 with 608,000 votes (1966 elections) against the *Blancos'* 497,000. Both parties include several factions. FIDEL – (*Frente Izquierda de Liberacion*) which includes Communists and *Fidelistas* (Castroists) got 70,000 votes in the 1966 elections. President Gestido (died Dec. 1967) was succeeded by the Vice-President Jorge Pacheco Areco. The emergence of the Tupamaros (left wing urban guerrillas) threatened political stability. In a bitter election campaign (Nov. 1971) *Colorado* candidate Bordaberry's victory was disputed and had to be ratified by the electoral supreme court.

USA (United States of America). Federal union of 50 States which has developed from the nucleus of 13 former British North American colonies that declared their independence on 4 July 1776. The newest members are Alaska and Hawaii, admitted 1959.

Area, including outlying territories – 3,619,655 sq. miles. *Population*, including armed forces abroad – 208 m. (of which approx. 53% are Protestants, 38% are Catholics, 5% are Jews, 11% are Negroes). *President* – Richard M. ⇨Nixon (1969–). *Vice-President* – Spiro T. Agnew.

Secretary of State – William P. ⇨ Rogers. *Secretary of Defense* – Melvin R. Laird. *Federal Budget*, 1971 – $212,000 m. *Defence* – $78,000 m. *Government* – The Constitution was drafted in 1787 to replace the original Articles of Confederation, and the ⇨ Bill of Rights, comprising the first ten amendments, was added in 1791. The fifteen subsequent amendments have not fundamentally altered the Constitution, although it has gradually evolved over the long period of its operation. The system is federal, and powers not granted to the Federal Government are reserved to the States or the people. In practice decentralization is carried even further; the most local units of government, which are legion, enjoy a high degree of autonomy, even in finance. The structure of the Federal Government, and of most inferior governments, is based on the doctrine of the ⇨ Separation of Powers; membership in any of the three co-ordinate branches of government – legislative, executive, judicial – is incompatible with membership in any other. The Constitution vests all legislative powers of the Federal Government in ⇨ Congress, comprising the Senate and House of Representatives. Congress also controls the raising and spending of funds. Executive power is granted to the President. He holds office for a four-year term which commences (in accordance with the ⇨ Lame Duck Amendment) on 20 January following the presidential elections (which take place in the November of each leap year). By the Twenty-Second Amendment to the Constitution (adopted 1951) a President is eligible for re-election once. On the death of the President, the Vice-President succeeds, and he also exercises the presidential powers during the President's legal incapacity. The Twenty-Fifth Amendment (1967) empowers a new President thus succeeding to appoint a new Vice-President with the concurrence of Congress. Members of the President's ⇨ Cabinet are responsible to him for the conduct of administration. They and other executive officials are appointed by the President with the consent of the Senate. The President is Commander-in-Chief of the armed forces, and he can call the ⇨ National Guard into Federal service. He makes military appointments, and has the personal advice of the ⇨ JCS. The Constitution provides for a ⇨ Presidential Veto of legislation, although this can be overridden by a two-thirds vote of both houses of Congress. The President also has powers relating to the third branch of government, the Judiciary. Judicial powers are vested in the ⇨ Supreme Court and inferior courts established by Act of Congress, but the Chief Justice and Associate Justices are appointed by the President with the consent of the Senate. They hold office during good behaviour. The courts have the power of judicial review whereby congressional and presidential acts can be declared unconstitutional, and hence null and void. Relations between the three branches of government are such that they tend to share in the exercise of governmental powers in a system of mutual ⟩Checks and Balances. Effective action requires their cooperation; and whilst minimum cooperation is ensured by the long-established two-party system, comprising the ⟩ Democratic Party and the ⟩ Republican Party, success depends on interpersonal more than inter-party accommodation. In this 'bargaining' process the President has come to play the leading part.

It was envisaged that the Legislature would have the dominant voice in national affairs; and for much of the nineteenth century something approximating congressional government existed. But the twentieth century has seen the emergence of the Executive as the dominant branch, the President, as Chief Executive, being the principal beneficiary. This has been due partly to constitutional adjustments whereby the President has come to be directly elected from a nation-wide constituency, rather than indirectly, as intended, by the ⟩ Electoral College. But probably more important has been the increasing involvement of the United States in world affairs (a field in which the President has always held the initiative, especially where the deployment of military forces is involved), and the increasing involvement of the Federal Government in economic management and social welfare (these being fields in which continuous executive and administrative action is required). The President now has the task, not merely of executing the laws, but, through the ⟩Executive Office of the President, the ⟩ State Department, the ⟩ Defense Department and other major agencies, of making national policy. He heads vast, complex administrative and military establishments. He has become the principal initiator of legislation, and without his lead Congress could scarcely proceed to action. Moreover, he can circumvent Congress's treaty-making power by entering into ⟩ Executive Agreements and its war-making power by embarking upon ⟩Executive War. And whilst Congress may hold the purse-strings, it is the President, through the ⟩Bureau of the Budget, who keeps the national accounts. The President is in every way the nation's political chief.

The conditions favouring this development have been summarised as 'warfare and welfare', and these have been the major themes of United States history during the present century. Theodore Roosevelt (President, 1901–09), with his theory of the President's 'stewardship', gave the office a prominence it had scarcely enjoyed since the assassination of Abraham Lincoln (1865), and brought the United States into the world arena. World War 1 further enhanced the President's status, at home and abroad; and President Woodrow Wilson (1913–21) took the fullest advantage of it to enlarge his role. After the war, however, the United States reverted to its traditional ⇔ Isolationism, rejecting the Treaty of Versailles and membership of the League of Nations, and many of the advantages gained by the President were lost. The momentum of presidential power was recovered during the Great Depression of the 1930s. When President Herbert ⇔ Hoover's projected return to prosperity failed to materialize, he was defeated at the polls by Franklin D. ⇔ Roosevelt (1932) who initiated the ⇔ New Deal. This proved as advantageous to the President as a successful war. Up to 1937, the President's measures were often opposed by the Supreme Court. Thereafter, the Court generally gave its blessing to social and economic reforms, and to the consequent enhancement of the powers of the Federal Government, now more than ever at the disposal of the Chief Executive. The later part of Roosevelt's term as President was dominated by ⇔ World War II. Whilst the war in Europe was in progress, the President won an unprecedented third term, making the presidency more personal than ever. When, despite United States attempts to remain non-involved (exemplified by the ⇔ Neutrality Acts), the Japanese attack on ⇔ Pearl Harbor brought her into the war (1941), the President assumed more or less full control, and personally directed his country's war effort.

The successful conclusion of the war did not bring a return to isolationism as before, though possession of the A-bomb might have encouraged it. The USA was committed to membership in UNO from the time of the ⇔ Dumbarton Oaks conversations (1944). Agreements entered into by Roosevelt at the ⇔ Yalta Conference shortly before he died (1945) ensured the continued presence of United States forces in Europe for some time, and this was immediately confirmed by his successor, Vice-President Harry S. ⇔ Truman, in the ⇔ Potsdam Agreement (1945). Japan was also to remain occupied. The United States commitment to Europe was made a regular peacetime one when Truman accepted the ⇔ Marshall Plan (1947); and before the completion of this commitment, the onset of the Cold War provided a new and continuing basis for American involvement. A permanent military commitment was foreshadowed in the ⇔ Truman Doctrine (1947), and the Anglo-American airlift to defeat the ⇔ Berlin Blockade (1948–49) confirmed the need for it. It was formalised in the establishment of ⇔ NATO (1949). The Cold War, and the policy of ⇔ Containment, entailed United States involvement in other areas of the world also, notably the Pacific and South-East Asia, especially after the establishment of the ⇔ Chinese People's Republic (1949). Truman immediately committed troops to the defence of South ⇔ Korea when it was invaded by the

North (1950), and the Korean War was his principal concern for the remainder of his term. One product of the war in Asia was the ⇨Anzus Treaty (1951). During the same period, United States technical and economic assistance was extended to the rest of the world, beginning with ⇨Point Four (1949) and developing into the ⇨Mutual Security Program (1951). In the Western Hemisphere, United States commitments were made more positive and regular by the ⇨Rio Treaty (1947) and the establishment of ⇨OAS (1948). At home, the Truman Administration continued and extended the policies of the New Deal in the ⇨Fair Deal (1949). In the field of industrial relations, however, the President was defeated by the passage of the ⇨Taft-Hartley Act over his veto (1947) by the first Republican congressional majority since 1932. The mood of the country and Congress was becoming less liberal at this time, more especially when the Korean conflict grew into a major war. This was shown by the passage of the McCarren Act establishing the ⇨Subversive Activities Control Board (1950) and the increased activities of ⇨HUAC. In general, however, the Truman Administration saw a further enhancement of the ascendancy of the President, internally and externally. The power of the President was demonstrated by Truman's dismissal of the popular General Douglas ⇨MacArthur (1951) for insubordination. The election of Dwight D. ⇨Eisenhower (1952), the first Republican President for 20 years, presaged a moderation, if not a reversal, of this trend. Eisenhower was not a professional politician and had no programme of proposed action except for ending the Korean War. When an armistice was concluded (1953), a period of disengagement seemed likely. Internally, the Eisenhower Administration was a period of relative inaction, at least on the part of the President. The early years, with the Republicans again in the majority in Congress, and holding the important committee chairmanships, saw the rise of Senator Joseph ⇨McCarthy and further action against 'internal subversion'. However, by the time the ⇨Communist Control Act was passed (1954), the mood was changing again, and the Act was not vigorously enforced. Eisenhower's second term saw the beginnings of Federal involvement in the Civil Rights field, heralded by the historic Supreme Court decision against school ⇨Segregation (in ⇨Brown v. Board of Education, 1954), with the despatch of Federal troops to ⇨Little Rock and the passage of the Civil Rights Act setting up the ⇨Civil Rights Commission (1957) to enforce the decision. In foreign affairs, whilst the President himself was generally inactive, his Secretary of State, John Foster ⇨Dulles, was far from being so. Though he threatened the Western Allies with an ⇨'Agonizing Reappraisal' of United States policy in the direction of 'going-it alone' he intensified the confrontation with communism, adding the threat of ⇨ 'Massive retaliation' and the promise of ⇨ 'Rollback'. Containment, however, remained the operative policy, and it was formally extended to South-East Asia with the establishment of ⇨ SEATO (1954) and the adoption of the ⇨ Formosa Resolution (1955), and to the Middle East with the enunciation of the ⇨ Eisenhower Doctrine (1957). This period, following the death of ⇨ Stalin (1953), saw a gradual improvement in relations between the USA and USSR, and meetings were held at the summit. This ended with the fiasco of the Geneva meeting following the ⇨ U-2 Incident (1960), the last international act of the retiring President.

The end of the Eisenhower Administration had also been marked by deteriorating relations with Castro's ⇨ Cuba, and this provided the opening scene for the incoming Administration. The administrations of John F. ⇨ Kennedy (1961–63) and Lyndon B. ⇨ Johnson (1963–69) saw a powerful reassertion of presidential leadership after the Eisenhower 'interlude'. But the return of the Democrats to the White House also saw yet another fulfilment of the prophecy that Democratic Presidents lead America into war – this time in Vietnam. President Kennedy began unpropitiously with the ⇨ Bay of Pigs fiasco (1961), but he largely made up for this by his handling of the ⇨ Cuba Missile Crisis (1962). Unexpectedly, this led to an improvement in relations with the Soviet Union, marked by the establishment of the ⇨ 'Hot Line' and agreement on the ⇨ Nuclear Test Ban Treaty (1963). It also gave strong impetus to the defence 'revolution' initiated by Secretary of Defense Robert ⇨ McNamara. But President Kennedy's real impact abroad was different in character from that of his predecessors, as was his impact at home. The President's invocation of the spirit of the ⇨ New Frontier, and the Administration's emphasis on youth and dynamism, set a style that aroused fresh aspirations everywhere, not least among the young Negroes who activated the ⇨ Civil Rights Movement. In keeping with his style was the establishment of the ⇨ Peace Corps (1961) and, in another way, the passage of the ⇨ Trade Expansion Act (1962) which led to the 'Kennedy Round' of tariff reductions. However, despite the Kennedy 'mystique' (which extended to the President's family, also, especially his brother, Robert ⇨ Kennedy), the Administration's positive and liberal proposals made little headway in the face of congressional conservatism, and much of the programme was still outstanding when John Kennedy was assassinated (1963). Much of this programme was subsequently enacted under the leadership of Kennedy's Vice-President and successor, Lyndon B. Johnson. This included the important 1964 Civil Rights Act which extended the scope of anti-discrimination laws far beyond the measure of 1960 and established the ⇨ Community Relations Service, and the Voting Rights Act (1965) which restricted ⇨ Literacy Tests. It also included ⇨ Medicare (1965). President Johnson's own idea of a ⇨ Great Society entailed action against poverty as well as discrimination (the two being intimately linked) and he introduced his ambitious ⇨ Anti-Poverty Program to deal with major social problems. To associate youth with the programme, he established ⇨ VISTA as a 'domestic Peace Corps' (1964). In 1964 Johnson won a resounding electoral victory over conservative Republican Barry ⇨ Goldwater; but the theme of the President's new term was set, not by this, but by the adoption, a few months earlier, of the ⇨ Tonkin Gulf Resolution. On its authority, Johnson increased United States military involvement in ⇨ Vietnam to the level of full-scale war, and then gradually escalated the war until its human and material costs became unacceptable to an increasing proportion of the nation, especially the young. Opposition to the war, and to the ⇨ Selective Service System that 'drafted' young men into it, increasingly took the form of direct action and civil disobedience as advocated by the growing ⇨ New Left. This, together with the increasing dissidence of militant Negroes, disenchanted with liberal remedies and demanding ⇨ Black Power, made Johnson one of the least supported Presidents of recent times. Though he took steps towards ending the Vietnam War, joining the ⇨ Paris Peace Conference and curtailing bombing of the North, he remained unpopular, and declined to stand for re-election in 1968. The Democratic candidate, Hubert ⇨ Humphrey, hampered by his association with Johnson as Vice-President, was narrowly defeated by Republican Richard M. ⇨ Nixon, who had been Vice-President under Eisenhower. The new President entered his term of office in a much more reticent and relaxed manner than either of his two predecessors. His ⇨ Inauguration (1969), when he declared it his task to unify the nation, seemed to mark the beginning of another 'interlude' in the growth of presidential leadership. However, actions of the President following the mid-term Congressional elections of 1970, both at home and abroad, tended rather to reinforce the long-term trend. In domestic affairs, after an initial phase of economic non-intervention, Nixon declared his commitment to Keynesian economics, and in 1971 he introduced his 'new economic policy' for containing inflation, diminishing unemployment, and reducing the American balance of payments policy. It began with a ninety-day wage–price–rent freeze, the suspension of gold convertibility of the US dollar, and a surcharge on imports. The surcharge was removed when the dollar was devalued in Dec. 1971. The freeze was instituted on the basis of the 1970 Economic Stabilization Act (extended

1971), the passage of which the President had originally opposed. 'Phase II' of the policy, which was initiated at the end of 1971, placed it on a regular basis through the agency of a Pay Board, a Price Commission, and a Cost of Living Council, all acting under the President's authority. The policy showed a measure of success in containing inflation, but not in reducing the balance of payments deficit. In foreign affairs, the President played an exceptionally active role, not only cultivating better relations with the Soviet Union, but reversing the longstanding American policy of not dealing with Communist China. The President visited Peking in Feb. 1972 for talks arranged by his close adviser, Henry ⟡ Kissinger, and followed this by a visit to Moscow in May, 1972. From the beginning of the Nixon Administration, the normalization of foreign relations took precedence over ⟡ Containment as the theme of American foreign policy. Most important was the progressive de-escalation of American involvement on the ground in Vietnam. However, the President ordered the resumption of the bombing of the North in April 1972 following fresh incursions of North Vietnamese troops. In this period the ⟡ Paris Peace Conference was temporarily broken off, but in Jan. 1973 a cease-fire agreement was announced. In all these actions, the central role has been played by the President and his advisers; and although Congress has been able in some measure to cajole and obstruct, the initiative has generally lain with the Executive in all major areas of policy. Nixon was reelected President in Nov. 1972.

USIA. United States Information Agency or Service – an ⟡ Independent Agency established in 1953 to administer all existing overseas information programmes of the Federal Government and develop new and more effective ones. To carry on the United States 'campaign of truth' it maintains field offices and libraries in most non-communist countries (frequently targets of anti-American riots), though its activities have been cut back in recent years because of the growing balance-of-payments problem. One of its agencies is the ⟡ Voice of America. Its Director is appointed by the President with the consent of the Senate, and he works under the general guidance of the ⟡ Secretary of State and the ⟡ NSC.

USSR (Union of Soviet Socialist Republics). *Area* – 8·65 m. sq. miles. *Population* (1971 est.) – 234,896,000. *Chairman, Presidium of the Supreme Soviet USSR* – N. V. ⟡ Podgorny (1965–). *Chairman, All-Union Council of Ministers* – A. N. ⟡ Kosygin (1964–). *General Secretary, CPSU Central Committee* – L. I. ⟡ Brezhnev (1964–).

The USSR has developed from the Russian Soviet Federal Socialist Republic (RSFSR), the first state to emerge from the October Revolution of 1917 on the territory of the former Tsarist Empire. In the course of the civil war further Soviet Republics were established, voluntarily or otherwise. Most of these Republics were later reorganized, and new Soviet Republics were set up after a series of cessions and annexations during and after World War II. These included: the territory which was formerly Eastern Poland; the three ⇨ Baltic States; the formerly Rumanian provinces of ⇨ Bessarabia and North Bukovina; the former Czechoslovak territory of Ruthenia; parts of East Prussia as well as certain border areas of ⇨ Finland. Since then the USSR has consisted of 15 Federal Soviet Republics: RSFSR, Ukraine, Belorussia, Uzbekistan, Kazakhstan, Georgia, Azerbaidjan, Lithuania, Moldavia, Latvia, Khirgizia, Tadjikstan, Armenia, Turkmenia and Estonia.

A new constitution has been in preparation since 1962. In the meantime, the constitution of 1936 (with minor amendments) remains formally in force. According to it, the highest organ of state power is the Supreme Soviet, the bi-cameral Legislature, consisting of the Soviet of Union and the Soviet of Nationalities. The Supreme Soviet is headed by a Presidium which takes over its functions in between sessions. The Chairman of the Presidium also acts as the Head of State of the USSR. The 1936 constitution guarantees all Soviet citizens comprehensive civil rights, and it guarantees the Federal Soviet Republic far-reaching rights of self-determination, including the right to secede freely from the USSR. At the same time, the constitution defines the Communist Party of the Soviet Union as the 'directing core of all organizations of the working people both public (voluntary) and state'. In practice, this clause can and does invalidate other constitutional provisions if and when desired.

The USSR came into being as the result of the ⇨ Bolshevik seizure of power in Oct. 1917, and the USSR has ever since been ruled by the leaders – or the one supreme leader – of the Communist Party (CPSU). The CPSU is the sole source of policy decisions and retains ultimate control over their execution in all fields of activities and on every level of authority. According to the party Statutes, the supreme organ of the CPSU is the party congress, which determines policy and elects a Central committee. In between congresses the Central Committee directs Party activities. The Central Committee in turn elects two smaller bodies, the Politbureau (short for Political Bureau) and the Secretariat. In practice, the elections of the Central Committee by the party congress and of the Politbureau and Secretariat by the Central Committee are – like the elections of Deputies for the Supreme Soviet – simple endorsements of previously prepared single lists of candidates without the choice of alternatives.

The Politbureau (or, as this body was called between 1952 and 1966, the Presidium) is the supreme policy-making authority and its decisions are unconditionally binding on the Party as a whole. The Secretariat, according to the Statutes, has the task of controlling work in hand, chiefly concerning the selection of cadres and the organization of checks on the execution of Party decisions. As the body in charge of the selection of cadres, the Secretariat in fact controls the appointment of all important officials both within the Party and without, i.e. the composition of the Party *apparatus* and of the institutions under its control. The Secretariat is headed by the General Secretary (known, during the ⇨ Khrushchev era, as the First Secretary) who is in charge of overall policy and organization. The General Secretary is assisted by a number of other Secretaries, each responsible for a special group of subjects. The Secretariat also includes a considerable number of specialized Departments with a permanent staff which transmit party decisions to the corresponding state and other institutions and supervise the execution of such decisions. Through specialized Departments of this kind, the Secretariat controls the Chief Political Directorate of the Soviet Army and Navy; the State Security Service, the police and the Judiciary ('Administrative Department'); international relations; relations with the ruling communist parties of other socialist countries; economic relations with other socialist countries; all the different branches of the Soviet economy; science and education; propaganda activities ('Agitprop'), Soviet personnel abroad; the appointment of party officials; and the preparation of lists of candidates subject to 'elections' both within the Party and without.

During the greater part of the history of the Soviet Union, the Secretariat – formerly in association with the now defunct Orgbureau (short for Organization Bureau) – has been the centre of power within the Party and, through the Party, within the USSR. It was chiefly through his control of the Secretariat and the Orgbureau that ⇨ Stalin, the party's General Secretary, accumulated sufficient power to defeat and oust all his rivals after Lenin's death. At a later period, he reinforced his powers by adding to the party Secretariat a special section in charge of Secret Police activities and by building up an additional personal secretariat of his own.

Stalin's first concern, after Lenin's death, was the removal of ⇨ Trotsky, his most renowned rival and enemy. By a series of skilful manoeuvres, he first isolated Trotsky and later secured his expulsion from the Party and his banishment to a remote area in Central Asia, followed by exile. Simultaneously or soon after, Stalin rid himself, one by one, of all his other critics and rivals in the party hierarchy. The task was accomplished by the end of 1930, when all the foremost old

Bolsheviks had been disgraced and ousted from the Party leadership, with the sole exception of Stalin himself.

Meanwhile, the first Five-Year Plan had been inaugurated (Oct. 1928) which launched the USSR on a course of rapid industrialization and the collectivization of agriculture. Collectivization, at first slow and voluntary, turned towards the end of 1929 into a campaign of wholesale terror against the peasantry. Within the space of five months nearly 60% of all peasant householders were forcibly collectivized against desperate resistance. Millions of peasants perished in this operation or were deported to forced labour camps. The direct and indirect effects of this campaign and its aftermath were so grave that farm output in the USSR remained, until the mid-1950s, below the level of the precollectivization period. Industrialization, by contrast, progressed rapidly. Between 1928 and 1938, the period covered by the first two Five-Year Plans, total industrial output nearly quadrupled. This spectacular expansion was, however, almost wholly confined to the development of heavy industries and large-scale new construction projects. Many of the latter were constructed by the unpaid work of forced labour camp inmates, while industrial expansion was generally accompanied by the rapid eradication of the last traces of the earlier egalitarianism, by an increasingly sharp differentiation in incomes, and, for the overwhelming majority of peasants and workers, increasingly harsh living and working conditions.

The second Five-Year Plan, launched in 1933, and the 17th Party Congress at the beginning of 1934 seemed to promise some measure of relief to the country's hard-pressed workers and peasants and some degree of moderation and reconciliation on the part of the country's leadership. The promise was not fulfilled. In Dec. 1934, S. M. ⇨Kirov, a rising star in the Party's Politbureau, was assassinated by a young communist. Whether or not – as Khrushchev later hinted – Kirov's murder had been organized from above, it became the signal and one of the excuses for the great purges which followed, culminating in the terror of the ⇨Yezhovshchina and the ⇨Moscow Trials of 1936, 1937 and 1938. In the course of these purges, almost the entire generation of party cadres who had been Lenin's associates in the revolution, the civil war and the direction of the ⇨Communist International were wiped out as 'enemies of the people'. The great Moscow show trials were merely the most spectacular manifestations of an operation which engulfed the entire political, military, economic and administrative leadership of the USSR and which turned the old Bolshevik Party of militant revolutionaries and civil war veterans into the instrument of rule of a largely new, privileged bureaucratic élite.

It was in the midst of the terror of the great purges (Dec. 1936) that the 'Stalin Constitution' was promulgated and propagated as the most democratic constitution in the world.

Externally, the years of the great purges coincided with the heightening menace emanating from Hitler-Germany and its ⇨ Axis partners, Japan and Italy. A tentative Soviet turn towards warding off this danger by a rapprochement with the Western powers and a policy of collective security, re-inforced by communist united front tactics, was again abandoned after the ⇨ Munich Agreement (Sept. 1938). In April 1939, the Soviet Ambassador in Berlin made the first Soviet overtures to the German Government. On 23.8.1939, one week before the outbreak of World War II, the USSR and Germany signed the ⇨ Hitler-Stalin Pact, by which the two signatory powers, among other things, agreed on a new division of ⇨ Poland among themselves. The Pact provided Stalin with the opportunity to annex most of the territories which had once formed part of the Tsarist Empire, and it provided the USSR with a breathing space until it itself became the victim of Hitler's aggression (22.6.1941).

The German invasion (⇨ World War II) transformed the USSR into an ally of the Western powers. The alliance barely survived the war. Differences within the anti-Hitler coalition about the future peace settlement had already come to the fore during the war-time conferences between ⇨ Roosevelt, ⇨ Churchill and Stalin. They were temporarily papered over by ambiguous formulas about divided zones of influence and all-round support for 'democratic' regimes in Europe and Asia, which, owing to their vagueness, subsequently became the subject of contradictory interpretations and the focus of renewed East-West conflict.

Conflict centred in the first place on the systematic ⇨ Sovietization which Stalin imposed during the final phase of the war and its immediate aftermath on all the countries of Eastern Europe which the Red Army had liberated or conquered. The exceptions were ⇨ Yugoslavia and ⇨ Albania where communist regimes came to power with no or, at most, marginal Soviet aid. Everywhere else in Eastern Europe, in Poland, ⇨ Hungary, ⇨ Rumania, ⇨ Bulgaria, ⇨ East Germany and, with only slight variations, in ⇨ Czechoslovakia, the imposition of communist regimes followed the strikingly uniform pattern of a planned stage-by-stage repression of all popular opposition forces, accomplished by the identical mixture of political deceit, Secret Police terror and direct Soviet intervention. It was this process of compulsory Sovietization and the Western counter-measures which it provoked, that gave rise to what subsequently became known as the Cold War.

Despite the appalling devastations, and human and material losses which it had suffered during the war, the Soviet Union recovered from this ordeal with remarkable speed. By 1948 production had begun to exceed the pre-war level and by 1952 it had grown two and a half times as much again. As in pre-war days, this expansion was almost wholly confined to the heavy industries, while agriculture continued to stagnate and living standards remained exceedingly low. Although Stalin's postwar foreign policies were to suffer a number of major set-backs, outstanding among them the failure of the Berlin Blockade (1948), the successful rebellion of communist Yugoslavia in the same year and the failure of the Soviet-instigated war in ⇨ Korea of 1950, the Soviet Union had by then emerged as the strongest single power in Europe and Asia, second only to the United States as one of the world's two Super-Powers.

Inside the USSR, Stalin's position had become stronger than ever. In 1941, he had for the first time assumed formal government responsibility by taking over the chairmanship of the Council of People's Commissars (renamed, after the war, Council of Ministers). The cult of his personality, highly developed even before the war, reached grotesque proportions in the post-war period. Purges and campaigns of repression which had been going on even during the war were again greatly stepped up after its end. During the war, the chief victims (of Stalin's rather than Hitler's actions) had been a number of national minorities who, from one day to the next, were deported from their traditional homesteads and dispersed all over Siberia and Central Asia. Among them were the Volga Germans, the Crimean Tatars, the Kalmyks, the Chechens, the Ingushi, the Balkars and the Karachai, more than a million people in all. The allegation made in connection with some of these deportations that they were necessary for war-time security reasons has been officially denied by Stalin's successors. In the post-war period, witchhunts and persecutions were in the first place directed against ideological heresies, real or imaginary, in the realm of literature, arts and science. The victims of these campaigns were officially described as 'rootless cosmopolitans' (meaning mainly Jewish writers and artists), 'bourgeois nationalists' (meaning members of the non-Russian nationalities of the USSR unwilling to accept Russification), and they included non-conformist intellectuals of every description deemed to offend against any of the ideological guidelines laid down by A. A. ⇨ Zhdanov, Stalin's spokesman on ideological and cultural affairs. In between, there were fresh party purges and victimizations, most noted among them the so-called ⇨ Leningrad Case. At the turn of the year 1952/53 there followed the alleged discovery of a terrorist murder plot by a group of eminent medical specialists (nearly all of them Jews) which ominously looked like the start of a new mass purge and blood bath.

Almost immediately after Stalin's death (5.3.1953), his heirs and successors began undoing some of his work. The 'doctors' plot' was exposed as a fabrication. The Secret Police was downgraded from its former position as a state within and above the state and subjected to party control. ⇨Beria, who succeeded ⇨Yezhov as Head of the Secret Police and who, for a brief period, participated in the post-Stalin 'collective leadership', was ousted by his colleagues and executed. Most of the surviving inmates of the forced labour camps were gradually set free, and some of the victims of Stalin's great purges were posthumously rehabilitated. A start was made with the revival of agriculture and the long delayed improvement of living standards by a planned expansion of consumer goods industries. G. M. ⇨Malenkov, Stalin's heir-apparent and his immediate successor as both Prime Minister and party leader, was ousted in stages by his principal rival, N. S. Khrushchev.

Under Khrushchev's leadership, the CPSU took a number of important new initiatives, in domestic and foreign affairs. Among the most noted in the first period was the ⇨Belgrade Declaration (1955), issued after Khrushchev's visit to ⇨Tito, and the denunciation of Stalin's terror and ⇨Personality Cult made in Khrushchev's 'secret speech' at a closed session of the 20th CPSU Congress (1956). The speech, which later became universally available, had a devastating effect both inside the USSR and in the wider realm of ⇨World Communism. It triggered off the chain of events which, soon afterwards, led to the ⇨Polish October and the Hungarian revolution, which – like the East German rising of June 1953 – was repressed by Soviet military intervention.

These and other unforeseen repercussions of the revelations made at the 20th CPSU Congress contributed to the gradual undermining of Khrushchev's authority among his own colleagues in the party leadership, but for a few years his powers continued to grow. In the summer of 1957, he succeeded in foiling an attempt to oust him made by the so-called ⇨Anti-Party Group, headed by Malenkov, ⇨Kaganovich and ⇨Molotov. In March 1958, Khrushchev took over the chairmanship of the Council of Ministers while remaining the Party's First Secretary and the dominating member of the party Presidium (later the Politbureau). But although by then he controlled all the main levers of power, he initiated policies and campaigns, both at home and abroad, which aroused increasing opposition either because they ended in failure and loss of prestige for the USSR (as the campaigns against West Berlin between 1958 and 1962; the ⇨Cuban Missile Crisis of 1962 and the handling of the ⇨Sino-Soviet Conflict) or because they undermined or threatened important vested interests inside the USSR, as did his ever-changing schemes for the revitalization of agriculture, his economic reforms of 1957 and his party re-organization of 1963. The most persistent and most successful reform pursued by Khrushchev during his years in power was the re-establishment of the absolute control of the party leadership over all rival networks of power of the Government, Army and Secret Police. The very success of this operation contributed in the end to his downfall. When the rest of the top party leaders combined in a conspiracy to depose him, he had no independent power base left to fall back on. In Oct. 1964, Khrushchev was ousted in a bloodless *coup d'état*, organized by his colleagues in the country's 'collective leadership'.

Since then, party and government leadership remained divided between L. I. Brezhnev in charge of the party and A. N. Kosygin in charge of the government, while official emphasis was consistently on 'collective leadership'. In the early 1970s, however, Brezhnev's personal status began to outstrip that of his colleagues. Under the rule of the new team, led by him, the earlier policies of ⇨ De-Stalinization, cautious liberalization and all-round innovation have been halted and partly reversed and have made way for fresh campaigns urging and enforcing intolerance against any and every form of ⇨ Dissent. The dangers allegedly inherent in dissent have also been quoted among several justifications offered for the invasion of Czechoslovakia (Aug. 1968) which constituted the third military Soviet intervention in another state since Stalin's death. (⇨ Bolshevism, ⇨ Brezhnev Doctrine, ⇨ Cominform, ⇨ Council for Mutual Economic Assistance, ⇨ Democratic Centralism, ⇨ Lenin's Testament, ⇨ Marxism-Leninism, ⇨ Purges, ⇨ Show Trials, ⇨ Soviet, ⇨ USSR State Security Service, ⇨ Warsaw Pact.)

USSR State Security Service. Until 1941, the Soviet Security Service (which includes the Secret Police) was under the control of a single department, and since then under the control of two separate departments with frequently changing names and initials. Originally called Cheka (Extraordinary Commission), the department was renamed (1922) GPU (State Political Directorate); (1923) OGPU (United State Political Directorate); and (1934) NKVD (People's Commissariat for Internal Affairs). The head of the department from 1917 to 1926 was F. E. Dzerzhinsky; from 1926 to 1934 V. R. Menzhinsky; from 1934 to 1936 G. G. ⇨ Yagoda; from 1936 to 1938 N. I. ⇨ Yezhov; from 1938 to 1953 L. P. ⇨ Beria. In 1941, the department was split up into the NKVD and the NKGB (People's Commissariat for State Security), renamed MVD and MGB (1946) when the People's Commissariats were re-established as Ministries. After Beria's execution (1953) and ⇨ Khrushchev's subsequent ascent to power, the MGB lost its status as a Ministry and became the KGB (Committee for State Security), while the MVD was dissolved and replaced by decentralized departments in the various Union Republics in charge of the militia (ordinary police). In 1965, after Khrushchev's dismissal, these departments in the Federal Republics were again brought under the centralized control of the All-Union Ministry for the Maintenance of Public Order. In Nov. 1968, this Ministry reverted to its pre-1953 name of MVD (Ministry for Internal Affairs).

Equipped with extensive powers since its foundation in 1917, the Security Service grew during the ⇨ Stalin era into the most powerful organization in the USSR, superior to party, state and army and responsible only to Stalin personally. The Security Service was in charge of all forms of censorship. It had unrestricted power to conduct searches and investigations. It acquired the power to arrest and, without trial, to execute by shooting or banish to forced labour camps (first set up in 1919). It controlled the militia as well as its own internal armed forces and a special corps of Border Guards. From the time of the mass arrests accompanying collectivization (1929/30) the Security Service also acquired considerable economic powers. Through the establishment of GULAG (Main Administration for Corrective Labour Camps) in 1930, the OGPU (and later the NKVD) became, in addition to its other functions, the contractor to the Government for lumbering, the mining of gold and other precious metals and for the construction of major economic projects, including the White Sea-Baltic Canal (1931–33), the Moscow-Volga Canal (1932–37), and a large number of new towns, whole new administrative areas and new railway lines in the climatically worst parts of the Soviet Far East. The Security Service was the organizer of repeated purges and a long series of political trials, both public and secret, which reached their climax in the terror of the ⇨ Yezhovshchina and the ⇨ Moscow Trials of 1936, 1937 and 1938.

After Stalin's death, the arbitrary powers of the Security Service were greatly reduced and, during the Khrushchev era, the Security Service was once again subjected to Party control. (⇨ Purges, ⇨ Show Trials, ⇨ USSR.)

U Thant (1909–). Secretary-General of the ⇨ United Nations (1961–71). He has expressed his greatest concern over the ⇨ Vietnam War. He was criticized for his decision to withdraw the UN peace-keeping force in the Middle East on ⇨ Nasser's request shortly before the ⇨ Arab-Israeli war of 1967. Formerly a Burmese civil servant, U Thant served as Secretary to the Ministry of Information (1949–57) and was his country's Permanent Representative to the UN (1957–61).

Uzbekistan. One of the 15 Federal Soviet Republics constituting the USSR. *Capital* – Tashkent. Uzbekistan is comprised of one Autonomous Region and nine Provinces.

V

VA. United States Veterans Administration – an ⇨ Independent Agency established in 1930 to administer Federal assistance to American ex-servicemen and their dependents, including the ⇨ 'GI Bill of Rights'. Its head is an administrator appointed by the President with the consent of the Senate.

Vargas, Getulio Dornelles (1883–1954). President of ⇨ Brazil (1930–45 and 1951–54) and the dominating personality in his country's politics for more than two decades. Opposed to the ruling oligarchies but dedicated to power and with a mass following, Vargas had established his claims to the presidency as the dynamic governor of Rio Grande do Sul. During his first, reformist but authoritarian regime, Brazil underwent a political and socio-economic revolution. His Brazilian doctrine of Fascism (*Estado Novo*) owed more to Portugal's than to Italy's example. Over the years, impatience with his authoritarian methods increased and after the war he was forced to resign. Still popular, he was elected as senator and congressman for several states and he chose to be senator from Rio Grande do Sul (1945). The failure of his second presidency has been ascribed to his own declining powers, corruption and scandal, but his supporters blamed the hostility of conservative forces and an army afraid of the growing power of the urban workers.

Vatican City State. Seat of the central government of the Roman Catholic Church, it is the smallest sovereign independent state in Europe – its independence was recognized by the Italian Government in the Lateran Treaties (1929). The Pope (since 1963 ⇨ Paul VI) is absolute ruler and enjoys full executive, legislative and judicial powers. The College of Cardinals, which elects the Pope from its members, acts as a Privy Council and Cabinet and the Curia is the administrative body of the Church, which commands the allegiance of more than 527 million Roman Catholics in virtually all countries of the world. The civil government of the state (population about 1,000) is in the hands of a lay Governor and a Council who are appointed by and are responsible to the Pope.

Vecheka. Russian abbreviation for All-Russian Extraordinary Commission, more usually called ⇨ Cheka.

Velasco Ibarra. ⇨ Ecuador.

Velchev, General D. ⇨ Bulgaria.

Venezuela. *Area* – 352,143 sq. miles. *Population* (1971 est.) – 10,778,051. *President* – Dr Raphael Caldera (1968–). *Constitution* (1961) – Federal Republic; executive power vested in an elected President. Legislature consists of a bi-cameral Congress – Senate and Chamber of Deputies – elected by universal adult suffrage.

Between 1908 and his death in 1935, Juan Vincente Gomez ruled Venezuela as an absolute tyrant. His repressive regime combined with the discovery of oil turned Venezuela into a land of riches for foreign investors. With little benefit to the mass of Venezuelans, oil revenues made fortunes for Gomez and those he favoured, and also enabled Venezuela to pay off the whole of its foreign and internal debt. For 27 years (up to 1935) political development had been stultified and an increasing number of people given cause to resent their government. For ten years they were barely held in check, though under the next two Presidents, General Lopez Contreras (1936–41) and General Medina Angarita (1941–45) a start was made at establishing constitutional government and social reforms undertaken. In 1945 Romulo ⇨ Betancourt – leader of the AD (*Accion Democratica*) led an army-based *coup d'état*. A new constitution was promulgated (1947) but despite an enormous majority for the AD candidate in the subsequent elections, the army again intervened, this time to depose the AD government (1948). Though the new junta permitted elections (1952) the winning (URD – *Union Republicana Democratica*) candidate was again deposed in an army coup. The new dictator Colonel Marcos ⇨ Perez Jimenez (1952–58) ruled in the Gomez tradition. There was some economic reconstruction, again largely through foreign investment, but the administration of Perez Jimenez was characterized by financial corruption and extensive repression. In 1958 Perez Jimenez was overthrown by a popular revolt supported by a section of the army. Betancourt was elected President (1959) and headed an AD-COPEI (Social Christian Party) coalition. He was succeeded by another AD President – Dr Raul Leoni (1964) who governed in coalition with the URD. The Communist Party has become an active force in Venezuelan politics, and in recent years there has been some 'Castroist' guerrilla activity. Venezuela is one of the South American countries most hostile to Cuba. As with many Latin American countries, the army plays a crucial part in Venezuelan politics. (In elections held (Dec. 1968) Dr Rafael Caldera was elected Venezuela's first Christian Democratic President.)

Verwoerd, Dr Hendrik Frensch (1901–66). The first Prime Minister of ⇨ South Africa (1958–66) born outside the country (in Holland), Verwoerd, despite his lack of family association with Afrikaaner tradition, dominated his party, Parliament and the country as no previous Prime Minister had ever done. As a university professor (1927–37), leading member of the ⇨Broederbond, editor of *Die Transvaaler* (1937–48), Minister of Native Affairs (1950–58) and finally as the Prime Minister who established the Republic, Verwoerd was the chief ideologist of ⇨*Apartheid*. His legacy is the repressive legislation which affects every aspect of South African life from the political to the purely personal. In 1936 he protested against the admission of German Jewish refugees into South Africa and in 1943 he lost a court case in which he sued a rival newspaper for referring to his own paper as 'a tool of the Nazis'. His vision of a future Afrikaaner Republic agreed significantly with European Fascist blue-prints. Anti-semitism has since been dropped as public policy, and with restricted electoral rolls and legislation that made opposition to his policies illegal, Verwoerd was happy to endorse a 'democracy' which was powerless to protect the liberty of its subjects. On ⇨Strijdom's death he was elected to the leadership of the party and became Prime Minister (2.9.1958). After ⇨Sharpeville, his belief in white supremacy unaltered by African discontent, he increased the range of discriminatory laws (*Apartheid*). Shot at point blank range by a white farmer (9.4.1960), his prestige was enhanced as his followers discerned the hand of God in his rapid recovery. For the establishment of the Republic and his handling of the Rhodesian crisis, where he efficiently bolstered Rhodesia's economy without disrupting relations with the United Kingdom, he was revered by White South Africa. His concept of separate development (*Bantustans*) remains unconvincing in a country where the economy depends on African labour and in which so little finance is made available for rural development. On 6 Sept. 1966, Verwoerd was stabbed to death in the House of Assembly by a deranged parliamentary messenger. Ruthless, a Calvinist claiming divine sanction for his actions, Verwoerd gave his followers what they most wanted, a moral and 'philosophic' justification for South Africa's doctrine and practice of racial inequality.

VFW. Veterans of Foreign Wars of the United States – second largest ex-servicemen's organization in the USA with between one-and-a-half and two million members who have served in campaigns and expeditions abroad. It combines with the ⇨ American Legion and similar groups to ⇨Lobby for public policies favourable to veterans, especially in connection with the ⇨VA. It also gives evidence before ⇨Congressional Committees on military and patriotic issues.

Vichy. The southern part of truncated ⇨France left unoccupied by the Germans after the armistice of 22 June 1940. Seat of ⇨ Pétain's semi-Fascist government (it dismantled the ⇨ Third Republic, dissolved trade unions, banned strikes, introduced anti-Jewish legislation, etc.), Vichy became openly collaborationist with the total occupation of France by the Germans (Nov. 1942) after the Allied landings in French North Africa. After D-Day the Vichy Government was removed to Germany (Sigmaringen).

Vienna Award. ⇨Transylvania.

Viet Cong. ⇨Vietnam.

Viet Minh. Abbreviation for the Vietnamese term *Viet Nam Doc Lap Dong Minh Hoi*, meaning Revolutionary League for the Independence of ⇨Vietnam. (⇨Ho Chi Minh.)

Vietnam. Politically partitioned Asian country to the south of China with an area of approximately 130,000 square miles and an estimated population of 39,000,000. (1969).

A nation developed under the all-pervasive influence of China's civilization and for nearly a millennium under Chinese suzerainty, Vietnam was conquered by France towards the end of the 19th century and, together with ⇨ Laos and ⇨ Cambodia, incorporated into the French dependency of Indochina.

In 1940, after the fall of France, the Japanese established bases in Indochina and exploited its resources, while leaving the French colonial administration nominally in charge. The French administrators collaborated in these arrangements until the spring of 1945, when the Japanese disarmed and imprisoned them. Thereafter Japan proclaimed the independence of the three Indochinese states and entrusted Vietnam to the nominal rule of the Emperor Bao Dai.

In the meantime, national resistance movements to French colonial rule had developed both inside Vietnam and among refugees abroad. The most influential of these resistance movements was the ⇨ Viet Minh, founded by the communist leader, ⇨ Ho Chi Minh. The Viet Minh was set up in May 1941 at a congress held in Kwangsi in Southern China. It included various left-wing patriotic refugee groups from Vietnam but was from the outset dominated by communists and the personality of Ho Chi Minh. Shortly afterwards, one of Ho Chi Minh's closest and ablest associates, Vo Nguyen ⇨ Giap (the future victor of Dien Bien Phu), was dispatched to Vietnam to organize bases for guerrilla activities. Ho Chi Minh followed him to Vietnam in 1944, and together they established Viet Minh strongholds over a wide area in the north of the country. The sudden power vacuum created in March 1945 by the Japanese arrest of the French administrators enabled the Viet

Minh to consolidate and spread its influence rapidly. Immediately after the Japanese surrender (Aug. 1945), the Viet Minh formed a coalition with other nationalist groups which refused to accept the authority of Bao Dai, and set up a Provisional Government of the Democratic Republic of Vietnam (VDR) at Hanoi. Ho Chi Minh used the following 15 months to impose his control both on his enemies without and on his various partners within the coalition government. When this was accomplished, a new government was set up (3.11.1946) with Ho Chi Minh as Prime Minister and Foreign Minister as well as President of the VDR.

The French meanwhile had re-established themselves in various areas of Vietnam and were determined to restore their former control over all Indochina. Various attempts at a compromise between the French government and the newly proclaimed VDR ended in deadlock, followed by a rise in tension and increasingly serious armed clashes. The turning point came in the winter of 1946. Ho Chi Minh's government evacuated Hanoi, re-established itself at a base in the countryside, and transformed itself into a centre for guerrilla warfare. Thereafter, the war began in earnest and dragged on for over six years. The French attempted to rally the country's anti-communist forces to a rival Vietnam Republic within the French Union, which they set up at Saigon under the ex-Emperor Bao Dai whom they recalled for that purpose from his self-chosen exile. But this move had no influence on the course of the war. The war reached its climax with the spectacular victory which General Vo Nguyen Giap, by then Ho Chi Minh's Commander-in-Chief, won at the French stronghold of Dien Bien Phu (7.5.1954) and which secured Viet Minh control over the whole of North Vietnam. Immediately afterwards, the international Geneva Conference, which had been called by Britain, France, the USA and the USSR, turned to the problem of peace in Indochina. The conference ended in the so-called ⇨ Geneva Agreements, which prepared the ground for the cessation of hostilities in Vietnam and the establishment of a temporary demarcation line between the communist-held north of the country and the southern half. Separate agreements dealt with Laos and Cambodia, while the Final Declaration of the conference provided for elections to be held throughout Vietnam by July 1956.

The Americans, still under the impact of recent developments in ⇨ Korea, refused to sign the Final Declaration. They prevailed, moreover, on Bao Dai, whose government depended on their economic aid, to appoint a new Prime Minister for South Vietnam. The man chosen for this post was Ngo Dinh Diem, a strongly anti-French nationalist and a right-wing, inflexible anti-communist. Diem began by getting rid of Bao Dai who was widely regarded as a French puppet, and to establish his own unchallengeable rule in the south. In Oct. 1955, South Vietnam was proclaimed an independent Republic with Saigon as its capital and Ngo Dinh Diem as its first President. Fearing that nation-wide elections would lead to a communist take-over of the South, Diem refused to take part in them, with the result that the cease-fire line between the two parts of the country hardened into a state frontier.

Nevertheless, a considerable stream of people crossed this frontier in both directions in the following years. Large numbers of anti-communists escaped from the North to seek refuge in the South, while many Southern communists made their way to the North. From 1959 onwards, increasing numbers of these originally Southern communists were sent back, after a period of military training, in order to make contact with sympathizers in the South, help in the establishment of an integrated opposition movement against the Diem regime, and in preparations for an eventual full-scale insurrection. Members of this movement – soon to be dubbed by outsiders as the 'Viet Cong' – engaged in guerrilla operations which Diem's Government failed to contain, despite harsh reprisals and considerable USA economic and military aid. Towards the end of 1960, the insurrectionist movement in the South, in collaboration with the communist leaders in the North, created a formal political framework for itself – the South Vietnam National Liberation Front (SVNLF or NLF) – which henceforth challenged the Republican Government in the South on the political as well as the military plane.

The NLF was, however, not the only enemy with which Diem had to contend. Increasingly, he became involved in bitter conflicts with Buddhist leaders who resented the privileges which Diem, himself a Roman Catholic, bestowed on the Catholic minority in the Republic. Eventually, Diem's own army turned against him. In Nov. 1963, Ngo Dinh Diem was overthrown by a military *coup d'état* and assassinated.

There followed some 18 months of political chaos, interspersed by countless *coups d'état* and accompanied by increasing Viet Cong successes, which threatened the collapse of South Vietnam. Some form of stability was eventually achieved after the start of the American military build-up. In June 1965, a new government was formed by the National Leadership Committee, composed of civilians as well as army leaders, under the overall direction of General Nguyen Van Thieu, who took over the presidency, and of Air Vice-Marshal Nguyen Cao Ky, who became Vice-President.

In North Vietnam, meanwhile, Ho Chi Minh's Government had re-established itself at Hanoi after the Geneva Agreements. The political and social changes initiated by Ho's regime were closely modelled on those promoted by ⊳ Mao Tse-tung in ⊳ China. In 1955, Ho Chi Minh surrendered the premiership to his old associate Pham Van Dong, retaining for himself the presidency of the VDR. As in other communist-ruled countries, real power in the VDR rests, however, neither in the state presidency nor in the government, let alone the nominally elected National Assembly, but in the leadership of the Communist Party. The Vietnam Workers' Party (*Lao Dong*), which is the successor to the former Indochinese Communist Party, differs from other ruling communist parties in having remained under the same leadership since its earliest beginnings without a major political purge. Ho Chi Minh's closest associates in the top hierarchy of the party had collaborated with him since the early 1930s or even the 1920s. They are all members of the Vietnam Workers' Party's Central Committee's Politbureau, over which Ho Chi Minh presided as Chairman. The most influential members of this closely-knit circle are: Le Duan, the Party's General Secretary; Truong Chinh, the Party's leading ideologist and propagandist; Pham Van Dong, the Prime Minister; Le Duc Tho, one of Ho's oldest associates; and General Vo Nguyen Giap, the Commander-in-Chief. This party leadership has maintained its cohesion even though it is divided into political factions – one of them with strong pro-Soviet leanings, another with equally strong pro-Chinese leanings, and a third one favouring an altogether independent form of national development.

Ho Chi Minh's toleration of this kind of factionalism within the party leadership reflected, on the one hand, a gradual change in his own role from the one-time unchallenged leader to a mainly counselling elder statesman and, on the other hand, the very acute dilemma into which the VDR has been placed by the exacerbation of the ⊳ Sino-Soviet Conflict. Although in no sense a 'satellite' of either Moscow or Peking, the VDR has yet remained dependent on outside aid and cannot afford to risk losing the support of either China or the USSR. Victory in the six-year-long war against France owed much to the facilities provided by Mao Tse-tung in the use of neighbouring Chinese territory as a base area for the training of Viet Minh forces, for the treatment of casualties and for stockpiling. Chinese aid, especially in the form of food supplies, became even more vital – and more abundant – in the 1960s, when the guerrilla operations in the South began to escalate into a full-scale war; but the same applied, even more forcefully, to Soviet military aid.

For South Vietnam, the provision of outside aid was, if anything, even more crucial. Yet, for many years, the kind of aid provided by the USA had, for all its lavishness, failed to produce the desired result. By the end of 1964, the Republic in the South seemed to be heading for total collapse. In this situation, the USA believed there was only one alternative left – to abandon South Vietnam altogether or to intervene directly. President Johnson opted for the latter course, and from 1965 onwards, the South Vietnamese armies were re-inforced by a massive US expeditionary force and by sustained US bombing raids on targets in North Vietnam. The VDR, in turn, increasingly supported the Viet Cong with contingents of its own regular army, while the USSR stepped up its support of the communist war effort with large-scale deliveries of up-to-date heavy military equipment, including large rockets and anti-aircraft ground-to-air missiles.

By the spring of 1968, both President Johnson of the United States and the North Vietnamese leaders seemed to have concluded that ever-increasing escalation was not necessarily a shortcut to either victory or a tolerable compromise. Neither was as yet willing to accept the other side's minimum conditions for the start of peace negotiations. But after President Johnson's announcement, in March 1968, that the areas of North Vietnam subject to US bombing raids would henceforth be drastically curtailed, Washington and Hanoi were able to agree that their representatives should meet at Paris to discuss – if not yet a cease-fire – then at least the conditions for the opening of peace talks. The first of these meetings was held on 13 May 1968.

In Sept. 1969 Ho Chi Minh died. His successor as President of the VDR was the former Vice-President, Ton Duc Thang. The withdrawal of American troops had already begun in June 1969 and a programme of 'Vietnamization' initiated, but in May 1970 President ⟡Nixon resumed the bombing of targets north of the 20th parallel, and a campaign in Cambodia found signs of Vietcong activity. In February 1971 South Vietnamese troops went into action in Laos. A fresh Vietcong offensive in April 1972 caused America to blockade North Vietnamese ports. Meanwhile, a series of secret negotiations had continued in Paris between Dr Henry ⟡Kissinger, President Nixon's national security adviser, and Le Duc Tho, the leading North Vietnamese negotiator, but at the end of 1972 reports of impending agreement were broken by renewed bombing of the north, including the biggest ever attack on Hanoi. However, in January 1973 a peace agreement was signed.

Virgin Land Campaign. A large-scale operation of land-reclamation in the USSR, initiated by N. S. ⟡Khrushchev in the 1950s to augment Soviet grain output.

VISTA. Volunteers in Service to America – a voluntary service organization in the USA, established by the Economic Opportunity Act of 1964. It was modelled on the ⇨ Peace Corps whose director, Sargent Shriver, was responsible for setting it up; but it is a 'domestic peace corps', operating within the United States at State and local level. Its members serve for one year and help in carrying out projects under the ⇨ Anti-Poverty Programme. They work among the poor in the cities on urban renewal projects, and in rural areas among Indians, migratory workers, and other poor communities, mainly in the fields of education and health.

Voice of America. Broadcasting service of the ⇨ USIA. It maintains stations in various parts of the world which are mainly engaged in relaying anti-communist programmes to communist and communist-influenced countries, interspersed with American 'pop' music. Two other radio networks are operated by the USA for similar purposes: Radio Free Europe, which broadcasts to Eastern Europe; and Radio Liberty, which broadcasts to the Soviet Union. Both use the local languages. These were both financed out of the ⇨ CIA budget until mid-1971, when, in the face of much Congressional opposition to continued American financing of them, funds for them were separately voted on a temporary basis up to mid-1972.

Vorkuta. ⇨ Forced Labour Camps.

Voroshilov, Marshal K. E. (1881–1969). Former Soviet Head of State. A ⇨ Bolshevik since 1903, Voroshilov distinguished himself as a commander in the Civil War. Commissar for Defence (1925–39) and created a Marshal in 1935, during the war he became a member of Stalin's inner Cabinet, the State Defence Committee. On Stalin's death (March 1953), he became Chairman of the Presidium of the USSR Supreme Soviet (Head of State), a post he relinquished in May 1960 on grounds of ill health. At the 22nd CPSU Congress (Oct. 1961) he was belatedly listed as a member of the ⇨ Anti-Party Group and charged with complicity in Stalin's purges in the 1930s. The matter was dropped after Khrushchev's personal intercession on his behalf, appealing for generosity in view of Voroshilov's repentance for his misdeeds and his past merits. He made several re-appearances on ceremonial occasions before his death.

Vorster, Balthazar Johannes (1915–). Prime Minister of ⇨ South Africa since 1966. His reputation for toughness and intransigence stood him in good stead when overtaking senior members. He won a majority in the ⇨ National Party caucus to succeed ⇨ Verwoerd as leader of the party and Prime Minister. During World War II he joined the pro-Nazi *Ossewabrandwag* (Ox-Wagon Sentinels). Arrested on suspicion of treason (1942), he was detained in custody until 1944. An MP from 1953, he was made Minister of Justice in 1961. He quadrupled the security police and through such legislation as the Sabotage Act (1962), the General Law Amendment Act (Ninety Day Law) (1963), empowered the police to arrest and imprison suspects without recourse to the courts. As Prime Minister he has insisted on the need to open and maintain diplomatic contacts with independent African states and the need for closer Afrikaans-English cooperation.

Vyshinsky, A. Y. (1883–1955). Former Soviet Procurator and Foreign Minister. A lawyer by profession and a Menshevik in his youth, Vyshinsky joined the Soviet Communist Party in 1920. A protégé of ⇨ Stalin's, he became Procurator (official custodian of the law) of the USSR (1935). He was prominently associated with many political ⇨ Show Trials, presiding over the Shakhty Trial of 1928 and acting as Public Prosecutor in the Metro-Vickers Trial of 1933 and in the three ⇨ Moscow Trials of 1936, 1937 and 1938. Between 1940 and 1949 and again from 1953 until his death in 1955 he was Deputy Foreign Minister under ⇨ Molotov and, between 1949 and 1953, Foreign Minister. He played an active part in the ⇨ Sovietization of Eastern Europe.

W

Wafd (Arabic – delegation). Egyptian political party which developed out of a delegation (1918) formed to negotiate with Britain for Egyptian independence, but which the U K government refused to receive. In the eyes of the post-war generation of Egyptian nationalists the *Wafdists* were compromised by their war-time cooperation with Britain when, from 1942–44, Nahas Pasha, with British backing, headed a *Wafd* government. After winning the elections (1950) Nahas vainly attempted to restore the authority of the *Wafdists*, but they were discredited by the corruption of their government. King ⇨ Farouk took advantage of serious rioting (1952) (⇨ U A R) to dismiss the *Wafd* government and later in the year the party was dissolved after ⇨ Neguib's Free Officers' coup.

Wagner Act. In the USA, the National Labor Relations Act of 1935 which regulated employer-employee relations, established the status of the unions in law, and created the ⇨ N L R B to enforce fair employment conditions. It re-enacted some of the provisions of the National Recovery Act (N R A) which was one of the early ⇨ New Deal measures invalidated by the ⇨ Supreme Court on the basis of a narrow interpretation of the ⇨ Commerce Clause in the period before 1937. In that year the Wagner Act was itself upheld by the Court, but some of its provisions were modified by the ⇨ Taft-Hartley Act in 1947.

Waldheim, Kurt (1918–). Secretary General, ⇨ United Nations, succeeding ⇨ U Thant in January 1972. Before and after becoming Austria's Foreign Minister (1968–70) he represented his country at the United Nations, chairing its Outer Space Committee (1965) and the International Atomic Energy Agency (1970).

Wallace, George C. (1919–). US Southern Democrat politician, Governor of Alabama (1963–67), and unsuccessful third-party candidate for President. He served in the Alabama State Legislature and as a circuit judge before being elected Governor of the State. A segregationist, he attempted to block the integration of Alabama schools. Finding some national support for his candidacy (1964), he launched a nation-wide campaign for the presidency in 1968 as leader of the 'American Independent Party' with former Air Force General Curtis E. LeMay as his running-mate. Wallace spoke out for 'law and order' and ⇨ States Rights and denounced intellectual elitism, civil rights legislation, the Federal ⇨ Anti-Poverty Program, and the opponents of the Vietnam War. While he succeeded in influencing the rhetoric of the campaign, he failed in his primary objective of gaining enough support to prevent any candidate securing a clear majority in the ⇨ Electoral College, thus throwing the election of the President into the House of Representatives where he might prevail. A candidate for the Democratic nomination again in 1972, he was seriously wounded in an assassination attempt during the campaign, but recovered sufficiently to address the Convention in Miami Beach in July from a wheelchair. He introduced the issue of ⇨ 'Busing' into the campaign at an early stage.

Wallace, Henry E. (1888–1965). Vice-President of the USA (1940–44) and unsuccessful third-party candidate for the presidency. He was Secretary of Agriculture during Franklin D. Roosevelt's first two terms (1933–40). After serving one term as Vice-President, Wallace was appointed Secretary of Commerce when ⇨ Truman took his place as Roosevelt's running-mate (1944). Soon after Truman succeeded to office, Wallace found himself in opposition to Administration foreign policy, and was forced to resign when he made his views public (1946). After a year as editor of the *New Republic*, he resigned and ran for President as the candidate of the Progressive Party – a third party formed to promote disarmament and closer ties with the Soviet Union. Wallace later broke with the Progressive Party and repudiated his pro-Soviet position.

Walloons. ⇨ Belgium.

'War on Poverty'. A slogan used in the USA, especially by President ⇨ Johnson, to advance the ⇨ Anti-Poverty Program.

Warren, Earl (1891–). Chief Justice of the US ⇨ Supreme Court (1953–69) and Governor of California (1942–53). Serving first as a district attorney (1925–38) and then Attorney General (1939–42) for California, he was three times elected Governor of the State and established a reputation as a defender of ⇨ Civil Rights. He ran unsuccessfully for the vice-presidency of the USA as the Republican nominee in 1948, and in 1953 was appointed Chief Justice by Dwight D. Eisenhower. Although his decisions have often supported the Federal Government in conflicts with big business, he has consistently supported individual rights against government infringement. Foremost among the many major decisions of the 'Warren Court' was that in ⇨ Brown v. Board of Education (1954) in which separate educational facilities were declared to be inherently unequal and therefore in violation of the ⇨ Fourth Amendment. Although some have criticized Warren as excessively liberal, many recognize in his judgments an attempt to make law more responsive to modern social realities. In 1963 he was appointed to head the ⇨Warren Commission which investigated the assassination of President Kennedy. He resigned as Chief Justice in 1969 to allow the incoming Republican President, Richard Nixon, to nominate his successor, having previously offered to do so to allow for his replacement by Abe Fortas, unsuccessfully nominated by President Johnson for the office.

Warren Commission. In the USA, commission of inquiry, headed by Chief Justice Earl ⇨ Warren, into the assassination of President Kennedy (Nov. 1963). After an extended investigation it concluded that the assassination was carried out by Lee Harvey Oswald acting alone. This conclusion has been persistently challenged by believers in a variety of conspiracy theories, but demands that the inquiry be reopened have been rejected.

Warsaw Pact. East European mutual assistance treaty, signed in Warsaw on 15 May 1955 and originally concluded as a Soviet countermove to the incorporation of the Federal German Republic into ⇨NATO. The founder-members of the Pact were Albania, Bulgaria, Czechoslovakia, the German Democratic Republic, Hungary, Poland, Rumania and the USSR. The Treaty binds the contracting parties to refrain from the threat or use of force and to settle their international disputes by peaceful means. It provides for cooperation, based on the principles of mutual respect for independence and sovereignty and non-intervention in internal affairs, and it restricts the obligation to mutual military assistance to 'the event of an armed attack in Europe on one or several of the signatory states by any state or group of states'.

The Treaty Organization is headed by a Unified Military Command, consisting of the Supreme Commander and the Ministers of Defence of the member states who act as his Deputies. The joint staff under the Supreme Commander has its headquarters in Moscow. The Chief of Staff also acts as the Secretary-General of the Warsaw Pact Political Consultative Committee in which all member states are represented. Both the Supreme Commanders and the Chiefs of Staff have invariably been Soviet officers. The Supreme Commanders were Marshal Konev (1955–60), Marshal Grechko (1960–67) and, since July 1967, Marshal Yakubovsky; Chiefs of Staff were General Antonov (1955–65), General Kazakov (1965–68) and, since Aug. 1968, General Shtemenko. Objections to the Soviet monopoly to these and other Warsaw Pact command posts were raised first by Rumanian and, in the early summer of 1968, by Czechoslovak spokesmen in the form of requests for a review and re-organization of the Pact's command structure, but were dropped after the invasion of Czechoslovakia.

From 1961 onwards, ⇨ Albania ceased to attend Warsaw Pact meetings and in Sept. 1968, formally withdrew from the Pact.

Warsaw Rising. ⇨ Poland.

Wedgwood Benn. ⇨ Benn, Anthony Wedgwood.

Weimar Republic. ⇨ Germany.

Weizmann, Chaim (1874–1952). First President of ⇨ Israel (1948–52), and from 1920 leader of the Zionist Movement. Born in Russia, Weizmann's attitudes were directly shaped by his experience and understanding of the plight of East European Jewry. Determined to find a practical solution, he understood the need for an 'organic Zionism' realizing that only a 'National Home' in Palestine would meet Jewish aspirations. A brilliant scientist and statesman, he made his greatest contributions to Zionism as a diplomatist, starting with the negotiations that resulted in the ⇨ Balfour Declaration. Even as an old man when the leadership had passed to others, he played a crucial role in the negotiations preceding the UN Resolutions of 1947 setting up a Jewish State.

Welensky, Sir Roy (1907–). Former Prime Minister of the Federation of ⇨ Rhodesia and Nyasaland (1956–63). Entered national politics through his membership of the Northern Rhodesia Executive Council. A strong advocate of the Federation, his own political position has slumped with its breakdown.

Welfare State. Refers to legislation and state-sponsored social insurance designed to raise minimum standards of living. It usually includes the provision of health services, housing, insurance against sickness and old age and relief for unemployment. Comprehensive welfare state legislation was passed in Britain by the ⇨ Attlee Government (1945–51) although many of its provisions had been anticipated in earlier social legislation. Welfare State legislation has become an accepted part of government activity in many countries, e.g. Scandinavia, Western Europe, New Zealand.

Western Samoa. *Area* – 1,097 sq. miles. *Population* – 131,552. An independent state and member of the ⇨ Commonwealth since 1962, Western Samoa was from 1919 a League of Nations Mandate Territory and from 1946 a UN Trust Territory, again under New Zealand administration. It is a constitutional monarchy with executive power vested in the Prime Minister and Cabinet, who are responsible to the Legislative Assembly, elected for a three-year term.

West Germany. ⇨ Germany, German Federal Republic.

West Indies Associated States. Comprise Antigua, St Kitts-Nevis-Anguilla, Dominica, Grenada and St Lucia. The dissolution of the ⇨West Indies Federation and subsequent independence of ⇨Jamaica, ⇨Trinidad and Tobago, and ⇨Barbados left the remaining colonies of the former Federation in an anomalous position. To provide for internal self-government, without the prohibitive costs of complete independence, the British Government proposed a system of Associated Statehood with the UK (1966), which came into operation during 1967. The states share certain common services and their premiers meet regularly at a Council of Ministers (1966). Each state enjoys internal self-government with its Prime Minister responsible to its Parliament, and there is universal adult suffrage. The Queen is represented by a Governor in each state. Citizens of the Associated States are also citizens of the UK. Association agreements may be terminated by any of the States or by the UK Parliament.

West Indies Federation (1958–62). Comprised the British Colonies of ⇨ Barbados, ⇨ Jamaica, ⇨ Trinidad and Tobago, The Leeward Islands (excluding the Virgin Islands) and the Windward Islands. At conferences in Barbados (1944) and Jamaica (1947) schemes for a Federation were put forward. In 1958 the UK Parliament passed the British Caribbean Federation Act. Elections were held, under the new Federal constitution, and Sir Grantley Adams (Barbados) became the first and only Prime Minister. A referendum in Jamaica (Sept. 1961) was won by the opponents of Federation. After their further victory in the Jamaican general elections (April 1962), the UK formally dissolved the Federation. In the same year, first Jamaica then Trinidad became independent members of the ⇨Commonwealth. Sheer distance between its members made Federal organization difficult, but it was destroyed by the fears of its two most populous and politically and economically advanced members that their own development would be handicapped by their association with the less developed islands. For some years attempts were made to form an Eastern Caribbean Federation centred on Barbados, but Barbadians eventually also opted for separate independence. The remaining members formed the ⇨ West Indies Associated States.

Westminster, Statute of. Enacted by UK Parliament (1931), formally recognized the sovereign, independent status of the British Dominions.

WEU. Western European Union – based on the 1948 Brussels Treaty, was formed (May 1955) to co-ordinate the defence policies and armaments as well as to promote general cooperation between its members – the ⇨EEC Six and the UK. Since most of its defence functions have been taken over by ⇨NATO, WEU's main importance now is political; it provides a formal link between the Common Market countries and Great Britain. Organizationally WEU consists of the Council, formed by the Foreign Ministers or their ambassadorial deputies, a Permanent Secretariat (London) and an Assembly (Paris). The latter, composed of delegates elected or appointed by the national Parliaments, meets twice yearly to pass recommendations to and receive the annual report from the Council; it also controls a number of Permanent Committees.

White Backlash. A reaction to recent ⇨ Civil Rights agitation and riots in the U S, especially in the summer of 1967. The white backlash has taken the form of open hostility to Negro efforts for equality and, more significantly, in voting for local and national officials who more or less openly oppose integration. It has been most apparent in the large northern cities. Its most recent manifestation has been the widespread opposition to ⇨ 'Busing' as a means of integrating schools, which became a major issue in 1972.

White Citizens Councils. Associations formed in the Southern States of the U S A to resist the ending of ⇨ Segregation following the 1954 decision of the Supreme Court in ⇨ Brown v. Board of Education. They were particularly strong in Mississippi where they were supported partly out of public funds. Resistance to school ⇨ Integration reached a climax at Little Rock, Arkansas, in 1957, when President Eisenhower had to send Federal troops to protect Black children going to a previously all-White school.

Whitehead, Sir Edgar (1905–). Prime Minister of Southern ⇨ Rhodesia (1958–62), Leader of the Opposition (1962–65). His belief in the necessity of increasing African representation in parliament and the inevitability of African majority rule as well as proposals to abolish discriminatory legislation (Land Apportionment Act) was used by the Rhodesian Front to ensure decisive victory (1962) by playing on traditional white fears of African domination.

White House. The official residence, in Washington D C, of the President of the U S A – hence, a familiar term for the US presidency. The building, which is a mile distant from the ⇨ Capitol, houses the offices of the President's closest advisers, the White House Staff or –

White House Office whose functions and membership are not specified, but it includes such officials as the President's Press Secretary, legal counsel, diplomatic and military aides, and administrative, legislative, and special assistants and consultants. The White House Office attained high importance under President Eisenhower and has continued as a 'power house' of American government. It is one of a number of bodies forming the ⇨ Executive Office of the President.

White Paper. A statement issued by the U K Government outlining proposed policy on a particular question, e.g. transport, trade union reform, defence. It differs from a bill presented to Parliament for its assent in that it does not incorporate final Cabinet decisions and often forms the basis for discussion by the House of Commons, as a result of which important changes may be made. A White Paper sometimes announces fundamental policy changes, e.g. the Defence White Paper (1957) which announced the end of conscription and the concentration on nuclear weapon development, the White Paper (1967) on the change to decimal currency, and the White Paper (1969) on trade union reform. The White Paper is so called because it is bound in the same white paper used for the text.

White Primary. A ⇨Primary Election in the USA restricted to White Voters. The ⇨Supreme Court invalidated the institution in 1944.

White Russia. ⇨Belorussia.

Williams, Rt. Hon. Dr Eric Eustace (1911–). First Prime Minister of an independent ⇨ Trinidad (1962–). Chief Minister (1956–61) and Prime Minister (1961–66) and again since 1966.

Willkie, Wendell L. (1892–1944). Unsuccessful Republican candidate for the US presidency (1940), Willkie took a leading position in the battle against government competition in the electrical industry and established a national reputation as an outspoken critic of ⇨New Deal policies. A ground-swell of support developed for his candidacy at the Republican Convention in 1940 and after six ballots he was chosen to oppose Franklin D. ⇨Roosevelt. Finding himself in agreement with the President on foreign policy objectives, he campaigned on domestic matters but was unsuccessful in stopping Roosevelt's re-election for a third term. Although he attempted to maintain his leadership of the Republican Party after his defeat, Willkie found his internationalist views incompatible with conservative Republican sentiment.

Wilson, Harold (1916–). British Prime Minister (1964–70) and Leader of the UK ⇨Labour Party since Feb. 1963. His administration was concerned at home with economic crisis and abroad with the second unsuccessful attempt to negotiate British entry into the ⇨EEC and the problem created by ⇨Rhodesia's UDI. An MP from 1945, his apointment as President of the Board of Trade in 1947 made him at 31 the youngest member of the Cabinet since Pitt. In 1951 he resigned from the Government with ⇨Bevan over Labour's budgetary policy and continued to be associated with the Bevanites during the fifties. Shadow Chancellor of the Exchequer and then Opposition Spokesman on Foreign Affairs, he opposed ⇨Gaitskell for the party leadership in 1960, losing by 166 votes to 81. In 1963 (after Gaitskell's death) he defeated George ⇨Brown for the party leadership by 144 votes to 103.

Labour was elected with a majority of five in 1964 but this was increased to 98 in the 1966 General Election. However, with continued economic crisis (despite devaluation (Nov. 1967)) the popularity of the government (as reflected in opinion polls, local and by-election results) slumped drastically, and it was defeated in June 1970 elections.

'Wind of Change'. Phrase taken from British Premier Harold ⇨Macmillan's speech to both Houses of Parliament in Capetown (S. Africa) on 3.2.1960. The speech, critical of ⇨ *Apartheid*, attempted to dissociate the UK from policies in which race was made the criterion for individual advancement and citizenship. (The phrase gained currency as new African states emerged, rapidly changing the map of the continent.)

Windsor, Duke of (1894–1972). Succeeded his father, George V, as King Edward VIII of England (20.1.1936) but abdicated (11.12.1936) on his decision to marry a twice-divorced commoner (⇨ Abdication Crisis). From 1940–45 he was Governor and Commander-in-Chief of the Bahamas.

World Communism. In the aftermath of World War II the formerly communist world movement underwent a process of fragmentation. The earlier uniformity had been sustained by the myth of ⇨ Stalin's infallibility as the leader of the only communist party ever to have made a successful revolution. This myth lost its basis after the war, when communist regimes came to power either wholly without or with merely marginal Soviet aid, first in ⇨ Yugoslavia and ⇨ Albania, then in ⇨ China and North ⇨ Vietnam and, at a later stage, in ⇨ Cuba. Their independent revolutionary achievements inevitably challenged Moscow's position as the sole commanding headquarters of world communism. The past practices of adjusting international communist policies to the state interests and aspirations of the USSR were bound to become unacceptable to new communist-ruled states with different or conflicting national interests and aspirations.

The first challenge came in 1948 with ⇨ Tito's successful rebellion against Stalin's treatment of Yugoslavia as a subject nation. The next stage, paradoxically, was reached as a result of ⇨ Khrushchev's bid to make amends for the maltreatment of Yugoslavia and to adjust Soviet policies generally to the new post-war realities. This bid began with the renunciation of certain Soviet privileges in its relations with China (including the right to a base in Port Arthur) and the dissolution of the 'mixed companies' in various East European states which had formerly served as a source of Soviet economic exploitation. The bid continued in 1955 with Khrushchev's public apology to Tito and the Soviet-Yugoslav ⇨ Belgrade Declaration, and it reached its climax with Khrushchev's denunciation of Stalin's crimes and ⇨ Personality Cult at the 20th CPSU Congress in Feb. 1956.

One objective of these initiatives, the reconciliation with Yugoslavia, was (temporarily) achieved, but there were unforeseen consequences. The most immediate and dramatic sequel was the chain of events which, from the 20th CPSU Congress, led to the rehabilitation of 'nationalist' and 'revisionist' communists in Eastern Europe and an unparalleled upsurge of uninhibited demands for national independence and individual freedom and which reached its climax in the ⇨ Polish October and the immediately following revolution in ⇨ Hungary. With these events, national self-assertion and the incipient revolt against domination by Moscow spread for the first time to the camp of Soviet satellites where communist regimes had been installed by direct Soviet intervention. In between, in June 1956, ⇨ Togliatti highlighted these developments by enunciating the new concept of ⇨ Polycentrism, which went rather further than Tito's and ⇨ Gomulka's thesis of 'each country's right to its own road to socialism' and, in fact, anticipated a later stage of development. The 20th CPSU Congress and the ensuing crisis in Eastern Europe also became the occasion for China's first ideological criticism of the CPSU leadership and her effective support of Gomulka against the threatening Soviet intervention in ⇨ Poland in Oct. 1956. The shock of the Hungarian revolution and its aftermath led to a fresh, if temporary, closing of the ranks. A meeting of ruling communist parties in Moscow in Nov. 1957 produced the compromise 'Moscow Declaration', which only the Yugoslavs refused to sign because it once again singled out ⇨ Revisionism as the 'main danger' and formally acknowledged the position of the USSR as the 'head' of the camp of socialist countries.

Relations between Yugoslavia and the Soviet bloc deteriorated further following the Hungarian revolution. Though backing the crucial second Soviet intervention in Hungary, the Yugoslavs blamed the first Soviet intervention for provoking the armed rising and gave asylum to Imre ⇨ Nagy and some of his supporters. After the Moscow conference of Nov. 1957, the USSR and its associates launched a new campaign against Yugoslav revisionism and its international influence, which reached its grim climax with the execution of Imre Nagy and others in June 1958. By that time, however, the fronts had already begun to shift. Peking had replaced Moscow as the pacemaker in the campaign against Yugoslavia. With the gradual unfolding of the overlapping ⇨ Sino-Soviet Conflict, this Chinese campaign imperceptibly changed its contents, with the result that Yugoslavia became eventually a mere substitute target for Chinese attacks aimed at the USSR. The aggravation of the Sino-Soviet conflict led, in turn, to new crises in inter-communist relations elsewhere. This emerged first in June 1960 at the

Bucharest Conference of the Rumanian communist party, which Khrushchev used for his attempt at creating an international communist front against China. The immediate result was Albania's open defiance of the Soviet leadership which soon afterwards led to a total rupture. The final break with China as well as Albania came at the second Moscow Conference of communist parties in Nov. 1960. For a time the break was concealed under the joint 'Moscow Statement' which the delegates from 81 communist parties eventually adopted after prolonged bitter debates and mutual denunciations. In contrast to the Moscow Declaration of 1957, the Statement of 1960 was not a compromise, but a thin paper cover for unresolved conflicts. After the 1960 Conference, polycentrism, which Togliatti had anticipated in 1956, became a fact. The leaders of the two great communist powers turned into irreconcilable rivals for the exclusive authority to interpret the common Marxist-Leninist doctrine in terms of international guidelines for communist policy and strategy. Yet another potential rival for this role emerged in 1966 in the person of Fidel ⇨ Castro who established a third 'Marxist-Leninist' centre with the organization of ⇨OLAS, created in deliberate opposition to both Moscow and Peking as an alternative authority for the revolutionary struggle in Latin America.

The Soviet leaders meanwhile tried to restore Moscow's shaken position. Firstly, to strengthen their hold over their East European neighbours, they launched a campaign for far-reaching economic integration which was designed amongst other things, to forestall any future breakaway. Secondly, they campaigned for another international communist conference designed to ex-communicate China by a majority decision and re-establish Soviet authority over the rest of the communist world. Both initiatives met with strong opposition particularly from ⇨ Rumania. Rumanian opposition effectively blocked repeated Soviet attempts at achieving economic integration in Eastern Europe through the transformation of ⇨ CMEA into a supra-national authority empowered to impose joint economic plans on all member countries. Rumania also played a prominent part in the more widespread opposition to the new world conference project. Public propaganda for this project began in the autumn of 1963 and a considerable number of communist parties were eventually induced to give it their formal backing. Most of them, however, were wholly insignificant and the opposition, though numerically much smaller, was formidable in terms of influence. It originally included, in addition to China and Albania, the communist party of Poland as well as the parties of Rumania, Vietnam, Korea, Cuba, Italy, Indonesia and Japan, i.e. a majority of the ruling parties (not counting Yugoslavia which was not invited) and the then largest and most influential non-ruling parties of Europe and Asia. Their motives for opposing the project varied. Some sympathized with the Chinese point of view but most of them were mainly concerned to preserve and re-inforce the chances for national autonomy and freedom of action provided by the Sino-Soviet schism. Despite this formidable opposition, the Soviet leaders went ahead with their plans. The 26 members of the Drafting Committee of the 1960 Conference were summoned to Moscow for a preliminary meeting to be held in Dec. 1964. Two months before the appointed date, Khrushchev was suddenly overthrown.

The manner of his removal and his transformation from one day to the next into an Unperson caused fresh dismay in the strife-torn communist world. Even Moscow's hitherto staunchest supporters publicly questioned the official version of the event and called for explanations which were not forthcoming. As soon as this issue had receded into the background, the new Soviet leaders revived the conference project. Encouraged by the growing isolation in which China found itself as a result of the Cultural Revolution, Soviet spokesmen declared from the autumn of 1966 onwards that the conditions were now right for a new conference. To overcome remaining misgivings they undertook not to ex-communicate anyone and to seek nothing but the restoration of unity. Opposition remained strong, but a preparatory meeting was finally held in Budapest in Feb. 1968. The meeting was boycotted by 6 of the 14 ruling communist parties, while Rumania walked out in protest in the midst of it. Those who remained finally decided to hold a new conference in Moscow in Nov. 1968.

Three months before the appointed date, the residual bonds of inter-communist unity were shattered by the invasion of ⇨ Czecho-slovakia. Despite the unprecedented flood of worldwide communist condemnations, Moscow attempted to proceed with the conference project. In June 1969, the conference was eventually held, but failed to make a difference to the existing divisions although, within Europe, inter-communist relations improved somewhat after Mr Brezhnev's visit to Yugoslavia (Sept. 1971), during which he re-endorsed the controversial ⇨ Belgrade Declaration of 1955.

World War II. Hitler's ambition to re-establish Germany as a dominant world power resulted in a European and then a world-wide conflict. War broke out when the ⇨ Third Reich, having purchased Russian neutrality (⇨ Hitler-Stalin Pact), attacked ⇨ Poland (1.9.1939) whose territorial integrity had been guaranteed by Britain and France (March/Aug. 1939). They declared war on Germany (3.9.1939). Poland was quickly defeated when the Allies failed to mount their promised counter-offensive. When Warsaw capitulated (27 Sept.), the country ceased to exist as an independent state. Russia had occupied eastern Poland (17 Sept.) when the Germans reached the demarcation line, agreed in the Hitler-Stalin Pact, while Germany annexed the western border regions. Poles were driven into the rump territory known as the Government General, a German-administered dependency. Here Germany liquidated the Polish leadership (academics, priests, politicians, doctors, engineers, etc.) and installed the death factories in which millions of Jews, gypsies and other 'non-Aryans' were killed. (⇨ Holocaust.)

While Hitler unsuccessfully appealed to Britain and France to accept the new *status quo* (*Reichstag* speech, 7.10.1939), the USSR secured bases in Estonia, Latvia and Lithuania (Sept./Oct. 1939). ⇨ Finland's refusal to make similar concessions led to the Russo-Finnish war (Dec. 1939–March 1940) and the USSR's expulsion from the ⇨ League of Nations (Dec. 1939). After inflicting some humiliating defeats on the Russians, Finland was eventually compelled to sue for peace and to accept Russian terms (Moscow Treaty, March 1940).

The War in the West. When, after the failure of a Belgian-Dutch peace appeal (Nov. 1939) and a similar Rumanian initiative, Germany decided to attack, strategic considerations and apprehensions about the Swedish ore supply persuaded her to strike at the northern flank first. While the Allies, by mining Norwegian waters, had anticipated Germany's sea and airborne invasion of ⇨ Denmark and ⇨ Norway (9 April 1940), they nevertheless failed to prevent it. Denmark was unable to offer resistance, but Norway, supported by Anglo-French landings (16/19 April) opposed the invaders, who helped by ⇨ Quisling collaborators, had established themselves in main towns (Oslo, Bergen, etc.) and at Narvik in the far north. In spite of heavy naval losses – ten destroyers sunk off Narvik by the British (10–13 April), three cruisers and four troopships sunk by coastal batteries – the German air-force succeeded in supplying and reinforcing the invading troops. When these, bisecting the country, linked up at Donbas (30 April) further Norwegian resistance became impossible. King Haakon VII and the Cabinet were evacuated with the Anglo-French expeditionary force (3 May) and formed a government-in-exile. In Norway a German *Reich-Kommissar* (Terboven) took over supported by Quisling's unpopular *Nasjonal Samling*. In Feb. 1942 Quisling became the country's nominal ruler.

The attack on the West (10 May 1940) repeated the giant enveloping manoeuvre which nearly defeated the French in World War I. Neutral ⇨ Belgium and Holland were attacked without warning while simultaneously powerful tank forces outflanking the Maginot Line struck at the French through ⇨ Luxembourg. Having broken through near Sedan (13 May), they raced towards the Channel – Boulogne fell (23 May),

Calais (26 May), Ostend (29 May) – cutting off the Anglo-French forces in northern ⇨ France and Belgium.

In the ⇨ Netherlands the Germans breached the Dutch border fortifications by dropping air-borne troops in their rear. After an air raid which flattened Rotterdam's city centre (14 May), the Dutch army surrendered, while the Government and the royal family continued the struggle from London. Similar tactics had pierced the Belgian defences; Brussels surrendered (17 May), and Antwerp a day later. Encircled near Ghent, the Belgian army led by the King capitulated (28 May), while the Government escaped first to France and then to England.

The encircled French and British forces, 338,000 men, were evacuated from the Dunkirk bridgehead (26 May–4 June) by every available British craft. Before they could be redeployed, the Germans had shattered General Weygand's new front (15/17 June). While one of the German armoured columns taking Dijon and Lyons reached the Swiss frontier (17 June), others fanned out towards the Atlantic coast. On 10 June ⇨ Italy declared war and invaded the south of France. Paris surrendered (14 June) and on 17 June Marshal ⇨Pétain, the new Premier, asked for and concluded an armistice (22 June) while General ⇨de Gaulle, in his London broadcast (23 June) asserted France's determination to fight on. Germany, at the cost of 45,000 killed and 111,000 wounded, had conquered France, taken close to 2 million prisoners and captured vast stocks of war material. Under ⇨ Churchill, who had succeeded ⇨Chamberlain (10.5.1940), Britain now faced the Axis alone. Failure to defeat the RAF in the Battle of Britain (Aug./Sept. 1940) forced the Germans to abandon Operation Sea-lion, the invasion of England, and with it the hope of quickly defeating an almost defenceless Britain. Prospects of a long war compelled Germany to look for raw material and industrial bases large enough to match those of the USA, increasingly mobilized as the 'arsenal of democracy' (transfer of 50 over-age destroyers, Sept. 1940; ⇨ Lend-Lease Act, March 1941). These considerations as well as fear of Russian intentions, induced Hitler to consider Operation Barbarossa, the invasion of the Soviet Union. It aimed at destroying the Red Army in six months, leaving Germany in control of Russia from Archangel to the Caspian.

While Germany was fighting in France, the USSR had annexed the ⇨ Baltic States (June/Aug. 1940) and forced ⇨ Rumania to cede Bessarabia and the northern Bukovina (June 1940). When ⇨ Molotov during his Berlin visit (Nov. 1940) demanded further concessions in the Balkans and Finland as the price for joining the ⇨Tripartite Pact (Sept. 1940), Hitler ordered preparations for Operation Barbarossa (Dec. 1940).

The North African Campaigns. Italy's belligerency had extended the war to the Mediterranean and North Africa where the attitude of the French fleet anchored off Oran caused concern. Its refusal to sail for a British or neutral port provoked a British attack which destroyed four battleships (July 1940). Although the naval balance was restored after the British had inflicted heavy losses on the originally superior Italian navy (carrier-borne attack on Taranto base, Nov. 1940; Battle of Matapan, March 1941), the Mediterranean became safe for Allied shipping only after the Allies dominated its southern shores.

⇨ Mussolini's intention to establish Italy as the dominant power in south-east Europe, North Africa and the Middle East led to the invasion of British Somaliland by the Duke of Aosta, viceroy of ⇨ Abyssinia (Aug. 1940). A month later an Italian army advanced from ⇨ Libya towards Egypt, which the British, notwithstanding the invasion threat had steadily reinforced. Employing their latest tanks, they struck back (Dec. 1940), and in a sweep that brought them 130,000 prisoners at the cost of 500 killed, chased the Italians past Tobruk (Jan. 1941) and Bengazi (Feb. 1941) to the border of Tripolitania. Italian requests for German help led to the formation of the Afrika Korps under Rommel. His counter-attack pushed the depleted British army (50,000 men had been sent to ⇨ Greece) back to the Egyptian border (May 1941). For two years the British and Axis forces surged backwards and forwards across these battle-grounds, until Montgomery's victory at El-Alamein (Oct. 1942) and the landing of General ⇨ Eisenhower's Anglo-American army in North Africa (Nov. 1942) caught the Axis forces in a giant pincer movement. Their surrender (Tunis, May 1943, 250,000 prisoners) enabled the Allies to attack southern Europe.

The Balkan Campaigns. Jealous of German successes, Mussolini attacked Greece (Oct. 1940), but was soon forced to halt and retreat. Fear that the three British divisions landed in Greece (March 1941) might imperil the flank of his intended attack on Russia, persuaded Hitler to invade Greece. He deployed his army in ⇨ Bulgaria, which had just joined the ⇨ Tripartite Pact (March 1941). When the Yugoslav Government, a signatory of the pact, was overthrown by an anti-German coup, the German plan of campaign was modified to include an attack on ⇨ Yugoslavia.

The invasions (6 April 1941) employing the well tried *Blitzkrieg* tactics (destruction of the air-force on the ground, deep thrusts of armoured divisions consolidated by fast-moving motorized infantry) again proved irresistible. The Yugoslav army (345,000 men) capitulated after ten days fighting. Only a further ten days were needed to defeat the Greek and British forces (270,000 men) on the Greek mainland. When Crete, to which the British had withdrawn, fell to a German parachute assault (May/June 1941), a second Dunkirk was imposed on Britain. But this time, lacking air support, the navy suffered grievously in rescuing the 16,000 remaining British troops.

The Russian Campaigns. For Operation Barbarossa (22 June 1941) Germany had assembled the mightiest forces so far deployed; 3·2 million men, 600,000 motor vehicles, 7,500 guns, 2,000 front-line aircraft and 3,500 tanks. In what was represented as an 'anti-communist crusade', Germany was joined by Rumania, Slovakia, Finland, Hungary and Italy. The USSR had about 4·7 million men with large if antiquated tank and air forces under arms in Europe, but was caught unprepared despite many warnings. Surprise and *Blitzkrieg* tactics resulted in deep *Wehrmacht* penetrations. By Dec. 1941 the Germans had captured more than 2 million prisoners in huge encirclement battles. They had overrun the Ukraine, the industrial Donetz basin and the Crimea; they were approaching the ice-free part of Murmansk, had besieged Leningrad and were within sight of Moscow, but remained unable to reach these objectives. Nor was the Red Army beaten, as its capture of Rostov (Dec.), Kalinin (Dec.), Mozhaisk (Feb. 1942) and Rzhev (March 1942) demonstrated. This inability to break Russian resistance doomed the Axis to ultimate defeat. For Japan's ⇨ Pearl Harbor attack (7.12.1941) brought the USA into a war specifically waged to counter-balance her industrial potential. In 1942, until the tide turned later that year, the Axis achieved the greatest extension of its power.

Resumed German offensives in Russia aimed at securing the vital Caucasian oilfields (Batum-Baku) and at cutting the Volga life-line at ⇨ Stalingrad (now Volgograd), which carried Allied supplies from Iran. The Germans, advancing past the Maikop oilfields (Aug. 1942), reached a point halfway between the Black Sea and the Caspian. They also occupied most of Stalingrad (Oct. 1942) before Russian counter-attacks forced the decimated Sixth Army to surrender (Feb. 1943, 90,000 prisoners). From then on, despite occasional German counter-strokes – recapture of Kharkov (March 1943), abortive summer offensive at Orel (July 1943) – the initiative remained with the Russians. By summer 1944 they had recaptured most of the territories previously yielded. Rumania, after being invaded by the Red Army, changed sides, declared war on Germany and signed an armistice with Russia (Sept. 1944). Finland did the same as did neutral, though Germanophile Bulgaria, after being overrun by Russia (Moscow armistice agreement, Oct. 1944). These defections, as well as the liberation of Belgrade (Oct. 1944) and most of Yugoslavia by ⇨ Tito's partisans and the Red Army hastened the German withdrawal from mainland Greece (Nov. 1944).

Soviet forces, however, proved unable to cross the Vistula in support of the Warsaw uprising of the non-communist Polish Home Army (Aug./Oct. 1944) which was completely annihilated. Warsaw fell to the Russians (Jan. 1945) in the course of their final assault on the German heartland. It carried them past Berlin, which they besieged, to the river Elbe where they linked up with the Americans at Torgau (22.4.1945). After Hitler's suicide (Berlin, 29.4.1945) and the capital's surrender (2.5.1945) Germany, now cut into two, surrendered unconditionally on 7 May at General Eisenhower's Rheims headquarters, and one day later to Marshal Zhukov in Berlin-Karlshorst.

The Italian Campaign. Having driven the Axis from North Africa (May 1943) the Allies decided to attack the 'soft underbelly of Europe' rather than the heavily fortified Channel Coast. Their successful landings on Sicily (10.7.1943) precipitated the collapse of the Fascist regime; Mussolini resigned and was arrested (25.7.1943). The new Prime Minister, Marshal Badoglio, negotiated an armistice which, although signed (3.9.1943) when the British invasion of Italy started, was only made public after the Americans had established their Salerno bridge-head south of Naples (9 Sept.). The Germans, expecting the defection, seized Rome (10 Sept.), disarmed the Italian forces and established a defensive front across the peninsula. They also freed Mussolini (12 Sept.) who, a captive ally, resuscitated his Fascist State as the *Republica Sociale Italiana*, while the 'legitimate' Badoglio government declared war on Germany (13 Oct.). The northward advance across the easily defendable Appenines was painfully slow. The Monte Cassino strong-hold delayed Allied progress from Oct. 1943 to May 1944, despite the establishment of the Anzio bridgehead (Jan. 1944) in its rear. Having overcome this obstacle, the Allies took Rome (June 1944), Pisa (July), Florence (Aug.), to be blocked again by a defence line running across the peninsula south of La Spezia. This position was held until the spring of 1945 when after an Allied breakthrough (21 April) the German forces surrendered (28 April), while Mussolini, trying to escape to Switzerland, was captured and shot by partisans.

The Liberation of Western Europe. Operation Overlord, the Channel coast landings which presaged the liberation of Western Europe and the conquest of Nazi Germany, was launched on D-Day (6.6.1944). An Anglo-American force under General Eisenhower, backed by an unpre-cedented concentration of naval and air power, established bridgeheads on the Normandy coast between Cherbourg and Caen. A breakthrough at Avranches (31 July) finally enabled the Americans under Patton to strike out towards Paris, where a simultaneous Resistance uprising (19 Aug.) opened the town for the triumphal entry of General de Gaulle's Free French forces (25 Aug.). Meanwhile, the British under General

Montgomery, having annihilated most of the German armour (Battle of Fallaise, 16 Aug.), liberated Brussels (4 Sept.) and Antwerp (5 Sept.) A second Allied landing near Nice (15 Aug.) compelled the Germans to withdraw from southern and central France. During these retreats two German C.-in-C.s, Generals Rommel and von Kluge, because of their alleged complicity in the ⇨Twentieth July attempt on Hitler's life, were faced with the alternatives of trial or suicide and chose the latter. Rommel was known to have insisted that Hitler end a war already lost after the Allies had established their Normandy bridgeheads. The Allied advance reached the German frontier near Trier and Aachen (Sept.) but was halted when a British air-borne bid to rush the Rhine bridges at Arnhem (17 Sept.) failed. A desperate German bid to separate the British from the American forces (Ardennes offensive, Dec.) was soon checked. Resumed Allied offensives, coinciding with Red Army drives in the east, carried them to the Rhine (Feb. 1945) which the Americans first crossed over the undamaged Remagen bridge (7 March) while the British forced a crossing further down river at Wesel (24 March). Brushing aside crumbling German resistance which disregarded Hitler's Nero Order (19 March), demanding a ruthless scorched earth policy, the British, American and French forces cut across Germany, linking up with the Russians at Torgau (25 April). Fanning out to the south, they reached the Alpine passes into Italy when Germany surrendered (8.5.1945). Holland, where strong German forces were isolated and by-passed, remained occupied until the German surrender.

The War at Sea. Naval operations in the European theatre of war, unless mounted in conjunction with specific military enterprises, basically aimed at blockading the opponent. Britain's superior naval power operated an effective long-range blockade while Germany relied on mines and submarines. Improved German U-boats and 'wolf pack' tactics of subjecting convoys to attacks of up to 40 submarines caused enormous shipping losses, and imperilled British supplies. Anti-submarine devices, and the provision after America's entry into the war of coast-to-coast air-umbrellas, eventually defeated the U-boat menace. Anglo-American losses running at over 4 million tons p.a. in 1941, more than doubled in 1942 when the Battle of the Atlantic was at its height; they were reduced to 3·5 m. tons in 1943 and thereafter declined dramatically. New tonnage, however, came off Allied slipways at a phenomenal annual rate in excess of 14 m. tons; hence the Anglo-American merchant navies with 40 m. tons between them were larger at the end of the war than at the beginning. Throughout the war Germany used her capital ships as surface raiders. The pocket battleship *Graf Spee*, was tracked down by British cruisers and scuttled in the River Plate (Dec.

1939). The *Bismarck*, Germany's most modern battleship, was sunk (May 1941) after having destroyed the British battleship *Hood*. Although British prestige suffered when a German flotilla led by the battle cruisers *Scharnhorst* and *Gneisenau* steamed through the Channel en route to Norway (Feb. 1942), the Royal Navy prevented any further attempts at convoy raiding by surface ships. German submarine losses were heavy. Of 1,170 U-boats commissioned, 974 were lost on active service; only 6,000 of her 39,000 submariners survived.

The Air War. The *Luftwaffe*, at the start of the war the strongest and most modern air-force in the world, was conceived as a tactical, close-support weapon. In this capacity it played a vital part in *Blitzkrieg* tactics. When defeated in the Battle of Britain (Aug./Sept. 1940), it had to assume the strategic task of bombing British industrial and communications centres for which it was not designed. The increasing demands from expanding battle lines as well as growing Allied superiority, both technical and numerical, caused a rapid decline in the strength of the *Luftwaffe*. By 1942 it was no longer able to defend Germany against Allied bombers although it could still inflict heavy losses on them. Raids of increasing frequency and intensity – first 1,000 bomber raid, Cologne, May 1942 – obliterated almost every major German town without, however, breaking German morale or gravely disorganizing the German war effort. In spite of air attacks it reached its peak in 1944. However, attacks on the Rumanian Ploesti oilfields (April 1944) and the Merseburg synthetic petrol plants (May 1944), caused severe fuel shortages, hampering *Luftwaffe* and tank activities. The Dresden raid (Feb. 1945) causing approximately 45,000 deaths, was perhaps the most devastating. The bomb tonnage dropped over Germany rose steeply from 14,500 t. in 1940 to 53,000 t. in 1942 and 1,188,000 t. in 1944; while the tonnage dropped over England declined from 37,000 t. in 1940 to 22,000 t. in 1941 and 9,000 t. in 1944, including the bombardment by 8,000 robot jets (Doodlebugs) and 1,100 V2 rockets, the first of their kind (approximate range 230 miles). About 60,000 British civilians were killed in air raids; the comparative German figure is put at 500,000.

The War in the Pacific. ⇨ Japan, formally neutral but a signatory to the ⇨ Anti-comintern Pact (Nov. 1936), hoped an Axis victory would give her control over the British, Dutch and French colonial empires in south-east Asia. These ambitions, crowning her bid for domination over China with whom she had been at war from 1937, inevitably antagonized the USA. America's pro-Allied sentiments combined with her economic interests and concern for her Philippine bases, made her a firm opponent of further Japanese expansion. The two countries were set on a collision course when Japan, immediately before joining the Tripartite Pact, occupied French Indochina (Sept. 1940) and, locking her back door, concluded a neutrality pact with Russia (April 1941). American reaction added the freezing of Japanese credits (July 1941) to previously ruptured trade relations. The failure of the comparatively moderate Premier, Prince Konoye, to secure American acquiescence in Japanese designs on the Dutch East Indies, brought the military under General ⇨ Tojo to power (Oct. 1941). When his request for re-opening trade relations was made dependent on Japan's withdrawal from China and Indochina, he ordered the attack on Pearl Harbor (7.12.1941). Italy and Germany transformed a mainly European war into a global one when they declared war on the USA (11 Dec.). The carrier-borne air attack on Pearl Harbor (five battleships, three cruisers sunk; three battleships and many smaller craft severely damaged) made it impossible for the US navy to oppose Japanese attacks which developed in a vast arc, extending from the Aleutian Islands to Mandalay. The main blow was directed against the Philippines (Manila surrendered Jan.; Bataan, April; Corregidor, May 1942) and the Dutch East Indies, which after the destruction of an Anglo-Dutch naval force (Battle of the Java Sea, Feb. 1942), quickly fell to the Japanese (Dutch capitulation 8 March).

Simultaneously with the attack on Pearl Harbor, Hong Kong was attacked (surrendered, 25.12.1941), and Japanese troops were landed on the northern end of the Malay peninsula. The battleships *Prince of Wales* and *Repulse* were caught without air-cover and sunk (10 Dec.) when they attempted to oppose these landings. Infiltrating through the jungle the Japanese captured Singapore from the unfortified landward side and took 60,000 British prisoners (Feb. 1942). When the British evacuated ⇨ Burma, Mandalay fell (May 1942), and the Burma Road, China's only remaining link with the outside world, was cut. To cover these conquests, Japan occupied the outlying archipelagos from the Solomon, Gilbert and Marshall Islands to the Aleutian Islands which, captured in June 1942, marked the furthest extension of Japanese power.

Within six months Japan had extended her rule over a huge area inhabited by 450 million people among whom she fostered anti-White anti-colonialist movements. Burma declared her independence (Aug. 1943), and Indonesia under Hatta and ⇨ Sukarno was granted independence towards the end of the war as was Vietnam.

The tide began to turn when, in the battles of the Coral Sea (May 1942) and Midway (June 1942) – fought exclusively by carrier-borne planes without the opposing fleets sighting each other – the Japanese lost their air-sea superiority (five carriers sunk). American counter-attacks, starting with the Guadalcanal landing (Aug. 1942), gathered momentum as they developed the technique of by-passing intermediate islands in their advance towards Japan. By the summer of 1944 American long-range bombers established on Saipan in the Marianas could attack Japan itself. Moreover, in defending her outlying bases, Japan sustained losses which, unlike the USA, she could no longer replace. When the Americans under General ⇨ MacArthur started to reoccupy the Philippines (Oct. 1944), the unsuccessful attempt to prevent the landings cost the Japanese 86 ships and 405 planes. Japanese air strength was similarly worn down, and when after the capture of Okinawa (April/June 1945) American air-bases were within 325 miles of Japan, no fighters were left to defend the homeland against the intensifying air assault. By Aug. 1945 more than 9 m. people from cities and industrial centres had been rendered homeless. After Japan's last naval squadron, the battleship *Yamato*, two cruisers and three destroyers were sunk while attempting to oppose the Okinawa landings, American ships ranged at will in Japanese waters.

In the spring of 1945 Admiral Mountbatten's forces broke the Japanese stranglehold on Burma entering Mandalay (March) and Rangoon (May 1945) after a campaign in which the Japanese lost an estimated 350,000 men. The dropping of the first atom bomb on Hiroshima (6.8.1945), Russia's declaration of war on Japan (8.8.1945) and simultaneous invasion of Manchuria, and the dropping of the second atom bomb on Nagasaki (9 Aug.) persuaded Japan to surrender (10 Aug.). World War II ended on 2 Sept., 1945 when the capitulation documents previously accepted (14 Aug.), were formally signed by the Japanese on board the USS *Missouri* in Tokyo Bay.

Wyszynski, Cardinal S. (1901–). Primate of ⇨ Poland. Wyszynski entered the priesthood in 1925 and later became a teacher at the Wloclawek training college for priests where he remained until the end of World War II. Appointed Bishop of Lublin in 1946, he succeeded Cardinal Hlond as Primate on the latter's death in 1949. Increasing pressures of the state authorities on the Church culminated in Cardinal Wyszynski's arrest (Sept. 1953) and his subsequent confinement in various monasteries. After ⇨ Gomulka's ascent to power in 1956, Cardinal Wyszynski was allowed to return to Warsaw and resume his office. A *modus vivendi* then established between the Church and the state was threatened by renewed tensions in 1966 when the Cardinal was prevented from going to Rome to attend the Pope's inauguration of the millennium of Polish Christianity.

Y

Yagoda, G. G. (1891–1938). Soviet Secret Police Chief. A ⇨ Bolshevik since his youth, Yagoda fought in the Red Army during the Russian civil war and soon after began to specialize in Secret Police activities for the ⇨ USSR State Security Service. A leading member of the ⇨ Cheka from 1920, he became the Deputy Head of the ⇨ GPU (1924) and People's Commissar for Internal Affairs (Head of the ⇨ NKVD) (1934). Entrusted with the preparation and conduct of the great ⇨ Purges which began after ⇨ Kirov's assassination (Dec. 1934), Yagoda was in charge of the first of the three ⇨ Moscow Trials but was, in ⇨ Stalin's opinion, insufficiently ruthless. In a telegram sent jointly with ⇨ Zhdanov to ⇨ Molotov, ⇨ Kaganovich and other members of the Politbureau, Stalin alleged (Sept. 1936) that the NKVD was four years behind in unmasking 'the enemies of the people' and insisted on Yagoda's immediate replacement by ⇨ Yezhov. In 1937, Yagoda was arrested and figured subsequently as one of the chief defendants in the third and last of the Moscow Trials. He was executed after the trial.

Yakhimovich, Ivan (1930?–). Soviet communist and former collective farm chairman in Latvia, sacked from his post for his repeated protests against restraints on freedom, unconstitutional trials of writers, and the invasion of Czechoslovakia. He was arrested in 1969.

Yalta Conference. War-time meeting held at Yalta in the Crimea between Churchill, Roosevelt and Stalin (Feb. 1945). Agreements reached at the conference included: (1) the division of ⇨ Germany into four zones of occupation and the establishment of an Allied Control Council in Berlin; (2) Germany's complete disarmament and obligation to reparation payments; (3) the re-establishment of ⇨ Poland within new frontiers, with eastern Poland to be ceded to the USSR and East German territories to be ceded to Poland by way of compensation; (4) the establishment of democratic governments in all liberated countries on the basis of free elections; (5) a Soviet declaration of war on ⇨ Japan and the cession of certain Japanese islands to the USSR; the re-establishment of the independence of ⇨ Korea after a period of joint

occupation by American and Soviet forces; (7) the endorsement of the
⇨ Atlantic Charter (originally issued by Churchill and Roosevelt in
Aug. 1941) as the basis of Allied post-war policy; (8) the convening of a
conference for the establishment of the United Nations.

Certain additional agreements were reached on the nature of the
post-war regimes in Poland and Yugoslavia and on the future division
between Soviet and Western zones of influence in Europe, the outlines of
which have become known only from unofficial records and memoirs.
Both the public and non-public agreements, like those later reached at
the ⇨ Potsdam Conference, became the subject of opposite interpretations and mutual charges of bad faith between the USSR and the
Western powers.

Yalta Memorandum. The 'political testament' of the Italian communist leader Palmiro ⇨ Togliatti, written at Yalta and originally
addressed to ⇨ Khrushchev. The memorandum was published shortly
after Togliatti's death in Aug. 1964.

Yemen. *Area* – 75,000 sq. miles. *Population* – 5 million. *Prime Minister*
– Muhsin al-Aini (1971–). *Constitution* (1970) – recognizes the Yemen as
an independent Islamic Republic, vests legislative authority in the
consultative Assembly and provides for a five man Presidential Council.

The Yemen was part of the Ottoman Empire until World War I but
its theocratic political structure under the rule of the *Imams* lasted until
the revolution of 1962, since when the country has been divided between
republicans and royalists. The *Imams* monopolized all government posts
and most businesses, but popular discontent led in 1948 to the assassination of the despotic and conservative Imam Yahya. His son Ahmad
(1948–62) defeated the insurgents and succeeded him. Although he
started developing the country with aid from the Western powers
(1951), there was no radical change in the political system – a formal
Cabinet was established in 1955 but only after an attempted *coup d'état*
against the *Imam*. In 1959 there were further disorders when the *Imam*
visited Europe. The Crown Prince introduced reforms, including the
innovation of a Representative Council, but these were rescinded after
the return of the *Imam*. After World War II the Yemen discarded her
isolationist foreign policy and joined the ⇨ Arab League (1945), the UN
(1947) and established diplomatic relations for the first time with foreign
powers including the USA, the UK and Egypt. In 1956 a military pact
was concluded with Egypt and ⇨ Saudi Arabia and in 1958 the Yemen
joined the ⇨ UAR in forming the United Arab States, but relations
between the two countries deteriorated when ⇨ Nasser dissolved this
federation and denounced the *Imam* as reactionary. In Sept. 1962 the
Imam died and was succeeded by Mohammed al-Badr, his son, but a

week later the latter was overthrown by a revolt of pro-Nasser army officers led by Colonel Abdullah ⇨ Sallal, who became head of the new republican government. This was the beginning of an extended civil war which assumed international importance. The UAR, which supported the republicans (a common military command was formed in 1964) had 60,000 forces in the Yemen (1965) while Saudi Arabia supplied the royalists with arms and financial help. The royalists had a force of 350,000 (superior in numbers but insufficiently equipped) and retained control over the mountainous area of the north. The republicans had control over the towns and the west coast. Their government was soon recognized by the Soviet Union and the USA and in 1963 was admitted to the UN. Various attempts were made to negotiate a peace. Nasser and King ⇨ Faisal met at Erkwit (1964), Jeddah (1965) and Khartoum (1967) but their agreements were hamstrung by a deadlock between the republicans and the royalists. The situation was not helped by growing divisions on both sides. Sallal (overthrown in 1967) had tried to implement a programme of social reforms but had been hampered by his preoccupation with fighting republican opposition. This split among the republicans diminished through 1968 and 1969 while the royalist cause was further weakened by internal feuds (there was a rival royalist government in exile), the defection of prominent royalists to the republicans, the illness of the *Imam* and, most important, the disenchantment of King Faisal with the royalists and his withdrawal of subsidies. The republican government has fostered closer relations with the UAR, e.g. a defence pact was concluded in 1962 and a common co-ordination committee for all political questions set up in 1964. Good relations with communist countries had already been encouraged before 1962, e.g. an economic agreement with the Soviet Union was signed in 1956 and a Friendship Treaty with China in 1958, but these were now strengthened. Friendship Treaties were concluded with the Soviet Union, Czechoslovakia, Rumania, Hungary and China in 1964 and in 1965 an economic agreement with East Germany was signed. In May 1970 the royalist faction finally made peace with the Republicans and accepted the establishment of the republic.

Yenan. ⇨ Mao Tse-tung's headquarters between Oct. 1935 and March 1947 (⇨ China).

Yezhov, N. I. (1895–?). Soviet Secret Police Chief. Between 1936 and 1938 Yezhov was the chief organizer of the great Soviet ⇨ Purges, named the ⇨ Yezhovshchina after him. Though a long-standing Communist Party member, he was almost unknown until 1933, when ⇨ Stalin began to sponsor his rapid promotion. On Stalin's personal insistence, Yezhov replaced ⇨ Yagoda as Head of the ⇨ NKVD (Sept.

1936) between the first and the second of the ⇨ Moscow Trials. When the great purges were brought to a halt, Yezhov, in turn, was replaced by L. P. ⇨ Beria (Dec. 1938). Yezhov's subsequent fate is unknown; according to some rumours he was shot; according to others he died insane.

Yezhovshchina. Russian term in international usage for the great Soviet purges of the 1930s, derived from the name of the Soviet Secret Police Chief, N. I. ⇨ Yezhov. The great purges began during the term of office of Yezhov's predecessor, G. G. ⇨ Yagoda, the organizer of the first of the three ⇨ Moscow Trials and himself a victim of the third of these trials; but it was during the Yezhov period, between 1936 and 1938, that the purges reached their climax with the mass extermination of the established political, military, economic and administrative élite of the ⇨ USSR.

Almost half the total officer corps, including practically the entire Supreme Military Command (75 out of 80 members) fell victim to the purge. So did the overwhelming majority of party officials at all levels and vast numbers of party members, including well over half the delegates to the 17th Party Congress of 1934 and 70% of the Central Committee elected by that Congress. The purge victims included the two former chiefs of the ⇨ Communist International, countless government officials and administrators, nearly all Soviet Ambassadors in Europe and Asia as well as foreign communists resident in the USSR and multitudes of ordinary hitherto obscure citizens. Official figures are not available, but according to non-Soviet estimates, some seven million political arrests were made during the two years of the *Yezhovshchina* alone. Of these about one million are estimated to have been executed as 'enemies of the people', while approximately another two million are estimated to have perished in forced labour camps during the same period. By the end of 1938, when the great purges had been brought to a halt, the total population of the Soviet forced labour camps (including both earlier political prisoners and the survivors of the *Yezhovshchina*) is believed to have been approximately nine million. (⇨ USSR State Security Service.)

Yugoslavia, Socialist Federal Republic of. *Area* – 98,725 sq. miles. *Population* (1971 est.) – 21,500,000. *President of the Republic* – Josip Broz ⇨ Tito. *President of the Federal Assembly* – Mijalko Todorovic (1972–). *President of the Federal Executive Council* – Djemal Bijedic (1972–). Yugoslavia is a Federation comprising the Socialist Republics of Bosnia-Herzegovina, Croatia, Macedonia, Montenegro, Serbia and Slovenia, which have considerable autonomy. Constitutional amendments adopted in 1971 by the five Chambers of the Federal

Assembly provided for the establishment of a collective State Presidency. Its members represent the Federation's constituent Republics and Autonomous Provinces. They are elected for five years, except for Marshal Tito who presides over the State Presidency for his own lifetime.

Yugoslavia developed from the Kingdom of Serbs, Croats and Slovenes, set up in 1918. In 1929, it was renamed Kingdom of Yugoslavia, when King Alexander established a royal dictatorship repressing the non-Serbian nationalities. After the assassination of King Alexander by a Macedonian terrorist (1934) his successor, the Regent Prince Paul, increasingly turned towards cooperation with the Axis powers. On 25 March 1941, his government joined the ⇨ Tripartite Pact of Germany, Italy and Japan. Two days later, the government was overthrown by a *coup d'état*. The Simovic government, which replaced it, exiled the Regent, declared the young King Peter a major and sought closer relations with the USSR. Ten days later, in retaliation, Germany and Italy, supported by Bulgaria and Hungary, invaded Yugoslavia. After a brief period of fierce fighting, King Peter and his government escaped to London. The invaders dismembered the country, annexing large parts of it and setting up quisling regimes in other parts. Military resistance developed soon afterwards from two centres – the Serbian *Chetniks*, led by Col. Draža Mihailovic, and the increasingly effective communist Partisans, led by Josip Broz Tito. In 1943, Winston Churchill withdrew British support from the more cautious *Chetniks* and sent a British mission to Yugoslavia to assist the Partisans. Despite the enormous military superiority of the enemy forces and the fearful atrocities committed by them, the Partisans liberated the greater part of the country by their own efforts and by their own revolutionary strategy to which they adhered against Soviet objections. Their victory over their *Chetnik* rivals as well as the enemy armies was all but assured, when the Soviet forces entered Yugoslavia to help them in the liberation of Belgrade and the rest of the country.

The nucleus of the post-war regime was created during the fighting. In Nov. 1943, the National Liberation Front – established and controlled by the Communist Party and, after the war, renamed People's Front – set up a provisional government headed by Tito, which deprived the London emigré government of its legal titles and prohibited the return of King Peter. On 29 Nov. 1945, Yugoslavia was proclaimed a People's Republic (renamed Socialist Republic, 1963) and subjected to a harsh communist dictatorship. Though seemingly similar to the regimes set up elsewhere in Eastern Europe by the USSR and even more fully Stalinist in its methods of rule, the Tito regime had already during the war begun to develop serious conflicts with ⇨ Stalin. The conflicts multiplied until the ⇨ Cominform announced its decision to expel the Yugoslav Communist Party for a long list of imputed crimes (28.6.1948). The basic cause of the conflict then and before was Stalin's contemptuous belittling of the Yugoslav communists' own national achievements and sacrifices in the Partisan war and his humiliating habit of treating them as underlings. Refusing to accept that role, Tito was driven onto a road which, in the rest of the communist world came to be denounced as 'nationalism' and ⇨ Revisionism. Stalin and his satellites attempted to subdue Tito by all means short of war, including economic boycott and diplomatic sanctions. Sustained by American and other Western economic aid and by a new upsurge of patriotism against the Soviet vilifications, the Yugoslav communists, gradually, by trial and error, evolved an altogether new communist practice and ideology of their own. Externally they opted for independence and non-alignment. Internally, they sought to combat the evils of bureaucracy by far-reaching measures of administrative and economic decentralization coupled with a system of workers' self-management. These experiments have produced a socialist market economy and a general atmosphere of increasing liberalization. This evolution still continues, but, in the opinion of many Yugoslavs, including Milovan ⇨ Djilas, Tito's former Vice-President, it progressed too slowly and was not nearly radical enough – a criticism which landed Djilas and some others in prison. Still, persecution for political or religious views has become the exception rather than the rule. The powers of the Secret Police have been drastically curtailed. The Yugoslav people now enjoy most democratic freedoms with the significant exception of the right to challenge the political monopoly of the League of Communists (as the Communist Party has been called since 1952). The role of the League differs, however, from that of other ruling communist parties. Its change of name symbolized its intention to transform itself from an instrument of centralized rule and direct intervention in economic, social and cultural life into a centre of political education and persuasion – an evolution which is still in progress.

Yugoslavia's international position changed rapidly after Stalin's death. Intent on re-establishing 'fraternal' relations with Yugoslavia, ⇨ Khrushchev travelled to Belgrade (May 1955) to apologize publicly for Stalin's treatment of Tito. Relations between the two countries deteriorated again after the Hungarian revolution in the autumn of 1956 and have since then had many sharp ups and downs. The Yugoslavs have consistently refused to join any *bloc*, East or West, and have opposed the hegemony of any great power over smaller powers. They have sought to establish friendly relations with all countries and the closest possible ties with other socialist and newly developing countries.

A notable exception from their general policy of 'active co-existence' and 'positive neutrality' was their all-out support for Moscow's condemnation of Israel in the Middle East war of 1967. The Soviet-led invasion of ⇨ Czechoslovakia (Aug. 1968) provoked a sharp deterioration in Belgrade's relations with the participants in the invasion and, at the same time, a yet greater intimacy with Bucharest and the beginning of a reconciliation with ⇨ China and ⇨ Albania. Relations with the USSR improved again after Mr Brezhnev's public re-endorsement of the ⇨ Belgrade Declaration during his visit to Yugoslavia in Sept. 1971.

Yugov, A. ⇨ Bulgaria.

Z

Zaire, Republic of ⇨ Congo (Kinshasa).
Zambia. *Area* – 288,130 sq. miles. *Population* (1969) – 4,054,000 of whom 50,000 are European. *President* – Dr Kenneth David ⇨ Kaunda (1964–). *Constitution* (1964) – An executive President is also Chairman of the Cabinet which is made up of the Vice-President and 14 members of the National Assembly. In addition to its 75 elected members, the President may appoint 5 additional members. There is an advisory House of Chiefs.

Formerly the British Protectorate of Northern Rhodesia (which in addition included the Protectorate of Barotseland), Zambia became an independent Republic within the Commonwealth in Oct. 1964. It was administered by the British South Africa Company from 1900 until 1924 when it came under the Crown. Less attractive to European settlement initially than Southern Rhodesia, Northern Rhodesian white settlers were unable to achieve the privileged status, i.e. responsible government, of their counterparts in Southern Rhodesia. African rights were protected by the doctrine of the paramountcy of African interests. Until the creation of the Federation of ⇨ Rhodesia and Nyasaland (1953–63), African political development was slow. Though an advisory council came into being in 1918, it took 30 years before two Africans entered the Legislature (1948). The dominant political figure, the leader of the European minority, Roy (later Sir Roy) ⇨ Welensky led the European demand for amalgamation with Southern Rhodesia. After a referendum in Southern Rhodesia, but despite opposition in Northern Rhodesia and without a referendum there, the Federation came into being (Aug. 1953). During the Federation period, Northern Rhodesia remained a British Protectorate and as in ⇨ Malawi there was increased African political opposition and unrest. Two African leaders emerged – Harry Nkumbula of the Northern Rhodesia African National Congress, and the man formerly one of his lieutenants who, as leader of the breakaway UNIP (United National Independent Party) later became Zambia's first President, Dr Kenneth Kaunda. Following complex constitutional developments (1945–59) a constitution (1962), designed to ensure racial parity in the legislative councils, resulted in an African majority by March 1963 despite a feud between Kaunda and Nkumbula. The UK explicitly recognized the principle of secession from the Federation which came to an end in Dec. 1963. Following Rhodesia's UDI, US, Canadian and British aircraft were used in an air-lift to supply Zambia with oil. UDI has strained relations between Zambia and the UK with Kaunda claiming that Zambia has borne the burden of Wilson's sanctions policy and that the UK Government is insufficiently determined to crush the rebel regime in Salisbury. Relations between Zambia and Rhodesia have been further strained by African guerrillas based in Zambia operating in Rhodesian territory. Zambian development depends on its copper industry which still relies on European technicians and will continue to do so until sufficient Africans are trained to replace them. There have been clashes between European mineworkers, many of whom are Rhodesians and South Africans, and African nationalists. To some extent political parties, despite UNIP's dominance, are affected by tribal considerations. The sectarian movement, led by the 'prophetess' (Alice Lenshina) was violently suppressed by Zambian forces. In the Dec. 1968 elections, the UNIP obtained an absolute majority of 81 out of 105 seats, and Dr Kaunda was re-elected.

ZANU. *Zimbabwe* African National Union – led by the Rev. Ndabaningi Sithole, broke away from ⇨ZAPU in 1963 and is also banned. The split seriously weakened the Rhodesian African nationalist movement at a decisive time in its history. Sithole, while in detention, was more recently charged (Nov. 1968) with continuing to engage in secret subversive activity while in prison. Both ZAPU and ZANU have claimed to have directed guerrilla activities in Rhodesia.

Zanzibar. ⇨ Tanzania.

Zapotocky, A. (1884–1957). Former President of ⇨Czechoslovakia. A founder-member of the Czechoslovak Communist Party in 1921 and, between 1923 and 1927, its General Secretary, Zapotocky's main field of activity was the trade union movement. Arrested by the Germans (March 1939), he was sent (1940) to Oranienburg concentration camp where he remained until the end of the war. In 1945, he became the Chairman of the 'Revolutionary Trade Union' organization and, later, the leading organizer of the workers' 'action committees', the principal force behind the communist coup of Feb. 1948. A Deputy Premier from 1946, he succeeded ⇨ Gottwald as Prime Minister in 1948. On Gottwald's death (1953), Zapotocky also became his successor as President of the Republic, a post he held until his death in 1957.

ZAPU. *Zimbabwe* African Peoples Union – Rhodesian African nationalist party led by Joshua Nkomo. It was formed in 1961 to replace the banned African National Congress and its successor the NDP. Nkomo has been in almost continuous imprisonment or restriction since 1963. ZAPU advocates universal suffrage – one man one vote – and opposes independence for Rhodesia without majority rule. Since it was banned in 1962 its headquarters have been in Tanzania.

Zhdanov, A. A. (1896–1948). A ⇨ Bolshevik from 1915, Zhdanov's rise to prominence in the USSR began in 1934, when he became a member of the party Secretariat and ⇨ Stalin's close associate. After ⇨ Kirov's assassination (Dec. 1934) Zhdanov succeeded him as head of the Leningrad party organization. As a member of the Politbureau from 1939 and Stalin's chief spokesman on ideology, Zhdanov embarked, soon after the end of the war, on a long series of campaigns and purges among members of the intelligentsia accused of displaying 'formalism' in the arts and literature, 'objectivism' in the social and natural sciences or other deviations suggesting bourgeois influences. Overshadowed for a period during the war by his principal rival G. M. ⇨ Malenkov, after the war Zhdanov recaptured his position as the most influential Soviet leader after Stalin. In 1947, he was the chief Soviet spokesman at the foundation meeting of the ⇨ Cominform. His sudden death (1948) inevitably provoked unanswered questions about its cause.

Zhivkov, T. (1911–). Prime Minister of ⇨ Bulgaria. A communist since 1930, Zhivkov made his career in the Party as a protégé of ⇨ Chervenkov. A member of the Central Committee from 1948, he was promoted to the Party Secretariat in 1950 and to the Politbureau in 1951. Following the pattern of changes in the USSR, he succeeded Chervenkov in 1954 as the Party's First Secretary. After a series of purges conducted with Soviet backing, he gained final ascendency over the Party and country at the 8th Party Congress (1962). After the Congress he assumed the premiership in addition to the party leadership, but later exchanged the Premiership for the new office of Chairman of the State Council (1971), while retaining the leading party post.

Zhukov, G. K. (1896–). Marshal of the Soviet Union. Zhukov joined the Communist Party in 1919 and made his career as a professional soldier. The most outstanding Soviet Commander in World War II, the victor of Stalingrad and of many other decisive battles, Zhukov became the most popular war hero in the USSR. Relegated by ⇨ Stalin to minor posts in the aftermath of the war, he re-emerged after Stalin's death first as deputy Minister and, in 1955, as Minister of Defence. A member of the CPSU Central Committee since 1953, he became a member of the party Presidium (later renamed Politbureau) in 1957 at the time of ⇨ Khrushchev's conflict with the ⇨ Anti-Party Group when he sided with Khrushchev. Four months later (Oct. 1957) he was deprived of both his party and government posts on the charge of having opposed party control of the armed forces and of having promoted a 'personality cult' of his own. Since then he has lived in retirement.

Zinoviev, G. Y. (1883–1936). Russian communist. A ⇨Bolshevik from 1903, between 1909 and 1917 Zinoviev was ⇨Lenin's chief lieutenant in the leadership of the Party. Though he clashed with Lenin in 1917 over the seizure of power, he remained a member of his inner circle in the Party's Politbureau, became the head of the Petrograd (later Leningrad) party organization and the first President of the ⇨Communist International. In the factional party struggles after Lenin's death, Zinoviev was (together with ⇨Kamenev) the chief leader of the 'left' opposition to ⇨Stalin although he was, at the same time, also a strong personal opponent of ⇨Trotsky. A subsequent attempt by Zinoviev, Kamenev, Trotsky and others to combine against Stalin ended in failure. They were all expelled in 1927. Though later re-admitted to the Party after public recantations, Zinoviev was arrested (Dec. 1934) after the murder of ⇨Kirov and, at a first (secret) trial (Jan. 1935) sentenced to ten years' imprisonment. He was re-tried in the following year as the leading defendant in the first of the public ⇨Moscow Trials and convicted and executed as an enemy of the people.

Zionism. The Jewish national movement to re-establish the Jewish nation in Palestine – the biblical homeland. The aspiration remained largely cultural and religious till the turn of the century when it was given a political impetus by Theodore Herzl, regarded as the founder of modern Zionism. An assimilated and non-religious Jew, he was profoundly shocked by manifestations of anti-semitism during the Dreyfus trials (1894–1906) which he reported for an Austrian newspaper. His pamphlet *Der Judenstaat* argued the case for a Jewish state as the only alternative to continual persecution, and he called the first World Zionist Congress (from which the modern movement developed) in Basle in 1897. Some early Zionists were anxious to establish a Jewish state even if it was not to be in Palestine. It was Chaim ⇨Weizmann and his followers who insisted that a Jewish nation could only be rebuilt in Palestine. The ⇨Balfour Declaration promising British government support for the idea of a Jewish National Home in Palestine was a crucial step in Zionism's political development. During the subsequent decades Zionist aims were increasingly to conflict with a growing Arab nationalism and the indigenous population of Palestine. Zionists disagreed as to the best way of achieving their ends and the movement was split into a number of factions from the extreme right to left-wing supporters of a bi-national Arab-Jewish state. Jewish settlement in

Palestine, in difficult circumstances, developed only slowly till the beginning of the thirties. The advent of Nazism with its threat to German Jewry and subsequently to all European Jewry presented Zionism with its greatest problem and profoundly affected its future course. For many Jews emigration to Palestine became not an ultimate political ideal, but an immediate necessity. The establishment of ⊳ Israel (1948), though in tragic circumstances and bitter conflict in Palestine, nevertheless represented a culmination of Zionist hopes. Since then, the importance of the movement has been in mobilizing aid for the developing state and recruiting and facilitating immigration.